LABOR IN THE ANCIENT WORLD

VOLUME V

in a series sponsored by the
Institute for the Study of Long-term Economic Trends
and the International Scholars Conference on
Ancient Near Eastern Economies

A Colloquium held at Hirschbach (Saxony), April 2005

EDITED BY

Piotr Steinkeller
Michael Hudson

ISLET
Dresden

COVER ART: A stone relief of the Pre-Sargonic ruler of Lagash named Ur-Nanshe (ca. 2400 BC = ED IIIa). AO 2344.

The upper register of the relief shows the construction of a temple, with Ur-Nanshe carrying a corvée basket (*tupšikku*). In the lower register, a feast culminating the construction is depicted.
Photo by Philipp Bernard. Courtesy of the Louvre Museum.

Labor in the ancient world / edited by Piotr Steinkeller and Michael Hudson. The International Scholars Conference on Ancient Near Eastern Economies, vol. 5

664 p. 23 x 15 cm

ISBN 978-3-9814842-3-6

Table of Contents

Participants: 1 Walther Sallaberger; 2 Carl Lamberg-Karlovsky; 3 Heather Baker; 4 Michael Jursa; 5 Lucio Milano; 6 Tom Palaima; 7 Seth Richardson; 8 Claus Ambos; 9 Karen Radner; 10; Dimitri Nakassis; 11 Michael Hudson; 12 Benjamin Studevent-Hickman; 13 Bob Englund; 14 Kristin Kleber; 15 Johannes Renger; 16 Piotr Steinkeller; 17 Geoffrey Gardiner; 18 Cornelia Wunsch

Hirschbach/Dresden, April 2005

Introduction

Labor in the Early States: An Early Mesopotamian Perspective

Piotr Steinkeller
Harvard University

> Labour was the first price, the original purchase-money that was paid for all things. It was not by gold or by silver, but by labour, that all the wealth of the world was originally purchased.
>
> Adam Smith, *An Inquiry into the Nature and Causes of the Wealth of Nations*, Book 1, Chapter 5, Paragraph 2, *Of the Real and Nominal Price of Commodities*, [1]1776.

1. As far as we know, the Sumerians were the first people in history to think of human work in abstract terms. Already at ca. 2400 BC, the Sumerian word á, whose basic and original meanings are "arm, strength, power, physical exertion," signified "labor" in exactly the same way we understand it today, namely, a quantifiable physical effort resulting in the creation of goods and services. The Sumerians measured labor in the units of time (days) needed by an average grown man to complete a particular task. The ability to count labor in abstract "work-days" (or "man-days") was a conceptual breakthrough in the history of accounting and administration, since it allowed the conversion of any form of productive human activity into a set of numbers, therefore opening up completely new managerial possibilities, particularly in the area of economic planning.

In a related development, the word á eventually came to mean also "wage, hire, rent."[1] This shows that even at that early date men realized

[1] The first certain example of this sense of á dates to the Sargonic period. See Yang Adab 297 A 663:1–5.

that labor not only was a function of time, but that it also had a measurable monetary value, which could be expressed in terms of silver or grain. Thus, the knowledge that "time is money" was likely shared by the ancient Sumerians as well.[2]

2. The huge body of written records that the civilizations of ancient Mesopotamia, Egypt, and the Aegean have bequeathed to us contains a great deal of firsthand information about the economies of early states. Although this information is of crucial importance to anyone wishing to understand how the essential traits of modern economy have come into being, a great number of economic historians (perhaps even the majority of them) still tend to think that the first expressions of rational economic behavior came with the civilizations of Greece and Rome, and that, therefore, all that preceded them was so primitive and rudimentary as not to deserve scientific scrutiny.

A good illustration of how defective the knowledge of ancient contributions in the area of economics continues to be is the recently published popular book by Jane Gleeson-White (2012), which attributes the invention of the double-entry book-keeping, in her words "one of the greatest advances in the history of business and commerce," to the merchants of the late 15th century Venice.[3] This "discovery" will come as a surprise to Assyriologists, however, since for many decades now it has been common knowledge among them that an early form of the double-entry account was known—and widely used in connection with all manner of economic activity, even an abstract one such as labor—to Babylonian administrators already at 2100 BC![4] Economic historians and general public are equally ignorant of the financial instruments and

[2] I am saying this without being facetious, merely to underscore the precocity and sophistication of ancient economic systems. Nota bene: while the Sumerians had a word for "labor," they apparently lacked the abstract notions of "time" and "money." But note that, already by 1,900 BC, the expression "to make money (lit.: silver)" (*kaspam epēšum*) was known to the Old Assyrian merchants (Veenhof 1997: 363).

[3] The same lack of understanding of the true nature of ancient book-keeping is displayed by the recent study of the history of accounting by Soll (2014: 2–3), who thinks that "ancient finance was limited to stores accounting, that is, basic inventorying," and that, in Mesopotamia specifically, accounting existed only "in its most rudimentary form." It is characteristic that Soll's bibliography does not contain even a single reference to the vast Assyriological literature dealing with this subject.

[4] See Hallo 2004.

operating procedures that were used, around 1,900 BC, by the Assyrian merchants, which, in terms of their complexity and sophistication, rivaled those employed two and a half millennia later in the banking houses of Renaissance Italy (Veenhof 1972; 1997; 1999; Larsen 1976: 92–102).

It was mainly in an effort to correct this situation that, back in 1994, Michael Hudson and C. C. Lamberg-Karlovsky formed an informal study-group, whose objective was systematically to investigate, via the medium of several colloquiums, various aspects of the economies of early states, and to make the results of these investigations available to broader audiences, especially economic historians, archaeologists, and anthropologists. Among the issues treated by the previous colloquia were the role of private economic activity (Hudson and Levine 1996), the forms of land-tenure and land ownership (Hudson and Levine 1999), the problem of debt and the native solutions to deal with it (Hudson and Van de Mieroop 2001), and record-keeping and accounting (Hudson and Wunsch 2004).

In April of 2005 our group convened again in Hirschbach near Dresden to tackle the issues related to human labor.[5] The objective of this colloquium was to offer a systematic discussion of the status of labor throughout the whole span of ancient Mesopotamian history, as well as to obtain comparative perspectives from other ancient civilizations of the Old World, such as Egypt and the Aegean. A secondary theme of the meeting was the use of corvée on large public projects.

The present volume grows from that meeting, presenting a number of papers that were originally read at Hirschbach, as well as a number of additional contributions, which were solicited subsequently to make the coverage more comprehensive.

The final result is a collection of twelve papers. Apart from this contribution, which is meant to serve as a general introduction, and focuses on third millennium Mesopotamia, there are six papers devoted to Mesopotamian labor. Thus C. C. Lamberg-Karlovsky treats the question of prehistoric labor in greater Mesopotamia; W. Sallaberger and A. Pruß study the labor-related issues in the Pre-Sargonic city of Nabada in the Khabur Region; P. Steinkeller and S. Richardson discuss the use of labor on large building projects, as documented in the Ur III and Old Baby-

[5] We were hosted there by Cornelia Wunsch, in her private house. Cornelia and her parents provided us with a truly ambient atmosphere, delicious food, and a perfect setting for our discussions. On behalf of all the participants of that meeting I extend to them our warmest thanks. Their wonderful hospitality will be remembered by us forever.

lonian periods respectively; K. Radner studies the hired labor in Neo-Assyrian times; M. Jursa offers an overview of labor and labor relations in Babylonia in the first millennium BC. In addition, the volume contains two papers devoted to ancient Egypt: M. Lehner investigates the use of labor invested in the construction of the Old Kingdom pyramids, while O. Goelet gives a characterization of labor in the period from the New Kingdom up to the beginning of the Hellenistic era. Two other contributions, by D. Nakassis and T. Palaima, study the organization, mobilization, and usages of labor in the Mycenaean Greece. The volume concludes with the summary observations by M. Hudson, which offer a modern economist's view of the role of labor in the development of the world's civilization.

In the following pages I offer a brief discussion of the principal sources of labor in the third millennium Mesopotamia, while also citing some comparative evidence (though only sparingly) and offering a bit of theoretical introduction. My objective here is to provide the reader with a basic historical framework against which later Mesopotamian manifestations of labor, such as those described in the contributions to this volume, may productively be compared and evaluated. Such a framework may likewise inform the understanding of the status of labor in the Egyptian and the Mycenaean worlds, which are also examined in this volume. The particular value of the third millennium economic records lies not only in their great antiquity (which obviously makes them of special interest for the universal history of labor, as they allow one to study the very beginnings of organized economic activity), but also in their quality, due to their enormous volume and mind-boggling detail.[6]

[6] The number of third millennium economic and legal records presently available may be put at ca. 120,000, of which nearly 100,000 come from the Ur III period. Similar documentation survives in abundance from all the later periods of Mesopotamian history, with the Neo-Babylonian and Old Babylonian records being particularly numerous (ca. 50,000 and 40,000 individual tablets respectively). Other large corpora of economic and legal records survive from Old Assyrian Kaneš in Anatolia (ca. 23,000 tablets) and first millennium Persepolis in Iran (ca. 15,000–18,000 tablets). See Streck 2010; Jones and Stolper 2008. This profusion of first-hand data provides Assyriologists with a huge advantage over the students of the economies of Greece and Rome, who for the most part must rely on secondary types of information. See the following characterization of the dilemma facing the historian of Roman economy: "The Romans recorded most of their day-to-day transactions by incising the wax covering of wooden oblongs about the size of

3. However true the adage that "gold is king" may be, the real foundation of the "wealth of nations" is human labor. To put it simply, labor is both the necessary prerequisite of any productive activity and the force that imbues a manufactured commodity or a completed service with economic value.

For an agrarian human group to develop any appreciable level of social complexity, most basically, labor specialization, surpluses in kind[7] are necessary. Without a surplus, that hypothetical group will have no crafts, nor will it be able to engage in economic exchanges with other communities. And, in order to produce agricultural surpluses, considerable labor investments, usually beyond the capacities of a single family, must be made. As Marshall Sahlins reminds us, the only way to obtain a surplus is through the intensification of labor: "getting people to work more, or more people to work."[8]

Since the capacity of a human being to produce labor is limited by natural constraints, throughout recorded history men intensified labor rather by getting more people to work. However, to make others—especially large numbers—to work for you is not a simple task. While it may be comparatively easy to mobilize an extended family or a tribe to work on a local communal project, the mobilization of workers that are not bound to each other by blood or social ties is fraught with difficulties of a completely different order. Invariably, the task of making large numbers of unconnected individuals to contribute their labor will call for some degree of coercion, usually tempered with economic and psychological inducements.

The fundamental difficulty of making free individuals to relinquish their labor is responsible for the fact that all ancient economies (and likewise modern underdeveloped economies of the Third World) were faced with a shortage of labor. This shortage was nearly always chronic, and

modern roof shingles. This medium was highly perishable, and we have almost no written records of such transactions after two millennia. We therefore are dependent on four kinds of evidence: casual remarks about the economy in works of literature that have been preserved for other reasons; proclamations or directives important enough to be chiseled into stone; archaeological evidence; and papyri from Egypt that were durable in the dry climate of that land. There is a lot of information, but hardly any of what economists call data" (Temin 2006: 134).

7 Or, in anthropological terms, "staple finance." See Earle 1991; D'Altroy and Earle 1985.

8 Sahlins 1972: 82. See also Lamberg-Karlovsky in this volume p. 59.

often profound. A widely held view in economic history is that a shortage of labor resulting from a high land-to-population ratio (low population density) invariably led individuals to force others to work for them. Thus, beginning with Herman J. Nieboer (1910), economists have speculated that slavery and various form of bondage (such as the serfdom of pre-modern Russia) invariably were adopted due to the shortage of labor via-à-vis low population densities.[9] As put by Nieboer (1900: 419),

> among peoples with open resources everybody is able to provide for himself; therefore free labourers do not offer themselves, at least not for employment in the common drudgery, the rudest and most despised work ... if therefore a man wants others to perform the necessary drudgery for him, and cannot impose it upon his wife, or wives, or other female dependants (either because women hold a high position, or because there is more mean work to be done that the women can possibly manage), he must compel other men to serve him; and this compulsion will often assume the form of slavery.[10]

In the context of bondage, the usual way of obtaining labor was debt-servitude, a practice that is in use even today.[11]

4. Slavery

One common method of extracting labor from other human beings, which was widely practiced both in ancient and modern times, is enslavement. Slavery is by far the most economical way of obtaining labor, since it comes essentially free (except for the cost of acquiring a slave and the subsequent outlays to maintain and to police him), and since it makes labor available at all times. In addition, slavery is self-reproducing.

However, in the period before classical antiquity (Greece and Rome) slavery played only a marginal role in the economies of early states. Although slaves are documented in Mesopotamia and Egypt since the end of fourth the millennium BC, their numbers were always small, and therefore this type of labor was never of much economic importance. In Mesopotamia slaves were predominantly those of the domestic or patri-

[9] This thesis has further been elaborated on by Williams 1994 and Domar 1970. See also Kolchin 1987: 17–18.

[10] Nieboer 1910: 419.

[11] See Steinkeller 2002a: 111–113.

monial variety. They usually worked as servants, and only rarely participated in productive labor or were trained as craftsmen.[12]

A great majority of them were debt-slaves, who stemmed from the free native population. As freemen and native-born, debt-slaves retained some legal rights; in particular, throughout the history of ancient Mesopotamia the law protected them from being resold abroad. Upon the repayment of their debts, debt-slaves could be manumitted and restored to their former status.

The true, outright slaves, who were completely deprived of social rights (though had some economic rights), were usually of foreign origin. The majority of them had been prisoners of war; less commonly, they had been acquired on international slave markets. Such foreign captives are documented since the earliest recorded history both in Mesopotamia and Egypt. The status of this social group can best be studied in Ur III Babylonia. Most of the foreign slaves who were brought to Babylonia during that period were women, who had been acquired by state institutions as part of foreign military operations. While some of them were presented as rewards to the members of the elite, the majority of these women (called géme), often together with their children, were distributed among temple households and other types of state-run economic institutions. Although primarily employed as weavers and in grain pro-

[12] In the Ur III texts from GARšana, a rural estate owned by the princess Simat-Ištaran and her husband Šu-Kabta, the personnel of the household are often referred to by the designation árad (é). In his discussion of these personnel, W. Heimpel (2009) translated árad indiscriminately as "slave." However, it is well known that árad, apart from meaning "slave," has a more general sense of "servant," particularly in the context of private and royal households. Thus, while some of the dependents of Simat-Ištaran and Šu-Kabta may indeed have been slaves (this point needs further study), the majority of them, as shown by various data pertaining to their professional status and activities, definitely were free individuals. See, *e.g.*, CUSAS 3 16, 30, and 33, in which árad é-a-me-éš, "household servants," together with lú-hun-gá-me-éš, "hirelings," are summarized as éren, "free royal dependents" (courtesy of M. Molina). For éren, see Steinkeller 2013a: 350–351.

Ancient terminology needs to be translated with caution and precision, since otherwise confusion and misunderstanding may arise, especially among those who are not intimately familiar with ancient texts. A case in point is a recent article by R. McC. Adams (2011), who follows Heimpel's translation and reaches on its basis various unwarranted conclusions. To his credit, however, Adams showed a doze of healthy skepticism in accepting some of Heimpel's ideas, asking, for example, "how could three scribal managers be slaves, as Heimpel now suspects?" (*ibid.* p. 6) (the answer is in the negative, of course).

cessing, these females intermittently worked as agricultural workers as well, most commonly maintaining irrigation systems and assisting with the harvest. They also served as carriers and occasionally even as boat-towers.

On the other hand, due to the absence in early states of security mechanisms allowing the utilization of large numbers of male slaves in productive labor, male prisoners of war were rarely turned into outright slaves. If they escaped slaughter—which was the usual method of dealing with them—they were blinded, and only then put to work, at certain specialized tasks.[13] In Babylonia, such blinded captives usually worked in orchards as gardeners' helpers, drawing water from the wells and irrigating fruit trees and vegetable plots.[14]

This gender-differentiated approach to the use of foreign captives as workers is nicely illustrated by an inscription of the Ur III king Šu-Suen, which describes how, following the pacification of the Iranian lands of Šimaški, the captured Šimaškian males were blinded, and subsequently put to work in the orchards of the main temple households of the realm. In contrast, the female Šimaškians were donated to the weaving houses of the same institutions:

> nam-guruš uru^{ki}-uru^{ki}-ba sá ba-ni-in-dug$_{4}$-[g]a-a igi-bi im-[ma]-an-du$_{8}$-du$_{8}$ ^{giš}kiri$_{6}$ ^{d}En-[líl] ^{d}Nin-líl-l[á] ù [^{giš}]kiri$_{6}$ dingir [gal]-⸢gal»-e-ne-[ka] ⸢gìr⸣-šè im-mi-in-sig$_{10}$ ù nam-g[éme] uru^{ki}-uru^{ki}-[ba] sá ba-ni-i[n]-dug$_{4}$-g[a] é-uš-b[ar] ^{d}En-líl ^{d}Nin-líl-lá ù é dingir gal-⸢gal⸣-e-ne-ka sag-⸢šè⸣ im-mi-[in-r]ig$_{7}$

> "He (*i.e.*, Šu-Suen) blinded the males of the conquered cities, and he assigned them to the personnel of the orchards of Enlil and Ninlil, and those of other great gods. And he donated the women of the conquered cities to the weaving houses of Enlil and Ninlil, and those of other great gods."[15]

Otherwise, when large groups of captive foreigners were transplanted to Mesopotamia, such individuals invariably were granted the status of state dependants. As such, they were settled on land and provided with field allotments, integrated into the local rural population, and made part of

[13] See Gelb 1973: 87; Steinkeller 2013b: 143–144.

[14] See Steinkeller 2013b: 143 n. 39.

[15] Frayne, RIME 3/2, 301–06 Šu-Sin 3 iv 15–31.

the royal economy.[16] This was a common practice in Ur III Babylonia. The same procedure was also used later in Assyria and the Neo-Babylonian empire.

5. Corvée

Since slaves were insignificant economically, the main source of labor in the early states necessarily was free population. This statement must be provided with a caveat, however, since, in addition to the slaves and the free, all ancient societies always included groups of people whose status fell somewhere between these two categories. While not legally slaves, such individuals lacked the social rights and the economic means of the free, being fully dependent for their livelihood either on various institutions or private individuals. They were permanently attached to those and worked for them all year round, usually performing various forms of unskilled labor. Such attached workers, who may best be classified as menials, were never very numerous. Accordingly, their contribution to the total labor picture was of secondary importance. A detailed discussion of this type of workforce in Mesopotamia will be offered later on.

Throughout history, the primary mechanism that was used—universally it seems—to extract work from free citizenry was the institution of forced labor or corvée. Corvée may be defined as a work duty of limited duration (usually several months per year) that is owed to the state or another governing body by the population at large. The people who were subject to corvée were almost always free. Another characteristic feature of corvée was its universal nature: unless subject to special exemptions, all free members of a given state or community were liable to perform it.

The corvée was done primarily on public projects or other undertakings that were of importance for the whole community and required large outlays of labor. The most important and typical tasks involved here were the maintenance of irrigation systems, harvest work, and major building operations, the last focusing mainly on the construction of palaces, temples, city-walls, and various other types of defensive structures. Military service, which was, *sensu stricto*, just another form of public works, counted as corvée as well.

It is characteristic that, in spite of its compulsory and seemingly exploitive nature, corvée was by no means a one-way proposition. The individuals subject to it were invariably beneficiaries of various economic

[16] Steinkeller 2013a: 357.

rewards from the state, most important of which was access to agricultural land and irrigation water. They also received protection from the state, as well as various rewards of psychological nature, such as a sense of accomplishment and the opportunity to share in the same system of ideological and cultural values.[17]

In view of corvée's universal nature, and the fact that it was typically used in connection with projects of value to the whole society, with its performance benefiting the participants in a tangible and often even economically calculable way (such as the dredging of a canal or the construction of a new temple), it will not be unreasonable to conclude that from a purely economic perspective corvée represented a primitive form of taxation—a proto "federal tax" of sorts.[18]

Outside the ancient Near East corvée was practiced—to offer just two examples—among the Incas and in ancient China. The Inca corvée, called *mit'a,* "turn" or "season" (cf. the Sumerian bala, "turn," discussed below p. 140), was a community service of specific duration (up to ten months per year) used for public projects, such as the construction of roads and monumental architecture. All able-bodied citizens were required to perform it. Like the Mesopotamian corvée, the *mit'a* obligation extended to military service (Murra 1982: 98–104; and the following pages).

For the corvée in China, see the following description by Mark E. Lewis (2007: 250):

[17] See Steinkeller in this volume, pp. 143–155, 203–204.

[18] Some anthropologists consider corvée to be the subcategory of a more general form of labor organization, which they term "custodial recruitment." See Abrams 1994: 99–101; Udy 1959: 78; Erasmus 1956: 445. According to Abrams 1994: 99–101, another subcategory of "custodial recruitment" is the "festive custodial" mode of labor procurement, which he defines as follows: "The more balanced form of custodial recruitment is what I would term festive custodial, equivalent of Erasmus' festive reciprocal system … In this system, labor is given to a socially more powerful individual in return for a feast or party upon completion of a project. The recipient of this labor generally does not offer his labor in return and does not contribute labor during the project, which is the critical distinction between this system and all forms of the familial recruitment system … Once the imbalance between host and participant becomes marked and the giving of labor is de facto obligatory (*i.e.,* a tax), a threshold has been crossed and the system may be considered corvée labor … Thus, a corvée system emerges from a festive custodial system as the degree of the instituted imbalance is increased."

> The early [Chinese] empires employed four types of manual labor: peasant corvée, hired, convict, and slave. Each of these had different legal and social characteristics and was consequently suitable for different types of work. Adult males in free households owed one month's labor per year. Such work was devoted to diverse tasks, and the legal texts mention repairing walls of government buildings, mending roads and bridges, excavating ponds, and digging or dredging canals. Corvée labor was frequently employed in local projects such as flood control, irrigation, or roads, but was also used to build imperial tomb mounds, construct walls around the capital, and repair breaks in the dikes of the Yellow River. However, such work crews changed each month, and peasants were unavailable during crucial agricultural work. If peasants were forced to work away from their native area, the state provided food and tools. Consequently, the use of corvée could lead to costly delays in major projects.

According to another author (Loewe 2005: 70), one month of Chinese corvée was due from all free male citizens between the ages of twenty-two and sixty-five. This labor was in addition to two years of obligatory military service. "It was also possible in certain circumstances to pay for a substitute to perform the work" (Loewe 2005: 70).

Ethnographic data suggest that in its most basic and ancient form corvée was a collective undertaking involving all the members of a community (such as a village or a tribal group), which was led and coordinated by the community's headman or a group of elders. The latter made the community to contribute its labor by using the "carrot and stick" approach. Since the labor was usually to be spent on projects that benefited the community directly (such as a canal or a ceremonial center), its members were motivated, both by their own personal interest and by altruistic considerations, to donate their labor freely. This favorable inclination toward the participation in a project was reinforced by various incentives of material nature, among which most characteristic was the ceremonial feast given out to the participants at the conclusion of the project. Indeed, feasts of this type, during which large volumes of food (especially meat) and drink are consumed are a characteristic feature of communal work in the so-called primitive societies. One finds ample evidence of them also in ancient Mesopotamia and Egypt, and in other early states as well.[19]

[19] See, in this volume, Lehner 407–411 and Steinkeller 199–203. Cf. also Abrams 1994: 99–100.

However, since the communal undertakings of this sort needed coordination and timetable (to make the members of the community show up for work, to assure that they work diligently and properly, to punish the ones who slack off, etc.), various coercive means were always necessary as well. Since most of the projects subject to corvée were of a seasonal or repetitive nature, compulsion must have become institutionalized from very early on. It is likely, therefore, that many of the coercive mechanisms and institutions one finds in the early states had their ultimate origin in communal work. Because of this, corvée undoubtedly mightily contributed toward the formation of elites and state institutions. In other words, without corvée there would no chiefs and kings.

In spite of corvée's paramount importance for the economies of the early states, textual information pertaining to it is scarce. In Mesopotamia, this is due primarily to the nature of documentation extant, which tends to concern the activities of the provincial (or "institutional") economies, concentrating therefore on small-scale projects that were done by local institutions with their own labor resources. In contrast, large-scale projects of national importance, which were conducted by the crown, are almost never documented directly. If such information is available, it is usually of secondary nature. Some references to corvée are also found in historical inscriptions, but this kind of information tends to be limited to very general statements only.

Economic sources, particularly those from the third millennium, also tend to privilege certain types of laborers, in particular, the menial workers who were permanently attached to the temple households and similar institutions. Since menials were alimented by their home institutions, they needed to be closely and regularly monitored—hence the great volume of textual information about them. For this type of workforce, see in detail below section 8. On the other hand, third millennium economic sources say considerably less about other categories of workers, especially wage laborers, who in actuality were economically much more important than menial workers. For the latter, see below section 7.

For these reasons, most of the surviving information on corvée pertains to its use in local, usually provincial contexts. Throughout the second half of the third millennium BC, all free members of temple and royal households were required to contribute corvée labor to their home institutions. This they did over a period of several months (probably never more than six months), in exchange for land allotments (or, more commonly, a share of harvest from the communally tilled land) and alimentation during their employment on corvée. This period of employment was called bala, "turn, cycle," an extremely important Sumerian term whose meanings also include those of "royal reign," "dynasty," and "cosmic cycle."[20] In the Ur III period bala came to designate in addition a proportional and rotational general tax, which was paid by all the provinces of the Ur III state in accordance with their individual economic capabilities.[21]

The individuals liable for corvée came from all economic and professional backgrounds. One finds among them craftsmen, shepherds, agricultural personnel, gardeners, foresters, merchants, and various types of administrative and cultic officials, as well as the most prominent members of local elites, such as the provincial governors and their kinsmen.[22] It is clear that the richest among them and many of the specialists did not perform corvée themselves. In all likelihood, such individuals provided substitutes in their stead, who may have been their junior kinsmen or dependent members of their private households, such as menial workers and perhaps even slaves. It is also possible that one could avoid corvée's performance by paying a corresponding monetary compensation.[23] Throughout the recorded history of Mesopotamia corvée was the main source of labor.[24] This was especially true of large construction projects. Steinkeller and Richardson show that such an employment of corvée is particularly well documented in the Ur III and Old Babylonian periods. Similar cases are known from the first millennium BCE. As examples here may serve the Neo-Assyrian constructions of royal palaces at Kalhu (modern Nimrud)[25] and Dur-Šarru-kin (modern Khorsabad),[26] and a similar undertaking at Babylon, which was conducted by Nebuchad-

[20] Characteristically, in reflection of the division of the year into two work cycles, in certain sources the free workforce at large is designated as either bala gub-ba, "performing to the bala duty," or bala tuš-a, "sitting out the bala duty."

[21] Sharlach 2004.

[22] See Steinkeller in this volume, pp.172–173.

[23] See Steinkeller in this volume 173 n. 145.

[24] For the third millennium and the Old Babylonian period, see Steinkeller and Richardson in this volume. For the Neo-Assyrian period, see Postgate 1974: 63–93, 218–229, 241–243. For the Neo-Babylonian period, see Jursa in this volume.

[25] Karlsson 2013: 166–167.

[26] Parpola 1995.

nezzar II.[27] There are strong reasons to think that the Egyptian building projects likewise were executed mainly through the use of corvée. See Lehner and Goelet. Such certainly was the case during the Old Kingdom, as demonstrated by the projects involving the construction of the Fourth Dynasty pyramids.

6. Corvée in Prehistoric Times

As we know from a variety of sources, the Mesopotamians considered corvée to be the cornerstone of human society. They even believed that the existence of corvée preceded the birth of human life itself.[28] This native opinion about the great antiquity of corvée is very revealing, if only as an indication of the importance the ancients attached to this institution. But, in point of fact, how far back in time can one detect the presence of corvée in the archaeological record?

In his contribution to this volume, Lamberg-Karlovsky argues that evidence of organized communal work—in other words, of corvée—is found already at ca. 9,000 BC, at Göbekli Tepe and similar sites in the vicinity of Urfa. Such a conclusion is inescapable, in my view, when one considers Göbekli's ceremonial center (in fact, the entire of site of Göbekli is one huge ceremonial center, only a part of which has so far been unearthed), since the creation of this large aggregate of stone architecture and sculpture must have involved a considerable investment of highly organized and coordinated labor. While this is clear, the question unavoidably arises: even if one assumes that the population of Göbekli had a social organization up to that task, how was a group of hunters and gatherers able to produce the surplus—a surplus of what!?—that apparently would have been needed to finance this undertaking? At the very least, one would expect that the agency in charge of it (whatever it may have been) commanded over huge supplies of food (meat?, beer?) that were required to feed the workforce during its employment on the project, as well as to feast them at the project's conclusion.

Although various chiefdoms have on occasion been able to mobilize sufficient labor resources to produce monumental architecture, such cases invariably involve agricultural societies. A good case in point here are the gigantic stone statues (called *moai*) and the massive stone platforms (called *ahu*) on which they stood, which were sculpted, transport-

[27] Beaulieu 2005.

[28] See Steinkeller in this volume, p. 138.

ed, and laboriously erected by the clans of Easter Island.[29] In terms of its scope and the volume of labor required, this project shares much similarity with Göbekli's ceremonial center. But the people of Easter Island had at their disposal, especially during the three centuries of this project's estimated duration, a highly intensive plantation agriculture, which produced large food surpluses.[30]

For this reason, the case of Göbekli seems to defy explanation. The only way to account for it would be to assume that social evolution did not, especially during its earliest history, always follow the same trajectory. If we follow this reasoning, we will be forced to accept that, in one case at least, large numbers of Neolithic hunters and gatherers periodically came together to contribute very significant volumes of labor toward the construction of a ritual center. This they did, apparently, entirely voluntarily, and with little, if any, remuneration, inducement, or reward of an economic nature. If so, the only reward they obtained in exchange for their labor could have been a spiritual one: the opportunity to partake in Göbekli's religious life. Are we allowed, accordingly, to conclude that the construction of Göbekli was permeated with a spirit not unlike that which guided the builders of medieval cathedrals?[31]

We are on a much safer ground when we move up in time to ca. 3,300 BC (Uruk IV period), and arrive at the site of Uruk in southern Babylonia. There, in an area traditionally identified as the precinct of Eanna one finds an architectural complex consisting of some nine large buildings, probably of religious character. One of these buildings is built entirely of limestone; several of them are adorned with a mosaic of colored stone cones, an expensive and very labor-intensive form of architectural decoration. These structures are provided with elaborate courtyards and surrounded, at least partially, with massive walls. To the west of the Eanna precinct, in an area thought to represent the ancient district of

[29] Diamond 2005: 79–119. Another recent book on this subject has argued that the construction of the *moai* and *ahu* was a strategy meant to keep the population levels down, by channeling the male population's sexual urges into another activity. See Hunt and Lipo 2011. But, as pointed out by Roger Atwood (2011), "to argue that [these people] preferred carving to sex is not an easy argument to sustain." Even more unsustainable is Hunt's and Lipo's idea that high cultures might develop without the presence of surplus economies.

[30] See Diamond 2005: 102.

[31] See Steinkeller in this volume, pp. 153–154.

Kullab,[32] another ceremonial center existed roughly around the same time. The latter complex, which belongs to the Uruk III period, included an enormous platform with a temple on its top (the so-called Anu Ziggurat), and, just next to it, another temple, which is made of stone.

It is evident that the construction of these ceremonial centers called for a great investment of labor. Alone the work on the platform of the Anu Ziggurat is estimated to have consumed the labor of 1,500 men working ten hours a day for five years.[33] One can be equally certain that the mechanism used to mobilize workers for this and other building projects at Uruk was the institution of corvée.

Since no private houses dating to those periods have ever been excavated at Uruk, the extent of such occupation and, with it, the total size of Uruk's population are difficult to estimate. On the face of it, it is even possible that, rather than forming a single urban agglomeration (= city), Uruk consisted essentially of two huge ceremonial centers, which were surrounded by several towns or villages interspersed with fields, orchards, and industrial areas.[34] In that case, Uruk's human resources would probably have been insufficient to supply all the labor needed for the construction work. The question thus must be asked: where did all the extra workers come from?

There is suggestive evidence that, during the Late Uruk period, the city-states (or their prototypes) of Babylonia formed a loose political alliance of cooperative nature.[35] It appears that this "federation" centered on Uruk and the cult of its chief deity Inana, imposing on the constituent members various obligations. One of them (in fact, the only documented one) was the duty to provide regular offerings for Inana's temple at Uruk. On the basis of similar arrangements that existed in Babylonia a millennium later,[36] it might be considered that, apart from

[32] Although commonly entertained by archaeologists, the idea that Kullab was situated in the western section of Uruk is not supported by any sound data. The actual location of Kullab is yet to be determined.

[33] Nissen 1988: 95.

[34] Such a picture would agree fairly closely with a description of Uruk's topography which is given in the first millennium BC version of the Gilgameš Epic, Tablet I 22–23, XI 327–328. According to that source, 28.5 % of Uruk's total area was occupied by the city, 14.5 % by the precinct of Eanna, 28.5 by date-palm orchards, and 28.5 % by clay pits.

[35] Steinkeller 2002b.

[36] The so-called bala system of Ur III times, for which see Sharlach 2004.

supplying offerings for Inana, the members of this early supra-Babylonian alliance were also required to contribute labor for Inana's temple and related structures. In this way, both the construction and the upkeep of Uruk's ceremonial centers would have equally been shared by all the members of the "federation." This in turn could explain how the huge volume of labor needed both for the construction and the subsequent maintenance of those centers had been obtained.

Be that as it may, however, one may be fully confident that corvée was known and practiced in Babylonia during the Late Uruk period.[37] Is it possible to trace its presence in Mesopotamia even farther back, perhaps down to the time when it was first employed?

I submit that the beginnings of corvée coincided with the introduction of irrigation-based agriculture on the alluvium, which must have happened sometime during the Obeid period. This suggestion will probably raise some brows, since there has been a tendency lately to downplay the role of irrigation works and their social dimensions in the growth of Mesopotamian urbanism. In reaction to Karl A. Wittfogel's "hydraulic theory," which attributed the rise of autocratic states in Mesopotamia, Egypt, India, and China to the need for a highly centralized control of irrigation systems,[38] some scholars are now inclined to believe that the earliest Mesopotamian farmers relied for their supplies of irrigation water exclusively on natural watercourses. As this view has it, such minimal irrigation works did not require any centralized means of management.[39]

37 For this conclusion, see also Nissen 1988: 95.

38 Wittfogel 1963.

39 For example, Nissen 1988: 58–60, 96, who thinks that "the existence of complicated irrigation systems can definitely be ruled out for the early periods (p. 59)," and that large canal systems came into being only in Late Uruk times (*ibid.* 96). The only evidence Nissen offers in support of this idea is the fact that, allegedly, the sea level in the Gulf during the Ubaid and Early Uruk periods (ca. 5,300–3,600 BC) was high, meaning that large areas of southern Babylonia were submerged under water. Based on this supposition, he further speculates that "even if the change in climate did, in the end, mean that large areas of the country were no longer under water ... for a long period of time there was so much water in the country that large areas were available for cultivation at a time when there still was sufficient water on hand in a profusion of small, even minute, creeks and waterways. Wherever artificial irrigation was necessary, there was, therefore, water available, without any great effort being needed to obtain it" (*ibid.* 59–60). However, recent studies of the geomorphology of the Persian Gulf indicate something considerably different: namely, that when the marine intrusions reached their peak at ca. 4,000 BC, the northern coastline of the Gulf ran as it did later during the third millennium

Wittfogel's thesis obviously is a huge oversimplification, for it dumps together a number of significantly different hydrological and ecological systems. Indeed, it may be true that Wittfogel was completely wrong about ancient Egypt, which relied on an inundation system based essentially on a single waterway, and where the agriculture depended on a largely predictable and dependable seasonal flooding, which, after the water had receded, left a layer of life-giving silt. There, the need of an extensive system of artificial canals probably was not, at least initially, a determining factor. However, things were dramatically different on the alluvial plain of the Euphrates and the Tigris, where no cereal cultivation is possible without the recourse to artificial irrigation works. Significantly, in Iraq irrigation water is not obtained through seasonal flooding, which comes too late in the agricultural cycle to be of any benefit. Just the opposite, the flood is a destructive force, which needs to be contained and diverted, since it will otherwise damage the growing crops. In that ecosystem, irrigation is done when the levels of the two rivers are generally low, which means that the water needs to be artificially lifted up and then directed into the fields via an intricate and extensive canal network.

It is true that in Iraq some cultivation can be carried out immediately adjacent to the two rivers, by cutting their levees and bringing the water down their slopes onto the neighboring fields. However, from an economic perspective this mode of farming is of marginal importance, since it yields subsistence gains at best, certainly lacking the potential of producing cereal surpluses, a condition *sine-qua-non* for the division of labor, and hence the birth of crafts and trade, and the establishment of an urban way of life. For this reason alone, the growth of Mesopotamian civilization was predicated on the presence of large-scale irrigation networks, which, as the need for surpluses steadily increased due to the population growth and various other societal pressures, became progressively more and more extensive and complex. An obvious consequence of these processes was the development of ever more efficient and centralized instruments of control, which were necessary to ensure the coordination and smooth running of all the component parts of the system.

BC (*i.e.*, just to the south of Eridu, Ur, and Lagaš), without the evidence of any substantial flooding farther north. See Lambeck 1996: 43–57; Sanlaville 2002: 133–50. Moreover, Nissen's theory is directly contradicted by the results of surface surveys, which show an unequivocal evidence of canal networks already in the Early and Middle Uruk periods. See Adams 1981: 65 fig. 13 (note that the caption belongs to fig. 12 and *vice versa*).

Here it must be realized that, as the dynamics of Babylonia's political history demonstrate it very clearly, in the Mesopotamian ecosystem the more remote parts of the irrigation system were totally dependent for their survival on the cooperation of the agencies in charge of the direct intakes of water from the Euphrates and the Tigris, to insure its regular flow to their fields. This fact also made them natural dependencies of those agencies (unless they were able to reverse the relationship, by assuming political control of the latter), a process that inevitably led to the formation of settlement clusters, and eventually, to the appearance of proto-city-states.

All these facts argue strongly that organized collective labor existed in Mesopotamia already during the Obeid period, and that its "invention" was directly connected with the appearance of extensive irrigation networks. It is impossible to say which of them came first. In all probability these two phenomena developed more or less concurrently, with the needs of agriculture dictating the use of labor force above that of a single family, and with the availability of labor so created enabling further expansion of irrigation works. This spiral process led to the formation of village clusters based on a shared irrigation system and subordinated to a single agency of control, eventually resulting in the appearance of urban centers and city-states.

7. Hired Labor

Since the corvée duty was of limited duration, it could satisfy only some of the existing labor needs. The shortage of labor was particularly pronounced during the harvest, when huge numbers of workers were needed over a brief period of time. Therefore, other sources of manpower had to be exploited. In Ur III Babylonia and earlier, significant volumes of labor were extracted from the dependent menial workers who were permanently attached to temple, royal, and private households. Although the menials worked full time, their numbers were comparatively small, and so their contribution to the total labor picture was of secondary importance at best. For this type of labor, see in detail below section 8.

Still another way of procuring extra labor was the antichretic loaning arrangement, in which the interest on a barley loan was repaid in human labor, usually in the form of harvest work. This practice was particularly common in Ur III times, especially within the provincial economies. The borrowers typically were various members of the royal sector,[40] though on occasion dependents of the provincial economies were part of such

[40] See Steinkeller 2002: 119, 129–133; 2013a: 382–383.

arrangements as well.[41] Although these transactions must have been of considerable help—particularly at harvest—they too, like the menial work mentioned earlier, could not alleviate fully the shortage of labor.

For this reason, both the provincial economies and the royal sector were forced to hire workers for wages.[42] Clearly, this was a measure of last resort, since the hired labor did not come cheaply: the standard wage of a male hireling was six liters of barley per day—though it could sometimes be as low as three liters or as high as ten liters.[43] While such wages were usually paid in barley, the occasional use of silver is documented as well.[44]

41 See the examples in Steinkeller 2013a: 407–408 Texts 13, 14, and 15, to which add the following example: 390 sar gišdìli ⌜10⌝-sar-ta á-bi ud 40 lá 1-kam á máš še ur_5-ra-ka, "(x field work representing) 39 man-days, the labor (in lieu) of the interest on a barley loan" (MCS 8 52 Liv. 51 63 13:25–26 + Orient 16 69 92 lines 25–26). Such antichrectic transactions were occasionally contracted also among private individuals. See, *e.g.*, TMH NF 1–2 32.

42 For the use of hirelings by the various components of the royal sector, see, *e.g.*, CUSAS 3 355:1–5, which deals with a project conducted at the royal estate at GARšana: [54 sar] ⌜5⌝ gín sahar ús-bi 72 nindan á guruš-a 2 ½ gín-ta guruš-bi 1,298 ud 1-šè še 6 sìla-ta ba-hun, "54 sar and ⌜5⌝ square 'fingers' of dirt (to be excavated); the length (of the retaining wall) is 72 nindan; at the rate of 2½ square 'fingers' (of dirt) per man, 1,298 men were hired for 1 day, at (the daily wage of) 6 liters of barley each." As a matter of fact, it appears that hired workers were *the main source of labor* at that estate. A search in BDTNS for lú-hun-gá, hun-gá, and hun in GARšana documentation yields a total of 286 attestations! Hired labor was commonly used also at the rural estate of Lugal-kugzu at Du-sabara. See, *e.g.*, NATN 451, 464; TMH NF 1–2 88, 316; MVN 15 68. The numbers of hirelings used in such contexts were very substantial. For example, on the royal estates in the area of Nippur, most of the field work was done by hirelings, with smaller numbers of workers being drawn from among the royal settlers (éren) of É-marza(ki) and Šimanum. See TMH NF 1–2 301, which lists 387 hirelings, 117 men of E-marza, and 50 men of Šimanum; TMH NF 1–2 300: 163 hirelings, 98 men of E-marza, and 49 men of Šimanum; TMH NF 1–2 304: 267 hirelings, 155 men of E-marza, and 52 men of Šimanum. Similar proportions are found in another sources belonging to this group (TMH NF 1–2 302; NATN 450; SNAT 233).

43 See Steinkeller 2002a: 119. Apart from the standard rate of 6 liters, the following rates are documented: 3 liters (TCTI 2 4264:7–10); 5 liters (TMH NF 1–2 86:1–4); 7 liters (TCL 5 5675 i 6–8); 7.5 liters (TMH NF 1–2 88:3–4); 8 liters (SNAT 511:21); 10 liters (RSO 83 361 no. 37:1–4:3–4).

44 ½ ma-na 7 gín igi-3-gál (kug-babbar) á lú-hun-gá ù ⌜á⌝ gud hun-gá (HSS 4 1 iv 16–17); 464 «GÍN» guruš ud 1-šè še-bi 15.2.2 gur 3,248 guruš ud 1-šè kug-bi ⅚ ma-na 4 gín 24 še, "464 men for 1 day, their barley is 4,640 liters (= 10 liters of barley per 1 man); 3,248 men for 1 day, their silver is 9,744 grains of silver (= 3 grains of silver per 1 man)" (RSO 83 361 no.

Although a systematic study of hired labor in Ur III times is yet to be written,[45] both the sheer number of references to the use of hirelings[46] and the extant records of the work contributed by them strongly suggest that this form of labor may have been nearly as important economically as the corvée, both within the provincial economies and the royal sector.

A good illustration of the extent to which institutional economies relied on hired labor for their regular operations is TUT 5, an estimate of the expenses incurred by all the major temple households of the province of Girsu/Lagaš in connection with the cultivation of their arable lands over a period of one year. In this source, 523,350 liters of barley are allocated for hired labor, an amount that, at the standard daily wage of six liters, would have been sufficient to purchase 87,225 man-days. This picture is collaborated by the testimony of many other sources, which routinely record purchases of thousands of man-days,[47] sometimes in connection with a single project.[48]

37:1–4); 1,415 guruš ud 1-šè éren dirig 1,533 guruš ud 1-šè kug-ta sa_{10}-a, "1,415 men for 1 day, the extra corvée labor; 1,533 men for 1 day, (the workers) 'purchased' for silver" (Princeton 1 396:1–4); 4.0.0 še gur lugal 10 gín kug-bar_6-bar_6 á lú-hun-gá gi zi zé-dè, "1,200 liters of barley (and) 10 shekels of silver, the wages of the hirelings pulling out fresh reeds" (Princeton 1 568:1–4); [60] guruš hun-gá á $šag_4$-gal-bi 0.3.0 še lugal-ta še-bi 36.0.0 gur Ur-$šag_5$-ga 20 guruš hun-gá kug-bi ½ gín-ta še-bi 0.1.0-ta [...]; "[60] hirelings, the wage of each (man) is 180 liters of barley; their (total) barley is 10,800 liters; (under) Ur-šaga; 20 hirelings, the wage of each (man) is ½ shekel of silver (and) 60 liters of barley" (Princeton 2 34:1–8); ½ gín 10 še kug-babbar kug á hun-gá (SNAT 132:1–2); 1/3 gin kug á lú-hun-gá še-gur_{10}-a (YOS 4 290:12).

45 In fact, I cannot think of any exhaustive discussion of this issue. One of the scholars who considers it briefly is K. Maekawa (1987: 69), who talks of "the recruitment of a vast number of hired laborers in the Ur III period," and concludes that "hired laborers constituted a major source of manpower in the Ur III period."

46 A search for lú-hun-gá, "hireling," in the online BDTNS database (http://bdtns.filol.csis.es/) yields 1,438 attestations. If one expands the search to hun-gá, "hired," the number of relevant examples rises to over 2,000.

47 See, *e.g.*, UDT 56, listing over 96,000 liters of barley = ca. 16,000 man-days (at 6 liters per day).

48 For instance, according to YOS 4 209 ii 8–10, 74,988 liters of barley was spent to purchase 12,498 days of hired labor as part of the earth-works done in the field Igi-É-mah-šè. Cf. further STA 28 iv 1, which records 11,420 liters of barley as á lú-hun-gá = 1,903+ man-days at 6 liters of barley; and MVN 12 192, recording 9,000 liters of barley as á lú-hun-gá = 1,500 man-days at 6 liters of barley.

It is clear that hired labor was predominantly used for unskilled tasks. The most common among those were harvesting, preparation of fields for cultivation, weeding, reed-collecting, irrigation works, transportation, and brick-making. However, there are also fairly frequent mentions of the hire of craftsmen, such as carpenters, reed-workers, leather-workers, felters, potters, and boat-caulkers.[49]

How and from where was the hired labor obtained? This question is not easy to answer, since the information about the hirelings usually is limited to their numbers and the volumes of their wages. Certain facts are clear, however. In the context of provincial economies, many of the hired workers were subordinates of temple households and other local organizations (such as the households of the governors), who, as described earlier, were liable for corvée. After their corvée service (bala) was over, during the remaining part of the year these individuals routinely hired themselves out for wages, most commonly, to the same institutions they were associated with, and to which they owed their corvée.[50] While this was one important source of hired labor, it may be conjectured that significant numbers of hirelings were additionally recruited from among the free populations of other provinces, either those associated with institutional economies or the members of the royal sector.

[49] For the hire of carpenters, see AUCT 1 353:6 (12 gín kug-babbar á šag$_4$-gal nagar); Hirose 343:1–2; SAT 3 1753:1, 2136:3; etc.; for reed-workers (ad-KID), see BPOA 6 1031:3; UTI 5 3151:4; MVN 18 543:4; CUSAS 3 518:2; etc.; for felters (túg-du$_8$), see UET 3 1475:27, 1483:14; etc.; for leather-workers (ašgab), see UET 3 1475:26, 1483:13; etc.; for potters (báhar), see MVN 1 232 i 34; for caulkers (má-GÍN), see AUCT 1 353 1 353:8 (8 gín kug-babbar á má-GÍN). Hires of various craftsmen are also mentioned in the "Laws of Ur-Namma," which stipulate that the daily wage of masons (šidim), carpenters (nagar), leather-workers (ašgab), reed-workers (ad-KID), felters (túg-du$_8$), smiths (simug), fullers (lú-ázlag), silver-smiths (kug-dím), and stone workers (bur-gul) should be 30 liters of barley in the summer, and 20 liters in the winter (Civil 2011: 244 § D1a). Another paragraph regulates the wages of skilled female weavers (géme-uš-bar) (Civil 2011: 244 § D8).

[50] In the sources from Girsu/Lagaš, this period of unemployment is described by the designation éren bala tuš-a, "workers sitting out the corvée duty."

[51] See, *e.g.*, BPOA 7 1669:1–3 (ŠS 3/-): 70 géme hun-gá á 3 sìla-ta géme hun-gá zíd àr-a.

[52] 5,532⅚ géme ud 1-šè géme hun-gá zíd àr-a (SAT 3 1397:1–3; ŠS 3/-). According to BPOA 7 1669 (see the preceding note), which appears to concern the same project, there were seventy géme involved. If so, the project lasted ca. 79 days.

Although the overwhelming majority of hired workers were male, there are also occasional instances of the hire of women. The status of female hirelings, who invariably are designated as géme, is uncertain. Since it is unlikely that they were free citizens (*i.e.*, wives, siblings, or daughters of the individuals bearing the status of éren or dumu-gir$_{15}$), one should probably identify them as dependent menial workers, who had been loaned by their home institutions to other temple households in exchange for wages. The daily wage of a hired female worker apparently was three liters of barley,[51] *i.e.*, one-half of what was received by male hirelings.

While the hires of géme appear to have been rare, the volumes of labor produced in this way could be substantial. In one instance, the hired géme spent 5,532⅚ days processing cereals.[52] In another case, 13,200 liters of barley was paid, over a period of two years, as wages of the géme hired to assist with beer-production.[53] Assuming that the standard daily wage of three liters of barley was used, this amount translated into 4,400 days of labor.[54]

The fact that during the Ur III period large numbers of free individuals regularly traded their labor for wages might perhaps suggest to some scholars that already at that early date there existed, in however a rudimentary form, a "labor market."[55] Such a conclusion would be a gross simplification, however, since the Ur III hires were contracted for the most part within an institutional setting, with both the wages and the mobility of hired workers being closely regulated and controlled by the state.[56] Free agents they certainly were not. A more significant historical-

53 á géme hun-gá lú-ŠIM-ke$_4$-ne (BPOA 1 562:1–9).

54 Other documented cases of hired géme involved smaller numbers of contributed days: 450 (BPOA 7 1590:1–2) and 500 [= 1,500 liters of barley at 3 liters per day] (Ontario 2 198:1–2).

55 See, *e.g.*, Adams 2011: 6–7.

56 It appears that in many such transactions, the "hire" amounted to a loan of labor made by one organization to another. A good illustration here is MVN 2 15, which describes the hire of a ship, a sailor, and ten boat-towers to transport grain from a field belonging to the domain of the Girsu/Lagaš province. One can be certain that neither the ship nor its crew had been hired on free market; rather, both of them had been loaned to the officials in charge of the field by another compartment of Girsu/Lagaš's economy. Thus, in this context "wage" is simply a reimbursement for the loaned labor and physical property (in this case, the ship). Since the individual compartments of the institutional economy had separate budgets, the administrators treated such

ly is the fact that, if hired labor indeed figured so prominently in Ur III times, the alleged contrast between the Ur III economy and that of the Old Babylonian period, in which the hire of workers was a norm, and where the presence of certain labor-market-like mechanisms may in fact be detected, would be considerably less than generally thought.

8. Menial Labor

Within institutional economies and sometimes also in private contexts, an additional source of labor were the menial workers who were permanently attached to temple households and other institutions. Since most of the surviving Ur III and earlier economic sources come from institutional contexts, the activities of the menials are particularly well documented. As a result of this, much of the previous study of the third millennium economy and society centered on this social group. However, the number of menials was comparatively small,[57] and thus their labor contribution was much less than that obtained from corvée or through hire.

The menial workers belonged to both sexes, with the numbers of men and women being roughly equal. The males of this class bore the designation UN-íl, which probably means "carrier." Their female counterparts were called géme, the term also used to describe slave women (see above p. **9**). While the men worked mainly as carriers and boat-towers, the women were employed primarily in weaving and cereal processing. Both groups were routinely assigned to various agricultural tasks as well. Only few of them appear to have been involved in crafts.[58]

It appears that the vast majority of these people were destitute natives (impoverished free men, widows, orphans, foundlings, etc.) who had been compelled by their circumstances to put themselves at the mercy of temples or private households. Some among them had been donated to tem-

internal transfers of labor and goods as "hires." But there are also documented cases of hires outside of institutional environments, in which both the hiring party and the worker clearly were private individuals. For the examples of such transactions, see Steinkeller 2002a: 129 n. 8; TMH NF 1–2 24, 32; NATN 98; AUCT 2 259.

57 *E.g.*, it may be estimated that the total of menials (both male and female) employed by Umma's institutional economy was in the range of ca. 3,000/4,000 individuals. See Steinkeller 2013a: 360.

58 1 UN<-íl> PN nagar tu-ra … á UN-íl tu-ra, "1 UN-íl worker, a carpenter, sick … wages of the sick UN-íl workers" (UET 3 1471:1, 13).

ples by their private patrons or by the state.[59] Most of them probably did not have family life.[60] The menials worked full time and were provided with food allotments. They almost never received land allotments. Because of their total dependence on their home institutions for their livelihood, the status of these individuals was not much different from that of domestic slaves. But, as natives, the menials could not be sold. They also seem to have possessed certain legal and social rights, which made their position somewhat closer to that of the free. But, unlike the latter, the menials had neither economic resources nor professional skills that would allow them to lead an independent existence.

Our data show that the menials (both men and women) worked non-stop throughout the year, being constantly shifted from one assignment to another.[61] In spite of this, because of their modest numbers the work that was extracted from these unfortunates could satisfy only a fraction of total labor needs.

Thus, in one instance a project used 100 man-days of UN-íl labor, as compared with 840 man-days that were contributed to the same undertaking by the hired workers (BE 3 83 iii 1–2). From another case we learn that the yearly labor available to a single agricultural unit (gána-gud) consisted of 9,360 man-days that were contributed by the permanent personnel of that unit (plowmen and their assistants) and of 628 ⅓ man-days that were extracted from the UN-íl workers. In addition, this unit needed to purchase 630 man-days of hired labor (TCL 5 5675 i 1–ii 18). A similar picture emerges from NATN 808:1–3, which seems to come from a royal estate. Among the expenditures recorded there, the barley allotments of the menials (še-ba šag$_4$ é-ne) and the agricultural personnel (še-ba engar-e-ne) amounted to 4,965 liters and 3,000 liters of barley respectively. In contrast, the cost of the hired labor was 9,240 liters of barley, *i.e.*, more than the other two expenditures combined.

It stands to reason that the phenomenon of menial workers was closely connected with the dominant role of temple households and other centralized institutions in economic life, especially in the sphere of agriculture, which was characteristic of southern Babylonia during the

59 See, in general, Gelb 1972.

60 Many of the grown UN-íl workers probably were sons of the unmarried géme. See ASJ 9 315 4:1–9, which concerns a runaway UN-íl, who was the son of a female miller (géme kikkin).

61 Good illustrations here are MVN 10 102 ([níg-ŠID]-ak á UN-íl ... iti 12-kam), UTI 6 3810 (IGI.GAR-ak á UN-íl), and TCL 5 6036 i 17–ii 27.

third millennium BC. To be able to take full advantage of their agricultural potential, these institutions needed to have at their disposal, apart from the plowing teams and other specialized agricultural workers, a permanent reservoir of unskilled laborers who could be used in various capacities throughout the season, mainly to maintain the irrigation system and as a means of transport. This situation changed significantly in Old Babylonian times, when both the temples and the palace ceased to be directly involved in the management of cereal production and other agricultural activity, with those tasks now being performed by private entrepreneurs in their employ. As a consequence, the menial workforce that used to be a permanent fixture of "big institutions" had disappeared, evolving into a class of impoverished—and usually landless—wage earners. Those individuals, known as *muškēnum*, now worked as hirelings for the agents of the palace and prosperous independent farmers, performing the same tasks as the earlier members of the menial class. Like their earlier counterparts, the *muškēnum* were comparatively few; their social status too hovered between that of slaves and free population.[62]

9. Laborers' Remuneration

The last issue that needs to be discussed in this connection are the forms of laborers' remuneration. In essence, the native terminology distinguished only between (1) the salary (usually yearly) that was paid to the workers and their families by their home institution in exchange for their labor contribution and (2) the wages that the same workers earned by hiring themselves out as a form of extra employment (comparable to the modern "overtime"), which they performed either for their home institution or some outside employer (institutional or private). These two forms of remuneration were in principle applicable only to the lower strata of a given institution's employees, who might be considered equivalents of our "blue collar workers." The primary form of remuneration of the higher-ranking employees, who were mainly comprised of administrative personnel, was the income from the land allotments that their home insti-

[62] I refer here to the narrow (legal) sense of *muškēnum*, which is used in the Hammurabi Code and other OB law collections. As the etymology of this term shows, *muškēnum*, "the one who prostrates himself," originally designated a person who assumes the status of dependence vis-à-vis another individual or some institution, most commonly, an impoverished freeman voluntarily agreeing to serve another person in exchange for upkeep and protection.

tution assigned to them in exchange for their services.[63] The size of such allotments—and accordingly, the income from them—depended on recipient's position within the institution in question.

The standard Sumerian word for first type of wages is še-ba, "barley allotment" or "barley share," with its variants siki-ba, "wool allotment," túg-ba, "garment allotment," and ì-ba, "(sesame) oil allotment." The corresponding Akkadian terms are *epru* and *kurummatu*.[64] Writing in 1965, Ignace J. Gelb famously argued that še-ba should be translated as "ration,"[65] in reflection of his position that the grain so distributed represented subsistence food that was used by the "great institutions" to sustain the dependent personnel in their care. This translation has since then been widely (and rather uncritically) adopted by Assyriologists, primarily for the reasons of convenience, since it provides scholars with a snap and easy designation of the various forms of the remuneration in kind that were used in the various periods of Mesopotamian history. In this way, the term "ration" has become deeply ingrained in Assyriology, and has even been adopted by some Egyptologists and students of the Mycenaean society.[66] In spite of its general acceptance and apparent usefulness, however, the word "ration" is highly inappropriate as a description of še-ba, primarily because it misrepresents the economic and social reality behind this phenomenon. As noted earlier, the še-ba was a salary (monthly or yearly) that a given employee received from his home institution as a payment for services rendered, and not a form of organized alimentation.[67] This point is made certain by the fact that the total

[63] Such allotments are designated by the term PAD (to be read šuku or simply pad).

[64] The Akkadian term *kurummatu*, attested since the Old Babylonian period, is commonly written with the Sumerian logogram PAD. It is characteristic that in Ur III times and earlier PAD described strictly land allotments, never referring to the wages paid in kind.

[65] Gelb 1965. Here it may be noted that the translation "barley ration" of še-ba was advocated already some years before the appearance of Gelb's article, in CAD I/J, 166 under *ipru* (1959).

[66] For Egyptology, see, *e.g.*, Kemp 2006: 171. For the Mycenaean studies, see, *e.g.*, Palmer 1989: 90, 117–118; 1992: 481 (references courtesy of Nakassis), who has differentiated between "rations" and "handouts"—the former being subsistence-level allocation of staples, usually grain and figs or olives, and the latter being small supplementary allocations that are below subsistence level.

[67] For this point, see the excellent discussion by Rosemary Prentice (2010), in reference to the conditions in Pre-Sargonic Lagaš.

amounts of grain received as še-ba by individual worker families[68] greatly exceeded their caloric needs, thus demonstrating that only a part of the allotment was actually consumed by a given family. The remainder of it must have been used by the family to acquire other foodstuffs and articles, either through purchase or barter. Moreover, while še-ba is usually mentioned in connection with the lower-ranking employees (most commonly, the menials, for whom see above section 8), not infrequently it was given out also to administrators, scribes, messengers, elite soldiers, and various other individuals enjoying the status of free citizens.[69] There

68 In the lists of worker grain-allotments (especially those from Girsu/Lagaš) one often finds volumes of grain that were additionally given out to the workers' children, some of whom were suckling babies. Such examples allow one to calculate the total compensation received by a given family.

N.b. the fact that the še-ba could be paid to infants and young children, who certainly were incapable of performing any productive work, was one of Gelb's arguments for analyzing the še-ba as a form of alimentation. However, this fact is immaterial for the question at hand. As one might expect from an ancient society, the concept of an autonomous "worker," who was abstracted from his kinship relationships, did not exist in ancient Mesopotamia. It was taken for granted, therefore, that the workers had dependants, and that the presence of such dependents necessitated supplementary increases in the worker's compensation, depending on their number and age. This was in agreement with the spirit of the third millennium socio-economic order, which viewed temple households and other "great organizations" as essentially communal organizations, in which the resources of the household and its income were proportionally shared by all its members, in accordance with their rank and particular contributions. Thus, even though the babies did not work, by virtue of being *bona fide* members of the community, they deserved full economic support.

69 See, *e.g.*, L'uomo 68: 1–3, which lists 102.4.2.5 sìla še-ba gìr-sè-ga énsi lú-níg-dab$_5$ ^{giš}kiri$_6$ èš dil-dil ù lú dil-dil, "30,865 liters of barley, (the monthly) barley allotments of the personnel of the governor, the men authorized to make withdrawals (= some of the top administrators), the orchards' (personnel), (the personnel of) the sundry shrines (in the countryside), and various other individuals"; še-ba dub-sar-e-ne, "the barley allotment of the scribes" (CUSAS 3 394:6–7, 408:2); še-ba A-da-làl dub-sar (UET 3 1094:2); še-ba dub-sar (OrSP 18 pl. 7 24 ii 24); 01.0 še-ba Tur-am-ì-lí sagi, "60 liters of barley, the allotment of Turam-ili, the cup-bearer" (MVN 21 236:1); 3.4.4 še gur še-ba rá-gaba-ne, "1,180 liters of barley, the allotment of the messengers" (Vicino Oriente 8/1 97:1–2); 395.0.0 še-ba nar-e-ne ki Á-bí-la-núm 10.1.0 še-ba àga-ús MAR.TU ki A-bu-ni, "28,500 liters of barley, the allotment of the singers stationed with Apilanum; 3,060 liters of barley, the allotment of the Amorite elite troops stationed with the (general) Abuni" (OrSP 18 pl. 7 24 iii 5–10).

are also instances where the employees usually compensated with land allotments are given the še-ba instead.[70] All these facts assure that še-ba was a form of salary or wages.

Another reason why "ration" is a bad translation of še-ba is the fact that, as universally understood, "rationing" denotes an artificial restriction of demand or consumption, an economic phenomenon that not only has nothing to do with the reality behind še-ba, but also one that taints negatively the nature of the relationship between the recipients of še-ba and the granting party. Because rationing by its very nature is restrictive— and therefore arbitrary and manipulative— that relationship unavoidably is perceived as an exploitive one.[71]

Neither applicable here is the nuance of "ration" as used in military contexts, since, unlike the še-ba, which was a regular form of compensation, military rations are issued ad-hoc to sustain soldiers on particular assignments of short (usually daily) duration.[72]

And last but not least, the translations "rationing" and "ration" should be avoided for the simple reason that, outside of ancient Mesopotamian studies (and to some extent Egyptology and Mycenaean studies), such

[70] See the following example: še-ba engar šag$_4$-gud lú šuku nu-dab$_5$-ba-me, "the barley allotments of the plowing personnel, (their) assistants, and (other) individuals who have not received land allotments" (UET 3 1377:25). A similar case is described in MVN 6 70, where thirty fullers of free-citizen status (which would qualify them to receive land allotments) are each paid 300 liters of barley as their yearly compensation, instead of receiving land allotments (lú-ázlag dumu-gir$_{15}$ šuku nu-dab$_5$-ba-me).

[71] Cf. the following comments by Prentice 2010: 94: "The choice of the word 'rations' to describe the regular distribution of barley (and wool) to the work-force is unfortunate, since, as commonly used, 'rations' have the negative connotation of either being distributed due to a shortage (as in modern times) or to maintain a subservient labour force at a subsistence level. This negative sense is transferred to the recipient of the rations; in one way or another they are 'deprived' persons. Thus, the use of 'rations' to describe the exchange of barley for labour, perhaps unconsciously, prejudices the view of the nature of the exchange which is taking place."

[72] The Sumerian term for this kind of daily sustenance is šag$_4$-gal, which describes both food and animal fodder. This term is particularly common as a description of barley and flour expended to mobilized work-forces (šag$_4$-gal éren bala gub-ba). See, *e.g.*, TUT 171:3; MVN 2 18:19, 72:12; MVN 9 125:2; et passim in Girsu/Lagaš sources. The šag$_4$-gal was also given out as sustenance to various individuals employed on particular assignments (including menial female workers among them), as well as to prisoners (*e.g.*, BE 3 40).

terminological usage is practically unknown. Although similar forms of remuneration in kind existed in many other ancient civilizations, both in the Old and New Worlds, I could not find, in the pertinent historical and anthropological literature, any instances of the use of this terminology in reference to similar phenomena.[73] Thus, if the students of ancient Mesopotamia wish to make themselves understood to the outside fields, they should abandon the term "ration" in favor of another, more appropriate translation. In my view, the best rendering of še-ba and the related terms (such as siki-ba, túg-ba, and ì-ba) is "x allotment," which approximates most closely both the etymology and the economic sense of the Sumerian word.

The question of the terminology describing the compensation earned as a result of hiring out (see above section 7) is much simpler and free of controversy. The Sumerian term here is á, corresponding to *idū* in Akkadian.[74] Both of these terms are to be translated as "wage." As noted at the beginning of this essay, the original sense of á was "arm, strength, power, physical exertion," hence "labor." The meaning "wage" of á was a later development, as were its derived meanings "hire" and "rent." The wages of hired labor were paid predominantly in grain, though, since the Ur III period, the use of silver is documented as well.[75]

10. The reader is now invited to read the individual contributions, which present various case studies of ancient labor. Though ranging widely both in time and space, these cases—at least as I read them—display the presence of remarkably similar threads and phenomena. This suggests that, before the advent of Classical Antiquity, in the states native to the Fertile Crescent and the Mediterranean human labor was

[73] Referring to the conditions in ancient Egypt, Barry J. Kemp (2006:171) suggested that "rations" may be understood as wages in kind, reasoning as follows: "Rations administration lay at the heart of the system. In the absence of money people were paid in kind, in commodities. In effect this was a 'wage,' but on account both of the commodity-based nature of the recompense and the modern connotations of personal economic freedom of the word 'wage,' the term 'rations' is preferable. But the distinction is somewhat artificial." However, this plaidoyer on behalf of "rations" is unconvincing, since, in the Mesopotamian situation at least, the use of commodities was by no means restricted to "rations." Also the wages of hired labor were usually paid in kind.

[74] Another Akkadian term for "wage" is *igru*, which also means "hire, rent."

[75] See above p. 20 and n. 44.

procured, managed, and exploited in very much the same ways. Among those shared characteristics, the immediately apparent are the following ones: the general insignificance of slave labor (all contributions); the prominence of corvée as the primary way of obtaining labor (Lamberg-Karlovsky, Lehner, Sallaberger and Pruß; Steinkeller, Richardson, Goelet); the role of large building projects as a tool of political integration (Lehner, Steinkeller, Richardson, Palaima); the use of hired workers as a way of dealing with the systemic shortage of labor (Steinkeller in this paper; Jursa); the practice of compensating the employees of "great organizations" with the salaries in kind and/or field allotments (Steinkeller Introduction; Sallaberger and Pruß; Goelet; Nakassis; Palaima). The reader, no doubt, will be able to detect many additional commonalities of this kind.

BIBLIOGRAPHY

Abrams, Eliot Marc (1994), *How the Maya Built Their World: Energetics and Ancient Architecture* (Austin: University of Texas).

Adams, Robert McC. (1981), *Heartland of Cities: Surveys of Ancient Settlement and Land Use on the Central Floodplain of the Euphrates* (Chicago: The University of Chicago Press).

— (2011), "Slavery and Freedom in the Third Dynasty of Ur: Implications of the Garšana Archives," in David I. Owen (ed.), *Garšana Studies*, CUSAS 6 (Bethesda MD: CDL Press): 1–9.

Atwood, Roger (2011), "The Real Lessons of Easter Island" (The Times Literary Supplement, 19 October).

Beaulieu, Paul-Alain (2005), "Eanna's Contribution to the Construction of the North Palace at Babylon," in Heather D. Baker and Michael Jursa (eds.), *Approaching the Babylonian Economy: Proceedings of the START Project Symposium, Held in Vienna, 1–3 July 2004*, AOAT 330 (Münster: Ugarit-Verlag): 45–73.

Carrasco, Pedro (1982), "The Political Economy of the Aztec and Inca States," in George A. Collier, Renato I. Rosaldo, and John D. Wirth (eds.), *The Inca and Aztec States, 1400–1800: Archaeology and History* (New York: Academic Press): 23–40.

Civil, Miguel (2011), "The Law Collection of Ur-Namma," in A. R. George (ed.), *Cuneiform Royal Inscriptions and Related Texts in the Schøyen Collection*, CUSAS 17 (Bethesda: CDL Press): 221–310.

Costin, Cathy L. (1996), "Craft Production and Mobilization Strategies in the Inka Empire," in Bernard Wailes (ed.), *Craft Specialization and Social Evolution: In Memory of V. Gordon Childe*, University Museum Monograph 93 (Philadelphia: The University Museum of Archaeology and Anthropology, University of Pennsylvania): 211–225.

D'Altroy, Terrence and Timothy K. Earle (1985), "Staple Finance, Wealth Finance, and Storage in the Inca Political Economy," *Current Anthropology* 26: 187–206.

Diamond, Jared (2005), *Collapse: How Societies Choose to Fail or to Succeed* (London: Penguin Books).

Dietler, Michael (2003), "Clearing the Table: Some Concluding Reflections on Commensal Politics and Imperial States," in Tamara L. Bray (ed.), *The Archaeology and Politics of Food and Feasting in Early States and Empires* (New York: Kluwer Academic / Plenum Publishers): 271–282.

Domar, Evsey D. (1970), "The Causes of Slavery or Serfdom: A Hypothesis," *The Journal of Economic History* 30: 18–32.

Earle, Timothy (1991), "Property Rights and the Evolution of Chiefdoms," in Timothy Earle (ed.), *Chiefdoms: Power, Economy, and Ideology* (Cambridge: Cambridge University Press): 71–99.

Erasmus, Charles J. (1956), "Cultural Structure and Process: The Occurrence and Disappearance of Reciprocal Farm Labor," *Southwestern Journal of Anthropology* 12: 444–471.

— (1965), "Monument Building: Some Field Experiments," *Southwestern Journal of Anthropology* 21: 277–301.

Gelb, Ignace J. (1965), "The Ancient Mesopotamian Ration System," *JNES* 24: 230–243.

— (1972), "The Arua Institution," *RA* 66: 1–32.

— (1973) "Prisoners of War in Early Mesopotamia," *JNES* 32: 70–98.

Gleeson-White, Jane (2012), *Double Entry: How the Merchants of Venice Created Modern Finance* (New York: Norton).

Hallo, William W. (2004), "Bookkeeping in the 21st Century BCE," in Michael Hudson and Cornelia Wunsch (eds.), *Creating Economic Order: Record-keeping, Standardization, and the Development of Accounting in the Ancient Near East* (Bethesda MD: CDL Press): 89–106.

Heimpel, Wolfgang (2009), *Workers and Construction at Garšana*, CUSAS 5 (Bethesda MD: CDL Press).

Hudson and Levine (1996), Michael Hudson and Baruch L. Levine (eds.), *Privatization in the Ancient Near East and Classical World*, Peabody Museum Bulletin 5 (Cambridge MA: Peabody Museum of Archaeology and Ethnology, Harvard University).

Hudson and Levine (1999), Michael Hudson and Baruch L. Levine (eds.), *Urbanization and Land Ownership in the Ancient Near East*, Peabody Museum Bulletin 7, (Cambridge MA: Peabody Museum of Archaeology and Ethnology, Harvard University).

Hudson and Van De Mieroop (2002), Michael Hudson and Marc Van de Mieroop (eds.), *Debt and Economic Renewal in the Ancient Near East* (Bethesda MD: CDL Press).

Hudson and Wunsch (2004), Michael Hudson and Cornelia Wunsch (eds.), *Creating Economic Order: Record-keeping, Standardization, and the Development of Accounting in the Ancient Near East* (Bethesda MD: CDL Press).

Hunt, Terry L. and Carl Lipo (2011), *The Statues that Walked: Unraveling the Mystery of Easter Island* (New York: Free Press).

Jones, Charles E. and Matthew W. Stolper (2008), "How Many Persepolis Fortification Tablets are There?," *Persica* 12: 27–50.

Karlsson, Mattias (2013), *Early Neo-Assyrian State Ideology: Relations of Power in the Inscriptions and Iconography of Ashurnasirpal II (883–859) and Shalmaneser III (858–824)* (Uppsala: Uppsala University).

Kemp, Barry J. (2006), *Ancient Egypt: Anatomy of a Civilization* (London: Routledge).

Kolchin, Peter (1987), *Unfree Labor: American Slavery and Russian Serfdom* (Cambridge MA: Harvard University Press).

Lambeck, Kurt (1996), "Shoreline Reconstructions for the Persian Gulf since the Last Glacial Maximum," *Earth and Planetary Science Letters* 142: 43–57.

Larsen, Mogens T. (1976), *The Old Assyrian City-State and Its Colonies*, Mesopotamia 4 (Copenhagen: Akademisk Forlag).

Lewis, Mark Edward (2007), *The Early Chinese Empires: Qin and Han* (Cambridge MA: Harvard University Press).

Loewe, Michael (2005), *Everyday Life in Early Imperial China during the Han Period 202 BC-AD 220* (Indianapolis: Hackett Publishing Co.).

Maekawa, Kazuya (1988), "Collective Labor Service in Girsu-Lagash: The Pre-Sargonic and Ur III Periods," in Marvin A. Powell (ed.), *Labor in the Ancient Near East*, American Oriental Series 68 (New Haven: American Oriental Society): 49–71.

Murra, John V. (1982), "The *Mit'a* Obligations of Ethnic Groups to the Inka State," in George A. Collier, Renato I. Rosaldo, and John D. Wirth (eds.), *The Inca and Aztec States, 1400–1800: Archaeology and History* (New York: Academic Press): 237–262.

Nieboer, Herman J. (1910), *Slavery as an Industrial System: Ethnological Researches,* 2nd revised ed. (The Hague: Martinus Nijhoff).

Nissen, Hans J. (1988), *The Early History of the Ancient Near East 9000–2000 B.C.* (Chicago: The University of Chicago Press).

Palmer, Ruth (1989), "Subsistence Rations at Pylos and Knossos," *Nibnos* 24: 89–124.

— (1992) "Wheat and Barley in Mycenaean Society," in J.-P. Olivier (ed.), *Mykenaïka. Actes du IXe Colloque international sur les textes mycéniens et égéens, Centre de l'Antiquité Grecque et Romaine de la Fondation Hellénique des Recherches Scientifiques et École française d'Athènes*, BCH Suppl. 25 (Paris: Diffusion de Boccard): 475–497.

Parpola, Simo (1995), "The Construction of Dur-Šarrukin in the Assyrian Royal Correspondence," in Annie Coubet (ed.), *Khorsabad, le palais de Sargon II, roi d'Assyrie*, Actes du colloque organisé au Musée du Louvre par le Services Culturel les 21 et 22 janvier 1994 (Paris: La documentation Française): 47–77.

Postgate, J. N. (1974), *Taxation and Conscription in the Assyrian Empire* (Rome: Biblical Institute Press).

Prentice, Rosemary (2010), *The Exchange of Goods and Services in Pre-Sargonic Lagash*, AOAT 368 (Münster: Ugarit-Verlag).

Sanlaville, Paul (2002), "The Deltaic Complex of the Lower Mesopotamian Plain and Its Evolution through Millennia," in Emma Nicholson and Peter Clark (eds), *The Iraqi Marshlands: A Human and Environmental Study* (London: Politico's Pub.): 133–150.

Sahlins, Marshall (1972), *Stone Age Economics* (Chicago: Aldine Publishing Company).

Sharlach, Tonia M. (2004), *Provincial Taxation and the Ur III State*, Cuneiform Monographs 26 (Leiden: Brill).

Soll, Jacob (2014), *The Reckoning: Financial Accountability and the Rise and Fall of Nations* (New York: Basic Books).

Steinkeller, Piotr (2002a), "Money Lending Practices in the Ur III Period: The Issue of Economic Motivation," in Michael Hudson and Marc Van de Mieroop (eds.), *Debt and Economic Renewal in the Ancient Near East* (Bethesda MD: CDL Press): 109–137.

— (2002b), "Archaic City Seals and the Question of Early Babylonian Unity," in Tzvi Abusch (ed.), *Riches Hidden in Secret Places: Ancient Near Eastern Studies in Memory of Thorkild Jacobsen* (Winona Lake IN: Eisenbrauns): 249–257.

— (2013a), "Corvée Labor in Ur III Times," in Steven Garfinkle and Manuel Molina (eds.), *From the 21st Century BC to the 21st Century AD: Proceedings of the International Conference on Neo-Sumerian Studies Held in Madrid, 22–24 July 2010* (Winona Lake IN: Eisenbrauns): 347–424.

— (2013b), "The Archaic 'Prisoner Plaque' from Kiš," *RA* 107: 131–157.

Stol, Marten (1995),"Old Babylonian Corvée (*tupšikkum*)," in Th. P. J. van den Hout and J. de Roos (eds.), *Studio Historiae Ardens: Ancient Near Eastern Studies Presented to Philo H. J. Houwink ten Cate on the Occasion of His 65th Birthday* (Leiden: Nederlands Historisch-Archaeologisch Instituut te Istanbul): 293–308.

Streck, Michael P. (2010), "Großes Fach Altorientalistik: Der Umfang des keilschriftlichen Textkorpus," *MDOG* 142: 35–58.

Temin, Peter (2006), "The Economy of the Early Roman Empire," *Journal of Economic Perspectives* 20: 133–151.

Udy, Stanley H. (1959), *Organization of Work: A Comparative Analysis of Production Among Nonindustrial Peoples* (New Haven CT: Human Relations Area Files Press).

Veenhof, Klaas R. (1972), *Aspects of Old Assyrian Trade and Its Terminology* (Leiden: Brill).

— (1997), "'Modern' Features in Old Assyrian Trade," *JESHO* 40: 337–366.

— (1999), "Silver and Credit in Old Assyrian Trade," in J. G. Dercksen (ed.), *Trade and Finance in Ancient Mesopotamia* (Leiden: Nederlands Historisch-Archaeologisch Instituut te Istanbul): 55–83.

Williams, Eric (1994), *Capitalism & Slavery*; with a new introduction by Colin A. Palmer; first published 1944 (Chapel Hill: University of North Carolina Press).

Wittfogel, Karl A. (1963), *Oriental Despotism: A Comparative Study of Total Power* (New Haven: Yale University Press).

1.

Labor, Social Formation and the Neolithic Revolution

C. C. Lamberg-Karlovsky
Harvard University

"All economic activities have their magic"
Bronislaw Malinowski 1961 (73)

The material world recovered by the archaeologist, whether biological remains, plants, animals, fish, shells, or manufactured artifacts, temples or tools, are all the product of labor. In laboring to produce these items whether for food or shelter humanity involves itself in the creation of a materialist world. Man's interaction with nature transforms it, provides his agricultural subsistence, and produces material life itself. Having said that, however, we have said nothing of the *structure* in which labor was organized within the community. Labor may be full-time or part-time. It may be skilled or unskilled, annual or seasonal. Or it may be attached, wherein the product of the labor is "owned" by an institution, *i.e.*, a temple household, feudal lord, or slave master; or labor may be unattached, as with a "commodity" that can be bought or bartered.

Labor within the modern context takes several perspectives: labor as enforced, plantation labor as colonized, labor as structured, labor as local or distant. Labor forms the crux for considering mercantilism, colonialism, capitalism, socialism, class formation and structure and is perceived as coercive, free, or unequally distributed. Labor can be considered as a site of social struggle involving gender, age, identity, agency, and class. In considering labor as intertwined with all of the above it is an experience of multiple and often contradictory relations. For an excellent discussion of labor in the modern context, see Anthony Giddens 1971. It is important to appreciate at the outset that the complexity of dealing with labor as reconstructed from the archaeological record, offers immediate constraints, particularly in the absence of written texts.

In recent decades our understanding of the Neolithic (ca. 10,000–5,000 BC) has been dramatically transformed. Indeed, in recent years few themes within archaeology as the "Neolithic Revolution" (Childe 1936), involving as it does the domestication of plants and animals and the concomitant transformation of village life, are subject to more research, dramatic recovery of new data, and creative theory. In mid-twentieth century the Neolithic began ca. 5,000 BC It was believed that the population of Neolithic villages numbered only in the hundreds, occurring in a restricted geographical region, referred to as a "nuclear area," from which it diffused throughout the rest of the Old World (Braidwood 1967). Neolithic villages were conceived of as self-sufficient egalitarian communities. Today, the Neolithic Revolution begins ca. 10,000 BC. The populations of Neolithic villages number in the thousandss, and the domestication of plants and animals occurs as independent processes in a number of regions throughout the Old World. Most dramatically, Neolithic villages are neither self-sufficient nor egalitarian. By 7,500 BC there is a settlement hierarchy of large villages in excess of 10 hectares to ones of a hectare; a network of trade unites the communities in the exchange of desirable resources, *i.e.*, obsidian, flint, limestone and shell, while some communities appear to be specialized with respect to ritual functions and the production of new materials, *i.e.*, copper implements. The Neolithic is no longer conceived of as a "Revolution" of short duration representing a rapid transformation from hunter-gatherer to farmer. The Neolithic is its own *longue durée*, a millennia long process of increasing population, social complexity and technological innovation. As discussed below there are even some archaeologists who refer to the Neolithic manifestation as characterized by "cities" with a distinctive "civilization." Agricultural adaptations, newly constructed ideological beliefs, and technological innovations are but three features that looked to and required new structures in the organization of specialized labor.

Recently, Steven Kuhn and Mary Stiner (2006) advanced an intriguing hypothesis that confronts the very origins of the division of labor. They suggest that the roots of Neanderthal extinction may be found in the difference in the division of gender/age related labor compared to modern *H. sapiens*. In this view, a gender- and age-based division of labor, emerging around 40,000–50,000 years ago, resulted in *H. sapiens* adopting a wider resource base, *i.e.*, the hunting of smaller prey. Thus, a shift from a narrow reliance on large game that continued to characterize Neanderthal subsistence, to a marked increase in the exploitation of small game provided a demographic advantage and an expanded population of *H. sapiens* throughout Eurasia. In this scenario males and females of the Middle Paleolithic, whether Neanderthal or *H. sapiens*, both were engaged in narrowly focused economies; the labor of men and women, of both hominins, was closely aligned. In the following Upper Paleolithic more broadly based economies emerge, signaling a wider range of economic and technological roles within *H. sapiens* populations. An emerging reliance on smaller animals, and a greater reliance on vegetal and seed resources, is believed to signal a gendered division of labor. Men hunt large prey; women and children hunt small animals and forage for consumables. This initial division of labor by gender and age in turn contributed to the evolutionary success of *H. sapiens.*

Within an evolutionary context the specialization of labor by gender is attested already among chimpanzees (Waal 2005). The alpha male maintains authority through his control of violence, by repeatedly facing down challenging subordinates. He protects the group-territory by consolidating co-operation for common defense. Females, on the other hand, cross group boundaries to mate, thereby assuring the dissemination of genes among larger groups. The role of labor in "the state of nature" was speculated upon by Thomas Hobbes (1997) in the middle of the seventeenth century:

> In such condition, there is no place for industry; because the fruit thereof is uncertain: and consequently no culture of the earth; no navigation, nor use of the commodities that may be imported by sea; no commodious building, no instruments of moving, and removing such things as require much force; no knowledge of the face of the earth; no account of time; no arts; no letters; no society; and which is worst of all, continual fear, and danger of violent death; and the life of man, solitary, poor, nasty, brutish and short.

Hobbes' perpetual state of war was replaced in the nineteenth century when cultural anthropologists situated non-industrial societies along an evolutionary time line in which bands, tribes, chiefdoms, states, kingdoms, empires and industrial states succeeded each other in a spiral of increasing cultural complexity. Such schemes encouraged both European ethnocentrism and a racism that the evolutionary hierarchy implied.

The division of labor on the basis of age and/or sex is related to the degree of labor specialization. V. Gordon Childe (1939) recognized only two forms of labor: specialized and unspecialized. Eliot Chapple and Carleton Coon (1942) refined this by defining three degrees of specialization:

1. None. Each individual performs the needs of labor utilizing the techniques known to all other members of the group irrespective of sex and age;
2. Part-time. An individual spends part of his/her time performing some specialized technique for the production of a commodity. This commodity can, in turn, be produced as a surplus utilized in exchange;
3. Full-time. The individual is a full-time specialist mastering specialized techniques for the production of a single commodity. He/she barters/trades/ or is given rations/wages in return for the commodity.

There is a second distinction to be made with regard to the full-time specialization of labor. This involves the segmentation of techniques. A distinction is made between those who perform only a part of a complete technique and those who carry an entire process to completion. The first type of specialist is by far the most common. In metallurgy, for example, it is seldom that a single specialist smelts the ore and forges it into a tool. Specialists at the site of the ore deposit typically do smelting while different specialists, who can be hundreds of miles away in a settlement, undertake forging. As the number of specialists and the complexity of techniques in a population increases, so does the segmentation of techniques. The complexity of the interaction of laborers, in turn, gives rise to the need for administering labor. The interaction, communication, and coordination of labor becomes necessary with increased labor specialization and a concomitant increase in its segmentation.

The division and specialization of labor is also related to trade. A specialist has to trade to get rid of his/her surplus. Such trade may be simple or complex. Simple direct trade is when one person gives another something he has gathered, raised, or made in return for a second person's product. There is a profound quantitative difference between this and complex indirect trade, which involves labor in the production of commodities within a market economy in which supply and demand are related to prices and wages. Several of the articles in this book discuss labor within that context. Lastly, the environment directly determines the degree to which a population develops a division of labor and trade. Jared Diamond (2005, 2006) points to the opportunities and constraints that environments play in the evolution and collapse of cultural complexity.

Differences in the complexity of technologies, that is, the adjustment of different cultures to their landscape are quantitative, functionally variable, and reflect differential complexity of human societies. A deciding factor in labor relations is the degree of specialization. Specialists working on a single technique develop advanced skills creating significant innovations. They can also produce a greater number of goods, thereby facilitating surplus, which in turn gives rise to exchange and specialists in trade. Thus, the degree of specialization and the extent of trade are functionally interrelated. As techniques are improved it may take hundreds of laborers to complete the full production process, while only an elite few may use or even see the final product. In the final analysis we can measure the relative complexity of a society in terms of the amount of time and energy expended in labor, specialization and commerce, and in the proportion of specialists and traders within a community (see White 1973 for further discussion).

Within the early Neolithic it is generally assumed that the ownership of land allowed for both communal ownership and an equal access to resources. In the absence of formal hierarchies the rights of possession were symmetrical. Fig. 1 (adopted from Sack 1986: 61) depicts the reciprocal circulation of resources, labor, and finished products.

The division of labor and the emergence of specialized labor for the production of commodities require a few words concerning the Labor Theory of Value (LTV). At the outset it is important to state that the LTV cannot profitably be investigated within the context of either the Paleolithic or the Neolithic. The archaeological evidence is insufficiently detailed to do justice to the theory. However, an understanding of the LTV allows us to *speculate* on the structure of labor within the Neolithic. This much discussed theory, central to the ideas of John Locke, Adam Smith, David Ricardo and Karl Marx, puts forth the following conceptual model:

In a given village everyone shares a set of skills and all products are derived from local resources. Each person pursues a particular trade, but is capable of pursuing any other trade undertaken in the village. Villagers exchange their products on a regular basis. The time necessary to produce their own products and the time needed to produce all other products are known to all villagers, along with how much of their product would be necessary to exchange for any other product. Thus, every commodity is proportionate to the quantity of labor needed for its production, thereby reducing different quantities of labor to a single standard of value.

The LTV leads to considerations of prices, exploitation, alienation, wages, supply and demand, all forming central components of classical economic theory. In the 20th century the LTV has been superseded by the theory of marginal utility. In examining labor within the context of an archaeologically reconstructed Neolithic village, the above concerns

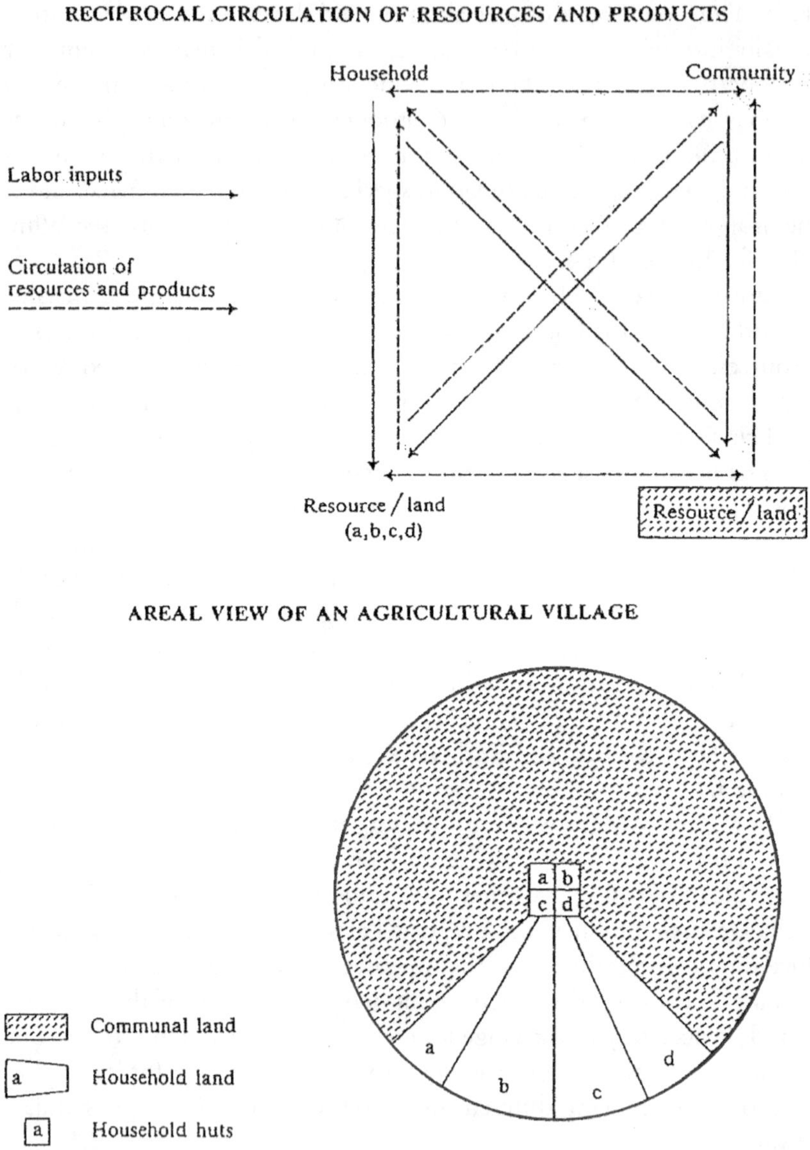

Fig. 1: Egalitarian Economics: reciprocity among household, community and resource(s)/land

have less than a marginal utility. Debates concerning LTV and its role in the evolution of economic theory are coherently reviewed by Joseph Schumpeter in his classic study *Capitalism, Socialism and Democracy* (1950, see also 1908). We can now move backward some 9,000 years ago to the reconstructed and imagined world of the Neolithic.

The presence of written texts offers a considerable opportunity for narrating the manner by which labor was structured in antiquity (Powell 1987). The essays in this volume attest to both the richness of such evidence and the contest of their interpretation. But what can we say in the absence of texts? How does the artifact transform itself into an interpretive object that allows for an understanding of its social context as labor?

Each society has embedded within it specific forms for the structure of labor. On the one hand, society defines the nature of labor while, on the other hand, the structure of labor defines the nature of society. Marx's notion that class struggle is the driving force of human history is enshrined in the first sentence of his Communist Manifesto: "The story of all human society is the history of the class struggle." Class struggle, however, is merely the outward expression of the development of the productive forces within society and these, in turn, have their origin within the "labor-power" of society. Labor, according to Marx, was not historical but a natural-biological force released through man's "metabolism with nature." For Marx's labor concept as "an eternal nature imposed necessity without which there can be no metabolism between man and nature, and therefore no life," see Capital vol. 1 part 1, Chapters 1 and 5. Marx and Darwin shared the mid-nineteenth century refusal to accept anything "as it is," favoring the interpretation that everything is only a stage of a further development. Darwin's idea of man as the product of a *natural* development is not unlike Marx's notion that *historical* development is the result of class struggle. The development of classes was intimately related to the development of different forms of labor that characterized, in turn, different stages of societal evolution. Darwin's introduction of the concept of development in nature—his insistence that in biology movement is not circular but linear—means that nature is being swept into history and that natural life can be considered historical. Marx turned this notion on its head and posited that historical life can be seen as part of nature. Thus the "natural" law of the survival of the fittest is just as much a historical law as the survival of the most progressive class. Engels could think of no greater compliment than to refer to Marx as the "Darwin of history … just as Darwin discovered the law of the development of organic life, so Marx discovered the law of the development of human history" (quoted in Arendt 2004: 597).

Prior to Marx most political philosophers viewed labor in a pejorative manner. Aristotle considered slaves and laborers as necessary but disqualified them from full citizenship, while Immanuel Kant took the view that working for a wage placed the laborer under someone else's will, thus disqualifying him from citizenship. For Marx the creative and revolutionary force in history is *homo faber*. The power of labor changes the material world and frees the individual. Marx was first to emphasize the fact that man works upon nature (agriculture) to satisfy his needs and comes to produce material life through the interaction of the physical world and labor: "The satisfaction of the first need (the action of satisfying, and the instrument of satisfaction which has been acquired), leads to new needs, and this production of new needs is the first historical act" (Marx, *German Ideology*, p. 156, quoted in Tucker 1972). It is within this recognition that the Marxist thesis holds that labor and the means of production are the primary movers of history.

Stages in the development of society are inextricably interwoven with that enduring canon of social evolution, the notion of "progress," the history of which is so well traced by Robert Nisbet (1980). The Paris Universal Exposition of 1889 underscored the principle of progress, "la marche générale de l'humanité." There, cultures and civilizations were divided into those that contributed to the march and those that did not. A single event separated the former from the latter, the Aryan invasion. The author of the exposition's catalogue, Charles Garnier, put it this way: "The people of the Aryan race ... were animated by a more liberal, more expansive spirit, and their discoveries, their progress has become the common good of humanity" (Ammann 1889: 28).

Progress of a distinctly technological sort belonged to the Gauls, Germans, Greek, Romans, Hindu and Persians, while "contemporary civilizations of primitive cultures" (*ibid.*) included Native Americans, Eskimos and the cultures of Africa, Japan, China, and the "immobilized" Semitic peoples. The exposition depicted "the stages of the genius of man" as the development from purely manual labor to the creation of specialized tools, and finally, the mechanical-industrial engines that transformed labor in the nineteenth century.

Long before the influence of Lewis Henry Morgan and V. Gordon Childe (1939), a modernist notion existed which has it that new technologies generate not only progress but also new social relations. Can we perhaps reverse this notion to suggest that new social relations, *i.e.*, new structures of labor create a need for new technologies? A consideration of the origins of agriculture allows us to posit the co-evolution of changing technologies and social structures as an intertwined narrative. The co-evolution of technology and social structure privileges neither as causal, but posits that society defines the nature of labor, while labor gives definition to a specific form of society.

It is not objects so much as images that are missing from the archaeological site, images that reflect theory portraying environmental reconstructions, climatic changes, demographic shifts, settlement pattern densities, and finally the very nature of a society and its organization. I wish to offer here an image of labor derived from my reading of the archaeological record of the late Neolithic (Pre-Pottery Neolithic B=PPNB, 10,600–8,400 BC). The transition from hunting and foraging to farming is one of the most transforming human events—the Neolithic Revolution. It is a process that endured in the eastern Mediterranean from the Natufian of the Levant (14,600–12,000 B.P.), planting the seeds of change to the Pre-Pottery Neolithic and the first farming communities. It was within the Pre-Pottery Neolithic A = PPNA, 12,000–10,500 B.P., communities that staple foods, cereals and legumes, were first cultivated. From an historical point of view, cereal domestication preceded animal domestication. The domestication of animals, *i.e.*, sheep, goat, and pig, seem not to be present before the middle of the ninth millennium, several centuries after some human groups began a sedentary life with cereal and legume domestication (Vigne 2008). Nevertheless, hunting still made up a considerable contribution of the Neolithic diet. The growth of population is documented by an increase in the size of the largest settlements, ca. 3.0 hectares, containing up to a hundred people within the PPNA community. Dramatic changes were at hand in the later PPNB.

For over a century it has been a canonical belief that the transition to agriculture was associated with a population increase. While this remains true, an understanding of the process and its complexity is a more recent advance (Bocquet-Appel and Bar-Yosef 2008). What is termed the "Neolithic Demographic Transition" (NDT) is now seen as a two-stage process. An initial stage of rapid population growth (within the earliest stages of the PPNB), lasting for less than a millennium, followed by a significant decline in population growth (the terminal phase of the PPNB and throughout the PPNC) (Bandy 2008). The first stage resulted in the development of "megasite" settlements, *e.g.*, Çatal Hüyük with a population of 3,000–8,000, or Basta and Abu Hureyra with populations of ca. 4,000, while the later sites of the PPNC never exceed 1,000 (Hershkovitz and Gopher 2008). Rapid population growth would have presented a challenge to the social organization of the community. Tensions involving possession or access to fertile land, water, seed, storage facilities, and emergent crafts would have led to increasing conflict both within and between communities. Such conflict would, in turn, necessitate management mechanisms for the control or exercise of hostilities. The archaeological record readily confirms that such mechanisms of management were of a religious and ritual character. Elaborate architecture, as at Göbekli Tepe, attest to entire communities dedicated, at least in part, to ritual (see below). Ritual, in turn, offered fabricators and practitioners controlling the sacred ideology an authoritative voice, namely power, in community affairs. That the transition to agriculture was not entirely a positive affair is suggested by the fact that there was a clear reduction in health status from the Natufian to the Neolithic. An increase in infectious diseases and nutritional deficiencies is well documented (Hershkovitz and Gopher 2008).

The Neolithic Revolution had a profound impact on changing patterns in the relationship of labor. The emergence of the PPNB was, in part, the result of economic intensification, a demographic growth, an optimizing climate, and new forms of labor organization. The emergence of food production required new craft specialists for the production of new agricultural implements: mortars, pestles, bifacial tools, sickles, hoes; for the manufacture of ceramic vessels for storage and cooking; for scheduling the planting and harvesting of the crops; for the construction of new architectural structures for storage and security for agricultural and animal products, as well as for elaborated ritual activities. In the late PPNB the archaeological record attests to a considerable expansion in both the number and the size of communities. Certain sites, *e.g.*, Basta, Ain Ghazal, and Çatal Hüyük, attain sizes of 10–15 hectares, more than doubling the size of earlier communities and attesting to both increased sedentism, population growth and subsistence intensification. Sites now indicate the presence of specialized storage facilities, two-story buildings, and structures clearly dedicated to ritual activities. Goat, sheep, cattle and pigs are domesticated while the transport of domesticated animals to Cyprus is indicated on the site of Shillourokambos. This early PPNB Cypriot site has pig, dog, cat, fallow deer, sheep, goat, cattle as well as barley, einkorn and emmer, all transported by boat from the mainland. The settlement consists of circular houses with wells dug to a depth of 5m and collective burials. The colonization of newly inhabited regions, as on Cyprus, are complimented by recent genetic studies that indicate the presence of multiple regions within the Near East that were involved in the process of domesticating animals and plants. Thus, three centers for domestication are postulated for goats (Joshi et al. 2004). For plants, Fuller (2008) observes: "Different species of wheat not only represent separate origins and dispersals but also present different potential in cooking and consumption." Thus, *T. aestivum* has superior bread-making qualities, being lighter and spongier, while *T. durum* is hardier and more drought resistant. One must imagine that the spread of such specialized knowledge, and the communication that allowed for sharing information among distant communities, unfolded as a punctuated process, one that allowed for different structures of organization and specialization of labor which, in turn, benefited and/or disadvantaged different communities.

Seed selection is an important matter of decision-making. Farming necessitates agro-ecological considerations, *i.e.*, productivity of the seed, soil, etc., but also socio-cultural concerns. David Mosse (2006: 92) put it well: crop development "is premised on the isolation of seed characteristics from the full range of factors involved in the social practice of cultivation, which include not only localized, contingent, and short term agro-ecological factors but also the negotiations of social relations for input supply and credit and managing debt relations, family obligations, gender relations, or market connections." Seed selection, and for that matter choices of animal use, are not merely matters of agro-ecology, but involve social functions driven by kin, political and economic concerns as well. Thus, seed selection stands as one of many examples that could be cited in which cultural practice may trump material gain. Within the agricultural community the manner in which the decision making plays out affects both the structure and the relations of labor (G. D. Stone 2006).

Evidence of the emergence of agriculture suggests a mosaic of processes involving a considerable geographic space, from southern Israel to central Anatolia, the upper Euphrates, and the Zagros Mountains of Iran and Iraq, as well as time, from ca. 10,000 to 8,000 BC Such processes involved local domestication(s) of plants and animals, the dispersal of agro-pastoral peoples between different regions and cultures, and the adoption of food production by indigenous hunters and gatherers. One can only imagine the profound impact these processes had on the transformation of labor. Agriculture required more specialized knowledge, greater full-time commitment to specific tasks, and the division of labor by gender, while allowing for greater numbers to live a sedentary existence within communities of emerging inequality, social hierarchy and conflict. The substantial changes in the PPNB archaeological record, evident in increasing settlement size, specialized architectural features (*i.e.*, storage facilities, ritual centers) or material remains (see below), suggest major shifts in the development of labor relations, property ownership, and population increase and/or aggregation.

Even before human history depended on the differentiation between villages and urban dweller, an important distinction took place *within* the village. A distinction that formed the nascent emergence of a hierarchy included, on the one hand, a village elite and on the other, commoners. Separate, isolated villages could not hope to secure their harvests or safeguard their territory unless a polity of specialists, including practitioners of the supernatural as well as of violence, were present to protect them. Equipping rituals with suitable artifacts brought about the need for artisan skills and specialist craftsmen. Protection from natural disasters by specialists claiming control of the supernatural mattered most, and was universally present. Supernatural sanction, confirmed and certified by specialist practitioners, offered not only the legitimacy of rule, but the structure of order within the earliest villages. If protection from natural disasters was essential, so was the efficient cooperation of the community in defense of its territory. In later times, within the Mesopotamian context (and many others), a symbiotic relationship wed priest to the military. On the one hand, supernatural sanctions were confirmed by priests who legitimated military rule and conquest. On the other hand, the military protected the priests from internal and external threats.

Within the agricultural villages of the PPNB issues of land tenure must have arisen. Who controlled access to the land? Were there formalized means of transferring land rights from one generation to the next? How was labor mobilized? Who controlled the acquisition and distribution of the resource that were obtained from a distance? On many of the sites one can distinguish distinctive activity areas: storage, craft production, cooking facilities, ritual vs. residential-domestic space, as well as resources procured from distant regions, *e.g.*, obsidian from Anatolia. In spite of such architectural and artifactual distinctions, Goring-Morris and Belfer-Cohen (2008: 156) conclude that within the PPNB "still we have no evidence whatsoever of any sort of hierarchical scale of domestic units." Similarly, Ian Kuijt (2011), Trevor Watkins (2008), among others, would have us believe in an egalitarian harmonious PPNB world in which conflict, hierarchy, emulation and competition did not exist. To the contrary, the archaeological evidence points to the emergence of a nascent "peer polity interaction" (Renfrew 1986), that is, the emergence of hierarchy in settlement, status, wealth and power. Given Alan Simmons

(2007: 124), admittedly conjectural but rather low PPNB settlement/population projections of over 200 villages of 200+ people and 15 mega sites of 3,500+ people, it is impossible to conceive, both within and between such settlements, the absence of conflict, hierarchy and "scaler stress" (Johnson 1977).

Raid and trade remained alternatives for obtaining goods from a distance. The presence of trade goods within the PPNB attests to an increased elastic demand for shells, minerals, flint and timber obtained from the hinterland. Demand for distant resources, organized by local elites, allowed for an increasing regional specialization in manufactured goods. The increasing integration of a web of communication and interaction altered older patterns. Hierarchies of command, both within and between villages, involved larger and larger numbers resulting in shifting patterns of self-assertion and submission. We need not await the village-urban continuum to confront the presence of hierarchy, labor specialization, inequality, violence and territoriality. They can be documented within the context of the PPNB. Steven LeBlanc (2011: 15) has correctly assessed the role of violence and warfare: "thus, stories that depict an age of peace in antiquity, or peaceful foragers, or warfare as a disease of modern society, or the ideal that human evolution took place in a peaceful environment are all erroneous." In later times, with the emergence of cities, the scale of such differences changes by several orders of magnitude—and with it the complexity of civilization.

The dramatic changes documented in the archaeological record of the PPNB, when contrasted with earlier periods, allow us to examine the material record and extrapolate the nature of an emerging social complexity dependent on an increasing specialization of labor. The existence of individual storage facilities within households suggests private ownership of agricultural produce. This does not, however, mean that the lands were privately owned. The stored produce may simply be an individual or a family share derived from communally-owned agricultural land. Given the archaeological evidence within the PPNB for specialized ritual activities, increased resource utilization and the emergence of wholly new technologies (see below), it is not inappropriate to suggest the emergence of social inequality. This inequality, in turn calls for class structures that both result from and cause different labor relations.

The questions asked are worthy of attention yet the answers can only be tentative, or even entirely speculative. Labor can be seen as organization and organization can result from directed labor. Typically within the Neolithic the household, the "oikos," is seen as the unit of labor and of organization. V. Gordon Childe (1936) viewed the Neolithic Revolution as a benign undertaking where land was communally owned, labor corporately organized and social organization egalitarian, *i.e.* wherein collective leadership dominated. Following Marx, Childe believed that the LTV structured production. However, within the PPNB there is evidence to suggest that collective leadership is becoming, if not already, hierarchical.

How does collective leadership become hierarchical? Competition for resources, warfare, military success, religion, ritual, and the role of legitimation are but a few of the avenues that give way to an emerging hierarchy. The evidence for any of the above is both limited and limiting. One may suggest competition for resources, but documenting its existence is elusive. Of warfare one can only say that the absence of evidence is not the evidence of absence. One might recall that for the third millennium, when conflict and warfare are thematic in the texts, the archaeological evidence for its prevalence is all but absent.

Was labor in the PPNB part-time or full-time? Was it specialized? Was it a commodity given in return for food allotments? Were there slaves? Was labor attached to an institution in return for subsistence? Was that institution a social unit, *i.e.*, a family, clan or administrative bureaucracy such as a temple? We are at a loss to answer any of the above questions in a specific manner. However, the evidence for an increasing specialization of labor results in wholly new and specialized activities that allow one to posit increasing social inequality. Labor and its structure shape the social landscape, organizes time, and calls forth a managerial class for its control. Labor can, on the one hand, be seen as the cause of social change and, on the other hand, the effect of social change. The difference is highly significant with regard to the role of labor within any society. Within the PPNB we are unable to distinguish the degree of full-time vs. part time labor, or the degree to which labor was specialized. We can, however, offer the following observations that lead to certain conclusions.

1. Agricultural labor refines the structure of time, necessitating more accurate calendrics for the harvesting and sowing of plants as well as for the managing of herds and their pasturelands.
2. New tools become essential for sowing and harvesting, as well as for tilling the soil, for reaping, winnowing, and grinding and for transport of the harvest.
3. Agriculture also requires storage facilities of a specialized and secure nature, free from insects, rodents, fire, theft, etc.

4. With the domestication of animals labor is invested in shelters, materials for tethering, provisioning of food, and care for their general maintenance.
5. The increase in both the size and the number of settlements in the PPNB required the construction of more houses, thus the production of more mudbrick, the collection of soil, water and temper, as well as the collection of suitable stone for the construction of very substantial stone houses, *e.g.*, at Basta.
6. The production of mudbricks and lime plaster on an industrial scale would have required a considerable labor force involved in a multiplicity of tasks. The lime plaster was used for coating (and multiple re-coatings) of the floors (and walls?) of houses. This labor-intensive enterprise involved the collecting of tons of limestone, crushing it to manageable size, collecting firewood to heat a kiln to over 800°F for several days in order to reduce the limestone to a powder. Limestone was additionally used to manufacture bowls and to produce figurines.
7. Land clearance (tree felling for fire wood, construction, tools, and for the pyrotechnology industry: lime plaster) was a labor-intensive undertaking that took different forms. Clearing open fields for community construction and agriculture differed from the deforestation that fueled pyrotechnological industries, *i.e.*, plaster production. Wood was also essential for the construction of houses, for the heating of homes, cooking of food, and for the manufacture of tools and utensils.
8. Stone tool production was a "profession" perhaps even older than the "oldest profession." Nevertheless, large scale tree felling was a Neolithic specialty that required high quality homogenous flint. The procurement of such flint as well as the increased use of obsidian and high quality bifacial tools argues for the specialized production of stone tools for felling trees, for harvesting cereals, and for grinding grains. Stone tool production implies the quarrying for appropriate quality flint as well as for the production of quality bifacial tools. The production of mortars and pestles, in turn, implies the time consuming, and heavy duty, labor of grinding cereals.
9. Obsidian, derived from the sources in Turkey, is only one of the many products that came to the PPNB communities of the Levant from a distant source. Mediterranean and Red Sea shells, turquoise, jet, jasper, and varieties of flint indicate a far more expansive net-

work of exchange and interaction with distant communities. How were these items obtained? What degree of specialization existed in the process of exchange and who controlled access to these commodities?

10. The industrial production of lime plaster was not the only technology calling upon new pyrotechnology skills. On several sites of PPNB date metal objects of cold hammered, as well as annealed copper, have been discovered, *e.g.*, at Çayonu, Basta, Çatal Hüyük, and Magzaliyah. The artifacts produced are referred to as a "trinket technology, for aside from what may pass as an awl or chisel, the majority of artifacts are for adornment: small beads, rings, bracelets, etc. Such items of status suggest differential wealth and the emergence of inequality (see below).
11. Lastly, we must consider archaeologically invisible commodities: textiles, reed matting, basketry, wooden tools, leather products, cordage, etc. In a community of several thousand, are we to believe that each household produced its own sandals? Made its own stone tools? Produced its own lime plaster? Constructed its own private cult structures?

It has been postulated that the different modes of food production, *i.e.*, grain agriculture and sheep-goat husbandry, became integrated as a single subsistence economy in the region of the northern Fertile Crescent (the Euphrates-Tigris basin) during the late PPNA and early PPNB (Peters et al. 2005: 120). At this time, in the northern Fertile Crescent a number of sites (Çayonu, Nevali Çori, Göbekli, Tell Halula) are characterized by residential and specialized workshops, ritual courtyards, and institutional buildings that are all distinguishable from domestic dwellings (Cauvin 1977; Özdogan and Özdogan 1998; Schmidt 2000; Hauptmann 1993). These architectural findings in combination with elaborate furnishings, plastered (terrazzo) floors, storage facilities, and a diverse set of art (ritual) objects are clearly suggestive of an increasingly hierarchical society and division of labor. The increased energy expended on the above together with the tilling and harvesting of cultivated land, the maintenance of animals, and the production of crafts produced from distant resources, may all have combined to promote the concept of territoriality and the ownership of land, animals, and built structures. With the intensification of agricultural productivity comes demographic growth and with the emergence of private property one can envision competition (conflict) between communities. Competition, in turn, leads to the strengthening and enlarging of kin units and the concept of identity tied to territorial integrity. The part-time, if not full-time, specialization of labor can be deduced readily from the specialized appearance of architecture, two storey houses at Beidha and Basta, the clear distinctions in wealth between larger and smaller houses at ąyonu, and in the industrial production of plaster as well as in the specialized manufacture of stone tools, metals, mortars and pestles, as well as the specialized knowledge required for seasonal planting, harvest, storage, irrigation, etc., and above all in the specialized ceremonial and ritual buildings of the PPNB. We do not suggest that within the PPNB (or within the entire Neolithic) labor, and/or craft production, was a full-time specialized activity. Steinkeller (1987; see also Wailes 1996 and Schloen 2001) has demonstrated that professional duties were part-time, rather than full-time, even under the managerial state of the Ur III period in Mesopotamia.

Recently Ofer Bar-Yosef (2001: 21) has written: "Excavations of PPNB sites ... in the Levant and Anatolia during the past decade have *uncovered the presence of a major civilization*. Large village sites elaborate building techniques, ceremonial centres, carved stone stelae and the like demonstrates that the 'PPNB civilization' deserves to have a different status in our archaeological literature and social interpretations." In concluding his paper Bar-Yosef states (p. 28): "This chapter thus joins other papers (as cited throughout) in contributing to efforts to reconstruct the social history of the Near East *prior to the emergence of chiefdoms and the states*" (emphasis mine). In this view we have "civilization" preceding chiefdoms and the emergence of the state.

What is truly special about the PPNA/PPNB is not the reconstruction of its material world, the foods procured, plaster produced and the architecture constructed, or the reconstructed environment and climate, but the artifacts and architecture that address a rich world of ideology and meaning. Labor exists in a social world that defines both its nature and structure. Whether labor is coerced or voluntary, it must be legitimized as must the emergence of inequalities of wealth and power. What separates the PPNB from preceding cultures is a veritable explosion in the symbols and structures of an ideology. Jacques Cauvin (2000) puts his finger on the heart of the matter in pointing to the PPNB as a period that restructures human mentality expressed in terms of new religious ideas and symbols, a period he posits as seeing "the birth of the gods." The new "mentality" is, in fact, a belief system, a religion, one imposed, constructed, enforced and subscribed to. The PPNB sees formalization of a new religious belief, and like all religious beliefs, they legitimize power, inequality, structure relations, and define the social value and relations of labor. In this manner, we define religion as a systematic structure of belief, a means by which social, economic and political relationships are negotiated.

We need mention but one remarkable site of late PPNA/PPNB date whose architecture and symbolism is richly devoted to ideology, Göbekli Tepe (ca. 9,000–8,500 BC), though numerous others exist (Çatal Hüyük, Çayonu, Nevali çri, Gürcü-Tepe, Qermez Dere, Ghazal, Jericho). For a valuable analysis of the dates and comparative archaeology of these sites see, http://www.canew.org/data.html). We cannot pretend that we understand the meaning of the symbolism but it is more than apparent that a considerable labor is invested in the construction of specialized buildings, art and artifacts found in the settlements of the PPNA and throughout the PPNB. If we cannot fully comprehend the meaning of the ideology, we can at least appreciate its message: the emergence of centralizing powers of authority within communities, an emergent network of interaction between elites of different communities, a nascent form of a managerial class/group controlling the means of production (labor), all managed by specialists, be they shamans or priests, promoting and enforcing an increasingly uniform ideology.

The site of Göbekli in Anatolia is remarkable for the monumentality of what Cauvin (2000: 217) calls "sacred art." Here, over twenty large cult buildings have been uncovered containing T-shaped pillars decorated in relief depicting bulls, lions, foxes(?), cranes, intertwined snakes, and human and mythological figures. The entire site of Göbekli was devoted to ritual behavior, a place of pilgrimage that assisted in centralizing belief and legitimized authority. Similar cult buildings have been uncovered at Nevali çri, where human heads of stone, masks, stellae and hundreds of clay figurines of lions, panthers, equids, bears, and vultures were found (for excellent illustrations of the above, see Özdogan and Basgelen 1999). The similarity of motifs, symbols, female figurines (frequently regarded as "Mother Goddesses") found on different sites, together with such shared practices as removing the human skull and of the placing of isolated crania in domestic buildings (as well as in cult buildings) from Jericho to Çatal Hüyük, attests to the shared ideology, perhaps of ancestor worship, that united the PPNB world. This shared network of ideology is complimented in the material world by the shared network in obsidian trade and technologies of production (M.-C. Cauvin et al. 1998). Ceremonial centers allowed for the ideological mobilization of labor, permitting us to perceive the presence of what

Bourdieu (1984) called "ideological capital." In the hands of elites such capital controlled labor and raw materials, converting it into commodity capital. What we see here, in nascent form, was fully realized in the ceremonial centers of southern Mesopotamia. There, monumental temple-hoeuseholds with large land-holdings mobilized labor for both agricultural and craft production.

The archaeological evidence derived from the PPNB attests to a strengthening of both socio-economic and ideological uniformity as well as of socio-religious authority. Defining the precise nature of this uniformity, and the structures of power that maintained the social order, remain elusive. If we move the chronological clock forward several millennia, to the Uruk Period of Mesopotamia, ca. 4,000–3,000 BC, where we have our first written records ca. 3,400 BC, what can we say then of their social structure? The dominant feature of the social landscape of the Uruk world was the temple. Each city-state would have its own patron divinity and each would be a large institutional landowner staffed by a cohort of priestly administrators. The temples administered labor; male and female workers were attached to the temple either part-time or full-time and were offered wages and, in some instances, land allotments, in return. Temples owned large tracts of land and herds of animals, as well as workshops for the production of beer, textiles, metals, wood objects, and importantly, the control of foreign trade.

We need not go into the complexity of the Mesopotamian world other than to indicate that initially the temples, and later the palace, dominated the social landscape. Power, authority and administration emanated from the temple and were legitimized by an elaborate religious ideology. The earliest writing was a specialized labor undertaken by temple administrators in order to monitor labor, production, and consumption. What Steinkeller (2007) has written for the Mesopotamian world holds equally true for the PPNB: "The importance of religion cannot be overestimated as a key element that made the southern Babylonian city-state work." Similarly, Robert McC. Adams (1971: 77) in reflecting on Mesopotamian society has forcefully argued for "a special role for religion, and religious institutions." In southern Mesopotamia the temple was a central institution coordinating labor. In like manner, we believe that within the PPNA/PPNB "the birth of the gods" allowed for centralizing, legitimizing, and expanding hierarchical patterns of community relations that brought forth greater integration as well as conflict.

The cult buildings of the PPNA/PPNB, the rich iconographic symbolism that united sites into a community of shared "meaning," the emergence of inequality, the evident part-time specialization of labor, the innovation of new technologies, such as metallurgy, the presence of long-distance exchange, even the "pictograms" on stone tablets from the site of PPNB Jerf el Ahmar, prefigure the much later Uruk world. In suggesting broad comparisons between the PPNB and the Uruk world we are reminded of the ahistorical assumption that quantitative differences (size) result in qualitative change (structure of social relations). Archaeological evidence recovered from PPNB settlements suggests that a substantial cultural landscape, from the southern Levant to central Anatolia and the Euphrates Valley, was united in shared symbols and rituals of belief. Ruth Amiran (1962) has even compared the manner by which PPNA statuary from Jericho was constructed, an outer skin of clay and plaster covering an inner core of reeds, to the identical description of the creation of humanity in the Sumerian and Akkadian literature. In reviewing the achievements of the PPNB Cauvin (2000: 219) joins Bar-Yosef in referring to the period as the "dawn of civilization."

Within the cultural complexity of the PPNB "progress" was trumped by "collapse." A stratigraphic gap characterizes the PPNB sites in the Levant and Anatolia. Following the PPNB there was a cultural "collapse" and an abandonment of settlements. Its cause has been the subject of considerable debate. Gary Rollefson (2010) argued that the large PPNB site of Ain Ghazal was abandoned as a result of the overexploitation of pastures and the deforestation of the landscape. Another perspective views the collapse as resulting from internal societal tensions: overexploitation and conflict between unequal villages. In response to this hypothesis Ofer Bar-Yosef (2001: 27) points out: "unfortunately we have no conspicuous archaeological evidence or the presence of a particular 'Big Man' or other kind of chief." Bar-Yosef is joined by a number of colleagues who prefer to implicate an abrupt climatic change, recorded in both the ice- and pollen-cores around 8,400–8,200 BP, as responsible for a worsening of the environmental conditions and the subsequent collapse of the PPNB. Shifts in patterns of seasonal precipitation would have resulted in labor's inability to accumulate the necessary surplus to sustain their large communities. Climatic change resulted in economic deterioration and a societal collapse expressed in the disappearance of the previously large towns and villages and the establishment of smaller communities and hamlets. LeBlanc (2011) suggests that there is "ample, unequivocal evidence: much warfare in the past was over scarce resources"; and "when viewing warfare in general across time, one can correlate it with climatic and technological transformations that led to changes in the level of resource stress." Thus, climate change, population increase and "technological transformations," all well attested toward the end of the PPNB, may implicate the presence of resource stress and increased interregional conflict and warfare all combining to bring down the PPNB.

In according the PPNB the status of a "civilization," we would have to acknowledge the PPNB as the first "civilization" done in by climatic and environmental change (for other examples, see Diamond 2006). I have little doubt that climatic change affected the PPNB. It may have even initiated adaptations to new forms of labor specialization and subsistence, *e.g.*, pastoral nomadism. Thus, the above scenario suggests that a challenging climatic change caused a "civilization" to "collapse." That the PPNB was followed by a period in which its cultural complexity was no longer evident is attested by the archaeological record. Settlements are fewer in number and smaller in size, while the materiality of cultural complexity—whether cult buildings, items of long distance exchange, or plastered skulls—do disappear.

Why would climatic change alter social behavior? Would one not expect to see the elements of cultural complexity continue in the face of environmental challenge? Complimenting climate change as the cause of collapse were the dramatic social changes that were brought about by the over-exploitation of society itself. Social tensions were brought about by an emerging elite, legitimized by an ideology that likely exploited and repressed the lower classes, *i.e.*, the laborers. In the "collapse" of the PPNB both climate and society may be implicated as causes. In this scenario climatic change *and* the social organization of the PPNB rather than bringing down a "civilization" failed to sustain a civilization. What of the use of the term "civilization" as an appropriate status for describing the PPNB? The word civilization is an obvious derivative of the Latin *civis* and *civilis* pertaining to a citizen. The author of the entry for *Civilization*, Henry Smith Williams, in the famed eleventh edition of the *Encyclopedia Britannica*, would appear to be in support of the use of the term "civilization" within a PPNB context:

> CIVILIZATION ... it would be putting no undue strain upon the word to interpret it as having to do with the entire period of human progress since mankind attained sufficient intelligence and social unity to develop a system of government ... Only very recently has it come to be understood that primitive societies vastly antedating the historical period had attained relatively high stages of development and fixity, socially and politically ... Nothing but an arbitrary

> and highly inconvenient restriction of meanings can prevent us from speaking of the citizens of these early societies as having attained certain stages of civilization. It will be convenient then to include under the comprehensive term "civilization" those long earlier periods of "savagery" and "barbarism" as well as the more recent period of higher development to which the word "civilization" is sometimes restricted.

This broad definition would allow for the incorporation of the PPNB as a "civilization." At the same time it recognizes the concept of "progress" and allows for earlier periods of "savagery" and "barbarism" as well as "stages of civilization." If, however, all social formations, following the adoption of a fully developed agriculture, are termed a "civilization," what terms are we to use for investigating the evolutionary changes that characterize different political stages (*e.g.*, chiefdom), and the state or economic (*e.g.*, feudalism) stages? If the PPNB is a "civilization" then our evolutionary trajectory goes from hunter-forager directly to civilization. Conflating social formations into two stages, hunter/foragers and civilization may say more about our modern era than the nature of our evolutionary past. In today's world, where diversity is cherished and where equality and an egalitarian spirit are celebrated within an imagined global community, rendering the remote past as a singularity of civilization has an appeal. We can now celebrate the diversity of our past within an egalitarian, universal social formation: civilization. This eliminates evolutionary hierarchies, celebrates equality, and does not dispossess the right of any social formation of the past 10,000 years, from being termed a "civilization."

In adopting such an approach we may comfortably retreat into a Boasian particularism concerned with documenting the similarities and differences within distinctive cultures while abjuring any evolutionary concerns for what brings about changes in stage and scale. Stage and scale matter! This is particularly true with regard to the organization of labor, as it is with settlement size, population densities, technological achievements, landscapes, energy sources, etc. One may well ask when do stage and scale not matter?

Positing the absence of a "Big Man" or "other kind of chief" while attributing the PPNB the status of a "civilization" "prior to the emergence of chiefs and states" confuses both stage and scale (Bar-Yosef 2000: 27–28). The PPNB most certainly had specialized labor, most certainly had forms of coercion within their communities of several hundred, most certainly had evidence of inequality, and most certainly had "Big

Men." These "Big Men" held religious authority that legitimized their right to rule. In this manner nascent shaman/priests held the means of coercion which when applied to the population became the means of production. They presided over ritual centers, the nascent forms of the later temples that were the focus of centralized political and economic power. Within such a context it is hardly comprehensible that the PPNB existed without intercommunity conflict and warfare. Sahlins (1972: 82) has argued that the only way to obtain a surplus is to get "people to work more or [get] more people to work."

Elizabeth Stone (2007: 219, 221) has offered recently a view of the ancient Near East within a perspective of the *longue durée*. She compares the rise and fall of notable families in third-millennium Mesopotamia to the manner described by Ibn Khaldun for early Islamic times. In like manner we suggest that an initial PPNB "oikumene," an initial ideological "horizon style," brought about a convergence of social complexity within the Near East. Gil Stein (2007) has recently written "A Tale of Two Oikumenai," comparing the Ubaid and Uruk Worlds within Mesopotamia. We suggest that both worlds find their structural origins in the PPNB. Within the PPNB the ritual and the domestic were not architecturally distinct. Ritual, religious ideology, feasting, and burial practices allowed for both cooperative behavior and coercive structures. Within the PPNB, for the first time, there is abundant archaeological evidence that ritual empowered individuals, established and privileged networks of kin, legitimized their authority, and allowed for the organization of communal labor, social hierarchies and inequality, within a significantly distributed geographical "oikumene". Within the context of the archaeological record, and economic anthropology, distinguishing between what is cooperative and what is coercive presents a false dichotomy. Ritual may be both cooperative and coercive. Bowles et al. (1997: 5–6) put it well in stating that a "predisposition to cooperate and to undertake costly punishment are probably related phenomenon," a dualism they refer to as "reciprocity fairness" (for more detail, see also Stanish 2004).

Malinowski (1971) and Mauss (2002) subscribed, albeit with reservations, to what Durkheim (1975a, b) referred to as "organic solidarity," which wed individual interests, the division of labor, and moral obligations as reciprocally responsible for collective well-being. Certainly within the PPNB one can imagine a division of labor in which reciprocity, a mix of exchange and moral obligation, constitute a kernel of social cohesion. Durkheim (1975b: 142) put it this way:

> … if division of labor produces solidarity, it is not only because it makes every individual someone who exchanges, as the economists

> like to say; it is because it creates between men an entire system of rights and duties that ties one to the other in a durable way.

Reciprocity, on the one hand, involves labor and exchange, and, on the other hand, rights, duties, and moral obligations. Reciprocity is thus situated at the juncture of economic activity (labor and exchange), political activity (rights and duties), and religious authority (moral obligations).

For Durkheim (1964) a Neolithic settlement would have represented a community of "organic solidarity"; a community based on the interdependence of people in an economy in which labor is increasingly specialized. He juxtaposed this to "mechanical solidarity" wherein people share a similar outlook or position within society. The former is a community in which the economy is socially embedded, the later a society in which the economy is based on contract. Bourdieu (1977: 172) has argued for a similar distinction, concluding that a shift from a traditional economy ("organic solidarity") to a capitalist ("mechanical solidarity") represents a shift in the balance of the two principles. Such ideal types, however, are of little help in ferreting out the nature of the Neolithic community. Typically the Neolithic community has been classed as a tribal society, a chiefdom, household based, egalitarian, and without specialization of labor. In recent years archaeological evidence and interpretation has challenged this representation. Kuijt (2000; 2011) has convincingly argued that an ideology within the Neolithic settlement masked profound differences in status, power, and wealth. Large public buildings as known from Göbekli Tepe, Nevali Çori, Ashikli Hüyük and Çayonu in Anatolia, Ain Ghazal and Jericho in Jordan, and Jerf el Ahmar in Syria, suggest social gatherings, elaborate rituals, and the organization of communal labor. The construction of communal buildings, irrespective of their function, has a great deal to do with the building of community and society. If the economy is socially embedded, its social embeddedness is constructed by what might be referred to as the "sociality of labor," the building of new social relations—new social collectives through shared manual labor. Bleda Düring (2006), while not emphasizing the role of labor, offers an excellent discussion concerning the "social construction" of the Neolithic community. The fact that Göbekli Tepe is dated to the PPNA, and stands alone as a specialized ritual settlement rather than a village community, suggests to the excavator, Mehmet Özdogan (1998, 2008), that monumental architecture in the construction of sacred space, elaborate rituals, a significant population density, and organized communal labor were already achieved by 9,000 BC in the early stages of the PPNA. It is of interest to note that similar cult sites have been identified around Göbekli in the vicinity of Urfa and within a 70 km radius of Göbekli (Çelik 2011).

Recently, E. B. Banning (2011) has challenged the notion that Göbekli Tepe constitutes a ritual site of "temples." Banning suggests that the binary opposition of "sacred" and "profane" and "household" and "temple" space may not have been so polarized within the Neolithic. He brings back into focus Mellaart's (1967) perspective in identifying the elaboration of wall paintings, statuary, and burials beneath domestic floors at Çatal Hüyük as evidencing "household shrines." Whether temple or household—and the evidence conspires to allow for both—Banning, uniquely within the context of neolithic studies, considers the considerable labor invested in the construction of the central stone T-pillars. The extensive labor involved in the construction of the buildings exceeded that spent on the construction of buildings on any other known Neolithic site. Banning estimates the labor involved in moving the stone pillars, which ranged from 2.0 to 5.0 meters in height, with volumes of 300,700 cm^3/ 800 kg to 4,218,000 cm^3/ 10,800 kg., would have been substantial. The quarrying, transport, dressing the sides of the pillars, carving the reliefs, and erecting the pillars as well as the associated stone walls of the buildings would have necessitated a coordinated labor force which, as the excavator acknowledges, "was not within the capability of a few people" (Schmidt 2006: 252). The buildings with their strong cultic associations also contained abundant evidence as centers for feasting activities. Feasting, which includes the preliminary evidence of imbibing beer, would have enhanced both the cultic activities and the collective work events (Dietrich et al. 2012). It took considerable collective labor to transport the megalithic central pillars of the buildings, some weighing 50 metric tons with a volume of 20 m^3. The collective work events at Göbekli Tepe were of a scale that would have required both the organization of labor and specialized skills for sculpting the reliefs on the pillars. A geomagnetic survey indicates that the site may have had 200 such T-shaped pillar buildings (Schmidt 2006). Whether households or temples, it is impossible to avoid the fact that they represent a considerable investment in labor, the accumulation of wealth, and the attainment of status—all pointing to a degree of centralized authority and a form of social hierarchy most likely embedded in a context of ritual belief and behavior. The Level III structures are several times larger than the "houses" of known Neolithic communities. They can be interpreted as large co-residential households inhabited by related kin, or as communal structures for ritual activities. The evidence from Göbekli Tepe underscores what has long been suspected: Neolithic societies within the Near East were settled within diverse environments and were characterized by a considerable cultural diversity, whose complexity remains a challenge to archaeological interpretation.[1]

The absence of the institutionalized temple households in northern Mesopotamia, Anatolia, and the Levant argues for different forms of labor organization within these regions—organization(s) of labor that were less centralized, bureaucratized, and coerced. In the final analysis labor is the energy source, the building block of all social complexity. The stage and scale of its development is directly related to the stage and scale of the organization of society. It is the different organization of labor that gives reality to such terms as feudalism, capitalism, commercialism, slavery, etc. The changing relations of labor are analogous to the S-curve of a phase transformation in materials, so well described by Cyril S. Smith (1977:6):

> There was a stage, invisible except in retrospect, wherein fluctuation from the status-quo involving only small localized distortions, began to interact and consolidate into a new structure; this nucleus grew into a more or less constant environment at an increasing rate because of the increasing interfacial opportunity, until finally its growth was slowed and stopped by depletion of material necessary

1 At times it is difficult to comprehend the nature (meaning?) of archaeological interpretation, as in the following example: "Göbekli is located near Urfa, in the heart of the Haran region, the sacred landscape where monotheism was born and God revealed himself to his chosen disciple, Abraham" (Goring-Morris and Belfer-Cohen 2011: 643). Whether attempting to reconstruct the social organization of Neolithic communities or Mesopotamian city-states, we contend that individual agency is given both constraint and opportunity by social structures that can be either coercive, cooperative, or a combination of both. At Degirmentepe in Anatolia, sacred structures and residential buildings remained one and the same throughout the Ubaid period (Stein 2007). One may posit a distinctive Anatolian-Levantine-Northern Mesopotamian continuity from the PPNB to Hassuna to Halaf/Ubaid in which the sacred was embedded in the domestic. The institutionalized temple, as a distinctive social institution and architectural template, was a much later occurrence. The organization of the temple complex was a Late Ubaid southern Mesopotamian invention—an invention with its own distinctive organization of labor, and one that was fully constituted within the Uruk period (for a comparison of land tenure and labor in southern and northern Mesopotamia see Steinkeller 1999 and Zaccagnini 1999.

for growth, or by the growing counter-pressure of other aspects of the environment. Any change in conditions (thermodynamic = social) may provide an opportunity for a new phase. We all know how the superposition of many small sequential S-curves themselves tend to add up to the giant S-curve of that new and larger structure we call civilization ... Because at any one time there are many overlapping competing sub-systems at different stages of maturity but each continually changing the environment of the others, it is often hard to see what is going on. Moreover, nucleation must in principle be invisible, for the germs of the future take their validity only from and in a larger system that has yet to exist. They are at first indistinguishable from mere foolish fluctuations destined to be erased. They begin in opposition to their environment, but upon reaching maturity they form the new environment by the balance of their multiple interactions. This change of scale and interface with time, of radical misfit turning into conservative interlock, is the essence of history or anything whatever, material, intellectual or social.

BIBLIOGRAPHY

Adams, Robert McC. (1981), *Heartland of Cities: Surveys of Ancient Settlement and Land Use on the Central Floodplain of the Euphrates* (Chicago: The University of Chicago Press).

Amiran, Ruth (1962), "Myths of the Creation of Man and the Jericho Statues," *Bulletin of the American Schools of Oriental Research* 167: 23–25.

Ammann, Auguste (1889), *Guide historique, a travers l'exposition des habitations humaines, reconstituées par Charles Garnier* (Paris: Librairie Hachette).

Arendt, Hannah (2004), *The Origins of Totalitarianism* (New York: Schocken Books).

Bandy, Matthew (2008), "Global Patterns of Early Village Development," in Jean-Pierre Bocquet-Appel and Ofer Bar-Yosef (*eds.*), *The Neolithic Demographic Transition and Its Consequences* (Munich: Springer): 129–144.

Banning, E. B. (2011), "So Fair a House: Göbekli Tepe and the Identification of Temples in the Pre-pottery Neolithic of the Near East," *Current Anthropology* 52: 619–660.

Bar-Yosef, Ofer (2000), "The Origins of Human Social Institutions," *Proceedings of the British Academy* 110: 1–38.

— (2001), "The World Around Cyprus: From Epi-Paleolithic Foragers to the Collapse of the PPNB Civilization," in *The Earliest Prehistory of Cyprus: From Civilization to Exploitation*, American Schools of Oriental Research, Archaeological Reports 5 (Boston: American Schools of Oriental Research): 129–142.

Bohrer, Frederick N. (2003), *Orientalism and Visual Culture. Imagining Mesopotamia in Nineteenth Century Europe* (Cambridge: Cambridge University Press).

Bourdieu, Pierre (1984), *Distinction: A Social Critique of the Judgement of Taste.* (Cambridge MA: Harvard University Press).

Bowles, Samuel, Robert Boyd, Ernst Fehr and Herbert Gintis (1997), *Homo reciprocans: A Research Initiative on the Origins. Dimensions, and Policy Implications of Reciprocity.* http://www.unix.oit.umass.edu/gintis/homo_ abst.html

Braidwood, Robert J. (1967), *Prehistoric Men* (Glenview IL: William Morrow Co.).

Cauvin, Jacques (1977), "Les Fouilles de Mureybit (1971–1974) et leur signification pour les origins de la sédentarisation au Proche Orient," *Annual of the School of Oriental Research* 44: 19–47.

— (2000), *The Birth of the Gods and the Origins of Agriculture* (Cambridge: Cambridge University Press).

Cauvin, M.-C. et al. (1998), L'obsidienne au Proche et Moyen Orient, *BAR International Series 738* (Oxford: Archaeopress).

Chapple, Eliot D. and Carleton S. Coon (1942), *Principles of Anthropology* (New York: Henry Holt).

Childe, V. Gordon (1936), *Man Makes Himself* (London: Watts and Co.).

Çelik, Bahattin (2008), "A New Early Neolithic Settlement in Southeastern Turkey: Hamzan Tepe," *NeoLithics* 2: 3–6.

— (2011), "Karahan Tepe: A New Cultural Center in the Urfa Area in Turkey," Documenta Praehistorica 38: 241–253.

Diamond, Jared (2005), *Guns, Germs and Steel: The Fates of Human Societies* (New York: Norton).

— (2006), *Collapse: How Societies Choose to Fall or Succeed* (New York: Viking).

Dietrich, Oliver, Manfred Heun, Jens Notroff, Klaus Schmidt and Martin Zarnkow (2012), "The Role of Cult and Feasting in the Emergence of Neolithic Communities. New Evidence from Göbekli Tepe, Southeastern Turkey," *Antiquity* 86: 674–695.

Düring, Bleda S. (2006), *Constructing Communities: Clustered Neighborhood Settlements of the Central Anatolian Neolithic ca. 8500–5500 Cal. BC* (Amsterdam: Nederlands Instituut voor het Nabije Oosten).

Durkheim, Émile (1964; 1893), *The Division of Labor in Society* (*De la division du travail social*), translated by George Simpson (New York: Free Press of Glencoe).

— (1975a; 1909),"Leçon sur la morale" in *Textes 2: Religion, morale, anomie* (*Paris: Éditions de Minuit*).

— (1975b; 1917), "Introduction á la morale" in *Textes 2: Religion, morale, anomie* (Paris: Éditions de Minuit).

Fuller, Dorian Q. (2008), "Agricultural Origins and Frontier in South Asia: A Working Synthesis," *Journal of World Prehistory* 20: 1–16.

Giddens, Anthony (1971), *Capitalism and Modern Social Theory: An Analysis of the Writings of Marx, Durkheim and Weber* (Cambridge: Cambridge University Press).

Goring-Morris, A. N. and A. Belfer-Cohen (2008), "A Roof Over One's Head: Developments in Near Eastern Residential Architecture Across the Epipaleolithic-Neolithic Transition," in Jean-Pierre Bocquet-Appel (eds.), *The Neolithic Demographic Transition and Its Consequences* (Munich: Springer): 239–286.

— (2011), "Comment," in E. B. Banning, "So Fair a House: Göbekli Tepe and the Identification of Temples in the Pre-pottery Neolithic of the Near East," *Current Anthropology* 52: 619–660.

Hauptmann, H. (1993), "Ein Kultgebäude in Nevali Çori," in M. Frangipane, H. Hauptmann, M. Liverani, P. Matthiae, and M. Mellink (eds.), *Between the Rivers and Over the Mountains, Archaeologica Anatolica et Mesopotamia Alba Palmieri Dedicata* (Rome: Università di Roma): 37–69.

Hershkovitz, I. and A. Gopher (2010), "Demographic, Biological and Cultural Aspects of the Neolithic Revolution: A View from the Southern Levant," in Jean Pierre Bocquet-Appel and Ofer Bar-Yosef (eds.), *The Neolithic Demographic Transition and Its Consequences* (Munich: Springer): 441–480.

Hobbes, Thomas (1997), *Leviathan: Authoratative Text, Backgrounds, Interpretations* (New York: W. W. Norton).

Johnson, Gregory (1977), "Aspects of Regional Analysis in Archaeology," *Annual Review in Archaeology* 6: 479–508.

Joshi, M. B. et al. (2004), "Phylogeography and Origin of Indian Domestic Goats," *Molecular Biology and Evolution* 2/3: 454–462.

Kuhn, Steven L. and Mary C. Stiner (2006), "What's a Mother to Do? A Division of Labor among Neandertals and Modern Humans in Eurasia," *Current Anthropology* 47: 953–980.

Kuijt, Ian (2000), *Life in Early Neolithic Farming Communities* (New York: Kluwer).

— (2011), *Daily Life, Materiality and Complexity in Early Urban Communities of the Southern Levant* (Winona Lake IN: Eisenbrauns).

LeBlanc, Steven (2011), "Why Warfare: Lessons from the Past," *Daedalus* 136: 13–21.

Malinowski, Bronislaw (1961; 1922), *Argonauts of the Western Pacific* (New York: Dutton).

— (1971; 1926), *Crimen y costumbre en la sociedad salvaje* (Barcelona: Ariel).

Mauss, Marcel (2002; 1923), *The Gift: The Form and Reason for Exchange in Archaic Socie*ties (*Essai sur le don: Forme et raison de l'échange dans les sociétés primitives*) (London: Routledge).

Mellaart, James (1967), *Çatal Hüyük: A Neolithic Town in Anatolia* (London: Thames & Hudson).

Mosse, David (2006), "Reply," p. 92 in Glenn Davis Stone, "Agricultural Deskilling and the Spread of Genetically Modified Cotton in Warangal," *Current Anthropology* 48: 67–105.

Nisbet, Robert (1980), *History of the Idea of Progress* (New York: Basic Books).

Özdogan, Mehmet (2008), "An Alternative Approach in Tracing Changes in Demographic Composition: The Westward Expansion of the Neolithic Way of Life," in Jean-Pierre Bocquet-Appel and Ofer Bar-Yosef (eds.), *The Neolithic Transition and Its Consequences* (Munich: Springer): 139–178.

Özdogan, Mehmet and Nezih Basgelen (1999), *Neolithic in Turkey: The Cradle of Civilization, New Discoveries*, (Istanbul: *Arkeoloji ve Sanat Yayinlari*).

Özdogan, Mehmet and A. Özdogan (1998), "Buildings of Cult and the Cult Buildings," in G. Arsebük, M. J. Mellink, and W. Schirmer (eds.), *Light on Top of the Black Hill, Studies Presented to Halet ąbel* (Istanbul: Ege Yayinlari): 581–601.

Peters, Joris, Angela von den Dreisch, and Daniel Helmer (2005), "The Upper Euphrates-Tigris Basin: Cradle of Agropastoralism," in J.-D. Vigne, J. Peters, and D. Helmer (eds.), *The First Steps of Animal Domestication*, Proceedings of the 9th Conference of the International Council of Archaeozoology (Oxford: Oxbow): 96–124.

Powell, Marvin A. (1987), *Labor in the Ancient Near East*, American Oriental Series 68 (New Haven CT: American Oriental Society).

Renfrew, Colin (1988), "Introduction: Peer-Polity Interaction and Social Change," in Colin Renfrew and John C. Cherry (eds.), *Peer Polity Interaction and Social Change* (Cambridge: Cambridge University Press): 13–24.

Rollefson, Gary O. (2010), "Ain Ghazal Excavation Reports 2," Bibliotheca Neolithica Asiae Meridionalis et Occidentalis (Berlin: Ex Oriente).

Sack, Robert Smith (1986), *Human Territoriality. Its Theory and History* (Cambridge: Cambridge University Press).

Sahlins, Marshall (1972), *Stone Age Economics* (New York: Aldine).

Schloen, David (2000), *The House of the Father as Fact and Symbol* (Winona Lake IN: Eisenbrauns).

Schmidt, Klaus (2001), "Zuerst kam der Tempel, dann die Stadt," Vorläufiger Bericht zu den Grabungen am Göbekli Tepe und am Gürcü-Tepe 1995–1999, *Istanbuler Mitteilungen* 49: 5–21.

— (2006), *Sie bauten die ersten Tempel: Das rätselhafte Heiligtum der Steinzeitjäger* (Munich: Deutscher Taschenbuch).

Schumpeter, Joseph (1908), "On the Concept of Social Value," *Quarterly Journal of Economics* 23: 213–232.

— (1950), *Capitalism, Socialism and Democracy,* 3rd edition (New York: Harper and Row).

Simmons, Alan H. (2007), *The Neolithic Revolution in the Near East: Transforming the Human Landscape* (Tuscon: University of Arizona Press).

Smith, Adam (1776), *An Inquiry into the Nature and Causes of the Wealth of Nations* (London: W. Stratham and T. Cadell).

Smith, Cyril S. (1977), *Metallurgy as a Human Experience* (Metals Park OH: American Society for Metals).

Stanish, Charles (2004), "Evolution of Chiefdoms. An Economic Anthropological Model," in Gary M. Feinman and Linda M. Nicholas (eds.), *The Archaeological Perspectives on Political Economics* (Salt Lake City: University of Utah Press): 7–24.

Stein, Gil (2008), A Tale of Two Oikumenai," in Elizabeth C. Stone (ed.), *Settlement and Society: Essays Dedicated to Robert McCormick Adams* (Los Angeles: Cotsen Institute of Archaeology, UCLA): 329–342.

Steinkeller, Piotr (1987), "The Foresters of Umma: Toward a Definition of Ur III Labor," in M. A. Powell (ed.), *Labor in the Ancient Near East*, American Oriental Series 68 (New Haven CT: American Oriental Society): 73–115.

— (1999), "Land Tenure Conditions in Third Millennium: The Problem of Regional Variation," in Michael Hudson and Baruch Levine (eds.), *Urbanization and Land Ownership in the Ancient Near East*, Peabody Museum Bulletin 7 (Cambridge MA: Peabody Museum, Harvard University): 289–329.

— (2007), "City and Countryside in Third Millennium Southern Babylonia," in Elizabeth C. Stone (ed.), in *Settlement and Society: Essays Dedicated to Robert McCormick Adams* (Los Angeles: Cotsen Institute of Archaeology, UCLA): 185–211.

Stone, Elizabeth C. (2007), "The Mesopotamian Urban Experience," in Elizabeth C. Stone (ed.), *Settlement and Society: Essays Dedicated to Robert McCormick Adams* (Los Angeles: Cotsen Institute of Archaeology, UCLA): 213–234.

Stone, Glenn Davis (2006), "Agricultural Deskilling and the Spread of Genetically Modified Cotton in Warangal," *Current Anthropology* 48: 67–105.

Tucker, Robert C. (1972), *The Marx-Engels Reader* (New York: Norton).

Vigne, Jean-Denis (2008), "Zooarchaeological Aspects of the Neolithic Diet Transition in the Near East and Europe and Their Putative Relationships with the Neolithic Demographic Transition," in Jean-Pierre Bocquet-Appel and Ofer Bar-Yosef (eds.), *The Neolithic Demographic Transition and Its Consequences* (Munich: Springer): 179–206.

Waal, F. B. M. de (2005), *Our Inner Ape: A Primatologist Explains Why We Are Who We Are* (*New York:* Riverhead Books).

Wailes, Bernard (1996), Craft Specialization and Social *Evolution: In Memory of V. Gordon Childe* (Philadelphia: University Museum of Archaeology and Anthropology, University of Pennsylvania).

Watkins, Trevor (2008), "Supra-Regional Networks in the Neolithic of Southwest Asia," *Journal of World Prehistory* 21: 139–171.

White, Leslie A. (1973), *The Concept of Culture* (Minneapolis: Burger Publishing Co.).

Zaccagnini, Carlo (2000), "Economic Aspects of Land Ownership and Land Use in Northern Mesopotamia and Syria from Late 3rd Millennium to the Neo-Assyrian Period," in Michael Hudson and Baruch Levine (*eds.*), *Urbanization and Land Ownership in the Ancient Near East*, Peabody Museum Bulletin 7 (Cambridge MA: Peabody Museum, Harvard University): 331–352.

2.

Home and Work in Early Bronze Age Mesopotamia: "Ration Lists" and "Private Houses" at Tell Beydar/Nabada

Walther Sallaberger and Alexander Pruß
Ludwig-Maximilians-Universität München

1. Home and Work: Defining the Research Question

The communal management of labor was one of the dominant features of the economy and society of third-millennium Mesopotamia, as testified by the existence of thousands of so-called "ration lists". These cuneiform documents, listing persons by name or profession with their monthly share of grain, stem from various sites and cover more than half a millennium, from the Fara period (ca. 26th century) to the time of the Third Dynasty of Ur (Ur III, 21st century). Their source were the various agencies concerned with the management of labor, situated at the palace, at temples, or other organizations, often labeled "households" in ancient Near Eastern studies. The specific perspective of the documents, namely the managerial view of the workforce, has greatly influenced the perspective of historical research, aiming at a reconstruction of the scope and hierarchy of the managing organizations.

Significantly, in recent years various scholars have shifted the focus away from the organizations and explanatory models, toward the governing principles of the exchange of goods and services. They have thus paved the way for a change from a managerial perspective, of the laborers as objects, to a view that treats them as subjects, as actors in the economy. The discussion thereby considers both evidence of the Presargonic and the Ur III periods, assuming that comparable socio-economic conditions prevailed throughout the latter half of the third millennium, especially regarding the situation of laborers; this is generally acknowledged at least since the detailed analysis of Maekawa,[1] but implicitly assumed already by scholars such as Gelb.[2]

The socio-economic situation of the persons covered by the "ration lists" has been dealt with repeatedly, mostly concentrating on the Ur III period. Minute differentiations in the notation of workers pertain to fundamental differences in economic condition, distinguishing, for example, persons holding a sustenance plot and those depending fully on the grain distributed by the communal organization.[3] Such observations are especially relevant, since the uniform listing of persons by number, profession or by name might lead to an impression of a mighty administration that directs collective laborers as unfree "serfs" obligated to work. This was the perspective, for example, of Gelb,[4] and similar views can still be found in the scholarly literature.[5]

More than twenty years ago Steinkeller had opened new paths on how to read such documents.[6] In his seminal study on the foresters of Umma, Steinkeller points to a certain social promotion within the group, which contributes to the "difficulty in detecting any clear social distinctions between the foresters who were directly engaged in productive labor and those who performed managerial functions", thus giving up a strict separation between "people involved in productive labor" and a "managerial group."[7] Even more relevant for the present study, the prosopographical evidence of stable work groups showing family relationships within teams of workers strongly indicates "that the Umma foresters *did* possess family life and that the dumu ['sons'] mentioned together with them were their blood relations and natural heirs."[8] Furthermore, the constant combination of some forests with specific teams of workers leads to the obvious but important conclusion "that the men employed in the Umma forests appear to have been recruited from the rural population permanently residing near the respective forests."[9]

1 Maekawa 1987.
2 Gelb 1965; 1976; 1979; 1980.
3 Koslova 2008.
4 Gelb 1965; 1979.
5 As an example we refer to Dahl 2010: 291, who characterizes ĝuruš, a term that literally means "men", as "'unskilled' workers" or "de-facto state-slaves" and who draws a dreadful picture of their living conditions.
6 Steinkeller 1987.
7 Steinkeller 1987: 100.
8 Steinkeller 1987: 99.
9 Steinkeller 1987: 102.

The observations of Steinkeller on social and living conditions have not been taken up in later research, mainly because the administrative textual documentation usually does not deal with such aspects. Although nobody doubts that the persons noted in the worker lists represent a large part of the population of Babylonia, evidence from administrative documents is usually missing from summaries on houses and household in Early Mesopotamia (which often concentrate on the testimony of legal documents). Basic questions thus remain unanswered: Where and how did the persons appearing in the worker lists live?[10] How does the system of the distribution of grain portions pertain to the setup and equipment of a private household? Is our impression of collective work simply based on the administrative perspective of the worker lists? What percentage of the population was reasonably subject to the redistribution of grain? Since the most substantial groups of worker lists come from archaeological excavations that did not record domestic architecture (the early expedition to Tello/Girsu did not yet recover mud-brick structures, Woolley did not excavate third millennium domestic quarters at Ur, etc.) — or from clandestine diggings (such as Ur III documents from Girsu, Umma etc.), these questions could not be answered. But they can be considered of great relevance, especially regarding the general shift of scholarly attention from communal organizations (*e.g.*, temples) and the managerial perspective (employees as objects) to internal economic dynamics, *i.e.*, the exchange of goods and services in an "entitlement system,"[11] and to employees as subjects (with, for example, their own family life).

On the other hand, archaeological research on third millennium or Early Bronze Age domestic quarters has been conducted in Upper Mesopotamia in the last decades. These investigations are often led by more general research questions like the increase of complexity in societies. So the study of Wattenmaker[12] on Early Bronze Age Kurban Höyük in the

[10] This question was also dealt with by Magid 2001, but based on the administrative texts with few clear results.

[11] Wilcke 2007 describes Ur III economy as an entitlement system. By this he takes up several trends to look at early Mesopotamian economy in terms of dynamic processes and not of rigid organizations; see in this regard for example Steinkeller 2004: 111 on private and state economy, Neumann 2002 on the limits of using only the *oikos* model, or Selz 1999/2000 on the "redistributive planned economy" as condition for a stable society; the examples could easily be multiplied.

[12] Wattenmaker 1998.

Karababa region of the Middle Euphrates observes an "increased involvement of households in specialized production, increasing reliance of households on pottery and textile producing specialists, and household production of surplus goods perhaps in order to provide tribute to the state."[13] The perspective of the single household also dominates the monograph by Pfälzner, who investigates houses and living conditions in Upper Mesopotamia in the Early Bronze Age.[14] The dominant type of house in the period of the Beydar tablets, Early Jezirah IIIb, is the so-called "allotment house" (*Parzellenhaus*).[15] Pfälzner assumes that its inhabitants were active in agriculture, in animal husbandry,[16] and in handicraft. His analysis starts from the individual excavated houses, and therefore his perspective (as Wattenmaker's) focuses on the household as the basic unit; the interpretation of the often meager archaeological remains is informed by modern ethnographic analogues. So the society that emerged from the interpretation of the excavated houses differed fundamentally from the contemporary society in Southern Mesopotamia reconstructed on the basis of written sources: according to Pfälzner the households of Upper Mesopotamia represented self-sufficient economic entities, the subsistence of a household was based on agricultural work on the family's own land or land taken in lease, the families were active in animal husbandry including sheep and goat pastoralism and they performed handicrafts on a domestic basis.[17]

[13] Matthews 2003: 178–79.

[14] Pfälzner 2001.

[15] Pfälzner 2001: 378–79; now also Pfälzner 2011, 152–164.

[16] This conclusion is, however, based only on the presence of sheep dung and of seeds of the ubiquitous *prosopis farcta*, which *can* also be used as fodder for animals, in a room of 3 square metres; see Pfälzner 2001: 271.

[17] Pfälzner 2001: 395 summarizes his results as follows: "Die Ergebnisse der vorliegenden Untersuchung tragen in einigen Punkten zur Beantwortung der oft diskutierten Frage nach den Existenzgrundlagen der urbanen Zentren des 3. Jtsds. in Nordmesopotamien bei [...]. Auf der Grundlage der Haushaltsanalysen ergibt sich für die nordmesopotamische Gesellschaft des 3. Jtsds. ein Bild, das deutlich von der geläufigen Theorie der ausschließlich staatswirtschaftlich geprägten (süd-)mesopotamischen Gesellschaft abweicht.

Ein großer Teil der nordmesopotamischen Haushalte bildete selbständig wirtschaftende Einheiten. Dabei bildete der landwirtschaftliche Anbau auf eigenem Land oder als Landpächter die grundlegende Subsistenzbasis. Daneben wurde Viehwirtschaft betrieben, die eine Weidewanderung mit den Schaf-/Ziegenherden einschloß. Da in einigen untersuchten Fällen nachweislich der gesamte Haushalt für die Weidewanderung die Wohnstätte temporär verließ und da während der Anwesenheit der Familien Tiere auch in den Häusern gehalten wurden, kann man davon ausgehen, daß die Haushalte die

This review of some recent scholarly literature on the place of work in Early Mesopotamia has presented two diametrically opposed reconstructions of the society: the philological study of "ration lists" has often lead to an image of collective laborers tightly controlled by the state, whereas the archaeological investigation of excavated "private houses" focuses on independent families and household production.[18] These "two societies", however, actually lived in the same world, as incontrovertibly demonstrated by the discovery of "ration lists" at Tell Beydar in Upper Mesopotamia, today's Syria, a site where large sectors of the ancient city with its "private houses" have been exposed. This evidence forces us to rethink our assumptions and to combine the philological and archaeological evidence. In this contribution we concentrate on a combined understanding of the two different sets of evidence, the cuneiform documents and the residential quarters at the town of Tell Beydar, ancient Nabada; the wider context evoked for the interpretation of the documentation indicates that this site can be taken as a paradigmatic example for early Mesopotamia.

Our study is organized as follows: Two short introductory sections present the contemporary "ration lists" from Girsu (section 2) and the site of Tell Beydar, ancient Nabada (section 3), in order to understand better the worker lists found at Tell Beydar (section 4). The question of how representative these lists are for the city's population leads to calculations of the size of Tell Beydar (section 5). Building on these results, the houses excavated at Tell Beydar can be seen as residences of the workers known from the lists and therefore a description of a house is provided (section 6). The conclusions (section 7) explore some features of the city's layout and the houses that are conditioned by the specific socio-economic situation of collective work and the "rations" system. Furthermore, the Beydar evidence forces us to be more exact about specialization in cities of various rank and finally to address the similarity of living conditions in Babylonia in the South and in Upper Mesopotamia in the North.

Viehwirtschaft ebenfalls in eigenverantwortlicher Weise betrieben haben. In den meisten Fällen war Viehzucht mit ackerbaulichen Tätigkeiten kombiniert. Als dritte mögliche Existenzbasis war häuslich durchgeführtes Handwerk vertreten. Dabei konnten unterschiedliche handwerkliche Tätigkeiten kombiniert werden. Das unabhängige Handwerk ermöglichte ebenfalls ein selbständiges Wirtschaften des Haushaltes."

18 The use of the very terms "ration lists" and "private houses" may have influenced the different reconstructions of early Mesopotamian society by philologists and archaeologists, respectively.

2. Early Dynastic Worker Lists and the Communal Workforce

2.1. Presargonic Girsu: Some Basic Facts

The classic example for an Early Dynastic organization is provided by the "female house", the Emunus,[19] of the lady of Girsu, the wife of the local ruler, an organization dedicated to the goddess Bawu in the years of king Urukagina. Here it suffices to recall some basic facts about the composition and size of the workforce active in the Emunus of Lagash for a comparison of the ration lists of Tell Beydar. The remains of the Emunus archive of nearly 1,800 tablets date to a span of twenty-three years[20] under the last Presargonic rulers of Lagash, Enentarzi, Lugalanda and Urukagina, thus being contemporary with the royal archives of Ebla and only a few years later than the Tell Beydar tablets (Table 6 below).[21] The texts cover all aspects of the organization's economy, first of all the management of the dependants and of its subsistence economy including agriculture, animal husbandry, horticulture, fishing, and the usufruct of forests. A total of ca. 600 to 800 persons depended directly on the Emunus, living on its grain and wool "rations" and contributing to its subsistence. The Emunus represented only one organization of its kind in the state's capital Girsu. The largest was the organization of the ruler, dedicated to the city-god Ninĝirsu. The "children's" households were partly attached to the Emunus, and also other cities like Lagash were subdivided into various temple households. Representatives from smaller settlements within the state of Lagash like Pasir or Urub were only identified by their place name, although these organizations could have been housed by temples as well, those of Enki and of Lugal-Urub respectively.[22] Representatives of the state's temples and settlements appear in the Emunus organization, when the wives of Lagash's elites were hosted as recipients of festival gifts designated as "holy milk and holy malt", which were distributed by the lady of Girsu and by the members of her

[19] The traditional reading é-mí is based on the assumption that this is the same word as á-mi etc.; see Attinger 1997: 116f.; the variant of *VS* 25, 23 iii 2 é-MUNUS-a-kam instead of common é-mí-kam, however, strongly favours a reading é-munus, which would allow the variation of the two writings of the genitive with and without extra -a- (I owe this observation and the argumentation to Vera Meyer-Laurin).

[20] Numbers after Foxvog 2011: 58; see also Schrakamp 2014 with ample documentation of relevant literature.

[21] The chronology used is the one established by Sallaberger and Schrakamp forthc.; for the dating of the Tell Beydar tablets see Sallaberger 2012.

[22] On the deities Selz 1995: 121 and 167–68.

organization; among these women appears the "wife of the administrator (saĝĝa) of Pasir (or of Urub)."[23]

The organizational unit is traditionally called "household," thereby referring to the *oikos* model.[24] The term "household" appears apt since it allows a link with the Mesopotamian terminology, with the frequent designation of organizations as é "house" and as "temple." However, the term might also imply the notion that the members of an *oikos* actually lived together in a building or a building complex. The Emunus community comprised c. 600–800 persons, who certainly could not all have inhabited a building of the types known from the Early Dynastic period. In order to acknowledge the presence of various designations and compositions of these organizations, such as temples, the palace, settlements, or city quarters, I will use the more neutral term "communal organization", implying the sociological use of the term "organization" without a further determination of the character or size of the "communities."[25] The use of this term should also underline the fact that these communal organizations act as largely self-sufficient entities, which were of course closely tied to the political center by their obligations toward the state, but in periods of political change survived and continued to function. This permanence is most fittingly expressed by the fact that the eternal gods were regarded as the patrons of the communal organizations called temples in Babylonia.

The management of persons and goods in the city state of Lagash reflects a multilevel system. The capital with the seat of the ruler dominated various further cities of the state, on which in turn the villages depended. Such a multilevel system is also indicated by the distribution of the ancient sites, and written sources allow identifying the political capital and the extent of a city state.[26] The various communal organizations were largely concerned with subsistence economy, but additionally they also fulfilled special functions which served wider segments of the community beyond the household. The Emunus of the lady of Girsu featured a prominent sector of textile industry, which can be considered

23 Selz 1995: 74–77; Prentice 2010: 183–184 (with lit.).

24 For a definition see Renger 2003–2005; see above section 1.

25 "Communal" is thus understood as "of a community" of whatever character. The neutral cover-term "communal organization" should not be confounded with the English translation of Max Weber's "kommunistische Leistungsvergemeinschaftung" (Weber [5]1972, 88, II. § 26) as "communal organization" (Weber 1947).

26 The system of settlements was studied by Sallaberger & Ur 2004 for Early Dynastic/Early Jezirah Nagar and by Steinkeller 2007 for Ur III Umma.

as characteristic for a household led by the queen or another high-ranking woman.[27] The palace, on the other hand, controlled the royal treasure, mainly of silver, including both its collection and its distribution, in order to secure the political stability of the state.[28]

The cuneiform documents written by a specific organization list persons grouped according to their professions and social status, and in this sense it is appropriate to speak of "collective labor": there exist no individual contracts between a person and the organization concerning specific service obligations.[29] The term "collective labor," however, does not indicate that all the persons listed in the respective documents necessarily worked or lived together.

The model of the "household" economy for third millennium Mesopotamia rests heavily on the Emunus archive of Girsu. The persons of the Emunus can be grouped in various categories according to their socio-economic status and the terminology used in the documents. They are listed in the documents as receiving monthly barley allotments: men 60 liters, women 30 liters.[30] According to the subscripts the workforce of the Emunus can be grouped as follows:[31]

A. = *Category* 1: lú šuku dab_5-ba "those who have received a sustenance field"; 189–267 persons, 49 different occupations, only males, receiving rations for 4–5 months per year

B. lú iti-da "persons of the month"; 266–436 persons, of various categories, including women and children, receiving "rations" for all 12 months, consisting of

[27] For the role of the textile industry cf., *e.g.*, Prentice 2010, chapter "Redistribution" p.13–95.

[28] Sallaberger 2013.

[29] Personal service contracts appear to be more typical in the Old Babylonian period, although similar contracts are known in the third millennium as well, especially concerning hired labor. In passing it should be stressed that "administrative" texts like worker lists represent *legal* obligations of service and its remuneration. Furthermore specific documents exist that list individuals who become members of a communal organization. A well-known example for the Emunus is DP 120 listing 43 individuals by name and filiation, a text that bears the following subscript: "Total of 43 men of 36 liters (of grain ration), persons belonging to the Bawu (temple) of Sasa, wife of Urukagina, king of Lagash: captain Eniggal took them over for the workforce" (ùŋ-šè e-dab_5). Note that also in this case the new status is fixed in an administrative document.

[30] Among the summaries of the Emunus organization see Gelb 1980: 34–35, Bauer 1998: 553–555, Prentice 2010, all with further literature.

[31] Prentice 2010. The fishermen as a special group (group 4 in Prentice 2010) are not considered here.

Category 2: igi-nu-du_8 íl šà-dub didli "who do not 'see', carriers, various people on the tablet"; 125–208 persons

Category 3: gemé dumu "women and children"; 159–229 persons, almost only women mainly in the textile sector

The first category lú šuku dab_5-ba "those who have received a sustenance field" includes 49 occupations with some professions appearing also in categories 2 and 3. In some cases the members of category 1 represent the foremen of the persons of categories 2 and 3, so the lú šuku dab_5-ba-group is composed of the more influential men. The composition of this group is exemplified by one text (Table 1).

general description	number	professions as listed
"farmers and warriors"	96+x	96+x RU lugal under 5 captains
activities in the fields	4+x	x engar ki-gub "plowmen at the plots," 4 RI.ḪU "?"
care of gardens and woods	9	2 lú-ter "foresters", 7 nu-$kiri_6$ "gardeners"
care of animals, herdsmen for donkeys, sheep, or pigs	22	1 sipa $šaha_x$ "herdsman of pigs," 2 sipa anše sur_x-ka "herdsmen of donkeys for the teams," 4 sipa AMA.GAN.ŠA, "herdsmen for breeding," 3+2 gáb-ra saĝ-apin "(who care for animals) for plowmen," 3+6 gáb-ra sipa udu siki-ka "... for the herdsmen of wool-sheep," 1 gáb-ra udu níĝ-gu_7-a, "... for the sheep for slaughter"
fishermen	4	4 ŠU.ḪA a du_{10}-ga "sweet water fishermen"
boat and wagons	21	13 má-$laḫ_5$ "boat-men", 8 persons with gáb-$kaš_4$ "responsible for equids, coachman"
overseers/foremen (ugula) for the subordinate workers in textile production	6	2 ugula ki-siki-ka "overseers at the wool place," 4 ugula íl "foremen of carriers"
textile production	20	16 azlàg "fullers," 4 tu_9-tan_x "cleaners of textiles"
managers	2	1 agrig "manager of household," 1 NU-bandà "captain"
food production	10+x	5+x LÚ.BAPPÌR "brewers," 1+4 muḫaldim "cooks"
care of beverages, oil and other goods	3	1 ka-$saman_4$ "responsible of oil vessels", 1 sagi "steward", 1 lú é-NÍĜ-ka "man of the house of goods"
care of persons and buildings	3	1 šu-i "barber," 1 $sugal_7$ "attendant," 1 ì-du_8 "doorkeeper"

administration and control	7	1 lú-ešé-gíd "field measurer," 1 lú zi-ga "the one for conscriptions(?)," 3 dub-sar "scribes," 2 lú igi-niĝén "overseers, inspectors"
craftsmen (ĝeš-kíĝ-ti)	32	4 SIMUG "casters", 3 naĝar "carpenters," 7 ašgab "skinners," 6 ^{ad}adgub(KID) "basket makers," 4 tu_9-du_8 "rope makers," 1 $saman_4$-kešé "who closes oil vessels," 7 bahár "potters"

Table 1: *Category* 1, lú šuku dab_5-ba "those who have received a sustenance field," example DP 121 (Urukagina year 6, month 6), total of 226 persons

RU lugal "subordinates(?) of the king" or "(who work on a) lot for the king" and àga-ùs "gendarmes" were the most important groups. They did the agricultural work on sustenance fields and furthermore fulfilled various duties for the community; they for example provided the Emunus with reed and firewood, produced baked bricks, or worked on canals and were integrated in building projects. Most importantly, they appear in conscription lists and thus formed the army. The RU lugal constituted the core of the Mesopotamian society, the people that were farmers and warriors.[32]

The groups of lú iti-da "persons of the month" are less diversified and can be summarized as follows (Tables 2 and 3).

igi-nu-du_8 "who do not 'see'"	87	51 with gardeners, 36 with fullers
íl "carriers"	38	male and female carriers
šà dub(-ba) é-gal "on the tablets, in the palace"	29	male and female personnel, relatively consistent group working in the personal household of the lady of Girsu, *i.e.*, in the palace, including various servants, attendants, and persons in charge of storerooms
šà dub didli "on the tablets, various"	42	mostly men, smiths and textile workers as craftsmen, door keeper, brewer, herdsmen, boatmen, and 2 cult priests, 3 different singers

Table 2: Category 2: igi-nu-du_8 íl šà-dub didli "who do not 'see', carriers, various people on the tablet", example numbers in year Urukagina 3 (STH 17, see Selz 1993; Prentice 2010: 23–52): total of 196 persons

[32] See e.g. Maekawa 1987, Schrakamp 2013 with further literature.

ki-siki "at the wool"	115	70 women + 45 children in 4 teams
ki-gu "at the flax"	11	6 women + 5 children
work mainly in provision and preparation of food	101	for regular provision, in the brewery, carrying firewood (also men), milling women, pig herding

Table 3: *Category* 3: gemé dumu "women and children", example text STH 21 (Urukagina year 2; see Selz 1993; Prentice 2010:52–64), total of 227 persons, namely 4 men, 143 women, 80 children

The Emunus has become the classic example for the economy of early Mesopotamia, where a large part of the workforce was employed to care for the daily needs or the subsistence of the community. The Emunus organization is also typical in the sense that it concentrated on a specific task, namely the textile industry, due to the role of the master of the household, the queen of Lagash. Queens and high-ranking women of ancient Mesopotamia usually controlled textile production. The textile sector of the Emunus included only the work of spinning and weaving, but not the production of wool, since it did not deal with an exceptionally high number of sheep. Furthermore the trading and distribution of the textiles was not controlled by the Emunus, but, as indicated by other archives, by the palace, the ruler of Lagash himself.[33]

2.2. Ration, salary, and redistribution: a short note on terminology

Ignace J. Gelb coined the term "ration" for the contribution of grain (še-ba), wool or clothes (siki-ba, tu_9-ba), and rarely oil, to persons.[34] He argued strongly against a translation "wages, *Lohn, salaire*", which was current in Assyriology before.[35] The position of Gelb has been generally accepted and the term "ration lists" is nowadays widespread in Assyriology. Dissenting voices concerning the use of the term "ration" are rare.[36] Recently, Rosemary Prentice has argued against the term "rationing", since it has "the negative connotation of either being distributed due to

33 Sallaberger 2013.

34 Gelb 1965.

35 Gelb 1965: 230.

36 However, the alleged strict link between social status and type of remuneration has been revisited most notably by Waetzoldt 1987: 119–121; Postgate 1992: 237–239.

a shortage (as in modern times) or to maintain a subservient labour force at a subsistence level."[37] Regarding the underlying hierarchy of the lists and the service of the persons involved, each of whom received a grain allotment depending on their work, status, gender and age, she argues in favor of "wages" that are related "to the degree to which they performed their service to the institution."[38] A third term hitherto not considered, but more fitting would be "salary", which denotes more clearly the type of remuneration Prentice is arguing for. The distinction is fundamental: compensation in terms of wages is given to workers for the completion of work, and compensation in terms of salary is given to employees and paid mensually.[39]

The grain portions distributed, however, are more than simply a remuneration for work, since all members of the communal organization, whether sick, small children or old people, received their share.[40] So besides the specific value of a laborer depending on gender, age, work and rank, the membership within an organization has to be regarded a defining feature of the Mesopotamian alltoment system. Grain was produced by the communal organizations themselves and thus, in a way, their members divided their harvest. Although barley could also be bartered for other commodities, the basic idea was surely to fulfill the daily needs of food (monthly distribution of barley) and clothing (annual distribution of wool or textiles).

Given the modern meaning of the term "ration", we will generally avoid it in the following discussion and use instead more neutral terms like allotment, portion or share; and instead of "ration lists" the respective cuneiform documents are called "worker lists", which are regularly organized according to profession and place of work.

[37] Prentice 2010: 94. Note the following Wikipedia definition: "Rationing is the controlled distribution of scarce resources, goods, or services. Rationing controls the size of the ration, one's allotted portion of the resources being distributed on a particular day or at a particular time" en.wikipedia.org, last accessed 08/04/2012. See also the introduction to this volume by Steinkeller.

[38] Prentice 2010: 94–95.

[39] Definition after Wikipedia (en.wikipedia.org s.v. wage, access 04/08/2012); note the terminology in German and Italian: wage of a worker = *Lohn eines Arbeiters* = *salario di un operaio;* salary of an employee = *Gehalt eines Angestellten* = *stipendio di un impiegato.*

[40] On children, see, *e.g.*, Gelb 1965; Waetzoldt 1987: 132–33.

3. Nabada/Tell Beydar

Despite the fragmentary nature of the textual evidence from Tell Beydar, this city provides a unique occasion to study socio-economic conditions, simply because a large part of the tell is excavated and therefore the study of the material remains can be combined with the textual evidence.

3.1. The Site Tell Beydar and the Archaeological Excavations

The site of Tell Beydar (fig. 1) covers an area of about 22 hectares. The tell is of roughly circular shape and consists of a circular central mound, the upper city, and an outer perimeter, the lower city. Settlements of this type have been called *Kranzhügel* or "cup-and-saucer" tells.[41] When the

Fig. 1: Aerial view of Tell Beydar in 1927 (Poidebard 1934: Pl. 135, 2)

city was founded in the first centuries of the third millennium (see Table 4), both parts were settled. However, the lower city wall and thus the whole lower city were abandoned before the middle of the third millennium.[42] In the following periods (including Beydar IIIb, the phase of the main archive), the settlement proper was located on the upper city with

[41] A *Kranzhügel* is defined as a circular or polygonal tell with a circular upper city in the center and an annular lower city around. Ca. 20 third-millennium sites in North-Eastern Syria and South-Eastern Turkey belong to this category. See Moortgat-Correns 1972: 25–52 for the first definition of the term, and Meyer 2010: 11–34 for a recent discussion of its significance.

[42] Bretschneider 1997: 194–95.

an area of 7 hectares. A massive city wall made of mud-brick walls and debris filling layers surrounded the upper city.[43] The street system (fig. 2) consisted of straight radial streets and circular connecting roads, making the street-map similar to the appearance of a dartboard.[44]

In the very center of the city (fig. 3) was an elevated area separated by terracing walls and artificial slopes, which is called the acropolis (Fields F, L, N, and O). This part of the city had a palace, several temples, storage buildings, a large bakery and a tower, but no private houses. The

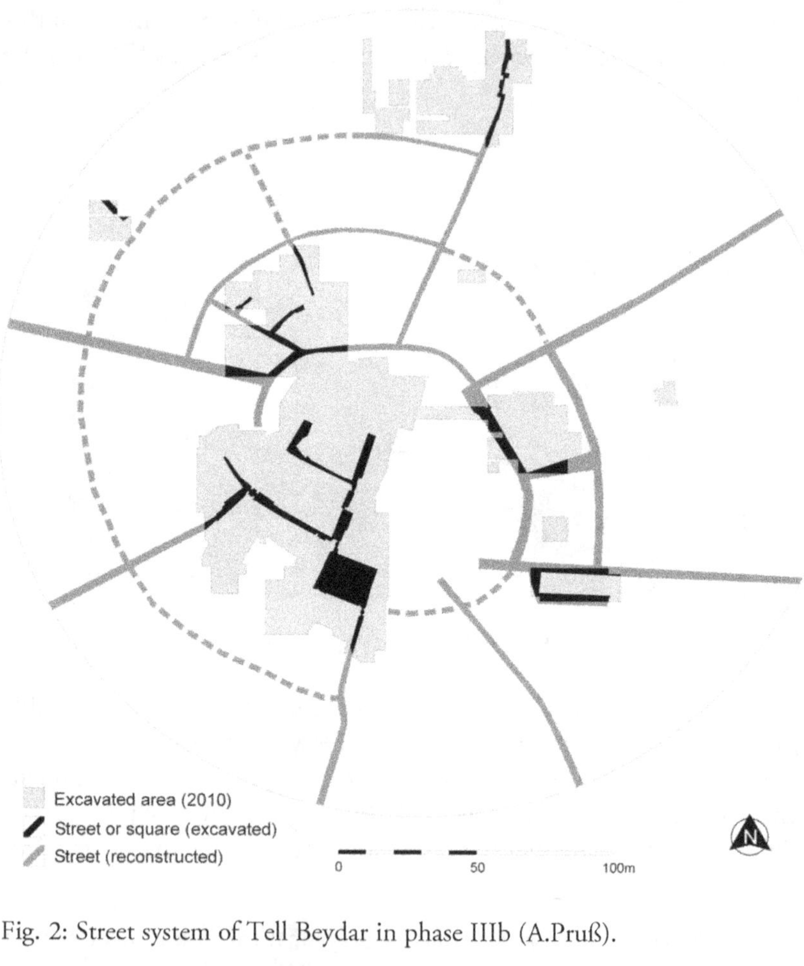

Fig. 2: Street system of Tell Beydar in phase IIIb (A.Pruß).

[43] Suleiman 2003; Milano and Rova 2003: 373–76.

[44] For a very similar street system, in the much larger contemporary site of Tell Khuera, see Meyer 2010: 199–221, especially Pl. 15.

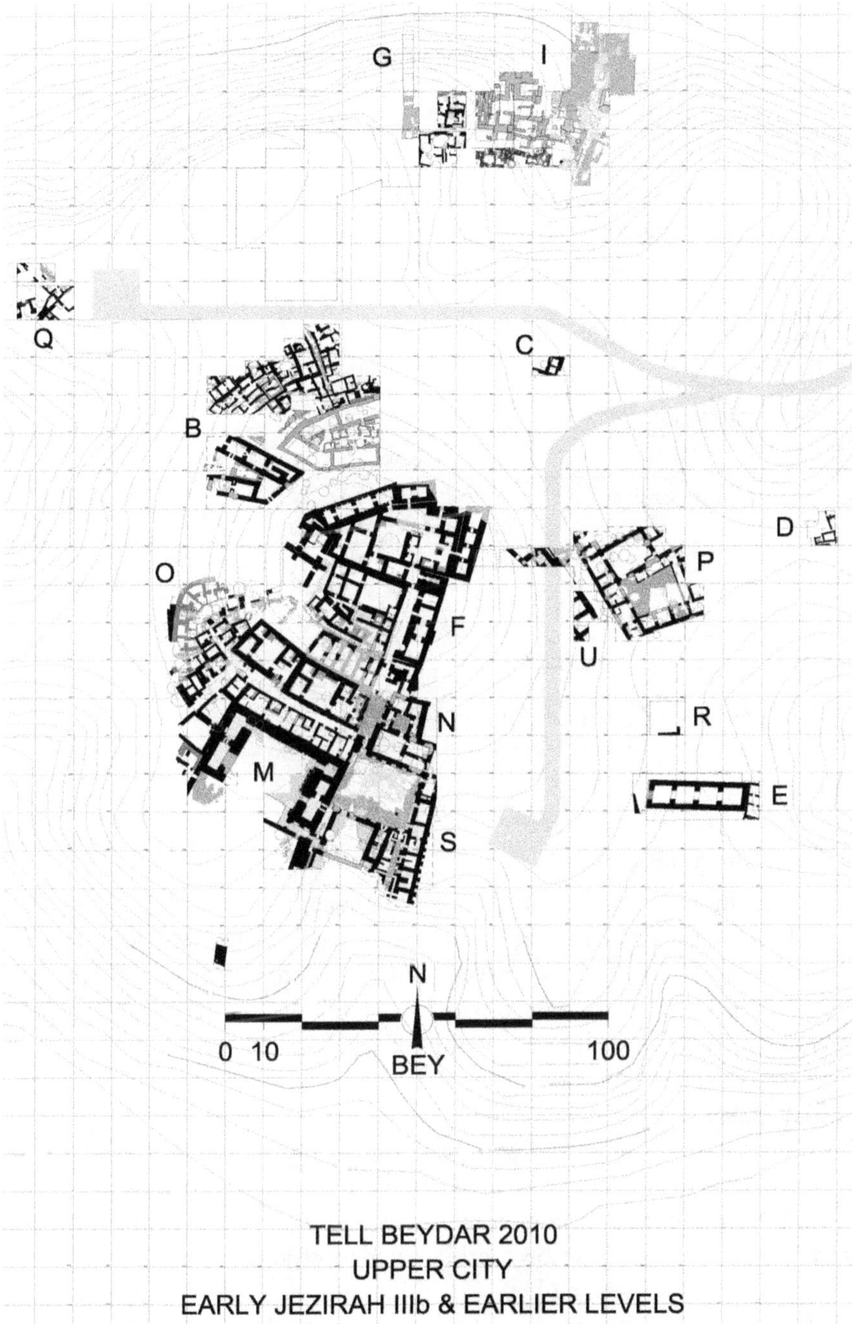

Fig.3: Excavated 3rd millennium remains in the Upper City of Tell Beydar (Mission Tell Beydar)

largest housing quarter uncovered so far is situated to the north of the acropolis, in Field B. Excavations in other Fields have revealed a large number of official or public buildings even outside the acropolis. These include: a temple (by far the largest temple of Tell Beydar known so far) (Field M), an open square surrounded by a large reception room and storerooms (Field S), a granary (Field E), a second palace (Field P), a massive building of still unexplained function (Field U), and a large building filled with many small workshops (Field I).

Beydar Period	Urban Development	Jazirah Period	South Mesopotamian Period	Date BC (ca.)
		EJZ 0		3100–2750
I	*Kranzhügel* settlement	EJZ 1	ED I	
II		EJZ 2	ED II	2750–2560
IIIa	Lower town abandoned	EJZ 3a		2560–2430
IIIb	Part of the Nagar kingdom; tablets	EJZ 3b	ED III	2430–2340
IV	Loss of urban features	EJZ 4a	Proto-Imperial	2340–2290
		EJZ 4b	Akkad	2290–2220
		EJZ 4c	Post-Akkad	2220–2100
Hiatus	Abandonment	EJZ 5	Ur III	2100–2000

Table 4: Periodization of Tell Beydar in the third millennium. The dates are taken from the Jazirah ARCANE volume (Lebeau ed. 2011).

3.2. Historical Context

The main archive of Nabada/Tell Beydar consists of 220 tablets (as of 2010) discovered in a secondary context mostly on the northern slope of the acropolis (Field B), but tablets stem also from the acropolis (Field F), and even from the granary (Field E) and the quarter near the Northern gate (Field I). According to the most recent periodization of the acropolis, the tablets do not belong to the latest monumental phase of the acropolis palace.

Some persons appear in similar functions in various tablets and sealed bullae. Thus the documents were once part of one archive, if an archive is defined as the documents belonging to one organization and disregarding their possibly accidental deposition or their actual find-spots. Although the Tell Beydar administration dealt generally with local affairs, the expenditure of fodder for the ruler's donkeys and the appearance of Nagar, modern Tell Brak, as first-rank capital on which Tell Beydar depended, allow to locate the archive within the general historical

EJZ Period	Beydar Period	Acropolis	Field P	
3b	IIIb	2	7	
			6	
		3a	5c	
			5a–b	Beydar tablets
		3b	4c–d	
		"Post-palatial"	4a–b	
4a	IVa	"Early Akkadian"	3	

Table 5: Placement of the main archive in the stratigraphy of Tell Beydar (after Sallaberger 2011:335).

situation.[45] The title of the ruler was written with the Sumerogram EN in the documents, perhaps to be read *mal(i)kum*, as in other states of Syria and Upper Mesopotamia during that period.

Nagar/Tell Brak as the capital of the region was the home of Mara'il, the first historical figure from the Jezirah, appearing in texts from Ebla and Mari at the time of Iplu(s)'il of Mari, *i.e.*, ca. fifty years or more before the destruction of Ebla (fig. 4). Mari's leading role must have ended soon after Iplu(s)'il, after the death of Enna-Dagan, thirty-five years before Ebla's end.[46] With the decline of Mari, Ebla gained more influence in Syria and Upper Mesopotamia. To this context belongs the phenomenon of gifts that were sent by Ebla to the ruler of Nagar and to the representatives of the seventeen cities forming Nagar's kingdom, among them Nabada (Tell Beydar's name during that time). These friendly relations culminated in a diplomatic marriage of a prince of Nagar with an Eblaite princess.

The geographical extent and internal layout of the state Nagar in the Habur triangle was reconstructed on the basis of archaeological survey data and the appearance of place names in documents from Ebla and Tell Beydar. The evidence of the Ebla gifts indicates that the capital Nagar/Tell Brak dominated seventeen second-rank provincial centers, among them Nabada. And the town Nabada itself controlled about 13 to 22 smaller settlements including two larger administrative sub-centers; the province's area covered between 300 and 500 km^2.[47]

[45] For the historical context, see in more detail Sallaberger 2011 with references to texts and studies.

[46] Archi and Biga 2003: 1–5.

[47] Sallaberger and Ur 2004.

Nagar was the dominant state in the Habur triangle, but only one of those existing in the region. The documents from the palace archives of Ebla clearly indicate political connections and commercial exchange between Ebla and the cities situated in the Euphrates valley down to Mari, in Northern Syria and in the Jezirah up to Nagar in the east, and even as far as Babylonian Kish. Whereas the Tigridian region was of marginal importance in the late Early Dynastic period, the politically and culturally closely linked city-states formed a continuous belt from Northern Babylonia to Upper Mesopotamia and to Northern Syria, as shown, for example, by the use of cuneiform writing and texts of Mesopotamian tradition at Tell Brak, Tell Beydar, Mari, and Ebla.

The main archive of Tell Beydar can be dated by its palaeography to the period about a generation or more before the fall of Ebla. This fits the historical situation of the domination of Mari. So the prominent appearance of Paba in a Beydar document, where she is listed even before the ruler of Nagar, may refer to the wife of Iplu(s)'il and the ruling queen of Mari, about fifty years before the destruction of Ebla.

Ebla and Mari	Tell Beydar	Babylonia	Sargon
Iplu(s)'il of Mari Igrishhalab of Ebla until c. 2353	*Main archive of Tell Beydar* around c. 2390/80–2355		
Irkabdamu c. 2353–2346			
Ish'ardamu c. 2345–2310		É-munus *archive, Girsu:* Enentarzi c. 2336–2331 Lugalanda c. 2330–2325	
		Urukagina c. 2324–2315	Sargon of Akkad c. 2324–2285
Ebla destroyed c. 2310			
		End of Lugalzagesi c. 2300	
Mari destroyed c. 2295			

Table 6: Historical context of the texts from Tell Beydar and from Girsu after Sallaberger & Schrakamp forthcoming, Middle Chronology dates. Note that the correlation with the archaeological chronology (based on radio-carbon; see table 4 above) is not absolutely clear.

Within the regional state of Nagar, which comprised a large part of the Habur basin in Upper Mesopotamia, Nabada/Tell Beydar represented a second rank town, or what we may call a "provincial center." The local economy was based on rain-fed agriculture and animal husbandry, sheep for the production of wool and oxen and donkeys as draught animals. The professions of Nabada's inhabitants are most clearly demonstrated by the worker lists.

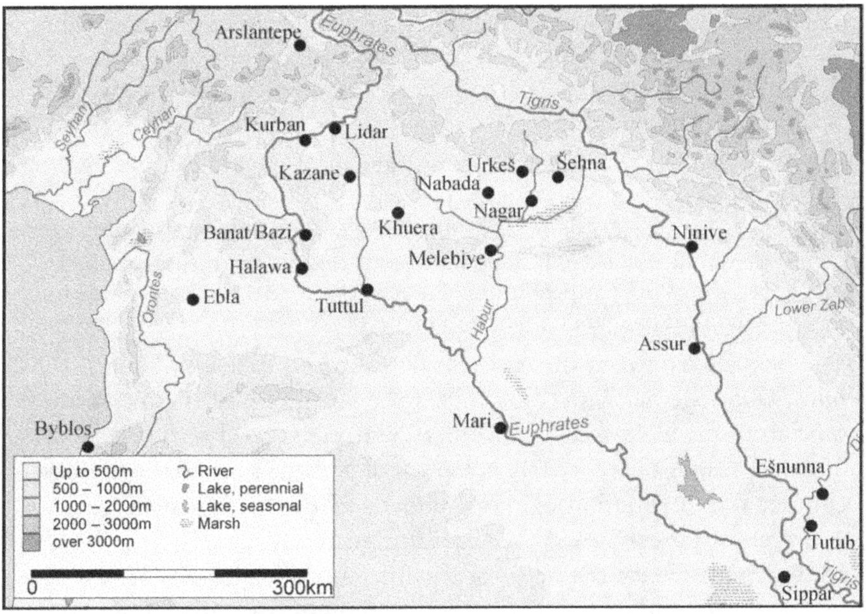

Fig. 4: Map of Syria and Upper Mesopotamia in the later 3rd millennium (A. Pruß).

4. Worker Lists from Tell Beydar

4.1. Structure and Scope of the Worker Lists

The management of workers is one of the dominant themes of third millennium administrative texts, and so it is of little surprise that some worker lists enrolling various professions with their monthly share of grain turned up among the tablets of Tell Beydar's main archive.[48] Several of the lists were found together in a fill under the last building phase in area B, room 2611, but also at a distance of ca. 80 m in area I.[49]

[48] The text group has been dealt with by Sallaberger 1996: 89–99. In Field I ration lists of the same character were excavated, but these tablets are of an earlier date; the tablets in question are *Subartu* 12, no. 216; Milano forthc. nos. 221(?), 223, 226, 233, 239.

[49] See Lebeau 1996 for the find-spots of the tablets published in *Subartu* 2; also *Subartu* 12, no. 209 comes from Field B: see Lebeau 2004: 3 ("couche de destruction"); 6, Pl. II a. Milano 2014, no. 239, however stems from Field I (see above fig. 3).

The following texts, many of them fragmentary, belong to this category:

Subartu 2, nos. 44, 54, 57, 58, 59, 71, 72, 119, 123, 131, 137, 140
Subartu 12, no. 209
Milano 2014, no. 239

The fourteen worker lists or fragments are all of the same structure:

- First entry: lú-ĝeš-DU, followed by the name of the "main official," number (of persons) + grain share, and additional grain (še-RU)
- list of professions, indicating number of persons and their grain share
- occasional other expenditures of barley (*e.g.*, fodder for donkeys or birds)
- Subscript: total of grain, month name

The persons named in the first entry are Arrum, Arši-aḫu, Ḫalti, KUR-ilum, who together with Tabla'alim form the group of the five leading officials of the archive of Tell Beydar; perhaps Išgi is also to be added.[50] They are responsible for various aspects of Nabada's economic life: agriculture, the distribution of metal tools, and the management of grain and even of fattened sheep.[51] According to the structure of the Beydar administrative texts, the name of the first entry is valid also for the following entries; other archives would use subscripts for this information. Therefore, the persons in a given list are linked to one of the main officials. Since in two cases two lists of the same official are dated to the same month, to the Sungod-month with Arrum and to the Ešḫara-month with Ḫalti, the ration lists stem at least from two different years. Albeit many texts are fragmentary, the grain totals indicate that each list covers ca. seventy-five to more than 200 persons.[52]

The combined evidence of the Tell Beydar archive suggests that five (or six) largely parallel groups of persons are concerned, each led by one official. There are two main arguments for this, namely the correspondence of the numbers of agricultural workers between worker lists and some agricultural documents, and secondly the total of persons under control of an official compared to an attestation elsewhere.

First, the numbers of the lú-ĝeš-DU and *ba-rí* udu in the worker lists agree largely with the number of the same professions in texts that document agricultural workers grouped with the main officials as representatives of the city of Nabada; the latter texts additionally identify workers assigned to small settlements in the city's countryside (*Subartu* 2, no. 3

[50] Section 4.2 below on *Subartu* 2, no. 123.
[51] Sallaberger 1996: 90–92; Van Lerberghe 1996: 115–16.
[52] Sallaberger 1996: 89.

and 39)[53]. As Table 7 clearly indicates, there are some fluctuations in the numbers of workmen per leading official; text *Subartu* 2, no. 3, the assignment of plough-teams, for example, features very small numbers of lú-ĝeš-DU; apparently few of them were employed in ploughing; and *Subartu* 2, no. 72 is a worker list of Arrum with very few laborers at hand. Nevertheless and despite the fragmentary data, it becomes evident that the work-groups listed in the agricultural texts as being employed at the same time pertain to the same groups under their officials in the monthly worker lists.

a) number of lú-ĝeš-DU per leading official in agricultural texts and worker lists

	Arrum	Arši-aḫu	Ḫalti	Tabla'alim	KUR-ilum
no. 3	3	2	7	[x]	0
no. 39 i–ii	30+[x]	35	45	[x]	[...]
agricultural texts		10 (no. 124)			
worker lists	38 (no. 54) 40 (no. 57) 17 (no. 72) 25 (no. 239)	36 (no. 59)	[x] (no. 58) 43 (no. 71)		34+[x] (no. 119)

b) number of *ba-rí* udu per leading official in agricultural texts and worker lists

	Arrum	Arši-aḫu	Ḫalti	Tabla'alim	KUR-ilum
no. 3	18	[x]	[x]+9	20	33
no. 39 iii-vi	[1]8	11	18	[x]+9	30
agricultural		23 (no. 53)			
worker lists	28 (no. 54) 27 (no. 57) 0 (no. 72) 28 (no. 239)	22 (no. 59)	[x] (no. 58) [x] (no. 71)		19 (no. 119)

Table 7: Correlations between worker lists (text numbers see above) and agricultural texts concerning number of laborers with leading officials (after Sallaberger 1996: 91–92; *Subartu* 2, no. 72 corrected after collation)

[53] See the tabulation concerning the place names in texts *Subartu* 2, nos. 3, 39 and 125 and the implications for the setup of the province of Nabada by Sallaberger and Ur 2004: 55–56.

Secondly, each of the five officials was responsible for at least 130 to ca. 240 persons, as can be seen from a list of persons engaged for harvesting (*Subartu* 2, no. 102; see Table 8). Since every person able and dispensable had to be employed for harvest, including even specialized workers as other archives demonstrate, the number of persons listed with each leading official may well represent a large part of his subordinates.

Leading official	Workers for harvest (*Subartu* 2, no. 102)		Worker lists
	Transliteration	Translation and reconstructed numbers[54]	Total number of persons
	Superscript: ki *šu* / bàd še al-gur$_{10}$-gur$_{10}$	"Placement of those of the wall/fortress: harvesting barley"	
Arrum	[1] *mi-at,* 30 (ii 6–iii 2)	[1]30	158 (no. 57) 158/161 (no. 54) 102/105 (no. 72)
Arši-aḫu	2 *mi-at* (ii 4–5)	200	134/136 (no. 59)
Ḫalti	2 [*mi-at*], 1,00[+x] (i 3–5)	260[+x] (max. 290, ≤ 299)	194+x, ca. 206 to 276 (no. 71)
Tabla'alim	2 *mi-at,* 40[+x] (ii 1–3)	240[+x] (max. 252, ≤ 259)	
KUR-ilum	2 *m*[*i-at*] (iii 6–iv 1)	200	(92+x) (no. 119, fragmentary)
[Išgi?][55]	[1] *mi-at,* 31+[(1/2)]	131 (max. 133)	
Total		1161 (max. 1205, ≤ 1221)	

Table 8: Total number of persons with leading officials according to list of workers for harvest (*Subartu* 2, no. 102) and to worker lists (same sequence of officials' names as in Table 7).

As the workers for harvest were needed at the same time, this proves that the five officials plus one unidentified person commanded a total of c. 1,160 to 1,200 persons. This corresponds by and large to the range of numbers of the worker lists, especially regarding the fact that Ḫalti is listed with

54 The numbers are reconstructed according to the probable maximum determined by the available space on the tablet and the possible maximum determined by the notation of numbers.

55 The missing personal name in no. 102 iii 3 apparently had a slightly different position than the other five leading officials; see Sallaberger 1996: 90 Table 1 as an overview of texts pertaining to the five main officials. One of the persons named Išgi (*iš*$_{11}$-*gi*) would be a possibility according to his appearance with other leading officials in *Subartu* 2, nos. 7 and 66; he is listed in the extra expenditures of the ration list *Subartu* 2, no. 123 v 2′, similarly as Arši-aḫu and Ḫalti in their ration lists (see section 4.2 below).

the largest number in both series. We can only speculate about the differences in the numbers: on the one hand, some men like guards may not have been allowed to leave their post for harvest work; on the other hand, the official may have included family members of his group of people for special tasks as harvest.

The evidence summarized in Tables 7 and 8 thus demonstrates that each of the five leading officials headed a group of ca. 150 to 270 persons. The lists of the same officials (Arrum and Ḫalti) display differences that hardly point to a fixed composition of their groups: two lists of Arrum (no. 54, 57) with 158 and 156/161 persons agree fairly well, whereas the third text (no. 72) lists only 102/105 persons. This suggests some fluctuation or a system of rotating services of which we are not yet aware; the texts themselves do not give any clues for an interpretation.

4.2. The Worker Lists: An Overview

The following list gives text number, leading officials, total of persons listed, the number of the lú-ĝeš-DU, the total of grain as preserved, expenditures other than for personnel, and the grain used for remuneration only. The restorations are based on the parallel lists.[56] The relation between amount of grain and numbers of persons allows a reconstruction of the numbers of persons involved in the more fragmentary texts. Note that the quantities of grain are indicated in the local system of capacity measures used at Tell Beydar:

1 kor = 10 bariga = 60 bán = 600 silà (liters)
Notation: 1.2.3 = 1 kor + 2 bariga + 3 bán = 600 + 120 + 30 = 750 silà (liters).

1. *Arrum*

Subartu 2, 57: Arrum, Month of Ba'li-Sulum: 158 persons

Total of grain: 22.[0.0] kor
Extra expenditures: total 0.7.3; 0.1.3 *dab$_6$-ḫir-tum* "collection"(?), 0.5.0 anše kungá equids, 0.1.0 birds, mušen-mušen
Grain for persons: 21.6.3 kor; per kor of grain 7.3 persons
Remarks: Restoration in vi 1: 2+[2] dub-sar; v 2 [bur]-gul(?)

Subartu 2, 54: Arrum, Month of AN.SAG: 155+[3 to 6(?)] = 158/161(?) persons

Total: [2$^?$]1.9.0 (probably some additional expenditures not preserved on the reverse)

[56] See Sallaberger 1996: 96–97 Table 3.

Extra expenditures: [x] *dab*$_6$-*ḫ*[*ir-tum*] "collection"(?); 0.1.0 onager, anše edin (or responsible person?); other entries not preserved
Remarks: Restorations according to parallel lists (entries for *šu* é-éš, *šu* ká?, ašgab, and *su-li-im* missing) and to missing indications of professions in i 6 (1 person), i 7 (x persons), iii 1 (1 person) and perhaps in gaps on the reverse.

Subartu 2, 72: Arrum, Month of Sungod (Utu): 99 [+3/6 aslag$_4$] persons

Total: 10.4.0 kor
No extra expenditures
Grain for persons: 10.4.0 kor; per kor of grain ca. 9.8 persons
Remarks: 3 or 6 fullers (aslag$_4$) in i 8 according to parallels. Note the low number of the lú-ĝeš-DU and the absence of *ba-rí* udu and their ugula (see above Table 7); this suggests a situation as recorded in agricultural text *Subartu* 2, no. 3 (Table 7), specific work assigned to these two groups. Read ⌜ugula⌝ é in ii 5 (already correct in Sallaberger 1996: 96 Table 3; transliteration to be corrected accordingly).

Milano 2014, 239: Arrum, Month of Sungod (Utu): 66+x persons (large gaps)

Total: [2?]7.2.0 kor
Extra expenditures: 0.1+x.3 [x]-*bù-tum*, 0.2.0 for *garà-sa* "leeks"(?), 0.2.0 for níĝ-è "expenditures", 0.1.0 for apin "plow (donkeys)."

2. *Arši-aḫu*

Subartu 2, 59: Arši-aḫu, Month of Ba'lim: 133 persons [+1/3 ugula *ba-rí* udu]

Total: 21.1.0 kor
Extra expenditures: total 3.8.5; 0.1.4 *dab*$_6$-*ḫir-tum* "collection (?)", 0.1.0 mušen-mušen "birds", 1.5.0 anše apin "plough equids," 1.0.0 Arši-aḫu, 0.0.3 AN.AN "gods"(?), 0.0.4 níĝ-è "expenditures"
Grain for persons: 17.2.1; per kor of grain ca. 7.8 persons

3. *Ḫalti*

Subartu 2, 58: Ḫalti, Month of Ešḫara: total not preserved, text with large gaps

Remarks: x + x + 1.6.0 for 2[+x] + x + 32 dumu-ninta "sons" (cf. no. 71 below), 0.2.0 for Muda and Enna'il

Subartu 2, 71: Ḫalti, Month of Ešḫara: 194+x persons (several gaps)

Extra expenditures: total 4.2.0; 2.2.0+[x] še [x], 2.0.0+[x] níĝ/ninda Ḫalti
Total: 32.4.0+x kor

Grain for persons: 28.2.0 kor (or less); calculating 7.3 (cf. no. 57)/7.8 (cf. no. 59)/9.8 (cf. no. 72) persons per kor: up to 206/220/276 persons

Remarks: The text includes besides the dumu "sons" with the carpenters (naĝar) another 5 + 2 dumu "sons" (cf. no. 58 above); 0.5.0 for dam lá-ŠÈ "...-women" (ii 5); 1 tibira "sculptor" at 60 liters (vi 2)

4. *KUR-ilum*

Subartu 2, 119: [KUR-i]lum in [x (x)]$^{ki?}$ (i 1): 92+x persons (several gaps, total not preserved)

Extra expenditures: 1.0.0 for MIN ud$_5$ "she-goats", x+0.3.0 for 100 uz-uz "ducks"(?); 0.4.4 for 10 uz-⸢x⸣ "ducks"(?); 0.[x].5 for x-mušen "birds", 0.1.0+x for AN.AN "gods"(?), and four personal names (x-muzu, Aba, Ḫulum, 'À-x-li)

Remarks: Note women in vi 3′–8′: [x] for lú x TUR munus 4+[x]; [x] for gemé *si-⸢a-ḫa*?⸣ "female servant(s) of Ši-aḫa(t)", x for 40 GÁ×MUNUS+GI "(women of the) 'locked quarter'/harem", x for 5 ⸢dumu munus? en⸣ "girls? of the sovereign (of Nagar)"; this provides a link with the women in the palace (more in detail Sallaberger 2004b: 45–47). KUR-ilum may thus be related closely to the acropolis (note the exceptional place name in i 1)

5. *Išgi*(?), anonymous lists and fragments

Subartu 2, 123: Išgi(?) (see fn. 55), fragment

Extra expenditures: 0.2.0 for Išgi, x for še gu$_7$, an[še ...] "grain fodder for [x] equids", 0.4.0 for 8 anše-IGI ninta "male donkeys"; 0.2.4 níĝ-è "expenditures"

Remark: 1 *ša* mušen-mušen "she of birds" iii 1′

Subartu 2, 44: Fragment

Extra expenditures: 1.3.3 for 10 tu "doves"; x *dab$_6$-ḫir-tum* "collection (?)"

Total: 16.3.2 kor

Grain for persons: max. 15.9.8, calculating 7.3/7.8/9.8 (cf. no. 71 above) persons per kor, up to 117/125/157 persons

Subartu 2, 140: Fragment

Total: 25.0.0 kor, thus probably in the range of 200 persons (cf. no. 71 above)

Subartu 2, 131: Fragment

Extra expenditure: 0.1.3 for *dab$_6$-ḫir-tum* "collection(?)"

Subartu 2, 137: Fragment

Subartu 12, 209: Fragment

4.3. The Professions

The Tell Beydar worker lists document the issues of grain to persons under the leading officials, whereby the recipients are identified and counted by profession with the total amount of grain indicated. This allows one to calculate the *rate* per person for a specific profession. Table 9 provides a summary of the number of persons per profession in the various Beydar lists; although various groups headed by different officials are concerned, the professions and the respective numbers are largely similar.[57] Single entries will also be discussed below.

The first, most numerous and best paid group are the lú-ĝeš-DU.[58] A literal translation of this term is hard to understand: the signs produce something like "person, bringing the wood(en implement)" or better (following a suggestion of P. Steinkeller) "person assigned to the wood(en implement)." The pertinent texts make clear that they were performing agricultural work and thereby served also as ploughmen (lú-ĝeš-DU APIN). The high number of persons, mostly around forty men, and the highest assignment, the first place in the lists, the organization with "foremen" (ugula), and finally their link with the political capital Nagar,[59] all these facts suggest that the lú-ĝeš-DU formed the fundamental component of ancient Mesopotamian societies: the group of holders of sustenance land that took care of the agricultural land and was obliged to perform public services, most importantly in the royal army. The best analogue here are the RU-lugal[60] of contemporary Girsu in the South, holders of sustenance land and performing services (see above). They are the ones that are called to the army by the king, as is underlined by their connection with the agà-ús "gendarmes" in Girsu; and similarly the gate-keepers

[57] For a more detailed listing of the data of the worker lists see Sallaberger 1996: 96–97 table 3; add there *Subartu* 12, no. 209 and Milano forthc. no. 239; correct the rations for the aslag$_4$ in no. 57 to 0.8.3 and in no. 59 to 0.9.3(?).

[58] Sallaberger 1996: 94.

[59] Sallaberger 1999: 399–400, especially on *Subartu* 2, nos. 107 and 111 and the so-called grain expenditure documents (Sallaberger 1996: 99–106).

[60] In Ukg. 4 x-xi the RU lugal is protected from the lú gu-la "the big/strong man". Maekawa 1987 argues that the Ur III éren can be seen as the successors of the Pre-Sargonic RU lugal; note that already the Presargonic RU lugal were called sur$_x$(ÉREN) "teams" in texts pertaining to workforce; their identification as RU lugal is possible by prosopography; see Bauer 1998: 483–87.

Profession	**Translation**	**Number**	**Ration** per head in liters (silà)
lú-ĝeš-DU	= ? (agriculture) (see Table 7)	17–43	120 + 10 še-RU
ugula lú-ĝeš-DU	overseer of lú-ĝeš-DU	3–7	80
ba-rí udu	"sheep-watcher"(?) (agriculture, see Table 7)	19–28	90
ugula *ba-rí* udu	overseer of "sheep-watchers"(?)	1/3	60–80
ḪAR-dú	(female) domestics	13–39	30
šu ká	he of the gate	1	60
ša ká	she of the gate	1	30
šu é-éš	he of the prison	1–2	60
šu KÍD.KÍD	(a doorkeeper?)	1	60
ugula é (šabrá)	overseer of a building	7–10	60
ugula kaš$_4$/maškim	overseer of runners/ commissioner	1	30
šu ŠE gud	he of the grain for(?)/grainfed(?) oxen	1	60
šu anše edin/eme$_6$	he of onagers/of she-asses	1	60
ša sila$_4$-sila$_4$	she of the lambs	1–2	30
nu-kiri$_6$	gardener	9–11	60
^{ad}adgub$_x$(KID)	basket weaver	2–5	60 (2–3) (+ 30 [1–2])
baḫár	potter	1–2	60
ašgab	leather worker	1	60
aslag$_4$	fuller	3–6	60
naĝar ^{ĝeš}gigir + dumu	cartwright, coach-maker + 'son'	6–8 1–4	60 30
mar-bala$_x$(NUMUN)	cart driver(?)	1	60
dub-sar	scribe	4	60
šu ḪAR.ḪAR	he of milling	1-2	60
sar-ra-bù	?	1–2	60
su-li-im	?	1	60

Table 9: Professions appearing regularly in the Tell Beydar worker lists

(*šu/ša* ká, *šu* KÍD.KÍD) and the keeper of the prison (*šu* é-éš) follow directly in the Tell Beydar lists,[61] sometimes even before their "foremen" (ugula; *e.g.*, 72).

The second group, which shares most features of the lú-ĝeš-DU, are the *ba-rí* udu, literally "sheep watchers". Our interpretation may be correct for the literal meaning, since in another text group from Tell Beydar we observe an alternation with *gu-li-sum*, perhaps "herdsman;"[62] and also the earlier worker lists from Field I use the term *gu-li-sum* instead of *ba-rí* udu.[63] But it can almost certainly be excluded that they all actually worked as shepherds, because of (1) the high number of 20–30 persons per text, which implies a total of about 100 persons;[64] (2) the fact that the few personal names for *ba-rí* udu do not at all agree with the names of the actual shepherds of Nabada;[65] (3) the *ba-rí* udu's organization with foremen (ugula) like that of the lú-ĝeš-DU; (4) their involvement in agriculture, again together with the lú-ĝeš-DU.[66] Like the latter, they turn up in the provisions for travelers and other services.[67] Disregarding whether or not the designation of this group really means "sheep watcher," they are unquestionably related to the lú-ĝeš-DU. Does this designation mean that they served as "guards" of animal herds, *i.e.*, the movable property of the community? Although this must remain speculative, such a situation would be appropriate in a world where the capture of sheep herds was an aspect of warfare.

The c. thirty herdsmen that actually herded the flocks of the palace, counting seven to eight thousand sheep and goats, are known from the animal inspection records and other texts;[68] they may or may not be summarized among the "sheep watchers," but there is no other entry in the worker lists that may pertain to these people. Therefore, it is not absolutely certain if the shepherds in the service of the town received monthly grain allotments or not.

61 *Subartu* 2, nos. 44, 57, 59, 71, 72, 131, 140
62 Sallaberger 1996: 102.
63 Milano 2014, nos. 223, 226, 233.
64 Adding the numbers of *Subartu* 2, no. 3 (Table 7) for the five officials: Arrum 18, Arši-aḫu [11], Ḫalti [1]9, Tabla'alim 19, KUR-ilum 33; total 100 persons (missing numbers reconstructed according to the parallels listed; see Table 7 above).
65 Names listed and relation of professions discussed by Sallaberger 2004a: 17–18.
66 Sallaberger 2004a: 18.
67 Sallaberger 1996: 101–02.
68 Sallaberger 2004a.

Professions in the worker lists dealing with animals are: "he of grain for cattle"; "she of lambs"; "he of the donkey of the steppe"; "he of the she-asses"; "he of ducks/geese" (*šu* uz-uz, *Subartu* 2, no. 119 iv 7); "she of birds" (*ša* mušen-mušen, no. 123 iii 1′). The nine to eleven documented gardeners (nu-kiri$_6$) apparently took care of fruit trees (such as the textually attested fig trees).

Administrative duties remained in the hands of the female ugula kaš$_4$ "overseer of the runners" (or maškim "commissioner"?), the three or four scribes (dub-sar), and the seven to ten "overseers of buildings" (ugula é), who probably served as managers of the various storehouses, so many of which were excavated in Tell Beydar (see Fig. 3 and section 5.2).[69]

The craftsmen included two to five basket weavers, two potters, five to eight cartwrights, one leather worker, three or six fullers, perhaps a single "seal cutter"(?) ([bur]-gul 57 v 2),[70] one "sculptor" (tibira, Ḫalti list 71 vi 2); transportation was perhaps entrusted to a mar-bala$_x$, "who transfers the carts" (if the term is correctly interpreted).

Remarkable is the high number of cartwrights among the craftsmen. Apparently, the Nabada community had a special service to take care of the manufacture and repair of wagons, an important means of traffic in the Habur basin and in Upper Mesopotamia. It is not without coincidence that carts appear dominantly in the glyptics of Tell Beydar, and in this way images in art refer to the most prestigious goods.[71]

Unclear remain the professions *su-li-im*, *sar-ra-bù*, and *šu* ḪAR-*da-nu*.[72]

The largest female group are the "domestics" (ḪAR-dú) of 13–39 persons per list, comprising a total of c. 150 women. It is safe to assume that they fulfilled the typical female duties mostly in the production of food like milling grain, baking bread and brewing beer. In the palace area the excavators found a milling place with two bread baking ovens in the corner between temple terrace and palace on the acropolis; furthermore in the ration lists one or two males are "men of the milling", thus listed as their supervisors. The ḪAR-dú may specially have served various organizations, not only the palace, since another center for food production was excavated in Field I at the northern fringe of the upper town (see below section 4.4.2).

69 Cf. Sjöberg 2003: 262 on the term ugula é.

70 Bonechi 2003: 56.

71 Bretschneider and Jans 1998.

72 The latter only in no. 119 iii 2, otherwise known from the grain expenditure documents.

Finally, it has to be emphasized that not all texts list the same professions or the same numbers. One text of Ḫalti (*Subartu* 2, no. 71), for example, features more craftsmen, the "sculptor" (tibira) and an exceedingly high number of cartwrights, who include "sons" (dumu-ninta). The "sons" are prominent in both his lists (no. 58, 71). The group perhaps to be assigned to Išgi (*Subartu* 2, no. 123) was seemingly more active in animal husbandry. The large but fragmentary list of KUR-ilum (*Subartu* 2, no. 119) includes forty "women of the locked house" (GÁ× MUNUS+GI) and the record furthermore provides prosopographic links with the lists of women from the palace area.[73] About forty women lived probably in the palace, among them "girls of the ruler," *i.e.*, the king of Nagar.[74] The preserved texts do not indicate directly whether the women were engaged in textile work. Incoming wool is documented in the administrative records of Nabada, but neither texts nor material remains can answer the question of where the production of textiles actually took place. The KUR-ilum list (no. 119), which through the women provides a link with the monumental complex on the acropolis, is fragmentary; also some other professions that are linked to the palace like blacksmiths or producers of perfumed oil could easily be fitted in the missing parts of the tablet.

4.4. Identifying Crafts in the Archaeological Record

4.4.1. The Metal Workshops

No metal workers are mentioned in the Beydar lists with the possible exception of the already mentioned tibira "sculptor" (Ḫalti-list no. 71 vi 2).[75] However, the archaeological evidence can help to define the relation between the metal workers and the central administration.

The best evidence for metal production in Beydar is a metal workshop uncovered in the former Eastern Palace in Field P.[76] The Eastern Palace, a large representative building, was erected shortly before the period of the main archive. After a rather short time of use it lost its representative function, though the building was still intact. The northern wing of the palace was abandoned, but the rest was transformed into a

[73] See above 4.2. remarks on the text.

[74] Sallaberger 2004b.

[75] See Pruß 2011a: 127 for the discussion of this professional and of his possible relation with the Field P metal workshop.

[76] Pruß 2011a: 121–28.

metal workshop. At least four kilns were installed in the former banquet hall, another one near the former entrance (see fig. 5). Crucible fragments and metal spills were found in the former banquet hall and the main courtyard of the building. No molds were found, but a trial piece impressed from a mold from which a male head of a composite figure could have been cast.[77]

Fig. 5: Location of kilns and crucible fragments in the former Eastern Palace of Beydar, Field P, level 5a–b (A. Pruß)

[77] See Pruß 2011b for a description of the trial piece and its role within the production process.

Several impressions of two very similar seals[78] were found on floors within the context of the metal workshop (fig. 6). One of the impressions is on a container sealing, the others on door sealings. Impressions of one of the seals were found on the Acropolis (Field F) in a context contemporary with the archive; both seals are frequently attested on the sealings from the floor of Temple E in the South of the town. These seals must have been owned by some officials of the town (one or two of the five leading officials of the ration lists?), who were responsible for the control of several large public buildings. The Field P seal impressions thus prove two things: the metal workshop is contemporary with the archive and it was controlled by the central administration.

Fig. 6: Location of sealings in the former Eastern Palace of Beydar, Field P, level 5a–b (A. Pruß)

[78] See Rova 2008: 72–73, no. 9–10, Fig. 8–9. The design of both seals is nearly identical: on one seal the boat-god and accompanying figures look to the left, on the other one to the right.

Another metal workshop existed in the center of the Acropolis in Field F.[79] Two molds and remains of a kiln were found in room 32861. This room is situated in the former Temple A and is dated to the "Early Akkadian" Phase IVa, *i.e.*, after the reduction of the city to a 1.5 ha village and the abandonment of the city wall, the palaces and most temples. The former Temple A, however, seems to have kept at least some of its functions, since the main room remained nearly unchanged in this phase. The setting of the workshop indicates thus some degree of administrative control for this metal-working location, too.

The archaeological evidence of metal-working at Tell Beydar contrasts with the evidence of the worker lists. Various reasons could be adduced for this mismatch: A few professions remain unidentified (*su-li-im*, *sar-ra-bù*), and many lists are fragmentary. Furthermore, it could well be that the metal workshop was directly related to the sovereign's palace at Nagar/Tell Brak, since metals, textiles, and other luxury goods were often directly controlled by rulers themselves. If that was the case, the craftsmen in question may not have belonged administratively to the local Nabada organization.[80]

4.4.2. Food Production

It is safe to assume that also the production of food was linked to the palace: here, one needed institutional kitchens and in fact such a milling place with two bread baking ovens was found in the angle between temple terrace and palace on the acropolis.[81] So a bakery may well be linked to the palace only, and therefore be managed in another administrative section than the communal workers. The same can apply to the brewers, and certainly a palace organization could hardly exist without the local production of beer.[82]

Another center for food production was excavated in Field I at the northern fringe of the upper town. A large workshop complex ("Northern Building") situated just inside the upper city wall contained one large room which was filled with the remains of eleven bread-ovens (*tannurs*), of which up to six were in use simultaneously (fig. 7).[83]

[79] Bretschneider, Jans, and Suleiman 2003: 151, Fig. 6.

[80] See already Sallaberger 1996: 99; for palatial archives of the period see Sallaberger 2013.

[81] Suleiman 2007: 87, Fig. 17–18.

[82] See section 6 below for the domestic production of food at Tell Beydar.

Fig. 7: Bakery room 61859 with many tannur ovens, seen from W (Beydar, field I; Photo L. Milano)

This bakery could feed a large number of people and was most probably integrated in the administration. One could hypothetically and for the sake of the argument assume that the grain allotments, which were calculated in sìla (of grain), were in reality distributed as bread, and not as unprocessed grain. The workers in the large workshop building thus would have received (parts of) their shares at their working place. However, the houses in the residential quarter (see below) regularly provide installations for domestic food preparation. So the bread produced in the Field I bakery was more likely provided for people at work and while on travel; this conforms exactly to the third-millennium textual evidence: Especially the location near the city gate can be related to the textually attested expenditure of beer and bread to messengers and travelers.[84]

Other industrial activities attested within the "Northern Building" of Field I are pottery and figurine production as well as food production and preparation other than milling and baking. These activities were situated in single rooms and small courtyards of the building which did not contain typical domestic installations.

[83] Room 61859, see Milano and Rova 2004: 10.

[84] The so-called bread-and-beer texts are expenditures of food to the persons present in a communal organization, *e.g.*, travellers, guests at a festival, but also workers, officials etc. Examples of these documents are the texts on cereals from the palace of Ebla (Milano 1990) or from Sargonic Umma (Foster 1982, especially group C.3.3 *ibid.*109–116).

5. The Size of Nabada/Tell Beydar

As argued above (section 4.1), the five or six leading officials directed an enormous workforce of about 1,200 persons. So an important question emerges from this evidence: what was the extent of the organization that issued the worker lists at Tell Beydar? If we want to compare the Upper Mesopotamian system of collective labor with the Babylonian one—as our ultimate goal is—we need first to estimate how many inhabitants of Tell Beydar belonged to the organization directed by the five or six leading officials.

5.1. The Number of Persons Involved

When the first discussion of the Tell Beydar worker lists appeared fifteen years ago,[85] the organization to which the workforce and the leading officials belonged was vaguely dubbed a "household," as one would do for any comparable third millennium corpus of administrative texts. In the case of Tell Beydar, however, the extent of the inhabited area is now known thanks to the archaeological excavations. It is within this particular area, therefore, that the individuals mentioned in the texts need to be placed.

The size of Nabada's population has already been discussed by Sallaberger and Ur.[86] Here, the main arguments are shortly summarized, and some new observations are added.

The worker lists under the five main officials document each about 150 to 270 persons; lower numbers are due to fluctuations in the labor duties (see above 4.1.). By comparing these figures with the numbers of laborers used for harvest (*Subartu* 2, no. 102), an estimate can be made that the total workforce numbered about 1,200 persons. Since about one third of persons listed in the worker lists are women, and since men and women are evenly distributed, one subsequently arrives at a figure of 1,200 (including 400 women) + 400 (additional women) = 1,600 persons. To this figure one must still add babies and small children that are not included in the lists.

A list of "men" (ninta, *Subartu* 2, no. 73 iii 2–4) allows another estimate: included in it are 605 "men" at Nabada and 240 persons designated as "free" (sikil-sikil, iii 5–iv 2). Assuming that the latter were likewise inhabitants of Nabada, probably temporarily not on duty (as often noted in third millennium texts dealing with workforce), this document thus

[85] Sallaberger 1996.
[86] Sallaberger and Ur 2004.

notes that 845 men were subject to the communal organization. This leads to a comparable number of 1,690 men and women at Nabada. The same text lists 1,001+x persons in the "land" (kalam), evidently the population of the rural settlements that depended on Nabada. Accordingly, between 2,200 and 2,300 persons lived in the villages around Nabada. For the sake of clarity it may be added that the number of working persons does not simply correspond to "grown-ups," since we may assume that people started to work as youths while still living with their parents, as comparable evidence from the Ur III period demonstrates.[87] So Nabada's 1,600–1,700 working persons may reflect a population of plus or minus 2,000 inhabitants, but hardly more than ca. 2,200 persons.

According to the available housing space and the agricultural possibilities of the Beydar sub-region (see below), the city of Nabada had about 2,000 or slightly more inhabitants. Comparing this figure with the totals of the harvesting texts and the worker lists, it becomes evident that we are not dealing with any "household" or a circumscribed "central organization." It is clear, instead, that the total (or at least the largest part) of the active workforce of the city of Nabada in fact figures in the worker lists produced by the five (or six) leading officials. Therefore, the professions appearing in the lists do quite reliably represent the workforce of Tell Beydar; and in this way they also provide a fairly representative picture of the socio-economic structure of a second-rank city. We will return to this point at the end of our paper.

There are other indications as well that the organization responsible for the Tell Beydar documents in fact managed the whole city. Some texts list persons according to city gates (ká), most probably referring to city quarters (*Subartu* 2, nos. 1, 5, 28, 29, 52). And the same administration supervised not only the urban center of Nabada, but also the personnel and agriculture of settlements in the reach of Tell Beydar.[88] Furthermore, we have seen in section 4.3 above that slight differences exist between the various worker lists: KUR-ilum shows strong connections with the monumental center at the acropolis; Išgi has certain links with animal husbandry; and Ḫalti employed more craftsmen and apprentices (dumu), which could place him in the city quarter around Field P (see 4.4.1.), although of course this must remain speculative.

87 Waetzoldt 1987.
88 Sallaberger and Ur 2004.

5.2. How Many Houses?

The excavations at the site of Tell Beydar aimed to expose a large area of the Beydar IIIb settlement, contemporary with phase 3 of the Beydar Acropolis sequence.[89] This is the period of the main administrative archive and the final period of a full-scale urban occupation of the site. In the following period Beydar IVa, the settlement was substantially reduced and the two palaces, most temples and the city wall were abandoned. The settled area inside the inner city wall comprised nearly 7 ha, of which ca. 1.2 ha were excavated until 2010.

The large-scale excavation of the settlement allows an attempt to reconstruct the number of houses at Tell Beydar—and thus an estimate of the overall population of the site as well. While some of the required parameters for such a calculation can be measured with some precision, others are just more or less plausible estimates.

Of the excavated area of 1.18 hectares, only 13.6% are covered with private houses, while official buildings (palaces and temples) cover 30.9% and buildings of economic use (storage buildings and workshops) another 28.8% (Table 10). Compared with other third millennium sites of comparable size (Table 11), this is a surprisingly high share of non-private architecture.

	Excavated area in ha	Share
City wall and gate	0.05	4.2%
Streets and open spaces	0.135	11.4%
Palaces	0.17	14.4%
Temples	0.195	16.5%
Storage buildings, workshops	0.34	28.8%
Houses	0.16	13.6%
Indistinguishable	0.13	11.0%
Total:	1.18	100%

Table 10: Use of the excavated area on the Upper City of Tell Beydar

One of the reasons for these percentages is the excavation strategy at Tell Beydar. For many years, the acropolis (where official buildings are concentrated and private houses are lacking completely) received the most attention and only later the Upper City outside the acropolis became the

[89] Lebeau and Suleiman 2003: Plans 6–9.

	Beydar IIIb	Halawa A 3[90]	Melebiye 2[91]
Site size	7 ha	11 ha	3.2 ha
Excavated	1.18 ha	0.39 ha	0.18 ha
City wall and gate	0.05 (4.2%)	0.065 (16.7%)	–
Houses	0.16 (13.6%)	0.19 (48.7%)	0.135 (75.6%)
Temples and Palaces	0.365 (30.9%)	0.065 (16.7%)	–
Storage buildings, workshops	0.34 (28.8%)	0.015 (3.8%)	–
Streets and open spaces	0.135 (11.4%)	0.045 (11.5%)	0.028 (15.7%)
indistinguishable	0.13 (11.0%)	0.01 (2.6%)	0.016 (8.7%)

Table 11: Share of different functional areas in the excavated areas of Beydar, Halawa A, and Melebiye

main focus of the excavations. The share of domestic architecture in the yet unexcavated parts of the Upper City is expected to be much higher. It seems proper to assume that large parts of the unexcavated area were covered with domestic quarters. However, as the results of the latest excavation seasons had made increasingly clear, the area outside the city center also has some large official (Eastern Palace) or economic (granary, workshop building of Field I) buildings.

For the following calculations, three alternative scenarios are used (Table 12). The first assumes that nearly all unexcavated space on the Upper City (5.8 ha) was filled with private houses, leaving only 0.2 ha for the remaining parts of partly excavated official buildings and 0.62 ha (11% of the remaining area) for streets and open spaces.[92] This would mean that 4.98 ha was occupied by additional private houses. Given the frequency of workshops and other buildings of economic use in the excavated parts of the Upper City, this scenario is extremely unlikely. But since it is the maximal possible figure, it gives an upper limit for the possible number of houses.

The second scenario assumes that a third of the available space is covered by official and economic buildings, which would leave 3.74 ha for domestic quarters and 3.33 ha for the houses themselves.

[90] Calculated on the base of the plans published in Orthmann 1989.
[91] Calculated from the plans published in Lebeau 1993.
[92] Following the share of 11.4% in the excavated parts of Tell Beydar. This agrees well with the data used by Postgate 1994: 56, who has 8.78–9.47% of street area for two quarters of Abu Salabikh. Postgate has noticed the absence of open areas in the samples chosen by him, which might explain the difference to Beydar, where some open areas were excavated (*e.g.*, the glacis north of the Acropolis Palace; for this, see Sténuit and Van der Stede 2003: 225, Fig. 1–3).

	All available space covered with houses	33% official and economic buildings	50% official and economic buildings
Domestic quarters	5.6 ha	3.74 ha	2.8 ha
Streets, open spaces	0.62 ha	0.41 ha	0.31 ha
Housing space	4.98 ha	3.33 ha	2.49 ha
Number of houses	830	555	415

Table 12: Available space for housing, according to different settlement patterns

The third scenario assumes that only 50% (2.8 ha) of the unexcavated area is built up with domestic quarters and the other half is covered with official and economic buildings and with some open areas (like dump sites). This would leave 2.49 ha for houses. This figure is used as the lower limit, since an even smaller share of houses appears to be very implausible.

As of 2010, 28 houses had been completely or partly excavated at Tell Beydar. The size of seventeen houses can be measured with certainty or with a high degree of probability. The average size of them (including walls) is 59 m^2. If the very large building B1 (358 m^2) is excluded, the remaining sixteen houses measure just 40.25 m^2 in average. Compared to other third millennium sites, both figures are remarkably low.[93]

One important reason for the small size of the houses is the partition of housing plots into two or more separate units. When constructed, each house had its own walls and the border between two houses was thus marked by a double wall. Later changes in the layout can be observed at several houses, e.g. at house 6 in Field B (fig. 7, see section 6.1 below).

If the double walls are interpreted as indicators of the original size of the house plots, these would have measured around 60 m^2. The distribution of these plots must have happened some time before the excavated state was reached, since a significant number of changes can be observed. The fact that the average house size shrank during the years

93 The mid-third millennium houses at Abu Salabikh measure 343 sq. m in average (Postgate 1994: 58), for roughly contemporary houses at Tell Khuera different averages were observed in different areas of the town: The excavated houses in area H ("Häuserviertel") have an average size of ca.135 sq. m. (Orthmann, Klein, and Lüth 1986: 25) while the houses of area K ("Kleiner Antentempel") measure just 48 sq. m. in average (Pfälzner 2001: Pl. 60).

before the excavated phase might indicate a shortage of available building space and probably also a population increase. It is unlikely that much unused space suitable for housing was available at Nabada at that time.

In Table 12, a figure of 60 m^2 is used as average for a house in Nabada at the time of the main administrative archive. This figure might turn out to be too low if much more elite residences similar to Building B1 show up in the future, but it seems adequate for the present. This results in 415–830 houses for the unexcavated part of the Upper City, to which twenty-five excavated houses[94] are to be added.

The figure of 60 m^2 for an average house including the walls agrees well with the average house-size postulated by Gelb, derived from a statistical evaluation of the size of houses based in sale documents, administrative texts, and court cases from the Fara to the Ur III period: the average size is ca. 1.33 *sar*, i.e. ca. 48 m^2, but probably excluding the walls.[95] The house sizes in sale contracts from Fara to the Sargonic period lead to the following average values:[96]

Fara period:	1.46 *sar* =	52.2 m^2
Presargonic period:	1.10 *sar* =	39.6 m^2
Sargonic period:	1.12 *sar* =	40.3 m^2
Ur III period:	3.48 *sar* =	125.3 m^2

Houses tend to be of varying size, and the evidence for the Ur III period is revealing in this regard: houses are between 36 and 732 m^2, but most often below 100 m^2.[97] In any case within the third millennium documentation, houses in the Presargonic period tend to be of the smallest size. This tendency apparently coincides with the archaeological trends.

5.3. How Many Families per House?

We know from the results of the excavations that the Beydar private houses had no second floor. No stairways had been found and the walls of the houses are too narrow (40 cm) to support more than 3 m of wall elevation, which is the normal height of a one-storied mud-brick house.

94 The figure is lower than the actually excavated 28 houses to adjust for only partly excavated houses.

95 Gelb 1976: 197.

96 The numbers are taken from the tables of Gelb et al. 1991: 269–273.

97 Collected by Waetzoldt 1996: 145–47. Piotr Steinkeller has kindly shown me two unpublished manuscripts concerning the size of houses in Ur III Umma, basically agreeing with the findings of Waetzoldt.

This means that the excavated rooms of the houses comprise all of the available space. Some activities, like the drying of cereal products, might have taken place on the roofs, but nobody really lived there.

Postgate has been very skeptical about the possibility of determining the number of families in a single house, since he considered it impossible to distinguish between nuclear and extended families in the archaeological record.[98] Stone and Henrickson were more optimistic when dealing with domestic quarters in Nippur and the Diyala region.[99] They assigned larger houses ("square houses" in Nippur) to extended family households and smaller ones ("linear houses") to nuclear families. This distinction might indeed be arbitrary, but in the specific case of Tell Beydar it is hardly conceivable that the small houses hosted more than a nuclear family.

Sources for the size of a nuclear family in third millennium Mesopotamia are rare. Waetzoldt has dealt with an Ur III text (BM 19972) from an unknown location in Southern Mesopotamia listing two to five persons per house.[100] Since the text mentions only the house-owners, their daughters and eventual slaves, Waetzoldt adds sons and one or two additional relatives and arrives at household sizes of five to nine persons for houses of 108 to 180 m^2. Gelb investigated various administrative documents from Presargonic to Ur III times,[101] and the most instructive example is the Presargonic text Nik I 19 with 55 persons in 12 families, *i.e.*, 4.5 persons/family including slaves.[102] Most researchers use figures between 3 and 6 persons.[103]

The Middle Assyrian "rations" lists from Tell Khuera/Ḫarbe give an indication for household sizes in the 13th century, since several of them list all recipients together with the head of the household, usually a married man. Twenty-eight households of people of local origin are listed, comprising of ca. 127 persons (4.53 persons/household). This includes a broad range of different household structures, from few single households and single parents to nuclear families with one to six children, some of them already adults. Servants (who occur rarely) were counted

98 Postgate 1994: 62.
99 Stone 1987: 126; Henrickson 1981: 76.
100 Waetzoldt 1996: 151–52.
101 Gelb 1979: 61–65.
102 Gelb 1979: 61–62; see also Magid 2001: 325.
103 Adams 1981: 144 uses 3.5 persons/family for Southern Mesopotamia; Pfälzner 2001: 33 uses modern ethnological data and arrives at an average of 5.5 persons per core family.

as household members, too. Another twelve households of Elamite deportees consisted of 43–45 persons (c. 3.67 persons/household).[104] The ration lists from Ḫarbe or contemporary Sabi Abyad indicate that roughly a third of the population were children.[105]

For the Middle Assyrian administration, a household was thus a group of people bound by kinship, marriage or service relations and receiving (and consuming) "rations" together.[106] This is basically the same definition as it is used today and it appears safe to use it also for third millennium contexts. We have every reason to believe that these economic groups actually lived together in one house. This does not exclude the possibility of several households, *i.e.*, families possibly including slaves, per house. In the archaeological record one should therefore expect at least storage facilities and a fireplace per household. The distribution of household installations, tools and pottery within the Beydar houses (see below) indicates clearly that a normal Beydar house was occupied by a single household or family only.

According to the sets of data just mentioned, the following calculations were thus made for 3, 4, or 5 persons per household, respectively. If one combines these data with the estimated number of houses, this results in a population of 1,320 (minimum) to 4,275 (maximum) people within the Upper city of Nabada. The more likely lower-to-medium calculations of house-covered space lead to the estimates of between 1,300

Number of houses	Housing space (as % of town)	3 persons/ household	4 persons/ household	5 persons/ household
855	5.14 ha (73%)	2565	3420	4275
570	3.49 ha (50%)	1710	2280	2850
440	2.65 ha (38%)	1320	1760	2200

Table 13: Estimate of the population of Tell Beydar/Nabada (Upper City) in the Beydar IIIb period using different parameters for housing space and household size.

[104] Jakob 2009: 17–18; 99–103, texts 70 and 71.

[105] Wiggermann 2000: 185–86 (Sabi Abyad, 34.5%); Jakob 2009: 18 (Ḫarbe, 33–38%).

[106] Jakob 2009: 17: Adult children with a finished professional training received their share through their father as long as they remained unmarried; this is different in the third millennium, where each recipient is listed individually.

and 2,900 inhabitants (see Table 13). These numbers are higher than 100–200 inhabitants per hectare, usually assumed by ethno-archaeological researchers and, following them, survey specialists,[107] but they are within the range of the estimates made by Postgate for Abu Salabikh.[108]

These calculations concern the Upper City of Tell Beydar, which was densely settled in the EJ IIIb period. Much less information is available on the Lower City (ca. 13 ha), situated in the outer perimeter of the *Kranzhügel.* The outer city wall, which encircled the Lower City, was abandoned already in the EJ II period, when the people of Nabada started to bury their deceased in the ruins of the abandoned wall.[109] Only few spots of the Lower City were excavated. Besides graves, only a small-scale workshop building in Field K has been uncovered so far.[110] A geomorphological study by Mauro Cremaschi (University of Milan) has led to the assumption that the Lower City was completely void of occupation.[111] As long as there is no proof of the existence of private houses in this part of the site, one can be confident that the domestic occupation in the period of the main archive of Tell Beydar did not extend beyond the walled Upper City.

5.4. Beydar's Population Versus Its Agricultural Base

A completely independent approach to the question of Beydar's population was used by Ur and Wilkinson, when they calculated the agricultural production of various sites in the region of Tell Beydar.[112] Ur and Wilkinson used surface structures, such as the hollow ways, which were still visible on satellite images taken during the 1960s, to determine the extent of agricultural land around various sites. With the assumption of certain parameters,[113] they arrived at the figure of 1,486 people, who could have been fed with the yield of Beydar's agricultural zone. These authors concluded that Beydar might have sustained a significantly larger

107 See Ur and Wikinson 2008: table 1 as being used for the Tell Beydar Survey (TBS); Adams 1981: 349–50; See Postgate 1994: 51, 63 with further references and a critical remark on the use of these numbers.

108 Postgate 1994: 62 gives a range of 248–1205 inhabitants/hectare.

109 Bretschneider 1997: 195.

110 Debruyne 2003.

111 Cremaschi and Perego 2014: 81–86.

112 Ur and Wilkinson 2008.

113 Biennial fallow; average cereal yield of 500 kg/ha and average yearly consumption of 250 kg/person; Ur and Wilkinson 2008: 313, table 1.

population by using the surplus of neighboring smaller sites (such as Tell Effendi). As they estimated, the latter sites produced enough grain to feed 2,744 individuals.

By grouping together the data from the entire survey area, Ur and Wilkinson reached a conclusion that the importation of food from its hinterland allowed a population of several thousand inhabitants at Tell Beydar.[114] This agrees well with the 1,300–2,900 inhabitants estimated according to the available building space (section 5.3), and the ±2,000 according to the textual evidence (section 5.1).

By using the actual records of grain yields and consumption in this region, one arrives at somewhat different figures. At Sabi Abyad in the Balikh region, one harvest in the Middle Asyrian period yielded 421 kg/ha.[115] Compared with the recent data from Near Eastern dry farming regions, this appears to be a rather bad harvest,[116] although other contemporary texts indicate even worse yields of 174 to 465 kg/ha.[117] However, the detailed study of Reculeau 2011 has demonstrated that the yields from Middle Assyrian Upper Mesopotamia are extremely low if compared with the yields in other periods and regions, this situation almost certainly having been due to the dry climate characteristic of that period. Therefore, the figure of 500 kg/ha used by Ur and Wilkinson is a much better estimate than of the low Middle Assyrian data, although it still might be too low. By using the figure in question, one obtains a yearly grain production of 375 tons for the agricultural zone around Tell Beydar, and 2,205 tons for the area covered by the Tell Beydar Survey. The Beydar texts record the grain "rations" in silà. This volume unit measured around one liter, according to Powell's calculations.[118] One liter of cleaned barley weighs ca. 0.62 kg.[119]

[114]Ur and Wilkinson 2008: 313. The authors remark that the Beydar region would have needed the import of additional workers during the harvest season.

[115]Wiggermann 2000: 193.

[116]Akkermans 1993: 214 assumes an average yield of 600 kg/ha for the prehistoric Balikh region. See for further data Wiggermann 2000: 193 with further references.

[117]Wiggermann 2000: Fig. 8.

[118]Powell 1984: 33, 41–42; Sallaberger 1996: 83.

[119]See the discussion by Wiggermann 2000: 186. He prefers to use 0.74 kg/l, which is at the upper end of the possible barley weights in modern times and above the 0.60–0.71 kg/l measured in the 19th century A.D. (Starke 2005: 48, note 96). The value of 0.62 kg/l used by van der Spek 1998 appears to be much more plausible.

Number of recipients	Monthly ration in liters (sìlà)	Total
206	130	26,780
129	90	11,610
42	80	3,360
257	60	15,420
6	30	180
Σ: 640	Average: 89.61	Σ: 57,350

Table 14: Monthly grain assignments for males in the Beydar worker lists (after Sallaberger 1996: 96f.)

The normal male professional in Nabada received 60 sìlà of grain per month, some professions (like the lú-ĝeš-DU, see 4.3. above) significantly more.[120] The average male rate thus was ca. 90 sìlà. Women received 30 sìlà, half the basic rate of males. The ratio of male to female grain recipients in the Beydar personnel lists is 3.28 : 1. Assuming that the numbers of adult males and females were roughly identical, this means that only about a third of the women received "rations" as payment for their work, and that the rest of them and the children received their grain from their husbands and fathers. The average yearly rate per inhabitant can thus be put at 248 kg; nearly the same value was used by Ur and Wilkinson.[121] At that rate, the 375,000 kg of grain from the fields around Tell Beydar could have sustained 1,512 individuals. Since the textual evidence treated above indicates a population of plus or minus 2,000 inhabitants (section 5.1), this figure highlights the importance of grain that was contributed by the rural satellites of Nabada. An independent indication of this importance is the fact that the agriculture of those sites was directly managed by Nabada's organization.[122]

[120] Sallaberger 1996: 93–98.

[121] Assuming that adult males, adult females and children each made up a third of the population and that only a third of the adult females received rations of their own. Thus the mean ration is based on an "average person" made up of a third each of 1 man (90 liters) + 1 woman (10 liters, a third of the women received rations) + 1 child (0 liters), thus 33.3 liters of grain per month, 400 liters per year.

[122] Sallaberger and Ur 2004.

6. Houses at Tell Beydar

According to its size and the evidence of non-residential buildings and open space (section 5.3), the site of Tell Beydar may have housed 2,000–2,500 persons. A similar picture emerges from the texts, which show the presence of least 1,200 persons, controlled by five chief officials. These data combined imply a workforce of 1,600 individuals, and, correspondingly, a total population of ±2,000 (assuming that only small children and perhaps some old people were not included in worker lists). All this proves that a large percentage of Nabada's population (if not its entirety) depended directly on a communal organization. This implies that there is hardly any room left for private enterprise, such as private business, handcrafts, etc.; and there is equally—as shown by the records of the sheep and goat herds—no room for independent, 'privately' organized nomads.[123] It follows, therefore, that the workmen appearing in the lists were inhabitants of Tell Beydar, who must have lived in the private houses excavated by the Tell Beydar archaeological mission.

6.1. What Did a Typical Beydar House Look Like?

An example of one of the houses excavated in Field B shall be considered here. House 6[124] is situated just south of the "Tablet House" and north of the U-shaped building (fig. 8). It covers an area of ca. 61 m^2 and is—like most of the buildings at Beydar—of trapezoid rather than rectangular shape due to the radial street system. The western part of the house is partly destroyed by a large Hellenistic pit, but its plan is clear.

At some time before the sudden abandonment of the quarter at the end of phase Beydar IIIb,[125] House 6 was divided. The two north-eastern rooms 2597 and 2558 (house 6a) were separated from the rest of the house and received a separate entrance from lane 2592. The remaining larger part (house 6b) was accessible from street 28936 in the south-west. The subdivision of a house into several subunits is a common phenom-

[123] See Pruß and Sallaberger 2003/04; Sallaberger 2004a on the integration of sheep husbandry in the urban economy, thus leaving no space in the region of Tell Beydar.

[124] Van der Stede 2007: 10–11, Fig. 6. 9. 11, Plans I–II.

[125] The whole Beydar IIIb settlement was obviously left in a hurry, since many buildings at different places of the site have yielded rich ceramic inventories from the occupation. There is, however, no evidence of a violent destruction or widespread burning.

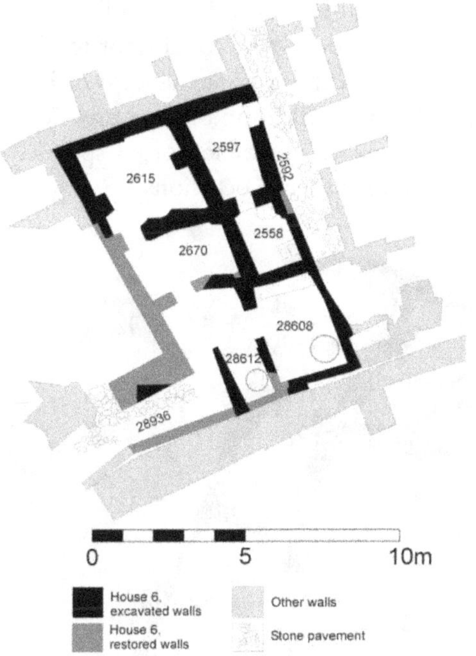

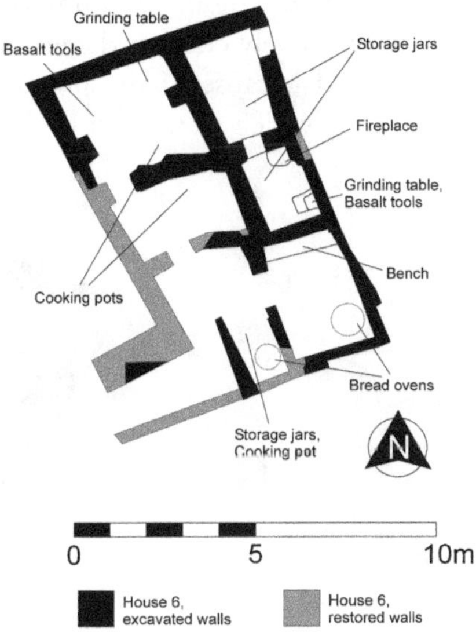

Fig. 8 and 9: Beydar house 6, layout and distribution of installations and domestic tools (A. Pruß after Van der Stede 2007: Plan II)

enon in densely inhabited settlements.[126] House divisions like this one might have happened when adult children received part of their parents' house upon marriage, when a house was divided by several heirs, or when some rooms of a house were sold. House 6a has an area of just 15 m^2; house 6b measures 46 m^2, which in both cases includes the walls. The actual space between the walls was considerably smaller (60–65% of the house area).

The presence of domestic installations (grinding stones; fireplace; storage vessels; fig. 9) proves that even the very small house 6a was indeed inhabited. It is possible that one of the two kitchen rooms (28608 and 28612) with a bread oven (*tannūr*) in the south of house 6b was actually used by the inhabitants of house 6a. In addition to the installations and finds mentioned in fig. 9, all rooms contained ordinary domestic pottery (bowls, goblets, and small and medium sized jars).

[126] See Pfälzner 2001: 97–100 for the development of an extended family's house in modern Syria.

The functional interpretation of the different rooms is shown in fig. 10. Both houses have space for storage, preparation, and cooking of food. Room 2670 of house 6b is interpreted as a reception room, since it is situated relatively close to the entrance, has no indication of food production, and because of the presence of some vessels of imported special wares,[127] which were most probably used for special occasions.

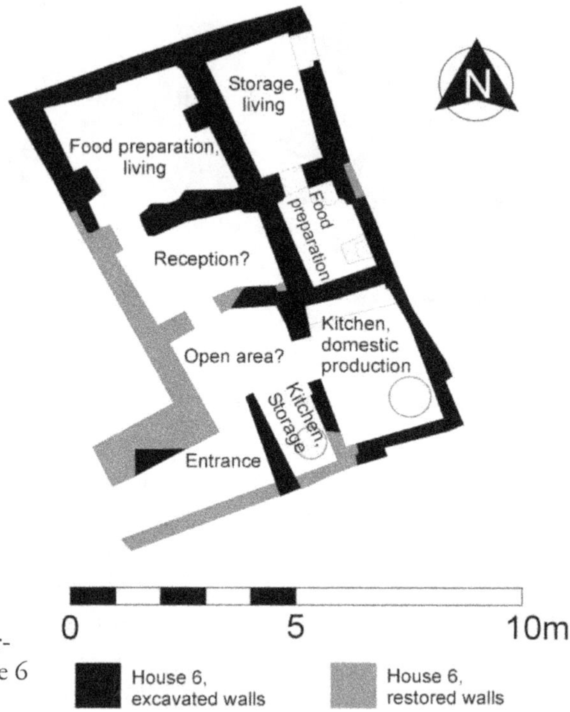

Fig. 10: Functional interpretation of Beydar house 6 (A. Pruß)

The storage capacity of the Beydar houses did not significantly exceed the size of the monthly "rations." There is rarely more than one large storage jar of 90–120 liters capacity. The inhabitants thus depended on the regular distribution of grain, since they simply could not store enough grain to wait for the next harvest.

The production capacities of the houses were sufficient to fulfill normal domestic needs, *i.e.*, mainly food production. But the excavated Beydar houses yielded no evidence for a production of professional craftsmen. These activities must have been situated elsewhere.

[127] In this case these vessels were made of Metallic Ware, a dense and clinky fabric typical for the late EJZ 2 and EJZ 3 periods. On this ware, see Pruß 2000.

6.2. An Elite Residence?

Building B1 in Field B[128] is so far the best candidate for an elite residence at Beydar (fig. 11). The building measures more than 350 m^2 and has rather thick walls of good quality. It is of trapezoid outer shape and consists of two rows of rectangular rooms on both sides of a trapezoid open space in the center. One room in the east of the building housed a large staircase, which proves the existence of a second floor. The building has three phases (B1/c to B1/a). The two later phases yielded a large amount of pottery, among it many storage vessels, but also typical domestic pottery.[129] This building is however not devoted exclusively to storage, since its layout differs fundamentally from the storage complexes known so far from Beydar (on them see 7.1. below). Nor is it a workshop, since it lacks the relevant installations. There is also no evidence for a representative or cultic function.

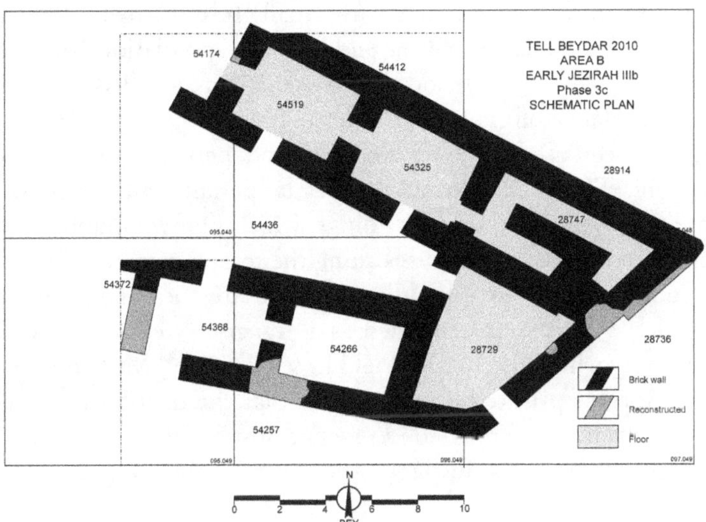

Fig. 11: Beydar, field B: building B1 (A. Pruß after Van der Stede and Devillers 2014: Plan III)

Two tablet fragments and a few sealings were found in the earliest phase of building B1, which might hint at a role in the city administration. But these objects were found in the fill of room 28729, not on the floor, and might have been discarded material from the nearby Acropolis Palace.

[128] Van der Stede and Devillers 2011: 16–22, Plans 2–4; *ead.* 2014: 11–31.
[129] Van der Stede and Devillers 2011: Fig. 45–51; *ead.* 2014: fig. 18–20.

The two later phases of building B1 yielded no tablets and only one door sealing found on the floor of room 54325.[130] A domestic use of building B1 seems thus the most convincing interpretation, at least for the two later phases. Considering the extent of the building and the wealth of its (ceramic) inventory one can safely assume that the head of the household was a member of the local elite, and one of the five leading officials would be a possible candidate. If that was the case, one could envision a larger number of servants actually living within the house.

7. Conclusions

7.1. Archaeological Evidence for the "Ration" System and Collective Labor

The cuneiform documentation reveals that the employees of Nabada's communal organization were paid according to rank, sex and age and to profession; as usual, the monthly portions were calculated in grain. The existence of a distributive system can actually be discerned in the archaeological record. Here, we will not address the speculations that beveled rim bowls of the Uruk period or the Akkadian so-called silà bowls[131] might be evidence of grain distribution. This is unlikely; the silà bowls might have been used for some prepared food, perhaps soup, a main dish of that time. The remains from Tell Beydar pertaining to grain distribution are large, central storage buildings, which point to public use: rows of storage rooms and warehouses along the temple terraces of the acropolis,[132] and a monumental building near the street leading to the eastern gate, which can be only explained as a granary,[133] even if it was completely empty when discovered (Field E, see fig. 3).[134] More importantly, the inventory of private houses suggests that the distributive system of monthly "rations" was realized in practice, just as the lists indicate: a private house contains only one large storage jar of 90–120 liters and several

130 The design of the seal used on this door sealing is different from the 'Brak style' seals typical for official contexts.

131 See Weiss and Senior 1992 on the silà-bowls from Leilan, where wasters were found in large quantities, giving the impression not only of mass production, but also of mass rationing. Similar bowls of ca. 1 liter were used at Beydar IIIb as well, but they are not of a standardized size and were not found in large quantities.

132 Bretschneider 2003: Pl. 9; Fig. 27. 39; Suleiman 2007: Pl. I–II.

133 Sténuit 2003.

134 For communal storage buildings in the EJZ III period see Pfälzner 2011: 197–199, listing only Tell Beydar for the period concerned.

small storage jars (section 6.1). This is in marked contrast to the storage facilities in the palace or the temple terraces. And the relevance of this distribution of storage facilities is underlined by a comparison with other periods, for example the Late Bronze Age private houses of Tall Bazi on the Middle Euphrates which always contained several large storage jars[135] and featured separate rooms for storage.[136] Furthermore, concerning the layout of the houses, it may be relevant that they are of a regular size and plan at least in their original form (section 6.1). These so-called "allotment houses" (*Parzellenhäuser*) were described by Pfälzner as the typical house of the Early Jezirah IIIa-b periods,[137] and they may well represent the appropriate housing for the inhabitants of a town with a collective urban management of labor.

Steinkeller has repeatedly pointed out that the administrative necessity to list people does not directly represent a social reality.[138] A list of workers under their foreman may in fact be the bureaucratic construct of a family specialized in some craft. The evidence of Tell Beydar adds another facet to this picture: the private living conditions of those on the worker lists. From the assyriologist's point of view, the administrative documentation of the third millennium has largely obscured a perspective on the role of the family and domestic life. In fact, most of the evidence concerning the laborers' private life is circumstantial, based for example on family traditions of professions, the religious sphere including the role of the family god, and the care of the dead,[139] or rare indications on the size of families.[140]

As argued in section 5, the persons summarized in the worker lists are the inhabitants of Tell Beydar. In this regard it is important to note that despite the urban character of the site (fig. 3) a large part of the population was engaged in agriculture (see Table 9, section 4.3). And since the field-work was organized collectively, no traces of it can be found in the houses of the town: the tools were kept in separate store-rooms, the harvested grain in granaries, and the oxen and equids used in the cultivation of the fields were assigned to work by the communal organization.[141]

135 Otto 2006: 93–94.
136 Otto 2006: 239–40.
137 Pfälzner 2001: 378–79; Pfälzner 2011: 152–164
138 See, *e.g.*, Steinkeller 1987, 1996, 1999: 294.
139 Selz 2006.
140 See above 5.2. on Nik 1 19.
141 Sallaberger 1996: 90–92.

Furthermore, the craftsmen and those fulfilling services must also have lived in the private houses exposed by the excavations. Generally, larger-scale domestic production is hardly attested in the residential areas of that time and region, known for example at Tell Khuera (areas H and K), Tell Melebiya and other places.[142] The houses excavated at Tell Beydar are mostly of modest dimensions. Usually, one house accommodates one family or household, as is evidenced by the single oven. And food production is the only work that can be documented in the houses themselves.

Work was therefore not only organized collectively, as the worker lists testify, but it must also have taken place in collectively run ergasteria. The strange U-shaped building[143] close to the acropolis, which was perhaps a place for fattening animals if it did not serve another purpose, would ideally fit the condition. We already mentioned the food production on the acropolis and the metal workshop in the former Eastern Palace (section 4.4).[144] In this regard also the storerooms and production areas along the temple terraces and in the acropolis palace become relevant, especially since there are no indications that many persons, if any, lived within the monumental buildings (see section 4.4). The enormous space used by workshops and storage buildings, almost 30% of the town in the excavated parts of Tell Beydar (Table 10), underlines the importance of places of collective labor in a city of that period.

To summarize: The inhabitants of ancient Nabada worked together with their peers in communal workshops, storerooms or in the fields, they received monthly barley portions from the communal granaries, and they prepared food and lived in their small houses of the densely inhabited city.

[142] See Lebeau 1993 and Pfälzner 2001: 295–305 for Melebiye; Orthmann, Klein, and Lüth 1986: 6–25 and Pfälzner 2001: 325–45 for Khuera H and K. The recent excavations in the lower town of Tell Khuera (area U) have however yielded buildings with a variety of installations, especially ovens (Meyer 2010: 176). These structures are interpreted as private houses with integrated workshops (J.-W. Meyer, personal communication).

[143] Sténuit and Van der Stede 2003: 226–29; Van der Stede 2007: 8–10, Plan I–II.

[144] Compare also the situation at Tell Khuera, where the just abandoned palace (F) was used as potter's workshop at the very end of the EJZ 3b period: Orthmann and Pruß 1995: 124–25.

7.2. The Communal Workforce in Context: Subsistence Economy and Specialized Crafts

The workforce of the city of Nabada, a provincial center of some 2,000 inhabitants, was organized into five parallel groups. Allowing some fluctuation and variation, this model appears similar to the management of workforce as we know it elsewhere from Early Mesopotamia. A good example is again provided by the Emunus of Girsu, the household of the ruler's wife (see section 2.1). The archive covers also partly the organizations of the governor's children, and for each single household a largely parallel list of professions is documented; the size of a household determines the number of persons and the presence or absence of various professions. In the case of Girsu, the households are named after their leaders, the wife or the children, or, after Urukagina's reforms, after the corresponding chief deities, the goddess Bawu and the divine children Sulshagana and Ig'alim.

In the case of Nabada, it is impossible to identify the role of the five officials at the top of the lists: the extremely laconic texts never assign titles to personal names. Thus, one might speculate that they were officials in the service of the ruler of Nagar, or members of a local elite bound to city quarters, or tribal chiefs, or even temple administrators— and it is possible to bring forth arguments in favor of each of these alternatives, which, in fact, are not mutually exclusive. The five leading officials are listed without any differentiation, so they could be regarded as officials of the same rank installed by the ruler of Nagar; however, the organization of work would more sensibly be entrusted to local persons of good standing, although loyalty towards the overlord was surely expected. The role of the city quarters designated by the city gates may indicate that the five groups in fact lived together in their own respective neighborhoods, but this must remain an assumption. Tribal organization has always been considered a relevant factor for early Upper Mesopotamia, although the texts give no indication at all in this regard. And finally, Tell Beydar boasts five large temples in the center of the city (Fields F and M), and the five officials could also have been related to them.

In any case, there is no doubt that the organization in question ran the city. There is no apparent dominating presence of a ruler or palace, and the temples appear only indirectly as recipients of sheep for sacrifices. Therefore, it is appropriate to speak of an urban organization that managed the economy including the workforce of Nabada. The contemporary documents of Mari provide a similar perspective.[144a] Be that as it

[144a] Sallaberger 2014.

may, it is evident that the five leading officials were subject to a superior political power, since they are listed together on the same tablets and their ration lists were found at the same place. This superior power may have been either a local representative of the regional ruler or more likely a city council (unken), the existence of which is demonstrated by the mentions, found in the Beydar documents, of the visits paid to it by the ruler of Nagar.[145] As an educated guess, one may therefore describe the hierarchy of control at Nabada as follows:

Ruler (EN) of Nagar
|
Nabada city council (unken) (?)
|
Five organizations, city quarters (?)

As concerns the composition of the workforce, the Beydar lists (Table 9) can be compared to the personnel of the Emunus of Presargonic Girsu (Table 1–3). By and large the same set of professions is included, and in this way the Tell Beydar organization can be described, like the Emunus, as an example of subsistence economy with a specialized sector (cartwrights and textile production, respectively). Both in Sumer and in the Habur basin by far the largest group was composed by men working in agriculture (RU lugal and lú-ĝeš-DU (APIN), respectively). Those men were evidently dependent on the ruler, thus providing soldiers for his army; in this direction points also their appearance together with groups functioning as police. One can add another example to this overview: at contemporary Early Dynastic Mari, the tablets from Chantier B similarly indicate that the respective organization was active in the subsistence economy of agriculture, food production and upkeep of the buildings.[146]

The differences in the composition of the workforce depended on two factors, the specific organization and the rank of the settlement. Concerning the organization, at Nabada, KUR-ilum was probably linked to the acropolis palace, and Ḫalti managed a larger group of craftsmen (see section 4.3); at Girsu, textile production was directed by the queen of Lagash; and at Early Dynastic Mari, one organization concentrated on providing offerings, another one on donkey breeding and riverine trade.[147]

[145] Sallaberger 1996: 106 ad (2).
[146] Sallaberger 2014.
[147] Sallaberger 2014.

Finally, it is clear that the rank of a city largely influenced the composition of its workforce. We use a simple three-tiered system with the capital of a state as the first rank; examples here include Girsu, Ebla, Nagar, Mari. Nabada is a rare representative of the second rank city, a provincial center. The smaller settlements are designated as the third rank, of which those in the province of Nabada provide textually attested examples.[148] To start with the third rank, the documents from Tell Beydar indicate that their agricultural production was organized by Nabada as well, whereas the five leading officials, which represent the provincial center of Nabada, were based in the town. So the diversification of labor and crafts appears to be a typical feature of the town, the center above the agricultural settlements.

The first rank city, the capital of the state, is first of all characterized by the presence of the ruler's palace. Although the palace with its own specific economy is based at the capital, the palace does not embrace the city itself, as most clearly expressed in the phrase SA.ZA$_x$^{ki} *wa ib-la*^{ki}, "Palace and Ebla".[149] The best example known for a palatial economy dealing mostly with the treasure of the state is provided by the texts of Ebla, whereas this specific focus transpires only rarely in the documents of the Emunus.[150]

The capital is apparently characterized by a more comprehensive differentiation of professions and crafts, including for example the management of prestige goods as silver and metals, specific textiles, equids,[151] or the control of overland trade. A comparison of the professions shows that the Sumerian Emunus organization is more diversified than Nabada, and it includes more specialized professions both in agriculture and horticulture and in crafts; additionally some persons are employed at the palace as attendants of the mistress of Lagash. The scope of crafts performed is significantly different: at Beydar, those dealing with prestige goods are completely or at least largely missing like black-smiths, producers of perfumed oil, and textile workers. Similar to the situation at Girsu, at Early Dynastic Mari the tablets from *Chantier* B reveal an urban organization that apparently managed overland trade by donkey and

148 Sallaberger and Ur 2004.

149 E.g. *ARET* 9, Index

150 Sallaberger 2013.

151 In this context note the specific link of equids to the capital Nagar as argued both on the archaeological and the textual evidence by Pruß and Sallaberger 2003/04.

riverine traffic by boat, a sector that generated high amounts of silver.[152] Although these organizations at Girsu and Mari devoted a large part of their workforce to subsistence economy, they were also specialized in crafts and services that benefitted the population of the city as a whole. This division of labor is at a lower level already visible between the second-rank city of Nabada and the agricultural settlements in the hinterland.[153]

Rank	*Description*	*Presargonic archives*
First rank: capital city	Palace with management of royal treasure	Ebla palace archives
	City: high diversification of crafts and services in urban organizations	Emunus of Girsu; Mari Chantier B
Second rank: provincial center	City: diversification of crafts and services	Tell Beydar/Nabada
Third rank settlements ("villages")	"Urban" high density in building, agricultural tasks	(no archives; an excavated site is, *e.g.*, Melebiye)

Table 15: Rank of settlements and internal differentiation

7.3. Communal Labor in Babylonia, Upper Mesopotamia, and Syria in the Early Bronze Age

The comparison with Girsu has demonstrated how the composition of the Beydar workforce conforms to the general picture of Early Mesopotamian communal organizations. The choice of Girsu is mainly dictated by the available evidence: other Mesopotamian archives are too fragmentary. The few documents from Mari have provided additional information on the setup of organizations at that period. The texts on cereals from Ebla,[154] however, do not list grain "rations," but are a documentation of the food given out to the people present at the palace at a given moment; in this way the Ebla texts are of the same type as the very common "bread and beer" texts from Early Mesopotamia. So the

152 Sallaberger 2014.
153 See also section 5.4 above and the reference to the study of Ur and Wilkinson 2008.
154 Milano 1990.

Beydar tablets help to place the Ebla documentation in the right perspective: the absence of worker lists in Ebla does not necessarily mean that the distributive system as known from Southern Mesopotamia was unknown in Syria and Northern Mesopotamia.

The cuneiform tablets from Tell Beydar are the first written documents that testify to the existence of collective labor and monthly grain assignments in Upper Mesopotamia in the third millennium, a fact previously unknown. Without the first-hand knowledge one had to rely on evidence from later periods, especially the second millennium, and extrapolate from the few facts known. This has resulted in the common opinion that Southern Sumer differed fundamentally in its social and economic organization from the North, Upper Mesopotamia and Syria. This widely accepted image has definitely influenced the archaeologists' investigations of private houses and their socio-economic interpretations based thereupon (see section 1).

Since the Beydar documents force us to rethink the assumed differences between Northern and Southern society and economy, we will very briefly review some evidence that has been brought forward in this regard. Gelb in his time linked the concept of the ration with his understanding of the society of Early Mesopotamia, and this picture has formed our conception not only of the "rationing" system, but also how one viewed a "working class" of Early Mesopotamia.[155] At that time, Gelb had postulated a strict difference between the society of third millennium Sumer and that of the Old Babylonian period.[156] Along similar lines, namely differentiating between a Sumerian South and the Semitic-speaking north, he characterized the economy of Ebla and thereby northern Syria as follows:

> Sheep raising was the mainstay of the local economy; thousands of sheep were raised, supplying the wool for the production of textiles, the main export product of Ebla. Thus wool was the basis of Ebla's commercial prosperity and political power. ...
>
> The closest parallel to Ebla, with its tremendous number of texts dealing with textiles and metal products, is Assyria in the much later "Cappadocian" period, where these two classes of texts also domi-

[155] Especially Gelb 1965.

[156] Note in this regard that Steinkeller in the introduction to this volume points to the important role of hired labor already in the Ur III period, which is another aspect of socio-economic continuity in Babylonia.

> nate. Old Assyria, like Ebla, was largely devoid of natural resources, had little grain and plenty of wool, and was forced to import metals in return for textiles.[157]

Gelb explained the difference between Lagash and Ebla as based on cultivation methods, whereby his negative impression of the climatic and soil conditions of Ebla is hardly compatible with the excellent situation in the region. This idea of a fundamental division between North and South, whereby the North span from Ebla to Northern Babylonia including Kish, was embraced by many, most prominently Steinkeller:

> These deep-rooted differences between the southern and northern economies, though progressively less and less distinct, survived well into the second millennium, and, in some places, much later. The dominance of temple households in the south, as contrasting their comparative insignificance in the north [*i.e.*, of Babylonia, W. S.], continued during Old Babylonian times [...]
>
> Although the organizing principle of northern Babylonian institutions contrasts sharply with that of southern ones, it shows close affinities with that of Pre-Sargonic Ebla. At Ebla, too, the dominant economic institution was the palace, which controlled extensive areas of agricultural land and was the main center for the production and distribution of goods. [...]
>
> Another characteristic feature of the Ebla organization, which I would suggest can also be detected in the organization of early northern Babylonia, is the markedly stratified nature of the Ebla society. This is demonstrated by the presence at Ebla of a fully developed aristocratic ruling class, the likes of which was unknown in southern Babylonia. Although the Ebla aristocracy was city based, its origins were likely tribal, as is strongly implied by the active involvement of its members in the economic and political life of the countryside. [...] A similar type of social organization is discernible, many centuries later, at Alalakh and Ugarit, in northern Syria, and, closer to Babylonia, at the city of Assur, where the power was shared by "the king and the City."[158]

Later, Steinkeller has further developed the contrast in the various systems of land tenure, the royal dominion at Ebla contrasted with the organization of the domain land by the temples in the Ur III period in the South.[159]

[157] Gelb 1986: 158, 163.
[158] Steinkeller 1993: 123–24.
[159] Steinkeller 1999.

Although the problems involved are highly complex and cannot even be touched in this article, we are obliged to address the wider implications of the Tell Beydar evidence concerning the current understanding of regional differences in the third millennium. Of course no simple solution for all existing data and models can be proposed here, so it will suffice (1) to discuss briefly the arguments behind the traditional understanding of the socio-economic conditions of Northern Mesopotamia and Syria; and (2) to address the context of the Ebla archives, the largest written contemporaneous corpus from the same region.

First, it has to be emphasized that most notions about the socio-economic structure of Assyria, Upper Mesopotamia and Syria in the third millennium were derived from or at least heavily influenced by later, second-millennium evidence, as demonstrated by the citations above. In this regard, however, more recent historical research based on data from archaeological surveys and the textual record has proven that the geo-political situation of the Presargonic period differed fundamentally from that of the early second millennium and later. In the mid-third millennium an uninterrupted series of city states with close political and cultural interaction among them reached from Babylonia through Upper Mesopotamia to Syria.[160] With the break-down of urban culture in Upper Mesopotamia at the end of the Early Jezirah IIIb period, the destruction of Mari by Sargon and its temporal decline and the emergence of the Amorites at the end of the third millennium these interconnections were interrupted forever and the situation changed completely.[161] This historical development helps to explain why the third millennium situation can be judged to have been as substantially different than the one in later periods.

Secondly, the Ebla data were regularly interpreted as evidence of a culture shaped by regional differences. However, the composition of the Ebla archives and their perspective is the best example of a palatial economy that concentrated on the management of the royal treasure, as it is found also, for example, in Ur III Puzrish-Dagan or the Old Babylonian Sînkashid texts from Uruk; also the Presargonic Emunus texts give some indications about the special economic role of the palace. This perspective includes the presence of certain sectors of the society that do not

[160] Interestingly the region on the Middle and Upper Tigris and to the East of the Tigris, including later Assyria, was of little importance at this time; this changed completely with the Sargonic period.

[161] Sallaberger 2007.

appear in documents on land and labor, such as the royal court, members of the army, or messengers.[162] Concerning the complex situation of land tenure, also here the apparently different situation is largely due to the perspective of the documentation: the Ebla archives highlight the royal sector, whereas the Ur III documents treat the provincial sector of the governor (ensí), albeit the royal sector was present as well to a considerable extent, even if not so well covered by the extant documentation.[163]

Steinkeller's article cited earlier was published in 1993, the same year when cuneiform tablets were discovered at Tell Beydar, ancient Nabada. These sources surprisingly demonstrated that the allotment system, the collective and communal cultivation of land were economic features at home both in Southern Sumer and in Northern Upper Mesopotamia, thus shattering the traditional view on third millennium Mesopotamia.[164] The similarities in the internal organization of labor do not exclude that regional differences may well have existed at a higher level, concerning the control of the land by temples, cities and/or the palace. In any case, the combination of the textual and archaeological record at Tell Beydar allows a more differentiated understanding of home and work in Early Dynastic Upper Mesopotamia. It will be the task of future research to investigate similar questions for other regions and periods as well, and to elaborate the regional, chronological and institutional variations of collective labor.

BIBLIOGRAPHY

Adams, Robert McC. (1981), *Heartland of Cities* (Chicago: University of Chicago Press).

Akkermans, Peter M. M. G. (1993), *Villages in the Steppe. Later Neolithic Settlement and Subsistence in the Balikh Valley, Northern Syria* (International Monographs in Prehistory 5; Ann Arbor: Oxbow Books).

Archi, Alfonso, and Biga, Maria Giovanna (2003), "A victory over Mari and the fall of Ebla," *Journal of Cuneiform Studies* 55: 1–44.

[162] Sallaberger 2013.
[163] Steinkeller 2013, section II, extensively discusses the royal sector and its relation to the institutional economies, as he calls it, for the Ur III period.
[164] As formulated, *e.g.*, by Pfälzner 2001, see fn. 17 above.

Attinger, Pascal (1997), [Review of The Sumerian Dictionary of the University Museum of the University of Pennsylvania. Vol. 1 A Part II], *Zeitschrift für Assyriologie und Vorderasiatische Archäologie* 87: 112–22.

Bauer, Josef (1998), "Der vorsargonische Abschnitt der mesopotamischen Geschichte," in P. Attinger and M. Wäfler (eds.), *Annäherungen 1: Mesopotamien, Späturuk-Zeit und Frühdynastische Zeit* (Orbis Biblicus et Orientalis 160/1; Freiburg/Schweiz: Universitätsverlag, and Göttingen: Vandenhoeck & Ruprecht): 429–585.

Bonechi, Marco (2003), "Leopards, cauldrons, and a beautiful stone. Notes on some early Syrian texts from Tell Beydar and Ebla," in *Semitic and Assyriological Studies Presented to Pelio Fronzaroli* (Wiesbaden: Harrassowitz): 75–96.

Bretschneider, Joachim (1997), "Untersuchungen an der äußeren Wallanlage (Feld H)," in Lebeau and Suleiman 1997: 193–207.

— (2003), "Der spätfrühdynastische „Palast-Tempel" auf der Akropolis von Tell Beydar: Die Bauschichten der Phase 3 a/b (Früh-Gezira IIIb)," in Lebeau and Suleiman 2003: 65–140.

Bretschneider, Joachim, and Jans, Greta (1998), "Wagon and chariot representations in the Early Dynastic glyptic", in M. Lebeau (ed.), *About Subartu. Studies Devoted to Upper Mesopotamia*, Vol. 2 (Subartu 4/2) Turnhout 1998): 155–78.

Bretschneider, Joachim; Jans, Greta, and Suleiman, Antoine (2003), "Die akkadzeitlichen Tempel auf der Akropolis von Tell Beydar: Die Bauschichten Früh Gezira IV-Zeit," in Lebeau and Suleiman 2003: 149–67.

Cremaschi, Mauro, and Perego, Alessandro (2014), "Tell Beydar in its Geomorphological Context," in Milano and Lebeau 2014: 75–89.

Dahl, Jacob (2010), "A Babylonian Gang of Potters. Reconstucting the Social Organization of Crafts Production in the Late Third Millennium BC Southern Mesopotamia," in L. Kogan *et al.* (eds.), *City Administration in the Ancient Near East. Proceedings of the 53*[e] *Rencontre Assyriologique Internationale* (Babel und Bibel 5; Winona Lake, Indiana: Eisenbrauns): 275–306.

Debruyne, Michel (2003), "Research on the Outer Rampart (Field K)," in Lebeau and Suleiman 2003: 387–94.

Englund, Robert K. (1990), *Organisation und Verwaltung der Ur III-Fischerei* (Berliner Beiträge zum Vorderen Orient 10; Berlin: Reimer).

Foster, Benjamin R. (1982), *Umma in the Sargonic Period* (Hamden, Ct.: Archon Books).

Foxvog, Dan A. (2011), "Aspects of Name-Giving in Presargonic Lagash," in W. Heimpel and G. Frantz-Szabó (eds.), *Strings and Threads. A Celebration of the Work of Anne Draffkorn Kilmer* (Winona Lake, Ind.: Eisenbrauns): 59–97.

Gelb, Ignace J. (1965), "The ancient Mesopotamian ration system," *Journal of Near Eastern Studies* 24: 230-43.

— (1976), "Quantitative evaluation of slavery and serfdom," in B. L. Eichler (ed.), *Kramer Anniversary Volume* (AOAT 25; Kevelaer: Butzon & Bercker, and Neukirchen-Vluyn: Neukirchener Verlag): 195–207.

— (1979), "Household and family in Early Mesopotamia," in E. Lipiński (ed.), *State and Temple Economy in the Ancient Near East* (OLA 5; Leuven: Department Orientalistiek): 1–97.

— (1980), "Comparative Method in the Study of the Society and Economy of the Ancient Near East," *Rocznik Orientalistyczny* 41: 29–36.

— (1986), "Ebla and Lagash: Environmental contrast," in H. Weiss (ed.), *The Origins of Cities in Dry-Farming Syria and Mesopotamia in the Third Millennium BC* (Guilford Ct.: Four Quarters): 157–67.

Gelb, Ignace J.; Steinkeller, Piotr, and Whiting, Robert M. (1991), *Earliest Land Tenure Systems in the Near East: Ancient Kudurrus* (OIP 104; Chicago: Oriental Institute of the University of Chicago).

Henrickson, Elizabeth F. (1981), "Non-Religious Residential Settlement Patterning in the Late Early Dynastic of the Diyala Region," *Mesopotamia* 16: 43–140.

Ismail, Farouk; Sallaberger, Walther; Talon, Philippe; and Van Lerberghe, Karel (1996), *Administrative Documents from Tell Beydar (Seasons 1993–1995)* (Subartu 2; Turnhout: Brepols).

Jakob, Stefan (2009), *Die mittelassyrischen Texte aus Tell Chuēra in Nordost-Syrien* (Vorderasiatische Forschungen der Max Freiherr von Oppenheim-Stiftung 2, III; Wiesbaden: Harrassowitz).

Koslova, Natalia (2008), "Bezeichnungen der Arbeitskräfte in Umma der Ur III-Zeit," in S.J. Garfinkle & J. Cale Johnson (eds.), *The Growth of an Early State in Mesopotamia: Studies in Ur III Administration* (Biblioteca del Próximo Oriente Antiguo 5; Madrid: Consejo Superior de Investigaciones Científicas): 149–206.

Lebeau, Marc (1993), *Tell Melebiya, Cinq campagnes de recherches sur le Moyen-Khabour (1984–1988)* (Akkadica Supplementum 9; Leuven: Peeters).

— (1996), "Le contexte archéologique et stratigraphique de la "Maison aux Tablettes" (Tell Beydar – chantier B – campagnes 1993 et 1994)," in Ismail *et al.* 1996: 3–29.

— (2004), "Le contexte archéologique et stratigraphique des documents épigraphiques découverts entre 1996 et 2002," in Milano *et al.* 2004: 1–11.

Lebeau, Marc (ed.) (2011), *Jazirah: Associated Regional Chronologies for the Ancient Near East and the Eastern Mediterranean* 1 (Turnhout: Brepols).

Lebeau, Marc and Suleiman, Antoine (eds.) (1997), *Tell Beydar, Three Seasons of Excavations (1992-1994). A Preliminary Report* (Subartu 3; Turnhout: Brepols).

— (2003), *Tell Beydar, the 1995–1999 Seasons of Excavations. A Preliminary Report* (Subartu 10; Turnhout: Brepols).

— (2007), *Tell Beydar, The 2000–2002 Seasons of Excavations, The 2003–2004 Seasons of Architectural Restoration. A Preliminary report* (Subartu 15; Turnhout: Brepols).

— (2011), *Tell Beydar, The 2004/2–2009 Seasons of Excavations, The 2004/2–2009 Seasons of Architectural Restoration. A Preliminary Report* (Subartu 29; Turnhout: Brepols).

— (2014), *Tell Beydar, The 2010 Season of Excavations and Architectural Restoration – A Preliminary Report* (Subartu 34; Turnhout: Brepols).

Maekawa, Kazuya (1987), "Collective labour service in Girsu-Lagash: the Pre-Sargonic and Ur III periods," in Powell 1987: 49–71.

Magid, Glenn (2001), "Micromanagement in the é-mi[sic]/^{d}Ba-ú: Notes on the Organization of Labor at Early Dynastic Lagash," in T. Abusch *et al.* (eds.), *Historiography in the cuneiform world. Proceedings of the XLVe Rencontre Assyriologique Internationale* (Bethesda Md.: CDL press): 313–28.

Matthews, Roger (2003), *The Archaeology of Mesopotamia. Theories and approaches* (London and New York: Routledge).

Meyer, Jan-Walke (ed.) (2010), *Tell Chuēra: Vorberichte zu den Grabungskampagnen 1998 bis 2005* (Vorderasiatische Forschungen der Max Freiherr von Oppenheim-Stiftung 2, II; Wiesbaden: Harrassowitz).

Milano, Lucio (1990), *Testi amministrativi: Assegnazioni di prodotti alimentari. Archivi reali di Ebla, testi* 9 (Roma: Missione Archaeologica Italiana in Siria).

— (2014), "The Earliest Epigraphical Documents and other Texts from Tell Beydar (Excavation Seasons 2004–2009)," in Milano and Lebeau 2014: 151–214.

Milano, Lucio, and Lebeau, Marc (2014), *Tell Beydar. Environmental and Technical Studies. Volume II* (Subartu 33; Turnhout: Brepols).

Milano, Lucio, and Rova, Elena (2003), "Tell Beydar – Field I Preliminary Report of the 1999 Season," in Lebeau and Suleiman 2003: 349–85.

— (2004), "Tell Beydar 2004 – Field I," in M. Lebeau and A. Suleiman (eds.), *Euro-Syrian Excavations at Tell Beydar. Report on the Twelfth Season of Excavations at Tell Beydar (2004)*: 10–12.
URL: http://www.beydar.org/pdf/Rapporto generale 2004 (B).pdf.

Milano, Lucio; Sallaberger, Walther; Talon, Philippe; and Van Lerberghe, Karel (2004), *Third Millennium Cuneiform Texts from Tell Beydar (Seasons 1996–2002)* (Subartu 12; Turnhout: Brepols).

Moortgat-Correns, Ursula (1972), *Die Bildwerke vom Djebelet el Bēdā in ihrer räumlichen und zeitlichen Umwelt* (Berlin and New York: de Gruyter).

Neumann, Hans (2002), "Die sogenannten *Oikos*-Ökonomie und das Problem der Privatwirtschaft im ausgehenden 3. Jahrtausend v. Chr. in Mesopotamien [...]," in A. Hausleiter *et al.* (eds.), *Material Culture and Mental Spheres. Rezeption archäologischer Denkrichtungen in der Vorderasiatischen Altertumskunde.* [...] (AOAT 293; Münster: Ugarit-Verlag): 273–82.

Oates, David; Oates, Joan, and McDonald, Helen (2001): *Excavations at Tell Brak 2: Nagar in the third millennium BC* (Cambridge and London: British School of Archaeology in Iraq).

Orthmann, Winfried (ed.) (1989), *Halawa 1980 bis 1986. Vorläufiger Bericht über die 4.–9. Grabungskampagne* (Saarbrücker Beiträge zur Altertumskunde 52; Bonn: Rudolf Habelt).

Orthmann, Winfried; Klein, Harald; and Lüth, Friedrich (1986), *Tell Chuēra in Nordost-Syrien. Vorläufiger Bericht über die neunte und zehnte Grabungskampagne 1982–1983* (Berlin: Mann).

Orthmann, Winfried, and Pruß, Alexander (1995), "Der Palast F," in W. Orthmann *et al.* (eds.), *Ausgrabungen in Tell Chuēra in Nordost-Syrien. Vorbericht über die Grabungskampagnen 1986 bis 1992* (Vorderasiatische Forschungen der Max Freiherr von Oppenheim-Stiftung 2, I; Saarbrücken: Saarbrücker Druckerei und Verlag): 121–72.

Otto, Adelheid (2006), *Alltag und Gesellschaft zur Spätbronzezeit: Eine Fallstudie aus Tall Bazi (Syrien)* (Subartu 19; Turnhout: Brepols).

Pfälzner, Peter (2001), *Haus und Haushalt. Wohnformen des dritten Jahrtausends vor Christus in Nordmesopotamien* (Damaszener Forschungen 9; Mainz: Zabern).

— (2011), "Architecture," in M. Lebeau (ed.), *Associated Regional Chronologies for the Ancient Near East and the Eastern Mediterranean vol. 1: Jezirah* (Turnhout: Brepols): 137–200

Poidebard, Antoine (1934), *La Trace de Rome dans le désert de Syrie, Le Limes de Trajan à la conquête arabe. Recherches aériennes* (1925–1932) (BAH 18; Paris: Geuthner).

Postgate, J. Nicholas (1992), *Early Mesopotamia. Society and economy at the dawn of history* (London and New York: Routledge).

— (1994), "How many Sumerians per hectare? Probing the anatomy of an early city, " *Cambridge Archaeological Journal* 4/1: 47–65.

Powell, Marvin A. (1984), "Late Babylonian Surface Mensuration. A Contribution to the History of Babylonian Agriculture and Arithmetic," *Archiv für Orientforschung* 31: 32–66.

Powell, Marvin A. (ed.) (1987), *Labor in the ancient Near East* (American Oriental Series 68, New Haven: American Oriental Society).

Prentice, Rosemary (2010), *The Exchange of Goods and Services in Pre-Sargonic Lagash* (AOAT 368; Münster: Ugarit-Verlag).

Pruß, Alexander (2000), "The Metallic Ware of Upper Mesopotamia: Definition, Chronology and Distribution," in C. Marro and H. Hauptmann (eds.), *Chronologies des Pays du Caucase et de l'Euphrate aux IVe-IIIe millenaires. Actes du colloque d'Istanbul, 16-19 décembre 1998* (Varia Anatolica 11; Paris: de Boccard): 193–203.

— (2011a), "Excavations in Field P in the years 2004–2009," in Lebeau and Suleiman 2011: 111–59.

— (2011b), "Finds from Field P," in Lebeau and Suleiman 2011: 161–208.

Pruß, Alexander, and Sallaberger, Walther (2003/04), "Tierhaltung in Nabada/Tell Beydar und die Bilderwelt der Terrakotten als Spiegel von Wirtschaft und Umwelt," *Archiv für Orientforschung* 50: 293–307.

Reculeau, Hervé (2011), *Climate, Environment and Agriculture in Assyria* (Studia Chaburensia 2; Wiesbaden: Harrassowitz).

Renger, Johannes (2003-05), "Oikos, Oikoswirtschaft," *Reallexikon der Assyriologie und Vorderasiatischen Archäologie* 10: 43–45.

Rova, Elena (2008), "Seal Impressions from Tell Beydar (2002-2006 Seasons)," in M. Lebeau and A. Suleiman (eds.), *Beydar Studies I* (Subartu 21; Turnhout: Brepols): 63–194.

Sallaberger, Walther (1996), "Grain Accounts: Personnel Lists and Expenditure Documents," in Ismail *et al.* 1996: 89–106.

— (2000), "Nagar in den frühdynastischen Texten aus Beydar," in K. Van Lerberghe and G. Voet (eds.), *Languages and Cultures in Contact. At the Crossroads of Civilizations in the Syro-Mesopotamian Realm. Proceedings of the 42th RAI* (Orientalia Lovaniensia Analecta 96; Leuven: Peeters): 393-407.

— (2004a), "A note on the sheep and goat flocks. Introduction to texts 151–167," in Milano *et al.* 2004: 13–21.

— (2004b), "Women at Beydar," in Milano *et al.* 2004: 43–49.

— (2007), "From Urban Culture to Nomadism. A History of Upper Mesopotamia in the Late Third Millennium," in: C. Kuzucuoglu and C. Marro (eds.), *Sociétés humaines et changement climatique à la fin du troisième millénaire: Une crise a-t-elle eu lieu en Haute Mésopotamie? Actes du Colloque de Lyon, 5-8 décembre 2005* (Paris: de Boccard): 417–456.

— (2011), "History and Philology," in M. Lebeau (ed.), *Associated Regional Chronologies for the Ancient Near East and the Eastern Mediterranean vol. 1: Jezirah* (Turnhout: Brepols): 327–342.

— (2013), "The Management of the Royal Treasure: Palace Archives and Palatial Economy in the Ancient Near East," in J. A. Hill, P. Jones and A.J. Morales (eds.), *Experiencing Power, Generating Authority.Cosmos, Politics, and the Ideology of Kingship in Ancient Egypt and Mesopotamia* (Philadelphia: University of Pennsylvania Museum): 219–225.

— (2014), "Urban Organizations for Offerings, Overland Traffic and the Euphrates Trade at Pre-Sargonic Mari", in *Mari, ni est, ni ouest? 75 ans de découvertes à Tell Hariri* (Syria, Supplement 2, Beyrouth: Ifpo): 341–354.

Sallaberger, Walther, and Schrakamp, Ingo (forthc.), "Philological Data for a Historical Chronology of Mesopotamia in the Third Millennium B.C.," in *iidem* (eds.), *Associated Regional Chronologies for the Ancient Near East and the Eastern Mediterranean vol. 3: History and Philology* (Turnhout: Brepols): 1–136.

Sallaberger, Walther, and Ur, Jason (2004): "Tell Beydar/Nabada in its regional setting," in Milano *et al.* 2004: 51–71.

Schrakamp, Ingo (2014), "Krieger und Bauern. RU-lugal und aga/aga$_3$-us$_2$ im Militär des altsumerischen Lagaš", in H. Neumann *et al.* (eds.), *Krieg und Frieden im Alten Vorderasien.* (Alter Orient und Altes Testament 401, Münster: Ugarit): 691–724.

Selz, Gebhard (1993), *Altsumerische Wirtschaftstexte aus Lagaš Teil 2: Altsumerische Wirtschaftsurkunden aus amerikanischen Sammlungen* (Freiburger altorientalische Studien 15,2; Stuttgart: Franz Steiner)

— (1995), *Untersuchungen zur Götterwelt des altsumerischen Stadtstaates von Lagaš* (OPSNKF 13; Philadelphia, PA: University of Pennsylvania Museum, The Samuel Noah Kramer Fund).

— (1999/2000), "'Wirtschaftskirse – Legitimationskrise – Staatskrise.' Zur Genese mesopotamischer Rechtsvorstellungen zwischen Planwirtschaft und Eigentumsverfassung," *Archiv für Orientforschung* 46/47: 1–44.

— (2006), "Was bleibt? Der sogenannte "Totengeist" und das Leben der Geschlechter," in E. Czerny *et al.* (eds.), *Timelines. Studies in Honour of Manfred Bietak Vol.* III (Orientalia Lovaniensia Analecta 149; Leuven: Peeters): 87–94.

Sjöberg, Åke W. (2003), "Notes on Selected Entries from the Ebla Vocabulary eš$_2$-bar-kin$_5$ (IV)," in W. Sallaberger *et al.* (eds.), *Literatur, Politik und Recht in Mesopotamien. Festschrift für Claus Wilcke* (Orientalia Biblica et Christiana 14; Wiesbaden: Harrassowitz): 251–266.

Spek, Robert J. van der (1998), "Cuneiform Documents on Parthian History: The Raḫimesu Archive. Materials for the Study of the Standard of Living," in J. Wiesehöfer (ed.), *Das Partherreich und seine Zeugnisse* (Historia, Einzelschriften 122; Stuttgart: Franz Steiner): 205–258.

Starke, Holger (2005), *Vom Brauerhandwerk zur Brauindustrie. Die Geschichte der Bierbrauerei in Dresden und Sachsen 1800 – 1914* (Köln: Böhlau).

Steinkeller, Piotr (1987), "The foresters of Umma. Towards a definition of Ur III labor," in Powell 1987:73–115.

— (1993), "Early Political Development in Mesopotamia and the Origins of the Sargonic Empire," in M. Liverani (ed.), *Akkad. The First World Empire. Structure, Ideology, Tradition* (History of the Ancient Near East / Studies 5, Padova: Sargon): 107–129.

— (1996), "The organization of crafts in third millennium Babylonia: The case of potters", *Altorientalische Forschungen* 23: 232–253.

— (1999), "Land-tenure conditions in Early Mesopotamia: The problem of regional variation," in M. Hudson and B. A. Levine (eds.), *Urbanization and Land Ownership in the Ancient Near East* (Cambridge MA: Peabody Museum): 289–329.

— (2004), "Toward a Definition of Private Economic Activity in Third Millennium Babylonia," in R. Rollinger and C. Ulf (eds.), *Commerce and Monetary Systems in the Ancient World: Means of Transmission and Cultural Interaction* (Melammu Symposia 5, Stuttgart: Franz Steiner): 91–111.

— (2007), "City and countryside in third-millennium Southern Babylonia," in E. C. Stone (ed.), *Settlement and Countryside. Essays dedicated to Robert McCormick Adams* (Los Angeles: Cotsen Institute of Archaeology, and Chicago: Oriental Institute of the University of Chicago): 185–211.

— (2013), "Corvée Labor in Ur III times", in S. J. Garfinkle amd M. Molina (eds.), *From the 21st Century B.C. to the 21st Century A.D.: The Present and Future of Neo-Sumerian Studies. Proceedings of the International Conference on Neo-Sumerian Studies Held in Madrid, 22–24 July 2010* (Winona Lake, Indiana: Eisenbrauns): 347–424.

Sténuit, Marie-Eve (2003), "L'entrepôt d'époque EJ IIIb. Étude architectural (chantier E – campagnes 1995-1996)," in Lebeau and Suleiman 2003: 243–268.

Sténuit, Marie-Eve, and Van der Stede, Véronique (2003), "Du Palais au quartier de maisons privées (jonction entre le chantier F et le chantier B – campagnes 1997-1999)," in Lebeau and Suleiman 2003: 225–241.

Stone, Elizabeth (1997), *Nippur Neighborhoods* (Studies in Ancient Oriental Civilization 44; Chicago: Oriental Institute of the University of Chicago).

Suleiman, Antoine (2003), "The Northern Stratigraphical Sounding (Field G)," in Lebeau and Suleiman 2003: 301–308.

— (2007), "Temples B and C, Storage Building and Artisanal Quarter (Fields F3, M & O, Seasons 2000 – 2002)," in Lebeau and Suleiman 2007: 85–98.

Ur, Jason A., and Tony J. Wilkinson (2008), "Settlement and Economic Landscapes of Tell Beydar and its Hinterland," in M. Lebeau and A. Suleiman (eds.), *Beydar Studies* I (Subartu 21; Turnhout: Brepols): 305–27.

Van der Stede, Véronique (2007), "Le chantier B: résultats des campagnes 2000–2002," in Lebeau and Suleiman 2007: 7–39.

Van der Stede, Véronique, and Anne Devillers (2011), "Le chantier B: résultats des campagnes 2004–2008," in Lebeau and Suleiman 2011: 15–76.

— (2014), "Le Chantier B: résultats de la campagne 2010," in Lebeau and Suleiman 2014: 11–40.

Van Lerberghe, Karel (1996), "The Livestock," in Ismail *et al.* 1996: 107–17.

Waetzoldt, Hartmut (1987), "Compensation of Craft Workers and Officials in the Ur III Period," in Powell 1987: 117–141.

— (1996), "Privathäuser. Ihre Größe, Einrichtung und die Zahl ihrer Bewohner," in K. R. Veenhof (ed.), *Houses and Households in Ancient Mesopotamia. Papers read at the 40e Rencontre Assyriologique Internationale, Leiden, July 5-8, 1993* (PIHANS 78; Leiden: NINO): 145–152.

Wattenmaker, Patricia (1998), *Household and State in Upper Mesopotamia: Specialized Economy and the Social Uses of Goods in an Early Complex Society* (Washington, D.C.: Smithsonian Institution Press).

Weber, Max (1947), *The Theory of Social and Economic Organization*, translated by A. M. Henderson and Talcott Parsons. Edited with an introduction by Talcott Parsons (New York: Free Press).

— ([5]1972), *Wirtschaft und Gesellschaft. Grundriß der verstehenden Soziologie.* Studienausg., 5., rev. Aufl. Besorgt von Johannes Winckelmann (Tübingen: Mohr).

Weiss, Harvey, and Senior, Louise (1992), "Tell Leilan "sila-bowls" and the Akkadian Reorganization of Subarian Agricultural Production," *Orient-Express* 1992/2: 16–23.

Wiggermann, Franciscus A. M. (2000), "Agriculture in the Northern Balikh Valley. The Case of Middle Assyrian Tell Sabi Abyad," in R.M. Jas (ed.), *Rainfall and Agriculture in Northern Mesopotamia* (MOS Studies 3; PIHANS 88; Leiden: NINO): 171–231.

3.

The Employment of Labor on National Building Projects in the Ur III Period

Piotr Steinkeller
Harvard University

1. Introduction

1.1. This paper studies the employment of labor on national building projects during the period of the Third Dynasty of Ur.[1] Such undertakings, which were concerned with the construction of temples, royal palaces, city walls, and other types of defensive structures, were but one part of what may be described as Ur III public works. By the latter designation I mean large, and therefore labor-intensive, projects that were planned, financed, and executed by the central government. Other important types of works included in this category were the excavation of new canals and major works on the existing irrigation and water-transportation systems; the building of roads and related infrastructure, such as the networks of roadhouses and relay stations; and certain types of agricultural activity, among which harvest work was by far the most important. To be technically correct, one needs to include here also military service *sensu stricto*, *i.e.*, participation in either defensive or offensive operations, since military service was just another form of public works.

[1] This article expands on Steinkeller 2013. In particular, the discussion of the Tummal project offered here is a much enlarged and updated version of Steinkeller 2013: 362–372. I wish to offer my warm thanks to Manuel Molina, who was kind enough to read repeatedly the original manuscript, providing additional references and offering corrections and improvements. Needless to say, the responsibility for the final product rest with me alone.

For the sources referred to as "Text 1," etc., see under Appendix at the end of this paper (pp. 211–236).

All of these works were done through the use of corvée labor. To quote one, popular definition, "corvée is labor, often unpaid, that is required of people of lower social standing and imposed on them by their superiors. It differs from chattel slavery in that the worker is not owned outright—and that the work is usually intermittent; typically only a certain number of days' or months' work is required each year."[2]

In fact, it was corvée labor that created Mesopotamian civilization. The ancients were well aware of the primordial and inevitable nature of corvée, as shown most eloquently by their creation stories, which connect the origin of corvée with that of humanity itself,[3] and even explain the creation of man as the gods' practical solution to the absence of suitable performers of corvée, an onerous task that the gods were reluctant to do themselves.[4] In other words, corvée preceded humanity's existence, being, like death and diseases, an unpleasant side-effect of the original creation.

1.2. A brief discussion of the native terminology for corvée is called for.[5] The Sumerian verb for conscripting or levying workers and soldiers is zi-(g) (Akk. *tebû*), whose basic meaning is "to rise, to raise." From that root derive the nouns zi-ga (Akk. = *tibûtu*), "conscription, general levy,"[6]

2 Wikipedia.

3 ama-mu mud-mu gar-ra-zu ì-gál-la-àm zub-sìg dingir-re-e-ne kéš-da-ì ... ama-mu za-e nam-bi ù-mu-e-tar ^{d}Nin-mah zub-sìg-bi hé-kéš, "(Enki speaking to Namma:) 'My mother, here is my blood set up for you — tie the corvée basket of the gods to it! ... My mother, after you determine (man's) destiny, may Ninmah tie the corvée basket to him!'" ("Enki and Ninmah" lines 30 and 37).

4 See "The Story of Atrahasis" Tablet 1, especially lines 240–241: *ka-ab-tam du-ul-la-ku-nu ⸢ú-ša-as⸣-sí-ik šu-up-ši-ik-ka-ku-nu a-wi-[l]am e-mi-id*, "I have removed your heavy toil, I have imposed your corvée basket on man."

5 Cf. Stol 1995: 293–295.

6 See, *e.g.*, Umma^{ki} e-ma-zi ... ^{d}Nin-gír-su-ke$_4$ Umma^{ki} zi-ga-bi ì-ku$_6$-lam (Frayne 2008: 269–275 UruKAgina 3 iv 10'-19'); zi-ga ba-ni-gar (Gudea Cylinder A xiv 7, 10, 13); zi-ga mu-na-gál (*ibid*. xiv 17, 22, 26); ^{d}Bìl-ga-mes uru-ni-a zi-ga [b]a-ni-ib-gar ("Gilgameš and Huwawa B" line 51); en-⸢e⸣ uru-ni-a zi-ga ba-ni-gar ... Unug$^{[ki]}$ zi-ga lugal-zu ba-ra-è-e Kul-ab$_4^{ki}$ zi-ga En-me-kár-ra hé-ús-e Unug^{ki}-⸢ga⸣ zi-ga-bi a-ma-⸢ru-kam⸣ Kul-ab$_4^{ki}$ an dungu gar-ra ("Lugalbanda 1" lines 24–29); Larsam^{ki}-ta zi-ga-mu-ne kur ki-⸢bala⸣-gá sag giš-bi hé-ni-ra (Volk 2011: 67–74 iii 22–25); ugnim zi-ga ma-da-mu-ta = *in ti-bu-ut um-ma-an ma-ti-ia* (Frayne 1990: 333–336 Hammurabi 2:36–37). For other examples of *tibûtu* being used in this sense, see CAD T, 391.

and lú-zi-ga, "conscript."[7] Another verb commonly used in the same sense is dab$_5$, "to seize, to take hold of." A nominal derivative of the latter is lú-dab$_5$-ba, "conscript," which, in fact, is the more common designation of conscripted workers in Ur III economic sources.[8]

The Sumerian word for "corvée" is $^{\text{(giš)}}$dubšig(ÍL) (Akk. *tupšikku/šupšikku*),[9] which primarily denotes the basket that customarily was used to carry earth on corvée projects. In fact, the sign ÍL, which, when standing for a verb means "to lift, to carry," shows in its original form the upper body of a worker supporting with his arm a basket over his head. See Fig. 1, showing this sign and the depictions of royal figures in exactly the same pose.

Fig. 1.
a. sign ÍL; b. foundation statue of Šulgi, the Metropolitan Museum of Art; Rogers Fund, 1959, 59.41.1.; c. Assurbanipal stela, probably from Babylon, after Börker-Klähn 1982a: pl. 224.

7 See Gudea Statue B iv 16, cited below p. 149.

8 For lú-dab$_5$-ba, which is used mainly in the sources from Girsu/Lagaš, see Steinkeller 2013: 350 n. 8. At the same time, lú-dab$_5$-ba carries also the sense "royal subject," which is most commonly expressed by the word éren.

9 See tu-ub-ši-ig ÍL = *tu-up-ši-ik-ku* (Arnaud Emar 6 545:265). Note the writing zub-sìg in "Enki and Ninmah" lines 30, 37. It is certain that, although not documented lexically, another equivalent of dubšig was *ilku*, which is the primary Akkadian word for corvée and similar types of obligations.

Contrary to what one might expect, mentions of dubšig in the sense of "corvée" are exceedingly rare in third millennium sources.[10] As far as I know, apart from Gudea Statue R ii 5, where the expression dubšig saharra, "dirt basket," is found (see below p. 5), the only other Ur III attestation of this word comes from a Nippur text, which records the transfer of an allotment field by the wife and daughter of the deceased holder of that field.[11] This term is equally rare in earlier texts. Here I can name only the attestations of it in a group of Sargonic sources from Nippur.[12]

The word dusu (probably better *dussu), which is another value of ÍL meaning "basket, corvée," appears to be a by-form of dubšig. See the gloss [d]u-si in A VIII/3 Comm. 22 (MSL 14, 507), which suggests the following development: dubšig > dussig > dus(s)i > dus(s)u.
Other Sumerian terms for "corvée" are dul-lum and kaskal. The former, which is a loan from the Akkadian *dullu*, "work, corvée labor, hardship," appears only in literary sources.[13] As for kaskal, whose meaning is "road, military campaign, commercial expedition," and which corresponds to Akkadian *ḫarrānu*, its sense "corvée" is a secondary development.[14]

Finally, one needs to mention in this connection the Sumerian word bala, "term, cycle," also "royal reign, dynasty, cosmic cycle." In Ur III times, this term also came to describe the period during which corvée was performed, as a result becoming practically synonymous with corvée itself. Thus, in the sources from Girsu/Lagaš, the workforce at large is designated as either bala gub-ba, "performing the bala duty," or bala tuš-a, "sitting out the bala duty."

[10] For the examples of *tupšikku*/*šupšikku*, see CAD T, 476–79. For dubšig in OB literary sources, see especially "Enki and Ninmah" lines 30 and 37 (cited above in n. 3), and "Enmerkar and Ensuhkešdana" lines 25 and 56: e-ne gá-a-ra gú ha-ma-an-gá-gá ^{giš}dubšig ha-ma-ab-íl-e, "he must submit to me! He must perform corvée for me!"

[11] NATN 258:7: ŠUKU-gá dubšig-bi íl-ba-ab, "take over the corvée obligation of my prebend!" Cf. Steinkeller and Postgate 1992: 99–100.

[12] OSP 2 46, 47, 48, and 62, all of which concern silver payments in lieu of the unfulfilled? corvée obligation that was due from the paternal estate of a certain Ur-Namma (kug ^{giš}dubšig é-ad-da-kam). Cf. also the Sargonic personal name Dub-si-ga (OIP 104 Texts 37 R. E. 15; 40 C vi 9 and passim in this source), which undoubtedly employs the same word.

[13] dumu-gir$_{15}$(-ra) dul-lum(-ma) la-ba-an-taka$_4$-taka$_4$, "a citizen cannot avoid corvée!" (Alster 1997: 147 SP 6.5); du-lum ur-gir$_{15}$-ra-àm egir-ra mu-un-du, "corvée is like a dog; it always follows one's back" (Alster 1997: 49 SP 2:14). For *dullu* in Akkadian texts, see CAD D, 173–177.

1.3. Throughout the documented history of ancient Mesopotamia, the obligation to perform corvée rested primarily (if not exclusively) with the free population. In the Ur III period, the source of corvée were all the free subjects of the crown, who were designated by the alternative terms éren, "royal subject," and dumu-gir$_{15}$, "citizen," and who included everybody from as low as craftsmen, shepherds, and oridinary farmers to as high as the top administrative and priestly officials and member's of the king's extended family. All of these individuals, who accounted for the majority of the population of the Ur III state, were required to do corvée for the crown, either by performing it themselves or by providing substitutes or monetary compensation.[15]

Depending on the political and practial exigencies, a ruler could exempt individuals or whole communities from corvée. An example of such an exemption is documented already in Pre-Sargonic times, when, following his conquest of the cities of Uruk, Larsa, and Patibira, a ruler of Lagaš by the name of Enmetena freed the populations of those cities from the obligation to perform corvée for Lagaš, reserving that right to their local institutions:

> dumu Unug^{ki} dumu Larsam^{ki} dumu Pa$_5$-ti-bir$_5$-ra-ka [ama]-gi$_4$-bi e-gar ^{d}Inana-ra Unug^{ki}-šè šu-na ì-ni-gi$_4$ ^{d}Utu-[ra] Larsam^{ki}-šè šu-na ì-ni-gi$_4$ Lugal-é-mùš-r[a] É-mùš-šè šu-na ì-ni-gi$_4$,
>
> "He freed the citizens of Unug, Larsa, and Patibira (from performing corvée for Lagaš); (accordingly) he restored them to Inana of Uruk, Utu of Larsa, and Lugal-emuš of Emuš, respectively" (Frayne 2008: 202–204 En-metena 4 v 4—vi 6).

Similar exemptions of cities and their populations are documented in the Isin-Larsa and Old Babylonian periods:[16]

> ud Nibru^{ki} ... gú-bi mu-un-du$_8$ éren-bi kaskal-ta ba-ra-an-zi-ga-a,
>
> "when he cancelled the taxes of Nippur, the beloved city of Enlil, (and) exempted its citizens from the corvée" (Frayne 1990: 31–32 Išme-Dagan 5:5–11);

[14] For this sense of kaskal, see the examples cited below. For the meaning "corvée" of *ḫarrānu*, see CAD Ḫ, 112–113.

[15] See below p. 173.

[16] As is well known, such exemptations were a standard royal policy in later times as well. During the first millennium kings frequently granted privileged status (*kidinnūtu*) to major cities, which mainly entailed the exemption from taxes and the obligation to perform corvée for the crown.

ud dumu Nibru^{ki} kaskal-ta ba-ra-an-zi ⌜é⌝ ^{d}En-líl ^{d}Nin-líl ù ^{d}Nin-urta-ke$_{4}$ ba-ra-an-g[ar] Ki-en-gi [Ki-uri] zag-10-[bi m]u-[un-du$_{8}$],

"when he exempted the citizens of Nippur from the corvée, he also removed (from the obligation to pay taxes) the temple households of Enlil, Ninlil, and Ninurta, and he cancelled the tithe of Sumer and [Akkad]" (Frayne 1990: 33–35 Išme-Dagan 6 ii 1–10);

Zimbir^{ki} uru^{ki} ul-la ^{d}Utu-ke$_{4}$ éren-bi ^{giš}dubšig-ta ^{d}Utu-ra hé-bí-zi = *Sippar*^{ki} URU.KI *ṣi-a-tim ša* ^{d}*Šamaš* ÉREN-*šu in* ^{giš}DUBŠIG *a-na* ^{d}*Šamaš lu-as-sú-úḫ*,

"for Šamaš I exempted from the corvée the citizens of Sippar, his ancient city" (Frayne 1990: 333–336 Hammurabi 2: 56–60).

A case of personal exemption from corvée is attested during the time of Gudea of Lagaš, which was granted by Gudea to one of his high cultic officials:

Nam-ha-ni gala-mah SAL-gil-sa-ka-ra kug-babbar zabar dubšig sahar-ra ù níg-en-na gál-la-aš é-a-na lú nu-ku$_{4}$-ku$_{4}$-dè ama-ar-gi$_{4}$-bi mu-n[a-gar] mu-bi-a 6(bùr) gibil ég-gaba gána inim mu-na-gi,

"(Gudea) 'established freedom' for Namhani, the great lamenter of the ..., in order that nobody enters his house (claiming taxes/dues on his) silver (and) bronze, (requesting him to perform) corvée and (claiming his allotments of) demesne land; during the same year he confirmed for him an allotment of 104 iku of new land, along the 'dike of the border'" (Gudea Statue R ii 2–10 = Edzard 1997: 59–60).

1.4. Although it is known that the Ur III period witnessed a massive program of governmentally sponsored construction, which focused on temples, palaces, city walls, and administrative structures, there survives comparatively little textual evidence bearing on these undertakings. Virtually none of it can be described as direct evidence, *i.e.*, sources that are purposely and primarily concerned with building projects, in the same way and to the same degree as there survive groups of sources concerned with particular aspects of the economic life, such as agriculture, for example. A notable exception here are the inscriptions of Gudea, which offer a completely unique body of evidence on the construction of Ningirsu's temple Eninnu (see in detail below pp. 146–153). However, most of the data bearing on public building projects are of secondary nature. Most commonly, these are records of human labor and materials that were spent as part of such undertakings. Such references usually have to be "fished out," so to speak, from among similar data.

Still, in spite of all these limitations, it is possible to obtain a good idea of the nature and scale of these works. There survives extensive evidence on at least three major buildings projects that were excecuted by the Ur III kings. These undertakings, which are the subject of this study, are the construction of the royal palace at Tummal in the second half of Šulgi's reign; the building of the temple of Nanna of Karzida during Amar-Suena's reign; and a similar construction involving the temple of Šara at Umma during Šu-Suen's reign.

1.5. The documentation extant makes it clear that such national projects involved active participation of the entire kingdom. In other words, all the provinces of the Ur III state were evidently required to support these undertakings with labor and material contributions. Of course, the main reason for such a broad participation was the fact that there was not enough manpower available locally to carry out the tasks at hand. Therefore, additional workers had to be brought from the outside. But there were also social and political reasons behind this arrangement. National building projects were an extremely important tool of political and cultural integration, in that they helped to create a community and interdependence between different regions of the state. As people from all over the country spent extensive periods of time working and living together, they not only identified with the project itself, but they also came to think of themselves as fellow members of a united Babylonia. Since, with the exception of the Sargonic period, Babylonia had never been united before, the need to create such a sense of unity must have been one of the main political objectives of the kings of Ur.

Similar political motivations may be detected behind the national building projects of later times. The royal inscriptions of the Isin-Larsa and Old Babylonian periods commemorating the construction of major city walls and temples sometimes include brief narratives, which describe how the ruler mobilized workers for the project in question, how those then produced bricks, and how eventually the project was completed. Such narratives are particularly common in the inscriptions of the rulers of Larsa. In two instances, the Larsa king Sin-iddinam claims to have raised one-fourth of the labor force of the entire country.[17] The length of the brick-making operation is sometimes specified. The attested fig-

[17] igi-4-gál ugnim kalam-ma-mu um-mi-zi (Steinkeller 2004b: 140–143 i 36–40; Volk 2011: 67–74 iii 78–80).

ures are one month,[18] five months,[19] and one year,[20] with the last figure probably representing the duration of the whole project.

In one of his inscriptions, Sin-iddinam makes a point of saying that he possessed an expertise of mobilizing large numbers of troops, attesting to the logistical complexities that such projects must have entailed: éren dagal-la mu-tùm-tùm-bi zi-dè-eš mu-zu-a-mu-šè nam-bi-šè ^{d}Nergal dumu ^{d}En-líl-lá-ke$_4$ ^{giš}al ^{giš}dubšig g[á$^{?}$-ra$^{?}$ ha$^{?}$-m]a$^{?}$-sum$^{?}$-sum$^{?}$, "because I had the true knowledge of mustering vast troops, on account of that, Nergal, son of Enlil, gave me a hoe and a basket."[21]

A characteristic and striking motif of these building narratives is the feeling of joy that accompanied such projects:

> "After (the gods) had sent down to me the holy hoe and the holy basket, from the lofty place of heaven which is the resting place of the basket, they determined destiny for them. And in order that the troops of Ur may be properly organized, and that they perform their work with joy, they gave respective instructions to Nanna, firstborn of Enlil."[22]

> "I completed the project with a happy face and with a joyous heart."[23]

> "At that time I baked the bricks of Ur in joy … they completed this project with joyous hearts."[24]

> "(Nergal) with joyous heart made complete the building instructions for me."[25]

[18] iti-da ud 30-ka sig$_4$-bi hé-em-mi-du$_8$ (Steinkeller 2004b: 140–143 i 39–40; Volk 2011: 67–74 iii 1–2).

[19] murub$_4$-ba iti 5-àm ba-ra-ab-zal sig$_4$-bi hu-mu-du$_8$ (Frayne 1990: 241–243 Rim-Sin 21:80–81).

[20] šag$_4$ mu dili-ka sig$_4$-al-ur$_5$-ra-bi hé-bí-du$_8$ (Frayne 1990: 164–166 Sin-iddinam 6:35–37); šag$_4$ mu dili-ka sig$_4$-bi hu-mu-dù bàd gal hu-mu-til (George 2011: 96–97 no. 44 ii 24–26).

[21] Steinkeller 2004b: 140–143 i 24–25.

[22] ki ⸢^{giš}⸣[du]bšig ki mah an-na-ta ^{giš}al kug ^{giš}dubšig kug um-ta-an-an-è-eš nam-bi im-mi-in-tar-re-eš ⸢ugnim⸣ Úrim^{ki}-ma si ⸢sá⸣-sá-a-da šag$_4$ húl-la kin-bi ak-a-da ^{d}Nanna dumu-sag ^{d}En-líl-lá-ra á-bi mu-un-da-an-ág-eš (Volk 2011: 67–74 ii 1–11; similarly in ii 50–58).

[23] sag-ki zalag šag$_4$ húl-la-ta kin-bi hu-mu-⸢til-til⸣ (Volk 2011: 67–74 iii 9–10).

[24] ud-bi-a sig$_4$ Úrim⸢^{ki}⸣-ma-ke$_4$ asila^{la} hu-mu-du$_8$ … šag$_4$ ⸢húl⸣-la kin-bi [hé-b]í-in-til (Volk 2011: 67–74 iv 23–30).

[25] šag$_4$ húl-la-ni-ta á-ág-ba ha-ma-ni-in-til (Steinkeller 2004: 140–143 i 34–35).

Equally characteristically, these building narratives also emphasize the fact that among the workers employed on such projects "no one received a higher or a lower wage,"[26] an indication of the remarkable— and quite unusual—degree of equality that existed among the participants of these undertakings. The wages themselves were very generous, since, apart from a monthly salary of between 30 and 60 liters of barley,[27] they included a daily food allowance, consisting of 2 liters of bread, 2 liters of beer, and 2 shekels (16.6 gram) of fat. One such listing also names 2 liters of dates, 2 liters of cheese, and 2 liters of sesame bran, "not including the food from the sheepfold."[28] If one can trust these statements, the remuneration given out as part of such projects was quite special, and completely unlike the wages the same laborers would receive in real life.

These facts suggest that the work conditions prevailing on important building projects differed significantly from the regular corvée. In view of their communal and egalitarian spirit, such projects should perhaps be understood, at least on one level, as social events, whose function was not unlike that of public festivals. Although the workers were no doubt forced to participate in them, they were treated decently, and it is likely that they even enjoyed the experience, being proud of their accomplishment, and partaking in a sense of civic pride. Indeed, in one of his inscriptions Sin-iddinam takes special credit for making his workers happy: ugnim Larsam^{ki}-ma aš-bi um-mi-tuš á šag$_4$-gal ì-šeš$_4$ šag$_4$ dùg-ga-bi-dè lú-kin-ak-bi-šè ha-ba-sum-sum, "after I had assembled the forces of Larsa, I gave them wages, food, and anointing oil to make them happy as its (*i.e.*, Ebabbar's) workers."[29]

As in the case of the Ur III building undertakings, it is likely that those of Isin-Larsa and Old Babylonian times too were meant to bring together the disparate parts of the country, creating a sense of political and cultural unity among their populations.[30] This sense of unity was formed not only by the fact of shared work, but equally by the pride the

[26] lú á lá lú á dah ba-ra-bí-tuku (Frayne 1990: 158–160 Sin-iddinam 2:60–62; George 2011: 104–105 no. 49:60–62).

[27] 30 liters in Frayne 1990: 147–149 Nur-Adad 7:67; 241–243 Warad-Sin 21:98. 40 liters in Steinkeller 2004: 140–43 ii 6; Volk 2011: 67–74 iv 17. 60 liters in George 2011: 104–105 no. 49:54.

[28] Frayne 1990: 164–166 Sin-iddinam 6:51–54.

[29] Frayne 1990: 164–166 Sin-iddinam 6:29–34.

[30] The royal inscriptions even know a term for it, which is kalam dím = *mātam banû*, "to unite, to consolidate the land." See kalam dím-dím-me = *ba-ni ma-tim*, describing Hammurabi (Frayne 1990: 347–349 Hammurabi 12:22).

builders felt about the fruits of their labor, which, as the royal inscriptions tell us, "were set up to be admired by the whole land."[31]

However, the source that gives us the best idea of the egaliterian and festive spirit that animated such undertakings is the hymnical composition describing the construction (more precisely: the rebuilding) of the Eninnu, Ningirsu's chief temple in the capital city of Girsu.[32]

After the project had received a divine sanction, Gudea undertook a boat trip to the cities of Lagaš and Nimin, where he visited the local temples and presented offerings to their divine owners. Ostensibly, Gudea's goal was to obtain from Nanše, the goddess of Nimin, an explanation of his oracular dreams, which had foretold the Eninnu's construction. But the true purpose of the trip clearly was to involve the entire state of Lagaš in the project: by consulting the main provincial centers and by honoring their main deities,[33] Gudea had sought to secure the cooperation of the whole land.[34] On a deeper level, by rallying his state behind the Eninnu project, Gudea had ultimately hoped to unify Lagaš politically and, no less importantly, to forge a sense of Lagašite cultural distinctiveness.[35]

Once the provincial centers had granted their consent and cooperation, the project could begin in earnest, its first act being the imposition

[31] u_6-di kalam-ma-ka bí-in-gub / hé-bí-gub (Frayne 1990: 209–210 Warad-Sin 6:23–24, 218–219 12:22–23); u_6-di kalam-ma-šè pa gal-le-eš hé-bí-in-è (Frayne 1990: 241–243 Warad-Sin 21:87–88); u_6-di un sár-ra-ba hé-bí-gub (Frayne 1990: 246–247 Warad-Sin 23:30).

[32] Gudea Cylinders A and B, Statue B. For the respective editions, see Edzard 1997.

[33] Here it is important to realize that the state of Lagaš had originated from a unification of at least three proto-city-states, which constituted the domains of Ningirsu, Nanše, and Inana respectively. See Selz 1990; Steinkeller 1999: 291 n. 7, 307 and n. 68. The memory of these prehistoric mini-states, which appear to have originally been territorial clans, and which should perhaps be compared to Egyptian nomes, survived down to Gudea's reign. This is shown by Cylinder A xiv 8–26 (see immediately below), where these territories are specifically identified as extended families or clans (im-ru-a). Given the fact that the presence of the representatives of these territories was required at the ceremony marking the beginning of Eninnu's construction, the autonomous and distinctive status of these "nomes" must still have been recognized at that time, though probably only on a ritual/symbolic level.

[34] Cf. Steinkeller 2007a: 207.

[35] Given the fact that Gudea's reign coincided with Ur-Namma's own — and much grander — unifying schemes, one of which was the promotion of Ur and its chief deity Nanna, it is likely that the Eninnu project had largely been undertaken in response to Ur-Namma's policies, as a way of strengthening Lagaš' political standing.

of a general levy (zi-ga) on the entire state of Lagaš.[36] At the symbolic ground-breaking ceremony, work contingents supplied by the three territorial clans or nomes (im-ru-a) of the state appeared in force and in full regalia, being lead by their commanders carrying the ceremonial standards (šu-nir) of their respective gods:

ma-da gú sag sár-sár-ra-na
Gú-eden-na ^{d}Nin-gír-su-ka-ka
zi-ga ba-ni-gar
uru dù-a á-dam gar-ra-na
gú giš bar-ra ^{d}Nanše-ka zi-ga ba-ni-gar ...
im-ru-a ^{d}Nin-gír-su-ka-ka zi-ga
mu-na-gál
šu-nir mah-bi Lugal-kur-dúb
sag-bi-a mu-gub ...
im-ru-a ^{d}Nanše-ka
zi-ga mu-na-gál
u_5 kug šu-nir ^{d}Nanše-kam sag-bi-a mu-gub ...
im-ru-a ^{d}Inana-ka zi-ga mu-na-gál
aš-me šu-nir ^{d}Inana-kam sag-bi-a mu-gub

"In his land of exceeding produce,
in Gu'edena of Ningirsu,
a conscription was established.
In his built-up towns and established villages,
in Gugišbara of Nanše, a conscription was established.
In the territorial clan of Ningirsu a levy rose up for him.
Lugal-kurdub, their great standard, stood in front of them.
In the territorial clan of Nanše a levy rose up for him.
The holy cormorant, the standard of Nanše, stood in front of them.
In the territorial clan of Inana a levy rose up for him.
The astral disk, the standard of Inana, stood in front of them."[37]

There survive, in fact, representations of this scene, which are depicted on the fragments of Gudea's stelae.[38] On three of these fragments,[39] there is shown the upper body of a standard-bearer, holding a tasseled standard (šu-nir), on top of which there is a bird, facing en face. The bird

[36] ud-ba énsi-ke_4 kalam-ma-na zi-ga ba-ni-gar, "at that time the governor established a conscription in his land" (Cylinder A xiv 7).

[37] Cylinder A xiv 8–26.

[38] See Suter 2000: 177–79.

[39] Cros 1910: 291 fig. 6 c and d; Suter 2000: 366 ST.23, 368 ST.24, 372 ST.28.

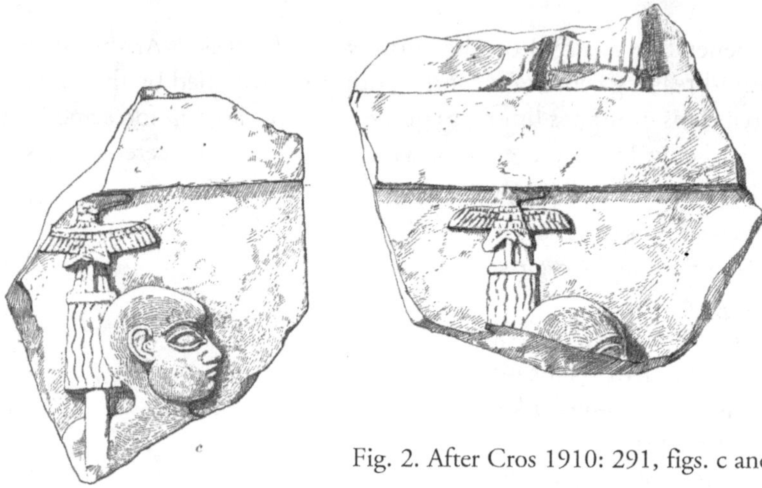

Fig. 2. After Cros 1910: 291, figs. c and d

has a long bill and outstretched wings, and it is perched on a pole. See fig. 2. This undoubtedly is Nanše's standard. Since the u_5[mušen], Nanše's holy bird and also her *alter ego* must have been a fisher,[40] the bird in question, in view of its long straight beak and its perching position, should probably be identified as the cormorant.[41]

Two other fragments[42] depict the standard of Inana, which is topped with a striding lioness. The lioness carries on her back an astral disk (aš-me), which is supported by the animal's upright tail. See fig. 3. Finally, on the fifth fragment[43] there is shown yet another standard, on whose

[40] This is evident from the fact that Nanše was the goddess of fish and water-fowl — and therefore also the patron of fishermen and fowlers. For this aspect of Nanše, see [dNanše] ku_6 mušen-e ki ág-me-en ... ama dNanše [zà]-mí-zu dùg-ga-àm ("Nanše and the Birds" Section D 29–32); ga-ša-an lú šu-ku_6-da [dNanše] za-ra hé-en-da-húl ("The Home of the Fish" Section C 16–17). Cf. Civil 1961: 175; Thomsen 1975: 197–200. The fundamental connection of Nanše with fish and fishing — and with the marshy environment of the southern reaches of the Lagaš/Girsu province more generally — is also reflected in the fact that the logogram used to write Nanše's name (and that of her city Nimin/Nina) is UNUG×HA, "city of the fish (goddess)." For this reason, the translation of u_5[mušen] as "goose," suggested by Veldhuis 2004a: 294–295, is certainly incorrect.

[41] See my unpublished paper, "Nanshe and the Birds," presented at the Symposium in Memory of Thorkild Jacobsen, Department of Western Asiatic Antiquities, The British Museum, London, April 5–7, 1994. A revised version of this paper is in preparation.

[42] Cros 1910: 291 figs. 6 a and b; Suter 2000: 368 ST.25, 390 ST.63.

[43] Cros 1910: 291 fig. 6 e; Suter 2000: 368 ST.26.

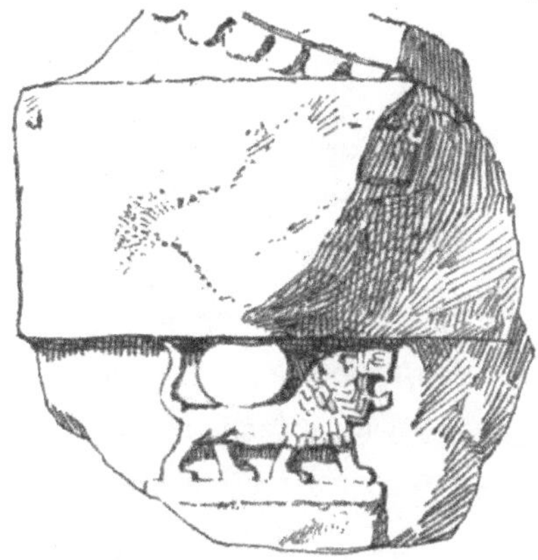

Fig. 3. After Cros 1910:291, fig. a

top there is a lion-headed eagle, with outstretched wings, and with a star at the end of its left wing; an identical star must have originally terminated its right wing. See fig. 4. One recognizes here the triumphant IM-dugud, Ningirsu's symbol and *alter ego*. I assume that this is the representation of Ningirsu as Lugal-kur-dúb, "Master who makes foreign lands tremble," whom the above passage mentions.[44]

Following the completion of the ritual preliminaries, the actual construction began. As the poet stresses, all the participating workers shared work equally irrespective of their position and rank—and with such an enthusiasm that no means of compulsion were necessary:

dubšig-bi munus-e nu-íl	"Women did not carry baskets,
sag ur-sag-e mu-na-dù ...	only the top warriors did the building
ùsan la-ba-sìg,	for him; the whip did not strike,
^{kuš}á-si la-ba-sìg	the leather strap did not strike;
ama dumu-ni níg nu-ma-ni-ra	mother did not hit her (disobedient) child;
šagina	The general,
nu-bànda	the colonel,
ugula	the captain,
lú-zi-ga	(and) the conscript,
kin a-rá ba-be$_4$(BA)	they (all) shared work equally[45];
siki ^{giš}gárig-ak	the supervision indeed was (like)
nam-ugula šu-ba mu-gál-àm	soft (lit: combed) wool in their (*i.e.* of the supervisors) hands."[46]

44 For a tentative reconstruction of the placement of this scene on Gudea's stelae, see Börker-Klähn 1982: pls. C, D, and E.

45 For a-rá, "equal(ly)," see [a-ra] [a-rá] *gít-ma-lum* (Aa I/1:200 = MSL 14, 206).

46 Statue B iv 5–19.

Fig. 4. After Cros 1910: 291, fig. e

This atmosphere of equality, peace, and general harmony, which, if we can trust the ancient author, permeated the building of the Eninnu, was equally characteristic of the seven-day period of ritual preliminaries, which preceded the actual construction.[47] During that time of ritual suspension a state of virtually paradisiac conditions prevailed, in which the whole city was of one heart and voice, slaves and servants became their masters' equals, children did not misbehave toward their parents, servants did not disobey their masters, women were exempted from physical work, debts were remitted, legal proceedings were halted, enmity and evil actions disappeard from the scene—and even death itself was put on hold:

ud É-ninnu	"When I erected the Eninnu,
é ki-ág-gá-ni	his beloved temple,
mu-na-dù-a	I cancelled the debts, cleared the hands
ur$_5$ mu-du$_8$ šu-šu mu-luh	(of all obligations);
ud imin-àm še la-ba-àr	for seven days grain was not ground (in the city).[48]
géme nin-a-ni mu-da-sá-àm	the slave-woman was an equal of her
árad-dè	mistress; the slave
lugal-ni zag mu-da-gin-àm	walked at his master's side;

[47] An identical period of seven-day observances occurred at the conclusion of the project, when Ningirsu and his spouse Bau re-entered the temple. See Cylinder B xvii 17–xviii 3, cited below pp. 19–20.

[48] Cf. munus kin dug$_4$-ga uru-ta im-ta-è, "the working slave-women he removed from the city" (Statue B iv 3–4). I assume that the same regulation is meant in either case, namely, that the griding of grain, which customarily

uru-gá ú-sig-ni	the impure ones[49] of my city
zag-ba mu-da-nú-àm	I made to sleep outside of it.
níg-érem é-bi-a	I sent evil back where it belongs.
im-mi-gi$_4$	
níg-gi-gi-na	I investigated the laws of Nanše and
^{d}Nanše	Ningirsu;
^{d}Nin-gír-su-ka-šè	
èn im-ma-ši-tar	(thus) the orphan was not delivered to
nu-siki lú-níg-tuku	the rich one;
nu-mu-na-gar	the widow was not delivered to the
na-ma-su lú-á-tuku	powerful one;
nu-na-gar	
é dumu-nita nu-tuku	in a household without a son,
dumu-munus-bi ì-bí-la-ba	I made its daughter to be its heir."[50]
mi-ni-ku$_4$	
ki-mah uru-ka al nu-gar	"No excavating was done in the city's
adda ki nu-túm	cemetery; no corpse was buried (there);
gala-e balag nu-de$_6$ ér nu-ta-è	the lamenter did not carry the harp, he
	did not emit laments
ama-ér-ke$_4$ ér nu-bí-dug$_4$	the dirge-mother did not perform
ki-sur-ra	lamentations.[51] Within the borders of
Lagaš^{ki}-ka	Lagaš
lú-di-tuku	the accused one was not taken to the
ki nam-érem-šè	place of oath-swearing;
lú nu-de$_6$	

was done by slave-women, was temporarily relegated to Girsu's suburbs, apparently to prevent the pollution of the temple's purified site. Cf. the following note.

49 Cf. lú úzug-ga im-gál lú si-gi$_4$-a NITA UD munus kin dug$_4$-ga uru-ta im-ta-è' "the ones being in impure condition, the castrated ones [taking si-gi$_4$-a for sa-gi$_4$-a, "fixed"], the …, and the working slave-women he removed from the city" (Statue B iii 15–iv 4).

50 Statue B vii 26–46.

51 For ama-ér-ra (which appears as um-ma-ér in DP 159 i 3), see PSD A/3, 213–114. As shown by comparative historical and ethnographic data, she was the chief lamenter, who directed the wailers in the manner of a choir conductor. Here it is interesting to note that such lamenters were known in medieval Armenia under the name "dirge-mothers," which bears remarkable resemblance to the Sumerian term. See Gaster 1975: 610.

lú-ur$_5$-ra é lú-ka nu-ku$_4$	the creditor did not enter one's house."[52]
du$_6$-du$_6$ mu-si-ig inim-gar mu-gi$_4$ ah dug$_4$-ga gír-ta im-ta-gar	"He removed inequities (lit.: he lowered the hills), he barred litigations, he removed lousy / bad actions from the path.[53]
énsi-ke$_4$ uru-na lú dili-gim na-ri ba-ni-gar	the governor has advised his city as if it were a single man—
ki Lagaš^{ki}-e dumu ama dili-a-gim šag$_4$ mu-na-aš-e	like the children of one mother the land of Lagaš is (now) united (lit.: is of a single heart) for him!
giš šu mu-du$_8$ ^{giš}kíšig mu-zi	He took up a stick and pulled out weeds (*i.e.*, he got rid of bad things),
^{ú}šakir mu-gar inim dug$_4$-ga bí-gi$_4$	placing fine herbs (*i.e.*, good things) instead.
šer$_7$-da é-ba im-ma-an-gi$_4$	He banned discord / legal disputes; he sent crime back where it belongs.
ù-sa-an bar-ús-sa eme ì-ḍu$_8$	He undid the tongue of the whip and the goad,
siki udu-⌈gan⌉-na-kam šu-a mi-ni-gar-gar	laying (instead) the (soft) wool of ewes in their (*i.e.*, of the supervisors) hands.
ama-a dumu-da gù n[u]-⌈ma-da⌉-dé	The mother and the child did not yell at each other;
dumu-ù ama-ni-ra KA dù-a nu-ma-na-dug$_4$	the child did speak sharp words to its mother;
árad á giš tag tuku-ra lugal-a-ni sag nu-ma-da-dúb géme lú nam-ara$_x$(DU) hul mu-na-ak nin-a-ni igi-na níg nu-mu-na-ni-ra	the master did not strike his slave on the head when he was neglecting? work; the mistress did not slap the face of the slave-woman when she was misbehaving toward her.
énsi É-ninnu dù-ra Gù-dé-a-ar inim-gar-bi lú-ù nu-ma-ni-gar	As the governor Gudea was erecting the Eninnu, no one submitted litigations to him."[54]
du$_6$-du$_6$ mu-si-ig inim-gar mu-gi$_4$	"He removed inequities (lit.: he lowered the hills), he barred litigations;
^{a}ah dug$_4$-ga gír-ta gar-àm	lousy /bad actions were removed from the path;

52 Statue B v 1–11.
53 Cylinder A viii 4–5.
54 Cylinder A xii 21–xiii 11.

uru-a ama-lú-tu-ra-ke$_4$	in the city it felt as if a nurse placed
a silim gar-ra-àm maš-anše	a healing potion over it; the wild
níg-zi-gál eden-na	beasts of the steppe all crouched
téš-bi-šè gurum-ma-àm	together;
ur-mah pirig ušumgal eden-na-ka	the lion, the panther, and the grif-
	fin of the steppe
ù dùg gar-ra-àm	lay (together) in sweet sleep."[55]
ur$_5$ mu-du$_8$ šu-šu mu-gar	He cancelled the debts, he freed the
ud lugal-ni é-a ku$_4$-ra	hands (of all obligations)[56];
ud imin-né-éš	for seven days
géme nin-a-ni mu-da-sá-àm	the slave-woman was an equal of
árad-dè lugal-e zag mu-da-gin-àm	her mistress; the slave walked at the
	side of his master.
uru-na ^{ú}uzug$_x$(KA×UD)-ni zag-bi-a	He made the impure ones of his
mu-da-a-nú-àm	city to sleep outside of it.
eme níg-hul-da inim ba-da-kúr	He removed evil (words) from the
níg-érem é-ba im-ma-an-g[i$_4$]	tongues; he sent evil back where it
	belongs."[57]

Although a skeptical modern mind may be naturally inclined to doubt the veracity of these descriptions, it may be noted that a strikingly similar spirit accompanied the construction of another famous shrine, which was built over three thousands years later in the heart of Europe. Writing in 1145 AD to the monks of Tutbury Abbey in England, Abbot Haimon, of Saint-Pierre-sur-Dives in Normandy, reported as follows:

> The inhabitants of Chartres have combined to aid in the construction of their church by transporting the materials ... Since then the faithful of our diocese and of other neighboring regions have formed associations for the same object; they admit no one into their company unless he has been to confession, has renounced enmities and revenges, and has reconciled himself with his enemies. That done, they elect a chief, under whose direction they conduct their wagons in silence and with humility...
>
> Who has ever seen!—Who has ever heard tell, in times past, that powerful princes of the world, that men brought up in honor and in wealth, that nobles, men and women, have bent their proud and haughty necks to the

55 Cylinder B iv 15–21.

56 The translation follows Statue B vii 29 (see above p. 16), which has šu-šu mu-luh. I assume that mu-gar is a mistake for mu-luh or, alternatively, that šu-šu mu-gar is meant to convey a similar sense.

57 Cylinder B xvii 17–xviii 3.

> harness of carts, and that, like beasts of burden, they have dragged to the abode of Christ these wagons, loaded with wines, grains, oil, stone, wood, and all that is necessary for the wants of life, or for the construction of the church? But while they draw these burdens, there is one thing admirable to observe; it is that often when a thousand persons and more are attached to the chariots—so great is the difficulty—yet they march in such silence that not a murmur is heard, and truly if one did not see the thing with one's eyes, one might believe that among such a multitude there was hardly a person present. When they halt on the road, nothing is heard but the confession of sins, and pure and suppliant prayer to God to obtain pardon. As the voice of the priests who exhort their hearts to peace, they forget all hatred, discord is thrown far aside, debts are remitted, the unity of hearts is established.[58]

Turning our attention back to ancient times, the ethos and working conditions we encountered in connection with Babylonian building projects find close parallels also in Egypt, especially during the Old Kigdom. I am referring here of course to the pyramid-building schemes at Giza. As we now know, the labor force employed on these undertakings was brought from all the parts of Egypt to work in rotating shifts of several months each. During their stay in Giza, the workers were housed in a special town or village, where an elaborate infrastructure had been set in place to support them: houses or barracks where they and their dependents lived temporarily, workshops, storehouses, breweries, slaughtering houses, bakeries, kitchens, and so forth.[59]

Contrary to the common belief (which goes back to Herodotus, who thought that the pyramids were built by an army of slaves numbering 100,000 individuals),[60] the workers employed on these projects were

58 Henry Adams 1913; 1959: 110–111.

59 Lehner 2002 (esp. 72–73); Morell 2001; Assmann 2003: 53–54; Shaw 2003.

60 This highly negative view of pyramid projects is deeply entrenched in Western cultural consciousness. Typical here is the reaction of Dominique-Vivant Denon, a participant of Bonaparte's Egyptian Campaign and the author of *Voyage dans la Basse et la Haute Égypte pendant les campagnes du general Bonaparte,* on seeing the pyramids for the first time: "One doesn't know what ought to astonish the most: the tyrannical madness that dared to order their construction, or the stupid obedience of the people willing to lend their labor to such edifices" (cited after *New York Review of Books* LVI no. 18 [Nov.19, 2009] 310). Much more recently, renowned architect Renzo Piano, when asked to give his views of the pyramids, opined as follows: "I never really loved them. To kill people by making them work so hard just to celebrate one man? I admire them, but with a kind of sadness" (*Time Magazine*, July 4, 2011, 76).

well treated and amply fed. "The people who built the pyramids were more likely a few thousand highly skilled and well-compensated full-time craftsmen and a cast of manual laborers."[61] Including the full-time specialists, the entire workforce employed at any given time at Giza probably consisted of only 20,000 to 30,000 men.

Great quantities of bones from cattle, sheep, and goats were discovered in the remains of that workers' town. According to Mark Lehner, "People were eating lots of meat … Our faunal specialist has estimated that there were enough cattle, goat and sheep to feed 6,000 to 7,000 people if they ate meat every day."[62] In addition, there are indications that the workers had access to medical care.

The pyramid builders were not slaves but free peasants and craftsmen, who, as one may surmise, did their work with a high degree of motivation—and perhaps even with enthusiasm. "They were proud of their work, yes … It's because they were not just building the tomb of their king. They were building Egypt. It was a national project, and everyone was a participant."[63]

One may even wonder as to the true objective of these projects. Was it the pyramids themselves? Or was it rather the goal of creating a sense of unity and common culture and ideology among the different parts of Egypt that contributed labor and other resources toward these undertakings? Perhaps it would not be too much of an exaggeration to suggest that it was the pyramids that built the Egyptian nation and its sense of shared culture. At the very least, one needs to recognize that these projects constituted an enormous integrating force, which must have contributed mightily toward the formation of the Egyptian national and cultural identity.[64]

61 Stille 2005: 64.
62 Stille 2005: 64.
63 Morell 2001: 82–83 (quoting Zawi Hawass.)
64 "… if we extend our purview to the material and administrative infrastructure required for the construction of such huge edifices, then the proposition that the entire Egyptian people was involved no longer looks quite so exaggerated. The laborers themselves were recruited from all over the country and lived in villages especially constructed for them. Although they certainly did not speak 'with one tongue' when they arrived at these settlements, they learned to do so in the course of joint effort and cohabitation" (Assmann 2003: 53).

2. The Tummal Project

2.1. Tummal and Its History

I begin my review with the Tummal[65] project, since this is by far the best documented Ur III public undertaking. Therefore, the conclusions we will be able to reach here should be representative of the other projects as well. The Tummal project is also the earliest among the cases treated in this study.

A group of sources from Umma and Girsu/Lagaš attest to a large-scale building activity at Tummal during the second half of Šulgi's reign. That activity appears to have culminated during years Šulgi 35–37. Although known to exist already in the Sargonic period,[66] Tummal probably came to prominence only in Ur III times, when it became the seat of a royal palace and the focus of the funerary cult of Ur-Namma. As indicated by the frequent references to the royal court and the high officials sojourning at Tummal,[67] this satellite of Nippur, and the immediate neighbor of Puzriš-Dagan (also known as E(-sag)-dana),[68] appears to have been, after the capital city of Ur, the most important administrative center of the Ur III state. There are reasons to suspect that it was there that some of the main offices of the Ur III state, such as the "war mininistry" and the "ministry of foreign affairs," were situated. However, this question will have to wait for the excavation of the site of Tell Dlehim, and of its neighbor Tell Drehem, the modern site of Puzriš-Dagan.

Tummal was the site of a major religious festival, which was celebrated yearly during the eight month.[69] This event, whose central part was Enlil's and Ninlil's boat-ride from Nippur to Tummal, was one of the

[65] Tummal is a conventional reading. The actual pronunciation of the toponym may have been /tumal/, but this remains unclear. The writing Tum-IMMAL (= TÙR) is rendered in this study as Tum-al$_x$—though the correct translation is probably ^{tum}Tummal$_x$(IMMAL).

[66] See ég Tum-al (OSP 2 148:4) and the PNs Ur-Tum-al$_6$ (OSP 2 93 iv 7′) and NIN-Tum-ma-al-e (BIN 8 168:21). It is likely that Tummal's history went even further back in time, but we have no textual proof of that. Here note that Tell Dlehim, the presumed modern site of Tummal (see below n. 68) shows an extensive Early Uruk und Jemdet Nasr occupation.

[67] See Sallaberger 1993: 131–144.

[68] In all likelihood, Tummal is identical with Tell Dlehim, site no. 1237 in R. McC. Adams 1981: 277–278. See Steinkeller 2001a: 68–71.

[69] Oh'e 1986: 123–132; Sallaberger 1993: 131–143.

most important cultic observances in Ur III times.[70] Its great significance is underscored by the fact that the fashioning of a new processional boat, which carried the divine couple on their journey, was deemed sufficiently weighty an event to be commemorated in one of the year-formulae.[71]

Yet another indication of Tummal's importance as a religious and political center is the fact that it was also the locus of the "great stela of Enlil and Ninlil." The instalation of this stela must have been a major national event, since it is mentioned in the formula of Šu-Suen's sixth regnal year.[72] That this event took place at Tummal is shown by an Umma tablet dating to precisely that year, which refers to the deliveries of flour for a stela in Tummal.[73]

An intriguing source bearing on Tummal in Ur III times is the so-called "Chronicle of Tummal,[74] which, as the current *communis opinio* has it, is a "school concoction,"[75] which purports to document the building activity at Nippur and Tummal, all the way from the hoary days of Gilgameš and Enmebaragesi down the reign of Išbi-Erra of Isin. The section describing the pre-Ur III phase of that activity is clearly a fabrication, since it directly derives from the standard version of the "Sumerian King List." However, the part dealing with the Ur III period (see Text 1), which attributes the building of the Ekur to Ur-Namma, and which makes Šulgi responsible for "making (things) in Tummal resplendent,"[76] is undoubtedly historical. To begin with, Ur-Namma's work on the Ekur is otherwise documented.[77] And, as we will see presently, there is ample evidence that Šulgi did indeed conduct major building operations at Tummal.

[70] The Tummal festival is described in an extraordinary group of literary, historical, and economic inscriptions. See in detail Sallaberger 1993: 139–143.

[71] Year Šu-Suen 9: mu ^{d}Šu-^{d}Suen ... má-gur$_8$ mah ^{d}En-líl ^{d}Nin-líl-ra mu-ne-dím.

[72] mu ^{d}Šu-^{d}Suen ... na-dù-a mah ^{d}En-líl ^{d}Nin-líl-ra mu-ne-dím.

[73] 10 workers ... ud 1-šè zíd munu$_4$ na-dù-a má-a «si» gá-ra ud 10-šè má gíd-da má dirig-ga ud 9-šè zíd munu$_4$ na-dù-a Tum-ma<-al> ku$_4$-ra, "10 workers for 1 day, loading the flour and malt of the stela on a boat; for 10 days, towing the boat (from Umma) upstream and floating it (subsequently) downstream; for 9 days, bringing the flour and malt of the stela into Tummal" (SAT 3 1710:1–8; ŠS 6/-). These foodstuffs undoubtedly were to be used in sacrificial offerings for the stela.

[74] For the most recent discussion and the partial edition of this composition, see Michalowski 2006b.

[75] See Michalowski 2006b: 162.

[76] Tum-ma-al^{ki}-e pa bí-i-è.

[77] Frayne 1997: 61 Ur-Namma 25.

Let us turn now to the specifics of Šulgi's building activity at Tummal. It appears that its main objective was the construction of a royal palace.[78] This residence, which is described as the "new palace" in a text from Ur,[79] housed the funerary chapels of Ur-Namma and his wife.[80] In two sources from Girsu/Lagaš, which record the assignments of laborers for various (mainly external) work-projects, the same structure is referred to as é Tum-ma-al Ur-^{d}Namma or é Ur-^{d}Namma, "the (Tummal) house of Ur-Namma."[81]

78 This building is usually is described as the "palace of Tummal." See Text 7:11; SNAT 81:15–16, 82:11–12, 528:11; MVN 1 79:2–6; MVN 5 153:4–5; MVN 13 136:2–3; SANTAG 7 31 ix' 3'; BPOA 7 1840:5; UTI 4 2770:8–9; etc. In Text 5 vi 28, it is called é-gal lugal.

79 0.3.2 ^{giš}hašhur duru$_5$ ^{giš}hašhur hád-bi 0.1.0 6 2/3 sìla 0.3.2 ^{giš}pèš duru$_5$ ^{giš}pèš še-[er]-gu-bi 13 1/3 é-gal gibil ki-a-nag ^{d}Ur-^{d}Namma-šè 900 ku$_6$ duru$_5$ nesag ezen-mah é-gal lugal-⸢kam?⸣ (rest broken off) (UET 3 76 i 2'-9'; date destr.). This text can be dated to Amar-Suen 5 based on iii 3′–5′: 2 sìla ì-giš dùg-ga 0.0.2 6 sìla ì-giš ^{giš}LUM má-gur$_8$ é-unu$_6$ ak-a, which correlates to the year-formula Amar-Suen 5. This "new palace" is also mentioned in "Ur-Namma A" line 149. See below p. 35 and n. 117.

80 13 […] níg-dab$_5$ ezem-ma dil-dil zag-mu ki-a-nag Ur-^{d}Namma ù ki-a-nag nin-šè ⸢x⸣ ba-sum mu 1-kam gìr ^{d}Nanna-ki-ág (UET 3 21 rev. 1′-6′; AS 5/-). Interestingly, a tablet dating to year Ibbi-Suen 1 records an offering for Apil-kin, a king of Mari and father of Ur-Namma's daughter-in-law (and the apparent wife of Šulgi) Taram-Uram, within Ur-Namma's "house," which was made together with those for Ur-Namma and Amar-Suen: 360 sa gi sá-dug$_4$ šu-a gi-na 20 sa gi u$_4$-sakar ù é-ud-15 ki-a-nag Ur-^{d}Namma 120 sa gi sá-dug$_4$ sá-dug$_4$ A-bíl-ki-[in] 150 sa gi sá-dug$_4$ ^{d}Amar-^{d}Suen šag$_4$ é Ur-^{d}Namma (AOF 23 27–28 VAT 7191:1–9; Umma?). [The same source records separate offerings for the ki-a-nag's of Šulgi, Amar-Suen, and Šu-Suen (lines 10–22), which must have been located at Ur; all of these offerings are summarized as sá-dug$_4$ ki-a-nag$^{!}$ 4-ba im sá-dug$_4$ lugal-ta, "the offerings of the four funerary chapels, (the information extracted) from the tablets (recording) royal offerings" (lines 24–25).] Cf. also 0.2.3 kaš sig$_5$ ki-a-nag A-bíl-gi-en$_8$ … [šag$_4$] bala-a (BCT 2 151:4–8; AS 6/-; Umma). For the ki-a-nag of Ur-^{d}Namma, see further UET 3 76 (cited in the preceding note) and the examples cited in nn. 81 and 83.

81 6 (men) é Tum-ma-al dù-dè Ur-^{d}Namma — following 2 (men) é ^{d}Šul-gi (TCTI 2 2796:11; AS 8/vi/15); 6 (men) é Tum-ma-[a]l dù<-dè> Ur-^{d}Namma — following [x (men) é] ^{d}Šul-gi (TCTI 1 949:11; AS 8/vii/24). In other documents of this type, the same work-assignment is alternatively designated as é Ur-^{d}Namma or ki-a-nag Ur-^{d}Namma, usually in conjuction with the é/ki-a-nag ^{d}Šul-gi and, after Amar-Suen's death, with the é ^{d}Amar-^{d}Suen as well:

(1) é ^{d}Šul-gi and é Ur-^{d}Namma (ITT 2 3503:8–9); (2) é Ur-^{d}Namma alone (ASJ 18 225 HSM 6435:15; Fs Sigrist no. 4:19, no. 5:17); (3) ki-a-

That the funerary chapel of Ur-Namma was located at Tummal is demonstrated, apart from the data supplied by the Girsu/Lagaš work-assignments,[82] by various other sources. The most important among them are two Umma texts from year Amar-Suen 6, which record expenditures of wooden rungs (^{giš}dal) for the ladder of Ur-Namma's ki-a-nag in Tummal.[83] Another Umma source, from Amar-Suen 2/viii, lists the doors that the Umma province supplied for a šutum warehouse[84] and Ur-Namma's ki-a-nag, the former of which is specifically said to have been at Tummal.[85] The same localization of Ur-Namma's ki-a-nag is also given in a Puzriš-Dagan tablet.[86]

nag Ur-^{d}Namma and ki-a-nag ^{d}Šul-gi (CT 7 47 BM 17775:10–11; DAS 55–67; MVN 5 240:7–8; AnOr 7 290:7–8; TUT 173:6–7; Fs Sigrist no. 1:6–7, no. 3:9–10, no. 6:6–7); (4) é ^{d}Šul-gi, é ^{d}Amar-^{d}Suen, and é Ur-^{d}Namma (UDT 41:9–11; ASJ 18 223 HSM 6425:12–14, 228 HSM 6495:9–11; ITT 2 970:10–12; HLC 3 175 (pl. 104) lines 7–9). The designation é Ur-^{d}Namma also appears in AOF 23 27–28 VAT 7191, cited in the preceding note.

82 See the preceding note.

83 11 ^{giš}dal ^{giš}kun$_5$ ki-a-nag Ur-^{d}Namma-šè šag$_4$ Tum-[a]l$_x^{ki}$ ki Ur-sila-luh-ta kišib A-gu šag$_4$ bala-a (RA 59 147 EO 14:1–6; AS 6/-) = 11 ^{giš}dal ^{giš}kun$_5$ ki-a-nag Ur-^{d}Namma-šè šag$_4$ Tum-al$_x^{ki}$ (MVN 10 230 iii 6–8; AS 6/-). For dal, Akk. *tallu*, "crosspiece, crossbeam, rung," see CAD T, 99–101.

84 In Ur III sources, this term, which represents the Akkadian *šutummu*, "warehouse, treasury," is written either syllabically (šu-tum or é-šu-tum) or logographically (é-GI.NA.AB.TUM = é-šútum; also é-GI.NA.TUM in GARšana sources). Later lexical texts use also the spellings É.GI.NA.AB.DU$_7$ = šutum and É.GI.NA.AB.DU$_{10}$. It appears that GI.NA.AB.TUM is a pseudo-Sumerian form, which plays on the term lú-gi-na-ab-túm, "guarantor," for which see Steinkeller 1989: 80–81. Heimpel (2009: 163–165) considers GI.NA(.AB).TUM to be an Akkadian term, which he identifies as *kinātum*, "servants." This etymology suggestes to him that the structure in question functioned as "barracks." In my view, both of these assumptions are incorrect. First, Heimpel's etymology is precluded by the element AB in the term (which he fails to explain). And second, there is no evidence whatsoever that the *šutummu* was used to house people.

85 1 ^{giš}ig ⸢é⸣-šútum(GI.NA.AB.TUM) [šag$_4$] Tum-al$_x^{ki}$ [1?] ^{giš}ig é 3 $^{\langle giš\rangle}$ig suh$_4$(KID) sal-la ki-a-nag Ur-^{d}Namma (BPOA 1 567:3–8; AS 2/viii). Cf. the following example, where the šutum of Tummal probably likewise is meant: 10 ^{giš}ù-suh$_5$ gal kùš 12-ta é-šu-tum šag$_4$ é-gal-ka-šè ... šag$_4$ bala-a (Orient 16 72 101:1–6; ŠS 3/vii).

86 2 udu niga 1 udu sá-dug$_4$ ki-a-nag Ur-^{d}Namma ... zi-ga šag$_4$ Tum-ma-al^{ki} (OIP 115 139:5–11; Š 42/vi/12).

Apart from the palace, other buildings affected by Šulgi's building operations were a sheepfold (é-udu)[87] and a šutum warehouse.[88] It appears that both of them belonged to the palace complex.

Tummal also housed the é-uz-ga sanctuary,[89] which, together with its counterpart at Nippur,[90] was a recipient of extensive animal offerings.[91] The operations of the two é-uz-ga's were regularly supported by

87 See Text 5 viii 2.

88 See Text 5 viii 22. For the šutum of Tummal, see also above note 85.

89 This sanctuary is plausibly mentioned in connection with Šulgi's building project at Tummal. See Text 5 vii 5–6, discussed below p. 180 and n. 163.

90 See Steinkeller 2001a: 68. For the é-uz-ga in Tummal, see also JCS 24 159 no. 51:7–11: 1 ⌜u_8 $sila_4$⌝ nú-a é-uz-ga Ur-^{d}Dumu-zi sipad ... zi-ga $šag_4$ Tum-ma-al. In the work-assignments from Girsu/Lagaš, these two sanctuaries are occasionally referred to as é-uz-ga 2-a-bi, "two é-uz-ga's" (ITT 2 970:6, 3503:6; TCTI 1 949:11; TCTI 2 2796:7; ASJ 18 223 HSM 6425:10; HLC 3 pl. 104 no. 175:5). The usual formulary in these sources is x (men) (gi íl) é-uz-ga, "x (men) reed carriers (for) the é-uz-ga," where the two sanctuaries apparently are treated as a single institution. A parallel case here is the work-assignments, included in the same sources, for the slaughterhouses of Puzriš-Dagan and Nippur. Although only one é-gud-gaz is usually listed, in some instances the é-gud-gaz É-$Puzur_4$-iš-^{d}Da-gan$^{an(ki)}$ and the é-gud-gaz Nibru^{ki} are specifically named (MCS 3 13 BM 1102105:9–10; MVN 11 83:11–12, 85:13–14; 104:10–11). Here note that in some texts É-$Puzur_4$-iš-^{d}Da-gan$^{an(ki)}$ is replaced by Sag-da-na (CT 7 47 BM 17775:12; MVN 4 240:10). Cf. é-gud-gaz-šè ... $šag_4$ É-te-na-ka (BPOA 1 1057:3–8; Umma).

91 See Michalowski 1989: 104–05; Sigrist 1992: 158–162; Wu 1996: 65–109; Sallaberger 2003/04: 58. It is characteristic that in literary sources the é-uz-ga and its personnel (uz-ga or lú-uz-ga) are consistently associated with lustrations. See "Curse of Akkade" line 256; "Lamentation over the Destruction of Sumer and Ur" line 447; and the examples cited by Sjöberg 1969: 120. That the é-uz-ga was a locus of cultic lustrations may find support in Text 5 vii 5–11, where timber is issued for the é-uz-ga and two bathrooms, one of which is identified as that of "ritual ablutions": 3 giš 6 [kùš]-ta é-uz$^!$(ŠE.RI)-g[a(-šè)] 2 giš 6 kùš-[ta] 2 giš ká 6 kùš-ta é-du_{10}-ús é-⌜gal» ús-sa-aš 5 ^{giš}šinig ⌜2?⌝ [kùš]-ta é-du_{10}-ús a-t[u_5-a(-šè)].

As for the etymology and reading of é-uz-ga, Sigrist (1992: 161 and n. 241) suggests a connection with /uzug/, "taboo," with a resulting reading é-ùzu-ga. A possible indication that the morphology of the term indeed is é-uzug-a(k), "place of taboos," is provided by the unique writing é-UZ.TUR-ga, which appears twice in an Umma tablet (Nisaba 11 45:5, 35). Since UZ.TUR, "duck," must be understood as a scribal whimsy for uz, also meaning "duck," this writing establishes, at the very least, that the term was read -uz-ga or -ùzu-ga. This is further confirmed by the writing é-uz-ga-aš (MCS 3 43 BM 105546:3; MVN 13 6:2; MVN 16 786:3; SNAT 539:2;

the provinces of Umma and Girsu/Lagaš, which sent there, in lieu of their bala duty toward the central government, foodstuffs,[92] fuel,[93] pots,[94] reed mats,[95] and various types of reed, leather, and wooden containers.[96] These two provinces (and almost certainly all the other provinces as well) also supplied the é-uz-ga with laborers,[97] who worked there in shifts, apparently on a rotating basis. While at Tummal, these laborers were responsible for the carrying of reeds (which undoubtedly served as fuel for cooking) and flour. Since the é-uz-ga's personnel included cooks,[98] this institution must have prepared substantial volumes of food, which, as it appears, was intended not only for sacrifices, but also to feed the resident population of the Tummal complex.[99]

Sharlach Taxation no. 36:3). Since any connection with "ducks" is impossible, of course, one may conclude that this writing is purely syllabic, with /uzug/ being the most likely referent here. A similar solution had been suggested already by Goetze (1963: 36 n. 30), who argued for a connection with uzug(ZAG.AN), *sukku*, "a small shrine."

92 See, *e.g.*, BPOA 7 2040:2 (mun-gazi).

93 See, *e.g.*, MVN 14 27; MVN 16 786; JCS 28 209 no. 4.

94 See, *e.g.*, MVN 14 359.

95 See, *e.g.*, BPOA 6 1058.

96 See, *e.g.*, BIN 3 433; Nikolski 2 218; BPOA 7 2040; SANTAG 6 277; BPOA 6 403, 1058; UTI 4 2532; CDLI P387651:10–11 (3 pisan-tab-ba kuš si-ga sá-dug$_4$ nin šag$_4$ é-uz-ga).

97 For Girsu/Lagaš, see the sources cited in nn. 81 and 90. For Umma, see the following examples: 1 (man) gi íl é-uz-ga (UCP 9/2 Part 1 no. 77:13); 2 guruš ud 1-šè 5 sìla ésir-é-a ... é-uz-ga gub-ba (MVN 14 317:1–5); 2 guruš zíd íl sá-dug$_4$ lugal 1 guruš zíd íl sá-dug$_4$ šagina é-uz-ga ... 1 guruš zíd íl sá-dug$_4$ lugal 1 guruš zíd íl sá-dug$_4$ šagina é-uz-ga (Nisaba 23 28 i 14–17, ii 2–6; collated by M. Molina); 21 guruš ugula Lú-^{d}Šára 1 Lugal-iti-da dumu In-ni-dar$^{?}$ 1 Lú-kal-la dumu Lú-^{d}Šára gi íl é-uz-ga 10 guruš ugula Lú-^{d}Šára 1 Ur-ama-na gi íl é-u[z-ga] (Nisaba 23 50 iii 18–24).

98 See UTI 4 2532:1–6 (AS 7/-; Umma): 30 ^{kuš}a-gá-lá é-uz-ga-šè muhaldim-e šu ba-ab ti ... šag$_4$ bala. The preparation of meat in the é-uz-ga is implied by an expenditure of "pegs for hanging sheep (carcasses)" (30 ^{giš}gag udu lá níg-dab$_5$ é-uz-ga; SANTAG 6 41 iii 16–17 (Š 41/-; Umma).

99 Here note three Nippur records of beer consumed as part of the "banquet of Tummal": 5 sìla kaš sig$_5$ sízkur ^{d}Inana gizbun$_x$(KI.BI) Tum-al (BPOA 7 2731:1–3; AS 9/viii); 0.0.3 kaš gin diri é-gud-gaz (+ various other issues of beer) gizbun$_x$(KI.BI) Tum-al-[(šè)] (NATN 883:1–14′; ŠS 6/viiii); 30.0.0 še gur še munu$_4$-šè gizbun$_x$(KI.BI) Tum-al-šè Ur-^{d}Šul-gi-ra munu$_4$-mú šu ba-ti (TMF NF 1/2 113:1–5; IS 3/vi). An Umma tablet notes supplies of fuel for gizbun$_x$ Ur-^{d}Namma^{ma}, probably at Tummal (Nisaba 9 20:1–3; undated; courtesy of M. Molina).

Although it is positively known that Tummal was a center of Ninlil's cult,[100] Ur III texts virtually never refer to her temple there.[101] It is particularly striking (and puzzling) that no such mentions are found in the sources concerned with the Tummal project. As a matter of fact, the same is true of the "Tummal Chronicle" as well, since that source talks only of "embellishing" Tummal (without naming any specific architectural feature), and of Ninlil's regular visits there from Nippur.[102] It appears quite certain, therefore, that Ninlil's true home was at Nippur, and that she, together with Enlil, only visited Tummal occasionally.[103] A possible explanation why her temple at Tummal is mentioned so rarely in Ur III texts is that the shrine in question usually hides behind the designation é-uz-ga. Although there is no conclusive evidence that the é-uz-ga was specifically connected with Ninlil's cult, the fact that the two documented Ur III é-uz-ga's were situated at Nippur and Tummal respectively, makes such a possibility fairly likely.

These facts bring us back to the "Tummal Chronicle," and the motivation behind the writing of this composition. In my view, the answer to

[100] See, in particular, "Sumerian Temple Hymns" no. 3 lines 39 and 46, which is dedicated to Ninlil: Tum-ma-al[ki] me nun-e gal pàd-da ... é Tum-ma-al[ki]. See also [ki]-tuš Tum-ma-al[ki] ⸢d⸣Nin-líl-lá-kam (Frayne 1997: 317–20 Šu-Suen 9 xi 9–10); (Ninlil) NIN Tum-ma-al[ki] ("Šulgi R" line 64).

[101] As far as I know, only three such attestations survive: 1 gud niga é [d]Nin-líl-šè šag$_4$ Tum-ma-al (SAT 2 259:2–3; Š 40/vi); foodstuffs é [d]Nin-líl ... šag$_4$ Tum-ma-al (SET 198:1–5, 23; Š 44/x); 1 gud niga 4 udu niga 1 máš é [d]Nin-líl ... 1 udu? ú [d]NIN-Tum-ma-al-la (Tel Aviv 1 56 Wadsworth Atheneum 22.350:5–7, 18; Š 40/viii/5). The offerings recorded in the Wadsworth Atheneum tablet can be placed at Tummal based on the parallels with SET 198. See Sallaberger 1993: 140. The [d]NIN-Tum-ma-al-la mentioned in the former text obviously is Ninlil (cf. the previous note).

[102] The latter information is confirmed by an inscription of Šu-Suen, which describes the fashioning of a barge for Enlil and Ninlil, which was subsequently used to transport this divine couple (actually, their cultic statues) from Nippur to Tummal. See Text 2. Further, note the formula of year Šulgi 8, which commemorates the caulking of Ninlil's boat (apparently in connection with her boat-trip to Tummal).

[103] Here is important to note that "Sumerian Temple Hymn" no. 3 line 47, which is devoted to é Tummal, and which identifies Ninlil as Tummal's mistress (lines 45–46), locates Ninlil's temple at *Nippur* (é [d]Nin-líl Nibru[ki]-a). A. R. George speculated that the é Tummal named in that composition is a "by-name for é-ki-ùr of Ninlil at Nippur ..., borrowed from her cult-center downstream of Nippur" (1993: 151 no. 1113).

this problem lies in its concluding lines, which cite a declaration made by a certain Lu-Inana, chief leather-worker (ašgab-gal) of Enlil, according to which Lu-Inana had, during the late part of the Ur III period, accompanied (lit.: "brought") Ninlil during her ceremonial travels from Nippur to Tummal.[104] As speculated by Michalowski,[105] Lu-Inana was a historical figure; he is possibly identical with an ašgab of that name who was active in Isin during the reign of Išbi-Erra. Lu-Inana's testimony is followed by a statement that Išbi-Erra built for Enlil a šutum storehouse[106] named É-kur-igi-gál.[107]

The structure in question is mentioned in an Ur III tablet from Nippur, where it is identified as a locus of the cult of Enlil and Ninlil.[108] There, its name is written É-kur-ra-igi-gál. The same writing is also attested in an Amar-Suen dedicatory inscription from Nippur,[109] as well as in the early Old Babylonian offering lists,[110] demonstrating that this is the original form.[111] As shown by the existence of an Ur III goddess named ᵈKur-ra-igi-gál or ᵈNin-kur-ra-igi-gál, "One/Lady present/standing in the Mountain (= É-kur?)," who was worshipped at Nippur and

[104] I follow here Michalowski's understanding of this crucial passage (2006b: 149–150).

[105] Michalowski 2006b: 160.

[106] É-šutum ᵈEn-líl-lá. For šutum and its various spellings, see above p. 159 and n. 84.

[107] For this structure in Old Babylonian and later sources, see Richter 1999: 32–35; Such-Gutierrez 2003: 94–95.

[108] ᵈEn-líl ᵈNin-líl šag$_4$ É-kur-ra-igi-gál (NATN 879:1–3).

[109] A brick inscription, excavated in the Inana temple, which commemorates the construction of ⸢Kur?-ra?⸣-igi-gál ⸢é?⸣-u$_6$-nir [é] ki ág-gá-ni for Enlil (Frayne 1997: 248 Amar-Suen 3).

[110] ᵈNin-líl šag$_4$ É-kur-ra-igi-gál (Fs Kramer 226 iii 21′–22′), 1 udu ᵈNin-líl É-kur-ra-igi-gál (*ibid.* 228 rev. vi 20′–21′), ká É-kur-ra-igi-gál (*ibid.* 229 rev. vii 10′), [É]-kur-ra-igi-gál (*ibid.* 228 rev. iv 24′). Note also Kur-ra-igi-gál é ᵈEn-líl, "Kura-igigal, the house of Enlil," in "Nanna/Suen's Journey to Nibru" line 315, and ᵈEn-líl-da Kur-ra-igi-gál-la-ka nam dùg tar-ra-me-en, "you (Enki), together with Enlil, determine favorable destiny in Kur-ra-igi-gál," in "Enki and the World Order" line 75. The writing É-kur-igi-gál was introduced in Old Babylonian times. See, *e.g.*, PBS 8/2 133:7, 8, 9, 17 (Samsuiluna) and the data collected by Richter 1999: 32–35.

[111] The underlying grammar must be é-kur-a igi-gál-ø, where -a is a locative. This fact precludes such translations as "House, Mountain Endowed with Sight" (George 1993: 117 no. 683) and "Tempel, der auf das Bergland blickt" (Sallaberger 1993: 53 and n. 223).

belonged to the circle of Enlil and Ninlil,[112] É-kur-ra-igi-gál was named after that goddess, probably representing the place of her worship. Given ^{d}Kur-ra-igi-gál's connection with Enlil and Ninlil, it is likely that she was a manifestation of Ninlil.

But where was the É-kur-ra-igi-gál situated? The data in hand—in particular the Nippur brick inscription cited earlier[113]—seem to assure that there was a structure called É-kur-ra-igi-gál at Nippur in Ur III times. On the other hand, the fact that there was a šutum at Tummal during the reigns of Šulgi and Amar-Suen[114] raises a possibility that there existed, at least during the Ur III period, *two separate* šutum's called É-kur-ra-igi-gál, both of them dedicated to Ninlil, which were located in Nippur and Tummal respectively.[115] The case of the two é-uz-ga's I discussed earlier would offer an obvious parallel here.

If there was a separate É-kur-ra-igi-gál at Tummal, it could actually have been this place that was the object of Išbi-Erra's building activity. Such a possibility is favored by the following consideration: had that construction taken place in Nippur (as is generally assumed), then the Chronicle's preoccupation with Tummal would otherwise be difficult to explain. In particular, there would be no logical connection between Lu-Inana's testimony (which describes Ninlil's boat-trips to Tummal) and the subsequent construction of É-kur-ra-igi-gál by Išbi-Erra.[116]

[112] Animal offerings for ^{d}Kur-ra-igi-gál (CT 32 50 BM 103409:27; YOS 18 13:31) and Kur-ra-igi-gál (Princeton 2 2 ii 23; YOS 18 12:16; MVN 10 169:20; UTI 6 3757:14′). In all these instances, coming from Puzriš-Dagan sources, the goddess is included among the Nippurean deities headed by Enlil and Ninlil. See further 4.3.0 še sá-dug$_{4}$ ^{d}Kur-ra-igi-gál ... kišib Ur-^{d}Ba-ú ^{d}Nin-kur-ra-igi-gál; seal of Ur-^{d}Ba-ú ⌜árad?⌝ ^{d}Ni[n]-kur-ra-[igi-gál] (YOS 4 248:3–7; Girsu/Lagaš); Ur-^{d}Ba-ú ^{d}Nin-kur-ra-igi-gál (SNAT 163:18; Girsu/Lagaš). This goddess appears already in a Sargonic god-list, where her name is spelled ^{d}Nin-kur-igi-gál (Sachs Mem. Vol. 259–60 BM 86271 i 15).

[113] See above n. 109.

[114] See above p. 163.

[115] An inscripion of Ur-Namma records the construction, in an unspecified location, of an unnamed šutum (é-šu-tum) of Ninlil (Frayne 1997: 74–75 Ur-Namma 37; two door sockets of unknown provenance). Given Ur-Namma's rebuilding of the Ekur (see above), this particular šutum was probably situated at Nippur. A šutum of Ninlil is also mentioned in the formula of Ibbi-Suen's "eighteenth" regnal year, but again its location is not identified: ^{d}Nin-líl ù ^{d}Inana é-šútum(GI.NA.AB.TUM) kug mu-ne-dù.

[116] Unless the É-kur-ra-igi-gál played some special role in those trips (as the place where Ninlil's boat was stored?).

If these assumptions are correct, the following (admittedly highly tentative) reconstruction of the events leading to the writing of the "Tummal Chronicle" could then be considered. During the planning phase of his work at Tummal, which may have been inspired by his desire to revive the Tummal festival and the ritual boat-ride of Enlil and Ninlil, Išbi-Erra requested information about the history of Tummal. This request prompted an investigation, which led to the discovery of Lu-Inana and the recording of his testimony. That record—we may further speculate—was then deposited in the royal archives. From there it somehow found its way into the Edubba, where, after it had been embelished with the information drawn from the "Sumerian King List," it became part of the Old Babylonian school curriculum.

2.2. Šulgi's Building Operations at Tummal

As indicated by the data extant, the main construction work on the palace of Tummal took place during years Šulgi 35–37. However, it is virtually certain that the project had begun much earlier. In all probability, the construction of the palace had been initiated by Ur-Namma, since the composition "Ur-Namma A" line 149 talks of Ur-Namma's "new palace," which he did not have time to enjoy.[117] That there existed a palace in Tummal before the main phase of Šulgi's construction is further demonstrated by the fact that a tablet from year Šulgi 34 already mentions Ur-Namma's funerary chapel.[118] The same locus may also be meant in two Puzriš-Dagan tablets from year Šulgi 32, which record expenditures of foodstuffs in Tummal.[119]

Whoever initiated the Tummal project—be that Ur-Namma or Šulgi—it is certain that the express purpose of this undertaking was to provide the Ur III state with a centrally-situated seat of government, as the capital city of Ur, because of its location in the southernmost reaches of Babylonia, was not well-suited for that purpose. As already noted, it

[117] é-gal gibil na-mu-un dù-a-ni nu-mu-un-húl-húl-⌈la⌉-ni, "he (*i.e.*, Ur-Namma) had indeed built a new palace, but he did not enjoy it (long enough)."

[118] 60 sa gi ki-a-nag Ur-^{d}Namma^{ma} ... šag$_4$ bala-a (Syracuse 130:1–5; Šulgi 34/-).

[119] Dates, raisins, and figs šag$_4$ Tum-ma-al^{ki} (MVN 2 171:1–8; Š 32/vi); 2 small gur-dub baskets with 175 *andaḫšum* (in-duh-šu-um) vegetables ⌈šag$_4$⌉ Tum-ma-al (TCL 5 5578; Š 32/vii). For the latter text, cf. AUCT 1 974:1–3 (Š 31/iv), recording a delivery of one small gur-dub with 50 *andahšum* to Esagdana-Nibru (= Puzriš-Dagan).

was likely there that some of the highest officials of the realm—such as the sukkalmah, and probably the king himself—worked and lived most of the time. Furthermore, it would seem that the construction at Tummal was closely connected with another massive project, which was the building of Puzriš-Dagan, less than 15 km away from Tummal. One might even consider that both undertakings were but parts of the same project.[120]

The works at Tummal continued beyond year Šulgi 37. For example, more additional construction was done on Ur-Namma's funerary chapel during the reign of Amar-Suen.[121] And the work on the palace continued as late as year Ibbi-Suen 1.[122] By and large, this was probably routine maintenance work, such as was regularly needed due to the mudbrick's inherent indurablity.

Rather surprisingly, Šulgi's activity at Tummal is not mentioned in any of his year-formulae. This is unexpected, since, as we will see in the following, it involved huge expenditures of labor and natural resources. I suspect, however, that the Tummal project is obliquely referred to in the formula of Šulgi's thirty-ninth year, which commemorates the construction of Puzriš-Dagan. Since Tummal and Puzriš-Dagan appear to have been parts of the same grand undertaking, it was apparently only when the whole project reached completion that it was deemed appropriate to commemorate it in a year formula.[123]

[120] The topography of Puzriš-Dagan/E(sag)dana is unknown. It appears that this state-run economic enterprise consisted of a number of highly specialized sub-units, housing animal corals, slaughtering houses and meat-processing offices, workshops devoted to leather and metal production, and various storing facilities for cereals and other agricultural products that were delivered to the government as bala contributions, which were probably physically separate from each other. This would mean that Puzriš-Dagan actually formed a chain of settlements, which stretched along the Euphrates over a sizable geographical area. According to this scenario, the territories of Puzriš-Dagan and Tummal would have been contiguous.

[121] See MVN 10 230 iii 6–8 (AS 6/-); TCTI 2 2796:11 (AS 8/vi/15); TCTI 1 949:11 (AS 8/vii/24).

[122] 138 logs (mostly giš-ùr) of gišimmar, ù-suh$_5$, ásal, and šinig (from ½ nindan 1 kùš to 1 nindan 2 kùš long), and some giš-ùr é-da - é-gal Tumma-al^{ki}-šè ki énsi Umma^{ki}-ta (SNAT 528:1–12; IS 1/iv).

[123] It is strange, though, that, none of the sources extant seem to bear specifically on the construction of Puzriš-Dagan. Should one assume, therefore, that the works at Puzriš-Dagan were administratively subsumed under the Tummal project?

Since the sources bearing on the Tummal project stem exclusively from Umma and Girsu/Lagaš, our information is essentially limited to the involvement of these two provinces. Luckily, these sources also contain accidental references to the contributions of other provinces. Thus, there survive records of the building materials that were supplied by the governors of Babylon, Adab, and Kutha in year Šulgi 36.[124] This information makes it certain that the whole core area of the Ur III state must have participated in this undertaking. It appears that each province was required to provide both human labor and materials goods, the latter consisting of building materials and food supplies to feed the workers.
Two aspects of the construction are primarily documented in sources extant: the types of labor used and the material goods supplied by individual provinces toward the project. The sources dealing with the latter also throw important light on the technical aspects of the construction itself. I begin my discussion with the review of the data bearing on the use of labor.

2.3. The Use of Labor on the Tummal Project

2.3.1. Labor Contribution of the Umma Province

Our best source of information on the employment of labor at Tummal is Text 6,[125] an Umma text dating to year Šulgi 37. This immense tablet, consisting of twenty-four columns with some 1,500 lines of writing, is a record of the labor (more precisely, man-days) that the Umma province contributed toward the Tummal project. That contribution was made over a period of five months—the second through the seventh month—

[124] See Text 5 i 4–6, ii 40–41, according to which the governor of Babylon contributed timber, while those of Adab and Kutha supplied straw, in the amounts of 120 and 60 bushels, respectively. This straw undoubtedly was used to make bricks. Another Umma source refers to the reeds provided by the governor of Adab (Text 10).

[125] Walters Art Gallery 48.1767. This exceedingly important source was published in transliteration by David I. Owen in MVN 15 390. An earlier study of this tablet had been done by Maureen Gallery Kovacs, who presented preliminary results of her work at the annunal meeting of the American Oriental Society at Cornell University in 1977. Kovacs later shared all her materials and notes with Owen. The great contribution of these two scholars toward the publication and understanding of this unique document must be acknowledged here.

[126] For the distinction between these these two types of state dependents, see in detail Steinkeller 2013: 351.

of year Šulgi 37. The laborers in question were exclusively the dependents of Umma's institutional economy. No members of Umma's royal sector appear in this text.[126]
Although the figures of the grand-totals (xxiii 48–xxiv 9) are preserved incompletely, it may be estimated, on the basis of the numbers given in the main body of the text, that it recorded ca. 45,000 man-days.[127]

The listing shows three major subdivisions, reflecting the employment of workers during three separate time-periods, which probably add up exactly to 100 days. The work was performed over five months, from the 3rd day of the third month through the 13th(?) day of the seventh month. No work was done during the sixth month:

(a) iti še-kar-gál-la (3rd month) ud 3-kam-a-kam iti nesag (4th month) ud 30-kam (i 1–vii 58);
(b) iti RI (5th month) (vii 59–xiv 52);
(c) iti šumun (6th month) ⌜ud 30⌝-[kam]
iti min-è[š (7th month) ud 13$^{?}$-kam] (xiv 53–xxii 28).

(a) iii/3 through iv/30 = 57 days;
(b) v = 30 days;
(c) vi/30 through vii/[13?] = [13?] days.

Many of the named individuals participated in two, or even three, periods of employment.

In addition, at the very end of the text (xxii 29–xxiii 46), there is listed separately the work that was expended to tow boats with building materials from the Umma province to Tummal.[128] This work was carried out concurrently with the building operations, from the third

[127] The surviving numbers of the grand-totals add up to only ca. 28,934+[x] man-days. However, by tallying the five main categories of workers, as recorded in the text, one obtains 42,550 ½ 10 gín + [x] man-days: (a) guruš gub-ba = 22,104 10 gín (vii 45, xiv 38, xxii 10); (b) guruš lá-NI = 14,067 ½ +[x] (vii 56, xiv 50, xxii 25); (c) UN-íl gub-ba = 3,734 (vii 46, xiv 39, xxii 11); (d) additional labor listed at the end of the text = 2,645 (xxiii 40).

Superficially, the figure of 45,000 man-days sounds very impressive, but, at the rate of 100 man-days per worker stipulated by this text (see below), it meant only 450 laborers working full time. Thus, in spite of the text's enormous size, the project described there involved a comparatively small expenditure of corvée labor.

[128] See, *e.g.*, 18 guruš ud 12-šè a-šag$_4$-^{d}Šára-ta ka íd-Tum-al$_x$^{ki}-ka-šè má in-u-da im-gíd gìr Lugal-me-è àga-ús (xxiii 1–6); 10 lá 1 guruš ud 10-[šè] Umma^{ki}-t[a] ka íd Tu[m]-al$_x$^{ki}-šè má ^{giš}šinig ^{giš}eren$^{?}$ im-gíd (xxiii 19–23).

through the sixth month of Šulgi 37. The transported materials included straw, timber (^{giš}šinig and ^{giš}eren?), wooden tools (^{giš}al and ^{giš}íl), and bitumen (ésir-hád). The total of this labor amounted to 2,601 man-days (guruš) and 44 days of labor provided by female servants/slaves working half-time (géme á-½).

Within the three major subdivisions, workers are identified in the following two alternative ways:

(1) by personal name and title or occupation: x guruš gub-ba lá-NI y PN (title/occupation), "x man-days performed; y man-days non-performed – (the obligation of) PN (title/occupation)";[129]

(2) by number, occupation, and name of the supervisor: x guruš gub-ba / x guruš occupation ugula PN, "x man-days performed / x professional man-days, under the supervision of PN."[130]

Although not identified as such in the text, the workers of category (1) are invariably éren. In contrast, category (2) comprises primarily menials (UN-íl and géme)[131], though some éren are included there as well.

The first major subdivision (i 1–vii 58) may serve as an illustration of the types of workers appearing in the present text. On the basis of the concluding tally (vii 45–58), the workers listed there (actually: man-days) may be grouped as follows:

(a) workers of the éren class:

7,461 10 gín	guruš gub-ba, "performed man-days"
3,907 ½	guruš lá-NI, "unperformed man-days"
78	guruš ugula, "man-days of the supervisors"
119	guruš ad-KID, "man-days of the reed-workers"
60	guruš nagar (gašam-me), "man-days of the carpenters (the craftsmen)"
66	guruš šidim, "man-days of the masons"
27	guruš lú-ninda, "man-days of the food-handlers"
30	guruš «UN»[132] tu-ra, "man-days of the sick"

[129] See, *e.g.*, 20 guruš gub-ba lá-NI 13 A-kal-la gáb-sar (i 27–28).

[130] See, *e.g.*, 53 guruš gub-ba 4 (guruš) á-½ ugula Ur-agrun (vi 67–68); 119 guruš ad-KID 48 guruš <UN-íl> ad-KID 60 guruš nagar gašam-me ugula Šeš-kal-la (vi 69–73); 45 guruš 13 guruš-ugula ugula Šeš-kal-la (vii 25–27).

[131] For the menials, bearing the designations UN-íl and géme, see Steinkeller 2013: 365.

[132] UN(-íl) is incorrect. These 30 sick were of the éren class. See 10 lá 1 guruš tu-ra (vii 7) plus 21 guruš tu-ra (vii 16).

(b) menials—UN-íl and géme:

790 UN-íl 2/3 gub-ba, "man-days of the UN-íl working 2/3 time"

29 géme <ù> lú á-½, "man-days of the slave-women and the individuals working half-time"

48 UN(-íl) ad-KID, "man-days of the UN-íl reedworkers"

48 UN(-íl) tu-ra, "man-days of the sick UN-íl"

The second and third subdivisions list the same types of workers, except that they also include guruš má-GÍN, "caulkers" (xxii 15), guruš má-lah$_4$ "boatmen" (xiv 45, xxii 16), and guruš nar, "singers" (xxii 19).

It is necessary to comment at this point on the social group identified here as "menials," whose members, as we just seen above, were also part of the project. The menials or the semi-free appear to have had some legal and economic rights, but they were not classed as citizens. They were much more numerous than chattel slaves, who had no legal or social rights, and constituted just another form of movable property. The most conspicuous among the menials were the males designated as UN-íl, "porters" or "coolies," and the females classified as géme, "servant / slave women." In principle, these individuals did not receive land allotments (though there were occasional exceptions to that rule). They worked all year round, usually as unskilled laborers, in exchange for food allotments. These are the individuals who did most of the agricultural work (except the specialized jobs of harrowing, plowing, and seeding) and who were primarily responsible for the transportation of agricultural and other products, either as porters or boat-towers. The géme were employed in grain-processing establishments (mostly grinding grain) and as weavers, but could also do the UN-íl work; thus they worked in agriculture and as porters—and occasionally even as towers. The contribution of this social group to the Tummal project was marginal—though see the important qualification below p. 175.

The labor force appearing in Text 6 was drawn from the four main districts of the Umma province, which were (Da-)Umma, Apišal, Mušbi'ana, and Gu'edena.[133] However, the overwhelming majority of the workers came from (Da-)Umma. Apišal and Mušbi'ana contributed considerably smaller contingents, with Gu'edena's contribution being so tiny as to be largely symbolic. This proportional relationship closely

[133] See, *e.g.*, in the first subdivision: šag$_4$ Umma^{ki} (iv 61); šag$_4$ A-pi$_4$-sal$_4$^{ki} ki Ur-e$_{11}$-e (vi 21–22); šag$_4$ Muš-bi-an-na ki Lugal-^{giš}kiri$_6$ (vi 54–55); šag$_4$ Gú-eden-na ki A-ab-ba (vi 66).

agrees with the distribution of arable land and other sources in the four districts.[134]

Very importantly, the named and titled individuals contributing labor in the present text, who, as already noted, undoubtedly had the status of éren, were required to provide 100 man-days each. This information is obtained if one calculates all the man-days that are assigned to each individual in this text; quite regularly, they add up to 100 days. See the following two examples:

	gub-ba	lá-NI	Attestations
Ad-da-gu-la	24	9	i 34
ugula-kín-kín	10	20	viii 11
	7	30	xv 16
	41	59	
Lú-kal-la sipad	22	11	i 30
	17	13	viii 7
	25	12	xv 21
	64	36	
Da-a-gi$_4$ ágar-nigin	16	17	i 69
	7	23	viii 45
	4	33	xv 51
	27	73	
Luga-nesag-e ì-du$_8$	16	17	iii 32
	6.5	23.5	x 35
	13.5	23.5	xvii 45
	36	64	
Da-da àga-ús	115	21.5	ii 76
	9	21	ix 68
	6	31	xvii 8
	26.5	73.5	

While the overwhelming majority of these individuals were liable for 100 man-days, some among them are assigned higher quotas. These elevated figures, which seem to oscillate around 200 man-days, are usually associated with high administrative officials, such as sabra, "majordo-

[134] See Steinkeller 2013: 358–359.

mo," and pisan-dub-ba, "head of the accounting."[135] It is possible, therefore, that there existed another, higher rate, which amounted to 200 man-days.

Among the individuals who provided corvée labor for the Tummal project, we find people of all walks of life and economic circumstances. They include some of the top administrators of the province, such as sabra, pisan-dub-ba, ka-guru$_7$, "granary superintendent," sag-du$_5$, "head keeper of real estate records," nu-bànda-gud, "head of plow-teams," dub-sar, "scribe," ugula-kín-kín, "supervisor of millers," ugula-uš-bar, "supervisor of weavers," ugula-UN-íl, "supervisor of menials," agar$_4$-nígin, "field assessor," SAHAR, "equerry," and santana, "head of gardeners." As a matter of fact, this group includes at least one member of the governor's family. The person in question is Ur-e'e, a brother of the governors Ur-Lisi and A'a-kala, who is known to have run the district of Apišal.[136] In the present text, Ur-e'e is designated both as a "worker" and as the person in charge of the workers from Apišal.[137]

Another likely relative of the governor is the unnamed granary superintendent.[138] Given the fact that only one such official is mentioned in this text, we almost certainly find here Arad, the chief official in charge of cereal storage and distribution, who too was a member of Umma's ruling family.[139]

Other individuals of high rank included in this group are the chief lamenters (gala-mah) of Umma and Zabalam and four merchants (dam-gàr).[140] Among the individuals of lower social standing, we can list the

[135] See the following examples (note that the first number represents the gub-ba man-days, with the second number representing the lá-NI days): Lugal-ezen sabra: 56/10 (i 32), 42/18 (viii 9), 50/24 (xv 14) – total: 148/52 = 200 man-days; Lú-gi-na sabra: 59/17 (ii 28), 43.5 / 16.5 (ix 11), 37/37 (xvi 21) – total: 139.5 / 70.5 = 210 man-days; A-ab-ba sabra: 59/7 (vi 57), 35.5 / 24.5 (xiii 41), 53/24 (xxi 8) – total: 203 man-days; Ur-^{d}Šára pisan-dub-ba: 56/10 (iii 22), 50/10 (x 25), xvii 36 – total 166.5 / 34 = 200.5 man-days.

[136] See Dahl 2007: 85–96.

[137] Ur-e$_{11}$-e SAHAR: 56/10 (v 23), 41/19 (xii 48), 0/0 (xx 1); šag$_4$ A-pi$_4$-sal$_4^{ki}$ ki Ur-e$_{11}$-e (vi 21–22, xii 87–88; xx 35–36)

[138] NN ka-guru$_7$: 40/26 (iii 48), 51/9 (x 54) – total: 91/35 = 126 man-days.

[139] See Dahl 2007: 115–121.

[140] Pàd-da dam-gàr: 27 ½ / 5 ½ (i 42), 7/30 (xv 26) – total: 61.5/38.5 = 100 man-days; Lugal-šag5-ga dam-gàr: 13/20 (iii 60), 6/24 (x 66), 0/37 (xviii 17) – 19/81 = 100 man-days; Lugal-é-mah-e dam-gàr: 18/15 (i 40), 25/12 (xv 22) – total: 67/33 = 100 man-days; Ur-^{d}Lama dam-gàr: 17/16 (i 44), 6/31 (xv 24) – total: 31/71 = 102 man-days (needs to be collated).

guda priests, shepherds (sipad, ùnu), craftsmen (simug, kug-dím, túg-du$_8$), masons (šidim), foresters (tir), fishermen (šu-ku$_6$), cooks (muhaldim), vegetable-growers (sum—for lú-sum-ma), brewers (lunga), elite soldiers (àga-ús), throne-carriers (gu-za-lá) and torch-carriers (lú-gi-zi). There are also the lowly doorkeepers (ì-du$_8$) and milk-carriers (ga-íl), and even one menial (UN-íl), named Kuli.[141]

The question obviously arises as to whether any of the people listed in MVN 15 actually worked *themselves* on the Tummal project. In the case of administrative officials and the high-status individuals such as merchants, the answer must of course be negative, not just because of their high social ranking, but simply due to the fact that their professional duties would not allow them to spend extended periods of time at Tummal. A good example here is the official Ur-silaluh,[142] who supervised the forest complex of the Umma province.[143] Clearly, Ur-silaluh had no time (and willingness) to toil at Tummal himself, a task calling for 100 days of back-breaking labor. Accordingly, we have to assume that, at least in the case of the higher-ranking people, the corvée work they were liable for was done by their substitutes.[144] Such substitutes may have been junior kinsmen of the individuals in question, or their servants or chattel slaves, or perhaps even hired menials. Unfortunately, our sources (as far as I know) throw no light on this matter. A reasonable assumption would be that the situation differed greatly, depending on the circumstances of each person.[145]

[141] Ku-li UN-íl: 25/5 (viii 63), 17/[?] (xv 73).

[142] Ur-sila-luh tir: 15/18 (iii 52), 30/0 (x 58), 16/21 (xviii 11) total: 61/39 = 100 man-days.

[143] See Steinkeller 1987a.

[144] For the hire of workers as corvée substitutes in Old Babylonian times, see Stol 1995: 298–300.

[145] It appears that one could even provide monetary compensation in lieu of performing corvée. A likely instance of such a substitution is found in BCT 2 83:1–4 (courtesy of X. Ouyang). According to this source, the well-known Umma merchant Pada paid to Umma's "Fiscal Office" two amounts of silver (1 and 4 shekels) as his "labor" (á) for the years Šu-Suen 9 and Ibbi-Suen 1 respectively. Here note that the same Pada contributed labor to the Tummal project (see above n. 140). Similar monetary substitutions for the unperformed corvée seem to be recorded in the following Umma texts, all from AS 6, in which the duration of labor invariably was 45 days, with its cost being 2 shekels of silver per worker: lá-NI 1 Ur-^{d}Ištaran dumu Du-du 1 Ur-é-mah ù Šeš-kal-la 1 A-tu 1 Ur-Suen enkud ud 45-šè á-bi 2 gín-ta šag$_4$ bala-a (AUCT 3 479:1–7); lá-NI 1 ^{d}Šára-za-me 1 Lugal-níg-lagar-e ud 45-šè á-bi 2 gín-ta Ur-^{d}Da-mu ugula su-su-dam šag$_4$ bala-a (TJSASE

On the other hand, it is likely that most of the lower-ranking individuals did actually work on the project, probably participating in the unskilled construction work, cutting straw for bricks, making bricks, coating the foundation walls with bitumen, and carrying various materials. However, here too, there may have been significant differences from one case to another, with some of these individuals providing substitutes instead of working themselves.

Among the workers identified only by number and occupation (see above p. 40), we find individuals who clearly were brought to Tummal because of their professional background. The examples here are masons (šidim), carpenters (nagar), reed-workers (ad-KID), caulkers (má-GÍN), and boatmen (má-lah$_4$).

One also notes the presence among the named "laborers" of the professionals who would be highly desirable on a building project. One such example is the silver smith (kug-dím) named (quite fittingly!) Kug-šaga.[146] This occupation is rare, and thus Kug-šaga's participation in the Tummal project may not have been accidental.[147] The same was probably true of the four metal-workers (simug) that were part of this under-

167:1–7); lá-NI 6 ½ guruš ud 45-šè á-bi 2 gín-ta lá-NI su-su nu-^{giš}kiri$_6$-[ke$_4$]-ne ugula Da-du šag$_4$ bala-a (ASJ 19 217 47:1–6); lá-NI 7 ½ guruš ud 45$^!$-šè á-bi 2 gín-ta lá-NI su-su-dam ugula Ur-^{d}A$^!$-hi$^!$ šag$_4$ bala-a (RSO 53 361 no. 36:1–5). Such transactions may also be suspected behind the payments of silver designated as á bala, "work/wages of the bala duty," which are recorded in Nik. 2 408:1–3; MVN 14 447:1–3; NABU 1989/95 12:1–2; and UTI 3 2144:3–5 (all courtesy of X. Ouyang). Among those of special interest is Nik. 2 408:1–3 (ŠS 7/ix), which lists ½ shekel of silver delivered, in lieu of á bala, by the gardener Lu-ibgal. Apparently the same Lu-ibgal appears among a group of men from the Gu'edena and Mušbi'ana districts who had failed to fulfill their corvée obligation (bala) in year Amar-Suen 7: 1 Lú-ib-gal nu-^{giš}kiri$_6$ ... šu-nígin 35 guruš lá-NI-àm šag$_4$ bala-a šag$_4$ Gú-eden-na ù Muš-bi-an-na (Nisaba 23 68:23, 27–29; AS 7/-). That the á and á bala payments refer to the same duty is indicated by the following two examples, which probably involve members of the same family: 10 gín kug-babbar á dumu Ur-^{d}Suen-ke$_4$-ne (BPOA 6 736:1–2; ŠS 5/-); ½ kug-babbar á bala-a ki Ur-^{d}Suen-ta (MVN 14 447:1–3; IS 2/-).

146 Kug-šag$_5$-ga kug-dím: 25/8 (ii 16), 15 ½ / 14 ½ (viii 77), 13 ½ / 23 ½ (xvi 9) – total: 54/46 = 100 man-days.

147 Attested as Kug-sig$_5$ kug-dím in Nisaba 24 37 rev. i 4–6, according to which he received, in year Š 45, 1 5/6 minas of silver for a gaba-gál, "wagon's front." He appears also as a witness in the sale document MVN 3 213:9 (Š 45/-). M. Molina informs me that Kug-šaga was the father of another kug-dím, named Ur-Šulpa'e (BRM 3 148:3 and seal; Š 47/ix).

taking.[148] Even rarer is the occupation gáb-sar, the writer of inscriptions on stone and clay. And there were two gáb-sar working at Tummal,[149] again suggesting that these professionals were brought there because of their particular skills.

But the rarest of all the occupations and titles appearing in the present text is kur-gá-ra,[150] a type of entertainer. Since there were also over forty singers (nar) participating in the Tummal project,[151] it is not inconceivable that this kur-gá-ra, as well as the singers, provided entertainment for the laborers and their supervisors, perhaps on the days free of work and during the festivals, which likely marked the different stages of the project. As a matter of fact, there is evidence that such building operations were accompanied by banquets (kaš-dé-a), which were meant specifically for the builders.[152]

In summary, it will be fair to conclude that a significant number (probably the majority) of the individuals listed in Text 6 did work on the Tummal project.

Less clear is the question of the workers who, by all indications, substituted for the higher-ranking éren. As I noted earlier, there are no data bearing either on them or their status. Since it is conceivable that at least some of those substitutes were menials, it is possible that the actual number of menials employed at Tummal was considerably higher than that appearing in Text 6.

But the main question raised by Text 6 is the figure of 100 man-days of labor that is assigned to most of the éren listed there. As we have seen earlier, 100 days was also the period that Umma's institutional economy contributed to the Tummal project in total. It would seem, therefore,

[148] One of them was Inim-Šara: Inim-^{d}Šára simug: 22.5 / 10.5 (iv 5), 26.5 / 3.5 (xi 4), 2/35 (xviii 35) – total: 51/49 = 100 man-days.

[149] Na-ú-a gáb-sar: 26 gub-ba / 7 lá-NI (i 13), 29 gub-ba / 1 lá-NI (x 3), 14 gub-ba / 23 lá-NI (xvii 14) – total: 69 gub-ba / 31 lá-NI = 100 man-days; A-kal-la gáb-sar: 20/13 (i 28).

[150] Lú-^{d}Utu kur-gá-ra: 18/15 (iii 14), 11/19, (x/23), 1 ½ / ⌜35 ½⌝ (xvii 32) – total: 30.5/69.5 = 100 man-days. As far as I know, the only other kur-gá-ras documented in Umma sources are A-kal-la (Nik 2 447:4), Ma-aš (NISABA 24 12 ii 3), and Lú-ga-mu (Nisaba 11 34 iii 14; courtesy of M. Molina).

[151] 43? guruš nar (xxii 19). Singers may have also been part of the Ga'eš project. See below p. 188.

[152] Text 35 iv 12–14 (AS 7/-), which deals with the Ga'eš project, lists three bushels of barley, beer, bread, and sesame oil that were used for a banquet (3.0.0 še kaš ninda gur 5 sìla ì-giš ud-e kaš-dé-a).

that those 100 days represented the corvée contribution that Umma's institutional economy owed to the crown. Was it a yearly contribution? Or was it an extraordinary obligation, which had been imposed on all the provinces because of the national character of the project? For the time being I favor the second solution.

At any rate, it appears that those 100 days of corvée were not directly related to the obligation that an individual éren owed personally to his institutional economy (in this particular case, the governor of Umma and his organization). Assuming that the latter obligation was 180 man-days per year,[153] during that particular year (Šulgi 37), a typical éren would still need to supply 80 man-days of work to the institutional economy.

Admittedly, the evidence of Text 6 is insufficient to answer this question conclusively. Since the corpus of published Umma texts has increased dramatically during the last decade, most of which yet await a systematic study, one may be confident that this problem will be solved eventually.

[153]Or, in practical terms, fifteen days per month. See Steinkeller 2003:45. Additional evidence that the free men were required to contribute 180 man-days of labor yearly to the state is provided by Ontario 2 190 (origin uncertain), according to which two free citizens (dumu-gir_{15}) contributed 180 man-days each over a period of six months: 2 guruš iti maš-dà-kú-ta (i) iti á-ki-ti-šè (vi) á-bi 360 guruš dumu-gir_{15} ud 1-šè iti 6-kam (lines 25–29). Elsewhere in the same text (lines 30–37), two dumu-gir_{15}, working at 2/3 capacity, contributed jointly, over a period of seven months, 140 man-days of labor: Ma-ku-ùb-ba Árad-dam 2/3 guruš iti ezen-[d]Šul-gi-ta (vii) iti še-sag_{11}-kud-šè (xii) á-bi 140 guruš dumu-gir_{15} ud 1-šè iti 7-kam $šag_4$-ba iti dirig 1-àm ì-gál. One may conclude that these two men too were required to contribute 180 man-days per year. Since two men working at 2/3 capacity for seven months would have contributed 420 man-days, it is clear that their actual joint contribution of 140 man-days over seven months (each man contributing ten days per month) assumed a yearly contribution of 180 man-days per worker (or 120 man-days when working at ⅔ capacity).

It is unclear whether or not those 180 days included the time free from work (ud du_8-a). If the former was the case, the actual mandatory number of man-days may have been thirteen or perhaps even twelve. Here it is important to note that, roughly 150 years after the fall of Ur, Enlil-bani of Isin claimed to have significantly reduced the obligations of subjects toward the state. While establishing that the corvée duty had been longer before Enlil-bani reduced it to four days per month, the source in question unfortunately does not specify its duration: še níg-kud-da igi-5-gál ì-me-a igi-10-gál-la hé-mi-ku_4 MAŠ.EN.GAG iti-da ud 4-àm hé-gub, "the grain tax (Akk. *miksu*) that used to be one-fifth (of the total produce) I changed to one-tenth; indeed, the commoner served (only) four days (of corvée) per month" (Frayne 1990: 87–90 Enlil-bani 1001 vi 12–19).

2.3.2. Labor Contributions of Other Provinces

Although one may be confident that many other (if not all) provinces of the Ur III state contributed labor toward the Tummal project, such evidence is available (apart from Umma) only for Girsu/Lagaš. Our evidence here is the records of the expenditures of foodstuffs for the Girsu/Lagaš masons and éren during their employment at Tummal. I review these data in the immediately following section.

2.3.3. Upkeep of Workforce During Its Employment at Tummal

A number of sources record food supplies that were given out to the Umma workers during their employment at Tummal. These supplies came from Umma itself. This shows that each province was responsible for the upkeep of its labor force during its employment on national projects.

A tablet from year Šulgi 35/i names huge numbers of cattle that were slaughtered to feed the masons (šidim) and the conscripted workers (éren) stationed at Tummal (Text 3). The expenditure for the masons was particularly large, as it amounted to 424 oxen and cows. The conscripted workers received considerably less meat, since only 21 heads of cattle were slaughtered for them. It appears certain that both the masons and the conscripts in question stemmed from the Umma province. This is corroborated by Text 6, discussed earlier, which names large numbers of mason man-days contributed by Umma. The expended meat came from Umma itself, and, without any doubt, was meant exclusively for Umma's native labor force.

Another expenditure of foodstuffs for Umma's laborers at Tummal is documented in a tablet from year Šulgi 37 (Text 9). The tablet in question records significant volumes of bread and beer (2.2.4 5 sìla ninda-šu gur and 3.3.4 3 sìla kaš gin gur) and a small quantity of flour, which were used to feed the carpenters (šag$_4$-gal nagar).[154] Their task was to fashion the doors of Tummal's palace (zi-ga ^{giš}ig é-gal).

[154]This text also mentions 180 liters of ordinary dried (dida) beer, which was expended in connection with some (additional?) work done on the door(s): giš-e šu de$_6$-a ù ^{giš}ig HI lá-a, "to treat/process the wood and to install the door(s)." For the difficult HI ... lá, see Veldhuis (2004b), who suggests the meaning "to close an opening by means of tying a hide." The beer in question clearly was meant for the workers who performed these jobs. Cf. MVN 13 378:1–2, where a leather-worker receives dida in connection with the HI-lá work.

A group of Girsu/Lagaš sources from year Šulgi 35 (with one dating to Šulgi 37) names barley and flour provisions that were given out to the Girsu/Lagaš laborers working on the same project. See Texts 4 and 8. One of these expenditures (Text 4) concerns the masons (šidim), who received 53 bushels (= 15,900 liters) of barley. At the monthly rate of 60 liters per one man, this amount would support 265 masons for one month.

The other sources from this group record the provisions of the éren. No numbers of the éren are ever specified, but, given the very substantial volumes of cereals involved, those numbers (= man-days) must have been quite large. If one adds up all the expenditures of barley made in year Šulgi 35, the result is ca. 270+ bushels of barley. At the monthly rate of 60 liters per man, this amount would translate into 1,350 man-days. The workers in question came from the main temple households of the Girsu/Lagaš province, and thus were part of the institutional economy. See, especially, Text 8 = MVN 6 15, where the workers are identified as belonging to the household of Nanše (in Nimin and Sirara), and to the sanctuaries of Lagaš. Note also Text 8 = MVN 7 549, where the supervisor (ugula) in charge of the workers is the head of the household of Gatumdug.

2.4. Building Operations

Our main source of information on the specifics of the construction at Tummal is Text 5, which dates to the first month of year Šulgi 36.[155] Formulated as a balanced account, this source is a very detailed and informative record of the building and related materials that were supplied to Tummal by Umma's institutional economy, and of how those materials were subsequently used. Since this information is of less relevance for the questions of labor, I will treat Text 5 only briefly here. But this source deserves utmost interest,[156] since it offers unique information on the Babylonian building methods and architectural terminology.[157]

The "capital" section of Text 5 (sag-níg-gur$_{11}$-ra-kam; i 1–v 5) lists the supplied materials. Most conspicuous among those are various

[155] This means that the information given in it actually pertains to the previous year, *i.e.*, Šulgi 35.

[156] No adequate edition and study of it are as yet available.

[157] For an exhaustive treatment of these issues and relevant terminology, see now Heimpel 2009: chapters 4–6.

types of timber, mostly pine (^{giš}ù-suh$_5$)[158] and tamarisk (^{giš}šinig), both unprocessed and processed.[159] One also notes huge volumes of straw (in-u) and chaff (èš-tum)[160]—1,200 gur and 60 gur respectively—which obviously were used as temper in brick production. Other products include bitumen, reeds and various reed products, ropes, date-palm fronds, various kinds of pots and jars, small volumes of sesame and lard, dyes and mordants (such as ú-háb and *allaḫaru*), various aromatics, as well as animal hides and metals.

In the "expenditures" part of Text 5 (zi-ga; v 6–xii 16),[161] which specifies how and where these materials were utilized, three building destinations are named. The first, and the most important of them, was é-gal lugal, "royal palace" (v 6–vi 28), within which a "large anteroom" (pa-pah gu-la), a "sitting/receiving room" (ki-tuš-lugal), a "bathroom" (du$_{10}$-ús), and a "great staircase" (kun gu-la)[162] are specifically named.

158 The identification of ^{giš}ù-suh$_5$, Akk *ašūḫu*, as "pine" is tentative only. While ^{giš}ù-suh$_5$ undoubtedly was some kind of a coniferous tree, its botanical identity is uncertain. See CAD A/1, 448–79 ("fir"); Heimpel 2011: 103–111 ("pine").

159 The latter include various types of building parts, such as ^{giš}é-da, "board," ^{giš}dal, "crosspiece," ^{giš}sag-kul, "door bolt," etc., and various wooden tools, such as ^{giš}ì-šub si-sá, "mold for regular bricks," ^{giš}ì-šub ar-ha, "mold for half-bricks," ^{giš}kun$_5$, "ladder," ^{giš}al, "hoe," ^{giš}íl, "lever," etc.

160 For èš-tum, Akk. *iltu*, which denotes finely chopped straw, see Steinkeller 2001c; Heimpel 2009: 191.

161 At least one receipt related to this section survives. See Text 5a, which corresponds to Text 5 v 10–13.

162 Bitumen, pots, sesame oil, and lard du$_{10}$-ús ù kun gu-la ba-ra-ab-du$_8$, "were used to caulk the bathroom and the great staircase" (vi 17–22). Another staircase is mentioned later in connection with the the é-uz-ga complex: 1 ^{giš}ù-suh$_5$ 4 kùš ^{giš}ar-gi$_4$-bí-lu kun-šè ba-dím, "1 pine log 4 cubits (long), was made into the *argibillu* of a staircase" (vii 20–21); 1 ^{giš}šinig 2 kùš sag-kul kun-šè ba-dím, "1 piece of tamarisk 2 cubits (long) was made into the bolt of a staircase" (vii 26–27). In these examples, kun is syllabic for kun$_5$, *simmiltu*. See Steinkeller 2007b: 225, 227–28 n. 20; Heimpel 2009: 176. kun$_5$/kun means both "staircase" (German *Treppenhaus*) and "wooden ladder." In the examples just cited, the former meaning is clearly meant. For the same sense of kun$_5$/kun, see bitumen and thread (níg-U.NU-a) of goat hair for é-kun-gá é-gal gu-la-šè, "the staircase of the great palace" (BIN 9 426:23): cord of palm-fiber $^{[giš]}$ig kun$_5$-šè, "for the door of a staircase" (CUSAS 3 472:12–13 [certainly not "ladder door," as translated by Heimpel 2009: 176]; wooden parts ésir-bi 2(bán) ká ^{giš}kun$_5$, "the (respective) bitumen is 20 liters, (for) the gate of a staircase" (BIN 10 193:1′–5′; followed by a similar expenditure for ká ^{d}Inana); x workers kun dù-a, "building a stair-

Although not mentioned here *expresis verbis*, this construction probably included the work on the funerary chapel (ki-a-nag) of Ur-Namma. As I noted earlier, the latter structure is positively known to have been part of Tummal's palace.

The second building destination (vi 29–viii 3) included the é-uz-ga sanctuary and two bathrooms,[163] a staircase (kun), the "great gate" (ká-mah), a retaining wall (ki-sá),[164] and a sheepfold (é-udu).[165]

The final destination (viii 4–18) is identified simply as "in Tummal." The only architectural feature named here is the "royal courtyard" (kisal lugal).

The materials that remained on hand were either stored in the palace (é-gal-la ku$_4$-ra; viii 19–x 25) or assigned to three individuals, two of whom were merchants (x 26–30). The materials deposited in the palace notably included timber from the governors of Babylon and of another province, whose name does not survive. The timber supplied by the latter official apparently was destined for a šu-tum warehouse.[166]

case" (CUSAS 3 146:31'); ^{giš}kun$_5$ (na$_4$) in the inscriptions of Puzur-Inšušinak, which actually come from the steps of a stone staircase (Gelb and Kienast 1990: 332–334 Elam 7:8, Elam 8:14). The main staircase of a building was called kun-sag. See Steinkeller 2007b: 228 n. 20; George 1993: 115 no. 671; Löhnert 2009: 217–218, for kun-sag, a part of Nippur's Ekur. For wooden ladders, see Text 5 i 25, 37, ii 3, iv 12; Text 24:7; 30 ^{giš}ga-lam ^{giš}kun$_5$, "30 steps of a ladder" (SANTAG 6 41 iv 8); 1 ^{giš}kun$_5$ ga-lam 8, "1 wooden ladder with 8 steps" (CUSAS 3 808:1); 2 ^{giš}kun$_5$ níg-gur$_{10}$ PN (MVN 14 340:1–2); and the examples from Pre-Sargonic sources cited in Steinkeller 2007b: 228 n. 20.

[163] 3 giš 6 [kùš]-ta é-uz$^!$(ŠE.GA)-g[a(-šè)] 2 giš 6 kùš-[t]a 2 giš ká 6 kùš-ta é-du$_{10}$-ús é-⌜gal⌝ ús-sa-aš 5 ^{giš}šinig ⌜2$^?$ kùš⌝-ta é-du$_{10}$-ús a-t[u$_5$-a(-šè)] (vii 5–11).

[164] It is likely that the staircase, the "great gate," and the retaining wall were likewise parts of the é-uz-ga. The same was probably true of the following "sheepfold" (é-udu) as well, since the é-uz-ga is known to have been a recipient of sacrificial animals (which means that it must have contained animal-keeping facilities of some sort).

[165] This section is summarized as zi-ga é-udu-ka, "expenditures of the sheepfold" (viii 3). However, this designation can hardly apply to all of the structures listed earlier, since features such as the é-uz-ga, the bathrooms, the staircase, and the "great gate" would not be expected in a sheepfold. It is possible, therefore, that é-udu refers only to the last items listed in this section. Alternatively, the end of column vii, which is now broken off, could have contained another, intervening designation.

[166] 30 giš 5 kùš-ta énsi Babilim^{ki} 2 giš 8 kùš-ta 5 giš 6 kùš-ta šu-tum énsi [GN] (viii 19–23).

Another text bearing on Umma's material contributions to the Tummal project is Text 9, which likewise dates to year Šulgi 37. This source lists various materials that were used to construct the door(s) of a palace. Although the text does not name Tummal, its date assures that Tummal's palace is meant. The articles named in Text 9 include an amount of zíd-GUM flour to produce glue, twenty heavy ropes (ébih) made of goat hair, as well as seven turtle carapaces (murgu$_2$-ba).[167]

3. The Construction of the gipar at Ga'eš

3.1. Introductory Remarks

Another Ur III public project that is amply documented in the surving textual record is the construction of the residence of the en priestess of Nanna in Ga'eš near Ur.[168] Ga'eš, also known under its poetic name Karzida, "the true quay," was the site of a shrine of Nanna.[169] It appears that this sanctuary housed the á-ki-ti building, where the spring (harvest) and the fall (sowing) á-ki-ti festivals were celebrated. As such, the Ga'eš sanctuary probably functioned as Nanna's countryside residence, which the god of Ur visited and temporarily resided in during the performance of the two á-ki-ti festivals. However, since a separate en priestess lived there permanently, it is clear that this sanctuary was a locus of Nanna's ongoing ritual activity. It appears that Ga'eš was also the site of a royal palace.[170]

The temple in question was erected, apparently for the first time, in year Šulgi 9, since the year-formula of that year talks of Nanna's entering his temple in Karzida.[171] Further works were conducted there in year Šulgi 36 (or, more likely, in the immediately preceding years), when Nanna is said to have entered Karzida for the second time.[172] As far as I can tell, neither of these operations is documented in economic sources.[173]

[167] Turtle carapaces appear also in Text 5 iii 16, xii 15 (2 múrgu-ba).

[168] The exact location of Ga'eš remains unknown.

[169] See Cohen 1993:150–153, 406–413; Sallaberger 1993: 171–190. To the sources discused there, add the important text BPOA 7 2856, which offers a detailed schedule of the á-ki-ti festivities.

[170] ½ ma-na igi-4-gál lá 5 še kug … é-gal-la ba-an-ku$_4$ šag$_4$ Ga-eš^{ki} (HSS 4 115:1–5; Girsu/Lagaš; AS 2/vi).

[171] mu Šul-gi … ^{d}Nanna Kar-zi-da /Ga-eš^{ki} é-a-na ba-(an-)ku$_4$.

[172] Year-formula Šulgi 36: mu ^{d}Nanna Kar-zi-da a-rá 2-kam é-a-na ba-an-ku$_4$.

[173] The only possible exception here are the Umma tablets Ontario 2 247, BIN 5 154, and SAT 3 2114, all from year Šulgi 36, which record huge expenditures of barley and flour, made at Ur, to the representatives of the governor

Although specific information to that effect is lacking, it appears that there was an en priestess—and therefore also her residence—at Karzida ever since the original construction of Nanna's temple in year Šulgi 9. That residence was restored—or possibly built completely anew—by Amar-Suen, as recorded in his inscriptions,[174] and the formula of his ninth regnal year, which commemorates the selection of Nanna's en priestess.[175] This residence must have been fully completed by the end of the preceding year, since it is known that the en priestess in question traveled (from Ur?) to Ga'eš to assume her office there on the fifth day of the first month of Amar-Suen 9.[176] Her oracular selection to that office had taken place either on that very day or on one of the four preceding days.[177]

The fact that three separate Ur III year-formulae are dedicated to Ga'eš underscores the importance of this sanctuary to the kings of Ur.

of Marad. [To those, add UTI 6 3704 (Š 36/viii), discussed below in n. 184.] As suggested by this author (Steinkeller 2013: 371 and n. 95), these cereals may have been used to feed the builders working at Ga'eš during that year.

[174] ^{d}Nanna Kar-zi-da lugal-a-ni-ir ^{d}Amar-^{d}Suen ... Kar-zi-da-a gi$_{6}$-par$_{4}$ (kug-ga-ni) mu-na-dù (Frayne 1997: 262–265 Amar-Suen 16:1–22, Amar-Suen 17:1–22).

[175] mu en ^{d}Nanna ^{d}Amar-^{d}Suen-ra ki-ág en ^{d}Nanna Kar-zi-da-ka / Ga-eš^{ki} ba-hun.

[176] 10 udu máš-da-ri-a lugal en ^{d}Nanna Eridu^{ki}<-šè> DU-ni Árad-mu maškim šag$_{4}$ Ga-eš^{ki} (Ontario 1 82:4–8; AS 9/i/5; Puzriš-Dagan). During that year (and probably also during the first month), a mašdaria offering (consisting of 10 oxen and 100 sheep and goats) was sent from Umma in connection with the very same event. See Text 62 (AS 9/-).

[177] This is demonstrated by an Umma tablet from AS 9/-, which records an expenditure of labor to produce flour and malt that were used as part of the selection of the en priestess — undoubtedly that of Nanna: [x]+90 géme ud 1-šè á zíd munu$_{4}$ en hun$^{!}$-e-da (MVN 16 1091:1–2). Although the month during which this event took place is not specified in the text, a comparison with Ontario 1 82 (see the preceding note) shows that it was the opening days of the first month.

There survive similar data on the selection the en priestess of Enki in Eridu, which is commemorated in the formula of year Amar-Suen 8: 1,660 sìla sá-dug$_{4}$ en uru Eridu^{ki} hun-e-dè Unug^{ki}-šè má-a gá-ra sìla gaz ⌜bala-šè⌝ (UTI 4 2742:1–4; AS 7/xi); 120 guruš ud 45-šè Unug^{ki} gub-ba en Eridu^{ki} hun-dè (UTI 4 2772:13–14; AS 8/-); 306 various pots en hun-e-dè (MVN 21 203 vi 22–29; AS 8/-). [M. Molina adds: BPOA 7 1925 (AS 8/vii), BIN 3 352 (AS 8/xi), and MVN 10 230 i 14 (AS 8/-).] Note also 2 guruš túg en hun-e-da Umma^{ki}-ta Úrim^{ki}-šè (MVN 14 14:1–5; AS 3/-). This passage must refer to the selection of the en of Nanna of Ur, which is commemorated in the formula of year Amar-Suen 4.

Another indication of this is the inclusion of Ga'eš in the collection of "Temple Hymns."[178] The reason why Ga'eš occupied such an important place in the Ur III religious and political life was probably related to the observance of the á-ki-ti festival there. As far as one can tell, the original á-ki-ti had been an Ur ritual of purely local interest, which acquired national significance only with the rise of Ur under Ur-Namma. There are grounds to think that Ur-Namma and his successors significantly altered the á-ki-ti's form and meaning—primarily by incorporating into it other traditional Sumerian observances (such as the Urukean "Sacred Marriage")—thereby turning it into a multifaceted celebration of the restoration of the cosmic order and of the renewal of kingship at the coming of the New Year.[179] It was probably during that time that the á-ki-ti became the most important Babylonian festival—and possibly the first ritual event in Babylonia's history to be observed on a truly national scale.

3.2. The Construction Work at Ga'eš/Karzida

The Ga'eš project is referred to in a few dozen of Umma and Girsu/Lagaš sources dating to Amar-Suen's reign (Texts 11–62a). While covering a period from Amar-Suen 4 to Amar-Suen 9, most of these sources belong to years Amar-Suen 7–8. This fact suggests that it was during those two years that the most intensive phase of the construction took place.

The building operations began already in year Amar-Suen 4, if not earlier. This is demonstrated by Text 11,[180] from that year, which is a record of bricks that Umma's institutional economy advanced to the chief administrators of several other provinces. Among those officials we find the representatives of the governors of Adab, Kazalu, Marda, and Sippar?, and the sabras of An (of Ur[181]), ^{d}Nin-gublaga (of Ki'abrig near

[178] Sjöberg 1969: 26 lines 158–168.

[179] This would involve primarily the more important "harvest á-ki-ti," which coincided with the spring equinox and the beginning of the New Year. In this connection note that the selection of the en priestess of Ga'eš in year Amar-Suen 9 occurred during the very beginning of the first month, *i.e.*, precisely at the time when the spring á-ki-ti should have been celebrated. If so, her selection and appointment at Ga'eš formed part of the New Year observances.

[180] RA 12 164–65 AO 7667.

[181] Since the other deities named in this group were associated with Ur and its region (Ki'abrig, Eridu, and Kisig?), the deity in question was probably the An of Ur. See PDT 2 797:7, which names a sabra of the An of Ur named Lú-^{d}Nin-šubur.

Ur), ^{d}En-ki (of Eridu), ^{d}Nin<-uru>-a-mu-DU (of Kisig?),[182] and ^{d}Nin-[…]. We can be confident that the bricks in questions were to be used by the labor forces of those provinces as part of their contribution to the Ga'eš project.

From a formal point of view, Text 11 is a list of individual brick expenditures, each group of expenditures being marked as kišib PN, "the receipt tablet of PN" (*i.e.*, "received by PN"). The receipts are divided into two groups, according to the two officials—Lugal-magure and Ludingira—via whom the bricks were distributed. See in detail the discussion of Text 11 in Appendix.

Six of the expenditures of bricks recorded in Text 11 are matched by the surving receipt tablets, which likewise date to year Amar-Suen 4. See Texts 12–16a. This shows that Text 11 is a digest of individual receipts, whose original number must have been fifteen (based on the number of kišib entries in Text 11). Since some of these receipts stipulate that the bricks were to be "returned" to Umma's administration, it is clear that these expenditures constituted loans, for which Umma expected to be fully reimbursed.

It would appear that these brick advancements were dictated by practical considerations: as the province of Umma was closer to Ga'eš than were Adab, Kazalu, and Sippar?, it would have made sense for the latter provinces to procure their bricks there, and so to reduce transportation costs. However, this reasoning fails to explain the issues of bricks to the representatives of Ur?, Ki'abrig, Eridu, and Kisig?, all of which were situated in the vicinity of Ga'eš. It is possible, therefore, that, while logistics was an important factor here, the reason behind these brick advancements had to do more with Umma's particular role within the Ur III

182 ^{d}Nin-uru-a-mu-DU belonged to the circle of deities associated with Ur. In PDT 2 797:20, an unnamed sabra of ^{d}Nin-uru-a-mu-DU is identified as one of the six sabras of Ur (the other five sabras being those of Nanna, An, Ningublaga, Ningal, and of the en priestess of Nanna). As is indicated by BPOA 6 111 ii 16, which names an animal offering for ^{d}Nin-uru-a-mu-DU BÀD^{ki}-šè, the home of this goddess was in BÀD. Since BÀD = Durum was situated near Uruk — and so at a considerable distance from Ur — BÀD possibly stands here for Kisig (but the sign is a clear BÀD, collated by this author), which was a close neighbor of Ur. Here note that the offerings recorded in BPOA 6 111 were destined exclusively for Ur and Ga'eš. ^{d}Nin-uru-a-mu-DU must have been a deity of some importance, since two sea-faring merchants (from Ur$^{?}$) dedicated a macehead to her for the life of Šulgi (Frayne 1997: 221–222 2036). She appears in TCL 15 pl. 28 line 224 as ^{d}Nin-uru-a-mu-un-DU; and in An:Anum IV 34 as ^{d}⸢Nin-uru⸣-mu-un-DU.

economic system. As I suggested elsewhere,[183] due to its central geographic position and the fact of its being the second most important (after Girsu/Lagaš) producer of cereals, the province of Umma was responsible for coordinating and supporting the work on public projects—at least the ones conducted in southern Babylonia. In fact, there survive extensive records of large volumes of cereals that the Umma adminstration advanced to the representatives of other provinces, almost certainly in connection with their participation in national corvée projects.[184]

As for other types of supplies, it is significant that one of the sources concerned with the Tummal project lists, among the building materials contributed by Umma, also those belonging to the provinces of Adab, Babylon, and Kutha.[185] While we cannot be certain that these were advancements, this evidence shows that, at the very least, Umma routinely handled such materials on behalf of other provinces.[186]

The final point raised by Text 11 concerns Lu-dingira, one of the two "transferors" (gìr) designated in this text. It is virtually certain that this official is identical with the general (šagina) Lu-dingira, who appears to have been the supreme commander in charge of large public projects during the reigns of Amar-Suen and Šu-Suen.[187] I will discuss him more extensively in connection with the temple of Šara project (see below p. 195). For now I note that Lu-dingira's participation in the Ga'eš project

[183] Steinkeller 2013: 370–372.

[184] See Steinkeller 2013: 371–372. To the sources discussed there, add UTI 6 3704 (Š 36/viii), which records an expenditure of 570.0.4 of barley made by the governor of Umma to a certain Ì-ṣur-DINGIR. This transaction can be matched with MVN 14 228:6–7: 572.04.4 še gur kišib-bi 2-àm kišib Ì-ṣur-DINGIR. Since the latter text is a summary of barley expenditures made by Umma to the representatives of various provinces (lú énsi ma-da-ke$_4$-ne), apparently in connection with some public project in southern Babylonia (see Steinkeller 2013: 371), Ì-ṣur-DINGIR too must have acted on behalf of some province (whose name remains unknown, however).

[185] Text 5, discussed above pp. 178–180.

[186] Another instance of such advancements may be recorded in Nisaba 9 139 (AS 2/v), in which a colonel (nu-bànda) by the name of Šarrum-ili receives 10 bushels of bitumen from the governor of Umma. Conceivably, the commander in question is identical with the colonel of the conscripts of Girsu of that name, who, in another source (AUCT 3 492; AS 7/–), borrows barley from Umma's administration. Given the large volume of bitumen involved, this expenditure may have been intended for a building project of some sort, perhaps even the intial stages of the Ga'eš construction.

[187] See Steinkeller 2013: 373, 376 and n. 112.

is also indicated by Text 44 (from AS 8/iii), which records food provisions (igi-kár) that were intended for him, as well as for Ilallum, another well-known Ur III general.

Paradoxically, as informative as it is, Text 11 says nothing about Umma's own contributions to the Ga'eš project. But Umma did actively participate in this project, supplying both building materials and labor. Its participation was particularly extensive during years Amar-Suen 6–8, when the main phase of the construction appears to have taken place. The documentation extant allows one to reconstruct the administrative procedure by which such supplies were obtained. It is clear that the officials in charge of the Ga'eš project had assigned to each of the participating provinces its share of materials and labor it was supposed to contribute. In the Umma sources, these contributions are called níg-gù-dé, "requests." Here of particular importance is Text 37 (probably from year AS 7), which lists the timber and other materials that the governor of Umma was requested to supply for the gipar of Ga'eš (níg-gù-dé gi_6-par_4 Ga-$eš^{ki}$-ka énsi $Umma^{ki}$). Among the items enumerated there are 180 roofbeams, 36 pine logs, 7 date-palm trunks, 46 doors and gates, and large volumes of various reedmats and related products. Upon receiving such "requests," the Umma officials then went about procurring the needed materials, in which they were assisted by the Umma merchants. One of the latter was Ur-nigingar, to whom, in two separate instances (Texts 19 and 40), the Umma administration issued substantial volumes of wool to purchase the requested items (of unspecified nature). Another Umma merchant, named Ur-Dumuzida, supplied bitumen for the project (Texts 23+24 and 32).

Once obtained and assembled, the requested materials were then delivered to Ga'eš. This last step is best illustrated by Texts 35, 36, and 47, which itemize many of the deliveries. The types and numbers of the delivered items (see in detail below) match closely the "requests" stipulated in Text 37.

The task of providing the materials and labor for the Ga'eš project was handled by a small group of Umma officials. The most visible among them is the scribe Abba-gina, son of Lugal-magure.[188] Abba-gina's

[188] In Text 28, Abba-gina is called the son of A-rí-bi. Cf. Text 51, where the same designation is applied to Abba-gina's brother Šeš-kala (in contrast to the seal, where Šeš-kala is said to be the son of Lugal-magure). Since A-rí-bi is a feminine name (see BPOA 7 1777:1–2), we find here the rare instance of a matronymic.

activities are documented in fourteen texts, dating to the years Amar-Suen 6–8.[189] During that period Abba-gina appears to have been the chief supplier of the building materials destined for Ga'eš.[190] He was also responsible for the transfer of workers there.[191] Among the other officials functioning in these capacities were his brother Šeš-kala[192] and the scribes Da'agi[193] and Dingira.[194]

While there is no evidence of a massive employment of Umma's institutional labor at Ga'eš—on the scale we have witnessed earlier in the case of the Tummal project, it is known that, during year Amar-Suen 6, Umma send there workers to make bricks. These workers were assigned to the "masons' house" (é-šidim), for the periods ranging from fifty to 180 days:

1 man for 50 days (Text 25);
2 men for 116 days (Text 26);
1 man for 85 days (Text 27);
5 men 120 days (Text 28);
1 man for 180 days (Text 29).

There are also records of the Umma carpenters, mat-makers, and other workers stationed in Ga'eš (Texts 29a, 50, and 56). We also read of the éren traveling to Ga'eš, doubtless to work there (Text 61). In addition, there survive records of the foodstuffs, such as barley, sesame oil, lard, bread, flour, and licorice (gazi), which were expended to feed the Umma masons and other laborers at Ga'eš (Text 35 iv 8–10, Texts 49, 50, 51, 57, 60 and 61).[195]

Text 35 also mentions barley, bread, and beer, which were spent "on the day of the banquet" (ud-e kaš-dé-a, iv 12–13). The banquet in question quite likely was meant for the workforce at large. As in the case of the Tummal project, such communal feats may have been accompanied by various forms of entertainment. This is suggested by the large expenditure (eleven bushels), in year Amar-Suen 8, of barley for the singers (nar) at Ur (Text 60). Since the same source mentions also an

[189] Texts 23, 24, 25, 26, 27, 28, 29, 29a, 35, 36, 47, 55, 56 and 57.
[190] Texts 35, 36 and 47.
[191] Texts 25, 26, 27, 28, 29, 29a, 55 and 56.
[192] Texts 51 and 57.
[193] Texts 32 and 39.
[194] Texts 45, 52a, 54 and 54a.
[195] See, especially, 6.2.3 še gur ⸢6?⸣ sìla ì-giš še-ba ì-ba šidim-ma (Text 35 iv 8–10).

expenditure of barley for Ga'eš, it is possible that the singers in question were actually stationed in Ga'eš (or at least performed there). This assumption finds support in the fact that, during the same year, the well-known Umma singer Ur-Suen transported eight bushels of licorice to Ga'eš (Text 49). Since Ur-Suen appears to have been the head of Umma's singer organization,[196] it is likely that the singers referred to in Text 60 were Umma natives, who had been sent to Ga'eš to entertain the Umma labor force working there. For this conclusion, note further that, likewise in year Amar-Suen 8, the aforementioned Abba-gina conscripted two men, whose task was to transport? the balag instruments to Ur (Text 55).

As for Umma's material contributions, the most informative source in this connection is Text 35. This record is an extensive listing of the bulding materials and foodstuffs, which Umma's institutional economy supplied to Ga'eš during year Amar-Suen 7 (zi-ga é Ga-eš, iv 17). Since these goods are grouped, by and large, according to their respective destinations and uses on the project, important information on the particulars of the construction is thus obtained. Among the structures affected by Amar-Suen's building operations were those following ones:

é-ki-tuš é-pa-pah kisal ù EN.DU, "the receiving room, the anteroom, the courtyard, and the walkway? (of the gipar)" (i 1–10);
du_{10}-ús $šag_{4}$ gi_{6}-par_{4}, "the bathroom, within the gipar" (i 11 – ii 16);
é-[šu]-tum-ma-šè, "the šutum warehouse" (ii 17 – iv 1).

Among the building materials supplied on that occasion to Ga'eš, we find pine logs, finished roofbeams, door bolts, bitumen, various items made of reed, ropes made of alfa grass and licorice fibers, two types of pots (both destined for the bathroom), salt, and licorice. Of special interest is the presence in this listing of 1,500 talents of straw, which, as the text tells us explicitly, was used as a temper to make bricks: im-ma ba-a-si, "it was mixed into the clay."

A related source is Text 36, which too dates to year Amar-Suen 7. Like Text 35, Text 36 is a listing of goods supplied by Umma for the gipar of Ga'eš. The latter source lists forty-one roof-beams, six ladders, and seventy brick moulds, plus various fats, licorice, salt, barley, bitumen, reeds, glue, and goat hair. Since none of these goods can readily be

[196] Ur-Suen is identified as nar énsi in MVN 21 199 rev. ii 40 (Š 47?). In TCL 5 6050 ii 10 (AS 7), he is listed among the chief officers of Umma's institutional economy. He is assigned there sixty bushels of barley, which was probably meant for the singers under his charge.

matched with those found in Text 35, a separate delivery must have been involved. This conclusion is further supported by the fact that neither ladders nor brickmolds are mentioned in Text 35.

Another extensive listing of the Ga'eš supplies is Text 47, from year AS 8/iv. This source records a variety of building materials, such pine and date-palm trunks, ladders, date-palm fibers (mangaga), and ropes. Included among these supplies are also ten bushels of licorice, as well as a small quanity of sheep fat (ì-udu).

Other sources listing Umma's supplies for the Ga'eš project mention straw (Texts 58 and 59), bitumen (Texts 23+24 and 32), ropes (Text 20), reeds (Texts 21 and 39), pots (Text 17), and charcoal (Text 48), as well as glue, the last to be used in the construction of the gipar's doors (Texts 45, 52a, 54, and 54a).

As noted earlier, there is also evidence of Girsu/Lagaš's participation in the Ga'eš project. Like Umma, during years Amar-Suen 6–8 Girsu/Lagaš contributed both labor and building materials toward this undertaking. Among the sources bearing on its labor contributions, particularly informative is Text 31, which lists two groups of Girsu/Lagaš workers that were stationed at Ga'eš. The first group of wokers, numbering forty-seven men, worked during thirty-five days; the assignment of the other group, numbering fifty-five men, lasted twenty days. In addition, we have records of Girsu/Lagaš workers collecting reeds for the Ga'eš project (Text 34), transporting various materials to Ga'eš and bringing the boats back (Texts 42, 43, 46, and 53), and performing unspecified tasks at Ga'eš (Texts 41 and 52).

Like Umma, Girsu/Lagaš too provided their workers with food during their employment at Ga'eš. Here our records mention barley (Texts 41, 42, 46, 52, and 53), flour (Texts 22, 30, and 42), and groats (Text 30). Among the building materials supplied by Girsu/Lagaš, one finds straw (Text 33), reeds (Text 34), and bitumen (Text 43).

One may confident that, apart from Umma and Girsu/Lagaš, many other Babylonian provinces took part in the Ge'eš project. We have already seen that, in year Amar-Suen 4, the provinces of Adab, Kazalu, Marda, and Sippar, and the cities of Ur, Eridu, Ki'abrig, and Kisig? supplied bricks for the construction of Ga'eš's gipar.[197] It is highly likely that these and many other places contributed labor as well. However, evidence for such contributions is lacking, except for the province of Babylon. According to Text 38, in year Amar-Suen 7 the governor of Babylon

[197] See above pp. 183–184.

received from Umma's institutional economy 1,800 bushels of barley, in all probability in connection with the Ga'eš project. Out of that total, 600 bushels were conveyed by the general Nir-idagal (lines 1–2), who may have commanded Babylon's workforce that was employed on the project. If so, the barley was to feed the workers under his command. Another 600 bushels were transferred to the granary superintendent of Nanna's temple (apparently that of Ga'eš), probably to be stored there for the troops' later use (lines 3–5). In addition, 420 bushels were allocated for the rations of the dù-a-kud personnel (meaning uncertain) (lines 6–8), while two smaller amounts (150 and 30 bushels respectively) were issued to the governor of Babylon and one of his representatives directly (lines 9–13).

4. The Construction of Šara's Temple at Umma

The erection of Šara's temple at Umma[198] is commemorated in the formula of Šu-Suen's ninth regnal year[199] and in Šu-Suen's dedicatory inscriptions.[200] Given its mention in a year-formula, we can be confident that this undertaking was a project of national importance. However, it is difficult to think of any specific theological or political reasons why the province of Umma and its chief deity Šara should have been treated in such a preferential way by the Ur III kings.

[198] This temple was partially excavated in the years 1999–2002, by the Iraqi archaeologists. See Al-Mutawalli 2009, 2010. The structure is 115 m long and 90 m wide. In Room 10, nineteen economic tablets were found. These date to a period between years Šu-Suen 9 and Ibbi-Suen 3, therefore after the construction of the temple in Šu-Suen 9. It is commonly thought that the name of this temple was É-šag$_4$-ge-pàd-da (see, *e.g.*, George 1993: 143 no. 1017). This assumption is based on the evidence of Šu-Suen's inscriptions (see below n. 200), and the inclusion of É-šag$_4$-ge-pàd-da among Šara's temples in the "Canonical Temple List" line 454. However, since this designation never appears in third millennium sources, a more likely solution is that in the Šu-Suen inscriptions in question one finds an epithet, and not a proper name. It was apparently these inscriptions that were mistakenly used by the author of the "Canonical Temple List." As for the temple's real name, it was almost certainly É-mah, which is richly documented in the third millennium sources, and which is identified as Šara's primary temple in the "Canonical Temple List" line 451.

[199] mu ^{d}Šu-^{d}Suen lugal Úrim^{ki}-ma-ke$_4$ é ^{d}Šára Umma^{ki} mu-dù.

[200] Frayne 1997: 326–328, Šu-Suen 16, 17 and 18, which commemorate the construction of Šara's é šag$_4$-ge pàd-da é ki-ág-gá-ni, "temple chosen in his heart, his beloved temple."

While the temple was completed in year Šu-Suen 9 (or possibly in the preceding year), the project had begun much earlier,[201] probably already in the last year of Amar-Suen's reign, when some preparatory work may have been carried out. This is suggested by Text 63, which records an expenditure of bitumen, which was applied to a sanctuary within the temple of Šara: 0.0.1 ésir é-a kug-bi 12 še gi é ^{d}LÀL.IB-ka é ^{d}Šára-ka-ke$_{4}$ ba-ab-su-ub, "10 liters of é-a bitumen,[202] valued at 10 grains of silver, (which) was pasted over the reed (structure?) of the sanctuary of ^{d}LÀL.IB of Šara's temple." Unfortunately, the meaning of this passage is unclear. If the mysterious ^{d}LÀL.IB[203]—who is attested only here, as far as I know—was some kind of a primeval creator-deity,[204]

[201] Apart from the data cited below, this fact is also indicated by one of Šu-Suen's inscriptions dealing with this project (Frayne 1997: 327–328 Šu-Suen 17), which dates the temple's erection to the time when the Muriq-Tidnim wall was constructed, an event securely datable to year Šu-Suen 4 (or the preceding year). This chronological discrepancy cannot be explained — unless one assumes that a significant part of the project had already been accomplished by that time.

[202] For this type of bitumen, see Heimpel 2009b: 55 and n. 47, who convincingly argues that é-a is to be understood as a reference to the god Ea (*i.e.*, the bitumen-producing underground springs).

[203] D. C. Snell (Snell and Lager 1991: 31), reads ^{d}Alammuš-uraš, translating "Alammuš of the earth?"

[204] Tentatively, I suggest that we find here ^{d}Làl-hur, one of the designations of the Sumerian birth-goddess. See ^{d}Làl-hur^{hu-ur}-gal-zu, "expert Làl-hur" = ^{d}*Be-lit-ì-li* (An II 40; following ^{d}Ama-du$_{10}$$^{du-ba-ad}$-bad = *um-mu pi-ti-a-at bir-ki*, "mother who opens the knees/womb"); ^{d}Làl-hur-ra-na ⌜alam⌝ sig$_{7}$-sig$_{7}$ = ^{d}MIN ⌜*ba*⌝*-na-at meš-re-e-ti* (*Mīs pî*, Incantation Tablet 4 line 31 = Walker and Dick 2001: 164). The word làl-hur otherwise means "bees wax." See Civil 1964: 74–75. Perhaps significantly, in "Ninkasi Hymn" lines 5–9 the same term designates a primeval (probably mythical) substance on which Ninkasi's city was founded by Ninhursag (which would fit our context perfectly): uru-zu làl-hur-re ki ús-sa / ezen gal-bi šu mu-ra-an-du$_{7}$-du$_{7}$ / ^{d}Nin-ka-si uru-zu làl-hur-re ki ús-sa / ezen gal-bi šu mu-ra-an-du$_{7}$-du$_{7}$, "having set up your city on 'wax,' she (*i.e.*, Ninhursag) perfected its great festivals for you; oh Ninkasi, having set up your city on 'wax,' she perfected its great festivals for you" (see now Sallaberger 2012, for a recent edition of this composition). Assuming that ^{d}LÀL.IB is to be read ^{d}Làl-uraš, "syrup of the earth (*i.e.*, honey?)," this name could be explained as a variant of làl-hur, with làl-uraš perhaps representing the original form: /làl-uraš / > /làl-ur(aš)/ > /làl-hur/.

perhaps some ritual action connected with the setting down of the temple's foundations may have been involved.[205]

Be that as it may, the construction began in earnest in year Šu-Suen 2. From that year we have a number of sources referring to the construction of the foundation platform (é-temen-na), the foundations (uš), as well as the records of the expended goat-hair thread, from which strings for laying the building's brickcourses were to be made (Texts 63a, 64, 65, 66, 67, 67a, 67b, 70, 70a, 70b, 71, 72, 73, and 74).[205a] From the same year there also survive two records of the timber that was harvested in the forests of the Umma province to be used as roofbeams in the building in question (Texts 76 and 77).

As it happens, these are the only texts referring directly to this project. It is rather clear that the main construction took place during years Šu-Suen 3–9, but, as far as I know, there do not survive any attestations of this activity. The only text that may indirectly refer to it is Text 78, dating to year Šu-Suen 7/iii and probably stemming from Puzriš-Dagan, which lists a very large shipment of grain from northern Babylonia, which was intended for Umma's cattle-raising establishment. Possibly, these were provisions for the foreign (non-Umma) workforce employed on the project. Such a possibility is suggested by the fact that such a large delivery of grain to Umma, one of the main producers and exporters of cereals in the Ur III state, would otherwise be very unusual.

In this connection, one also needs to mention an undated Umma text (YBC 9819), which offers calculations of bricks that were used to construct the temples of Šara and Ninura.[206] Contrary to Heimpel, who

[205] A tablet from year Šu-Suen 1 records expenditures of [gi]hal kin-gi$_4$-a baskets during the first, fourth, sixth, eighth, and eleventh months of that year for the temple of Šara (BPOA 6 1262). As I will argue elsewhere, these baskets were used in the extispicy procedure (kin-gi$_4$-a), probably to hold the sacrificial exta. Possibly, these particular [gi]hal kin-gi$_4$-a baskets were meant for the extispicies performed in preparation for the construction of Šara's temple.

[205a] 2⅚ ma-na níg-U-NU-a siki ùz gu kin-e ra-ra é [d]Šára-ka, "2⅚ minas of goat-hair thread (for) strings that are to be laid/struck in the work on Šara's temple" (Text 63a:1–4); 1 gú níg-U.NU-a siki ùz gu dím-e-dè é [d]Šára-ka-šè, "1 talent of goat-hair thread to make strings for the temple of Šara" (Text 70b: 1–3). For gu … ra, "to measure with a rope, to strike a rope," cf. gu mu-ba-ra (for barag$_3$), "he spread the string" (Gudea Cylinder A xx 13); sig$_4$-ga gu bí-dúb, "he struck the brickcourse with a string" (*ibid.* xx 27).

[206] RA 32 127–28 YBC 9819 = RA 76 28–29 (sig$_4$ é [d]Šára ù é [d]Nin-ur$_4$-ra; iv 3–4). For the most recent discussion of this well-known and extensively studied source, see Heimpel and Hillard: 2008: 71–74. YBC 9818 calculates the bricks for the walls (iz-zi), retaining walls (ki-sá), and bàd gìr DU é an-ka, "rampart? of the upper temple" (found only in Ninura's temple).

considers this source to be a school exercise,[207] I would rather think that it is a *bona fide* estimate (probably only one of several such estimates), which had been made in preparation for the project.

As concerns the building activity in year Šu-Suen 2, the sources in question offer information on two aspects or phases of the project: the rituals that initated the construction, and the construction itself. The former are illustrated by the expenditures of cattle and various substances, which were to be used as sacrifices. Thus we learn that one cow, three sheep, and seventeen goats were expended—undoubtedly to be slaughtered—in connection with the "striking down into the ground of the foundation of the temple of Šara" (uš ki giš ra) (Text 66). In addition, Text 70a lists pots and leather bags that were expended for the same occasion (uš é ^{d}Šára-ka ki gá-ra).

A related rite of the "placing of the foundation deposits (temen) in the temple of Šara"[208] called for the use of cedar, cypress, and juniper (za-ba-lum) resins (or oils), cream (ì-dùg-nun-na), sweet butter (ì-nun-dùg-ga), fine date syrup (làl sig$_5$), various flours, bread (Texts 71 and 72), and linen sheets (Text 73), the last probably serving as a wrapping. Also expended on this occasion was combed wool, which was part of the materials (níg-dab$_5$) used to install (or to re-install) the foundation deposits: temen é ^{d}Šára-ka ki$^{?}$-a šu gi$_4$-da, "to return? the foundation deposits of the temple Šara into (their) place?" (Text 67).

Additionaly, a sheep and flour were presented as part of the sízkur and sá-dug$_4$ offerings for the "retaining wall" (ki-sá, Akk. *kisû*) (Text 67a and 70).[209] Clearly, a similar rite, which commenced the work on the tem-

207 Heimpel and Hillard 2008: 72.

208 é ^{d}Šára-ka temen-aš si-ga (Text 71); é ^{d}Šára(-ka) temen si-ga (Texts 72 and 73). For the difficult term temen, see most recently my discussion, with earlier literature, in Steinkeller 2004b: 136 and n. 6. As noted there, when used in conjunction with the verb si-(g), temen invariably means "foundation deposit." However, the same term also describes "foundation platform." This meaning is certain in our Texts 64 and 65 (see below), where the word in question appears as é-temen-na, and where huge volumes of bitumen (64+ and 25 bushels respectively) are being applied to it as caulking. This sense of temen is also clear in a number temple names, such as é-temen-ní-gùr(-ru), é-temen-bi-nu-kúr, etc. (see George 1993: 149 nos. 1088–1093).

209 For this meaning, see CAD K, 429–30 ("supporting wall against a building"); Dunham 1982: 38 ("a supporting abutment [built against the lower part of a wall]"). This interpretation has recently been questioned by W. Heimpel (Heimpel and Hillard 2008: 72–73; Heimpel 2009: 171), who argues that ki-sá actually denotes "foundation platform / terrace." Heimpel's evidence is the huge volume of bricks that are assigned to the ki-sá of the

ple's platform, must be meant here. It is interesting to note here that virtually all of the substances appearing in this group of sources are found also in Gudea's Cylinder A, in the famous passage describing the ritual of the fashioning of the "first brick."[210]

The construction itself is illustrated by two expenditures of bitumen to caulk the foundation platform (é-temen-na) of Šara's temple (Texts 64 and 65). The volumes of the bitumen used were huge: over 64 talents and 25 talents respectively. An aditional 10 bushels of bitumen were applied to the (outer) sides of the temple's three foundations (da uš 3-àm ba-ra-ab-du$_8$ šag$_4$ é ^{d}Šára-ka) (Text 74). Bitumen was also used to caulk the mats and other objects made of reeds, which probably served

Šara and Ninura's temples in YBC 9819 (for which see above). However, as we have seen above, the Sumerian word for temple platform/terrace is é-temen-na (or simply temen). That ki-sá means "retaining wall / abutment" is also shown (apart the from ample evidence cited in CAD K, 429–30) by an inscription of Warad-Sin, where a translation "foundation platform" is out of question: Úrim^{ki} dagal-e-dè ki-sá-a-bi šu peš(HA)-e-dè ... bàd gal ... mu-na-dù, "in order to enlage Ur, to expand its retaining walls, ... a great (city) wall he erected for him" (Frayne 1990: 237–238 Warad-Sin 19:8–16). Further, see the following examples from Isin texts, which show that the ki-sá had openings provided with doors: hides for ^{giš}ig dib pa-pah-šè šag$_4$ ki-sá-a, "the passage (dib) door (leading to) the ante-room, in the retaining wall" (BIN 9 171:1–4, 175:1–4, 176:1–4); hides for ^{giš}ig dib-šè šag$_4$ ki-sá-a, "the door passage in the retaining wall" (BIN 9 165:1–5, 166:1–4, 170:1–3; BIN 10 192:1–3); glue for ^{giš}ig dib-šè šag$_4$ ki-sá-a (BIN 9 164:1–9, 167:1–4, 168:1–4); glue mu ^{giš}ig-šè šag$_4$ ki-sá-a (BIN 9 157:1–8; Ferwerda TLB/SLB 5 no. 11:1–4); hides mu ^{giš}ig-šè šag$_4$ ki-sá-a (JAOS 98 253 no. 4:1–3); 8 ebih(ÉŠ.MAH) gíd 2 ½ nindan-ta ki-lá-bi 43 2/3 ma-na mu ^{giš}ig dib-šè šag$_4$ ki-sá-a (BIN 10 81:1–5). The function of the ki-sá, which ran along foundation platforms and city walls, was to protect the structures in question from underground water. Therefore, the ki-sá was impregnated with massive amounts of bitumen. See Gudea Statue B vi 51–56: Ma-ad-ga^{ki} hur-sag íd-lú-ru-da-ta ésir gú 216,000$^{?}$ im-ta-e$_{11}$ ki-sá É-ninnu-ka mu-ni-dù, "from Madga, the mountain range of the Ordeal River, he brought down bitumen, a load of 216,000$^{?}$ (bushels$^{?}$); into the retaining walls of the Eninnu he built it." Since the ki-sá was for all practical purposes a part of the foundation platform (or of the city wall), it is not surprising that it might occasionally describe the latter structure as well (as it could be the case in YBC 9819).

210 See gud d[u$_7$] máš du$_7$-re$_6$ giš bí-tag (xviii 7); làl ì-nun ì-dùg-nun-na al im-ma-ni-tag ŠIM×ÙH šimbi$_x$(ŠIM×PI) giš hi-a UH-šè im-mi-ak (xviii 20–22); šimbi$_x$(ŠIM×PI) ha-šu-úr ŠIM×ÙH-a sag im<-ma>-ni-du$_8$ (xix 6–7).

as a covering or insulation of the substructure (gi-KWU-844 ù kid é ^{d}Šára-ka-ke$_4$ ba-ab-su-u[b]; Text 72).[211]

Finally, there survives a record of 20 liters of *allaḫaru* mordant, which was used to bleach some large textile or fabric of the god Šara (túg IM gal ^{d}Šára-šè; Text 72). Unfortunately, as the meaning of túg IM is unknown, there is no assurance that the textile in question was in fact part of the building materials.

Among the officials who authorized or supervised these operations, one finds, apart from the governor of Umma and a son of the majordomo (sabra) of Šara, two other officials: a chief mason named Ur-Igalim (Texts 64 and 66) and the general Lu-dingira (Texts 64, 66, 68, 69, 70, and 75). Lu-dingira, whom we already encountered in connection with the construction at Ga'eš,[212] appears to have been the head of the entire project. In three instances, Lu-dingira conveyed the *materia magica* used in the earlier-discussed building rituals (Texts 64, 66, and 70). His involvement in the construction of Šara's temple is further indicated by the issues of pots and fats to him, at Umma, during the same year (Text 68 and 75). Lu-dingira's presence at Umma during that time is confirmed by Text 69, which records the expenditure of a sheep to a mounted messenger, who came to visit Lu-dingira in his Umma residence. The same Lu-dingira may also appear in Text 78, dating to year Šu-Suen 7. This source records a huge shippment of barley, which was possibly meant to feed the workers employed on the Šara project.

Concurrently with the construction work, the members of the royal sector harvested, in the forests belonging to Umma's institutional economy, large number of poplar trees. This project is described in Texts 76 and 77,[213] which record 1,434 and 2,700 harvested poplars respectively. Assuming that two separate operations were involved, the total number of logs was 4,134.

[211] Another job performed in this connection is possibly mentioned in MVN 16 1136, which likewise dates to year Šu-Suen 2. This tablet lists an expenditure of ten talents of reeds for KAS$_4$ ak šag$_4$ é-temen-ka (line 1–2). If the sign KAS$_4$ stands here for SUHUŠ, "root, foundation" (Akk. *šuršu, uššu*), the job in question may have focused on the platform's substructure.

[212] This official very likely was also engaged on the corvée project indirectly described in the Umma text TCL 5 6041. See Steinkeller 2013: 376.

[213] For these two sources, cf. also Steinkeller 2013: 373, 385–386 Texts 1 and 2.

Text 76 identifies the logs as giš é ^{d}Šára gá-nun-na$^{!}$ ku$_{4}^{!}$-ra, "timber of/ for the temple of Šara; it was brought into the warehouse." This indicates that, following the loging operation, the timber was first deposited in a warehouse, to be subsequently processed into roofbeams of Šara's temple.[214]

The workers (éren) partaking in these operations were led by the chancellor Aradmu (who also served as the general of the town of GARšana), his son Ahuni, and eight generals (šagina): Dada, Huba'a, Hun-Šulgi, Iddin-Dagan, Igi-anakezu, Lu-Nanna, Nur-Šulgi, and Ṣeluš-Dagan. Four of the latter are known to have had local appointments: the city of Umma (Hun-Šulgi) and the towns of Zabalam (Dada), NAGsu (Lu-Nanna), and Uṣar-dagi (Nur-Šulgi). Evidently, it was those settlements that supplied workers to harvest the trees. The bulk of the work thus was done by the local Umma population.

The remaining four generals—Huba'a, Iddin-Dagan, Igi-Anakezu, and Ṣeluš-Dagan —very likely commanded éren contingents stemming from other provinces. If so, the construction of the Šara temple involved the participation of the entire country.

5. Ur III Defensive Fortifications

The reader may justifiably wonder why I have not thus far considered the projects involving the construction of defensive fortifications. And it is well known, of course, that Ur III times saw the construction of two important "walls," the "wall of the periphery" (Bàd-ma-da) and the "wall holding the Amorites at bay" (Bàd-MAR.TU/Mu-ri-ik-Ti-id-nim).[215] Both of them are commemorated in the Ur III year-formulae,[216] which means that they were thought to be highly significant accomplishments by their royal builders. It is also clear that these two projects must have involved great expenditures of labor and other resources.

The reason behind this omission is quite simple: as far as I know, neither of these two undertakings is in any way reflected in the surviving administrative record. This is a major problem, of course. Here the case of Bàd-ma-da is particularly perplexing, since this "wall" was completed in year Šulgi 37 (or in the preceding year), that is precisely at the time when the Tummal project reached its most intensive phase. I will study this issue systematically in a forthcoming monograph, along with the

214 The destination of the timber is specified in Text 76:11: ^{giš}ásal giš-ùr$^{!}$ hi-a.
215 See, most recently, Michalowski 2011: 125–129, 153–169.
216 Year Šulgi 37 and year Šu-Suen 4 respectively.

topographical questions raised by Bàd-ma-da and Bàd-MAR.TU.[217] For now I provisionally submit that, because these two lines of fortifications (as I understand their true nature) were situated in the periphery (*i.e.*, beyond the borders of core Babylonia), the so-called institutional economies of Babylonia (represented by the provincial governors and their organizations) were not required directly to contribute toward these undertakings. Instead, the workers employed on them were exclusively members of the royal military organization and the crown sector more generally. If correct, this assumption could explain the absence of references to these two projects in the documentation in hand (which comes predominantly from the provincial economies of Umma and Girsu/Lagaš).

6. Conclusions

As demonstrated by the three cases studied in this article, in the Ur III period large building projects of national importance were supported by the contributions incoming from the entire state. Those contributions consisted both of building materials and labor. The former are known to have come from the provinces of Umma, Girsu/Lagaš, Adab, Babylon, Kutha and Sippar. The question of labor is more elusive, since only the contributions of Umma and Girsu/Lagaš are explicitly documented. But this, I believe, is due to the bias of the surviving documentation. Since, as it seems, contributions toward building projects were part of the general bala-taxation system, which was rotational and involved all the core provinces of the Ur III state, we can be quite confident that all the provinces were required to provide labor (or a monetary substitute in its lieu) for such undertakings.

The data extant attest only to the use of institutional laborers (both éren and menials) on such projects. Royal dependants (éren) may have been part of these operations as well, but we lack any certain examples of this. As we have seen earlier in connection with the construction of Šara's temple at Umma, the royal éren (stemming mainly—if not exclusively—from the royal settlements within the Umma province) were involved in this project in a marginal way, in that they harvested timber for the temple's roofbeams. That timber came from the forests belonging to Umma's institutional economy, indicating that the work in question was done on behalf of the governor of Umma and his administration. It

217 "The Grand Strategy of the Ur III Empire: Babylonia's Foreign Policy and Territorial Expansion at the End of the Third Millennium BC" (in preparation).

remains unclear, however, whether Umma's institutional economy was expected to reimburse the crown for this job (as was the usual practice in such instances[218]), or whether this was a direct contribution of the royal component of the province toward the construction of the temple.

If the case of Umma is representative of the system behind the labor procurement for such projects, the institutional éren were expected to provide 100 days of labor per person during a given year. Unfortunately, the significance of this figure is unclear. As I noted earlier, it is impossible to determine whether those 100 days were paid *in addition* to the regular obligation of the éren toward the state or simply as part of the latter.

As shown by Text 6, which records the labor contribution of Umma's institutional economy toward the Tummal project, such dues could be paid in installments. In this particular instance, Umma made three separate labor contributions, which were spread over a six-month period. This fact supports the conclusion that the system was rotational in nature, with the total labor obligation being shared proportionally by the provinces according to their size and economic capabilities (as it was characteristic of the bala system in general).

The labor used on these projects comprised essentially two groups of workers: a comparatively small body of specialized craftsmen and a large force of unskilled laborers. Among the former one finds primarily builders (šidim), carpenters (nagar), reed-workers (ad-KID), caulkers (má-GÍN), and "food-handlers" (lú-ninda). The last probably included the cooks, bakers, butchers, and brewers that were responsible for the preparation and distribution of the food and beer meant for the workforce at large. Also participating in such projects were (though in smaller numbers) smiths (simug), silversmiths (kug-dím), and the writers of brick and dedicatory inscriptions (gáb-sar).

The unskilled labor, which was provided either by the éren themselves, or, as it appears more likely, by their various substitutes (such as their kinsmen and personal slaves and hired menials),[219] involved the transportation of building materials to the building site and various types of unskilled work on the building site itself, such as brick-making, carrying and lifting, assisting builders in laying down the walls and impregnating them with bitumen, and helping with the preparation of meals and drink for the workforce.

[218] See Steinkeller 2013: 382–383.

[219] This was probably true of the higher-ranking éren, who were fully employed. See above p. 173.

During their employment on building projects, workers were fed with food and drink provided by their native provinces. These provisions were unusually generous, since they included significant amounts of meat. Here the volumes of meat consumed at Tummal stand out. According to Text 3, the builders (šidim) from Umma consumed, apparently during one year, 424 heads of cattle. During the same time-period additional twenty-one heads of cattle were given out as food to the Umma éren.

These large expenditures of meat are noteworthy, and so they deserve a further comment. As it happens, the provisioning of workers with meat was actually quite common in Ur III times, especially in the context of public projects and the operations of the central government more generally.[220] This phenomenon may have been unique to Ur III times, probably because of the abundance and ready availability of cattle and sheep in that period, which were due primarily to the gún mada taxation system. It is characteristic that expenditures of meat to common workers otherwise were rare in ancient Mesopotamia. In this connection, it may be significant that in the Isin-Larsa royal inscriptions that boast of the generous food allotments given to the labor employed on public projects,[221] meat is never mentioned.

[220] Thus, Puzriš-Dagan sources record regular and massive expenditures of cattle, sheep, and goats to Tummal's kitchen (é-muhaldim) on behalf of professional soldiers (àga-ús), runners (kas$_4$), and holders of allotment fields (lú-PAD-ra-ke$_4$-ne) (see, *e.g.*, Fs. Levine 132–138; PDT 1 529; and passim in the BDTNS databse). Further, it is known that the diet of the employees of the Puzriš-Dagan complex included, on a daily basis, meat broth and various types of cooked meat. See Steinkeller 2008: 188–190. Meat and meat broth were routinely given out also to messengers and other types of royal personnel at Urusagrig (Brunke 2013). Similar expenditures are documented at GARšana (see, especially, CUSAS 3 1025). An especially poignant case is presented by a group of sources recording the expenditures of sheep carcasses to the soldiers stationed in Nemzi'um in northern Babylonia, where the numbers of carcasses issued are as high as 1,472 in a single transaction; other expenditures amounted to 554, 600, and 1,235 carcasses (BPOA 7 3022+3023 [AS 5/iti NI-ik-mu-um]; BPOA 6 906 [AS 6/vii]; JCS 10 29 nos. 7 [AS 9/vii]; JCS 10 29 no. 8 [undated]). Significantly, meat was often distributed also among the menial types of workers, such as géme and UN-íl. See, *e.g.*, 92 áb hi-a ba-úš mu géme-uš-bar-e-ne-šè ... 27 áb hi-a ba-úš mu géme UN-íl MAR.TU-ne-šè (Nikolski 2 481 v 28–29, v 36–37); 100 adda udu ki Gù-dé-a-ta géme-uš-bar Uru-sag-rig$_7^{ki}$ íb-kú ugula A-lí-[ni-su] kišib Ù-zé-nu-[ri] ugula uš-bar (ITT 5 6799:1–5; for the officials cf. ITT 3 5630); 100 adda udu ki Lugal-hi-li-ta géme-uš-bar zú-si ba-ab-kú (ITT 3 5417:1–4).

[221] See above p. 145.

The workforce employed on Ur III building undertakings was also treated to banquets or drinking parties (kaš-dé-a),[222] during which large quantities of beer, bread, barley, and sesame oil were consumed. The presence at Tummal and Ga'eš of singers (nar) and kur-gá-ra performers even suggests that these banquets were accompanied by various forms of entertainment. It is fair to assume that such events were a regular feature of building projects, especially at the point of their conclusion, where they were likely mandatory.

Indeed, it is generally recognized that in the ancient and premodern societies feasts constituted an exceedingly important strategy to mobilize labor for public projects. As stated by Michael Dietler and Ingrid Herbich at the ouset of their exhaustive study of this subject, "The use of feasts to mobilize collective labor has been a widespread and fundamental economic practice of societies around the world. In fact, variants of the practice are so strikingly omnipresent in the ethnographic and historical literature that a good case can be made for acknowledging it both as virtually a universal feature among the agrarian societies and as nearly exclusive means of mobilizing large voluntary work projects before the spread of the monetary economy and the capitalist accommodation of labor and creation of a wage labor market."[223] These authors argue for the need of "a fully theorized understanding of the specific range of practices that enable voluntary labor to be mobilized on a scale above the household level, how the possibility for labor exploitation inheres in some of these practices, and, crucially, the ways that feasting operates as a mechanism of conversation within this realm."[224] They further define "work feast" as "a particular form of the 'empowering feast' mode in which commensal hospitality is used to orchestrate voluntary collective labor."[225] Although Dietler and Herbich focus on the feast as a means to mobilize *voluntary* labor for communal works, it is certain that their conclusions are equally applicable to the societies in which participation in such operations was outright obligatory or, at the very least, sanctioned by custom —such as the Mesopotamian and Egyptian ones.[226] Even though the

[222] See, especially, Text 35 iv 12–14.
[223] Dietler and Herbich 2001.
[224] Dietler and Herbich 2001: 241.
[225] Dietler and Herbich 2001: 241.
[226] In fact, this point is explicitly acknowledged by Dietler and Herbich. Arguing against "simplistic correlations between the existence of large-scale earthworks and the necessity of centralized political organization," these authors assert that "the idea that such projects must be the result of tributary

builders of Tummal and the pyramids of Giza were compelled by their governments to work on these projects, the expectation of communal feasts must have been an important inducement for them to work on such undertakings with a positive attitude.[227] As I argued in the begin-

corvée labor is simply not warranted, as it is clear that work feasts can mobilize voluntary work groups on a similar scale for similar kinds of projects. Indeed, it should be evident at this point that *corvée* labor can only be understood when it is properly situated in the context of the full range of voluntary 'collective work events' because it operates as a kind of variant of the work feast. *Even large state-directed projects, at least those that depend upon the labor of free subjects rather than slaves, will usually take the organizational form of work feasts* [emphasis mine]" (*ibid.*, 257). Writing two years later in another place, Dietler elaborates the same point in even stronger terms: "The 'work-feast' was a nearly universal practice among agrarian societies because it was one of the only means possible of mobilizing large numbers of workers across familial lines, aside from slavery ... Moreover, it operated at all levels of society, serving as a crucial means of organizing interhousehold flows of labor and, sometimes, of labor exploitation. Although state rulers and institutions often had recourse to a form of the work-feast known as corvée in which participation was obligatory (as a form of labor tribute) rather than voluntary, it was still necessary to conduct the labor exchanges in the idiom of commensality that governed other non-obligatory forms of work-feast: that is a meal or drinking party hosted by the beneficiary of the labor project. Coercion is a poor tool for maintaining long-term labor cooperation, and rulers who failed to honor this code of symbolic exchange would find it increasingly difficult to maintain the authority of their right to corvée labor or to count on work being done properly by those participating ... Hence, there is very good reason to view corvée labor simply as a variant of the work feast in which the composition of the labor force is pre-determined by an ideology of obligation and authority" (Dietler 2003: 277–78).

227 Among various data showing that the ancient Babylonians believed feasting to be an integral part of communal work-projects, especially illuminating is the passage from Gilgameš Epic describing the construction of Uta-napištim's "ark." As part of this undertaking, on which the entire population of the city of Šuruppak was actively employed, huge quantities of meat, beer, ale, wine, and sesame oil were given out to the workers. Those, in the words of the poet, "celebrated as on the New Year festival itself!" (Tablet XI 71–74). Another (this time historically documented) case of feasting as part of a building project is the enormous banquet given by the Neo-Assyrian king Ashurnasirpal II at the conclusion of the construction of his palace at Kalhu (modern Nimrud). According to an ancient account, this banquet was attended by 47,074 men and women from all the lands held by Assyria at that time, 5,000 foreign dignitaries and envoys, 16,000 inhabitants of Kalhu, and 1,500 officials of all Ashurnasirpal's palaces, altogether 69,574 invited guests. Those were given choice food and drink, and were bathed and anointed with oil for a period of ten days. See Wiseman 1952; Oppenheim 1969;

ning of this study, their attitude was even more influenced by the purely psychological rewards that such participaton brought to them: a pride derived from their accomplishment and a satisfaction of partaking with their co-workers in the same system of ideological values.

Remarkably, similar patterns of collective work and the role of feasting and psychological inducements as a means of compelling individuals to contribute their labor toward communal building projects may be discerned already at Göbekli Tepe, a monumental ceremonial center in south-eastern Turkey, which dates to the Pre-Pottery Neolithic A and B (10,000–8,000 BC). The builders of this cultic center were disparate groups of hunters-gatherers, who, over a period many generations, were drawn periodically from a wide geographical area to participate in repeated construction work. As recently argued by Oliver Dietrich and his co-authors, a prerequisite for the long life of this ceremonial center and its complex symbolic system "must have been an extensive network of supra-regional contacts sustained on a regular basis. For the large amount of quarrying, stone-carving and construction work required to build a monumental sanctuary like Göbekli Tepe, there had to be a means of bringing together groups from different areas and organizing communal work. An answer on how this was achieved lies in the widespread evidence for extensive feasting, including the consumption of—most likely alcoholic—beverages, in the PPN archaeological record."[228] In view of the patently religious character of that center, it is virtually certain that the feasts that took place at Göbekli Tepe, and the various festive activities (such as dancing and musical performances) that undoubdely were associated with them, had a "strong cultic significance."[229] Because of this, what motivated the builders of Göbekli Tepe to contribute their labor likely was not just the expectation of free food and drink. An equal-

Karlsson 2013: 166–167. Importantly, the same inscription also notes that the among the workers employed on the Kalhu project were contingents of people coming from all of Ashurnasirpal's foreign possessions. The participation of these foreigners in the project was probaly due more to symbolic than economic considerations. By making them part of this undertaking, Assurnasirpal apparently aimed to foster a sense of unity among the conquered territories and their identification with Assyria and its ideology.

[228] Dietrich *et al.* 2012: 684–687. For the implications of Göbekli Tepe for the history of collective labor, see also, in the present volume, Lamberg-Karlovsky's contribution and my "Labor in the Early States: An Early Mesopotamian Perspective."

[229] Dietrich *et al.* 2012: 690.

ly (if not more) important motivation in that respect must have been the possibility of participating in Göbekli's cultic rituals and, through that, of coming into the direct contact with the divine world—or, in other words, of partaking in a profound religious experience.

I stressed earlier that the Ur III national building projects involving participation of the entire country were an important political tool, in that they strengthened social cohesion, thereby significantly contributing toward the creation of a sense of national identity and a unified ideological system. Elementary forms of such social strategies may have been at work already in Göbekli Tepe. As Dietrich and his co-authors write: "At the dawn of the Neolithic, hunters-gathers congregating at Göbekli Tepe created social and ideological cohesion through the carving of decorated pillars, dancing, feasting—and, almost certainly, the drinking of beer made from fermented wild crops."[230]

No less important, the architectural structures that such communal projects brought forth were vocal messengers of the prescribed ideology in their own right. As was the case in ancient Egypt and throughout the ancient world, the main means of disseminating ideological messages were monumental architecture and public ritual.[231] Since both art and display inscriptions that had a propagandistic intent were usually inaccessible to the population at large,[232] it was official buildings—such as temples, palaces, and city-walls—that tried to persuade the ordinary folk about the unique qualities and attributes of their rulers, their intimate relations with the gods, their love for their subjects, and their power and ability to nurture and to protect them.[233] The same messages were spread

[230] Dietrich et al. 2012: 674.

[231] See, *e.g.*, Baines 1989; Trigger 1990.

[232] This is due to the fact that their primary audience was the divine realm. As such, these materials were most commonly buried in the buildings' foundations and walls. This applies equally to temples and secular structures, such as palaces and city walls.

[233] This fact is not broadly acknowledged in Assyriological literature (and in the studies of ancient Mesopotamia more generally). Due to their preoccupation with texts, Assyriologists tend to see written messages—be it dedicatory inscriptions, hymns to gods, temples, and deified kings, or literary compositions—as the primary vehicles of political propaganda. While some of such materials may in fact have served propaganda purposes occasionally—the cases of the "Sumerian King List" and the hymns of Šulgi come to mind here —such instances were rare, and their impact was highly limited and never direct, because, even in such cases, the audience *physically* exposed to such messages was essentially confined to the courtiers and the *literati*.

through the staging of communal cultic events—the innumerable festivals, processions, and divine travels that marked the passage of seasons and high points of the agricultural cycle, during which ordinary people could, at least for a brief moment, become one with the world of gods and kings and share in its splendors.

If, as it appears quite likely, Gudea's hymns were actually sung at the completion of the Eninnu, their words may have reached some people in the attendance, and perhaps even convinced them of Gudea's greatness. The same may have been true of the images on the stelae that depicted the construction (if those were in fact accessible to the public). But the main means of conveying Gudea's message were the temple itself and the array of cultic occurrences that accompanied the entire project—from its planning phase, through all the building operations, down to the temple's eventual consecration.

BIBLIOGRAPHY

Adams, Henry (1913; 1959), *Mont-Saint-Michel and Chartres* (Garden City NY: Doubleday).

Adams, Robert McC. (1981), *Heartland Of Cities: Surveys of Ancient Settlement and Land Use on the Central Floodplain of the Euphrates* (Chicago: The University of Chicago Press).

Al-Mutawalli, N. A. (2009), "Jukha (Umma): The First and Second Seasons 1999–2000," *Sumer* 54: 53–82.

— (2010), "Administrative Cuneiform from Umma in the Iraq Museum; Excavation of Shara Temple (1999–2000)," *Sumer* 55: 45–86.

Alster, Bendt (1997), *Proverbs of Ancient Sumer* (Bethesda MD: CDL Press).

Assmann, Jan (2003), *The Mind of Egypt: History and Meaning in the Time of the Pharaohs* (Cambridge MA: Harvard University Press).

Baines, John (1989), "Communication and Display: The Integration of Early Egyptian Art and Writing," *Antiquity* 63: 471–482.

Beaulieu, Paul-Alain (2005), "Eanna's Contribution to the Construction of the North Palace at Babylon," in Heather D. Baker and Michael Jursa (eds.), *Approaching the Babylonian Economy: Proceedings of the START Project Symposium, Held in Vienna, 1–3 July 2004*, AOAT 330 (Münster: Ugarit-Verlag): 45–73.

Börker-Klähn, Jutta (1982), *Altvorderasiatische Bildstelen und vergleichbare Felsreliefs*, BaF 4 (Mainz: Philipp von Zabern).

Brunke, Hagan (2013), in David I. Owen (ed.), "Rations in the *Al-Šarrākī* Messenger Texts," in *Cuneiform Texts Primarily from Iri-sağrig / Al-Šarrākī and the History of the Ur III Period*, Volume 1, Commentary and Indexes, NISABA 15 (Bethesda MD: CDL Press): 207–334.

Civil, Miguel (1961), "The Home of the Fish: A New Sumerian Literary Composition," *Iraq* 23: 154–175.

— (1964), "A Hymn to the Beer Goddess and a Drinking Song," in *Studies Presented to A. Leo Oppenheim, June 7, 1964*, From the Workshop of the Chicago Assyrian Dictionary [1] (Chicago: The Oriental Institute of the University of Chicago): 67–89.

Cohen, Mark E. (1993), *The Cultic Calendars of the Ancient Near East* (Bethesda MD: CDL Press).

Cros, Gaston (1910), *Nouvelles fouilles de Tello, publiées avec le concours de Léon Heuzey, F[ois] Thureau-Dangin* (Paris: E. Leroux).

Dahl, Jacob L. (2007), *The Ruling Family of Ur III Umma: A Prosopographical Analysis of an Elite Family in Southern Iraq 4000 Years Ago*, PIHANS CVIII (Leiden: Nederlands Instituut voor het Nabije Oosten).

Dietler, Michael (2003), "Clearing the Table: Some Concluding Reflections on Commensal Politics and Imperial States," in Tamara L. Bray (ed.), *The Archaeology and Politics of Food and Feasting in Early States and Empires* (New York: Kluwer Academic / Plenum Publishers): 271–282.

Dietler, Michael, and Ingrid Herbich (2001), "Feasts and Labor Mobilization: Dissecting a Fundamental Economic Pracice," in M. Dietler and Brian Hayden (eds.), *Feasts: Archaeological and Ethnographic Perspectives on Food, Politics, and Power* (Washington DC: Smithsonian Institution Press): 240–264.

Dietrich, Oliver, Manfred Heun, Jens Notroff, Klaus Schmidt, and Martin Zarnkow (2012), "The Role of Cult and Feasting in the Emergence of Neolithic Communities. New Evidence from Göbekli Tepe, South-Eastern Turkey." *Antiquity* 86:674–695.

Dunham, Sally (1982), "Bricks for the Temples of Shara and Ninurra," *RA* 76: 27–41.

Edzard, Dietz O. (1997), *Gudea and His Dynasty*, The Royal Inscriptions of Mesopotamia, Early Periods 3/1 (Toronto: University of Toronto Press).

Frayne, Douglas R. (1990), *Old Babylonian Period (2003–1595 BC)*, The Royal Inscriptions of Mesopotamia, Early Periods 4 (Toronto: University of Toronto Press).

— (1997), *Ur III Period (2112–2004 BC)*, The Royal Inscriptions of Mesopotamia, Early Periods 3/2 (Toronto: University of Toronto Press).

— (2008), *Presargonic Period (2700–2350 BC)*, The Royal Inscriptions of Mesopotamia, Early Periods 1 (Toronto: University of Toronto Press).

Gaster, Theodor H. (1975), *Myth, Legend, and Custom in the Old Testament* (New York: Harper & Row).

Gelb, Ignace J., Piotr Steinkeller, and Robert M. Whiting (1989/91), *Earliest Land Tenure Systems in the Near East: Ancient Kudurrus*, OIP 104 (Chicago: The Oriental Institute of the University of Chicago).

Gelb, Ignace J. and Burkhart Kienast (1990), *Die altakkadischen Königsinschriften des dritten Jahrtausends v. Chr.*, FAOS 7 (Stuttgart: Franz Steiner).

George, Andrew R. (1993), *House Most High: The Temples of Ancient Mesopotamia*, Mesopotamian Civilizations 5 (Winona Lake: Eisenbrauns).

— (2011), *Cuneiform Royal Inscriptions and Related Texts in the Schøyen Collection*, CUSAS 17 (Bethesda: CDL Press).

Goetze, Albrecht (1963), "Šakkanakkus of the Ur III Empire," *JCS* 17: 1–31.

Heimpel, Wolfgang (2004), "AO 7667 and the Meaning of ba-an-gi$_4$," *Cuneiform Digital Library Journal* 1: 1–13.

— (2009a), *Workers and Construction Work at Garšana*, CUSAS 5 (Bethesda: CDL Press).

— (2009b), "The Location of Madga," *JCS* 61: 1–61.

— (2011), "Twenty-Eight Trees Growing in Sumer," in David I. Owen (ed.), *Garšana Studies*, CUSAS 5 (Bethesda: CDL Press): 75–152.

Heimpel, Wolfgang, and Kent Hillard (2008), "Fact and Fiction in YBC 9819 and SET 188 as Sources for the Reality behind the Name of Year 6 of King Shu-Sin of Ur," in Piotr Michalowski (ed.), *On the Third Dynasty of Ur: Studies in Honor of Marcel Sigrist*, The Journal of Cuneiform Studies, Supplemental Series 1 (Boston: American Schools of Oriental Research): 71–76.

Karlsson, Mattias (2013), *Early Neo-Assyrian State Ideology: Relations of Power in the Inscriptions and Iconography of Ashurnasirpal II (883–859) and Shalmaneser III (858–824)* (Uppsala: Uppsala University).

Koslova, Natalia (2008), "Bezeichnungen der Arbeitskräfte in Umma der Ur III-Zeit," in Steven J. Garfinkle and J. Cale Johnson (eds.), *The Growth of an Early State in Mesopotamia: Studies in Ur III Administration*, BPOA 5 (Madrid: Consejo Superior de Investigaciones Científicas): 145–201.

Lafont, Bertrand (2009), "The Army of the Kings of Ur: The Textual Evidence." *Cuneiform Digital Library Journal* 5: 1–25.

Michalowski, Piotr (1989), *The Lamentation over the Destruction of Sumer and Ur*,

— (2006a), "Love or Death? Observations on the Role of the Gala in Ur III Ceremonial Life," *JCS* 58: 49–61.

— (2006b), "The Strange History of Tumal," in P. Michalowski and Niek Veldhuis (eds.), *Approaches to Sumerian Literature: Studies in Honour of Stip (H. L J. Vanstiphout)*, Cuneiform Monographs 35 (Leiden: Brill): 145–165.

— (2011), *The Correspondence of the Kings of Ur*, Mesopotamian Civilizations 15 (Winona Lake IN: Eisenbrauns).

Lehner, Mark (2002), "The Pyramid Age Settlement of the Southern Mount at Giza," *Journal of the American Research Center in Egypt* 39: 27–74.

Löhnert, Anne (2009), *'Wie die Sonne tritt heraus!": Eine Klage zum Auszug Enlils mit einer Untersuchung zur Komposition und Tradition sumerischen Klagelieder in altbabylonicher Zeit*, AOAT 365 (Münster: Ugarit-Verlag).

Molina, Manuel (2009), "New Ur III Court Records Concerning Slavery," in P. Michalowski (ed.), *On the Third Dynasty of Ur: Studies in Honor of Marcel Sigrist*, The Journal of Cuneiform Studies, Supplemental Series 1 (Boston: American Schools of Oriental Research): 125–143.

— (2010), "Court Records from Umma," in Alexandra Kleinerman and Jack M. Sasson (eds.), *Why Should Someone Who Knows Something Conceal It? Cuneiform Studies in Honor of David I. Owen on His 70th Birthday* (Bethesda MD: CDL Press): 201–217.

Morell, Virginia (2001), "The Pyramid Builders," *National Geographic Magazine* (November): 79–99.

Nissen, Hans J. (1988), *The Early History of the Ancient Near East, 9000–2000 B.C.* (Chicago: The University of Chicago Press).

Oh'e, Setsuko (1986), "An Agricultural Festival in Tummal in the Ur III Period," *ASJ* 8: 121–132.

Owen, David I., and Rudolf H. Mayr (2007), *The Garšana Archives*, CUSAS 3 (Bethesda MD: CDL Press).

Oppenheim, A. Leo (1969), "The Banquet of Ashurnasirpal II," in James B. Pritchard (ed.), *Ancient Near Eastern Texts Relating to the Old Testament*, 3rd ed. with Supplement (Princeton: Princeton University Press): 558–560.

Richter, Thomas (1999), *Untersuchungen zu den lokalen Panthea Süd- und Mittelbabyloniens in altbabylonischer Zeit*, AOAT 257 (Münster: Ugarit-Verlag).

Sallaberger, Walther (1993), *Der kultische Kalender der Ur III-Zeit*, UAVA 7 (Berlin: Walther de Gruyter).

— (1996), *Der babylonische Töpfer und seine Gefässe*, Mesopotamian History and Environment, Series 2, Memoirs 3 (Ghent: The University of Ghent).

— (1999), "Ur III-Zeit," in Pascal Attinger and Markus Wäfler (eds.), *Mesopotamien: Akkade-Zeit und Ur III-Zeit*, Annäherungen 3, OBO 160/3 (Freiburg Schweiz: Universitätsverlag): 121–390.

— (2003/04), "Schlachtvieh aus Puzriš-Dagan: Zur Bedeutung dieses königlichen Archivs," *Jaarbericht "Ex Oriente Lux"* 38: 45–62.

— (2012), "Bierbrauen in Versen: Eine neue Edition und Interpretation die Ninkasi-Hymne," in Catherine Mittermayer and Sabine Ecklin, Altorientalische Studien zu Ehren von Pascal Attinger, OBO 256 (Fribourg: Academic Press Fribourg).

Schramm, Wolfgang (2001), *Bann, Bann! Eine Sumerisch-Akkadische Beschwörungsserie* (Göttingen: Seminar für Keilschriftforschung Göttingen).

Selz, Gebhard J. (1990), "Studies in Early Syncretism: The Development of the Pantheon of Lagaš – Examples for Inner-Sumerian Syncretism," *ASJ* 12: 111–142.

Shaw, Jonathan (2003), "Who Built the Pyramids? Not slaves. Archaeologist Mark Lehner, digging deeper, discovers a city of privileged workers," *Harvard Magazine* (July-August): 42–49, 99.

Sigrist, Marcel (1992), *Drehem* (Bethesda MD: CDL Press).

Sjöberg, Åke W. (1969), *The Collection of the Sumerian Temple Hymns*, TCS 3 (Locust Valley NY: J. J. Augustin).

Snell, Daniel C., and Carl H. Lager (1991), *Economic Texts from Sumer*, YOS 18 (New Haven: Yale University Press).

Steinkeller, Piotr (1987a), "The Foresters of Umma: Toward a Definiton of Ur III Labor," in M. A. Powell (ed.), *Labor in the Ancient Near East*, American Oriental Series 68 (New Haven: American Oriental Society): 73–116.

— (1987b), "The Administrative and Economic Organization of the Ur III State: The Core and the Periphery," in McG. Gibson and R.D. Biggs (eds.), *The Organization of Power: Aspects of Bureaucracy in the Ancient Near East*, Studies in Ancient Oriental Civilization 46 (Chicago: The Oriental Institute of the University of Chicago): 19–41.

— (1989), *Sale Documents of the Ur III Period*, FAOS 17 (Stuttgart: Franz Steiner).

— (1999), "Land-Tenure Conditions in Third Millennium Babylonia: The Problem of Regional Variation," in Michael Hudson and Baruch A. Levine (eds.), *Urbanization and Land Ownership in the Ancient Near East*, Peabody Museum Bulletin 7 (Cambridge MA: Peabody Museum of Archaeology and Ethnology, Harvard University): 289–329.

— (2001a), "New Light on the Hydrology and Topography of Southern Babylonia in the Third Millennium," *ZA* 91: 22–84.

— (2001b),"Security for Loans in the Ur III Period," in Raymond Westbrook and Richard Jasnow (eds.), *Security for Debt in Ancient Near Eastern Law* Culture and History of the Ancient Near East 9 (Leiden: Brill): 47–62.

— (2001c), "AB-tum = èš-tum/*iltu*," *NABU* 2001/35.

— (2002), "Money Lending Practices in the Ur III Period: The Issue of Economic Motivation," in Michael Hudson and Marc Van de Mieroop (eds.), *Debt and Economic Renewal in the Ancient Near East* (Bethesda MD: CDL Press): 109–137.

— (2003), "Archival Practices at Babylonia in the Third Millennium," in Maria Brosius (ed.), *Ancient Archives and Archival Traditions: Concepts of Record-keeping in the Ancient World* (Oxford: Oxford University Press): 37–58.

— (2004a), "Toward a Definition of Private Economic Activity in Third Millennium Babylonia," in Robert Rollinger and Christoph Ulf (eds.), *Monetary Systems in the Ancient World: Means of Transmission and Cultural Interaction*, Oriens et Occidens: Studien zu antiken Kulturkontakten und ihrem Nachleben 6 (Stuttgart: Franz Steiner): 91–111.

— (2004b), "An Inscription of Sin-iddinam and Other Inscribed Materials from Abu Duwari," in Elizabeth C. Stone and Paul Zimansky, *The Anatomy of a Mesopotamian City: The Survey and Soundings at Mashkan-shapir* (Winona Lake IN: Eisenbrauns): 135–152.

— (2007a) "City and Countryside in Third Millennium Southern Babylonia," in Elizabeth C. Stone (ed.), *Settlement and Society: Essays Dedicated to Robert McC. Adams* (Los Angeles and Chicago: Cotsen Institute of Archaeology and the Oriental Institute of the University of Chicago): 185–211.

— (2007b), "On Sand Dunes, Mountain Ranges, and Mountain Peaks," in Martha T. Roth et al. (eds.), *Studies Presented to Robert D. Biggs*, From the Workshop of the Chicago Assyrian Dictionary 2 (Chicago: The Oriental Institute of the University of Chicago): 219–232.

— (2008), "Joys of Cooking in Ur III Babylonia," in Piotr Michalowski (ed.), *On the Third Dynasty of Ur: Studies in Honor of Marcel Sigrist*, The Journal of Cuneiform Studies, Supplemental Series 1 (Boston: American Schools of Oriental Research): 185–192.

— (2010) "On the Location of the Towns of Ur-Zababa and Dimat-Enlil and on the Course of the Arahtum," in Jeanette C. Fincke (ed.), *Festschrift für Gernot Wilhelm anlässlich seines 65. Geburstags am 28. Januar 2010* (Dresden: ISLET): 369–382.

— (2013), "Corvée Labor in Ur III times," in Steven J. Garfinkle and Manuel Molina (eds.), From the 21s Century BC to the 21st Century AD: Proceedings of the International Conference on Neo-Sumerian Studies Held in Madrid, 22–24 July 2010, (Winona Lake IN: Eisenbrauns):

Steinkeller, Piotr and J. N. Postgate (1992), *Third-Millennium Legal and Administrative Texts in the Iraq Museum, Baghdad*, Mesopotamian Civilizations 4 (Winona Lake IN: Eisenbrauns).

Stille, Alexander (2005), "Mark Lehner," *Smithsonian* (November): 62–64.

Stol, Marten(1995),"Old Babylonian Corvée (*tupšikkum*)," in Th. P. J. van den Hout and J. de Roos (eds.), *Studio Historiae Ardens: Ancient Near Eastern Studies Presented to Philo H. J. Houwink ten Cate on the Occasion of His 65th Birthday* (Leiden: Nederlands Historisch-Archaeologisch Instituut te Istanbul): 293–308.

Such-Gutiérrez, Marco (2003), *Beiträge zum Pantheon von Nippur im 3. Jahrtausend vor Christus*, Materiali per il Vocabolario Sumerico, vol. 9/1–9/2 (Rome: Università degli studi di Roma "La Sapienza," Dipartimento di studi orientali).

Suter, Claudia (2000), *Gudea's Temple Building: The Representation of an Early Mesopotamian Ruler in Text and Image*, Cuneifrom Monographs 17 (Groningen: STYX).

Thomsen, Marie-Louise (1975), "'The Home of the Fish': A New Interpretation," *JCS* 27: 197–200.

Trigger, Bruce G. (1990), "Monumental Architecture: A Thermodynamic Explanation of Symbolic Behaviour." *World Archaeology* 22: 117–130.

Veldhuis, Niek (2004a), *Religion, Literature, and Scholarship: The Sumerian Composition Nanše and the Birds*, Cuneiform Monographs 22 (Leiden: Brill).

— (2004b), "Ḫi-(še$_3$) la$_2$," *Cuneiform Digital Library Bulletin* 2004:4.

Volk, Konrad (2011), "Eine neue Inschrift des Königs Sin-iddinam von Larsa," Andrew R. George, *Cuneiform Royal Inscriptions and Related Texts in the Schøyen Collection*, CUSAS 17 (Bethesda MD: CDL Press): 59–88.

Walker, Christopher, and Michael Dick (2001), *The Induction of the Cult Image in Ancient Mesopotamia: The Mesopotamian Mīs Pī Ritual*, State Archives of Assyria Literary Texts 1 (Helsinki: The Neo-Assyrian Text Corpus Project).

Wiseman, D. J. (1952), "A New Stela of Aššur-naṣir-pal II," *Iraq* 14 (1952) 24–44.

Wu, Yuhong (1996),"The Ewes without Lambs and Lambs Cooked in é-uz-ga, 'The Private House of the Kings,' in the Drehem Archives," *JAC* 11: 65–109.

Appendix: Documentation

A. Tummal Documentation

(1) "Tummal Chronicle" lines 22–33.

Ur-^{d}Namma-ke$_{4}$ É-kur in-dù ^{d}Šul-gi dumu Ur-^{d}Namma-ke$_{4}$ Tum-ma-al^{ki}-e pa bí-i-è ^{d}Nin-líl Tum-ma-al^{ki}-šè in-de$_{6}$/tùm a-rá 5-a-kam Tum-ma-al^{ki} ba-šub

"Ur-Namma built the Ekur; Šulgi, son of Ur-Namma, made (everything) in Tummal resplendent; he brought Ninlil to Tummal regularly. For the fifth time Tummal was abandoned."

mu ^{d}Amar-^{d}Suen-ka-ta (var.: ^{d}Šu-^{d}Suen-ka-ta) en-na mu ^{d}I-bí-^{d}Suen lugal-e En-am-gal-an-na (var.: En-me-gal-an-na) (= Ibbi-Suen 4) en ^{d}Inana Unug^{ki}-ga máš-e in-pàd-dè ^{d}Nin-líl Tum-ma-al^{ki}-šè ì-DU.DU-en inim Lú-^{d}Inana ašgab-gal ^{d}En-líl-lá-šè sar-re

"'From the (first) year of Amar-Suen till year Ibbi-Suen 4, I regularly carried/accompanied Ninlil to Tummal'—written according to the words of Lu-Inana, chief leather-worker of Enlil."

^{d}Iš-bi-Èr-ra É-kur-igi-gál-la é-šutum/šútum ^{d}En-líl-lá in-dù

"Išbi-Erra built (in Tummal?) the Ekur-igigala, a šutum building of Enlil."

(2) Frayne, RIME 3/2, 317–20 xi 4–xii 24.

má-gur$_{8}$ mah íd mah-e hé-du$_{7}$ kar èš-e kar ^{d}Nin-líl-lá-kam men dalla-bi [ki]-tuš Tum-ma-al^{ki} ⸢^{d}⸣Nin-líl-lá-kam … giš-gi Tum-ma-al^{ki} ^{d}En-líl-lá-šè ki šag$_{4}$ húl-la ^{d}Nin-líl-⸢lá⸣-šè ^{d}En-líl ^{d}Nin-líl-da mu-dì-ni-in-u$_{5}$ … íd-bi íd-Nin mu-DU-zal-le mu p[àd-d]a un-e [… má-gur$_{8}$]-bi [Tum-m]a-al-e [im-ma]-ti-a-ta, *etc.*

Cf. year-formula Šu-Suen 8: mu ^{d}Šu-^{d}Suen má-gur$_{8}$ mah ^{d}En-líl ^{d}Nin-líl-ra mu-ne-dím.

(3) Nikolski 2 481 v 12–14, vi 7–9, 13–15, 29. Umma; Šulgi 35/i.

šu-nígin 424 gud áb hi-a ba-úš mu šidim Tum-ma-al gub-ba-ne-šè Níg!(U)-^{d}Ba-ú nu-bànda šidim šu ba-ti… šu-nígin 10 gud áb hi-a ba-úš mu éren Tum-ma-al gub-ba-ne-šè […]-úr-ki šu ba-ti… šu-nígin 11 gud áb hi-a ba-úš mu éren Tum-ma-al gub-ba-ne-šè I-dur-DINGIR šu ba-ti ... zi-ga iti še-gur_{10}-kud ba-a-kéš.

Apparently the same Nig-Bau, a supervisor of masons, is mentioned in MVN 13 756:4, an Umma tablet from ŠS 9/– (courtesy of M. Molina).

(4) CT 1 pls. 4–5 iii 10–11. Girsu/Lagaš; Š 35/–.

53.0.0 (še) gur šidim Tum-ma-al-la gub-ba-me.

(5) RA 16 19–20 = AAICAB 4 pls. 318–319. Umma; Šulgi 36/ix.

A balanced account of the building materials that Umma's institutional economy contributed to the Tummal project during year Šulgi 36. The colophon reads: níg-ŠID-ak Mu-zu-da $šag_4$ Tum-ma-al^{ki}, "balanced account of Muzuda in Tummal" (xiii 16–17). The identity of Muzuda is unknown; he appears as gìr Mu-zu-da in ii 18.

(A) Capital— sag-níg-gur_{11}-ra-kam (i 1 – v 3).

Listed first are the materials on hand (giš sumun-àm, i 21), among them the timber supplied by the governor of Babylon (i 4–6). Then follow the new deliveries made by various individuals are spelled out (giš gibil-àm, i 24); those are untitled, except in the last two lines of column ii, where the governors of Adab and Gudua deliver 120 and 60 bushels of straw (in-u) respectively. Columns iv 1–v 3 name the totals.

Among these materials especially conspicuous are various kinds of timber, unprocessed and processed: šinig, ù-suh_5, giš gal, giš-ùr, "roofbeam," ^{giš}da, "plank," ^{giš}a-ra, $^{giš}kun_5$ "ladder" (i 25, 40, ii 3), mi-rí-za (*parīsu*), ^{giš}me-te-LUM (probably *medelu*, rather than *metenu*, as in CAD M/2, 43, "narrow plank"), ^{giš}íl, "lever," ^{giš}al, "hoe," ^{giš}zú-al, ^{giš}ni-ru, ^{giš}sag-kul gal, "large door-bolt," $šag_4$-si-ig, and ^{giš}šu-a-DI.

Other types of materials listed in this section include bitumen (very small amounts), straw (1,200 bushels of in-u and 60 bushels of èš-tum), ropes (éš má-gíd, éš-giš-zi-da, and éš-gána), various types of pots (dug-gur-háb, dug-sìla-bànda^{da}, dug-DU.DU.KAL, and dug-DU.DU.KAL gíd-da), reeds (gi ŠID and gi NE), date-palm midribs (murgu-peš), turtle carapaces ($murgu_3$-ba), oils (small amounts of ì-giš and ì-šáh), mordants (ú-háb, al-la-ha-ru, and ŠE.KUR), copper and the su-gan metal, and animal hides (very small volumes).

(B) Expenditures—zi-ga (iv 4′–x; totals in xi–xii 16)

This section specifies how and where the materials listed in A were utilized. Three building destinations are named here: (1) é-gal lugal, "royal palace" (v 6–vi 28), within which a "large anteroom" (pa-pah gu-la), a "sitting/receiving room" (ki-tuš-lugal), a "bathroom" (du_{10}-ús), and a "great staircase" (kun gu-la) were situated; (2) the é-uz-ga sanctuary, two bathrooms, a staircase (kun), the "great gate" (ká-mah), a retaining wall (ki-sá), and a sheepfold (é-udu) (vi 29–viii 3); (3) "in Tummal"; the only architectural feature identified here is the "royal courtyard" (kisal lugal) (viii 4–18). The materials that remained on hand were either stored in the palace (é-gal-la ku_4-ra; viii 19–x 25), or assigned to three individuals, two of whom were merchants (x 26–30).

This part of Text 5 contains extremely important information on the architectural elements used as part of the building operations. However, due to the considerable length of this section and the difficulty in reading and identifying many of the items appearing there, I have chosen not to discuss it in any detail.

(C) Negative balance—lá-NI (xii 17–25)

(D) Positive balance—dirig (xii 26–xiii 15)

(5a) SANTAG 6 30:1–4 = Text 5 v 10–13. Umma; Šulgi 36/–.

3 ma-na 11 gín urudu kin til-la har dub-KA-ab-ba-ka ba-a-kéš é-gal Tum-ma-al^{ki} gìr Lugal-nesag-e.

The corresponding entry in Text 5 reads: 3 ma-na 10 gín urudu izi-kú$^{!}$(A.KA)-bi 1$^{!}$ gín 5 gín su-gan har dub-ab-ba-ka-šè ba-dím.

(6) MVN 15 390. Umma; Š 37/ii-vii.

For a full transliteration and photographs, see D. I. Owen, MVN 15, 141–750 no. 390. Because of the great length of the text, it has been impossible to transliterate it here. I offer instead a synopsis of its contents. See also my detailed discussion of this text above pp. 38–50.

Text 6 is a record of the labor that Umma's institutional economy was required to contribute toward the Tummal project during year Šulgi 37. The labor was provided in three installments, spread over the second through the seventh month. Although the grand-totals recorded in the colophon are preserved incompletely, on the basis of the figures recorded in the body of the text it may be estimated that the total of man-days (both performed and non-performed) was roughly 45,000.

Individual entries of Text 6 show the following two alternative patterns:

(1) x guruš gub-ba lá-NI y PN (title/occupation) "x man-days performed; y man-days non-performed—(the obligation of) PN (title/occupation)";

(2) x guruš gub-ba / x guruš occupation ugula PN, "x man-days performed / x professional man-days, under the supervision of PN."

The text is divided into three main sections, in reflection of the three periods during which the workers were employed (i 1–vii 58; vii 59–xiv 52; xiv 53–xxii 28). Each section concludes with the totals of workers supplied within individual work-periods.

The workers came from the four main districts of the Umma province:

šag$_4$ Umma^{ki} (iv 61, xi 65, xix 7)
šag$_4$ A-pi$_4$-sal$_4$^{ki} ki Ur-e$_{11}$-e (vi 21–22, xii 87–88, xx 35–36)

šag$_4$ Muš-bi-an-na ki Lugal-^{giš}kiri$_6$ (vi 54–55, xiii 39–40, xxi 5–6)
šag$_4$ Gú-eden-na ki A-ab-ba (vi 66, xiii 53–54, xxi 17–18).

The three groups of totals and the types of workers identified there are as follows:

Totals of Section 1 (vii 45–58)

7,461 10 gín guruš gub-ba
790 UN-íl ⅔ gub-ba
29 géme <ù> lú á-½
119 guruš ad-KID
60 guruš nagar
48 UN(-íl) ad-KID
30 guruš <<UN>> tu-ra
48 UN(-íl) tu-ra
27 lú-ninda
78 guruš ugula
66 guruš šidim
3,907 ½ guruš lá-NI
iti še-kar-gál-la ud 3-kam-a-kam
iti nesag ud 30-kam

Totals of Section 2 (xiv 38–52)

8,779 guruš gub-ba
1,259 UN-íl á gub-ba
540+[x$^?$] géme ù l[ú] á-½
150 guruš ad-KID
60 UN<-íl> ad-KID á
90 guruš nagar
78 šidim
480 guruš má-lah$_4$
106 lú-ninda
180+⌜15⌝ guruš ugula
[…] guruš tu-ra
[102] UN<-íl> tu-ra
[x]+1,100 guruš lá-NI
[x]+40 UN<-íl> lá-NI
iti RI

Totals of Section 3 (xxii 10–28)

5,864 guruš gub-ba
1,685 UN<-íl> á gub-ba
251 guruš ad-KID

113 UN<-íl> ad-KID
157 guruš nagar
78 guruš GÍN:má
20+[x] guruš má-lah$_4$
50 guruš na[gar]
76 šidim
43$^{?}$ guruš nar
360+[x ...]
⸢30⸣+[x ...]
120+[x ...]
120+[x guruš tu-ra]
275 ⸢UN-íl tu-ra⸣
9,060 ⸢guruš lá⸣-[NI]
550+[x] guruš UN<-íl> [lá-NI]
iti šumun ⸢ud 30⸣-[kam]
iti min-è[š ud 13$^{?}$-kam]

Note: the notations á, á-½, and ⅔ signify full-time employment, 50%-time employment, and 66%-time employment respectively; tu-ra means "sick."

Following these three sections, Text 6 records the labor spent to transport building materials (mostly straw, but also bitumen and timber) from Umma to Tummal (xxii 29–xxiii 46). These operations were carried out during the third through the sixth month of year Šulgi 37, *i.e.*, concurrently with the building activity. The total labor expended in this way was 2,601 man-days (guruš) and 44 days provided by female workers working half-time (géme á-½).

The text concludes with the grand-totals of man-days expended, designated as [guruš] gub-ba Tum-ma-al^{ki}, and the year-formula (xxiii 47–xxiv 11).

(7) YOS 4 274. Umma; Šulgi 37/iii.

1 5 giš 13 kùš-ta
2 6 giš 12 kùš-ta
3 7 giš 11 kùš-ta
4 30 giš 10 kùš-ta
5 12 giš 10 lá 1 kùš-ta
6 11 giš 8 kùš-ta
7 7 giš 7 kùš-ta
8 2 giš 6 kùš-ta
9 tir Ti-im-KU.KU^{ki}-ta
10 ki Ab-ba sig$_5$-ta

11 é-gal Tum-al$_x$^{ki}-šè
12 gìr Lugal-KA-gi-na
13 má še-ka ba-a-gar
14 iti še-kar-ra-gál-la
15 mu ^{d}Šul-gi lugal Bàd ma-da mu-dù

In all probability this transaction corresponds to Text 6 xxii 42–47: [...]⌜ki⌝-šè ⌜má⌝ [še/giš im-gí]d gìr [Lugal]-KA-gi-na, during month iii.

(8) Girsu/Lagaš grain expenditures for the workers employed at Tummal. Šulgi 35, 37.

17.4.2 5 sìla še gur lugal ... mu éren-na-šè ... šag$_4$-gal éren Tum-ma-al gub-ba (MVN 6 448:1–6; Š 35/–).
3.1.5 8 ½ sìla še gur lugal ... mu éren-na-šè ... šag$_4$ Tum-ma-al (MVN 6 156:1–5; Š 35/–).
141.4.0 ⅓ sìla še ù zíd gur lugal ... šag$_4$ Tum-ma-al (MVN 6 450:1–6; Š 35/–).
3.0.0 še gur lugal ... 0.0.4 2 sìla zíd ... 0.2.0 zíd ... 3.0.0 zíd 1.0.0 še gur ... šag$_4$ Tum-ma-al (MVN 7 175:1–10; Š 35/–).
24.0.0 9 sìla še gur lugal ... mu éren-na-šè ... šag$_4$ Tum-ma-al (MVN 7 285:1–7; Š 35/–).
10.4.1 8 sìla še gur lugal ... mu éren-na-šè ... šag$_4$ Tum-ma-al (MVN 7 333:1–7; Š 35/–).
15.1.4 še gur lugal ... mu éren-na-šè ... šag$_4$ Tum-ma-al (MVN 7 498:1–6; Š 35/–).
15.3.0 9 sìla še gur lugal mu éren-na-šè ... šag$_4$ Tum-ma-al (MVN 7 521:1–6; Š 35/–).
5.1.2 4 ½ sìla še gur lugal ... mu éren-na-šè ... šag$_4$ Tum-ma-al (MVN 7 532:1–7; Š 35/–).
8.4.2 4 ⅓ sìla še gur lugal ... mu éren-na-šè ... ugula sanga ^{d}Gá-tùm-dùg šag$_4$ Tum-ma-al (MVN 7 549:1–7; Š 35/–).
12.4.0 še gur lugal ... mu éren-na-šè ... šag$_4$ Tum-ma-al (MVN 7 580:1–5; Š 35/).
5.3.4 še gur lugal šag$_4$ Gír-su^{ki} 0.4.0 šag$_4$ Tum-ma-al iti šu-numun ... še éren bala é ^{d}Nanše ù éren bala èš dingir Lagaš^{ki} (MVN 6 15:1–11; Š 37/–).

(9) BPOA 1 444. Umma; Šulgi 37/–.

1 0.0.2 4 sìla zíd-GUM še-gín-šè
2 0.0.1 eša

3 2.2.4 5 sìla ninda-šu gur
4 3.3.4 3 sìla kaš gin gur
5 šag$_4$-gal nagar
6 0.0.3 kaš-dida gin
7 giš-e šu de$_6$-a ù ^{giš}ig HI-lá-a
8 5 sìla zíd gú-gal
9 0.0.1 5 sìla NI.UD.KA
10 7 múrgu-ba
11 20 ébih siki ùz
12 ki-lá-bi 1 gú 4 ma-na
13 zi-ga ^{giš}ig é-gal
14 kišib Arad$_2$ dumu Šeš-kal-la
15 mu bàd ba-dù

Seal of Lu[gal-...] / dub-[sar] / dumu Lugal$^?$-AN-[...]

9. As far as I know, the rare commodity NI.UD.KA, which is measured in capacity measures, is attested only in the Ur III texts from Umma. See 2 sìla NI.UD.KA (Text 23 = Text 24); 2 sìla NI.UD.KA (Text 36:4); ⅔ sìla NI.UD.KA$^!$ (UTI 3 2004:2); etc. A possibility that this term designates a type of oil (ì-UD-ka$^?$) is not very likely, because of the final -KA, which is difficult to justify grammatically.

(10) BPOA 6 1174. Umma; Šulgi 37/–.

1 1,740 sa gi NE
2 [...] ⸢sa⸣ gi šid
3 kug-bi 5 gín
4 2,700 gi NE
5 gu-kilib-ba 20 sa-ta ì gál
6 gi énsi Adab^{ki}
7 gi-sal$_4$ é-gal-šè
8 En-dingir-mu šu ba-ti
9 gìr Si-ri lú-kas$_4$
10 mu bàd ba-dù

B. Ga'eš Documentation

(11) RA 12 164–65 AO 7667. Umma; Amar-Suen 4/–.

For a partial edition and detailed discussion of this text, see Heimpel 2004.

A record of bricks that Umma's institutional economy advanced to the governors of several other provinces (Adab, Kazalu, Marda, Sippar?), as well as to the sabras of An (of Ur?), Nin-gublaga (of Ki'abrig near Ur),

Enki (of Eridu), ^{d}Nin-a-mu-DU (of Kisig?), and Nin-[...], as part of their contribution to the Gaeš project. Formally, the text is a list of individual brick expenditures, each group of expenditures marked as kišib PN, "the receipt tablet of PN." The receipts are divided into two groups, according to the two officials—Lugal-magure and Lu-dingira—via whom the bricks were distributed. The recipients of the bricks were as follows:

(**a**) kišib-bi 2-àm kišib ⌜Níg⌝-^{d}Nin-gal (i 1–9); kišib Árad-^{d}Nan[na] šeš sabra ^{d}Nin-[...] (i 15–16); kišib Bí-lí-a lú sabra An-na-ka (i 22–23); kišib-bi 2-àm kišib I-ti-É-a lú ^{d}En-ki-ka (ii 7–8); kišib Gìr-ni-ì-šag$_{5}$ (ii 14); [kišib] Lú-kal-la sabra (ii 20); [kišib] ^{d}Šul-gi-ezen lú ^{d}Nin-a-mu-DU-me-éš (ii 22–23); kišib Šu-lu-lu lú ^{d}Nin-gublaga (iii 4); gìr Lugal-má-[gur$_{8}$-re] (iii 7).

(**b**) kišib Šu-lu-lu lú UD.KIB$^{?}$.NUN$^{?ki}$ (iii 14); kišib-bi 2-àm kišib DI-ì-lí lú énsi Adab^{ki}-ka (iv 1); kišib Šu-lu-lu lú énsi Már-da^{ki}-ka (iv 8); kišib Ri-iš-be-lí lú énsi Ka-zal-lu^{ki}-ka (iv 10–11); gìr Lú-dingir-ra (iv 13).

The name DI-ì-lí, which appears also in Texts 16 and 16a, probably should be transliterated *Di-ni-lí* (*i.e.*, Dīn-ilī). But note that in the seal impressed on these two sources, the name of the same person apparently is written DI.KUD-ì-lí.

The text concludes with the totals of bricks, and a statement that the bricks in question were expended in Ga'eš:
[šu-n]ígin 142 sar 12 gín sig$_{4}$-ù-ku-ru-um [šu-nígin 11]+2 sar sig$_{4}$-za-rí-in [zi-g]a$^{?}$ šag$_{4}$ Ga-eš^{ki} (iv 14–16).

(12) PDT 2 1370:1–7 = Text 11 ii 1–8. Umma; Amar-Suen 4/vi.

3 kùš gíd ½ nindan ⅓ kùš dagal 2 kùš sukud a-rá 1-kam 3 kùš gíd 4 kùš dagal 4 kùš sukud a-rá 2-kam I-ti-É-a lú ^{d}En-ki-ka-ke$_{4}$ šu ba-an-ti. Seals of I-ti-[É-a] / árad ^{d}En-ki; and Ur-^{d}Nin-⌜šubur⌝ / dub-sar / dumu Níg-pàd-[da].

(13) PDT 2 1377:1–11 = Text 11 ii 9–14. Umma; Amar-Suen 4/vi.

1 nindan gíd ½ nindan ⅓ kùš dagal 2 kùš sukud a-rá 1-kam 1 nindan gíd 4 kùš dagal 4 kùš sukud a-rá 2-kam SIG$_{4}$.ANŠE ar-hu ù-ku-ru-um-ma Lú-kal-la sabra ^{d}Nin-URU-a-mu-DU šu ba-ti kišib Gìr-ni-ì-šag$_{5}$-ga íb-ra. Seal of Gìr-ni-ì-šag$_{5}$ / dub-sar / dumu ⌜x⌝-[...].

(14) UTI 5 3394:1–16 = Text 11 ii 15–20. Umma; Amar-Suen 4/–.

3 nindan gíd ½ nindan dagal 2 kùš sukud a-rá 1-kam ½ nindan dagal 1 kùš ba-an-gi$_{4}$ 4 kùš sukud a-rá 2-kam šag$_{4}$ SIG$_{4}$.ANŠE 1-a-kam sig$_{4}$-ù-ku-ru-um-bi 17½ sar sig$_{4}$ énsi Umma^{ki}-ka inim Níg-^{d}Ba-ú ⌜nu-bànda⌝-

ta Lú-kal-la šu ba-ti bala$^{?}$-ta [...] iti-ezen-^{d}Š[ul!-gi ud 1-kam? gi$_4$-g[i$_4$-dam] mu lugal-⸢bi⸣ ⸢pàd⸣. Seal of Lú-kal-la dub-sar / dumu I-ta-e$_{11}$-a / dub-sar.

(15) SNAT 346:1–7 = Text 11 ii 21–23. Umma; Amar-Suen 4/–.

1 sar 160 sig$_4$-ù-ku-ru-um ki énsi Umma^{ki}-ka-ta ^{d}Šul-gi-⸢ezen⸣ lú ^{d}Nin-a-mu-DU-ke$_4$ šu ba-ti gi$_4$-gi$_4$-dam é-gi$_6$-par$_4$ Ga-eš⸢^{ki}⸣. Seal of ^{d}Šul-gi-[ezen] / dub-sar / dumu Ur-^{d}⸢Dumu$^{?}$⸣-[zi$^{?}$].

(16) PDT 2 1353:1–6 = Text 11 iii 15–iv 1. Umma; Amar-Suen 4/vi.

2 sar sig$_4$-ù-ku-ru-um ki énsi Umma^{ki}-ta DI-ì-lí lú Adab^{ki}-ke$_4$ šu ba-ti sig$_4$ ki-ba gi$_4$-gi$_4$-dam é-gi$_6$-par$_4$ Ga-eš^{ki}-šè. Seal of DI.KUD-ì-lí / dub-sar / dumu Šeš-ka-la gu-za-lá.

(16a) BDTNS 193721, an unpublished tablet in a private collection, (courtesy of M. Molina). Umma; Amar-Suen 4/–.

⸢½$^{?}$⸣ nindan gíd ½ nindan 2½ kùš dagal 3 kùš sukud a-rá 1-kam ½ nindan gíd ½ nindan 2½ kùš dagal 1 k[ùš ba]-an-gi$_4$ 5 ⅓ kùš sukud ki énsi Umma^{ki}-ta DI-ì-lí lú Adab^{ki} šu ba-ti sig$_4$ ki-ba gi$_4$-gi$_4$-dam é-gi$_6$-par$_4$ ⸢Ga⸣-eš^{ki}. Seal of DI.KUD-ì-lí / dub-sar / dumu Šeš-kal-la gu-za-lá.

(17) MVN 1 231 ii 16–18. Umma; [Amar-Suen 4/–]).

24 dug 0.0.3 25 dug 0.0.2 Ga-eš^{ki}-šè.

(18) MVN 16 878:1–10. Umma; Amar-Suen 5/–.

3.0.0 zíd munu$_4$ hi-a gur 2 sìla ì-nun 2 sìla ga muru$_{13}$ 2 sìla ì-giš 3 ma-na siki ùz Ga-eš-šè ... ki Ur-^{d}Šul-pa-è-ta kišib énsi-ka. Seal of Ur-Lisi, governor of Umma, dedicated to Amar-Suen.

(19) UNT 75:1–5. Umma; Amar-Suen 6/iv.

10 gú siki GI níg-sám níg-gù-dé é Ga-eš^{ki}-šè é-kišib-ba gu-la-ta Ur-nìgin-gar dumu Lú-^{d}Ba-ú dam-gàr šu ba-ti, "10 talents of ordinary wool was received from the Great Warehouse by Ur-nigingar, son of Lu-Bau, the merchant, as the purchase price of the requested (materials) for the temple of Ga'eš."

The merchant Ur-nigingar receives wool to purchase materials for the Ga'eš project also in Text 40. For the role of Umma merchants in procuring materials for the Ga'eš project, see above p. 62.

(20) SACT 2 183:1–5. Umma; Amar-Suen 6/v.

270 ^{gi}gilim gazi Á.AN.TUR 30 gíd 1 nindan 4 kùš Ga-eš^{ki}-šè ki Ur-^{d}Šul-pa-è-ta kišib Da-a-gi. Seal of Da-a-gi / dub-[sar] / [...].

The meaning of the term Á.AN.TUR, which describes the ropes or cables (gilim) made of the plaited gazi fibers (apparently the licorice plant = *Glycyrrhiza glabra*, whose rootes are known to be a source of fibers, used in modern times as an insulation and as an ingredient of wallboards), is unclear. This term is occasionally qualified by the numerals 30 and 20. See the following examples: 30 gilim gazi Á.AN.TUR 30 gíd 1½ nindan-ta (NATN 481:1–3); 105 ^{gi}gilim gal KA Á.AN.TUR 30 gíd 5 nindan-ta 900 ^{gi}gilim gazi Á.AN.TUR 20 gíd 1½ nindan-ta (UTI 4 2493:1–3); 4 ^{gi}gilim ⸢gal⸣ KA Á.<AN.>TUR 30 4½ nindan-ta 60 ^{gi}gilim gazi 1½ nindan-ta (UCP 9 2/2/2 63:1–3); 7 ^{gi}gilim Á.AN.TUR 30 2 nindan-ta (MVN 16 1356:2); x gilim gazi Á.AN.TUR 1½ nindan-ta (Text 35 ii 2, iii 11). Á.AN.TUR is possibly to be analyzed as á-an tur, "small spadix." However, as far as I know, the term á-an is used only in connection with the date palm.

(21) YOS 4 81:1–6. Umma; Amar-Suen 6/v.

31+[x g]u-kilib gi gi-ta$^{?}$ BU A A gá-nun kar$^{!}$-ta$^{!}$ ki Šeš-kal-la-ta kišib Da-a-gi [G]a-eš^{ki}-šè. Seal of Da-a-g[i] / dub-[sar].

(22) HSS 4 132:1–6. Girsu/Lagaš; Amar-Suen 6/vi.

2.1.0 dabin ⸢gur⸣ lugal é-kín-kín gu-la-ta$^{!}$ ki Lú-^{d}Nin-šubur-ta Ur-^{d}Ig-alim dumu Lú-gu-la šu ba-ti Ga-eš^{ki}-šè.

(23) Ledgers pl. 15 9 vi 1–6 = Text 19d. Umma; Amar-Suen 6/xi.

0.0.2 ésir é-a kug-bi 24 še 2 sìla NI.UD.KA kug-bi igi-6-gál Ga-eš^{ki}-šè kišib Ab-ba-gi-na.

This text is a silver account of the merchant Ur-Dumuzida. In the corresponding receipt tablet (Text 24), the said commodities are received by Abba-gina from Ur-Dumuzida. Ur-Dumuzida procures bitumen for the Ga'eš project also in Text 32.

For the official Abba-gina, who routinely handled materials and labor destined for the Ga'eš project, see above p. 186–187.

(24) BPOA 7 2288:1–5 = Text 19c. Umma; Amar-Suen 6/–.

0.0.2 ésir é-a 2 sìla NI.UD.[KA] Ga-eš^{ki}-šè ki Ur-^{d}Dumu-zi-da kišib Ab-ba-gi-na. Seal of Ab-ba-gi-na / dub-sar / dumu Lugal-má-gur$_{8}$-re.

(25) BPOA 6 1458:1–5. Umma; Amar-Suen 6/–.

50 guruš ud 1-šè é-šidim gub-ba Ga-eš^{ki}-ka gub-ba ugula [...] kišib Ab-ba-[gi-na]).

An assignment of one worker for fifty days of labor is apparently meant.

(26) Syracuse 5:1–5. Umma; Amar-Suen 6/–.

2 guruš ud 116-šè é-šidim gub-ba Ga-eš gub-ba ugula Lú-^{d}Da-mu kišib Ab-ba-gi-na.

(27) YOS 4 179:1–5. Umma; Amar-Suen 6/–.

1 guruš ud 85-šè é-šidim gub-ba Ga-eš^{ki}-ka gub-ba ugula Lugal-ne-sag-e kišib Ab-ba-gi-na. Seal of Ab-ba-gi-na / dub-sar / dumu Lugal-má-gur$_8$-re.

(28) AAICAB 1/1 Ashm. 1924–665 iv 20–v 2. Umma; Amar-Suen 6/–.

5 guruš ud 120-šè á-bi ud 600-kam é-šidim gub-ba Ga-eš^{ki} gub-ba kišib Ab-ba-gi-na dumu A-rí-bi.

(29) BPOA 7 2300:1–5. Umma; Amar-Suen 6/–.

1 guruš ud 180-šè é-šidim gub-ba Ga-eš^{ki}-ka gub-ba ugula Árad-mu kišib Ab-ba-gi-na. Seal of Ab-ba-gi-na / dub-sar / dumu Lugal-má-gur$_8$-re.

(29a) BPOA 6 322. Umma; Amar-Suen 6/–.

5 guruš ud 124-šè 2 guruš ud 105-šè guruš nagar ad-KID Ga-eš-a gub-ba ki A-gu-ta kišib Ab-ba-gi-na. Seal of Ab-ba-gi-na / dub-sar / dumu Lugal-má-gur$_8$-re.

(30) Amherst 87:1–8. Girsu/Lagaš; Amar-Suen 7/iii.

22.3.0 níg-àr-ra sig$_5$ gur lugal 5.0.0 dabin gur Ga-eš^{ki}-šè ⌜ki⌝ Lugal-igi-huš-ta ⌜...⌝ šu ba-[ti] gìr [...] é-kín-kín ⌜gibil⌝-ta.

(31) DAS 361. Girsu/Lagaš; Amar-Suen 7/vi.

A listing of two groups of workers assigned to work in Ga'eš (šag$_4$ Ga-eš^{ki}, line 26). The first group, numbering forty-seven men and led by six foremen (ugula) worked for thirty-five days. The second group, numbering fifty-five men and led by four formen, worked for 20 days. The whole contingent was supervised by the nu-bànda Ba-ad-da-rí.

(32) Ledgers pl. 17 10 v 11–14. Umma; Amar-Suen 7/vii.

0.3.0 ésir é-a kug-bi 1 ⅔ gín 24 še é Ga-eš^{ki}-šè kišib Da-a-gi.

This source is a silver account of the merchant Ur-Dumuzida. Cf. Text 23 = Text 24.

(33) TCTI 2 3254. Girsu/Lagaš; Amar-Suen 7/ix.

120(gur) in-nu èš-tum Ga-eš^{ki}-šè á éren é-sukkal ^{d}Utu-bar-ra ugula Ur-^{giš}gigir.

The same Ur-gigir supervises a delivery for Ga'eš also in Text 34.

(34) ITT 2 3672:1–8. Girsu/Lagaš; Amar-Suen 7/ix.

3,180 <sa> gi šid guruš-e 10 sa-ta 1,340 <sa> gi NE guruš-e 13 sa-ta gi zé-a Ga-eš^{ki}-šè éren é sukkal-m[ah] ugula Ur-^{giš}[gigir].

(35) YOS 4 256. Umma; Amar-Suen 7/–. Collated.

i	1	3 ^{giš}ù-suh$_5$ 1 nindan-ta
	2	8 ^{giš}ù-suh$_5$ 6 kùš-ta
	3	10 lá 1 giš-ùr 8 kùš-ta
	4	14 giš-ùr 4 kùš-ta
	5	16 ^{giš}zi-gur$_8$-ru-um 1½ kùš-ta
	6	0.1.0 5 sìla ésir-é-a giš-ùr-e ba-ab-su-ub
	7	0.0.1 1 sìla ì-giš
	8	33.1.0 ésir-hád gur
	9	1.1.0 ésir-é-a gur
	10	é-ki-tuš é-pa-pah kisal ù EN.DU ba-ra-ab-du$_8$
	11	15 ma-na siki ùz
	12	3 sar kid-gi-sal$_4$
	13	[g]i-bi 108 sa
	14	⌜á⌝-bi ud 18-kam
ii	1	5 sa ^{gi}ti-um-ma
	2	5 gilim gazi Á.AN.TUR 1½ nindan-ta
	3	gi-bi 75 sa
	4	á-bi ud 20
	5	30 ^{gi}guru$_5$
	6	gi-bi 15 sa
	7	^{ú}GUG$_4$(A.ZI+ZI) níg-ub-ba-bi 1 gún
	8	á-bi ud 3
	9	0.0.4 mun
	10	0.0.3 5 sìla gazi
	11	šu giš-ùr-ka ba-a-si
	12	31 dug-gur-pú
	13	630 dug 0.0.1 5 sìla
	14	á-bi ud 346
	15	du$_{10}$-ús-šè
	16	šag$_4$ gi$_6$-par$_4$

17 10! ${}^{[g]iš}$ù-suh$_5$ gal! 10 lá 1 kùš-ta
18 11 ^{giš}ù-suh$_5$ ⸢8⸣ [kùš-t]a
iii 1 18 giš-ùr 10 lá 1 kùš-ta
2 15 giš-ùr 7 kùš-ta
3 32 giš-ùr 4 kùš-ta
4 6 ^{giš}dal ⸢x⸣ 4 kùš-ta
5 13 ^{giš}zi-gur$_8$-ru-um 2 kùš-ta
6 0.1.4 2 sìla ésir-é-a giš-ùr-e ba-ab-su-ub
7 26 2/3 sar kid-gi-sal$_4$
8 gi-bi 960 s[a]
9 á-bi ud 160
10 12 sa ^{gi}ti-um-ma
11 70 gilim gazi Á.AN.TUR 1 ½ nindan-ta
12 gi-bi 150 <sa>
13 ⸢á⸣-bi ud 40
14 50 ^{gi}guru$_5$
15 gi-bi 25 sa
16 ^{ú}GUG$_4$ níg-ub-ba-bi 1 ½ gún
17 á-bi ud 5
iv 1 [x m]a-na siki ùz é-[šu]-tum-ma-šè
2 [x] mun
3 0.0.3 gazi
4 šu giš-ùr-ka ba-a-si
5 8 ma-na še-gín
6 ⸢x⸣ na$_4$?-ka-šè
7 ⸢é?-ŠIM?⸣-šè
8 6.2.3 še gur
9 ⸢6?⸣ sìla ì-giš
10 še-ba ì-ba šidim-ma
11 5 sìla ì-giš giš mu-sar múrgu ar-za-gá ba-⸢ab-šeš$_4$⸣
12 3.0.0 še kaš ninda gur
13 5 sìla ì-giš
14 ud-e kaš-dé-a
15 1500.0.0 in-u gur
16 im-ma ba-a-si
17 zi-ga é Ga-eš
18 mu kišib Ur-mu TÚG sum-mu-da-šè
19 mu Ab-ba-gi-na
l.e.20 mu Hu-úh-nu-ri^{ki} ba-hul
Seal: Ab-ba-g[i-na] / dub-[sar] / dumu Lugal-má-gur$_8$-[re]

i 5, iii 5. zi-gur$_8$-ru-um is an unusual writting of *sikkūrum*, "bolt, bar." See CAD S, 256–59.

i 10. I assume that EN.DU, which is attested only here and in NATN 471 (see below), is to be connected with the lexical KI.EN.DU = *mālaku*, "passage, processional road," for which see MSL 15, 44 Diri Oxford line 340: KI.EN.DU = *ma-la-kum*; CAD M/2, 158 *mālaku* A. See also ki-en-du mah [...] ^{d}En-ki-ga-ke$_4$ [si] im-sá-e-ne, "they are setting straight the great processional road of [Eridu/Abzu] of Enki" ("Enki and the World Order" line 150). A meaning "processional road" or "passway" would fit the present context quite well. Interestingly, the *mālaku* in question is likely mentioned in another Umma tablet: 200 sar é 25 sar pú gìr lugal-ke$_4$ ús-sa ma-la-ku-um énsi Ummaki-ka, "200 sar (of bricks for) the building, 25 sar (of bricks for) the well in front of the building; (located) at the royal road adjoning the passway of the governor of Umma" (Nisaba 9 100:1–5). For EN.DU, see also NATN 471:1–4, where it is mentioned in connection with a gate: ká é-ŠIM EN.DU-a lá-a gíd-bi 7½ kùš dagal-bi 2 kùš 3 šu-si, "a gate of the brewery which is suspended in a passway; its length is 7½ cubits, its width is 2 cubits and 3 fingers."

i 12, iii 7. I assume that kid-gi-sal$_4$ is the same as gi-sal, *gisallu*, a reed screen or fence along the edge of a flat roof. See CAD G, 97 *gisallu* A; Heimpel 2009a: 258–266; Schramm 2001: 24–25 lines 103–104, 107–108. Note the expenditure of a very large volume of reeds, supplied by the governor of Adab as part of the Tummal project, for gi-sal$_4$ é-gal-šè, "roof-screen of the palace" (Text 10:1–7). For the reading gi-sal$_4$, see [x] sa gi gi-sal$_4^{al}$ É-maš-šè (MVN 13 165:1–3).

ii 1, iii 10. For ti-um, a type of reed structure, see Heimpel 2009a: 177–179.

ii 2, iii 11. For the term Á.AN.TUR, see the commentary to Text 20.

ii 5, iii 14. For ^{gi}guru$_5$, a type of reed bundle, see Heimpel 2009a: 179–180. To the examples cited there, add Gudea Cylinder A xxii 22: é giguru$_5$-bi muš kur-ra téš-ba nú-àm, "the guru$_5$ of the temple looked like mountain snakes rolled together (in a pit)."

ii 7, iii 16. The meaning of níg-ub-ba, which was made of GUG$_4$ = *elpetu, šuppatu* "alfa grass," is unclear. Heimpel 2009a: 179, 216, suggests the meaning "corner piece."

ii 11, iv 4. Based on B. R. Foster's collations, Heimpel 2009a: 214 and n. 156, reads the first sign as éš, "rope." However, my own collation has shown that the sign in question is a pretty clear ŠU (in both instances, it is wider than the sign ÉŠ found in the same text), as it appears in C. E. Keiser's original copy. Thus, one needs to translate: "licorice and salt filled the 'hands' of the roof-beams," where "hands" are clearly the craftsmen who fashioned the roof-beams. This interpretion is also dictated by the fact that the production of ropes could hardly have involved the use of spices (against Heimpel 2009a: 214, who speculates that "perhaps roots, stems, and other parts were woven into the ropes"). Here note that šu-a ... si, lit.: "to fill the hands (with something)," means "to receive." See Gelb, Steinkeller, and Whiting 1989/91: 229, 239. Here note that the food consumed by builders is frequently mentioned in such contexts, as in Text 9:6–7, which lists 0.0.3 kaš-dida gin giš-e šu de$_6$-a ù ^{giš}ig HI lá-a, "30 liters of ordinary dida-beer (for the carpenters) treating the wood and installing doors" (following the flour, bread, and ordinary beer issued as the "food of the carpenters"). For similar examples, see Heimpel 2009a: 113.

ii 12. For this jar, see Sallaberger 1996: 101 under ^{dug}gur-túl(-lá), "Trog für den Brunnen." Contrary to Sallaberger's reading, however, in the Ur III attestations of this term the last sign is consistently PÚ and not TÚL (as in the present example and Text 5 vi 19).

ii 17. The numeral 10 is followed by an erased 2 (or 4).

iv 6–7. Alternatively, na$_4^?$-ka-šè could be read NI.UD.KA-šè, since NI.UD.KA is otherwise attested in similar contexts. See 0.0.1 5 sìla NI.UD-ka (Text 9:9); 2 sìla NI.UD.KA (Text 36:4); ⅔ sìla NI.UD.KA$^!$ (UTI 3 2004:2); etc.

iv 11. The line is possibly to translated: "5 liters of sesame oil were used to anoint the wooden inscriptions in the back of the ar-za-gá." However, I am not aware of any other attestions of ar-za-gá.

iv 12–14. The beer and sesame oil in question were expended "on the day of the banquet."

(36) ARRIM 7 [1989] 16 no. 12. Umma; Amar-Suen 7/–.

1 lá-NI 0.0.3 2 sìla giš-ì
2 57 ma-na siki ùz
3 0.3.2 5 sìla gazi
4 2 sìla NI.UD.KA
5 30 giš-ùr 8 kùš-ta
6 11 giš-ùr 10 lá 1 kùš-ta
7 6 ^{giš}kun$_5$
8 70 ^{giš}ì-šub
9 ⌜0.0.2$^?$⌝ ésir é-a
10 2 giš ⌜x⌝-[x] gíd-bi ⌜3 kùš-ta⌝
11 5 gi [...]
(space)
12 lá-NI-àm
13 šu nígin 1,715 [...]
14 4.0.0 še gu[r]
15 0.1.3 mun
16 0.2.0 ésir hád
17 3 ma-na še-gín
18 4,289 [sa gi]
19 3.0.0 [... gur]
20 [...]
21 dirig-ga-àm
22 dirig lá-NI Dug$_4$-ga-gi-na
23 é-gi$_6$<-par$_4$> Ga-eš^{ki}
24 kišib Ab-ba-gi-na dumu Lugal-má-gur$_8$-re
25) mu Hu-úh-nu-ri^{ki} ba-hul

A list of the building materials delivered by Umma for the Ga'eš project.

Lines 1–12 enummerate the deliveries still outstanding (lá-NI-àm), as compared with the volumes that had been requested by the central government (in Text 37 and similar records). Lines 13–21 record the deliveries made in excess (dirig-àm) of the original requests.

(37) SNAT 534. Umma; undated (Amar-Suen 7 based on the contents).

1	6 ^{giš}ig dib
2	7 ^{giš}gišimmar gíd-bi 15 kùš-ta
3	23 giš-ùr gal gíd-bi 12 kùš-ta
4	20+⸢2? giš⸣-ùr gíd-bi 10 kùš-ta
5	67 giš-ùr gíd-bi 8 kùš-ta
6	44 giš-ùr gíd-bi 7 kùš-ta
7	22 giš-ùr gíd-bi 5 kùš-ta
8	12 ^{giš}ù-suh$_5$ gíd-bi 12 kùš-ta
9	12 ^{giš}ù-suh$_5$ gíd-bi 10 kùš-ta
10	12 ^{giš}ù-suh$_5$ gíd-bi 8 kùš-ta
11	40 ^{giš}ká
12	83 sar kid-gi-[sal$_4$]
13	2,690 ⸢lá⸣ [x] Á.⸢AN⸣.[TUR]
14	gíd-⸢bi⸣ [...]
15	7,800+[x] kid Á.⸢AN⸣.[TUR]
16	2,640+[x] ⸢kid⸣ [^{gi}]ti-um-ma
	(space)
17	níg-gù-dé gi$_6$-par$_4$ Ga-eš^{ki}-ka
18	énsi Umma^{ki}

A list of building materials, which the central government requested of Umma's institutional economy to contribute toward the Ga'eš project. See the discussion above p. 186. Since the materials in question were delivered by Umma during year Amar-Suen 7 (see Texts 35 and 36), the present text must date to Amar-Suen 7 (or the preceding year).

1. ^{giš}ig dib probably means "passage dooor." Among the extant attestations, note especially the following ones: ^{giš}ig dib sig$_5$ gíd-bi ½ ninda 4 kùš-ta dagal-bi 3 kùš-ta á-bi ud 6-ta šag$_4$ É-maš-a-ka gál-la (BIN 5 274:1–22); a copper *armatum* for ^{giš}ig dib ká du$_{10}$-⸢ús⸣ lugal-ka (Santag 6 316:1–2; cf. MVN 18 245:1–3); materials for ^{giš}ig dib tab-tab-ba "a double passage door" é-^{giš}gigir (SA 58:1–4; MVN 20 23:1–5); materials ^{giš}ig dib tab-tab-ba ká ki-[...] (RA 14 180:1–7); and the examples cited above in n. 209.

4. The number is probably 20+⸢4⸣, since, if so reconstructed, the total number of roofbeams would result in a round figure of 180.

12. Reconstructed on the basis of Text 35 i 12, iii 7.

13. Reconstructed on the basis of Text 35 ii 2, iii 11.

(38) BPOA 1 381. Umma; Amar-Suen 7/–.

1 600.0.0 še gur
2 gìr Nir-ì-da-gál
3 600.0.0 še gur
4 kišib A-ab-ba-mu ka-guru$_7$ é ^{d}Nanna
5 é ^{d}Nanna-šè
6 420.0.0 gur
7 še-ba dù-a-kud
8 ki Nam-ha-ni šeš Lugal-má-gur$_8$-re
9 30.0.0 gur
10 Lú-^{d}Nanna dumu DINGIR-ba-ni
11 150.0.0 gur
12 énsi Babilim-ma^{ki}
13 gìr Lú-kal-la dub-sar
(space)
14 šu-nígin 1,800 še gur
15 zi-ga mu énsi Babilim-ma^{ki}-šè
16 mu Hu-úh-nu-ri^{ki} ba-hul

A record of 1,800 bushels of barley which was expended by Umma's institutional economy to the governor Babylon, apparently in connection with the Ga'eš project. See above pp. 189–190.

2. For the general Nir-idagal, see Steinkeller 2013: 398.

(39) MVN 18 208:1–5. Umma; Amar-Suen 7/–.

[x] sa g[i] gu-kilib-ba 15 s[a-ta] é Ga-eš^{ki}-šè ki Šeš-kal-la-t[a] kišib Da-a-g[i]. Seal of Da-a-gi / dub-sar / [...].

(40) TSDU 34bis:1–7. Umma; Amar-Suen 8/ii.

3 gú siki GI níg-gù-dé Ga-eš^{ki}-šè ki Lú-^{d}Nin-gír-su-ta Ur-nìgin-gar dam-gàr šu ba-ti gìr ^{d}Utu-bar-ra ra-gaba.

The same Ur-nigingar procures materials for the Ga'eš project also in Text 19.

(41) TCTI 2 3939:1–8 (tablet and envelope). Girsu/Lagaš; Amar-Suen 8/iii.

0.3.2 še lugal ugula Ur-^{d}Dumu-zi 0.1.0 še ugula Ur-mes šag$_4$-gal éren dumu-dab$_5$-ba-šè ki Lú-ba-ta Ur-^{d}Dumu-zi ugula šu ba-ti šag$_4$ Ga-eš^{ki}. Seal of Ur-^{d}Dumu-zi / ugula dumu-dab$_5$-ba.

(42) TCTI 2 3393:1–7. Girsu/Lagaš; Amar-Suen 8/iii.

0.2.3 dabin lugal 0.3.3 še šag$_4$-gal éren é-gu-za-lá ki Lú-ba-ta Lú-dingir-ra ugula šu ba-ti š[ag$_4$] Ga-eš^{ki}.

The flour and barley expended in this receipt appartently was intended for the boat-towers mentioned in Text 43. Note that the ugula Lu-dingira appears there as well.

(43) ITT 5 8222:1–6. Girsu/Lagaš; Amar-Suen 8/iii.

6 guruš ud 13-šè má ésir Ga-eš$_8$^{ki}-[šè] gíd-⌜da⌝ gìr Lú-^{d}Gù-dé-a àga-ús énsi é-gu-za-lá-me ugula Lú-dingir-[ra] nu-bànda Ur-^{d}Nun-[gal].

(44) BPOA 6 1278:1–10. Umma; Amar-Suen 8/iii.

15 ^{gi}kaskal gal 1 ^{gi}pisan gazi ga su-ba igi-kár Lú-dingir-ra 14 ^{gi}gur-dub 0.1.0-ta 7 ^{gi}kaskal ^{giš}hašhur 0.0.3-ta gìr dù-a igi-kár Ì-làl-lum-ma ki Ur-^{d}Šul-pa-è-ta kišib Lú-kal-la. Seal of Lú-kal-la / dub-sar / dumu Ur-e$_{11}$-e SAHAR.

(45) MVN 16 1563:1–3. Umma; Amar-Suen 8/iv.

⌜⅓⌝ ma-na še-⌜gín⌝ ki A-kal-la-ta ^{giš}ig Ga-eš^{ki}-šè kišib Dingir-ra. Seal of [Dingir]-ra / dub-sar / dumu Lú-ga.

The same A-kala and Dingira appear also in Texts 54 and 54a.

(46) TÉL 9:1–7. Girsu/Lagaš; Amar-Suen 8/iv.

0.0.2 še lugal šag$_4$-gal éren bala tuš-[a] Ga-eš^{ki}-ta má-gur$_8$ gíd-da ki Ùnu-ta [kišib$^?$ ...]-zu èš-dil-dil-me.

(47) MCS 8 90 BM 105417 + Orient 17 42. Umma; Amar-Suen 8/iv.

1 0.0.1 8 sìla ì-udu
2 8.0.0 gazi gur
3 1 ébih ⌜siki ùz⌝ 15 nindan
4 20 gir-ga mangaga!(KA×SA$^!$)
5 1 ^{giš}ù-suh$_5$ gi
6 [x gi$^?$]-muš gal
7 [x] ^{giš}kun$_5$
8 ⌜3⌝ ^{giš}gišimmar 13 kùš-ta
9 12 éš šag$_4$$^?$-ga gíd-bi 10 nindan-ta
10 10 gú mangaga
11 Ga-eš^{ki}-šè
12 ki Lú-kal-la-ta

13 kišib Ab-ba-gi-na
14 iti nesag mu en Eridu^{ki} ba-hun
Seal of Ab-ba-gi-[na] / dub-sar / Lugal-⸢má⸣-[gur$_8$-re].

4. Cf. 12 gir-ga ma-an-ga-ga, "12 rolls of fibers" (YOS 4 238:4); 5 gir-ga mangaga (UTI 3 2030:2). For gir-ga, a loan from Akk. *girrigû/girgû, kirku,* "roll," see CAD K, 408 under *kirku* B.

(48) BPOA 2 2605:1–7. Umma; Amar-Suen 8/iv.

260 gú giš ú-bíl-la mu ^{giš}ig níg<-gù>-dé-a gi$_6$-par$_4$ é Ga-eš^{ki}-ka-šè giš-kin-ti ku$_4$-ra ki énsi Umma^{ki}-ka-ta kišib A-a-mu gìr Šu-Eš-dar lú-kin-gi$_4$-a lugal.

It appears that this huge volume of charcoal represented fuel that was to be used in the production of the gipar's doors. For ú-bíl-la, *upillû,* see CAD U/W, 179b.

(49) MVN 20 105:1–7. Umma; Amar-Suen 8/iv.

5.0.0 gazi gur gìr Kas$_4$ 8.0.0 gazi gur gìr Ur-^{d}Suen nar Ga-eš^{ki}-šè má-a ba-gar é-kišib-ba énsi-ta.

(50) BCT 2 236. Umma; Amar-Suen 8/iv.

A record of the barley allotments (0.2.0 or 120 liters per person) issued to six named individuals working at Ga'eš (Ga-eš^{ki}-šè, lines 1–8). The total, amounting to 2.2.0 of barley, is designated as še-ba zag-mu-ka, "allotments of the New Year" (lines 9–10). Seal of ⸢Bí⸣-dug$_4$-ga / dub-sar / dumu La-a-šag$_5$.

(51) MVN 14 369:1–2. Umma; Amar-Suen 8/v.

3.3.0 še gur šag$_4$-gal šidim Ga-eš^{ki} ki-sur$_{12}$ É-duru$_5$-gu-la-ta ki Lú-^{d}Šul-gi-ra-ta kišib Šeš-kal-la dumu A-rí-bi. Seal of Šeš-kal-la / dub-sar / dumu Lugal-má-gur$_8$-[re].

(52) SAT 1 26:1–6. Girsu/Lagaš; Amar-Suen 8/v.

0.3.2 5 sìla še lugal šag$_4$-gal éren èš dil-dil bala tuš-a ki Lú-ba$^!$-ta Lú-dingir-ra ugula dumu Ka-kug šu ba-ti šag$_4$ Ga-eš^{ki}.

For the foreman Lu-dingira, see Texts 42 and 43.

(52a) BPOA 1 1636:1–4. Umma; Amar-Suen 8/v.

⅓ ma-na še-gín ki A-kal-la-ta ig giš-gur$_8$-ra-šè kišib Dingir-ra. Seal of Dingir-ra / dub-[sar] / dumu Lú-ga.

The meaning of the term giš-gur$_8$-ra, which qualifies doors also in Texts 54a and 56, is uncertain. Other attestations of this term known to me are as follows: 2 ^{giš}ig giš-gur$_8$-ra ésir su-ba gíd-bi ½ nindan 1 kùš-ta dagal-bi 2 kùš-ta á-bi ud 90<-ta$^?$> 2 ^{giš}nu-kùš á-bi ud 1 ús é-níg-lagar-ka gub-ba; 3 ^{giš}ig giš-gur$_8$-ra sig$_5$ gíd-bi ½ nindan 4 kùš-ta dagal-bi 2 ½ kùš-ta á-bi ud 90–ta é-ki-tuš gibil é-a-ka gub-ba ^{giš}ig é-a gub-ba (as part of Umma's building É-maš) (BIN 5 274:1–17); 2 ^{giš}ù-suh$_5$ suh ù-SAR ^{giš}ig giš-gur$_8$-ra kug-bi ⅔ gín (TCL 5 6037 iv 2–3).

The same A-kala and Digira appear also in Texts 52a, 54, and 54a.

(53) TCTI 1 980. Girsu/Lagaš; AS 8/vi.

0.0.1 še lugal ki Lú-ba-ta Lú-gi-na má-lah$_4$ šu ba-ti šag$_4$ Ga-eš$^{[ki]}$. Seal of Lú-gi-na / má-lah$_4$ / dumu Lú-$^{d⌜}$Iškur$^{?⌝}$.

(54) BPOA 7 2254:1–4. Umma; Amar-Suen 8/vi.

1 ma-na še-gín ^{giš}ig é Ga-eš^{ki} ki A-kal-la-ta kišib Dingir-ra. Seal of Dingir-ra / dub-sar / dumu Lú-ga.

The same A-kala and Dingira appear also in Texts 52a, 45 and 54a.

(54a) MVN 16 988:1–5. Umma; Amar-Suen 8/vi.

1 ma-na še-gín ^{giš}ig giš-gur$_8$-ra-šè ki A-kal-la-ta kišib Dingir-ra. Seal of Dingir-ra / dub-[sar] / dumu Lú-ga.

The same A-kala and Dingira appear also in Texts 52a, 45 and 54.

(55) BPOA 7 1872:1–5. Umma; Amar-Suen 8/x.

2 guruš ud 60-šè Úrim-ma^{ki}-šè ^{giš}balag-balag x-a ugula Ur-^{d}Šul-pa-è kišib Ab-ba-gi-na. Seal of Ab-ba-gi-na / dub-sar / dumu Lugal-má-gur$_8$-re.

The reading of x-a is uncertain.

(56) UTI 4 2867. Umma; Amar-Suen 8/–.

1 2 guruš nagar
2 6 guruš ad-KID
3 ud 125-šè
4 1 ^{giš}ig giš-gur$_8$-ra sig$_5$
5 gíd-bi 1 nindan dagal-bi ⌜x⌝
6 á-bi ud 90-šè
7 gi$_6$-par$_4$ Ga$^!$-eš$^{!ki}$
8 ugula A-gu-⌜gu⌝
9 kišib Ab-ba-gi-na
10 mu en Eridu^{ki}

Seal of Ab-ba-gi-na / dub-sar / dumu Lugal-má-gur$_8$-re.

Two carpenters and six mat-makers are sent to Ga'eš to fashion the gipar's door. Cf. Texts 45, 52a, 54, and 54a also dating to Amar-Suen 8, where glue is issued, undoubtedly for the same door. Cf. also Texts 48 and 62a.

In line 4, the editors read the numeral as 60, but almost certainly a single door is meant. As is indicated by its great height (1 nindan = ca. 6 m.), it must have been the gipar's main door. For the term giš-gur$_8$-ra, see the commentary to Text 52a.

(57) SNAT 395:1–5. Umma; Amar-Suen 8/–.

5.0.0 gazi gur 1.0.0 zíd munu$_4$ hi-a gur kišib Ab-ba-gi-na 3.3.0 gur kišib Šeš-kal-la 11.0.0 kišib Ur-^{d}Ùr-bar-tab šag$_4$-gal šidim Ga-eš^{ki}.

Note that the same Ur-Urbartab receives supplies for Ga'eš also in Text 60. Because of the identicial volume (11.0.0), the same transaction is probably meant.

(58) BPOA 2 2277:1–5. Umma; Amar-Suen 8/–.

5 ^{gi}gur in-u-da Ga-eš^{ki}-šè ki Ur-^{d}Šul-pa-è-ta kišib Lú-kìri-zal. Seal of Lú-kìri-zal / dub-sar / dumu Da-DU-mu.

(59) Nisaba 9 58:1–4. Umma; Amar-Suen 8/–.

5 ^{gi}gur in-u-da Ga-eš^{ki}-šè ki Ur-^{d}⸢Šul⸣-pa-è-[ta] kišib Lugal-iti-d[a]. Seal of Inim-^{d}Šára / dub-sar / dumu Lugal-iti-da.

(60) Nisaba 11 21 iii 3–5, 23–24 = BIN 5 iii 74–76, iv 128–131. Umma; Amar-Suen 8/–.

300.0.0 še-ba nar gur šag$_4$ Úrim^{ki}-ma kišib Lú-dùg-ga ... 4.0.0 <še> gur Ga-eš-šè kišib Lugal-iti-da 11.0.0 <še> gur Ga-eš-šè kišib Ur-^{d}Ùr-bar-tab.

Note that the same Ur-Urbartab receives supplies for Ga'eš also in Text 57. Because of the identicial volume (11.0.0), the same transaction is probably meant.

(61) BPOA 1 1389:1–6. Umma; Amar-Suen 8/–.

0.0.1 kaš gin 1½ sìla ì-šáh 0.0.3 ninda šu-ùr-ra éren Ga-eš^{ki}-šè du-a šu ba-ab-ti kišib A-kal-la. Seal of A-kal-la / dub-sar / dumu Ur-nìgin-gar SAHAR.

(62) Nisaba 9 51:1–8. Umma; Amar-Suen 9/–.

10 áb hi-a 80 u$_8$ bar-gál 20 máš máš-da-re$_6$-a en Ga-eš^{ki} hun-gá gìr Nu-úr-Eš$_4$-dar lú-kin-gi$_4$-a ki Uš-mu-ta kišib énsi-ka.

(62a) UDT 84:1–3. Girsu/Lagaš; no year/vi/12.

5 sìla kaš 5 sìla ninda Bur-^{d}Adad ig Ga-eš-šè gin.

Food rations for a man traveling to Ga'eš regarding the (gipar's) door—apparently to work on it. This text probably dates to year AS 8, when the gipar's door was fashioned. See Text 56 and the related sources cited there.

C. Temple of Šara Documentation

(63) YOS 18 123 viii 39–42. Umma; Amar-Suen 9/–.

0.0.1 ésir é-a kug-bi 12 še gi é ^{d}LÀL.IB-ka é ^{d}Šára-ka-ke$_{4}$ ba-ab-su-ub kišib Lugal-nir.

(63a) AnOr 1 165. Umma; Šu-Suen 2/v.

2⅚ ma-na níg-U-NU-a siki ùz gu kin-e ra-ra é ^{d}Šára-ka ki ⸢Lú⸣-^{d}Šul-pa-è-ta kišib Dingir-ra. Seal of Dingir-ra / dub-sar/ dumu Lú-ga.

(64) ASJ 7 126 no. 30:1–8. Umma; Šu-Suen 2/vi.

64.1.0 ésir hád gu[r] 1(bán) 2 sìla ì-giš é-temen-na ⸢ba⸣-ab-du$_{8}$ zi-ga é ⸢^{d}Šára-ka⸣ ki A-a-kal-la énsi-ta gìr Lú-dingir-ra šagina ù Ur-^{d}IG^{da}-alim šidim bar-ta gál-la šag$_{4}$ ^{kuš}dùg-gan-na.

The spelling -^{d}IG-^{d}a-alim found in this text suggests that the divine name in question is to be read ^{d}Da$_{11}$-alim.

(65) MVN 15 26:1–6 = Forde, South Dakota 8. Umma; Šu-Suen 2/vi.

25 gú ésir gul-gul é-temen-na é ^{d}Šára-ka du$_{8}$-dè ki Ur-^{d}Šul-pa-è-ta kišib Lú-^{d}Nin-šubur. Seal of Lú-^{d}Nin-šubur / dub-sar / dumu Dùg-ga / sabra ^{d}Šára.

(66) AAICAB 4 Bod. S 418:1–12. Umma; Šu-Suen 2/vi.

1 áb bar$_{6}$-bar$_{6}$ 1 u$_{8}$ gi$_{6}$ bar ⸢su-ga⸣ 1 ùz sig$_{17}$ 1 udu niga bar su-g[a] 1 udu ú bar su-ga 16 máš níg-dab$_{5}$ uš ki giš ra é ^{d}Šára-ka gìr Ur-^{d}IG-alim šidim-gal Lú-dingir-ra šagina maškim ki ⸢Uš-mu-⸢ta⸣ kišib énsi-⸢ka⸣. Seal of A'a-kala governor of Umma, dedicated to Šu-Suen.

(67) MCS 8 95 BM 105548:1–6; collated by T. Gomi, Orient 17 43. Umma; Šu-Suen 2/vi.

1 ma-na siki kur-ra ^{giš}ga-rig$_{6}$-ak níg-dab$_{5}$ temen é ^{d}Šára-ka ki$^{?}$-a šu gi$_{4}$-da ki Ur-^{d}Nin-tu-ta kišib Lú-^{d}Nin-šubur. Seal of Lú-^{d}Nin-[šubur] / dub-sar / dumu Dùg-ga / sabra [^{d}Šára-ka].

Since in the related Texts 64 and 65 the temple-platform is described as é-temen(-na), in the present example temen apparently means "foundation deposits." Cf. Texts 71, 72, and 73.

(67a) BPOA 1 741. Umma; Šu-Suen 2/vi.

1 udu sízkur ki-sá-a é ^{d}Šára-ka kišib énsi. Seal of A-a-kal-la, énsi Umma^{ki}, dedicated to Šu-Suen.

(67b) MVN 14 287. Umma; Šu-Suen 2/vii.

3 ma-na še-gín ^{giš}ba-KA-KA$^{?}$ é ^{d}Šára-ka ba-ra-ab-du$_8$ ki A-kal-la ašgab-ta kišib Dingir-ra. Seal of Dingir-ra / dub-sar/ dumu Lú-ga.

(68) BPOA 6 422:1–11. Umma; Šu-Suen 2/viii.

2 dug-šagan 5 sìla-ta kuš si-ga 2 dug-šagan dùg-gan igi-kár Lú-dingir-ra šagina ... ki A-a-kal-la-ta kišib Dingir-ra. Seal of Dingir-ra / dub-sar / dumu Lú-ga.

(69) BPOA 1 522:10–11. Umma; Šu-Suen 2/viii.

1 udu Du-ú-du [ra-ga]ba$^{?}$ lú é Lú-dingir-ra šagina-šè im-gin-na; also igi-kár sukkal-mah (line 2) and igi-kár Šag$_4$-kug-ge šagina (line 4).

The general Šagkuge was associated with the Umma province. See Steinkeller 2013: 391. His presence in the city of Umma at that time was likely connected with the construction of Šara's temple. The same was probably true of the chancellor as well (who is referred to in this source).

(70) AnOr 1 163:1–13. Umma; Šu-Suen 2/v–ix.

[...] 2 sìla eša 3 sìla [zíd] šu-a gi-na iti RI-ta ud 26 zal-la-ta iti ^{d}Li$_9$-si$_4$ ud 5-šè eša-bi 0.3.1 8 sìla zíd-bi 0.4.5 7 sìla sá-dug$_4$ ki-sá-a gìr Lú-dingir-ra šagina kišib énsi-ka.

(70a) BPOA 1 1353. Umma; Šu-Suen 2/–.

2 ^{dug}saman$_4$ ^{kuš}dùg-gan kuš si-ga uš é ^{d}Šára-ka ki gá-ra ki A-kal-la-ta kišib Lugal-nir. Seal of Lugal-nir / dub-sar / dumu Ur-^{d}Šára / pisan-dub-ba-ka.

(70b) UTI 4 2594 = UTI 5 3239. Umma; Šu-Suen 2/–.

1 gú níg-U.NU-a siki ùz gu dím-e-dè é ^{d}Šára-ka-šè ki Ur-^{d}Šul-pa-è-ta kišib énsi-ka. Seal of A-a-kal-la, énsi Umma^{ki}, dedicated to Šu-Suen.

(71) UTI 3 1837:1–9. Umma; Šu-Suen 2/–.

0.1.0 zíd-sig$_{15}$ 0.0.5 5 sìla eša 0.1.5 zíd-gu 0.1.3 ninda šu$^{?}$ 1 sila ì-dùg-nun-na 1 sìla làl [s]ig$_{5}$ é ^{d}Šára-ka temen-aš si-ga ki Lú-kal-la-ta kišib Lú-^{d}Nin-šubur. Seal of Lú-^{d}Nin-šubur / dub-sar / dumu Dùg-ga / sabra ^{d}Šára-ka.

(72) TCL 5 5680 iii 29–32, v 25–vi 1. Umma; Šu-Suen 2/–.

2.1.3 ésir-é-a gur kug-bi 6⅚ gín gi-KWU-844(É×ŠÚ) ù kid é ^{d}Šára-ka-ke$_{4}$ ba-ab-su-u[b] kišib Lugal-[...] ... 0.0.2 al-la-ha-ru kug-bi 1 ⅓ gín$^{!}$ túg IM gal ^{d}Šára-šè kišib ra-ra Lú-^{d}Nin-šubur 4 ma-na eren kug-bi ⅓ gín 12 še 8 ma-na šu-úr-me kug-bi ⅔ gín 24 še 8 ma-na za-ba-lum kug-bi ⅔ gín é ^{d}Šára temen si-ga kišib Lú-kal-la.

gi-KWU-844, a reed object of some kind, appears also in Text 5 xii 2. The reading and meaning of KWU-844 are unknown.

(73) BPOA 1 732:5–11. Umma; Šu-Suen 2/–.

2 gada gin 1 gada sag-gá 4-kam-ús é ^{d}Šára-ka temen si-ga ... ki Ì-kal-la kišib énsi-ka.

(74) BPOA 7 2244:1–4. Umma; Šu-Suen 2/–.

10 gú ésir hád da uš 3-àm ba-ra-ab-du$_{8}$ šag$_{4}$ é ^{d}Šára-ka kišib Ur-e$_{11}$-e. Seal of Ur-e$_{11}$-e / dub-sar / dumu Ur-nìgin-gar.

(75) BPOA 7 2206:1–7. Umma; Šu-Suen 2/–.

3 ½ sìla ì-nun dùg-ga 5 sìla ì-giš dùg-ga igi-kár Lú-dingir-ra šagina Ur-^{d}Šul-pa-è-ra níg-ŠID-a ba-an-na-zi mu dub ^{d}Šul-gi-uru-mu tùm-da-šè kišib Ur-^{d}Šul-pa-è. Seal of Ur-^{d}Šul-pa-è / dub-sar / dumu Lugal-kug-ga-ni.

(76) TIM 6 48. Umma; Šu-Suen 2/–.

1 ⸢x$^{?}$⸣+3 ^{giš}ásal
2 ugula Da-da
3 50 lá 1 ^{giš}ásal
4 ugula Zé-lu-uš-^{d}Da-gan
5 30 lá 1 ^{giš}ásal
6 ugula A-hu-ni
7 6 ^{giš}ásal
8 ugula Hu-un-^{d}Šul-gi
9 mu má ^{d}En-ki-ka ba-ab-du$_{8}$
10 682 (or 1,212) ^{giš}ásal

(space)
11 šu-nígin 1,434 ^{giš}ásal giš-ùr$^{!}$ hi-a
12 giš é ^{d}Šára$^{!}$
13 gá-nun-na$^{!}$ ku$_{4}$$^{!}$-ra

A record of 1,434 poplar roof beams, which were harvested in Umma's forests (see Text 50) by the workforce led by four military commanders: Dada (the general of Zabalam), Ṣilluš-Dagan, Aḫuni (son of the sukkal-mah Aradmu), and Hun-Šulgi (the general of the city of Umma).

For the identities of the individuals appearing here, see Steinkeller 2013: Appendix, commentary to Text 1.

(77) Forde 1 3. Umma; undated – year Šu-Suen 2 based on Text 76.

1 720 ^{giš}ásal
2 tir Giš-gi-gal^{ki}
3 360 tir GAR-ša-na^{ki}
4 ugula sukal-[mah]
5 240 tir ⸢x⸣-[...]
6 ugula Nu-úr-^{d}Šu[l-gi]
7 180 tir Gir$_{13}$-giš^{ki}
8 ugula Hu-ba-a
9 120 tir Ti-im-KU.KU
10 ugula I-ti-Da-gan
11 240 tir igi NAG-su^{ki}
12 ugula Lú-^{d}Nanna
13 360 tir A-kun-NE
14 ugula Igi-an-na-ke$_{4}$-zu
15 360 tir A-kun-NE
16 ugula Zé-lu-uš-^{d}Da-gan
17 240 tir É-lugal
18 ugula Hu-un-^{d}Šul-gi
19 240 tir Ti-im-KU.KU
20 ugula Da-da

A record of 2,700 logs of poplar, which were harvested, in eight forests of the Umma province, by the chancellor Aradmu (who also served as the general of GARšana) and eight military commanders: Nur-Šulgi (general of Uṣar-dagi), Huba'a, Iddin-Dagan, Lu-Nanna (general of NAGsu), Igi-Anakezu, Ṣilluš-Dagan, Hun-Šulgi (general of the city of Umma), and Dada (general of Zabalam). Of those, Hun-Šulgi, Ṣilluš-Dagan, and Dada appear also in Text 76.

The eight forests mentioned here belonged to the complex of thirty forests that were managed by Umma' Forest Sector. See Steinkeller, 1987a. For the identities of the individuals appearing here, see Steinkeller 2013: Appendix, Commentary to Text 2.

The restoration of the forest's name in line 5 is uncertain. The first sign could be either Š[u- or D[a-, yielding alternative restorations (tir) Šu-na-mu-gi$_4$ and (tir) Da-gu-na/ma.

(78) AUCT 2 307:2–4. Puzriš-Dagan?; Šu-Suen 7/iii.

1 12.2.3 še gu[r]
2 á má hun-g[á] še 150.0.0 gur
3 0.5.0$^?$ GA AR SAR M[A$^?$]
4 é-amar é-^{d}Šára^{ki}-šè
5 kaskal-bi 25 da-na
6 da-na-a á še 1.0.0 gur 1 sìla-ta
7 ki Lú-dingir-ra-ta ba-z[i]
8 iti šeš-da-k[ú]
9 mu ^{d}Šu-^{d}Suen [lugal] Úrim^{ki}-ma-k[e$_4$]
10 ma-da Za-ab-ša-li^{ki} mu-hu[l]

For an edition and discussion of this text, see Steinkeller 2010: 378–379.

4.

Building Larsa: Labor-Value, Scale and Scope-of-Economy in Ancient Mesopotamia

Seth Richardson
The University of Chicago*

Prospect

The working group at Hirschbach met to address a set of comparative historical questions about how ancient labor (often, a rubric for mass or forced labor) was compelled or procured in ancient economies. This paper will interrogate some of the premises for those questions themselves, by way of an econometric exercise. What are the grounds for assuming that coercion or inequality (political, social, or economic) should be the determining theoretical problems for research? Are either social and legal degrees of "unfreedom" or political and economic inequality the crucial explanatory forms to seek out and examine? In what other contexts of political economy could ancient mass labor be understood? What tools can we use to think about the largest possible formal representations of the ancient economy, given the massive methodological and documentary challenges presented by the sources?

* This essay was helped immeasurably by advice and input over the years from Benjamin Foster, Steven Garfinkle, Cornelia Wunsch, J.-L. Huot, Stephanie Rost, Piotr Steinkeller, Benjamin Studevent-Hickman, Marc Van De Mieroop, and Magnus Widell; both Stephanie Dalley and Tina Breckwoldt shared some of their unpublished work with me. I am particularly indebted to Carrie Hritz, whose ideas made portions of this analysis possible (see nn. 140, 144). All errors are, of course, my own.

Abbreviations used in this essay include: AbB I = Kraus 1964; AbB II = Frankena 1966; AbB IV = Kraus 1968; AbB IX = Stol 1981; AbB XIII = van Soldt 1994; ARM 26/2 = Charpin *et al.* 1988; ETCSL = The Electronic Text Corpus of Sumerian Literature (http://etcsl.orinst.ox.ac.uk); *FI* = Civil 1994; RIMA 2 = Grayson 1991; RGTC 3 = Groneberg 1980. Other sigla follow CAD.

Our interest in "forced labor" mischaracterizes or ignores political ideologies of consensualism in early states and their mutually supporting feedbacks. (Unless otherwise qualified, the term "forced labor" in this paper refers to all forms of labor which were compelled by extra-economic means, and where the consent of the laborer was of secondary importance.) Forced labor arose as a topic for modern research in the first place because it was mostly mass labor which was ever necessary for states to document in antiquity—thus the sources for it are relatively plentiful—and so produced source-mimesis. Beneath this, however, lies our very modern assumption that labor is fundamentally a social and economic disutility; our everyday understanding of value itself is a realized market price minus deprivation of costs, labor being chief among them.[1]

My argument is twofold: one, that the social and political benefits of community labor were *perceived* as shared rather than coerced in antiquity (notwithstanding the probability of unequally shared benefits) and labor investment as something other than a deprivation or disutility; two, that the *scale* of mass-labor projects deliberately and programmatically obscured (then as now) the fact that they were economic products of distinctly minor importance relative to dispersed labor inputs in the larger economy. The very success of monumental architecture in persuading ancient populations of the power of the state has been equally successful in persuading modern scholars of state-labor's essential character as both compelled *and* economically important, thus reifying in modernity a set of political relations first propagated in antiquity (as ARM 26/2 238 puts it, "Kingship is his brickmold and (his) dynasty is his wall."). Correspondingly, the low-status and spatially dispersed farming work which formed the backbone of the Mesopotamian economy left few traces in the archaeological record, and had less of a role to play in state ideology. To us, farming seems an essential but quotidian part of ancient economic life—important but, frankly, boring.[2]

Why does monumental architecture fascinate us? City-walls, temples, and canals, were projects with high public profiles, but exceedingly low costs within the scope of the larger economy (approximating a "Gross

[1] See the distinction made by Giampietro *et al.* 1993: 230–31 of productivity as constituted both by work accomplished and "costs" such as time, energy consumed, wages paid, *etc.*

[2] Arguing for the centrality of agriculture, Rothman 1994: 150 wrote: "Irrigation agriculture and to a lesser extent pastoralism were the bedrocks of economic life for the state institutions of palace and temples as well as for all other sectors of society .... agriculture is *the* most critical economic enterprise in the society as a whole."

State Product" or the like). Even assuming certain production bottlenecks, these costs were in fact so low that we should assume that compulsion would normally have been not only unnecessary, but counterproductive to the larger ideological goal of mass-labor, which was to construct the imagined community of the city-state through participatory enactments of authority and compliance,[3] and the complementary social goals of individuals to build self, identity, and status in relation to other groups. Through the case studies below, I will demonstrate that formal economic analysis can prove this.[4] The econometric utility of one of the most consistent, emic standards of Mesopotamian valuation, the labor-day, offers a formal structure leading to a more authentic index of value than prices and wages for the ancient economy. Before diving headlong into my historical analysis, however, it is necessary to contextualize it within theoretical positions about economic value in classical economics, the study of ancient economics, and their relation to one another. Readers who wish to skip ahead to the experiment may go to p. 261.

Scale, Value, and Scope-of-Economy

In modernity

One of the most intractable problems in ancient economics is the question of scale; one of the most durable questions in modern economics is the problem of value. Of the vast number of documented transactions we have at our disposal from Mesopotamian antiquity, not one is uncompromised by some question of its originary social circumstance, its repre-

[3] Bretschneider *et al.* 2007: 1 recognized precisely these social capacities of monumental architecture (and similarly Uziel 2010): "By making particular use of the natural landscape and the artificially created environment, the monumentality of public buildings helped to improve social cohesion and legitimated a particular societal system. Moreover, their intergenerational use gave such buildings great potential for communication and remembrance, especially during specific ceremonies"; see now also Baker 2014. The works in the volume, however, more or less assume the monumentality of associated labor-costs; for instance Ristvet 2007, though eschewing monumentalism as an index of power (p. 198), and even estimating low labor costs likely required for Tell Leilan's wall (pp. 200–201), nevertheless writes that the building of the wall "would have required a massive mobilization of labor" (p. 203).

[4] In this sense, "formal" denotes the econometric use of express values for the analysis of economic practices which may have intersected with the sphere of textuality and accountability (*e.g.*, with tablets, tokens, seals, *etc.*)—or not. The evaluation of irreduceably physical, embodied or socially-embedded economic phenomena (*e.g.*, labor, material, utility) is of course the problem that characterizes the so-called "transformation problem."

sentativeness, or its importance relative to the wider economy. How can we defend or question in economic terms what "a lot" or "a little" really is? Big and small numbers may be big and small numbers, but without context or comparison, their importance is impossible to evalute. Beyond this, inequalities (social, economic, political, and legal), transaction costs,[5] and institutional imperatives[6] lay behind many commercial exchanges without having been specified in the documents themselves. Even assuming that some given contract or administrative document did not obscure socially-embedded conditions—that the text more or less "said what it meant"—our ability to compute the value of one GÍN of silver, one BUR of field, or one GUR of barley is still entirely lost amidst our inability to determine those products' relative value in the context of the volume problem—its place relative to production, exchange, or use. "Values" are not figures we are simply unable to compute for lack of data or ancient systems of valuation—on occasion, there are plenty of comparanda—but they are figures for which we are unable to establish a sense of scale relative to the aggregate of value realized outside of the restricted scope of a formal and usually institutional economy.[7]

For many neo-Classical modern schools, value was identified as the expression of pricing and market mechanisms. For scholars of neo-Marxist and other substantivist schools, on the other hand, the exclusive realization of value through exchange was part of an (ultimately political) deception which deliberately obscured the real and fundamental source of value, which was labor. Substantivists produced a diversity of theoretics, emphasizing "that there is no autonomous category 'economy' as a separate sphere of social life in precapitalist societies,"[8] while classical economics provided more methodologically consistent avenues of research by relying on values derived from exchange contexts.[9] But labor remained difficult to analyze—primarily because most of its economic volume was embedded outside of the formally documented market, but also because where labor *did* appear in texts, it was *de facto* undervalued.[10]

5 North 1984; Michael Smith 2004:78, 92.

6 Steinkeller 2004a; Jursa 2004.

7 For considerations of the value problem, see Grewal, forthcoming, and Papadopoulos and Urton, eds. 2010.

8 Gledhill and Larsen 1982:198.

9 *Ibid.*, 197–200, however, point out that even Polanyi imagined socioeconomic integration primarily arising from acts of exchange rather than production.

10 Englund 1991.

The quest for a "substance of value" stretches back to the early modern period. A brief sketch of its importance and theoretical range helps to situate why I privilege labor-time as the critical working method for my study, and what that implies about other approaches and results. The issue of value formed the irreduceable point from which many schools of early modern economic theory argued. The mercantilist ethos of the pre-classical modern period, for instance, privileged commerical trade surpluses and bullion reserves as the substance of value. Quesnay and the physiocrats, meantime, championed agricultural production and land as primary to establishing value. At the later, Neo-classical turn, Smith posited the "natural price" generated by the "invisible hand" of the marketplace as the ideal manifestation of value. A generation later, Ricardo countered with his critical "labor theory of value," which was subsequently renovated by Marx, who identified labor as the "sole substance" of value.

Common to these otherwise opposed conceptions of value was a predisposition to see of labor itself as a disutility or deprivation of other natural goods, *i.e.*, that labor itself was an opportunity or sunk cost relative to value, and *de facto* its opposite. Even Marx only hoped to restore labor's standing as a preeminent index, identifying an "immanent measure" of labor value in addition to a conception of it as value's "sole substance." This remained a thorn in the side of later Marxist theory, and some neo-Marxists found the idea not only logically inconsistent (Boss 1986, Mongin 1989, Smith 1991), but utterly dualistic in not answering the so-called "transformation problem" by which labor-value is revalued in the marketplace. Others, however, chose to see "immanence" as a mere formal articulation of an otherwise immutable essence (Pilling 1986), especially those following Sraffa, committed to the analysis of "equilibrium prices," "value-forms" valid only within particular economic systems (Fine, 1986).

"Value theory" has gone on to have a life of its own in several other disciplines, from sociology to environmental science to philosophy. The term remains as protean as its interlocutors, but we can usefully distinguish between discussions about "moral goods" (*e.g.*, the debate about "personhood" echoing through a half-dozen and more fields) and "natural goods," those which are economic, if in a rather wide sense of the word. Some of the latter conversations consider environmental inputs as the ultimate substances of economic value—from biophysical human energy and work physiology (Giampietro *et al.* 1993, Rappaport 1971), to environment as a "public good" (Holland and Cox 1992, Weaver 1994), even to solar inputs and total embodied energy (*i.e.*, the concept of "emergy," see especially Brown *et al.* 1995, also Garrod and Willis 1999). These econometrics, using the total environment as the delimiting scope (*i.e.*, hereafter meaning the "boundary") of the economy, clearly represent a widespread effort to incorporate substances-of-value well outside the reach of the formal, documented economy.[11]

Despite these continuing efforts to define a substance of value, the study of economic systems remains closely allied in both the academic and public imagination with formal evidence and analysis.[12] To this extent, modernist views about the ancient economy have largely prevailed in Assyriology where research itself is largely defined and bounded by work with documents.[13] "Economies," in this modernist articulation, are nearly the same thing as the documentary systems which represented them. My essentially Sraffan exercise locates "equilibrium prices" in the form of labor-time units, and thus does not have to contend with the transformation problem at all, since its measures are explicitly comparable in original (that is, emic) and equal value-forms.[14] The critical contribution of the methodology is that it avoids the incommensurability of ancient formal and substantial metrics. More optimistically, it may claim—either by dint of being culturally local or, objectively, the true basis of value—to be a more accurate and relevant basis for evaluation than artificial values in silver[15] or barley.[16]

[11] One 1997 study (see Zimmer 2014) was able to estimate the economic value of world ecosystems at $33 trillion—twice the amount of the GNP of every country in the world. On the Roman economy and an excellent statement of the theoretical problem, see Scheidel and Friesen 2009; within ancient Near Eastern studies, the Oriental Institute's MASS project, pioneered by Tony Wilkinson, comes closest to a model of the total environment as the basis for economic life. See now especially Wilkinson et al., eds., 2012.

[12] See Warburton 2006: 15–16 on the tendency to circumscribe what constituted the ancient economy.

[13] Englund 2012.

[14] Labor-time does, however, carry a transformation problem in the valuation of labor by time rather than, say, actual biophysical inputs (see Giampietro, *et al.* 1993) or any external metric of actual work achieved. Nor can there be much doubt that the administrative abstraction of labor-time itself, as Englund 1991 has argued, was created by and for the benefit of institutions. Neither of those factors, however, has much bearing on the labor-day unit's comparability in assessing relative "equilibrium prices."

[15] See van Driel 2002.

[16] *Contra* Walters 1970: xix, who believed that "wages in silver or barley can be converted into work-days, from work-days into volume of earth, and from volume into canal dimensions" (cf. Kozyreva 1988: 204, who argues that the term KAR at Larsa was meant to become a universal conventional valuator).

Concerning antiquity

In ancient Near Eastern studies, the use of the formal economic textual evidence which at first seemed so promising came under fire in two distinct phases. In the 1950s and 1960s, Karl Polanyi among others[17] argued for the primacy of traditional economic forms which relied on value-indices outside the scope of documentation—a substantivist position. Village economies of reciprocity, they argued, were unlikely to have produced any documentary apparatus (and therefore witnesses/precipitates) in the first place, let alone those employing the accounting methods created by urban institutions to maintain their non-egalitarian social orders. Neither these systems nor these standards would have been of much use to the non-urban populations of Mesopotamia, and so the majority of the economic world is quite simply hidden from the eyes of the modern scholar. Critics of the Polanyites, for their part, seized on an early iteration of the theory in which it was asserted that markets were non-existent in Mesopotamia[18]—a position retracted by Polanyi himself more than thirty years ago now.Too often this reductionist view has been used as an excuse to ignore or develop any robust research scheme for the study of the undocumented economy, the central concern of the substantivists.

Both substantivism and its detractors now seem long in the tooth compared to the more recent approaches of scholars who aim their second-phase critiques at the shortcomings of the evidence which *does* exist. These scholars argue that the very ability and intent of texts to represent phenomena external to themselves is fatally hampered (in terms of objectivity) by the conventions of the scribal system itself.[19] It can be doubted, according to this view, whether the accounting system itself was semiologically geared to represent a set of facts so much as an idealized realm of institutional practices and relationships, principally those of domination and subalternity. For example, Englund has noted that institutional

This is too optimistic a view, in my opinion, of what accounting systems can represent of value; such statements confuse "conversions" with the transformations of value which formal systems accomplish. That the sophisticated and consistent mathematical and accounting systems worked in their own terms must be acknowledged (see especially Powell 1990), but this does not mean that they were neutral representations of economic reality.

17 See especially Steinkeller 2004a.

18 *E.g.*, Silver 1983; cf. Kirk 2007: 184–88, with a more nuanced look at Polanyi's contribution; and see now especially van der Spek *et al.* 2015.

19 *E.g.*, Englund 1991; Glassner 2003; Steinkeller 2004a.

accounting assumed both a 360-day working year and a normal complement of "time off" ($U_4.DU_8.A$);[20] and that worker credits were calculated by real performance, whereas debits were produced by performance norms rather than by, say, overdrawals on real goods such as wages or rations.[21] Studying Egyptian texts, Janssen noted that although labor costs were sometimes expressed as part of the value of objects in exchange, the fact that this was not done systematically rendered its expressions enigmatic.[22] Where Polanyi had questioned the scope of writing's accounts of the external world, these scholars questioned the nature of writing itself as a system strictly concerned with accountability.

Of course, substantivists have been particularly at pains to assert their model through research because they work with so little textual data to begin with. These scholars must turn for evidence to anthropological models and ethnoarchaeology comparanda, but their studies remain theory-rich and data-poor. They can suggest, but not prove, especially in the kinds of ways formalists would want to see. Could the purely theoretical observations of substantivists be integrated with formal analyses into a picture of the unified, whole "economy" that we all suspect exists as some external reality?[23] An opportunity arises in returning to uses of "form" and "substance" closer to an Aristotelian meaning, distinct but not exclusive terms connoting *process* and *content*. In such a sense, historians

[20] Englund 1988: 126f. and 1991: 275–77, citing Ur III examples of time off calculated at rates between ⅕ and ⅒.

[21] Englund 1991: 258–59, 263–64, 276, 280; he thus argued that the accounting use of labor-time functioned not as a neutral, value-free system of accountability, but as a site of exploitation since "the expected labor performance was in all likelihood simply beyond the capabilities of the normal worker," and noting that "a very large majority of known Ur III accounts result in a deficit" which compounded over time. I am aware that others disagree with this view (*e.g.*, Robson 1999; Walters 1970: 153, opined that it was unclear whether the chief purpose of the archive he studied was to track labor performance [*i.e.*, the obligations of people] or project management [*i.e.*, the canal work]. My opinion is that that the institutional bias of the accounting system, whether accidental or deliberate, is already evident in the fact that institutions preferred it, and that any system of valuation is inherently arbitrary (and thus its "accuracy" or "neutrality" is impossible). The solution to this argument, however, is simply not relevant to my conclusions which compare two products in terms of the same institutional valuations. If I were to insist on an institutional bias that *was* crucial to my argument, it would be in the geographic dispersal of the majority of value and the concentration of a particular minority of it.

[22] Janssen 1988: 15.

[23] Cumberpatch 2001; see also Hansen 2006, on "shotgun" demography.

of economic antiquity need not choose between "formalism" and "substantivism" as mutually opposed theoretical camps, but must recognize the dual usage of "formal" as referring to both the corpus of economic documentation and the analytic methods used to study them.

Between these two types of criticism, every published analysis based on economic data (outside the protective, almost quasi-magical authority of archival studies) runs the risk of being criticized as either a) documenting only the minority of the economy visible in texts, unintegratable within any wider economic tableau, or b) reproducing and magnifying a series of positivist fallacies about data, even misunderstanding the inner nature of economic documents themselves (which then invariably seem to turn out to be about something other than economics altogether). Thus in ancient Near East studies there arose a long standoff on accepted methodology for economic analysis.[24] The debates of the 1950s–1960s too often cast (consensual) reciprocity and (coerceive) redistribution/markets in early state communities as mutually exclusive systems. The resulting theoretical stalemate produced sometimes cartoonish images of an antiquity populated by either Polanyi-esque networks of harmonious, neighborly small households or a grim succession of increasingly powerful palace estates imposing malign and parasitic economic demands on their host populations, with a few isolated historical episodes of private enterprise. The critiques of the 1980s–1990s then deflated both those stances as reifying tendentious and self-interested economic and administrative genres (yes, "genres": the texts' subject matter do not excempt them from being read as a literature of a kind). Today most scholars see these methodological concerns as responses to different, but overlapping sectors of the ancient economy as it undoubtedly existed: different systems coexisting within segmentary early states, sectors whose relative importance waxed and waned in any given political epoch, though some excellent work has been directed towards breaking past a merely accommodationist position.[25]

24 *E.g.*, Pearson 1957: 8, arguing that any opposition of an *oikos* to a market system was a false one: "The question is how were these elements of economic life institutionalized to produce the continuous goods and person movements essential to a stable economy?"

25 *E.g.*, Cumberpatch 2001 and Kirk 2007. See now Grewel (forthcoming) specifically on the analysis of ancient valuation systems outside of exchange and use contexts, including discussions of Douglass North's location of value in institutional contexts. It has otherwise been assumed that the overall trend, from the fourth to first millennia BC, was a gradual marginalization of reciprocal exchange systems and communitarianism.

This tacit and practical compromise arose precisely because no proponents of any perspective were ever able, with even the best-documented ancient economy at hand (undoubtedly that of Mesopotamia between ca. 2500–1500 BC), to support or debunk the substantivist argument through *formal, quantitative analyses*. Thus the debate—long on theories, short on methods—settled into its dotage on a note of methodological insufficiency. And indeed the methodological obstacles are legion: Mesopotamian texts document only a specific subset of economic activities; only elite and urban concerns are recorded; mechanisms for valuation are more absent than present; the accidents of recovery do not permit us to know what fraction of the formal data we possess anyway—the list of problems is seemingly endless.

This study uses an input-output model for a specific, local, and bounded ancient city-state economy, that of Old Babylonian Larsa, in order to define the first-order problem of measuring scope-of-economy (something like GNP). I will reconstruct the relative value of two major economic projects in Larsa—annual barley production and the construction of the city wall—by employing labor-time as the unit of comparative value. Labor-time has several advantages as a metric: for one thing, it is emic to these Babylonian social economies, which routinely used—even preferred—this method of valuation and accounting to prices and wages. Second, where our textual record has gaps, the data is reconstructable from a wealth of other sources, from cuneiform texts to modern biometrics in order to establish dependable *minimum inputs*. Third, since it results in statements of relative value (if this is not already redundant), it renders a true *order of magnitude* for different sectors of the economy, to give a proportional sense of what "social embeddedness" we ought to be looking for in contextualizing the formal economic data we see.

The economic events used in this study privilege labor-inputs as the common valuator for economic products. Since this valuator was, in fact, an central feature of Mesopotamian accountancy—*i.e.*, an explicitly formal economic expression—it is surprising that labor-time has not, as yet, itself been the subject of much theoretical study. We have in labor-time a cliometric tool with the capacity to reveal the determining balances of production, by gross volume-share, in the ancient economy. I do not intend to cast substantivism as "the big picture" and formalism as an overly narrow view, but the results do strongly argue for seeing the undocumented, substantial economy as the locus of most economic value, demonstrating the validity of Polanyite claims about the non-formal rural economy as the overwhelmingly dominant system within which other systems of exchange and use were secondarily formed.

Cliometrics and Case Studies: A First Attempt

This origin of the present project lay in a 1997 student paper about the Neo-Assyrian imperial economy. Though that study depends too much on unsecure data, it still serves to illustrate my larger project, and warrants a brief description here. Wanting to illustrate an argument about the secondary importance of Neo-Assyrian palace-building within the larger fund of labor commanded by the imperial center, I made a thumbnail sketch of the claims of Aššurnaṣirpal II about his Nimrud palace workforce and compared them to subsistence provisioning for all imperial forces.

The claims of royal inscriptions, of course, must be used with utmost caution as any approximation of fact, but we can make a virtue of one of their worst vices by assuming that Assyrian royal rhetoric typically amplified (rather than reduced) the amounts of manpower used for these projects. That is: labor-value estimates made by royal sources were either accurate or inflated, but never minimized. This being the case, we can argue that labor-value estimates are always equal-to-or-greater-than, but never less-than, what such sources claim. Aššurnaṣirpal was relatively specific in his claims about the dates, sizes, and origins of deportee labor forces specifically expropriated to Kalḫu for building work—from the 1,200 Zamuan troops (ERÉN.MEŠ) deported in his Year 3 (881 BC) to the 3,000 captives (*šallātu*) from Bīt-Zamāni and Šubrû in his tenth campaign (probably 866 BC).[26] One could even assume that other deportations in those same fifteen years not specifically earmarked for Kalḫu also ended up there for building work: from the 332 troops of Nirbu in Year 3 to 3,000 captives from the city Udu in the tenth campaign.[27] Assuming that all those people from eleven deportations worked from the time of their deportation to the completion of the Kalḫu palace in Aššurnaṣirpal's Year 18, one would come to a staggering figure of more than 49 million labor-days invested on the building of Kalḫu. That is a big number; but it is an aggregation across a fifteen-year period of time, averaging 3.2 million labor-days per year. That is still a big number of some kind; but what was the scalar value of that number in the wider economy?

What if we compare that value to another product representative of the imperial economy, the labor value of basic subsistence rations for the

26 RIMA 2, *passim*; also: 3,050 from Suḫu and an unknown number from Sirqu (Year 6, 878 BC); 500 form Laqû (Campaign 7, probably 877 BC); 2,500 from Bīt-Adini (Campaign 8, 876 BC); unknown numbers from "Ḫatti" and Patinu (Campaign 9, 875 BC).

27 *Ibid.*; also: 300 troops from Bāru (Year 3); fifty Dirru troops, 2,000 captives from Arbakku, and 2,000 more from Ḫanigalbat (all Year 5).

Assyrian army and other support personnel? Supposing, as has been proposed, that the number of troops Šalmaneser III claimed to have fielded in his fourteenth year was not the actual size of his army, but was instead a number which roughly comprised all Assyrian imperial personnel, from the *turtānu* on down to the youngest groom to curry a donkey in Tušḫan. The minimum annual caloric value required to support a workforce of this size, at a mere (starvation-level) 1,000 kilocalories per man per day, would be 43.8 billion kilocalories. What labor-value was necessary to produce this raw energy? Assuming a surplus production rate of 2,142 kilocalories per man per day (*i.e.*, after subtracting the thousand kilocalories a farmer himself would need), one comes to about 20.5 million labor-days needed simply to sustain Assyrian forces and personnel at the *most* basic subsistence level.

Starvation-level support of Assyrian personnel already required more than six times the labor of palace-building annually. By this sketch, the annual economic cost of symbolic and occasional monumental architecture in the imperial metropole was clearly inferior to the annual and geographically dispersed costs for the most minimal subsistence—provisioning for imperial forces spread throughout the territories of the empire. In terms of gross labor-value, we can say that the imperial economy was primarily concerned with investment and expenditure *throughout the periphery* (perpetuating or promoting inequality and underdevelopment in the periphery, an underdevelopment argument), and only secondarily and for symbolic purposes concerned with draining capital from the periphery to the center (the dependency-theory model). This finding is consonant with a theoretical postulate that high or late (*i.e.*, post-reform) imperial states normally operated for the benefit of their territorial systems as a whole, and not primarily for the benefit of the core, because at some point the gross political inequality of producers to consumers would require readjustment.

Getting to Larsa: A Second Attempt

The results of this first experiment were interesting and promising for the study of value within orders-of-magnitude. But the variables involved were simply too numerous to gain a stable read on precisely *how* inferior investments in monumentality were. In particular, I was uncomfortable in relying on royal inscriptions as an almost exclusive textual data source for building work. It seemed natural in a next phase to think of research targets which offered a broader array of documentary types, and the Ur III and early Old Babylonian periods came quickly to mind for their bountiful quantities and varied types of written records concerning labor. Among many choices, Old Babylonian Larsa eventually presented itself as a superior case study for its coincidence of rich historical, administrative, *and* archaeological evidence on exactly the kinds of products I wished to compare.

Two economic products from the Old Babylonian city-state of Larsa will be my points of comparison in the remainder of this paper: I will make two estimated valuations of labor-value, first in that city's perimeter wall, and second in its annual barley harvest. Several bodies of evidence make such a study feasible and more convincing than the Neo-Assyrian case. On first glance, the most advantageous texts for the Larsa case might also be its royal inscriptions, which recorded several episodes of the rebuilding of the city wall, often in tandem with explicit (if idealized) delineations of wages paid to project workers and/or the prices that set these wages in some economic context. This dataset superficially seems tailor-made for accounting. But a study of those price-and-wage schedules makes it quickly apparent that they reflected neither market conditions nor even economic capacity. These were idealizing documents aimed at political persuasion, not the documentation of economic reality.[28] The royal inscriptions only really become useful in their characterization of the social setting of economic regulation—in their rhetorical equation of standards with public happiness.

But four other lines and aspects of evidence provide opportunities for research and create a set of checks and balances on each other. First, we can first note the basic fact of historical coincidence: that the Larsa city wall and its barley harvest were products created in the same historical environment—in the same population catchment, in the same period (roughly the 19th/18th centuries BC), and that these products were both abundantly documented. While we can point to potentially superior amounts of information for single projects from other Mesopotamian corpora (say, the labor-texts from Umma or GARšana,[29] or the still-standing (in gross terms) ziggurats of Ur, Choga Zanbil, and Babylon,[30] or the better-documented floor plans of Larsa temples and palaces), few such projects are known from both texts *and* surviving physical remains.

28 Richardson 2012; Scheidel 2010.

29 On Garšana, see Owen and Mayr 2007; Kleinerman and Owen 2009; Heimpel 2009. On Umma, see van Driel 2000, Steinkeller 2007a and 2012, Adams 2008.

30 Woolley, 1939; Ghirshman *et al.* 1994; George 1995.

Yet in the case of Larsa, we have some site-specific administrative, historical, art historical and archaeological information about both farming and building at this time and in this place. No one source of data is beyond reproach in its own right, but the diversity of textual genres allow us to check normative figures against real production and vice-versa, the existing fragments of wall permit us to grasp the basic scope of work, and so forth. Also helpful is the fact that Larsa lies squarely within the boundaries of an intensive landscape survey, latterly supplemented by satellite survey, so we have a better-than-average ability to compare textual and archaeological evidence for the city-state's settlement system and thus its productive capacity.

Second, Larsa's wall and barley crop were manifestly the major products of their respective economic sectors, of civic-works and agriculture. This is not to say that other types of products were insignificant: many other buildings, of course, were built and many other canals dug, many other crops grown and animals raised. Taking the correspondence of just one Larsa official—a certain Bēlšunu—as an example, agricultural administrators could be responsible for not only barley, but wood, wine, dung, flour, malt, beer, vegetable oil, ground peas, hides, grapes, leeks, garments, house-building, land claims, sesame, and wool.[31] And building work entailed not only city-walls but canals, temples, gates, fortresses, warehouses, food-processing and -storage facilities, institutional residences for priests and priestesses and, lest we forget, palaces. But the sheer size of barley harvests and city walls establishes their dominance within their respective sectors: no piece of architecture was anywhere near as large as the city wall (consider, for instance, that it was large enough to have kept 40,000 of Hammurabi's troops at bay for six months), and the product focus of state records on barley is overwhelming.[32] In short, we do not really have to wonder whether Larsa's city wall was its largest piece of civic architecture or whether perhaps the city was in fact devoting more labor to animal management or some other form of primary production.

Third, the cuneiform record shows that Larsa's administrators not only had familiarity with, but regularly used labor-time as an accounting tool for both types of work. The administrative apparatus of the city not

[31] AbB IX nos. 20, 28, 51, 58, 85, 99, 103, 137, 142, 274, and 275.

[32] Rothman 1994: 160: "[T]he subject of the state records we actually have is almost always barley seed and returns in barley." Barley formed the backbone of the state's in-kind tax, with quantities of other products lagging far behind. In the case of the wall, the only other piece of civic architecture to receive so much attention in Larsa's royal inscriptions and rebuilding episodes was the Šamaš temple, but this structure was much smaller.

only used these evaluative methods, but the metrics were cross-applicable for individual tasks in each area, *e.g.*, earth-hauling labor rates used to evaluate agricultural canal-digging were similar to those used for building ramparts, *etc.* Crucially, these accounting devices show up in different phases of project management—normative labor-time rates show up in mathematical texts or ideal figures,[33] in projected manpower estimates, in balanced accounts comparing work expected versus work performed (U$_4$ versus U$_4$ ZAL-LA-ŠÈ),[34] even in semi-narrativized form, in almanacs such as the *Farmer's Instructions.*[35] For many types of work represented in these projects, we can actually see the evaluation of labor time proceed from theory to estimate to final accounting in the ancient record, and beyond into the cultural lexicon. Of course, this does not certify the metric as infallible—as Englund has argued, the scribal use of labor-time "acted at once to simplify calculations and, collaterally, to increase the state's demands on labor"[36]—only to say that its application (and degree of error) was roughly isometric across different types and stages of work. Moreover, not only do we have the widespread use of the metric, we also have a large array of data documenting labor-time for most of the same tasks associated with wall-building and farming.

Fourth, we are extremely fortunate in the ancient scribes' choice of labor-time as the primary unit of value because it is naturally bounded at its maximum limit. Not only does labor-time provide methodological consistency over wages or commodities as equivalent forms, and a common framework for theoretical questions about substance-of-value, it has the practical benefit of restricting focus to inputs and outputs with technological and environmental boundaries. This is not to say that intensive production might not, say, temporarily increase ancient labor outputs by some percentage, or that certain organizational dynamics might lessen labor inputs through efficiency measures to some degree. But barley-farming and mud-brick building are types of work which have essentially changed very little over the millennia, especially relative to the mercurial inputs of the market. Labor costs might inflate or deflate by 25 per cent,

33 *E.g.*, Goetze 1962: 13–15, that the rate of removal of wet earth evaluated by labor-time used in Ur III texts—10 GÍN per man-day—"is exactly [the] figure which is given in Old Babylonian mathematical texts"; also Walters 1970: 148.

34 Englund 1988: 126–27, suggesting that such figures were typically inflated by modest amounts (ca. 10%), thus reflecting the self-interested nature of accounting by institutions *vis-à-vis* their workers.

35 Civil 1994.

36 Englund 1988: 124.

but they would not—could not—do so by 1000 per cent, as prices might. Not only is the metric relatively stable, it permits a reconstructibility through analogy and experimental archaeology[37] that is impossible to carry out for prices, markets, or use contexts.

Thus, though this paper makes every effort to do due diligence to specific accounting data, it is in the end the methodological stability of a labor-time approach, relative to other types of formal analysis, that provides a convincing result. Above all, it is important to bear in mind throughout that this is an experiment of *proportion*:[38] I am not seeking absolute and historically-reconstructable labor figures specific to, say, the 1912 BC building of the Larsa wall by Gungunum—a figure for the sake of a figure. How much work is a "lot" of work, anyway? A comparative model reflects my original contention that values only begin to attain meaning in comparison to other values. In isolation, values are impossible to isolate in economic terms. Many scholars, of course, have made heroic efforts to document the labor, price, or value of individual commodities or projects in antiquity, but though they may establish process and form, such studies cannot define their findings in terms of economic scale or scope. My goal is to assess the proportion of value between two archetypal economic products and consider the broader implications of those relations.

To emphasize another important aspect of my experiment: I will deliberately skew the evaluation in favor of an assumption that monumental architecture represents "a huge amount of work." That is, *for the purposes of argument*, I will consciously inflate the value of labor inputs for the city wall and underestimate the amount of labor invested in barley production; I will assume that construction was as hard as we might imagine, and farming was as easy as we might think. Since (to be clear) my goal is to demonstrate that monumental architecture is actually economically cheap—and therefore ideologically efficient—I want to show that the methodology stands up against interpretive bias. Therefore, countervailing assumptions about end value will be coded into this work

[37] Perhaps the most successful such enterprise recently is documented in the lavishly illustrated and consummately scholarly work of Seeher 2007. This project carried experimental archaeology to its logical conclusion by actually building sixty-five meters of ancient city wall using mostly ancient and native building materials and techniques. Indeed, all of the building steps I mention here and more are discussed in this work; my discussion is stripped down to assess value rather than building as such.

[38] On parametric modeling, see, *e.g.*, Jongman 2000.

to show that, even given the benefit of the doubt, barley farming is in reality a far larger economic product than civic-architecture on an order of magnitude of twenty times or more. I will make explicit as I go along just how and where these assumptions affect my calculations, in the interest of keeping contact with real costs, but absolute numbers are not my real quarry here; magnitude estimates are.

Historical Background

Before we get down to accounting, let us set the historical stage. By the Old Babylonian period, Larsa was already among Mesopotamia's oldest cities. The oldest settlement remains there come from the ʿUbaid period (sixth millennium BC) and continue through the Uruk period and beyond. Larsa's symbol was among the repertoire of the so-called Jemdet Nasr period "city seals," testifying to its political stature at an early date. Large teams of Larsa workers appear on texts from Early Dynastic IIIa Šuruppak, and the city's independent political status may perhaps be implied by its mention in a list of oaths sworn to major gods in the period's most famous monumental text, Eanatum's "Stele of the Vultures." The city's fortunes waned over the succeeding centuries, as Akkad and Ur came to the fore,[39] and Larsa did not re-emerge from relative obscurity until the late 20th century BC under the leadership of Gungunum, the first king to record the construction of the city's wall. Larsa then flourished for more than a century and a half until it fell to Hammurabi's forces in 1763. The city then maintained an uneasy existence as a subject city for a generation until the revolt of Rīm-Sîn II,[40] whereafter evidence for occupation at the site becomes spottier. Some Kassite remains and references testify to the town's continued existence,[41] but Larsa really only re-emerged as a center of any importance towards the middle of the first millennium, when it played some role in the political and military history of imperial states.

Larsa's heyday was clearly the early Old Babylonian period.[42] The first phase of this epoch was characterized by continuous tensions between Isin

39 Fitzgerald 2002: 6f.

40 Charpin 2004: 319–24, 337–43; Charpin 1991.

41 A *kudurru* of Nazimaruttaš (ca. 1300 BC), for instance, seems to refer to Larsa's city wall (Arnaud 1972b: 163–69). Dunham 1990: 350 notes that the neo-Babylonian walls of Larsa's Ebabbar temple were in one area directly atop Kassite and perhaps even Ur III foundations, pointing towards a disposition to re-use older lines; see also Frayne 1990: RIME 4 2.13.19 (p. 238) on the redeposition of foundation tablets at Larsa.

42 See Steinkeller 2004b on Larsa's political history in this period.

and Larsa, resulting in the gradual expansion of the Larsa state to include about a dozen middle and lower Babylonian cities. Finally, Larsa took control of Isin in 1793, only thirty short years before Larsa itself fell to Babylon.[43] Despite its regional successes, Larsa was hardly internally stable: during this 170-year period, Larsa had seven changes of dynasty, and underwent at least two openly political revolutions, those of Nūr-Adad, who assumed power around sixty-five years after Gungunum came to the throne,[44] and of Kudur-mabuk's sons, Warad-Sîn and Rīm-Sîn, who took the throne thirty years after the Nūr-Adad coup and ushered in a period of political contact with Elam. None of these dynastic shifts may be said to have substantially altered the geographic integrity of the Larsa city-state, an issue which has much to do with the assessment of its productive capacity undertaken below. The state generally grew over time, with few territorial losses, including the development of a kind of second capital at Maškan-šapir. This northern reach of the state was closely tied to the Emutbal tribe, to the Kudur-mabuk "dynasty" (Kudur-mabuk occupied a position at this city while his sons ruled at Larsa), and to Elam.[45]

Perhaps the single-best documented event in the city's history, however, was its siege, conquest, and occupation by Hammurabi of Babylon. Aided by the king of Mari, Hammurabi brought something fewer than 40,000 troops to the walls of Larsa for six months, prevailing over Larsa's apparently superior forces.[46] Word was eventually sent to Zimri-Lim, the king of Mari, that "... the weapon of the wicked and of the enemy is broken. The city of Larsa is fallen."[47] Yet despite the construction of a ramp intended to breach the city walls, it appears that the city primarily

[43] Van De Mieroop 1993: 57, quoting the famous Mari letter that "ten or fifteen kings ... follow Rīm-Sîn of Larsa"; *ibid.*, p. 49, that texts dated to Rīm-Sîn are known from six subject cities (Larsa, Girsu, Kisurra, Kutalla, Nippur, and Ur), while Isin, Umma, Uruk, and Zabalam were probably also under his control.

[44] Van Dijk 1965: 5–7, 13: Nūr-Adad claimed that Larsa had been conquered by an unnamed enemy, and that its canals had been obstructed and its gate blocked; the city revolted against its king (presumably Sumu-El) and elected Nūr-Adad, "taken from amongst the crowded multitude"; he then drove out the strangers and opened the city's great gate; *cf.* Charpin 2004: 103; see also Adams and Nissen 1972: 48–49; Dalton 1983: 82–83.

[45] Steinkeller 2004b; Van De Mieroop 1993: 50.

[46] Charpin in Huot *et al.* 1989: 194.

[47] ARM 26/2 386 and 379 & note d: the reports discuss Hammurabi's troops in terms suggesting it to be "en nombre inférieur" to the 40,000 at Rīm-Sîn's disposal.

fell because it ran out of food;[48] one Mari letter elegaically described the fallen city as prostrate—cast down—a ruined place where people "shelter their cows and sheep within their houses."[49] The wall of Larsa was then systematically demolished (ARM 27 158). The extent of the destruction seems to have been absolute, despite later references to fields located near the city gates and even Middle-Babylonian references to a city-wall; but the nearly complete absence of standing wall in the archaeological record testifies to a fairly thorough destructive event.[50]

Despite the destruction of its wall, however, Larsa was not subjected to the treatment Mari later received—a wholesale destruction of palace and city.[51] Instead, Hammurabi directed the kind of attention to Larsa that made clear his intention to govern it: he carried out restoration work on the Ebabbar temple,[52] made offerings there,[53] and installed himself briefly in its palace;[54] documents from the city in those early post-conquest years bore a new series of Hammurabi's year-names, independent of his Babylonian ones. More importantly, Babylon installed its own officials in Larsa, responsible for the reorganization of taxation and production; their instructions were to "determine the state of the spirit of the population"[55] and proceed with a redistribution of land, probably to reward Babylonian colonists and collaborators with the new regime. There

48 ARM 27 156, ll. 6–10: people fleeing the city reported "instead of grain, there is (only) straw"; note, however, that some crucial parts of the text have been restored for this translation.

49 ARM 27 158 and 161.

50 According to Huot *et al.* 1989: 40, evidence for Larsa's wall is "completely missing today, with the exception of a few rare traces visible above the ground." Against this, see AbB IV no. 1 and Arnaud 1972b: 163–69. References to gates, however, are not inconsistent with the individual baked-brick towers and piers which survived to today.

51 Hammurabi may have been imitating the magnanimity of Rīm-Sîn, who claimed to have spared the lives of the inhabitants of Isin when he conquered it in his thirtieth year.

52 Frayne 1990: RIME 4 3.6.13–14 (pp. 349–51); the years of this work are uncertain, however, and unfortunately Hammurabi's inscriptions contain no discussion of prices, wages, workers, or process.

53 Van De Mieroop 1993: 60, pointing to records dated Hammurabi 31 of sheep offerings to Šamaš of Larsa.

54 Van De Mieroop 1993: 60, citing ARM 27 158.

55 Frayne 1990: RIME 4 3.6.13–14 (pp. 349–51), inscriptions of restoration work and 3.6.2017 (p. 369) for a seal of one of his officials; Van De Mieroop 1993: 60 cites texts dated as early as Hammurapi 31 for offerings at the Ebabbar. Birot 1993: 263 (referring to ARM 27 157) specifies that Hammurapi's residence was in the city of Larsa.

is every indication that Hammurabi's intent was to rebuild the city's prosperity. The cornerstone of this effort was his enactment of a debt-annulment edict in the first year following the conquest.[56] The Babylonian king's letters display concern for the restitution of lands of Larsaeans improperly redistributed in the wake of the conquest,[57] mitigating political conflict, and for continuing various maintenance and repair projects to irrigation works which Rīm-Sîn had begun.[58] Ellis and Buccellati have each voiced concerns about the possible "irregularity" of economic information from the immediate post-conquest period (with especial reference to the Šamaš-ḫazir archive), but the former, at least, concluded that Hammurabi's changes "seem to be primarily ... in personnel, and in intensity of organization," rather than in any punitive actions or radical restructuring of the economy.[59]

The Work and the Site

Building Programmes

The political history of the city is more than incidental to the economic forms we wish to study; in that context, let us have a closer look at the types of work under consideration. First, the building: for the most part we can consider Larsa's production of civic architecture to have formed a relatively stable set of obligations, with some expansion in its construction of defensive walls as its territorial power grew. To go by Larsa's year-names recording monumental architecture projects, we can point to fourteen episodes of wall- or fortification-building, twenty episodes of canal-excavation, and seventeen episodes of temple-building carried out within

[56] Charpin 1991: 71; Birot 1993: 263; Ellis 1976: 44–45 followed Kraus in understanding the edict to have honored a pre-existing edict of Rīm-Sîn's, presumably promulgated for the jubilee of his sixtieth year.

[57] *E.g.*, AbB XIII no. 13, in which a man attempts to claim ownership of a "squat" which he has been working on behalf of another person (despite his existing possession already of another tax-field of 5 BÙR); cf. AbB IV no. 1, in which Hammurabi instructs Šamaš-ḫazir to award land to an individual at the gate of Larsa.

[58] AbB IV nos. 3 and 57; no. 80 specifies work needing completion at the "mouth of the canals," the KA ÍD.HI.A— the region of the troublesome villages of Pi-Naratim (KA ÍD.DA.MEŠ), whose conquest was celebrated in Sumuel 8, Sîn-iqišam 2 and Rīm-Sîn 15; see Richardson 2012: 18–20.

[59] Ellis 1976: 12: "our [post-conquest] evidence may be coloured by circumstances arising from that conquest, so that it might not really be representative of the period"; also pp. 21 and 44–45 n. 60 (cf. Buccellati 1972: 151–52).

the 140 years between Gungunum's accession and Rīm-Sîn's thirtieth year, when his year-names left off with the recording of annual events; in all, roughly fifty "major," celebrated projects.[60] In terms of royal building obligations, we are looking at something like a major building project celebrated once every three years by the Larsa kings. Of course this is no more than a heuristic device: more projects were carried out than were celebrated in the year-names alone (including construction episodes of the Larsa city-wall itself, some of which we know from other sources), and some of these projects may have been either re-buildings (*e.g.*, Rīm-Sîn's rebuilding of Larsa's Inanna temple) or partial projects (*e.g.*, Gungunum's construction of a gate at Ur, as against Warad-Sîn's reconstruction of Ur's entire city-wall). Unsurprisingly, the majority of urban building took place in Larsa itself (ten projects), with fewer projects at Ur (four),[61] Maškan-šāpir (three), and Zarbilum (two).[62] About a dozen other places in the kingdom were the focus of single building events, both cities (Adab, Eridu, Kutalla, Zabalam) and non-urban sites (Iškun-Nergal, Iškun-Šamaš, and Ka-Geštinanna).

The balance of the state's city-wall constructions kingdom-wide were at the site of Larsa proper. No fewer than five major building episodes of Larsa's city wall were part of its steady construction program, undoubtedly along with many minor repair and augmentation projects. For military architecture outside of the capital, Larsa first fortified Ur in the very south, and then Dunnum, Šarrakum, and Maškan-šāpir, all along the north-eastern reaches of the Tigris. Only in Rīm-Sîn's time did Larsa give attention to militarizing the western border of the Euphrates, just when that king was opening up the eastern part of his kingdom to new cultivation.

Agricultural production

Larsa's agricultural production seems to have expanded to a greater degree over this same period, through the opening of new canals, the reclamation of old farmlands, and the acquisition of territory through conquest. The area of land in the kingdom under primary production was obviously not all only in the vicinity of Larsa (*i.e.*, in the many villages within its local settlement hierarchy), but also surrounding Larsa's many subject cities, which at various points included Eridu, Ur, Bad-tibira, Uruk, Girsu,

60 Van De Mieroop 1993: 67 notes that we have virtually no evidence outside the year-names for building at Ur in the second half of Rīm-Sîn's reign, either.

61 See Frayne 1990: 236–37 (RIME 4.2.13.18) on the size of bricks and bastions.

62 Dalton 1983: 202–203.

Zabalam, Kisurra, Šarakkum, Adab, and Maškan-šāpir.[63] At Larsa, some portion of land was under institutional control, chiefly by the palace, but also by temples,[64] although the latter are not abundantly documented.

Palace land was sometimes under the control of specific high officials: in Rīm-Sîn's time, this included such men as Ṣilli-Šamaš, Sin-eriš, Nanna-imaḫ and Sin-magir;[65] under Hammurabi, the reins were handed over to officers such as Šamaš-ḫazir and estate supervisors such as Bēlšunu.[66] Crown units are perhaps the best-documented types of land under production, and we are privy to evidence that some of these units produced hundred of thousands of liters of barley every year. It is exactly this body of textual documentation which makes our evaluation of minimum barley production possible. Nor did the work associated with barley end with production: storage and redistribution were also major Crown obligations as barley was collected and expended throughout the kingdom.[67] As Stol concludes in his study of "State and Private Business in Larsa," the central government "was interested in only two commodities: barley and silver";[68] it seems clear that the production of surpluses or reserves of these commodities was an institutional goal.[69]

There were also individual producers, including tenant farmers with either in-kind or service obligations (*i.e.*, *šukussu*- and *ṣibtum*-fiefs). Such holdings were sometimes subsets of the larger Crown estates, but they could also be located elsewhere in the kingdom (and more unevenly documented). We know less of true freeholders, since they came into

[63] Van De Mieroop 1993: 54 Fig. 1 shows thirteen cities under Rīm-Sîn's control; compare with the famous Mari letter (discussed p. 57) which enumerates Rīm-Sîn's vassals as "ten or fifteen kings."

[64] *E.g.* OECT XV 126: 14, locating land in the A.GÀR *a-ḫi-bi* É [d]UTU.

[65] For Ṣilli-Šamaš, see, *e.g.*, AbB I 90, IX 94 (dated Rīm-Sîn 2) and 110, TCL 17, YOS 5 181; Sin-eriš, YOS 5 209; Sin-magir and Nanna-imaḫ, TCL 10 28 and Riftin 54, *etc.* For earlier examples, *e.g.*, see the letters of Nūr-Adad concerning barley deliveries and production, AbB IX 23, 56, and 91. Compare with the men identified in Text No. 9 discussed by Westenholz 2006: 123–29 as the LÚ.GIŠ.GU.ZA.(MEŠ) ("chair-bearers"?).

[66] The correspondence of Šamaš-ḫazir is too voluminous to cite in full here, but see now the newer texts of YOS XV 24–37; for his correspondence with Bēlšunu see, *e.g.* AbB IX 20, 28, 51, 58, 85(?), 99, 103 and note a, 137, 142, 274–75; see also Frayne 1990: RIME 4 3.6.2018 (p. 369), the seal of one of Hammurabi's officials at Larsa.

[67] Goetze 1950b: 94–95.

[68] Stol 1982: 141.

[69] Breckwoldt 1995/96.

contact with the textuality of institutional orders less frequently and systematically. If I am not engaging in circular reasoning, the documentation seems to diminish in direct proportion to lower institutional control and geographic dispersal (on the distribution of cadastral and harvest yield data by toponyms, see below).

Finally, we can point to individual economic actors whose roles were more complex or interstitial than categorical terms such as "private" or "institutional" might suggest—men such as Balmunamḫe, who seemed to have their fingers in every corner of the economy (in immoveables, in staples, in craft production, in tax collection), often profiting by converting commodities through marketing into the silver and barley the palace wanted. Some have preferred to see such actors as fundamentally institutional actors who employed market instruments to achieve their ends;[70] others have cast them as essentially independent profiteers capitalizing on a particular niche in the economy between institutions and markets.[71] I have no interest in claiming at the outset that one or another sector of production was predominant, though my conclusions have necessary implications on the question; here, I only emphasize the diversity and co-existence of institutional and non-institutional mechanisms of production and exchange. This diversity puts in context that barley production and consumption was a larger and more complex economic sector than that of monumental architecture.

Studies of Larsa

Finally, I must very briefly sketch the history of Larsa studies. The city and area of Larsa were first investigated in earnest by Parrot in 1932, whose general description of the urban layout was reproduced in many future campaign reports. To paraphrase: Larsa was an immense oval, roughly 2 km measured North to South and 1.8 km measured East to West, with an occupied area totalling about 190 hectares, rising about 7 meters above the alluvium, with occasional low "buttes" rising as high as 11.5 meters; on the southeast periphery of the site was a mound dubbed the "Chameau" (18.5 meters high), and, most prominently, in the interior, were the ruins of the Ebabbar, with the remains of the ziggurat

[70] *E.g.*, Dyckhoff 1998: 123, on *Palastgeschäfte*.

[71] See Garfinkle 2005; Van De Mieroop 1993: 67 argued that, among other reforms, Rīm-Sîn attempted to put "provinicial entrepreneurs … out of business" in a bid to centralize state power.

standing at 22 meters in height.[72] Parrot did not return for a second campaign until 1967,[73] at which time he decided to concentrate work on the Ebabbar temple, as later described by Huot:

> Larsa is an enormous site, on the scale of the great agglomerations of its neighbors (Ur and Uruk, for example). Without attaining the gigantism of Uruk, the ruins of Larsa measure 1.5 km in diameter. With such a vast surface as this, the urban study required recourse to aerial photography, [the results of] which are at the present time inaccessible. For these reasons, the mission has preferred to concentrate its efforts, for the past ten years, on the exploration of a sole building, the most important in the city, the sanctuary of the god Šamaš .... to trace the history of the Ebabbar is to trace the history of the city.[74]

Aside from this focus on the Ebabbar, only very small forays away from the temple were ever hazarded. Margueron excavated the palace and the ziggurat adjacent to the Ebabbar in the third campaign.[75] In the fifth campaign, he assigned Huot a test trench nearer the center of the mound, and another trench was sunk to the south-west of the Ebabbar, in the "artisanal zone," but these endeavors were never as intensive as the work at the center of the mound.[76] From Calvet's fifth campaign onwards, the Larsa excavation team would focus almost entirely on the temple mound.[77] Only with the full clearance of the temple in the mid-1980s could Huot begin to speak of excavations in the larger *intramuros*—but no subsequent expedition accomplished this due to the changing political situation.[78]

Extramurally, another set of relevant investigations were the areal surveys of Robert McC. Adams; were it not for this mapping of the larger area, any attempt to estimate the size of the city-state's production catchment would be largely theoretical, reconstructed from textual documentation without the hope of linking it to evidence on the ground. Adams'

[72] Parrot 1933; in 1968: 3–4, he worried that "l'immensité de la ville ... laisse perplexe lorsqu'on y doit commencer le travail"; see also Frayne 1990: RIME 4 2.9.5–6 (pp. 162–66) on Sîn-iddinam's construction of the Ebabbar.

[73] Parrot, *ibid.*, estimated the city circumference at about eight kilometers; a later estimate (Huot *et al.* 1989) made out a perimeter of 5.1 kilometers and an urban area of around 190 hectares, obviously a rather great disparity.

[74] Huot 1985: 309–11.

[75] Parrot 1968: 262, 268.

[76] Margueron 1971: 271, 285–86.

[77] Calvet *et al.* 1976; the campaigns of the late '70s to late '80s focused on later, Neo-Babylonian and Parthian reconstructions of the temple.

[78] Huot 1987b: 37.

survey already identified almost four dozen settlements in Larsa's hinterland (*i.e.*, closer to Larsa than to any other city). These surveys have, a generation later, been confirmed, corrected, and mapped onto sites visible on CORONA and other satellite images of the region, which have added information about numerous small sites. The specific function of these settlements remains unknown, but the range of sizes suggests differentiated use.

Finally, we should make mention of a few crucial works which have contributed to the study of Larsa's economy from cuneiform texts. Several text editions (with commentary) must be included here, such as Grice (1919), Faust (1941), Kozyreva (1988), Arnaud (1994), Dalley (2005), and especially Birot's thoughtful editions of (1969). Ellis' (1976) study of state agricultural practices remains relevant in some respects;[79] Walters' (1970) analysis is still an important consideration of work standards and practices, despite Stol's (1971) determination that the case-study site was Lagaš rather than Larsa; the unpublished dissertation of Tina Breckwoldt (1994) not only took a bold stab at understanding grain production, storage, and distribution at the level of the whole system, but helpfully gathered together many of the relevant documents in transcription and translation; Fitzgerald's (2002) unpublished dissertation on Larsa also stands as a useful background work. From these texts and analyses come many of the working nuts and bolts for this present study. A great deal of supporting evidence has been appendicized to facilitate ease of reading; readers wishing to ground their understanding in the details should avail themselves of the charts and notes following the main text.

Case Study One: The City Wall of Larsa

Dates of construction

To figure out how much labor-value went into the wall, we have to begin with a history of the object. From Larsa, forty-seven year-names record fifty-one separate construction projects; a partially overlapping corpus of about four dozen royal inscriptions also mention building work.[80] From these sources, we can identify five episodes of building or repairing the city wall of Larsa, only three of which appear to have been full-scale building projects.

[79] Mostly for discussion of production processes than for hard facts and figures; cf. Stol 1982.

[80] See especially Frayne 1990: RIME 4 2.5.3 (pp. 117–18), 2.6.2 (pp. 124–25), 2.8.7 (pp. 147–49), 2.9.11–13 (pp. 171–75), and 2.13.18–21 (pp. 236–43); see also CUSAS 17 44–50.

The first claim to have built the Larsa wall was made by Gungunum in 1912 BC, documented in brick-inscriptions and his twenty-first year-name, the former elaborating: "in the course of one year he made the bricks and built the great wall of Larsa named Utu-kibale-sadi ('the god Utu overtakes the rebellious land')."[81] It is impossible to know whether Gungunum meant that he built the wall anew, or merely repaired an existing wall. As Civil has noted, terms describing work often "do not make an explicit distinction between tasks being done for the first time and for subsequent enlargements or reconstructions ..... [for instance] the verb DÙ 'to build' in the royal inscriptions, where it can mean 'to build for the first time,' but also 'to rebuild.'"[82]

It would be hard to believe that Gungunum's wall was entirely new, top to bottom. But even if Gungunum were merely repairing an existing wall, it was probably not very old, and primary construction may have been in the not-too-distant past. Larsa played an exceedingly small role in third millennium political history, with little to suggest that it had ever wielded military power; mostly it was a place with a modest temple establishment and a healthy agricultural capacity.[83] Isin's early year-names do not suggest that Larsa was a military enemy until late in the 20th century BC, when inter-city warfare begain to gain momentum in the region[84]— and Larsa year-names only seem to begin with Gungunum in any event.

81 Brick-inscriptions: Frayne 1990: RIME 4 2.5.3 (pp. 117–18); Arnaud 1972a: 34 and ns. 2–3, noting that the unusual expression of time taken to both assemble materials and finish building (ŠÀ.MU.DIDLI.KA SIG$_4$.GA / Ù BÀD.BI MU.DÙ) was reprised by Sîn-iddinam for work on the Ebabbar (Frayne 1990: RIME 4 2.9.6 [pp. 164–66]: "I baked its baked brick in the course of one year"); see also the temporal phrase in Abi-sare's inscription. It is difficult to know if the use of the phrase marks it as an unusual expression of a usual pace of work, or as an unusually fast building episode.

82 Civil 1994: 110; cf. rarer cases in which walls were said to have been "restored" (BÍ-IN-GI$_4$-A; Warad-Sîn 11, the city wall of Šarrakum) or a "wall [which] had not been built for a long time" (U$_4$-NA-ME BÀD-BI NU MU-UN-DÙ-A; Rīm-Sîn 28, the city wall of Zarbilum).

83 Fitzgerald 2002: 6–14; the only work known to have been done at Larsa by the Ur III dynasty was a renovation of the Ebabbar by Ur-Namma; Huot *et al.* 1989: 32; Frayne 1997 (RIME 3/2.1.1.35, exs. 7–9).

84 Following the wars fought in the reign of Išbi-Erra (years 4, 8, 16, and 27 = 2015–1992 BC), no Isin year-name again mentioned a military conflict until the year Lipit-Ištar "i," at least 58 years later and roughly coincident with the accession of Gungunum. Išbi-Erra did record the building of Isin's city wall in his twelfth year (2007 BC), however, and this wall was rebuilt five times: by Šu-ilišu (Year 7 = 1979 BC), Išme-Dagan (ca. 1940, Frayne 1990: RIME 4 1.4.5 [pp. 31–32]), Enlil-bani (ca. 1850, *ibid.*, 1.10.2–3 [pp. 78–80]),

The next known episode of work at the Larsa wall probably dates to only a dozen years later, in 1901 BC, when Abi-sare recorded in his fifth year-name that he "dug the ditch of the rampart," ¹⁷*ḫirītum* BÀD LARSA[ki]-MA BA-BA-AL. This is probably to be connected to a brick inscription in which he stated that, "in the course of one year" he "strengthened" (*eli ša … udannin*) the great wall at Larsa.[85] Indeed, if Gungunum's work on the wall was only a dozen years before Abi-sare's, it seems probable that the latter did not do much more than finish off or maintain recently completed work.[86]

Nūr-Adad made the third claim to building Larsa's city wall in a year-name (year "i") about forty years later. Unfortunately, because this king's year-names remain unordered, we cannot fix an exact date for the work. Excluding his first two years, both identified as accession years (*i.e.*, years 1 and "a"), the work could have been accomplished anytime between 1863 and 1850.[87] The work was also memorialized in a royal inscription. After characterizing the wall as "like a mountain range in a pure place," Nūr-Adad wrote:

> In order to establish my name forever, I determined the holy perimeter of this great wall (and) named it Utu-umani-sa-bindu ('The god Utu had achieved his triumph'). By the true judgement of the god Utu, I counted among the ruins the wall of the city … with which

Zambija (ca. 1837, *ibid.*, 1.11.1 [p. 92]), and Damiq-ilišu (Year 13 =1804 BC; cf. *ibid.*, 1.15.1 [pp. 102–103). Though Isin's wall seems to have survived the Babylonian assaults celebrated in years Sîn-muballiṭ 17 and Hammurabi 7, it is less clear whether it survived Rīm-Sîn's assault, since Samsuiluna subsequently claimed to have "restored" it (Dalton 1983: 178; she also believes the wall to have predated Išbi-Erra). See also Fitzgerald 2002: 10 on Isin's military record as early as the Sargonic period. Although Isin's record of building seems superior to the Larsa case, virtually no excavation work was undertaken by B. Hrouda to locate that city-wall (see reports in *Iraq* 35, 37, 38, 41, 47, 49, 51 and 53); Hrouda 1973: 192 reported only that no part of the mound was higher than 8 m off the surrounding plain, a fairly low site compared to Larsa with its remaining gates and features such as the "Chameau," at 18.5 m high.

85 Frayne 1990: RIME 4 2.6.2 (pp. 124–25): here the wall is also called Utu-kibale-sadi; Abi-sare also claims in this inscription to have "built the palace of his settlement"; caution is noted as the translation is a conflation of two broken exemplars.

86 Abi-sare's work on the Baba canal, recorded in royal inscriptions, was probably also a continuation of Gungunum's excavation of that canal in his penultimate, twenty-seventh year-name; Dalton 1983: 56, 69; Sigrist 1990: 12.

87 Frayne 1990: 147 has argued that the alternate name for the wall-building year was MU-ÚS-SA É [d]EN-KI; cf. Sigrist 1990: 22–23.

> I had joined battle. I made its (inhabitants) who did not submit bow down at the feet of the god Utu, my lord. I restored there the boundary of the god Utu, my lord.[88]

The inscription does not explicitly mention a wall-rebuilding—only the delineation of its "holy perimeter" (TEMEN-KÙ)[89]—but it seems probable that it alludes to rebuilding work following the revolt through which Nūr-Adad took power. In the course of that revolt, Nūr-Adad had "re-opened" the city gate which had been "barred."[90] If it is correct to associate these events, we should probably see his work taking place closer to 1863 than 1850, soon after his accession; I will use a conventional date of 1860.

Only a generation later, in 1837 BC, Sîn-iqīšam celebrated the rebuilding of the Larsa wall in his third year-name. Unfortunately, although Sîn-iddinam before him left lengthy descriptions of wall-building episodes at Ur and Maškan-šāpir in the previous decade, Sîn-iqīšam left no such detailed commentary—just the brief claim that the work was done.[91] Following this, the only other mention we have of building work at the Larsa wall was made by Kudur-mabuk, who reports having "opened the great gate in the wall of Larsa."[92] Larsa, of course, in subsequent years built city walls at Ur (Warad-Sîn 10), Šarrakum (Warad-Sîn 11), Iškun-Šamaš (Rīm-Sîn 10), Iškun-Nergal (Rīm-Sîn 13), and Zarbilum (Rīm-Sîn 28)—and two large gates at Maškan-šāpir (Rīm-Sîn 7). Still, this was a tepid pace of military preparedness: in the year-names following the last building of the Larsa wall, when Babylon built at least sixteen major fortifications, Larsa had built only six.[93]

88 Frayne 1990: RIME 4 2.8.7 (p. 149); Steinkeller 2007b: 224–26 distinguishes ḪUR.SAG, "mountain range," from KUR, "mountain," against Frayne's translation here and in other cited cases, *passim*. Also against Frayne, see Steinkeller 2004c: 136, where he understands not "I determined the holy perimeter of this great wall," but "I embedded holy foundation inscriptions in that great wall."

89 Frayne 1990: RIME 4 2.5.3 (pp. 117–18), 2.8.7 (p. 149); the significance of the renaming of the wall from Utu-kibale-sadi is unknown; it may have "rebranded" the wall as his work and/or identified an altered or enlarged footprint of the wall. Again, cf. Steinkeller 2004c: 136.

90 Van Dijk 1965: 5–7, 13.

91 Sigrist 1990: 28.

92 Frayne 1990: 209–20 (RIME 4.2.13.6 ll. 10–13); on his building at Ur, see Dalton 1983: 190. Unless the fortifications built in years Rīm-Sîn 10 and 13 were in the immediate neighborhood of Larsa, this is the last we hear of defensive building within the city-state environment altogether.

93 Years Apil-Sîn 1c, 2, 5, 12, 16, Sîn-muballiṭ 1, 7, 10–12, 15, 18 and Hammurabi 19, 21, 23, and 25.

It is more the quality than the quantity of information the Larsa inscriptions provide that makes the site a good case study. In addition to our ability to date the building episodes, Larsa's royal inscriptions sometimes include statements about (idealized) wages and prices, construction methods and schedules, and the relative scale of projects (*e.g.*, "I made it higher than before"). Also, like temples, stele, divine weapons and other sanctified objects, city walls in this period bore names, such as Utu-kibale-sadi or Nanna-suḫuš-mada-ĝenĝen, a practice which alerts us to the perceived status of the walls as agents; they were endowed with both anthropomorphic attributes (*e.g.*, the gates had "heads") and supernatural qualities beyond what mere baked bricks carried.[94] As Steinkeller has pointed out, these attributes are further reflected in the fact that city walls of this period, like temples, were commissioned by the gods themselves, and supplied with foundation deposits and inscriptions.[95]

A variety of epithets also provides a window into both the physical appearance and aesthetic reception of the walls; a sampling of these from Larsa inscriptions includes:

- The great wall, which like a mountain range raised high cannot be touched, which comes forth on its own accord …
- I asked [Nanna about] … reinforcing its supporting wall, about making its foundation greater than it had been previously.
- Like a verdant mountain I caused [the wall] to grow up there in a pure place. I lifted its head … I caused it to shine forth splendidly …
- In the course of that (year) five months had not passed (when) I baked its bricks. I finished that great wall and raised up its parapet.
- I chose the place for my royal foundation inscription in its foundation, (and) raised the head of its gate there. I made its fosse strong, circled it with bricks, (and) dug its moat.[96]

Such descriptions shared the poetics used for temples—they were pure, they shone like silver, lightning, or lapis lazuli, were covered in greenery; city walls were piled up like cloudbanks,[97] rose like mountains, to heaven, untouchably splendid. Their analogs were natural, precious, and uncreated by man. This is hardly the place for a full analysis of such phrases; here it

94 See further Bretschneider, *et al.* 2007.

95 Piotr Steinkeller, personal communication.

96 Frayne 1990: RIME 4 2.13.18–21 (pp. 236–43); Sigrist 1990: 35; Dalton 1983: 200, quoting Warad-Sîn's boast that the wall at Ur "could not be tunneled" (cf. Frayne 1990: RIME 4 2.13.20 [p. 240]).

97 *E.g.*, Gilgameš and Agga (ETCSL 1.8.1.1, l. 39): BÀD GAL MURU$_9$ ÚS-SA-A-BA.

is enough to point out that the visible and public nature of the structures under examination marks them as qualitatively different from other kinds of economic products, in communitarian and ideological terms. As Steinkeller has remarked, since Larsa was not itself so directly threatened militarily during the "long" nineteenth-century BC, the repeated wall-building "could not have been motivated solely by purely defensive considerations," but must have had much to do with a symbolic project designed to turn people from all over the kingdom "into 'Larsans'" (personal communication).

To sum up, we know of three major building episodes in the life history of the Larsa city wall, in 1912, 1860, and 1837—at intervals of fifty-two and twenty-three years—with smaller projects undertaken around 1901 and sometime in the early 18th century. The last event in the life of the wall was its death at the hands of Hammurabi in 1763 BC, a project which, no less than the building phases, involved some commitment of labor (see nn. 110, 184, below). Any undocumented routine maintenance or rebuilding would, of course, add to any tally of labor-value, but it is impossible to assess this unknown.

Size of the product: how big was the Utu-kibale-sadi?

How big was the wall? What we require first are workable measurements for all three dimensions of the object, to create a schematic plan, section, and elevation. Huot's original assessment of the potential for reconstruction was bleak: "[the wall is] completely missing today, with the exception of a few rare traces visible above the ground."[98] Notwithstanding, enough information remains to permit our particular over-estimate, archaeological, textual, and art historical. My final calculation assumes a wall 5.2 kilometers long, composed of two parts: a rampart of packed earth in the form of a trapezoidal prism, about 12 m high, a little more than 50 m thick at its base tapering to about 10 m thick at its apex, with a total volume of 1,934,400 m^3; and a fortification wall surmounting it, 6 m high and 10 m thick, about 312,000 m^3 of masonry exclusive of the major gates.

[98] Huot *et al.* 1989: 40.

[99] See Dolce 2000; Charpin, 1993; Heinrich and Seidl 1967; Müller 2001.

[100] A tablet published by Arnaud 1994: 11, no. 77 showing something like a city plan is too unlike Larsa to represent it: its area is less than a quarter the size of Larsa and represents more of a regular, rectilinear shape. With the prominent feature of the ramp in the plan, one might suggest it represents a city other than Larsa—perhaps a town, fortress, or *dimtu*-settlement.

How do I arrive at such numbers, inflated as they are? Let us take the dimensions one by one, beginning with the plan. Actual city plans are few and far between in the cuneiform record,[99] and none is known to exist for Larsa. Fortunately, a string of ruined gate piers still stand around about half of the city, from the northwest to southeast corners of the tell. Continuing clockwise, the remains of houses, streets, debitage, and brick scatters align along an arc for the other half, from the southeast back to the northwest corner, enough to provide the rough perimeter of the ancient wall. This reconstruction assumes these traces form the remains of one basic perimeter, though we cannot exclude the possibility that they are the remains of different walls (see, for instance, the above mention of a possible new layout by Nūr-Adad).

The reconstructed plan appears overlaying Huot's site plan in Figure 1a (next page); its segments and vertices are discussed in Appendix 1 (working clockwise from the northwest corner of the tell). The segments lengths tally up to 5,200 meters of wall, not taking into account the gates themselves. We have no way to confirm this estimate,[100] but the enclosed area conforms closely to the edge of the tell; the reconstruction is based on archaeological features found *in situ*, and happens to align very closely with the perimeter estimate of Huot *et al.* 1989 of 5.1 km. By way of comparison, the Middle Bronze city wall of Mari was around 5,970 m in length; Šubat-Enlil's lower town walls were around 3,700 m; Qatna's walls were about 3,980 m long; an unnamed rampart represented in a plan from Mari can be calculated at 4,021.5 m; the wall at Hattuša was 4,500 m.[101] Among Larsa's peer cities, a 5,200 m long wall was by no means unusual.

The width of the fortification walls is more difficult to work out, and the width of the rampart almost impossible. For one thing, we must engage with the knotty problem of distinguishing rampart from glacis from fortification wall.[102] For another thing, different types of fortification wall are represented in the archaeology. Segment A, for instance, with its parallel features, suggests a possible casemate or double wall, but this method of construction is not found among the five other visible segments of wall (C, D, E, F, or I).[103] We must proceed on the assumption that segment A is an anamoly in this regard. Yet another problem: only segment A preserves the full width of any wall feature (10 m thick per wall); thus, though the excavators were able to document the dimensions of the piers of large gates, 10 m is our only datum on a fully-preserved wall. This size

[101] Burke 2008: 175–76, 213; Charpin 1993: 197; see ARM 27 59.
[102] Burke 2008: 48–56.
[103] *Ibid.*, 61–63.

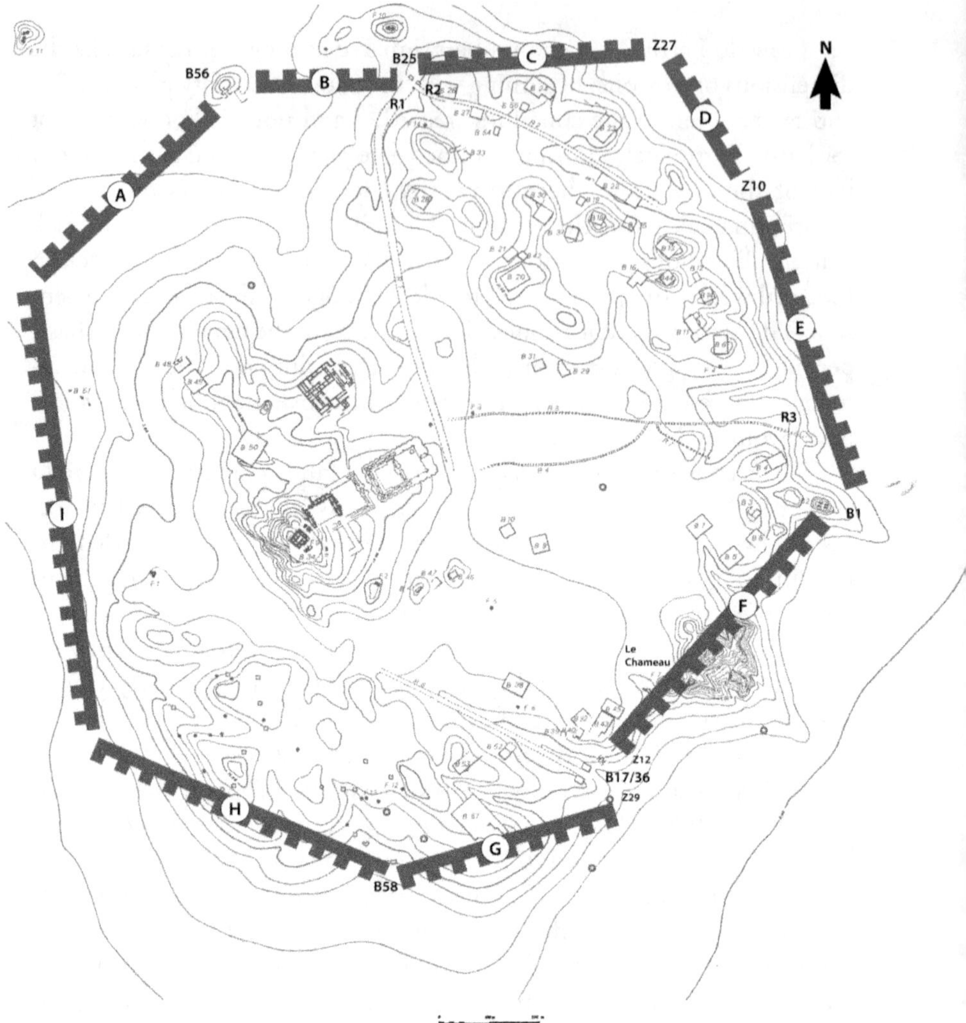

Figure 1a: Plan of Larsa (after Huot *et al.* 1989) showing proposed city wall segments A–I. Permission courtesy of J.-L. Huot; copyright: Mission archéologique de Larsa, DR. Image by Leslie Schramer.

is large, but not really out of keeping with other Middle Bronze walls: the walls at Mari mostly ranged between six and ten meters thick (and as much as seventeen meters, but only at points where the walls joined the gates); at Šubat-Enlil, the walls were generally five meters thick; at Qatna, probably smaller still.[104] We can safely assume that the Larsa walls were nowhere thicker than the city's gate piers (up to 18 m thick), and 10 m

[104] *Ibid.*, 173–76, 214.

thick walls already outpace the average width of the Syro-Levantine walls surveyed by Burke (2008: 62–63), generally between two and four meters thick. In the spirit of overestimating, let us assume that the Larsa fortification walls stood ten meters thick at all points. On the subject of the ramps, however, the width dimension must be considered in tandem with the height of the total structure.

So, how high was the wall? Of course few ancient mudbrick structures survive to their original height, and Larsa is no different in this regard. We must distinguish between the heights of natural landscape features (*i.e.*, the buttes), the rampart walls on which the fortification walls sat (on which, more below), and the fortification wall proper. This is a tricky affair. We know that Gates B36 and B17 already sat raised four meters off the plain, and wall segment I two meters—but we cannot reconstruct the total height of the built wall. Conversely, the wall atop the Chameau reached at least 18.5 meters—but it is not clear from the report how much of the footing was butte. Turning again to comparanda (per Burke 2008), Margueron thought the Mari wall eight meters high; Weiss guessed that the Šubat-Enlil wall ranged between five and fifteen meters high depending on the landscape; al-Maqdissi estimated Qatna's wall to have been as high as fifteen to twenty meters off the plain; Schachner that the Hattuša wall was ten meters high. What all this obscures, of course, is how much of that elevation was brick-built, and how much was earthen rampart and footing.

At this point, we must touch on two pieces of art historical evidence which speak to both the height and width of the wall. The first is a clay plaque found at Larsa, depicting Ištar trampling a fallen enemy atop a gated tower.[105] Though the specific form of the merlons cannot be identified, it clearly shows a battlemented (– *samītu*?) wall and a city gate.[106] It is of course in no way clear that the plaque depicts the wall of Larsa or any other specific city, nor can we assume that such a depiction aimed at realism or accuracy. Indeed, the depiction may be good for just one purpose here (see Fig. 1b): as the top of the gate in this depiction sits at the same height as the adjoining section of walls, we may take this image as a jumping-off point for a second maximizing *assumption* about the city wall, *i.e.*, that the height of the wall can be assumed to have been more or less the same height as the gates, or even the highest remaining feature

[105] Parrot 1961: ill. 358c and 1969: 64 and Pl. VIIIa; the glyptic motif may reflect Sumerian tropes, *e.g.*, Šulgi D: "I shall smite on the walls those who lie on the walls" (ETCSL 2.4.2.04 l. 212).

[106] Porada 1967: 2–3 and n. 13.

along the entire circuit, about 18 meters high, though this almost certainly overestimates the average height of the rampart and fortification wall.

Another piece of evidence comes in the form of a beautifully-carved steatite cylinder seal: IM 15218, excavated at Larsa. The seal has been published many times, not only for its fine carving but also for the fact that it bears an inscription of a servant of Abi-sare. Like the plaque discussed above, the seal depicts Nergal trampling a fallen enemy, recumbent against a structure of some kind, identified by both Parrot and others as a "mountain."[107] Unfortunately, the base of the structure is mostly broken away, obscuring most of its decorative composition. Yet a close examination of the subject is still rewarding (see Fig. 1c): the enemy figure lies diagonally against the slope, while the mound-shaped structure against which it lies is surmounted by a rectilinear feature emerging *from* it, perpendicular to the groundline. Just enough of the mound remains to show that it was made up of cobbles—just like the rectilinear feature, which was composed of two vertical rows of five cobbles or bricks. Cobble patterns were a common method of depicting mountains in Mesopotamian art, but the two constituent shapes of this "mountain" differs from other depictions.[108] Once this distinction is noted, the mound and the rectilinear feature resemble a cross-section of a fortification wall atop a rampart too much to ignore.[109] Thus, where site topography preserves an outline of the *plan* of the Larsa wall; and the plaque suggests the *elevation*, this small cylinder seal leaves us a view of the fortification wall and rampart in *section*.

Any attempt to reconstruct the rampart at Larsa must take several features into account, all having to do with the interplay between water and earth. Earthen foundation walls were functionally necessary beneath (brick) fortification walls for several reasons: they acted as a barrier between groundwater and the foundation, both by their magnitude and their relatively salt-free earthen content; they were a cheap and effective way to magnify the height of smaller brickwork structures; and they were all the easier since they were typically byproducts of moat (*ḫirītum*)

[107] Parrot 1933: 179; Parrot 1954: 55–56, 77, and ill. 260; Parrot 1969: 65 and Pl. VIIIc; cf. Arnaud 1994: 12, who does not remark on the structure at all; Porada and Basmachi 1951: 68: "With his right foot, [Nergal] steps on a small human figure which reclines on a mountain." For bibliography, see Frayne 1990: RIME 4 2.6.2 (pp. 124–25).

[108] The "fish-scale" type of patterning, however, is far more common in glyptic; compare the images in Digard 1975: 287, fig. 24.2, "Montagnes."

[109] Compare with Burke 2008: 51 Figure 6 and Gasche 1990.

Fig. 1b: Wall elevation (after Parrot 1961: ill. 358c). Image by Leslie Schramer.

Fig. 1c: Wall section (after IM 15218). Image by Leslie Schramer.

dredging excavations, which piled up masses of low-salinity wet earth precisely along the wall perimeter. The coincidence of work location, optimal building material, and labor efficiency aggregated in architectural forms which differed in degree more than in kind between dikes, levees, ramparts, and glacis.

We have no specific reference to the construction of a rampart at Larsa (though, importantly, there was a *ḫirītum*-moat[110]), but neither does any description of the wall identify its total composition, either. Other wall-building descriptions do seem to point to earthen ramparts in their terminology and metaphors. A 19th-century hymn of Ninšatapada identified Larsa as a "city lofty like a mountain" and derided Uruk as "the heaped-up earth" (or "rubbish heap").[111] Such imagery was common, but Warad-Sîn's description of the wall of Ur was more specific, mentioning a supporting wall (KI-SÁ) set below a foundation (KI-GAR) and above its fosse (E-EK-SUR-RA-BI) which contained a surrounding moat (*ḫirītum*).[112] Hammurabi described the Sippar wall as having a clay foundation, and that the

[110] Dalton 1983: 103; Larsa, Kiš, Nippur, and Ur (among others), all had I_7 or E *ḫirītum*'s; see also Frayne 1990: RIME 4 2.13.21 (p. 243). It is tempting to speculate, in fact, that the reason few remains of the Larsa wall are visible today is that, rather than being dispersed, the earth was simply backfilled into the *ḫiritum* from which it had originally been dug.

[111] Hallo 1991: 387: the latter term was SAḪAR-DUB-BA MU-UN-DÁB-BÉ.

[112] Frayne 1990: RIME 4 2.13.19–21 (pp. 238, 240, 243, respectively).

summit of the wall was raised "with earth like a great mountain."[113] That this earth supported a brick wall explains the otherwise difficult concept that the *foundation* of the wall (*uššī* BÀD) was raised with earth.[114]

This Sippar wall is an important case because the archaeological situation is the opposite of Larsa, preserving heaped-up earthen "walls" without any remaining brickwork. Gasche insisted that the successive layers of built-up earth there were dikes intended to protect against Euphrates flooding, with only ancillary military uses. This accords well with Sippar's particular non-military history, but Gasche further dismissed other earthen walls elsewhere as military on the same basis, including the old third millennium walls at Uruk as "not convincing" fortifications.[115] Such objections had much to do with Gasche's larger arguments about the impact of fluvatile regimes on settlement and economy, however, and did not seriously present evidence disproving the military use of such walls.

The distinction of military versus non-military use on the basis of present evidence seems arbitrary; there is little in the presence or structure of earthen mounds that is inconsistent with defense architecture,[116] and much to support it. Inscriptions of Samsuiluna describing his fortifications of Kiš and Dūr-Samsuiluna, for instance, are quite explicit in distinguishing earthen ramparts from brickwork, with both as integral parts of city walls:

> He built the city of Kiš, dug its moat, surrounded it with a lagoon, made its foundation firm as a mountain with masses of earth, caused its bricks to be moulded, (and) built its wall. In the span of one year he raised its top higher than before.[117]

[113] Dalton 1983: 146: BÀD *ṣiram in ebiri rabutim ša rišašunu kima satîm eliya*, "a lofty wall, with much earth, the top of which reaches as high as a mountain"; also pp. 148–49; see Hammurabi's 43rd year-name, that the wall of Sippar was "made out of great masses of earth" (BÀD-BI SAHAR-GAL-TA IN-GAR-RA; Akkadian: *šanat eper* ZIMBIR[ki] *iššapku*).

[114] Dalton 1983: 146; Frayne 1990: RIME 4 3.6.2 (p. 335), 3.6.7 (p. 341).

[115] Gasche 1990: 593; the earthen wall at Sippar measures around 1200 m × 800 m, enclosing about 96 hectares. Gasche himself has noted, *ibid.*, 591, that fortification walls were traditionally placed on the shoulders of supporting or buttressing walls, and so it is difficult to understand his insistence on Sippar's walls as (purely) levee walls.

[116] Equally arbitrary, Dalton's election (1983: 150–51) to see the city wall (BÀD *ša* ZIMBIR([ki])) and the river wall (KAR *šu-ul-mi-im*) as physically and functionally separate structures ("one (wall) which guarded the city and one which guarded the city's water supply") does not seem grounded in any archaeological evidence.

[117] After *ibid.*, 187.

> He dug its moat, he piled high its embankment, he molded its bricks and he built its wall.[118]

Not only were earthen ramparts known features of defensive walls, they were tied into the ecology of ancient Near Eastern city planning. Earthen ramparts and supporting walls composed of canal mud not only raised brick walls above groundwater and flooding, they were naturally free of the salts which otherwise absorbed water upward and created cracks in the bricks themselves. Excavation texts sometimes distinguished excavated earth (SAḪAR ZI-GA) for building from "salty dirt" (SAḪAR MUN).[119] As Wright noted,

> [Mud bricks were] usually made and dried on a canal bank, a source of relatively salt-free mud and water ... [and] used in the foundation, watertable or doors ... The lifetime of such a building depends on the speed with which salt is drawn into the foundations by capillary action. This is turn depends on the dampness and salinity of the building site.[120]

The use of canal excavation as a source of building material also vastly reduced labor costs. "Digging a ditch and making an embankment," Civil noted pragmatically, "are, up to a point, complementary activities."[121] Certainly in royal inscriptions the building of walls and moats are frequently paired, spoken of almost as a single act, a merism. As Iaḫdun-Lim

[118] *Ibid.*, 160–61; see also Paulus 1979/81: 131, on traditional Sumerian defensive walls: "The crude walls of rammed and patted clay were superseded by a more solid form of building using sun-dried clay bricks."

[119] Heimpel 2009: 241.

[120] Wright 1969: 17–18, pointing out that salts are filtered out by surrounding moats as water entering from a larger river channel drops its heavier particles near the intake point in the form of silting. See also Oates 1990: 388–89 on the unsuitability of saline earth for brick production. McHenry 1989: 61: "Water from virtually any source will be satisfactory, but it should be low in dissolved salts." The idomatic insistence on "purity" in Mesopotamian building accounts (pure places (KI SIKIL), pure foundations, pure bricks, *etc.*) may allude, among other qualities, to the use of relatively salt-free soil, though no attested useage supports the conjecture.

[121] Civil 1994: 110; see also Burke 2008: 145; cf. Dalton 1983: 133–37, 144, who segregates these types of building activities as different projects, though noting the common nomenclature shared by many walls and canals, and a large number of walls built on the banks of canals and rivers, *e.g.*, Hammurabi's Rapiqum wall, Ammiditana's Kar-Šamaš wall, Ammiṣaduqa's Dūr-Ammiṣadqua wall and Rīm-Sîn's Iškūn-Šamaš wall, all on the banks of the Euphrates, and, on the Tigris, Hammurabi's wall at Dūr-Šamaš and Abi-ešuḫ's at Dūr-Abi-ešuḫ.

wrote: "I built the wall of Mari and dug its moat. I built the wall of Terqa and dug its moat"; Ammiditana's 35th year name was for a fortress wall built alongside (GÚ, on the bank) the canal "Divine-Strength-of-Enlil"; and Anam of Uruk boasted that he "restored the wall of Uruk ... in baked bricks in order that water might roar in its surrounding moat."[122] One can see in both textually attested cases of walls "piled up higher than before" and in the multiple strata revealed by cross-sections of ancient levees that the regular heightening of walls was consistent with both canal-dredging and wall reinforcement. Nor need we wonder if canal excavation could produce the needed masses of earth. Levee walls known from Umma tablets in the time of Šulgi and Amar-Sîn include heaped-up embankments as high as nine meters,[123] which agrees with Dalton's assertion that canal dredging could routinely produce earthen walls from "five to eight meters high."[124] Mud walls (IM-DU$_8$-A) in Ur III work-assignment texts are known in lengths exceeding four kilometers,[125] and one canal-excavation text from Old Babylonian Lagaš records 131 barges of excavated earth (SAḪAR) from a canal with a total volume of 2,358 cubic meters.[126]

Yet even assuming the presence of a rampart or supporting wall at Larsa, how are we to estimate its specific size (especially when nothing is left of it)? And what was the size of the brick-built fortification wall atop *that*? The seal of the wall in cross-section shows a fortification wall around half the height of the mound on which it sits, though again this is not a depiction on which we can rely for accuracy. Still another suggestion comes by way of the famous inscription of Naram-Sîn about the walls of Armanum, describing the height of two ramparts (SA-DU, lit. "hill") and their respective walls (BÀD). Though the numbers are clearly fantastical, they reveal an *expectation of proportion*: the first rampart was said to be 130 cubits (ca. 52 m) high, running up to a wall 44 cubits (17.6 m) high; the second rampart was 180 cubits (72 m) high supporting a wall 30 cubits (12 m) high. The fortification walls described by the

[122] Dalton 1983: 51, 65–66; Frayne 1990: RIME 4 4.6.4 (pp. 474–75), 6.8.1 (p. 603).

[123] Civil 1987.

[124] Dalton 1983: 7.

[125] Civil 1987: 70, citing CT 7 43.

[126] Walters 1970: 117–19, Text 88; he calculates the labor-value of this excavated earth as 1,935.25 labor-days; cf. Englund 1988: 179, estimating that the labor-value of constructing a pisé wall of 1,791m^3 volume was 1,592 labor-days. Both estimates assume a work rate of around 1.1–1.2 m^3 of earth moved per labor-day.

inscription are one-third and one-sixth, respectively, of the height of the ramparts on which they sit.[127]

My goal is not to find the exact dimensions of the Larsa wall, but to make a reasonable estimate while giving the benefit of the doubt towards maximum size and scope of the wall-building work. On this basis, and on the demonstrable premise (see below) that heaped-earthen ramparts were less labor-intensive than masonry walls, let us assume that the fortification wall was no more than one-third of the assumed height of 18.5 meters (roughly a six-meter fortification wall sitting atop a twelve-meter rampart). Working from the height dimension, we will follow Burke (2008: 50) in assuming that the slope of the rampart was 30°; this leaves us with a form with a section in the form of an isosceles trapezoid. By the dimensions we know (10 m wide at the top, 12 m height, and base angles at 30° each (*q.e.d.*, top angles = 150°)), we can calculate a base of about 52 m (rounding up from 51.56 m), giving us an area of 372 square meters for the section. At a length of 5,200 m, the volume of the Larsa rampart wall comes to 1,934,400 m^3 of packed earth. The fortification wall, meantime, at 5.2 km length, 6 m height and 10 m thick, occupied a volume of 312,000 m^3 of masonry. It cannot be stressed enough, of course, that it is exceedingly unlikely that the Larsa wall was actually this large.[128]

Labor value of the wall

Before we try to account for the building of the Larsa wall task by task, we can take note of some "wholesale" estimates of rates for brickwork construction. An early experiment came from the observation of construction at the Tell Brak dighouse. The dighouse measured roughly 25 m × 5 m × 4 m, built by one master-builder and four laborers in four weeks (with five days

[127] Frayne 1993: RIME 2 1.4.26 (p. 135) iv.20-v.16; later in the same inscription, vi.10–17, Naram-Sîn mentions two other proportions for ramparts: walls as about 10:1 and 5:1. That these proportions are mostly near-exact, it is difficult to tell how much these numbers were being idealized. It is also not impossible to imagine that the inscription refers to height in two different ways: that the "height" of the walls were absolute, while the "height" of the hills referred to the length of the slope. If that is the case, the numbers are not so clearly fantastical. Burke 2008: 50 has estimated the average slope of ramparts to be about 30°, with attested widths of up to 70–90 m—dimensions which are not inconsistent with Naram-Sîn's claims.

[128] Cf. Burke 2008: 144, with estimated rampart volume for Levantine cities averaging around 200,000 m^3 and never exceeding 1,000,000 m^3; and Charpin 1989: 197, who calculates a rampart wall about 80% the length of Larsa's wall (4021.5 m), but only 3% of the volume estimated here (60,322.5 m^3).

of work a week),[129] *i.e.*, 100 labor-days invested for 116 m^3 of brickwork. In crude terms, for all tasks from start to finish, 1.16 m^3 of finished brickwork was produced per labor-day. Extrapolating from this, we could produce other metrics: with Larsa bricks averaging 32 × 32 × 6 cm (*i.e.*, 235 bricks/m^3), the dighouse would have used about 27,260 bricks, or 272.6 bricks per labor-day. A single brick therefore represents something like 0.00367 labor-days (or 0.367 % of a labor-day). In a larger and more recent experiment, Jürgen Seeher's team invested 2,990 man-days in producing 64,000 larger mudbricks (each 45 × 45 × 10 cm) in a partial reconstruction of the Hattuša city wall; this works out to something like 0.43 m^3 of bricks produced per labor-day, quite slow considering it did not include construction.[130] Still, these figures bracket the range of wall-construction rates in other studies, which range between 0.67–0.96 m^3 of finished brickwork produced per labor-day.[131] If we were to take the low end of Burke's rates (*i.e.*, assuming the most labor-intensive rates), this would produce a labor-cost of 465,672 labor-days for the brick wall volume alone (312,000 m^3).

Overall rates may not be accurate enough for us: for instance, masonry building is substantially more complex than rampart-building, while overall rates may not account for labor-costs lying outside the immediate scope of construction. What, for instance of clearing the site? Growing the straw to mix into the bricks? Building the brick-molds to be ready for production? Reed-gathering for interleaving? It is not obvious how much such tasks would substantially add to the labor-value of any given wall—or whether some or all tasks were not already folded in to overall rates[132]—nor that any given work rate is so easily transferable from one specific context to another.[133]

The best way to make a more accurate assessment is to break down the individual tasks required for work and cost them out at known or analogous labor-rates. Having recourse to specialized terminologies and

[129] Oates 1990: 389–90. Total building time was six weeks, but two weeks were for brick-drying, with no labor costs.

[130] Seeher 2007: 47, 219.

[131] Gathered helpfully by Burke 2008: 146, 152; cf. Ristvet 2007: 200 and n. 30, estimating c. 0.32 m^3 per labor-day for finished brickwork.

[132] The overall responsibility for building a wall was not divided by so many individualized functions from the perspective of either worker or institution; texts documenting individual types of work were essentially interesting in accounting, not documentation of work; see Mosely 1975: 194.

[133] See Heimpel 2009: 224 for known work norms for brickmaking at 80, 120, 240 and 250 bricks per day.

the Mesopotamian affinity for taskwork-accounting allows us to check these overall rates against a line-item audit. The GARšana texts discussed by Heimpel (2009) are most helpful for these purposes. These documents discuss more than three dozen separate tasks making up the larger project we think of as "building a brick wall"—everything from site clearing to trimming GISAL-mats for layering into the brickwork.[134] I have particularized the taskwork for the Larsa wall after Heimpel's list, slightly reordering tasks for clarity of process; omitting a few that cannot be meaningfully worked into the calculations,[135] are redundant to other terms,[136] or which are not relevant to city-wall building;[137] and adding a few others that seem not to be represented by that corpus of texts. We have already estimated the largest wall likely to have been situated at Larsa; what gross labor inputs would be necessary to build it, assuming a single-episode building?

Based on taskwork analysis (see Table 1 for the tallied costs, and Appendix 2, p. 299, for notes on individual tasks), we can estimate that the labor value invested in the Larsa wall was just shy of two million labor-days (**1,957,095**). The labor-value in the fortification wall (*i.e.*, without the rampart) comes to 1,312,295 labor-days, almost three times the estimate that would be produced by the Mallowan model (*i.e.*, 465,672 labor-days).[138] I have assumed a wall much larger than what probably existed; estimated some labor rates on the slow side; and, most importantly, employed a model reflecting the idea that the rampart and brickwork were

[134] *Ibid.*, 221–22; see now also Anastasio 2011.

[135] *Ibid.* Several terms fail to specify what actual work was being done, therefore not only are there no rates known, but none can be generated by comparison; this includes 6.1.2, "employed at the brickyard"; 6.1.5 "work on brick stacks"; 6.7.6, "making GI-SAL GI-IR," which Heimpel thinks may be a type of apron to keep water off of the upper wall; and 6.11.1, "moving dirt," which seems redundant to "carrying/hauling earth."

[136] *Ibid.*, 256 concluding, for instance, that "twinning" bricks (SIG_4 TAB) was "not descriptive of a particular method of brick laying, but the general designation of building with bricks." His extensive consideration of what differentiates different types of "delivering earth" suggests that "making *du*ʾ*um*" (*du-ú-um* AKA) was a task subsumed under what is here calculated as "carrying" and "mixing" earth.

[137] *Ibid.*; tasks not relevant to wall-building are, *e.g.*, 6.2.2, "stripping" (*i.e.*, bitumen from a roof: ZIL) and 6.3.4, "making" (AK in this context would be redundant to DÙ, "constructing").

[138] Of course, Mallowan's (1966) observation of building did not take into account the (enormous) labor costs hidden from on-site building, *e.g.*, straw production or carrying earth to the production site.

Table 1: Tasks for construction of rampart and brick fortification wall

task	material / activity	known day-rate	analog day-rate	Labor Days
RAMPART				
Rampart: excavation and heaping-up	SAḪAR ZI-GA+ KA-ALA SI-GA	10 GÍN	—	644,800
BRICK FORTIFICATION WALL				
Site clearing	IZ-ZI GUL[a]	—	10 SAR	149
Straw harvested*	IN-U	1 GUR	—	124,800
Straw carried	IN-U GA_6-ĜÁ	—	18 m^3	2,080
Dirt work (excavation)	SAḪAR ZI	10 GÍN	—	91,520
Pouring water	A BAL	—	3600 kg	21,667
Carrying earth[b]	IM GA_6-ĜÁ	—	10 GÍN	91,520
Mixing earth	IM LU	—	1.725 m^3	180,870
Molding bricks	SIG_4 DU_8	240 bricks	—	52,000
Baking bricks	$ŠEG_6$[c]	—	[10%]	5,200
Carrying bricks	SIG_4 GA_6-ĜÁ	3.75 GÍN	—	277,333
Building[d]	ŠU DÍM	—	1.16 m^3	268,965
Delivering reeds	GI-SAL GA_6-ĜÁ[e]	26 m^2	—	36,000
Laying reeds[f]	GI-SAL ĜÁ-ĜÁ	6 m^2	—	156,000
Trimming reeds	GI-SAL GUL	—	288 m^2	217
PLASTERING				
Plaster production	SUMUR	—	0.8625 m^3	1,326
Plastering reeds[g]	GI-SAL IM SUMUR AK	—	360 m^2	2,600
Plastering brickwork	IM SUMUR AKA	—	360 m^2	318
TOTAL				**1,957,095**

a Lit., "razing walls."

b Heimpel 2009: 249–250 theorizes that an alternative term, "hauling earth" (IM GÍD), may have referred to hauling by sledge; that it was used next to IM GA_6-ĜÁ shows that it was considered a separate activity.

c *Cf.* Walters' 1970: 125–126 (Text 99), which gives the term DU_8-IGI-NIGIN against DU_8-DÙ-AN, "sun dried."

d The task of "construction" (DÙ) was either a subset of "building" (ŠU DÍM) and/or was differentiated from the skilled labor required of masonry, *i.e.*, for the construction of not just architecture, but reed huts, ovens, mats, *etc.* (Heimpel 2009: 235–237).

e Lit., "carrying reeds."

f *I.e.*, as lattices or screens.

g Heimpel 2009 266–274 distinguishes "plaster" (SUMUR) as the material used for the tops of walls and "stucco" (IM; "stuccoing" = IM SUMUR TAG) as that used for the vertical parts of the walls. For the purposes of estimating labor inputs, such distinctions are mostly unimportant.

built all at once, and not gradually in stages, as was almost certainly the case. These and other factors will be considered again in the conclusion, after we consider the labor-value of the Larsa barley havest.

Case Study Two: Larsa's Barley Production

The scale of barley production

Larsa's agricultural productive capacity was enormous even by the standards of lower Mesopotamia; barley-farming was carried out on a massive scale there as early as the Uruk period. Primary production in Old Babylonian Larsa took place on Crown lands, eponymous estates, temple farms, and small freeholdings, with a diverse textual record reflecting that state of affairs. Accordingly, it is impossible to arrive at anything like a single "snapshot" of land under production close to what, for instance, Steinkeller has been able to determine for Ur III's centralized administration of the Umma province.[139] As far as we can analyze Larsa's lands, we will have to settle for a subset of verified and documented agricultural capacity, well below the total labor investments. Fortunately, such an "under-estimate" is in perfect accordance with my methodology: overvaluing the labor-costs of monumental architecture and undervaluing the labor-costs of agricultural outputs. First, I will report on the scale of land under the plow; and then harness those areas of land to known labor-rates for farming tasks.

We might begin, as we did for wall-building, with a look at some existing templates for the estimating the carrying capacity of Bronze Age city-states in southern Iraq, for instance the model of Robert Hunt (1987). Hunt assumed 29% of hinterland under production in Lower Mesopotamian environments within a 12.4 km radius for a single-tier environment centered on a dominant urban site.[140] Tweaking this model for Larsa's particular settlement distribution (the shape of an inverted chevron), the 29% figure produces a "V" shape roughly 7 km thick north to south and 20 km east to west. We are looking at something like an overall area of 318.3 km^2, 29% of which is 92.31 km^2 under production (= 9,231 hectares). Assuming, for example, barley production of 1,050 liters/hectare

[139] Steinkeller 2007a.

[140] Hunt 1987: 165–66, with another 29% of land in fallow and 42% not under production; cf. Civil 1987: 49–51, who opined that smaller plot-holders would have left less land in fallow than large estates. Wilkinson's 1994 model is much more sophisticated, but is unfortunately too specific to Upper Mesopotamia to do us much good here; this work, however, has guided much of C. Hritz's modeling, discussed below. For an example of Hritz's approach, see her several contributions in Wilkinson *et al.* eds. (2013).

(see below) and Hunt's very conservative estimate that barley production returned only a 9% surplus on invested labor (measured by kilocalorie; *i.e.*, 1 man-day of farming labor = 1.09 liters barley[141]), we would find:

9,231 ha. = 7,408,801 liters barley = 6,797,065 labor-days *per annum*

A model more specific to the Larsa region was devised by Carrie Hritz in support of earlier working versions of this study; it is presented here for heuristic purposes, not as the definitive conclusions of finished research. Hritz's model was based on standards developed by Tony Wilkinson's MASS project at the Oriental Institute of the University of Chicago, which in turn built on Wilkinson's 1994 study. Hritz was also able to correlate topographical and settlement data to both archaeological surveys and declassified Corona satellite imagery of the immediate Larsa area. The results of this estimate assume lower rates than Hunt's model for both population density and barley yields, but expands the overall amount of settled area, partly by identifying dozens of smaller settlements in addition to those identified by Adams and Nissen (see n. 151 below).

Larsa's rank-size based on occupied urban area relative to its neighbors was enormous: at 270 hectares, it was more than twice as large as Bad-Tibira to the east (121 ha.) and almost eight times as large as Uruk (35 ha.). Accordingly, Larsa's productive zone would have intruded beyond the geographical halfway points between these cities, especially to the east, where Larsa's productive zone enveloped Tell Abla, the most sizable second-tier settlement in the area.[142] This population-based subsistence model anticipates not only the productive sphere of its central zone (*i.e.*, a simple radius mapped out from the Larsa tell), but also the numerous small sites lying outside it. Assuming an occupation rate of 150 persons per hectare[143] and known yields of 881 kg grain per hectare, Larsa proper required a

[141] Hunt 1987: 166; his idea was based on the proposal that 9% represented the minimum surplus needed for primary producers to support "non-productive" households.

[142] To judge by the toponymic analysis following, Tell Abla is most likely to be identified as ancient Raḫabum, Ḫanṣipatanu, or Dimat-Kunanim according to rank-size and geographical orientation; further research should be able to identify some of the sites in the Larsa city-state.

[143] Wilkinson 1994: 499 concluded that populations up to 150 pph in urban environments in the Jezirah would produce equilibrium with production, but that 200 pph models would require imported food. Given that southern Mesopotamia could rely on much greater yields of barley per hectare, a 150 pph settlement density model seems quite a minimal and dependable boundary.

minimum of 15,161 ha. productive land,[144] another 2,170 hectares of land supporting its smaller sites, mostly lying along the northwestern edge of the state, and 2,283 belonging to Tell Abla and a few third-tier settlements. This gives a total of 19,614 hectares under production, an estimate obviously much larger than Hunt's. At that size:

19,614 ha. = 17,999,931 liters = 16,513,698 labor-days *per annum*

Hunt's and Hritz's models might be only "eyeball" estimates, but, at three-and-a-half and eight times the size of the city-wall labor value estimate, they begin to suggest the order of magnitude and interpretive problems we are dealing with.[145] But let us check these estimates against the data we have on actual production and normative labor-rates for associated tasks.

Size of the product: how big was the Larsa barley harvest?

As with the city-wall building, our twin tasks are to figure out

a) how big the job was, and

b) how much work would attach to a job that size.

Larsa texts, both published and unpublished, offer excellent information on agricultural production in terms of toponyms, yields, and cadastral measures of productive land. Larsa's storage-and-redistributive economy was also the subject of an important study by Breckwoldt (1995/1996), distilled from her earlier unpublished dissertation. That study focused on some relatively well-known texts reporting on lands and harvests of towns within the local orbit of the Larsa city-state. (Under normal circumstances, "local" means towns close enough to deliver grain to Larsa on a regular basis; my study also assumes this local region is the same population catchment from which corvée labor would have been drawn for city-wall building.) Despite this wealth of information, we must remain conscious of the fact that nothing like a full accounting of agricultural production from cuneiform evidence will be possible to the same degree that it is possible to re-imagine the size of the city wall. All we will ever have in the way of

[144] Incidentally, this estimate matches a "linear zone" model Hritz also produced, which assumed most productive lands lying along visible canal lines rather than in an ordered, tiered settlement system arrayed in neat circles. Estimating the total lands lying along canals and levees, the Larsa state takes on a much more oblong shape, running along a SW-NE axis, with the available land totaling 15,388 hectares—virtually identical to the 15,161 hectare estimate.

[145] Compare with Ur III Girsu, which had at least 24,266 ha. under production (Maekawa 1984: 90–91; cf. Steinkeller 2007a); see also Foster's (1982) discussion of hectarage in Girsu, Umma, Adab, Nippur, and other Sargonic estates.

hard data are subsets of a larger and unknown total capacity. Fortunately, this state of affairs is perfectly consonant with my model: the job is to discover the largest known *minimum* of production and compare that smaller product to the civil-sector work.

There are essentially two ways to build a portrait of Larsa's barley production: one is to get a handle on the size of the productive lands from field accounts; the other is to reconstruct the size of those lands retrospectively from known barley yields. The first method is clearly the more dependable one, doubly so because most labor rates for farming were tied to the area of land being worked, not the barley yielded. But it is not obvious without examining the data whether barley yields would not by their preponderance give us the better information in the end. To date, most scholarly attention has been directed to a few suggestive texts reporting millions of liters of grain (see, *e.g.*, YOS 5 176, a distribution of 5276.1.0,6 ŠE.GUR, more than 1.5 million liters of grain).[146] We will therefore have a look at both the fields and yields of the Larsa city-state.

Toponyms of the Larsa area within the territorial kingdom

More than two hundred toponyms can be associated with the Larsa state; their location on the ground is made problematic, however, partly by the fact that Larsa's territorial ambitions brought it to control a wide swath of places in lower Mesopotamia—from Maškan-šāpir in the north to Ur in the south—many of which did not routinely bring grain to Larsa. This was a sizeable territory that included large cities not in Larsa's immediate ambit, *e.g.*, Lagaš, Umma, Adab, Šarakkum, and portions of Malgium and Emutbal. The precondition for finding measures of either our target lands or yields, then, is establishing a base list of toponyms close to Larsa proper.

This entails two separate stages. The first is to discover the set of toponyms which can be firmly anchored for proximity to Larsa. Breckwoldt's study focused on a few of the best-documented towns in the immediate Larsa region, but we can expand this list to at least twenty-two "anchored" toponyms: Aḫanuta, Abisare, Ašdubba, Dimat-Balmunamhe, Dimat-

[146] It must also be acknowledged that amounts of grain in Larsa texts do not always clearly spell out the connection between distributed/stored amounts of barley, and actual harvested yields. This is a potentially large methodological problem which I unfortunately have to sidestep for the moment. In the main, the routinized administration of large amounts of barley distributed annually speaks against them being reserves, i.e., the stored yields of multiple years; and amounts going into storage were (perhaps obviously) not being brought there *from* storage; thus I feel these quantities probably correlate closely to yields.

Kunanim,[147] Dunnum,[148] lands "harvested by the crown,"[149] Eduru-Šulgi, Ḫanṣipatanu, Ḫašur, Ḫumsirum, Iddi-Uraš, Iškun-Ea, KA.AN, Masabum, MÁŠ.ZI, Pakakaya, Raḫabum, Sin-KAL, Sin-nūr-mātim, Širimtum, and Zarbilum. This list forms the basis for the results seen in Table 2, fifty-two more towns and watering districts which can be correlated to these toponymic anchors.[150] It must be emphasized that I am making no claims about the relative importance of the anchors or the secondarily-correlated toponyms. The table reflects only that the "anchors" can be directly located at Larsa, while the secondary ones are located in turn by the anchors (locational data to be found in the cited texts, among others); they are correlates of adjacency and not rank or size.

In all, seventy-four toponyms can be tied with confidence to the Larsa city-state.[151] Many more toponyms in the Larsa corpus are either certainly not, or not clearly, within the city-state.[152] Some of the borderline cases could potentially add quite serious totals of land to our surveys, but must be disallowed for various reasons: some seem likely to be close, but cannot be definitively proven so;[153] other texts present information about towns

[147] See Koliński 2001: 26–27 and Table 8; his conjecture was that this and other *dimtu* housed "scattered people."

[148] On Dunnum, see Dalton 1983: 90, on a letter of Gungunum he interprets as an order for the army to refortify that site and dredge its canal.

[149] Fourteen watering districts are not individually listed on Table 2, but subsumed under "É.GAL [lands];" these derive from one list, YBC 7238 (RS 3).

[150] Ḫumsirum, which appears in Fig. 2, but not Table 2, is assigned to the Larsa region on the basis of YBC 7248; alone among the "anchors," this town cannot be correlated to Larsa by geographic information, but only by the text's date and format, which it shares with NBC 8161. Note also that the hundred plus fields of URU.KI Ḫumsirum on YBC 7248 are categorized as under "the hoe of Šamaš-ḫāzir" (GIŠ.AL PN) — in the time of Rīm-Sîn (Year 22). See also Koliński 2001: 28 for possible additional toponyms, including Dimat-Kattim.

[151] Adams and Nissen 1972 identified thirty-four Isin-Larsa period sites within seven kilometers of Senkere, numbered 414–24, 428–430, 433–447, and 457–460.

[152] Several dozen toponyms appearing in Larsa texts cannot be located certainly within the Larsa city-state, either for lack of information by geography (*e.g.*, situation along a known canal or road), prosopography (*e.g.*, by the management of its resources by an official otherwise known to have controlled land or grain in Larsa towns), or adjacency (*e.g.*, by its mention together with another known Larsa town).

[153] The excluded data here is quite substantial. For instance, (Dūr)-Etellum (AbB IV 102 and 108 give 1.0.0.0 IKU land) and Mašmašene (AbB IV 24: 6.0.0 IKU land), both frequent toponyms in Larsa texts, may have been closer to Lagaš (see the PA$_5$ Etellum in many of the texts from Walters 1970: esp. 197),

Table 2: Toponymic anchors and associates

Anchors	**co-anchors**	***associates***
Aḫanuta (OECT XV 27)	Raḫabum	Kubatum[a] (OECT XV 27)
Abisare[b] (YBC 6663 and 6974)	Ašdubba	*none*
Ašdubba[b,c] (Birot 69; VS 13 100)	Abisare	Enlil-garra (OECT XV 112), Nabrara[c] (TCL 11 158; cf. AbB IX 150), Rakabat (AbB XIV 163)
Dimat-Balmunam-he[c] (YBC 5585)	KA.AN and Širimtum	*none*
Dimat-Kunanim (YOS 8 100; VS 13 104)	KA.AN and Raḫabum	Āl-Kubbukum, Āl-Iddin-Ea, Dimat-Nutuptum, Dimat-Warad-ili, Ewirnum, Til-Ḫatudum, Til-Mer[rik?], Til?-Dukanum (all NBC 8161)
Dunnum[c] (TCL 11 175, VS 13 104)	Ḫanṣipatanu, Raḫabum, and KA.AN	*none*
É.GAL lands (YBC 7238)	Kururu	[comprised of fourteen otherwise unknown *ūgarū*]
Eduru-Šulgi (Birot 69)	*none*	*none*
Ḫanṣipatanu (TCL 11 174)	Dunnum	All *ūgarū* except Kururu (see JCS 11 31b 9): Akulṣi-làl (=Akulim?), Aluratum, Ašdiša, Diḫlani, DUB.SAR, Garubum (= Gabburum/ Gubrum?), Kuštanu, ÍD-UL-SI-TA and Kururu (all OECT XV 80); Ḫupatum and Raḫinuru (both OECT XV 13).
Hašur (OECT XV 18; TEBA 107; Birot 69; on the "kaskal Larsa")	*none*	Zawar (OECT XV 18)
Iddi-Uraš[d] (YOS 5 166)	MÁŠ.ZI	*none*
Iškun-Ea[b] (TCL 10 28)	*none*	*none*

Anchors	**co-anchors**	*associates*
KA.AN[b] (SVD 54; VS 13 104)	Dimat-Balmunamḫe and Dimat-Kunanim	Al-Warad-Sin[a] (VS 13 104), Dūr-Diḫutim[a] (YOS 5 181), Tilla[a] (AbB IV 109, VS 13 104)
Masabum (YOS 5 170 and 185)	*none*	*none*
MÁŠ.ZI[d] (YOS 5 166)	Iddi-Uraš	*none*
Pakakaya (YOS 14 226)	*none*	Ubarriya (YOS 14 226)
Raḫabum[c] (AbB XIV 3; OECT XV 22)	Aḫanuta	Al-Warad-Sin[a], Bela, Tilla, Zibnatu[a] (all VS 13 104); Šunnamu(n)gi(m) (also VS 13 104, but *cf.* AbB IX 150 and OECT XV 121) Erra-UR.SAG, Ki-Utušua (see also SVJAD 137), Sin-māšmāš and A.GÀR Igruru (all OECT XV 76); Nanna-GÚ.GAL (cf. RGTC 2), Ḫarab-kare, Ki-Utuea, Šubat-ilim and the *ūgarū* Kazazanu, Warḫu, and GIŠ.BAR (all OECT XV 22); Mašum and Nūr-libi (both TCL 11 156).
Sin-KAL (YOS 14 223)	*none*	*none*
Sin-nūr-mātim[b] (YBC 7194)	*none*	Dūr-Diḫutim[a] (YOS 5 181)
Širimtum[b,c] (Birot 69)	Dimat-Balmunamḫe	Six fields (A.ŠÀ) from AbB XIV 56: Munḫiatim, Hiššar (also YOS 15 67), IGI.URU, A.GÀR Gula, *ṣerum,* and Pi-ilim
Zarbilum[c] (YOS 5 207)	*none*	*none*

[a]co-associated elsewhere
[b] Breckwoldt 1995/1996: at Larsa.
[c] RGTC 3: at Larsa
[d] independently located

which are probably within the city-state, but in a format which does not permit data to be extracted clearly enough to prevent overlaps and double-counting of land or yields from other places already on the list;[154] a number of toponyms close to Larsa provide amounts of substantial land, but only for the specialized production of dates[155] and sesame[156] instead of barley. What is not possible at this point is to create anything like a map of the Larsa state, nor is this the place for a major study of its historical geography. However, we can sketch the following picture: clusters of villages flanked the northeast and northwest shoulders of the city-state, forming a rough "V" shape, with the probable extension of the state's major canal branch leading from Bad-tibira in the northeast all the way to the Euphrates in the southwest. These are two indications of basic orientation: Ašdubba perhaps lay to the west of Larsa, towards Uruk (per VS 13 100), and Raḫabum lay perhaps to the east, since one of its local villages, Erra-Ursag, lay on the Lagašitum canal.[157]

In addition, we can speculate that the appearance of toponyms under the control of similar officials and/or together in the same accounts of land or grain also suggest their physical adjacency (see Fig. 2). Some of these correlations are more insistent than others, but an adjacency theorem (*i.e.*, that toponyms appearing together in accounts were likely in proximity to one another) cannot really as yet be proven. Still, as a general rule, "account adjacency" and physical adjacency are not *counter*indicated—anchors which correlate to other anchors tend to correlate to them consistently and not to others. At this point, I can identify five "super-clusters" of anchored toponyms with correlated adjacencies:

according to Stol's review (1971: 365–66). OECT XV 1 and 2 account for, respectively, 4.2.1.7.2.2 and 1.1.1.7.5.2 IKU of ÉŠ.GÀR.HI.A lands, 2343 ha. probably within the Larsa state, but do not include any unimpeachably Larsaean toponyms; see also TCL 11 155 and 185.

[154] OECT XV 22 gives 3.0.0.0 IKU of lands in nine places near to and including Raḫabum, all certainly within Larsa, but only two can be localized (Raḫabum itself and Ki-Utuèa), and so only a fraction of the land can be assigned to specific places.

[155] *E.g.*, Nabrara, Dunnum, Ašdubba, Nanna-GÚ.GAL, and Rakabat (TCL 11 167A, 175, 190, 247); such lands could be substantial in size: TCL 11 158 gives 6.2.3 IKU of GIŠ.ŠAR in Nabrara alone.

[156] Although sesame was one of the select commodities regularly tracked by the state (along with dates, barley, and wool), delivery sizes were small relative to those other products.

[157] Unpublished Yale cadasters suggest that Rīm-Sîn ordered a survey of Girsu lands in his Year 21 and Larsa lands in Year 22 (see Richardson 2008).

Figure 2: Super-clusters of anchored Larsa toponyms

Cluster A (all east of Larsa?):
Raḫabum — Aḫanuta — Dimat-Kunanim

Cluster B (all west of Larsa?):
Abisare — Ašdubba[158] — Eduru-Šulgi — Ḫašur — Širimtum

Cluster C:
Dimat-Balmunamḫe[159] — KA.AN — Dimat-Kunanim

Cluster D:
Dunnum — Ḫanṣipatanu

Cluster E:
MÁŠ.ZI — Iddi-Uraš

The anomaly among these fifteen toponyms is Dimat-Kunanim, which correlates sometimes to cluster A and sometimes to cluster C (perhaps as a pivot between those two clusters); otherwise these adjacency principles seem fairly stable. A similar clustering stability occurs among the secondarily classified toponyms as well; of the fifty-two, only six correlate to more than one anchor (though many are also only known from one locating text). As a general statement, most Larsa toponyms appearing with other toponyms do so within a small, fixed range of others; this tends to suggest the clearly tiered settlement system (both geographically and administratively) already predicted by archaeological models and surveys.

Productive lands and known yields in the Larsa city-state

With the known local towns and villages accounted for by name, we can look for known totals of productive land. There are two ways to go about this: by actual statements of productive land; and by harvest yields from which supporting lands can be reconstructed. As mentioned above, the former category of data is more dependable, but the latter is more abudant. Looking to the first, the sizes of large productive tracts come primarily from cadastral texts, though a surprising number come from administrative letters. Just under half (thirty-five of seventy-four) of the located toponyms preserve information about measured land; these total 1.4.0.6.2.2, 60 SAR, about 5,378 hectares (Table 3, col. 3). These represent the largest unique field measurements (that is, within a single cuneiform text, thus avoiding the possible redundance of identical lands

[158] But cf. YOS XV 95, which mentions Ašdubba with Kutalla and Bad-tibira, both to the north-east of Larsa.

[159] Co-anchored to KA.AN, but also Širimtum (*e.g.*, YBC 5585).

added from multiple texts) in each locality, as small as the 1.8 hectares of Nanna-gugal in OECT XV 22, and as large as the 1,263.8 hectares of the "lands harvested by the palace" in YBC 7238.

5,378 hectares is less than what Hunt and Hritz estimated, and a known minimum rather than a projected maximum. Without doubt, the total amount of productive land was much larger: some places with massive harvest yields documented have no preserved information on the size of land (see Table 3: Dimat-Balmunamḫe, Iškun-Ea, Masabum, MÁŠ.ZI, Sin-nūr-mātim, and the Gula, Hiššar, and Munḫiatim fields). In fact the inverse seems to hold true as well: more than two-thirds (twenty-five) of toponyms with lands surveyed have no documented harvest yields. One might speculate on this basis that fields under institutional control were unnecessary to survey because their sizes were known and implied by their real and expected yields, whereas freeholdings and service-lands were documented in terms of size because they were alienable/ transferable and because their dues were calculated on the basis of size.[160]

Nor does any cadastral record indicate that the land for which it accounts represents the total land of that place—perhaps just some of it. For instance, were the town of Abisare to have farmed *only* the 2.0.0 IKU of land mentioned in OECT XV 112, one would have to explain how it those 12.7 hectares could have produced the yield of 415.4.0 ŠE.GUR listed in YOS 5 175; this would require a fantastic yield rate of 9,822 liters per hectare. Nor again is there any reason to believe that the lands documented by the state economy were anything near the total land under production:[161] individual ŠUKU-plots and private non-institutional lands are poorly represented among these documents.[162] In short, we can be very confident that the count of 5,378 hectares is a secure and minimal count of known lands.

So what can yields tell us about the size of their fields? This is more difficult to answer responsibly, since the answer rests on the all-important "x-factor" of what average barley yields were. We already have Hritz's

[160] This conjecture is also supported by the fact that, in the six cases in which both field sizes and yields are known for toponyms *from separate documents*, the barley yields uniformly imply much larger amounts of land than their otherwise documented field sizes (Abisare, KA.AN, Širimtum, A.ŠÀ IGI.URU, A.ŠÀ Pi-ilim, and A.ŠÀ *ṣērim*).

[161] Kozyreva 1988: 203 estimated that only a third of Larsa's cultivated area belonged to the "state economy," though as far as I am aware there is no way to externally confirm this estimate.

[162] Halstead 1990: 192.

working standard of 846 liters/hectare.[163] Figure 3, below, abstracts a number of Larsa texts also give a good idea of actual yields on large estates and farms:[164]

Figure 3: Some documented yields from Larsa fields

text	**land**	(in hectares)	**yield**	(in liters)	**rate** (l./ha.)	**date**
Jacobsen (1982)[165]		(430.47)		(386,132)	897.0	Ha
OECT XV 106:7–9	2.7.0.4	(172.88)	260.2.4,6	(78,166)	452.1	Ha 32
OECT XV 106:11–13	3.2.2	(23.99)	33.1.4	(10,000)	416.8	Ha 32
OECT XV 106:14–16	1.8.2.2	(119.58)	77.4.4,8	(23,388)	195.5	Ha 32
YBC 7238:17[166]	3.1.9.0.0	(1,263.85)	2716.0.0	(814,800)	644.7	RS 3
YBC 7238:23	1.0.0.0.0	(381.06)	1000.0.0	(300,000)	787.3	RS 3
Birot, *Tablettes* 1[167]	6.0.5	(39.87)	110.2.0,5	(33,125)	830.8	Ha 32
Birot, *Tablettes* 2	5.2.0, 75 SAR	(36.6)	164.4.3,7	(49,477)	1,351.8	Ha 32
Birot, *Tablettes* 3	8.0.0, 75 SAR	(51.0)	184.4.2,7	(55,467)	1,087.6	Ha 32
Birot, *Tablettes* 4	8.1.0, 1 UBU	(53.1)	223.1.4	(67,000)	1,261.7	Ha 32
Birot, *Tablettes* 5	1.1.0.1	(70.2)	266.3.2	(55,467)	790.1	Ha 32
Birot, *Tablettes* 6	9.2.3	(62.4)	211.3.2	(63,500)	1,017.6	Ha 32
Birot, *Tablettes* 7	9.0.2, 20 SAR	(57.9)	156.1.0,7	(46,867)	809.4	Ha 32
Birot, *Tablettes* 8	4.1.2, 1 UBU	(28.4)	38.1.2	(11,480)	404.2	Ha 32
Birot, *Tablettes* 9	1.2.1.4, 1 UBU	(79.9)	201.2.4,3	(60,463)	756.7	Ha 32
Birot, *Tablettes* 10	1.1.2.4	(75.5)	198.4.3,5	(59,675)	790.3	Ha 32
Birot, *Tablettes* 11	1.1.4.0.2	(470.6)	1,805.2.4,7	(541,667)	1,151.0	Ha 32

163 Powell 1985: 28–29 cites modern Iraqi yields from as low as 56 to as high as 121 GUR per BUR.

164 Cf. OECT XV 121 and 134, which report yields on smaller plots, some as small as 15 SAR ($^{1}/_{20}$th of a hectare).

165 This total from Jacobsen 1982: 39, 43 (Appendix 18) combines data from three Larsa texts (n.d., Ha 35 and Ha 39), each of which measures multiple fields, with individual yields ranging from as low as 462 to as high as 2,315 liters per hectare.

166 The yields from this text are conceivably higher: amounts of barley are represented in columns two and three of this text, following a first column giving field size. Column three is headed ŠE NÌ.KU$_5$, but the header for column two is broken. The amounts in column two are consistently twice the amounts in column three, but the relationship between the two amounts is unclear; the neat 2:1 ratio is too ideal to represent expected versus actual yields. For the moment, the only certainty is that the amount called ŠE NÌ.KU$_5$ was an actual amount harvested; see Powell 1985: 32 and n. 94.

167 Birot himself (1969: 44–46) believed that the totals in these eleven texts, from *iššakkum* land, represented either $^{2}/_{3}$ of total production, or that they were totals from which a rent or levy was subsequently derived (cf. Ellis 1976: 12–13, 31; p. 28, opining that these tablets might have come from Lagaš and not Larsa; but cf. *ibid.*, 30 n. 100).

Table 3: Larsa toponyms with known field-sizes and/or yields with minimum hectare estimates

Toponym		largest known record of land	largest single yield of grain (ŠE.GUR)[a]	minimum land in hectares
Aḫanuta	1	NBC 8161: 6.2.3*	*none*	43.4
Kubatum	1.1	AbB IV 35, XI 165: 7.0.0	*none*	44.4
Abisare	2	OECT XV 112: 2.0.0	YOS 5 175: 415.4.0	155.4
Ašdubba	3	*none*	VS 13 100: 96.0.0	35.8
Dimat-Balmunamḫe	4	*none*	YBC 5585: 938.2.0	350.7
Dimat-Kunanim	5	NBC 8161: 1.2.6.1.5*	*none*	550
Dimat-Nutuptum	5.3	NBC 8161: 6.1.2	*none*	40.9
Dimat-Warad-ili	5.4	NBC 8161: 1.2.2.1	*none*	80.8
Ewirnum	5.5	NBC 8161: 1.4.0.0	*none*	88.9
Til-Ḫatudum	5.7	NBC 8161: 2.2.6.2.0	*none*	931.4
Til-Mer[rik?]	5.8	NBC 8161: 1.0.3	*none*	7.4
É.GAL **lands**	7	YBC 7238: 3.1.9.0.0	[➛ at least 2716.0.0]	1263.8
Eduru-Šulgi	8	TCL 11 171: 2.1.5, 75 SAR	[➛ 76.0.3]	16.8
Ḫanṣipatanu	9	OECT XV 80: 1.1.0	*none*	8.4
A.GÀR Aluratum	9.2	OECT XV 80: 0.2.0	*none*	4.2
A.GÀR Diḫlani	9.4	OECT XV 80: 1.1.0	*none*	8.4
A.GÀR Ḫupatum	9.7	OECT XV 80: 0.1.0	*none*	2.1
A.GÀR Kuštanu	9.8	OECT XV 80: 1.0.0	*none*	6.3
A.GÀR/URU Kururu	9.9	YBC 7238: 1.0.0.0.0	[➛ at least 1000.0.0]	381
A.GÀR Raḫinuru	9.10	OECT XV 13: 0.2.0	*none*	4.2
Ḫašur	10	TCL 11 146: 3.1.1.3	*none*	200
Iddi-Uraš	11	*none*	YOS 5 166: 60.0.0	22.4
Iškun-Ea	12	*none*	YOS 5 201: 972.0.0	363.3
KA.AN	13	TCL 17 5: 5.0.0	YBC 5585: 840.0.0	313.9
Tilla	13.3	AbB IV 109: 2.6.0.0	*none*	165.1
Masabum	14	*none*	YOS 5 185: 597.4.0	223.4
MÁŠ.ZI	15	*none*	YOS 5 166: 609.0.0	227.6
Raḫabum	17	OECT XV 22: 6.0.0	*none*	38.1
Bela	17.2	NBC 8161: 1.6.0.0	*none*	101.6
Ḫarab-kare	17.6	OECT XV 22: 6.0.2	*none*	38.8
Ki-Utuèa	17.8	OECT XV 106: 1.0.2.2.5	[➛ 503.3.1]	399.7
Ki-Utušua	17.9	OECT XV 128: 4.0.0	*none*	25.4
Nanna-gugal	17.10	OECT XV 22: 0.0.5, 15	*none*	1.8
Šunnamungim	17.15	OECT XV 121: 6.2.4, 70 sar	*none*	52.1
Mašum	17.16	TCL 10 133: 4.6.1.1	AbB XI 185: 100.0.0	294.6
Nūr-libi	17.17	TCL 10 133: 1.0.2.2	*none*	68.4
Sin-nūr-mātim	19	*none*	YOS 5 181: 922.0.0	344.6
Širimtum	20	AbB XIV 49: 6.0.0	AbB XIV 63 (=TCL 17 1): 840.0.0	313.9
A.ŠÀ DU$_6$	20.1	*none*	TCL 17 4: 120.0.0	44.8
A.ŠÀ Gula	20.2	*none*	AbB XIV 56: 110.0.0	41.1
A.ŠÀ Hiššar	20.3	*none*	AbB XIV 64: 160.0.0	59.8
A.ŠÀ IGI.URU	20.4	TCL 17 10: 8.1.0	AbB XIV 56: 174.0.0	65
A.ŠÀ Munḫiatim	20.5	*none*	AbB XIV 58: 504.0.0	188.3
A.ŠÀ Pi-ilim	20.6	AbB XIV 59: 2.0.0	AbB XIV 57: 210.0.0	78.4
A.ŠÀ *ṣērim*	20.7	AbB XIV 59: 3.0.0	AbB XIV 56: 470.0.0	175.6
Ḫumsirum	22	YBC 7248: 5.5.0.5	*none*	351
			TOTAL HECTARES:	8223 ha.

[a] Estimated field sizes are reconstructed from the rate of 802 liters/hectare (see below); the 415.4.0 ŠE.GUR of Abisare from YOS 5 175, for instance, gives 124,740 liters of grain, with an implied result of 155.4 hectares, much larger than OECT XV 112's 12.7 hectares (= 2.0.0 IKU A.ŠÀ).

* Indicates that the number is a fragmentary minimum; actual size of field or yield is larger, but the actual total is unreconstructable

➛ Indicates a barley yield reported directly from the same land enumerated in the previous column.

The seventeen figures in Fig. 3 all derive from institutional texts; their average yield is 802.6 liters per hectare, which is unexpectedly close to Hammurabi's famous boast about pocketing "18 GUR per BUR" (ca. 844 liters per hectare) as in-kind levies.[168] We must keep in mind, too, that such rates likely reflect the tax burden on fields rather than total production, with an unspecified portion unaccounted for. Once again, we cannot depend on such numbers to be right in any absolute sense, but they are perfectly dependable as known minimums.

Adopting this 802.6 liters/hectare figure as an estimated *minimal* rate of production, then, what would known yields tell us about the commensurately minimum sizes of the lands producing them? We most often know attested quantities of harvested barley without knowing the size of the land they are grown on (cf. figures for É-GAL lands, Eduru-Šulgi, Kururu, and Ki-Utuea on Table 3, where the opposite situation pertains), and all of the towns for which both types of data exist show yields much larger than known fields could produce. Looking at the known amounts of barley irrespective of documented land, we find 12,257.4.5 ŠE.GUR, some 3,677,390 liters. At the 802.6 liter per hectare rate, this implies 4,581.8 hectares of land under production (Table 3, col. 4), fairly close the known areas of land (5,378 hectares, col. 3).

On present evidence, we cannot really hope to be more substantially accurate by using one type of information over the other, from either field sizes or barley yields. And once again we are setting aside factors that we know would add massive quantities of land to our estimate. Twenty-eight of seventy-four known Larsa toponyms preserve neither production figures

[168] Stated field rental rates of the period put the tax rate at 16–18 GUR per BUR: Ellis 1976: 57 n. 228; Birot 1969: 44–46; cf. Wright 1969: 13–14.

or field sizes, for one thing;[169] and some of the largest documented barley yields come from texts which do not even mention the location of the productive fields at all, only the names of the overseeing officials. And—an overarching problem—many of the documented yields may represent quantities due as taxes, and not statements of entire yields.[170]

Fortunately, this is not a "completist" project. Since we do have these forty-six toponyms with known, unique data for lands and/or yields (see Table 3), I will collate both, avoiding overlaps, to arrive at a known minimum of Larsa land. That is, for any toponym with a statistic of either kind, I will use the larger amount of land reported either in the form of a field size or implied from a harvest yield. This produces a documented area of land of 8,223 hectares (Table 3, col. 5; at 3,528.36 m^2 per IKU, this comes to 23,305 IKU), an estimate about 89% of what Hunt might have assumed, but only about 42% of the MASS estimate. I will make my assessment of invested labor-value on that amount of land.

Labor value of the harvest

We find ourselves happily equipped with an even better set of normative work rates for farming than we were for building. (The superior standardization of work rates in the agricultural sector as against the construction sector is by itself suggestive of its greater institutional importance.) With such normative rates in hand, it is a relatively straightforward business to attach them to the land base estimate of 8,223 hectares. But what are the expected tasks of barley farming? We can begin by comparing some of the steps observed in modern barley farming by Hillman, and those found in the didactic Sumerian work called the *Farmer's Instructions* (hereafter, *FI*). Tasks for which accounting rates are known or reconstructable are in bold; tasks for which I have been unable to account labor-values appear in italics.

[169] It is possible that the clustering of data for harvest yields and cadastral field-sizes in particular toponyms reflects a localization of the institutional sector within the Larsa state. That is, toponyms without (or without much) data for these categories (even including such towns as Ašdubba, Nabrara, and Warad-Sîn (but see now Owen 2012: 450-51), often mentioned in other contexts) may reflect a sector of villages and towns in which freeholders predominated, whereas well-documented towns had greater institutional affinities. The distribution may also, however, be purely accidental, a consequence of our uneven recovery of the sources. The question is promising (or troubling) enough to warrant further study.

[170] Powell 1985: 8–10, opined that GÚ-NA-BI "probably means 'its revenue,' not 'its yield'."

Figure 4: Barley farming taskwork

Hillman[171]	Farmer's Instructions[172]
Manuring	**Inspection of Irrigation**
Tilling	**Field-flooding**
Harrowing	**Guarding Crops** (from cattle)
Clearing Irrigation Channels	**Weeding**
Clod-Breaking	**Hoeing / Smoothing**
Hoeing Grooves	*Assemble / Repair Tools*
Sowing	**Plow Once with Oxen**
Covering Seed	**Second Plowing**
Repeated Irrigations	**Harrow 3 Times**
Repeated Weedings	**"Flatten Stubborn Spots"**
Culling Green Crops	**Sowing**
Guarding Ripening Crops	**Clod-Breaking**
Harvesting	**"Pest Control"**
Temporary Field Storage	**3 Irrigations**
Transport to Threshing Floor	**Optional 4th Irrigation**
Preparation of Threshing Floor	**Harvest**
Root Removal	**Lay Down Sheaves**
Threshing	*Rest the Sheaves*
Raking Straw	**Transport Sheaves**
Heaping Grain	*Clean Threshing Room Floor*
Winnowing (Once)	**Thresh**
Re-Threshing and **Winnowing of Straw**	**Winnow**
First Sieving	**"Move Grain Around"**
Second Sieving	*Measure Grain*
Grain Washing	*"Release the Grain"*
Grain Storage	
Straw Transport and Storage	

Table 4 represents the collation of these two lists, though a few tasks have been lightly re-titled. Indeed, not all of the above steps so clearly correspond to one another, nor do normative rates exist for all of them. What we can do is to pick out the core tasks for which rates exist, set aside those that don't (*e.g.*, root removal, repairing tools, resting sheaves) and

171 Hillman 1984: *passim*; 1985: 1–11; similarly, see Charles 1990. The situation with these articles is similar to Seeher's work: while they are exhaustive studies of labor processes, they do not offer consistent or actionable econometric data for our purposes.

Table 4: Tasks for Larsa barley farming on 8223.0 hectares (23,305 IKU); expected yield at 802.6 liters/hectare[a]

task	term	known rate[b]	laborers per operation	Labor Days
PREPARATION				
"Trough" clearing	KÁB-KU$_5$	10 GÍN	1 man	54,820
Plowing × 1.5	GEŠ-TÚG-GUR	1 IKU	3 men, 2 oxen[c]	174,787
Harrowing × 3	GEŠ-ÙR-RA	5 IKU	3 men, 2 oxen	69,915
Clod-clearing	NÌ-GUL	20 SAR	1 man	116,525
Smoothing	TÉŠ … SIG$_{10}$	12 SAR	1 man	194,208
PLANTING				
Furrowing / Sowing	GEŠ-APIN	2 IKU	3 men, 1 ox	46,609
Hoeing[d]	AL / AL DÙ	7 SAR	1 man	332,928
MAINTENANCE				
Weeding × 3	Ú ZÉ-A	20 SAR	1 man	116,525
Irrigations × 4	A DÉ	[see notes]	4–5 men	90,561
Guarding Crops × 120	(*FI*, ll. 65–66[e])	—	[1/8 man]	291,312
HARVEST				
Harvesting	ŠE GUR$_{10}$	1 GUR	1 man	21,999
Sheaf-binding	ZAR KÉŠE/SÁ	1 IKU	2 men	46,610
Bringing-in	ŠE DE$_5$	[see notes]	n/a	46,610
Threshing	ŠE GEŠ RÁḪ	4 BARIGA	2 men	54,998
Winnowing × 1.5	ŠE LÁL	2 BARIGA	2 men	164,994
Transport	Á MÁ.ḪI.A *maštitum* & Á LÚ.ŠE.ÍL	[5%]	n/a	91,170
TOTAL labor-days				1,914,571

[a] 23,305 IKU ➛ 6,599,780 liters (= 21,999⁺ GUR). See also Robson 1999: 163–165.
[b] Analogous rates appear in brackets.
[c] Englund 2012: 451–452.
[d] *I.e.*, seed-covering.
[e] ETCSL 5.6.3, ll. 65–66: "After the seedlings break open the ground, perform the rites against the mice. Turn away the teeth of the locusts" (SIZKÚR ^{d}NIN-KILIM-KE$_4$ [*sic*?] DUG$_4$-GA-AB / ZÚ BIR$_5$ MUŠEN-RA BAL-E-EB).

build a portrait of the labor-value invested in that subset of tasks. Behind virtually every task listed in Fig. 4 (above) lay also the work of building and maintaining equipment and infrastructure for it—plows, harrows, hoes, mauls, boats, threshing sheds—the labor-value of which cannot be accounted for here. The labor value of animals, on the other hand, can and must be costed into our analysis if only for the reason that they consumed at least as much food as human laborers (and probably a lot more[173]), and directly impacted the source-value of that labor's very object, *i.e.*, grain; each animal will therefore be accounted for here as one person. (See Appendix 3, p. 312, for notes on tasks accounted for in Table 4.)

The estimated labor value of the annual Larsa barley harvest comes to **1,914,571** labor-days, virtually the same as the estimated labor value of the city wall (**1,957,095** labor-days) from a particularized account of taskwork. In crude terms, city-states invested as much labor in producing a barley crop as they did in building a city wall; yet my labor estimate is only a fraction of what the Hunt and Hritz estimates assumed for this city-state (ca. 6.8-8 million labor-days).

Now it is worth recapitulating several premises of this part of the study. This barley-harvest estimate represents only a subset of all barley being grown in the Larsa state; this barley only represents a subset of all agricultural production (dates[174] and sesame[175] in particular were bulk-produced crops well-represented in state documents). Second, I have used, where available, the fastest-known work rates for farming tasks and omitted all labor investments related to infrastructure and tools. Third, it cannot be said strongly enough that the addition of labor-values for the excavation, dredging, and maintenance of the larger irrigation canals would add easily tens if not hundreds of thousands of more labor-days to my estimate for farming.

This study cannot account for important historical questions about farming and building as they were actually done *in process terms*—*e.g.*, the question of intensified production under Rīm-Sîn and Hammurabi (*i.e.*, adding labor costs), or of institutional abilities to streamline and ease production bottlenecks (*i.e.*, reducing labor costs through efficient allocations of labor). Most importantly, seasonality must be reintroduced to the equation. "Farming versus building" poses a false opposition in terms of opportunity costs or other disutilities: the work slotted into different parts of the year for the most part; the satisfaction of one type of work did not as a rule negatively impact the other. Different types of work were compartmentalized and pursued intensively and sequentially

172 Civil 1994: 28–33.

173 See, *e.g.* YOS 5 184, in which the grain expenses for the plow-teams in Iškun-Ea and Abisare in Rīm-Sîn 7 outstrip (hired) workers' wages by almost 10:1 (see also YOS 5 181).

174 *E.g.*, VS 13 96; TCL 11 153, 158, 160, 180, 182, 192; on labor costs for date versus grain production, see Rothman 1994: 154–56.

175 Goetze 1950b: 83–84.

in different parts of the year, mitigating the accumulation of tasks. The various Babylonian calendars, which were built around the seasonality of the agricultural year, featured such month names as "month of [cutting barley with] the sickle (*i.e.*, harvest),"[176] "the month the brick (is placed in the brick mold)," and so forth.[177] Preparing and tending crops, occupied the ninth through eleventh months, while it was the third month in which bricks were made, late summertime when canalwork was generally undertaken, *etc.*[178]

Administrative texts also used work rotations as an organizational principle,[179] and it is clear that irrigation work was compartmentalized into a fairly narrow section of the year.[180] The division of large projects into multiple phases is even attested in royal inscriptions. Tattanum of Tutub named one year for the making of bricks for a project, and the following year for the building; similarly, Sin-iddinam made the unusual claim for the Ebabbar that he "baked its baked brick in the course of one year;" Warad-Sîn claimed to have baked the bricks for the wall of Ur in only five months of a year;[181] cf. Samsuiluna, who tells us that he rebuilt the brickwork of six fortresses "in two months."[182] As little time as building work took, it is clear that it could be arranged in ways that did not interfere with the larger demands of the argicultural work year.

[176] Cohen 1993: 266.

[177] *Ibid.*, 93, 314–15, noting that *simanu* itself came to mean (simply) "season"; Englund 1988: 127; Jacobsen 1982: 57–60. Despite the fact that these month names are difficult to correlate to absolute seasons of the tropical year, the heuristic value, that different types of work were seasonally-appropriate, remains the same.

[178] Walters 1970: xiii, 103 n. 27, and 112; see also see CAD L s.v. *labānu* v., with references to "the month for making bricks and building houses and cities."

[179] Compare UET 5 866–71 and 875, timetables for scheduled work service; see also AbB IX 264.

[180] Inundations normally were done in January-March, according to Stephanie Rost (personal communication) with an earlier irrigation in October. The heavy work of dredging, however, was generally concentrated just before this, in August/September.

[181] Dalton 1983: 176; note that only one year-name of Tattanum is presently known; Frayne 1990: RIME 4 2.9.6 (pp. 164–165), ll. 35–37, and 2.13.21 (pp. 242–43), ll. 80–95; also note the last year-name of Sîn-iddinam and the first of Sîn-eribam, both named for the building of the wall at Maškan-šapir (Sigrist 1990: 25–26).

[182] Dalton 1983: 165.

Conclusion

The comparison does not pretend to accuracy in absolute terms; yet still the results are telling. I have come to an almost identical estimate of labor-value (ca. 1.9 millon labor-days) for both products under study. Of course, the terms of the study are deliberately skewed: I have imagined an absurdly large city-wall and assumed the slowest work-rates, and set that result against a fancifully small area of farmland worked at fast rates with a good deal of important tasks omitted from the accounting (including the excavation of canals). But let us imagine we *could* establish a level-playing field; what would an honest accounting find? That barley entails twice the labor of the wall? Maybe four times?

No: the truly equalizing condition was that growing the barley crop was an annual affair, while the city-wall was essentially built only once, with a few episodes of rebuildings, repairs, and maintenance. Even if we were to follow our argument to its final, illogical conclusion, and assume that the three major (re-)building episodes we know of between 1912 and 1837 were full and complete rebuildings of the city wall, we would still find (for those seventy-five years) only 5.7 million labor-days spent on wall-building, against 142.5 million labor-days on barley farming. Thus even maintaining the fantastic terms of the study, institutional building work still only comes to something like 4% of the farming work—not more than a week of work compared to six months of farming in any given year—and the real figure would be even smaller (compare to the United States' annual 4.7%-of-GDP spending on its military).

This disparity of value indicates a truth which may seem counter-intuitive or even uncomfortable, but must be stated bluntly: monumental architecture was cheap and easy to build,[183] despite the fact that it clearly had the persuasive ability to convey the opposite because it was visible, public, and durable.[184] Meanwhile, the brutal, back-breaking labor in-

[183] Seeher 2007: 222–24, came to much the same conclusion: "Whether 900, 1000, or 1,100 laborers were at work on the walls is beside the question; what is important here is to demonstrate that the Hittites would not have needed to supply and sustain hoards [sic] of several thousand workmen to build their city walls."

[184] Nor should we be impressed by the many episodes of wall-demolition that took place during this era, *e.g.* Warad-Sîn against Kazallu (Year 2), Iaḫdun-Lim against Samanum (Frayne 1990: RIME 4 6.8.2 [p. 606]), Zimri-Lim against Mišlan and Samanum (Year "i"), Hammurabi against Mari and

vested every day in ancient farming was hidden away by its spatial and social dispersement, and its low-status in terms of political messaging.[185] The shell game of ancient agricultural states was to privilege attention on the monumental, to imply its political and social importance in (false) economic terms, and to re-valorize the community labor it marshalled as a festival of royal largesse put on *by* the state for the benefit of the people. It was a consummate political triple-deception, one we reproduce n scholarship when we attend too closely to the focus and claims of the institutional sources. Old Babylonian kings uniformly attached visible public happiness (rather than safety and use) as the primary value of corvée labor for civic work: "I had my people eat food of all kinds and drink abundant water"; "[I] caused rejoicing in my city"; "My workforce did its work amid plenty"; and so forth. Even if we dismiss this as rank propaganda, we still must take note of the *focus* of that propaganda: public joy rather than public safety or royal prerogative. [186]

The exposure of labor-value disparity and a consideration of seasonality and other process issues makes the point that labor-demands for building were in fact *so* small in comparison to farming that they expose some assumptions about its social and legal contexts as ridiculous. Would it even be *possible* to create a corps of "forced," "unfree" or "semi-free" laborers to toil under adverse conditions—for no more than one week a year? Would workers who had toiled for 150 days of the year in the dirt and mud to grow barley for state and bare survival choose to resent a few days of collective labor, in the company of neighbors and with the prospect of feasting and song? Should we really imagine teams of tens of thousands groaning under the weight of massive building blocks under the stern eyes of whip-wielding overseers, when the average work-

Malgium, Samsuiluna against Ur and Uruk (Year 11), *etc.* Were one to assume that Hammurabi's army was at least half the size of Larsa's 40,000 men, and an accepted 20 GÍN/day rate for earth-movement above ground-level, the entire wall-mass (2,246,400m^3) of both Larsa's rampart and fortification wall could have been dispersed to nothingness—presumably refilling the moat or fosse—in as little as eighteen days by the Babylonian forces.

[185] But note the preponderant use of CAD A/1 s.v. *alāla* interj., the "refrain of a [joyous] work song," in farming rather than building contexts.

[186] On the rhetoric of a visibly happy (working) public, see Richardson 2012: 42; cf. the Sumerian proverb SPC 3.92, É ^{d}EN-LÍL-LA PA_4-HAR ADDIR-ÀM: "Enlil's temple is a gathering(?) of wages" (ETCSL 6.1.03).

account text deals with teams of workers numbering four dozen men?[187] These prospects seems ludicrous once we look at them this way.

I can imagine the challenges to such a reconstruction from a number of directions. No doubt there are ancient historians who know more about the types of work I have discussed. From the vantage point of value theory, it could be argued that I have measured one incommensurable against another, that these use-values cannot really be compared, *e.g.*, that city-walls defended the very life of the *polis*, a use for which no "price" could or (morally) should be put.[188] From an econometric view, it could be argued that the unit of labor-time is itself flawed, because basic energy inputs in one human labor hour "can differ up to 100-fold."[189] Or one could make a theoretical objection that labor-time was no more inherently dependeable an index of value than wages or prices.[190] A semantic association of wages with "presents" and "rewards" may also be worth investigating further; what we perceive as work and remuneration may have been considered performances of social responsibility and gratuity. From the perspective of organizational dynamics, it could be maintained that institutionally-directed projects had a unique capacity to aggregate and organize labor to ends that atomistic, non-centrally managed projects could not; or that the efficient allocation of

[187] Fully quantifying this description is beyond the scope of this paper, but see, *e.g.*, Walters' (1970) texts nos. 102, 103, 107, 108, 114 and 115, numbering 65, 45+, 165, 111, 122, and 169 workers, respectively (cf. text 98) — and especially texts 117–118, which cover 27 days of gang-labor averaging 46 men per gang. Walters concluded, *ibid.*, 152, that crews of workers could range from one to 32 men, but that "6 could be regarded as an average." Kienast 1978: 156, listing 90 workers; UET 5 721 (66 workmen in five gangs), and 722 (six gangs averaging 59 men per gang). Though labor-day estimates might run into the thousands (Walters, 1970: 149), we obviously need not imagine this implied thousands of workers.

[188] Frayne 1990: RIME 2.13.20 (p. 240), Warad-Sin on the city-wall of Ur: "... at whose base the black-headed people multiply (and) are able to save their lives — I built its great wall." One could, of course, make the same argument about the use-value of food; in 1763, it was the food-stores of Larsa that saved the lives of its citizens, and not its wall. Conversely, one can note the ironies of the "Lamentation Over the Destruction of Sumer and Ur" which presents the grim scene of breaching forced using the city wall to attack the defenders within, ll. 406–407b: "In Ur (people) were smashed as if they were clay pots / Its refugees were (unable) to flee, they were trapped inside the walls ..."

[189] Giampietro *et al.* 1993: 231.

[190] Janssen 1988 14–15 came down heavily in favor of use-value as a determining factor for prices.

resources by bureaucracies could streamline and transform productivity; or that competition between managers had similar effects.[191] On the worker side, it could also be argued that the objectification of both labor and laborer by administrative processes resulted in something very like a change in value itself; as Englund put it, "It is important to realize that these workers, who in the accounts are converted to workdays, really are dealt with in parallel fashion to the material they are to process."[192] All these considerations deserve more study in their own right.

But they cannot erase the fact of a massive disproportion of one type of labor to another. Proportion is by itself determinant of mode of production, with important implications for the social and political meaning of different types of labor. Farming was simply twenty-five times more work for the community than temple-building, palace-building, or city-wall building—and no market condition, no administrative system, no rhetoric would do anything to significantly alter that basic fact.[193] That being the case, a new conceptualization of mass labor must not only be articulated as a performance of polity-building in social terms as is now being done, but in economic terms as well. Given the relatively light demands of building labor, the participation of the community, and the state's efforts to invest such occasions with an atmosphere of feasting and plenty, we have to lay aside the presumption of mass labor as a disutility and consider it something closer to a prebend, an opportunity, a festival of inclusion and identity. It is not at all a necessary deduction that the absence of coercion meant that communitarian consensualism was based on pure altruism and principles of reciprocity, rather that it could be produced by incentives such as feasting, social approbation, and the production of group membership. That being the case, labor itself was perceived

[191] The various authors cited above comment on these organizational dynamics in passing: Walters 1970: 148–49; Hunt 1987: 161–62, 167; Fales and Postgate 1995: 16f.; cf. Wright 1969: 4 on "labor redundancy" in hierarchical/complex systems. An excellent case study of labor-organization is Moseley's (1975), on the pre-Columbian Moche Valley, esp. 191–93.

[192] Englund 1991: 258, 272; Walters 1970: 151–52 also noted that workers could be delivered (MU-TÚM) just like other commodities.

[193] Among other things, power levels in pre-industrial societies were limited to a low range. Giampietro *et al.* 1993: 239–41 point out: "The only process of conversion available … is the physiological conversion of food into applied power by human muscles." Shortages could be coped with only by strategies of changing the population structure, animal power, and a limited range of exosomatic (i.e., technological) instruments.

to have social, political, and economic values (whether they were "worth it" is quite another question), and labor cannot be isolated as a disutility; indeed few ancient sources represent it as such.[194] Beyond this, I have shown that a proportional look at the scope of the economy in its entirety is not a utopian idea, especially when the medium of that analysis maintains fidelity to ancient formal methods; and that substantive approaches need not (indeed, should not!) avoid formal econometric analysis. Nothing like a full formal analysis of the substance of value could be produced for any society, and Mesopotamia is no exception. But it is possible to achieve some perspective in terms of the largest components of the economy by comparing products through equilibrium pricing, through the determination of value-forms valid within their original contexts.

[194] Recent research into the so-called "IKEA Effect" has shown that there is a perceived increase in the valuation of products, both "utilitarian and hedonic," when they are self-made: see, *e.g.*, Norton *et al.*, 2011.

Appendix 1 (for use with Figure 1)

Notes on the reconstructed segments of the Larsa city wall[195]

Feature	Comments
Segment A	Running away to the southwest of Gate B56 are two sections of preserved wall, parallel to one another but spaced apart at 11 m, each no less than 10 m thick. It is proposed that segments A and I probably extended to insect one another at a point to the north of Z42, near the edge of the tell.[196] Length: 500 meters.
Gate B56	Situated atop a butte lying somewhat outside the main tell, composed of two piers of unequal size; the passage is 3.6 m wide and 19 m deep. The bricks in these features appear to match others used in Nūr-Adad's time, and so this feature may date to the 1860 rebuilding; but it also includes some types of bricks found in other structures, including B2, B15, B17, and B53.[197]
Segment B	Hypothetically connects Gates B 56 to Gate B25; of this segment nothing remains on the ground. Length: 350 meters.
Gate B25	A set of double gates at the north-central edge of the tell. The exterior, larger gates were formed by two 7×10 m piers set apart to allow a passage 8 m wide; a smaller "pincer-gate" in the interior was substantially narrower. All parts of this feature were made with baked brick. The gate was clearly one of the main entrances to the city, with two of the longest sections of street running directly to it, one (R1) running more or less directly south to the Ebabbar and the Nūr-Adad palace; the other (R2) running south-easterly through a neighborhood of buildings in the northeast quarter of the city (the "Quartier d'Habitat").[198]

[195] This reconstruction is mostly based on the report of Huot 1989 *et al.*

[196] On feature Z42, see Suire 2003.

[197] *Ibid.*, 42–45, 49; such bricks also match features B50 (in the monumental quarter), Gate B56, and B58, at the southern extremity of the tell. These "Nūr-Adad" bricks (Huot's "group 3" bricks, 34.5 × 36cm) are the smallest but most homogeneous type of brick found at the site. Note Birot's (1969: 47–48) Text 13, dated Hammurabi 38 and provenanced to the Larsa region: the text is an order for pine wood for the construction of a gate ca. 3.5 m wide, which would obviously fit this gate opening rather nicely.

[198] See Calvet 2001 on the layout of Larsa generally.

Segments C–E	Few features lie between Gates B25 and B1, but the wall connecting them cannot have been straight, since it would have cut right through the residential neighborhood. Two small sections of wall were found by the excavators at points Z27 (north of building B23 and lying a little outside the tell) and Z10 (due east of B22 at the tell's edge). A crude arc formed by points B25–Z27–Z10–B1 would form about a quarter of the entire city wall, consistent with the assumption of Huot *et al.* 1989 that the wall more or less conformed to the edge of the tell.[199] Lengths: 420, 330, and 680 meters, respectively.
Gate B1[200]	Made of the same type of Nūr-Adad-period baked bricks as B56, Gate B1 seems to have been built atop the ruins of a smaller, earlier gate, with an extremely narrow passageway of not more than a meter. The new passage was widened to about four meters between two massive towers each measuring 12×18 m. Presumably this formed the main eastern entrance to the city, although in this case the nearest street (R3) is much smaller than (R1) and (R2), and terminates at a point along the wall about 125 m to the north.[201]
Segment F	The most prominent perimeter feature, the "Chameau" was thus built on top of the rampart wall, and so plainly forms the connection between Gates B1 and B 36/17. Length: 690 meters.
Gates B36/17	These twin gates sit just a few meters from each other at the SSE edge of the tell. Gate B36 is formed by two U-shaped towers roughly 5×5.5 m each; the passage between them is 2 m wide and 15 m in length. This pincer-gate is situated on a low rise at a height barely higher than the (remnants of the) top of the rampart. Gate B17

[199] Huot *et al.* 1989: 40, "a peripheral band … delimited by the zone of construction;" an alternative hypothesis of the excavator, however, was that the wall was actually even bigger here, with some other traces suggesting repaired wall substantially beyond this area, around the so-called "Rue 5," and enclosing more structures. Unfortunately, since this road does not appear on Huot's plan, it is impossible to accommodate this conjecture in my reconstruction.

[200] This gate is the same one excavated by Parrot (1933: 177), labeled "QX."

[201] Huot *et al.* 1989: 32, 40–41.

	is a much larger affair: here the towers were 16m square, with a grand 10m wide passage, opening onto street (R6). The bricks of B17 differ from the "Nūr-Adad" type, and are similar to features B2, B15, B17, B53, and Gate B56.[202] Smaller wall segments adjacent to the gate likely formed a series of terraces and "anchor walls" that improved the field of fire, with parts of the wall jutting out from these gates to points Z12 and Z29.[203]
Segment G	The building B57 anchors this wall segment by its alignment to the wall at exposure Z12, and Huot guessed that it extended along a number of similarly aligned buildings at least as far as the small structure B58 at the extreme southern tip of the tell.[204] Length: 480 meters.
Segment H	Largely a matter of conjecture: that a wall enclosing the buildings in the southwest corner of the tell, extending westward from near B58, might have passed through feature Z36 to intersect with Segment I.[205] Length: 620 meters.
Segment I	Centered on probable remains of excavated city wall—a segment of butte 20m thick and running for around 50 m in length; the excavators suspect it may locate the remains of a gate (Z43).[206] The position of the wall is also marked by a line of kiln slag.[207] Length: 1,130 meters.

[202] *Ibid.*, 42.
[203] *Ibid.*, 47 fig. 17; Burke 2008: 83 fig. 9.
[204] *Ibid.*, 50.
[205] See Suire 2003: 11 fig. 1.
[206] *Ibid.*, 10–11, 13, and fig. 1.
[207] Huot and Calvet 2003: 10–11; another straight line of slag and ash was also noted to the west of Segment I at feature Z20, but unassociated with any brickwork. It lay further out from the tell, and ran in a NNE-SSW direction less likely to join Segments A and H to any purpose—unless it was to enclose feature 32, a three hectare necropolis, probably in use from the fourth to the first millennium BC (*ibid.*, 13).

Appendix 2 (for use with Table 1)

Notes on wall-building labor costs

- **Rampart excavation and heaping-up**: The normal term for excavation work was SAHAR ZI-GA; its complementary activity was KA-ALA SI-GA, literally only "opening (made by) the hoe" but, in context, the piling-up of the earth produced thereby.[208] Earth-moving rates for moving dirt are among the best-attested and most consistent work-rates in the cuneiform record, usually at 10 GÍN (3 m^3) per man-day for canal excavation work, though rates as fast as 20 GÍN per man-day are known for work at the uppermost-levels of the ground.[209] Unlike brickwork, Syro-Mesopotamian ramparts show no evidence of having required the mixing of earth with straw or stone, or of forming-work as *terre pisée*, *i.e.*, beaten, molded or packed down.[210] Thus "heaping up" was relatively uncomplicated, if heavy, work; consider that at the siege of Larsa, Hammurabi assigned only 450 men to the task of heaping up a siege ramp out of earth;[211] such work could be carried out piecemeal, by relatively small groups of workers over time. The following assumptions are built into the calculation: the proximity of the excavated *ḫirītum* to the rampart (SA-DU), thus no additional transport costs[212] and the binding of the two tasks as one;[213] and that earth for the ram-

208 Heimpel 2009: 239–40, discussing the difficulty of the term; Wright 1969: 18–19.

209 *Ibid.*, 285; Goetze 1962: 15; Walters 1970: xix; Englund 1988: 169 n. 42; Burke 2008 144f., with literature; cf. Wright 1969: 20; Charpin 1989: 197, employs a slower metric of 7.5 GÍN per man-day. At a weight of ca. 1202 kg per 3 m^3 earth, the weight of this earth moved is about 3606 kg per man per day.

210 Englund 1988: 169 n. 42 proposes a rate of 3.75 GÍN of pisée wall construction per man-day, reflecting the rate of actual work in four textual exemplars—but it is archaeologically unattested for city walls. See Burke 2008: 50–51: notwithstanding, many such ramparts have revealed (unmixed) *layers* of material other than earth, *e.g.* gravel, testifying "to the unsuitability of a rampart composed solely of earth or soil."

211 ARM 26/2 378 and 379.

212 Heimpel 2009: 285, documents some of the accounting devices used to alter work rate projections when distance (*nazbalum*, "carriage") was at issue.

213 The combined task probably lies behind ÉG SI-GA, the piling up of levee banks (Civil 1994: 115, 121); it should not be confused with the deeper, heavier work of dredging canals by basket (see *e.g.*, Walters 1970: 96 n. 14, Text 70 on *tupšikkum*, "forced labor"). See also Kingsbury 1977: 15 n. 4, commenting on soldiers guarding workers moving É.DURU$_5$.Ì.SÀ, "wet earth": such work was probably extremely unpleasant and reserved for prisoners or other truly forced laborers.

part was not obtained by digging purposely deep pits: I use an average of 10 GÍN per man-day to arrive at the 644,800 labor-days embedded in 1,934,400 m^3 of heaped-up earthen rampart.

- **Site clearing**: Mostly absent from Old Babylonian records, clearing building sites of old structure and rubble is nevertheless well-attested in Ur III and Neo-Assyrian[214] texts, though without identified work rates. With Heimpel,[215] one could assume a rate comparable to clod-clearing, *i.e.*, 45 SAR (1575 m^2) per day of surface area in agricultural work. Applied to the ca. 10m wide top of the 5.2 km rampart wall, this would produce a labor cost of a mere 33 days. However, I assume that the process included both minor demolition of existing brickwork and clearing, and compared it to clearing rates for more difficult terrain,[216] so I have lowered this rate to 10 SAR/day, to arrive at 149 labor-days.
- **Straw, Earth & Water**: The amounts of straw and earth in molded bricks is crucial to calculating many of the subsequent tasks. Oates was informed that every 100 bricks for the Tell Brak dighouse required 60 kg of straw, *i.e.*, about two standard American bales of hay (total 0.3 m^3). Unfortunately, Oates did not inform us of the size of the dighouse's bricks. We know, however, that the total size of the dighouse was 116m^3. If we assume a standard of 720 bricks/sar (18 m^3), then we can estimate that 100 bricks had a mass of 2.5 m^3, only 0.3 m^3 of which was made up of straw, about 12%.[217] The estimated amount of materials for 312,000 m^3 of brick wall, then comes to 274,560 m^3 of earth (by weight, 330,021 metric tons, at ca. 1,202 kg/m^3) and 37,440 m^3 of straw (by weight, 7,488 metric tons, at ca. 200 kg/m^3). I assume that not more than 25% of mixed earth above the finished (*i.e.*, dried) brick volume would have been water, commensurate with modern adobe brick-making practice. Oates' conjecture that ash was included in the Tell Brak bricks is not corroborated by ancient texts, and is so excluded; likewise, any suggestion of bitumen mixed into the bricks.[218]
- **Straw harvesting**: Englund gives a normative rate of 1 GUR (=.3 m^3) of straw harvested per man-day.[219] The decay of straw was probably

214 Parpola 1987: 112–13.

215 Heimpel 2009: 240; Civil 1994: 86.

216 Goetze 1962: 15–16 cites an Ur III rate for clearing thorn bush at only 10 SAR/day.

217 Cf. Seeher 2007: 38 who used less than 4% straw.

218 Oates 1990: 388–89.

219 Englund 1988: 171, n. 45.

the single largest reason for the eventual crumbling of brickwork, but the material was necessary to providing matrix to the structure, and its durability was greatly improved by modest amounts of maintenance.[220]

- **Straw transport**: My presumption (see below) is that brickmaking took place at a number of locations both on and offsite; accordingly, straw was carried to a number of local production centers. Both Ur III and Old Babylonian texts show that straw was normally transported by boat, but sometimes hauled overland, perhaps by sledges.[221] It is impossible to know what distances were involved, and no normative rates for these procedures exist. At a minimum, however, we could assume that a worker could portage at least as much straw by weight as he could excavate earth (10 GÍN of straw, or 3606 kg) in a day. At 200 kg/m^3, that works out to the daily rate of about 18m^3 (=1 SAR).
- **Excavation**: This rate is identical to that used for procuring earth for the rampart wall; it assumes earth procurement at the site of brick production.
- **Pouring Water**: It is assumed that it was far easier to either produce bricks near available water or to dig an extension canal to a building site than to haul water to it. Yet it is not clear that the provision of water was not a task already subsumed under the heading of "mixing earth;"[222] nor that the excavated earth was not already wet. Yet it may also be that *du*ʾ*um* (a term whose etymology Heimpel expressed some puzzlement towards) alludes to the further "darkening" (> *daʾāmu*), as the addition of water to already damp earth changed its color. For our purposes, we will assume that drawing and pouring water was a necessary task. At 25% above finished volume, I assume 78,000 m^3 (78,000,000 liters or kilograms) of water drawn for the bricks of the Larsa fortification wall. I assume that weight was once again the bounding factor for labor inputs,[223] and a worker could be expected to portage about 3600 kg/day at close range (in practical terms, this implies a more or less constant rate of carrying about 7.5 kg/minute through an eight-hour workday).
- **Carrying earth**: The labor costs for this activity more or less reduplicate excavation work. Earth was carried in baskets holding a dry weight of

[220] Oates 1990: 388–89 and Gasche 1981: 44–47 and n. 7; cf. Seeher 2007: 221, who cites a much faster rate of 200–500 kg (1–2.5 m^3) per day.

[221] Heimpel 2009: 304–308; Walters 1970.

[222] Heimpel 2009: 241–42.

[223] Civil 1994: 69 refers to a carrying-jar with a capacity of about 30 liters.

about 13.3 kg or a wet weight of 22.5 kg,[224] apportioned into batches for mixing. Seeher cites a study for carrying earth across a 100 m distance at 0.35 m^3 per hour, or 2.8 m^3 for an eight-hour day.[225]

- **Mixing earth**: Since rates for this task are usually subsumed under brick-making as a single activity, it can be difficult to break it out individually. Research into traditional methods of mixing emphasizes manual mixing (actually, by foot) as preferential because small rocks can be removed and fine consistency achieved. A single worker might effectively process 0.23 m^3 every 90 minutes or so; assuming something like an eight hour workday, we arrive at a working rate of 1.725 m^3 per labor-day.[226] This rate is applied to the full mass of the brick wall (*i.e.*, both straw and earth together).
- **Molding bricks**: Assuming the use of the standard 720 brick per SAR, we anticipate the molding of 12,480,000 bricks total.[227] A number of known rates can be derived from either rations keyed to normative rates[228] or records of actual production,[229] all of which fall between 216–245 bricks molded per man-day. An Old Babylonian text from Kisurra, however, calls for 360 men to mold 10 IKU of bricks in five days.[230] Assuming 72,000 bricks per IKU, this rate comes out substantially higher at 400 bricks/day, but the tone of the letter seems to acknowledge this rate as an accelerated one: "The work of an entire month must be done in five days! You are required not to be indolent!"[231]

[224] Baskets probably also aided in standardizing proportions of ingredients (Powell 1990: 490). Why Heimpel (2009: 250) assumes water was added to earth before it was carried is unclear. Note large deliveries of baskets in UET V (519, 642–663) which may reflect preparations for institutional building activity.

[225] Seeher 2007: 219–20.

[226] Keefe 2005: 62–64; cf. Seeher 2007: 219, citing a faster rate of 0.5 m^3 per hour.

[227] If such numbers seem daunting, compare with a single delivery for a canal wall cited by Dalton (1983: 138), calling for 1.3 million bricks, or Jacobsen's (1982: 62) discussion of hundreds of thousands of liters and millions of bricks used in Early Dynastic building projects. The best-known surviving bricks from Larsa, *i.e.*, those with royal inscriptions, were substantially smaller (c. 2700 bricks/SAR) than the bricks assumed by mathematical and accounting texts (720 bricks/SAR).

[228] Heimpel 2009: 223–24.

[229] Walters 1970: 127–28 (Text 101) and 133 (Text 109).

[230] Kienast 1978: 143–44 (Text 154).

[231] A preceding task, wooden mold-making, is not folded in here. Paulus (1979/81: 130) hazards that molds might have been kept as the property of individual gangs from year to year; cf. Moseley (1975: 194) on Peruvian work-teams: "The association of segments, brick symbols, and soils [in the bricks] implies that makers' marks identified specific groups of individuals who not only produced adobes but transported them to the construction site..."

- **Baking bricks**: It is my assumption that most bricks of the fortification wall were sun-dried, and only a small proportion actually fired; that proportion seems reflected in the survival of only specific features, especially the gates. Certainly no more than 10% of the wall remains (and probably less), and I have assumed this mass for the proportion of fired bricks (*i.e.*, 1,248,000 bricks). It is clear that such quantities of baked brick could be produced at one time: one large inventory related to the construction of a canal wall near contemporary Lagaš, lists 512,640 baked bricks among a total consignment of 1,310,320, roughly 39% of the whole.[232] I will assume that it did not take more labor to fire bricks than to mold them in the first place.
- **Carrying bricks**: Most bricks were not made on the building site. For the Larsa wall, there is significant evidence to suggest brick production both at Larsa[233] and elsewhere,[234] near watercourses, and the numerous brick-delivery texts from the Walters[235] and Heimpel[236] volumes attest

232 Walters 1970: 125–26 no. 99.

233 A number of kilns were identified by Huot *et al.* 1989: 34–36, 38 at Larsa; these may have had several purposes (*e.g.*, for ceramics, metalworking, or cooking), but three ovens out on the plain were associated with deformed, cast-off bricks: F10, F11, and F15. Similarly, at Ur, most surviving exemplars of Warad-Sîn Year 10 bricks (Frayne 1990: RIME 4 2.13.18 [pp. 236–37]) were found at the easternmost edge of the tell.

234 Of two stamped brick exemplars of Gungunum's Year 21 inscription, one was found at Larsa, and one at Umm al-Wawiya, a small site between Larsa and Uruk (Frayne 1990: RIME4 2.5.2 [p. 117]). Adams and Nissen (1972: 54, 217) proposed to identify the site (no. 439) as Enegi, and concluded that, "since traces of defensive systems are rather rare in connection with settlements of this size … we feel that it may be a town on the border between two city states." However, since there is not, in fact, any trace of coherent military architecture here—just ten loose fragmentary bricks of Gungunum and Amar-Sîn—it seems to me to make more sense to think of it as a specialized production site. Compare with other specialized production sites in the Larsa hinterlands, *e.g.* sites 428 and 429 (ceramics production, *ibid.*, p. 236). Frayne (1990: RIME 4 2.5.2 [pp. 117–18]) certifies that the Gungunum inscription is, in fact, the one for his Year 21 building of the Larsa city wall (l. 9: "in the course of one year, I made its bricks"); cf. Birot 1968: 242 col. 2. See also Dalton 1983: 90, on the possibility of brick-production at Dunnum; compare also with Lanfranchi and Parpola 1990: 206–210 and nos. 291 and 296.

235 *E.g.*, Walters 1970: 96 and nos. 17 and 21 (no. 70); *ibid.*, 135 (no. 112), and 140 (nos. 117–19), specifying men carrying bricks (ERÍN LÚ-SIG$_4$-ÍL-ÍL) and boatmen (ERÍN LÚ-MÁ-LAḪ$_4$-LAḪ$_4$).

236 Heimpel 2009: 161–62, citing thirteen texts listing the delivery of almost 300,000 bricks (more than 1,500 m^3).

to off-site production as a widespread practice.[237] Unfortunately, the distance and multiplicity of production sites precludes any normative value. In the absence of this, we must rely on an anecdotal example. Walters' texts 112 and 113 provide both a number of men (six) delivering quantities of brick by boat. In addition to the six workers, we must count an overseer (one Mr. Sasiya) and, per Walters' text 118, a boatman. Thus, eight men were required to deliver the (smaller) delivery in text 112 of ½ SAR of bricks, providing our labor rate of 3.75 GÍN/day (or $1.125m^3$).[238]

- **Building**: The task of bricklaying and working with mortar (NAGÀ/*esittu*) is subsumed under the rubric ŠU DÍM. Following Heimpel, I understand the term to include associated tasks such as "handing up bricks" (SIG_4 ŠU DÍM-MA SUM) and "lifting earth" (IM Ì-LI-DE_9, *i.e.*, as mortar). It is too difficult to incorporate here a principle the ancient accountants understood, namely that the work pace slowed the higher the work on the wall had to reach. I derive the all-important rate of bricklaying on one simple principle: that, having separated out all other tasks related to preparing the site and the bricks, bricklaying could not have proceeded at a rate *slower* than the overall rate cited by Mallowan for the Tell Brak dighouse.
- **Delivering reeds**: A known rate of 2 bundles of reeds gathered per man-day, each bundle representing about $1m^2$ when laid out.[239] As determined below, the total number of reeds required would be $936{,}000m^2$; also known is the consistent makeup of one reed bundle (SA-GI) per $1\ m^2$ of finished matting.[240] Reed-cutting was almost always accounted for in terms of area cleared rather than bundled product, but TCL 5 5675 (Umma, AS 04) gives two figures averaging 26 SA-GI per day, or $26\ m^2$ per man-day.

[237] See also Kienast 1978: Bd. 1 1–5, positing that brick production at Kisurra was for Isin, 20 km distant; and examples in CAD L s.v. *labānu* A 1b: "BE 9 51 and Watelin Kish 3 pl. 14." Of course, the actual building of barges is not folded into this calculation; see Englund 1988: 169 n. 42 for a boat-building rate between 10 and 15 workdays per GUR-capacity.

[238] cf. AbB IX no. 132.

[239] Englund 1988: 171, n. 45.

[240] Goetze 1948: 182; Stephanie Rost (personal communication) has directed my attention, however, to Sallaberger 1989 and Waetzoldt 1992, who argue for slower labor rates than Goetze assumed; their observations would tend to inflate some of the labor costs for some of the reed-related tasks discussed here.

- **Laying reeds**: Englund cites an Ur III period rate stating that six 1×1 m reed mats could be produced in one man-day, and Heimpel cites two GARšana texts which reflect exactly that same day-rate (6 m^2/day).[241] Though some excavated structures reveal the use of GISAL-mats every fourteen or eighteen courses interspersed in the brickwork, I will assume the low (*i.e.*, more labor-intensive) rate of every five courses. For a wall 6 m high, and assuming a brick height of 6 cm, that would require a course of reed mats every 30 cm, or 18 courses of reed matting (excluding the very bottom and the very top of the wall). Each course would require 52,000 m^2 of GISAL-mat (for a wall 10 m thick and 5200 m long), *i.e.*, 936,000 m^2 of GISAL-mat at the 6 m^2/day rate.
- **Trimming reeds**: This activity has no known directly-attested work rates, but the slowest rate for trimming (horizontally, one assumes) is about 8 SAR (288 m^2) per day (SNAT 457, Umma ŠS 02), a rate applied here for the inner and outer façade of the wall (total 62,400 m^2).
- **Plaster production**: I assume a layer of plaster 1 cm thick across the façades and the top of the wall, which should come to 1,144 m^3 of required plaster. I assume this work involved processing gypsum: crushing it to powder from its crystalline form; heating it to a low temperature; and combining it with water to form "a material that sets and finally becomes very hard" and water-resistant.[242] I have thus assumed a production rate half as fast as that for mixing earth.
- **Plastering reeds**: We encounter some difficulty in that the activity of "slapping on" plaster, as Heimpel translates it, is neither an attested work rate, nor is it easily likened to some other type of work. For heuristic purposes, however, I cannot imagine that this work went more slowly than the act of weeding, which was carried out at a rate of 10 SAR (360 m^2) per man-day on 936,000 m^2 of interleaved reed mats.
- **Wall plastering**: See above; the same rate would be applied for plastering the inner and outer façades and top of the wall (and area of 114,400m^2).[243]

[241] Englund 1988: 169–70 n. 43; Heimpel 2009: 258–59.
[242] Lucas 1989: 76–79.
[243] Kienast 1978: Text 155.

Appendix 3 (for use with Table 4)

Notes on farming labor costs

- **Canal clearing:** The first task of any season was the clearing of the small canal branches below the level of institutional responsibility[244] in anticipation of a pre-plowing irrigation (the labor cost of which is included below under "Irrigations"). One way to try to measure this is by the assumption that every field was associated with a small ditch regulated by a water-distribution gate (KÁB-KU$_5$); Hunt shows the volume of the ditches might be around 499 m^3 per one hectare of land to be irrigated.[245] The width and depth of these was relatively stable (ca. 5 m wide and 2.5 m deep), while lengths varied according to the size of the fields, but averaging about 40 m per hectare. I have assumed that exacavation work to dredge 10 cm of silt from them would entail the removal of 20 m^3 per hectare (*i.e.*, 164,460 m^3 in all) at the 10 GÍR (3 m^3)/day rate. Stephanie Rost, however, has pointed out in a personal communication how problematic it would be to associate KÁB-KU$_5$ (or KUN-ZI-DA) water control devices exclusively with non-institutional use, since much institutional work (including SAḪAR ZI-GA/SI-GA/ŠU-TI-A, and KIN Ú SAḪAR-BA) also used them. Having said that, the resulting costs here assume nothing of maintenance of much larger canals, and is heuristically valid as a *minimum* cost.
- **Plowing:** Some sources suggest three plowings (*FI*, ll. 30-34: once each with the ^{giš}BAR-DILI, ^{giš}APIN-TÚG-SAGA$_{11}$, and TÚG-GUR plows), while others[246] suggest only one. Michael Jursa has suggested to me that second plowings were only necessary to open up new fields (*i.e.*, new to cultivation, coming out of fallow, or with difficult soil); but cf. AbB IX 151, which discusses fields "that have been harrowed, broken up, *ploughed three times* [emphasis mine]; fit for seeder-ploughing and soaked with water." I will split the difference, assuming that half of the fields needed both a "soft-soil" and a preparatory plowing for one reason or another. At least three persons were required for the job.

[244] See especially Rost 2011 on the variability in labor organization for irrigation work. AbB II 147 gives a window onto the delicate line between collective versus state responsibility for labor: an overseer writes requesting more workers after the workmen of a village are unable to clear their local canal; cf. Walters 1970: 14.

[245] Hunt 1988: 195 Chart 2; on the reading KÁB-KU$_5$, see Selz 1989.

[246] Englund 2012: 451–52.

Ur III documents employed rates of between 75–82 SAR/day,[247] but I have used a faster rate of 1 IKU/day.

- **Harrowing:** This task also required three people, though often one of these was a boy "employed" to sit on the harrow to add weight. The harrow moved much faster than the plow, sometimes as fast as 6 IKU per day, but normally with a rate of 5 IKU /day, sometimes sinking as low as 4.5 IKU;[248] I will use the 5 IKU rate.
- **Clod-clearing:** Rates as low as 8–10 SAR/day are known from Umma documents; most common are 10–20 SAR/day,[249] though rates as fast as 45 SAR/day are also known.[250] I have adopted a quick rate of 20 SAR/day.
- **Smoothing:** The last stage in field preparation would have been to smooth or level the remaining uneven places left by the previous tasks. Field-leveling was a slow, painstaking business, usually at a rate of 10–12 SAR/day;[251] I will use the quicker rate of 12 SAR/day.
- **Furrowing and sowing**: I will assume that all fields were planted with a seeder-plow, though this was likely only available to a minority of cultivators; many would have used a slower and more labor-intensive method of hoe-planting at 10–20 SAR/day. A light seeder-plow would have required either one or two oxen (I have assumed one) and three men working, covering up to 2 IKU/day.[252]
- **Hoeing:** *i.e.*, covering seed. Whatever the availability of seeder-plows, covering seed had to be done by hoe. Attested rates range between ½ and 10 (but most commonly between 5–7) SAR per day.[253] I will assume the fastest known rate of 10 SAR (353 m^2) per day.
- **Weeding:** The growing season for barley lasted four months; weeding is heavily correlated to higher yields. I have assumed three weeding operations at four-week intervals within the four months. Known rates

[247] Civil 1994: 75–77.

[248] *Ibid.*, 77.

[249] Englund 1991: 265; and the CDL Wiki page on attested work rates, in particular here for NÍG-GUL work (hereafter: "CDLI work rates Wiki"): http://128.97.154.151/wiki/doku.php/ur_iii_equivalency_values.

[250] Civil 1994: 86.

[251] *Ibid.*, 78.

[252] Maekawa 1984: 82; Civil 1994: 75–76, 83; Jacobsen 1982: 59–60.

[253] CDLI work rates Wiki; see also Civil 1994: 79–80, adducing 128 examples of hoeing rates, averaging 5.2 SAR/day, and noting the difference between AL DÙ and AL AK work.

range between 10–20 SAR/day, but the faster rate for Ú ZÉ-A is better attested; SIG_7 normally refers to reed.[254]

- **Irrigation:** This task is much less standardized than others and difficult to assess. Central bureaucracies were mostly involved in the construction and maintenance of irrigation works, not in the operation of the small feeder canals used for actual individual inundations.[255] In principle, the inundation of individual plots seems easy work: one opens a sluice, the water pours in, and one closes it. Civil, however, details some of the types of work associated with controlled flooding, and argues against seeing the "workmen as passive spectators": there were berms, dams and outlets to be built, quaternary channels to be prepared, and equipment to be manned.[256] Stephanie Rost (personal communication) has pointed out the continuous vigilance required to guard against levee breaks and the wasteage of water, including during night-time; a commonly-used term associated with inundations, A-DA GUB-BA ("stationed at the water") may refer to this kind of general watchfulness or a more specific task.

I have used the average of two methods to estimate the labor-value for inundations. First, I followed van Driel in assuming 1.2 ha. as an average-sized plot (6,853 notional "plots"; cf. Rothman, who assumes 5 ha. plots[257]). Each plot required three men working each of three irrigations following weeding, plus a preceding irrigation prior to plowing; a fourth man was necessary to work any relevant equipment (sluice, *shaduf*, *etc.*) and supervise adherance to water-rights procedures.[258] This method gave 109,648 labor-days. Second, I followed Maekawa, who documented five irrigations of (at their largest) 8.15-IKU plots at Lagaš (numbering 2,859 plots); each involved five men, presumably over the course of a growing season; this gives the lower figure of 71,475 labor-days.[259] The figure on Table 4 (p. 294) is the simple average of these two rates.[260] Neither the van Driel nor the Maekawa model includes any labor costs from preparatory canal digging or maintenance.

[254] Englund 2012: 450.
[255] Hunt 1987: 173.
[256] Civil 1994: 68; see Rost and Hamdani 2011 on traditional dam construction.
[257] Rothman 1994: 160, 163, fig. 5; his assumption seems to be drawn from his reading of TCL 10 133, which document institutional plots at Mašum and Nūr-libi.
[258] Van Driel 2002: 86.
[259] Maekawa 1990: 127–28 and 141, Table 6.2.
[260] Incidental evidence might come from Walters 1990: 149, Text 24, which details "irrigation work" involving "60 workers (on every) 2 BUR"—but the

- **Guarding crops:**[261] Characterized by what we might think of as "heavy looking on," it seems difficult to acknowledge these as labor inputs. But crops were subject to predation by birds, infestation by insects, trampling by cattle and, at a certain point, theft by people; certainly the concern is echoed in the ancient texts. Assuming again the average 1.2 ha. plot size and a 120-day growing season, I acknowledge that this was hardly a full-time job, and might have been done by a young boy. Notwithstanding, even assuming that only an hour of the workday (1/8 labor-day) was devoted to this activity by someone over the growing season, the labor-inputs were substantial.
- **Harvesting:** One of the best documented activities of Babylonian antiquity, there were two ways to account for labor inputs: one was by field area, the other by finished harvested amount. Reaping (ŠE-GUR$_{10}$) ranges between ½ and 1½ IKU/day; a volumetric 1 GUR/day rate is also attested.[262] These rates give very similar results in terms of labor-time. At the volumetric rate, we come to 21,999 labor-days; at the areal rate, we get 23,305 labor-days. I will use the quicker rate here.
- **Sheaf-binding:** Working behind the reaper were two other men, a sheaf-binder and a man "to arrange the cut handfuls of grain before the latter" (*FI* ll. 74–80, one man as the sheaf-binder and another to "apportion the sheaves"). Assuming these men kept pace with the reaper, they also worked at a rate of 1 IKU/day.[263]
- **Bringing-in:** No attested rates are known for this activity. I have to assume that the delivery of sheaves to the threshing-room floor could not have entailed any less labor than binding them in the first place, and so I use that estimate as a minimal cost.
- **Threshing**: Attested rates for threshing ran well behind the pace of the bringing-in, at an attested 4 BARIGA (240 liters)/day. Two men were required, one to thresh and another to turn and shift the sheaves (what the *FI* calls "moving the grain around").[264]

nature of the work described is not clearly irrigation (the work is just called KIN; cf. Text 31, where KIN refers to canal excavation, not inundations), and the information is thus undependable.

261 For this and subsequent tasks, as well as others not considered here, see Hillman 1985: 5–11, steps 12–30.

262 Powell 1985: 9 and n. 13; Civil 1994: 90; Englund 2012: 449; CDLI work rates Wiki.

263 Civil 1994: 91 understood a 1 GUR/day rate for "stacking sheaves," but that total is not so different from the first.

264 Englund 2012: 449; Civil 1994: 95.

- **Winnowing:** Unlike other grains, barley requires only one winnowing;[265] an attested rate is the same for threshing, requiring two men for the operation.[266] A second threshing of leftover straw was a normal procedure, but would have gone faster, perhaps at twice the speed, so I count 1.5 operations.
- **Transport:** This is a highly variable labor cost, dependent on both equipment (sledges v. boats) and distance. In bulk, however, transport costs are well represented by manifests documenting the cost of porters, their drinks (*maštītum*), and boat hires. As a sample, six such Larsa manifests (YBC 6231 and YOS 5 168, 169, 182, 185 and 209) together record 3,510 GUR moved to storage. From this "capital" (SAG-NÍG-GUR$_{10}$), 147.4.0 GUR was expended on ship hires, 18.0.2,6 on porters' wages, and 10.0.5,8 on *maštītum*. 52,814 liters of grain was thus the "cost" of moving 1,053,000 liters of grain, a stable 5% rate.[267] I thus apply a 5% labor-cost "tariff" on all labor preceding this final step (*i.e.*, 5% of 1,823,401). This is the only labor-cost in this project reconstructed from an exchange rather than a labor value, but I feel confident of its general accuracy because the expenditures were in-kind and identical to the end-product (*i.e.*, grain was paid for grain).

[265] Hillman 1985.
[266] Civil 1994: 96.
[267] Cf. Breckwoldt 1995/96: 71, citing transport costs between 2.08% and 7.24%.

BIBLIOGRAPHY

Adams, Robert McC. (2008), "An Interdisciplinary Overview of a Mesopotamian City in the Third Millennium BC." *Cuneiform Digital Library Journal* 2008/1: 1–23.

Adams, Robert McC. and Hans J. Nissen (1972), *The Uruk Countryside: The Natural Setting of Urban Societies*. Chicago: University of Chicago Press.

Anastasio, Stefano (2011), *Costruire tra i due fiumi: Introduzione all'edilizia in Mesopotamia tra Neolitico ed età del Ferro* (Millenni 8). Firenze: Istituto Italiano di Preistoria e Protostoria.

Arnaud, Daniel (1972a), "Quelques Nouvelles Briques Inscrites de Larsa," *RA* 66: 33–38.

— (1972b), "Deux Kudurru de Larsa: II Étude Épigraphique," *RA* 66: 163–76.

— (1984), "Larsa. A. Philologisch," *RLA* VI: 496–500.

— (1994), *Texte Aus Larsa: Die epigraphischen Funde der 1. Kampagne in Senkereh-Larsa 1933*. Berlin: Dietrich Reimer.

Baker, Heather (2014), "Babylonian City Walls in a Historical and Cross-Cultural Perspective," in *Krieg und Frieden im Alten Vorderasien*, ed. H. Neumann *et al.*, 87–96. Münster: Ugarit-Verlag.

Birot, Maurice (1968), "Découvertes épigraphiques à Larsa," *Syria* 45: 241–47.

— (1969), *Tablettes Économiques et Administratives d'Époque Babylonienne Ancienne*. Paris: Librairie Orientaliste Paul Geunther.

— (1993), "Lettres de Zimri-Addu," in *Correspondence des gouverneurs de Qaṭṭunân* (ARM 27), ed. M. Birot, nos. 155–64. Paris: Éditions Recherche sur les Civilisations.

Boss, Helen (1986), "A Reappraisal of Marxian Economics: The Productive-Labour Theory of Value and Its Corollaries," *Historical Reflections* 13/2–3: 335–75.

Bretschneider, J., J. Driessen, and K. van Lerberghe (2007), *Power and Architecture. Monumental Public Architecture in the Bronze Age Near East and Aegean*. Orientalia Lovaniensia Analecta 156. Leuven: Peeters.

Breckwoldt, Tina (1995/1996), "Management of Grain Storage in Old Babylonian Larsa," *Archiv für Orientforschung* 42–43: 64–88.

Brown, Mark T. and Sergio Ulgiati (1999), "Emergy evaluation of the biosphere and natural capital," *Ambio* 28/6: 486–93.

Buccellati, Giorgio, 1972, review of [Kraus 1968], *OrAn* XI/2: 147–52.

Burke, Aaron (2008). *Walled Up To Heaven: The Evolution of Middle Bronze Age Fortification Strategies in the Levant*. Studies in the Archaeology and History of the Levant 4. Harvard Semitic Museum Publications. Winona Lake, IN: Eisenbrauns.

Calvet, Yves (2001), "Remarques sur l'urbanisme de Larsa à l'époque paléo-Babylonienne," in *Études Mésopotamiennes: Recueil de textes offert à Jean-Louis Huot*, ed. C. Breniquet and C. Kepinski, 57–67. Paris: Éditions Recherche sur les Civilisations.

Calvet, Yves *et al.* (1976), "Larsa: Rapport préliminaire sur la sixième campagne de fouilles," *Syria* LIII/1–2: 1–45.

Charles, M. P. (1990), "Traditional Crop Husbandry in Southern Iraq 1900–1960 A.D.," *Bulletin on Sumerian Agriculture* 5: 47–64.

Charpin, Dominique (1989), "Données nouvelles sur l'histoire de Larsa," in *Larsa: Travaux de 1985*, ed. J.-L. Huot *et al.*, 191–195. Paris: Éditions Recherche sur les Civilisations.

— (1991), "La mîšarum d'Hammu-rabi après la conquête de Larsa: un nouvel indice." *NABU* (no. 4–Décembre): 71.

— (1993), "Données nouvelles sur la Poliocétique à l'époque paléo-babylonienne." *MARI, Annales de Recherches Interdisciplinaires* 7: 193–204.

— (2004), "Histoire Politique du Proche-Orient Amorrite (2002–1595)," in *Mesopotamien: Die altbabylonische Zeit*, ed. D. Charpin *et al.*, 23–482. OBO 160/4. Fribourg: Academic Press.

Charpin, Dominique *et al.* (1988), *Archives Épistolaires de Mari* (ARM XXVI/2). Paris: Éditions Recherche sur les Civilisations.

Civil, Miguel (1987), "Ur III Bureaucracy: Quantitative Aspects," in *The Organization of Power: Aspects of Bureaucracy in the Ancient Near East*, ed. McG. Gibson and R. D. Biggs, 43–53. SAOC 46. Chicago: The Oriental Institute.

— (1994), *The Farmer's Instructions: A Sumerian Agricultural Manual.* Aula Orientalis Supplementa V. Barcelona: Editorial Ausa.

Cohen, Mark (1993), *The Cultic Calendars of the Ancient Near East.* Bethesda, MD: CDL Press.

Cohen, G. A. (1983), "More on Exploitation and the Labour Theory of Value." *Inquiry* 26/3: 309–32.

Cumberpatch, Chris G. (2001) "Some Observations on the Concept of 'Embedded' and 'Disembedded' Economies in Archaeological Discourse," *Assemblage* 6.
http://www.assemblage.group.shef.ac.uk/issue6/Cumberpatch_Econ_web.html

Dalley, Stephanie (2005), *Old Babylonian Texts in the Ashmolean Museum Mainly from Larsa, Sippir, Kish, and Lagaba* (OECT XV), Oxford: Oxford University.

Dalton, Shannah Smoller (1983), *Canal, Wall and Temple Names of the Old Babylonian Period.* Ph.D. Dissertation, Brandeis University.

Digard, Françoise (1975), *Répertoire analytique des cylindres orientaux*, v. 2. Paris: Éditions du Centre national de la recherche scientifique.

Dolce, Rita (2000), "Some Architectural Drawings on Clay Tablets: Examples of Planning Activity or Sketches?" in *Proceedings of the First International Congress on the Archaeology of the Ancient Near East, Rome, May 18th–23rd 1998.* vol I, ed. P. Matthiae *et al.*, 365–96. Rome: Universite degli studi di Roma "La Sapienza."

Dunham, Sally (1990), "Review of [Huot *et al.*, eds. 1989]," *JAOS* 110/2: 349–51.

Durand, J.-M. (1977), "Notes sur l'histoire de Larsa," *RA* 71: 17–34.

Dyckhoff, Christian (1998), "Balmunamḫe von Larsa—eine altbabylonische Existenz zwischen Ökonomie, Kultus, und Wissenschaft," in *Intellectual Life of the Ancient Near East*, ed. Jiří Prosecký, 117–24. Prague: Academy of Sciences.

Ellis, Maria deJ. (1976), *Agriculture and the State in Ancient Mesopotamia.* Occasional Publications of the Babylonian Fund No. 1. Philadelphia: University Museum.

Englund, Robert K. (1988), "Administrative Timekeeping in Ancient Mesopotamia." *JESHO* XXXI/2: 121–86.

— (1991), "Hard Work—Where Will It Get You? Labor Management in Ur III Mesopotamia." *JNES* 50/4: 255–80.

— (2012), "Equivalency Values and the Command Economy of the Ur III Period in Mesopotamia," in *The Construction of Value in the Ancient World*, ed. J. Papadopoulos & G. Urton, 427–458. Los Angeles: Cotsen Institute.

Fales, F. M. and J. N. Postgate, eds. (1995), *Imperial Administrative Records, PartII: Provincial and Military Administration.* SAA XI. Helsinki: Helsinki University Press

Faust, David Earl (1941), *Contracts from Larsa Dated in the Reign of Rim-Sin.* YOS VIII. New Haven: Yale University Press.

Figulla, Heinrich H. and W. J. Martin (1953), *Ur Excavation Texts Vol. V: Letters and Documents of the Old Babylonian Period.* Philadelphia: The University Museum.

Fine, Ben, (1986), "Introduction" in Ben Fine, ed. (1986), *The Value Dimension: Marx versus Ricardo and Sraffa.* London: Routledge & Kegan Paul.

Fitzgerald, Madeleine (2002), *The Rulers of Larsa.* Ph.D. Dissertation, Yale University.

Foster, Benjamin (1982), *Administration and Use of Institutional Land in Sargonic Sumer*. Mesopotamia 9. Copenhagen: Akademisk Forlag.

Frankena, R. (1966), *Briefe aus dem British Museum*. Altbabylonische Briefe II. Leiden: Brill.

Frayne, Douglas (1990), *Old Babylonian Period (2003–1595 BC)*. Royal Inscriptions of Mesopotamia (Early Periods) 4. Toronto: University of Toronto.

— (1993), *Sargonic and Gutian Periods (2334–2113 BC)*. Royal Inscriptions of Mesopotamia (Early Periods) 2. Toronto: University of Toronto.

— (1997), *Ur III Period (2112–2004 BC)*. Royal Inscriptions of Mesopotamia (Early Periods) 3/2. Toronto: University of Toronto.

Garfinkle, Steven (2005), "Public versus Private in the Ancient Near East," in *A Companion to the Ancient Near East*, ed. D. Snell, 384–396. Malden, MA: Blackwell.

Garrod, G. and K. G. Willis (1999), *Economic Valuation of the Environment: Methods and Case Studies*. Cheltenham: Edward Elgar.

Gasche, Hermann (1990), "Mauer (mur). B. Archäologisch." *RLA* VII: 591–95.

George, Andrew (1995), "The Bricks of E-Sagil." *Iraq* 57: 173–97.

Ghirshman R., *et al.* (1994), *Tchoga Zanbil (Dur Untash), Volume I: La Ziggurat.* Tehran: Cultural Heritage Organization of Iran.

Giampietro, Mario *et al.* (1993), "Labor Productivity: A Biophysical Definition and Assessment." *Human Ecology* XXI/3: 229–60.

Glassner, J.-J. (2003), *The Invention of Cuneiform: Writing in Sumer*. trans. Z. Bahrani and M. Van De Mieroop. Baltimore: The Johns Hopkins University Press.

Gledhill, John and Mogen Larsen (1982), "The Polanyi Paradigm and a Dynamic Analysis of Archaic States," in *Theory and Explanation in Archaeology: The Southampton Conference*, ed. C. Renfrew *et al.*, 197–229. New York: Academic Press.

Goetze, Albrecht (1948), "Umma Texts Concerning Reed Mats," *JCS* 2/3: 165–202.

— (1950a), "Sumu-yamutbal, a Local Ruler of the Old-Babylonian Period." *JCS* 4: 65–76.

— (1950b), "Sin-iddinam of Larsa: New Tablets from his Reign," *JCS* 4: 83–117.

— (1962), "Two Ur-Dynasty Tablets Dealing with Labor," *JCS* 16: 13–16.

Grayson, Albert Kirk (1991), *Assyrian Rulers of the Early First Millennium BC, I (1114-859 BC)*. Toronto: University of Toronto Press.

Grewal, David Singh (forthcoming). *The Invention of the Economy.* Cambridge, MA: Harvard University Press.

Grice, Ettalene Mears (1919), *Records from Ur and Larsa Dated in the Larsa Dynasty.* YOS V. New Haven, CT: Yale University Press.

Groneberg, Brigitte (1980), *Die Orts- und Gewässernamen der altbabylonischen Zeit* (Répertoire Géographique des Textes Cunéiformes 3). Wiesbaden: Reichert Verlag.

Hallo, William, (1991), "The Royal Correspondence of Larsa: III. The Princess and the Plea," in *Marchands, Diplomates et Empereurs,* ed. D. Charpin and F. Joannès, 377–88. Paris: Éditions recherche sur les Civilisations.

Halperin, Rhoda (1984), "Polanyi, Marx and the Institutional Paradigm," in *Research in Economic Anthropology* 6: 245–72.

Halstead, P. (1990), "Quantifying Sumerian Agriculture." *Bulletin on Sumerian Agriculture* 5: 187–95.

Hansen, Mogens H. (2006), *The Shotgun Method: The Demography of the Ancient Greek City-State Culture.* Columbia: University of Missouri Press.

Heimpel, Wolfgang (2009), *Workers and Construction Work at Garšana.* CUSAS 5. Bethesda, MD: CDL Press.

Heinrich, E. and U. Seidl (1967), "Grundrisszeichnungen aus dem Alten Orient." *Mitteilungen der Deutschen Orient-Gesellschaft zu Berlin* 98: 24–25.

Hillman, Gordon (1984 and 1985), "Traditional Husbandry and Processing of Archaic Cereals in Recent Times: The Operations, Products and Equipment which might feature in Sumerian Texts," in two parts: "Part I: The Glume Wheats," *Bulletin on Sumerian Agriculture* I: 114–52; and "Part II: The Free-Threshing Cereals," *Bulletin on Sumerian Agriculture* II: 1–31.

Holland, Alan and Jeremy Roxbee Cox (1992), "The Valuing of Environmental Goods: A Modest Proposal," in *Valuing the Environment,* ed. A. Coker and C. Richards. London: Belhaven Press.

Holmstrom, Nancy (1983), "Marx and Cohen on Exploitation and the Labor Theory of Value." *Inquiry* XVI/3: 287–308.

Hrouda, B. (1973), "Isin (Ishan al-Bahriyat)," in "Excavation in Iraq 1972–73," *Iraq* 35/2: 188–204.

Hunt, Robert C. (1987), "The Role of Bureaucracy in the Provisioning of Cities: A Framework for Analysis of the Ancient Near East," in *The Organization of Power: Aspects of Bureaucracy in the Ancient Near East,* (SAOC 46), ed. McG. Gibson and R. D. Biggs. Chicago: The Oriental Institute, 161–92.

— (1988), "Hydraulic Management in Southern Mesopotamia in Sumerian Times: Some Observations," *Bulletin on Sumerian Agriculture* IV: 189–206.

Huot, Jean-Louis, ed. (1978), "Larsa: Rapport préliminaire sur la septième campagne à Larsa et la première campagne à Tell el 'Oueili (1976)," *Syria* LV/3–4: 183–223.

— (1983), *Larsa et 'Oueili: Travaux de 1978–81*. Paris: Éditions Recherche sur les Civilisations.

— (1985), "Travaux en Basse Mésopotamie: Les Fouilles Français à Larsa et 'Oueli." *Compte Rendus des Seances de l'Académie des Inscriptions & Belles-Lettres* 129/2: 300–18.

— (1987a), *Larsa: 10e Campagne, 1983, et 'Oueili, 4e Campagne, 1983: Rapport Préliminaire*. Paris: Éditions Recherche sur les Civilisations.

— (1987b), "Larsa: Cité de Basse Mésopotamie," *Dossiers Histoire et Archéologie* (Dijon) 122: 37.

Huot, Jean-Louis *et. al.* eds. (1989), *Larsa: Travaux de 1985*. Paris: Éditions Recherche sur les Civilisations.

Huot, Jean-Louis and Yves Calvet (2003), *Larsa: Travaux de 1987 et 1989*. Paris: Institut français d'archéologie du Proche-Orient.

Jacobsen, Thorkild (1982), *Salinity and Irrigation Agriculture in Antiquity* (Bibliotheca Mesopotamica 14). Malibu: Undena Publications.

Janssen, Jac. J. (1988), "Prices and Wages in Ancient Egypt." *Altorientalische Forschungen* 15/1: 1–23.

Jongman, W. M. (2000) "Hunger and Power: Theories, Models and Methods in Roman Economic History," in *Interdependency of Institutions and Private Entrepreneurs*, ed. A.C.V.M. Bongenaar, 259–284. PIHANS 87, MOS Studies 2. Leiden: Nederlands Historisch-Archaologisch Instituut te Istanbul.

Jursa, Michael (2004), "Accounting in Neo-Babylonian Institutional Archives: Structure, Useage, and Implications," in *Creating Economic Order*, ed. M. Hudson and C. Wunsch, 145–98. Bethesda, MD: CDL Press.

Keefe, Laurence (2005), *Earth Building: Methods and Materials, Repair and Conservation*. New York: Routledge.

Kienast, Burkhart (1978), *Die Altbabylonischen Briefe und Urkunden aus Kisurra*. Teil II, Bds. 1 & 2. Wiesbaden: Franz Steiner.

Kingsbury, Edwin (1977), "La Dixième Année de Sumu-el." *RA* 71: 9–16.

Kirk, Alan (2007), "Karl Polanyi, Marshall Sahlins, and the Study of Ancient Social Relations," *Journal of Biblical Literature*, 126/1: 182–91.

Kleinerman, Alexandra and David I. Owen (2009), *Analytical Concordance to the Garšana Archives* (CUSAS 4). Bethesda, MD: CDL Press.

Koliński, Rafal (2001), *Mesopotamian* dimātu *of the Second Millennium BC* (BAR International Series 1004). Oxford: Archaeopress.

Kozyreva, N. V. (1988), *Drevniaia Larsa* [*Ancient Larsa*]. Moscow: Glav. red. vostochnoi lit-ry. (English summary, pp. 203–05 and tables on pp. 53 and 144).

Kraus, F. R. (1964), *Briefe aus dem British Museum* (*CT 43 und 44*). Altbabylonische Briefe I. Leiden: Brill.

— (1968), *Briefe aus dem Archive des Šamaš-ḫazir in Paris und Oxford* Altbabylonische Briefe IV. Leiden: Brill.

Lanfranchi, Giovanni B. and Simo Parpola, eds. (1990), *The Correspondence of Sargon II, Part II: Letters from the Northern and Northeastern Provinces* (State Archives of Assyria V). Helsinki: Helsinki University Press.

Lucas, A. (1989), *Ancient Egyptian Materials and Industries.* London: Histories & Mysteries.

Maekawa, Kazuya (1984), "Cereal Cultivation in the Ur III Period," *Bulletin on Sumerian Agriculture* I: 73–96.

— (1987), "Collective Labor-Service in Girsu-Lagash: The Pre-Sargonic and Ur III Periods," in *Labor in the Ancient Near East*, ed. M. Powell, 49–71. New Haven: American Oriental Society.

— (1989), "Rations, Wages and Economic Trends in the Ur III Period," *Altorientalische Forschungen* 16/1: 42–50.

— (1990), "Cultivation Methods in the Ur III Period," *Bulletin on Sumerian Agriculture* V: 115–45.

Mallowan, Max (1966), *Nimrud and Its Remains*, vol. I. New York: Dodd & Mead.

Margueron, Jean (1970), "Larsa: Rapport Préliminaire sur la Quatrième Campagne," *Syria* XLVII/3–4: 261–77.

— (1971), "Larsa: Rapport Préliminaire sur la Cinquième Campagne," *Syria* XLVIII/3–4: 271–87.

— (1984), "Larsa. B. Archäologisch," *RLA* VI: 500–506.

McHenry, Paul (1989), *Adobe and Rammed Earth Buildings: Design and Construction.* Tucson: University of Arizona Press.

Mongin, Philippe (1989), "Les Deux Théories Marxiennes de la Valeur-Travail et le Problème de la Mesure Immanente," *Archives de Philosophie* 52: 247–66.

Moseley, M. Edward (1975), "Prehistoric Principles of Labor Organization in the Moche Valley, Peru," *American Antiquity* 40/2: 191–95.

Müller, Béatrice (2001), "Maquettes en Mésopotamie," in *Études Mésopotamiennes: Recueil de textes offert à Jean-Louis Huot*, ed. C. Breniquet and C. Kepinski, 377–88. Paris: Éditions Recherche sur les Civilisations.

North, Douglass (1984), "Transaction Costs, Institutions, and Economic History," *Journal of Institutional and Theoretical Economics* 140/1: 7–17.

Norton, M. I. *et al.*, "The 'IKEA Effect': When Labor Leads to Love," Harvard Business School Marketing Unit Working Paper No. 11–091 (March, 2011): http://papers.ssrn.com/sol3/papers.cfm?abstract_id=1777100; accessed July 2013.

Oates, David (1990), "Innovations in Mud-Brick: Decorative and Structural Techniques in Ancient Mesopotamia," *World Archaeology* XXI/3: 388–406.

Owen, David (2012), "Three Old Babylonian Accounts," in *The Ancient Near East: A Life! Festschrift Karel Van Lerberghe*, ed. T Boiy *et al.*, 445–56. (OLA 220). Leuven: Peeters.

Owen, David and Rudolf Mayr (2007), *The Garšana Archives* (CUSAS 3). Bethesda, MD: CDL Press.

Papadopoulos, John and G. Urton, eds. (2010), *The Construction of Value in the Ancient World*. Albuquerque, NM: University of New Mexico Press.

Parpola, Simo, ed. (1987) *The Correspondence of Sargon II, Part I: Letters from Assyria and the West* (State Archives of Assyria I). Helsinki: Helsinki University Press.

Parrot, André (1933), "Les Fouilles de Tello et de Senkereh-Larsa, Campagne 1932–33 (Rapport Préliminaire)," *RA* XXX: 169–82.

— (1954), *Glyptique Mésopotamienne, fouilles de Lagash* (*Tello*) *et de Larsa* (*Senkereh*) (*1931-1933*). Paris: Geuthner.

— (1961), *Sumer: The Dawn of Art*, trans. S. Gilbert and J. Emmons. New York: Golden Press.

— (1968), "Les Fouilles de Larsa: Deuxième et troisième campagnes (1967)," *Syria* XLV/3–4: 205–33.

— (1969), "Scenes de Guerre à Larsa," *Iraq* XXXI/1: 64–67.

Paulus, Marcel J. (1979/81), "Traditional Building Materials in Ancient Mesopotamian Architecture," *Sumer* 41/1–2: 130–32.

Pearson, Harry (1957), "The Secular Debate on Economic Primitivism," in *Trade and Market in Early Empires: Economics in History and Theory*, ed. K. Polanyi *et al.*, 3–11. Chicago: Henry Regner Co.

Pilling, G. (1986), "The law of value in Ricardo and Marx," in *The Value Dimension: Marx versus Ricardo and Sraffa*, ed. Ben Fine, 18–44. London: Routledge & Kegan Paul.

Porada, Edith (1967), "Battlements in the Military Architecture and in the Symbolism of the Ancient Near East," in *Essays in the History of Architecture Presented to Rudolf Wittkower*, ed. D. Fraser *et al.*, 1–12. London: Phaidon.

Porada, Edith and F. Basmachi (1951), "Nergal in the Old Babylonian Period," *Sumer* 7: 66–68.

Powell, Marvin A. (1985), "Salt, Seed, and Yields in Sumerian Agriculture. A Critique of the Theory of Progressive Salinization," *ZA* 75/1: 7–38.

— ed., (1987), *Labor in the Ancient Near East*. New Haven, CT: American Oriental Society.

— (1990), "Masse und Gewichte [§III.4 – IIIC]," *RLA* VII: 490–91.

Rappaport, R. A. (1971), "The flow of energy in an agricultural society," *Scientific American* 225/3: 117–21.

Richardson, Seth (2008), "Ningirsu Returns to his Plow: Lagaš and Girsu Take Leave of Ur," in *On the Third Dynasty of Ur*, ed. P. Michalowski, 153–57. Boston: ASOR.

— (2012), "Early Mesopotamia: The Presumptive State," *Past and Present* 215: 3–49.

Ristvet, Lauren (2007), "The Third Millennium Wall at Tell Leilan, Syria: Identity, Authority, and Urbanism," in *Power and Architecture: Monumental Public Architecture in the Bronze Age Near East and Aegean*, ed. J. Bretschneider, *et al.*, 183–211. Leuven: Peeters.

Robson, Eleanor (1999), *Mesopotamian Mathematics, 2100-1600 BC: Technical Constants in Bureaucracy and Education* (OECT XIV). Oxford: Oxford University Press.

Rost, Stephanie (2011), "Irrigation Management in the Ur III Period: A Reconsideration Based on a Case Study of Maintenance of the ÍD-NINA-ŠÈ-DU canal of the Province Lagaš," in *The Empirical Dimension of Ancient Near Eastern Studies*, ed. G. Selz, 211–69 (Wiener Offene Orientalistik 6). Wien: Lit Verlag GmbH & Co.

Rost, Stephanie and Abdulamir Hamdani (2011), "Traditional Dam Construction in Modern Iraq: A Possible Analogy for Ancient Mesopotamian Irrigation Practices," *Iraq* 73: 201–20.

Rothman, Mitchell S. (1994), "Palace and Private Agricultural Decision-making in the Early 2nd Millennium B.C. City-State of Larsa, Iraq," in *The Economic Anthropology of the State*, ed. Elizabeth M. Brumfiel, 149–67 (Monographs in Economic Anthropology 11). Lanham, MD: Society for Economic Anthropology.

Sallaberger, W. (1989), "Zum Schilfrohr als Rohstoff in Babylonien," in *Der Orientalische Mensch und seine Beziehung zur Umwelt*, ed. B. Scholz, 311–30. Graz: RM-Druck & Verl.-Ges.

Scheidel, Walter (2010), "Real Wages in Early Economies: Evidence for Living Standards from 1800 BCE to 1300 CE," *JESHO* 53: 425–62.

Scheidel, Walter and Steven J. Friesen (2009), "The Size of the Economy and the Distribution of Income in the Roman Empire," *Princeton/Stanford Working Papers in Classics* (January 22, 2009).
Available at: http://dx.doi.org/10.2139/ssrn.1299313.

Seeher, Jürgen (2007), *A Mudbrick City Wall at Hattuša: Diary of a Reconstruction*. Istanbul: Yainlari.

Selz, G. (1989), *Die altsumerische Wirtschaftsurkunden der Ermitage zu Leningrad: Altsumerische Verwaltungstexte aus Lagaš* (FAOS 15/1). Stuttgart: F. Steiner.

— (2011), ed. *The Empirical Dimension of Ancient Near Eastern Studies* (Wiener Offene Orientalistik 6). Wien: Lit Verlag GmbH & Co.

Sigrist, Marcel (1990), *Larsa Year Names*. Andrews University Press: Institute of Archaeology Publications.

Silver, Morris (1983), "Karl Polanyi and Markets in the Ancient Near East: The Challenge of the Evidence," *The Journal of Economic History* 43/4: 795–829.

Smith, Michael (2004), "The Archaeology of Ancient State Economies," *Annual Review of Anthropology* 33: 73–102.

Smith, Murray E. G. (1991), "Understanding Marx's theory of value: an assessment of the controversy," *Canadian Review of Sociology and Anthropology* 28/3: 357–376.

Steinkeller, Piotr (1987), "The Administrative and Economic Organization of the Ur III State: The Core and the Periphery," in *The Organization of Power: Aspects of Bureaucracy in the Ancient Near East*, ed. McG. Gibson and R. D. Biggs, 19–41 (SAOC 46). Chicago: The Oriental Institute.

— (2004a), "The Function of Written Documentation in the Administrative Praxis of Early Mesopotamia," in *Creating Economic Order*, ed. M. Hudson and C. Wunsch, 65–88. Bethesda, MD: CDL Press.

— (2004b), "A History of Maškan-šapir and its Role in the Kingdom of Larsa," in *The Anatomy of a Mesopotamian City: Survey and Soundings at Maškan-šapir* by E. Stone, 26–42. Winona Lake, IN: Eisenbrauns.

— (2004c), "An Inscription of Sin-iddinam and Other Inscribed Materials from Abu Duwari," in *The Anatomy of a Mesopotamian City: Survey and Soundings at Maškan-šapir* by E. Stone, 135–52. Winona Lake, IN: Eisenbrauns.

— (2007a), "City and Countryside in Third Millennium Southern Babylonia," in *Settlement and Society: Essays Dedicated to Robert McCormick Adams*, ed. E. Stone, 185–211. Los Angeles: Cotsen Institute.

— (2007b), "On Sand Dunes, Mountain Ranges, and Mountain Peaks," in *Studies Presented to Robert D. Biggs, June 4, 2004*, ed. M. T. Roth *et al.*, 219–32. Chicago: The Oriental Institute.

— (2012), "More on the Reading of the Toponym GARšana," NABU 2012/3: 42.

Stol, Marten (1971), review of [Walters, 1970], *BiOr* XXVIII: 5/6: 365–69.

— (1981), *Letters From Yale: Transliterated and Translated.* Altbabylonische Briefe IX. Leiden: E. J. Brill.

— (1982), "State and Private Business in Larsa," *JCS* 34 3/4: 127–230.

Suire, Joel (2003), "Larsa: nouvelles observations de surface," in *Larsa: Travaux de 1987 et 1989*, ed. J.-L. Huot and Y. Calvet, 9-14. Beyrouth: Institut français d'archéologie du Proche-Orient.

Uziel, Joe (2010), "Middle Bronze Age Ramparts: Functional and Symbolic Structures," *PEQ* 142/1: 24–30.

Van De Mieroop, Marc (1987), "The Archive of Balmunamhe," *Archiv für Orientforschung* XXXIV: 1–29.

— (1993), "The Reign of Rim-Sin," *RA* 87: 47–69.

— (1992), *Society and Enterprise in Old Babylonian Ur* (Berliner Beiträge zum Vorderen Orient 12). Berlin: Dietrich Reimer Verlag.

van der Spek, R. J. (2015), "An Introduction: Markets from Ancient Babylonia to the Modern World," in *A History of Market Performance: From Ancient Babylonia to the Modern World*, ed. R. J. van der Spek *et al.*, 1–16. London: Routledge

van Dijk, J. (1965), "Une insurrection générale au pays de Larsa avant l'avènement de Nuradad," *JCS* 19: 1–25.

van Driel, G. (2000), "Institutional and Non-Institutional Economy in Ancient Mesopotamia," in *Interdependency of Institutions and Private Entrepreneurs. Proceedings of the 2nd MOS Symposium*, ed. A. C. V. M. Bongenaar, 5–23. Leiden: Nederlands Historisch-Archaologisch Instituut te Istanbul.

— (2002), *Elusive Silver: In Search of a Role for a Market in an Agrarian Environment—Aspects of Mesopotamia's Society* (PIHANS 95). Leiden: Nederlands Historisch-Archaologisch Instituut te Istanbul.

van Soldt, W. H. (1994), *Letters in the British Museum, Part 2.* Altbabylonische Briefe XIII. Leiden: E. J. Brill.

Waetzoldt, Hartmut (1992), "'Rohr' und dessen Verwendungsweisen anhand der neusumerischen Texte aus Umma," *Bulletin on Sumerian Agriculture* VI: 125–46.

Walters, Stanley D. (1970), *Water for Larsa: An Old Babylonian Archive Dealing with Irrigation* (YNER 4). New Haven: Yale University Press.

Warburton, D. A. (2006), "The Institutionalization of Social Evolution," *Akkadica* 127/1: 13–40.

Weaver, R. D. (1994), "Economic valuation of biodiversity," in *Biodiversity and Landscapes*, ed. K. C. Kim and R. D. Weaver, 255–69. New York: Cambridge University Press.

Westenholz, J. (2006), *Cuneiform Inscriptions in the Collection of the Bible Lands Museum Jerusalem: The Old Babylonian Inscriptions*. Leiden: Brill.

Wilkinson, T. J. (1994), "The Structure and Dynamics of Dry-Farming States in Upper Mesopotamia," *Current Anthropology* 35/5: 483–520.

Wilkinson, T. J., McG. Gibson, and Magnus Widell, eds., (2013), *Models of Mesopotamian Landscapes: How Small-scale Processes Contributed to the Growth of Early Civilizations*. BAR International Series 2552. Oxford: Archaeopress.

Woolley, C. Leonard. (1939), *The Ziggurat and Its Surroundings* (Ur Excavations V). London: Oxford University Press.

Wright, Henry T. (1969), *The Administration of Rural Production in a Mesopotamian Town* (Anthropological Papers 38). Ann Arbor, MI: University of Michigan.

Zimmer, Carl (2014), "The Price Tag on Nature's Defenses," *The New York Times*, June 10, 2014, D3.

5.

Hired Labor in the Neo-Assyrian Empire

Karen Radner
University College London

1. Introductory Remarks

For the understanding of any state and any society it is vital to have a grasp of the key principles of its economic basis. Yet for the Neo-Assyrian Empire our knowledge is still severely limited, in contrast to the Neo-Babylonian Empire where the field of economic history has long enjoyed popularity among modern scholars.

At the root of this problem lies the extremely differential nature of the available primary documentation. The business records of temple households and private family firms from several major Babylonian cities, which constitute the vast majority of the known Neo-Babylonian sources and offer a wealth of information for the economic historian (see now Jursa 2010), have no parallel among the texts from the main Neo-Assyrian archival sources of Nineveh and Kalhu. These cities served as the centers of the Empire and were intimately linked to the Assyrian kings and their courts. They are certainly not representative of all of Assyria or even all of its urban environments. Most of the texts unearthed in Nineveh and Kalhu come from palace contexts. They have shaped the perception of Assyria in the first millennium BC more than any other bodies of texts, and their focus and limitations explain in part why key economic issues, such as the very nature of labor in Assyria's economy, have found relatively little attention.

To survey "labor in the Assyrian Empire" is beyond the scope of the present paper which limits itself to a discussion of labor for hire.[1] The

1 I wish to thank the organizers of the 2005 symposium, Piotr Steinkeller and Michael Hudson, for the kind invitation and Cornelia Wunsch for hosting us in beautiful Hirschbach. An earlier version of this paper was published as Radner 2007a.

terminology that the Assyrians employed to refer to hired labor is derived from the verb *agāru* "to hire" which is used in the *G* stem and the *N* stem (passive). Attested forms include the terms *munnagru* "hired worker," *nāgurtu* "labor as a hired worker" and, by far the most widely used, *igrē* "wages (for hired labor)". The present paper draws on all known attestations for these terms.

2. Working for a salary, from the reign of Tiglath-pileser to Assurbanipal

The evidence for hired labor in the Neo-Assyrian period currently available to us covers a period of about 120 years. The earliest reference dates to the reign of Tiglath-pileser III (r. 744–725 BC). It is a legal document from the Governor's Palace in Kalhu (738 BC; Postgate 1973: no. 98; Radner 2007a: no. 1) in the form of a receipt for a sum of copper which is described as compensation for the recipient's wages. It is impossible to know from what kind of work arrangement the financial claim had resulted and who satisfied it but the phrasing of the text indicates a dispute that was resolved by this new arrangement.

Some letters from the state correspondence of Sargon II (r. 721–705 BC) provide more detailed information. Due to the nature of this correspondence there is a focus on military personnel for hire. A bodyguard is mentioned in a dispatch of the governor of Arrapha: "Concerning the guard about whom the king, my lord, wrote to me and whom the servants of the king, my lord, have hired for me: He will set forth tomorrow." (Fuchs and Parpola 2001: no. 2: 4–7). As the letter continues with information on a planned journey by boat, leading through dangerous territory to Babylonia, the guard is likely to have been hired as protection for this specific enterprise.

Scouts, too, are attested as hiring out their services to Sargon's men. An official informs his king about the reaction of Ariyê and Ariṣâ, the co-regents of the small mountain kingdom of Kumme, Assyria's northern neighbor and vassal state (Radner 2011), to a royal order to resettle those of their subjects residing in Assyria to locations elsewhere in the Empire: "The king, our lord, he is the master of all. What can we say (against his orders)? The king, our lord, may take the men from Kumme who hold houses in the countries (*i.e.*, who live in the provinces of the Assyrian Empire) to wherever is good (in the king's opinion), but the scouts from Kumme who have gone away from Kumme in hired service have not yet come back. They are still there (*i.e.*, in Assyria). The king, our lord, should ask and investigate—maybe they are among those (*i.e.*, the men from Kumme living in Assyria) who are getting deported." (Lanfranchi and Parpola 1990: no. 105: 11–23).

The author of the letter then counsels Sargon to take this request seriously as these scouts were valuable assets when stationed at home in Kumme, from where they braved the difficult mountain lands between Assyria and its northern arch enemy Urartu in order to gather intelligence on Assyria's behalf: "The king, my lord, should return them to Kumme. The king, my lord, knows how they are withdrawn from (their regular working environment in) Urartu and that they are in Assyria (only) in hired service." (Lanfranchi and Parpola 1990: no. 105: 24–rev. 3). The scouts from Kumme were quite clearly compensated for their services with payment, and this highlights the important role of mercenaries in the Assyrian army in the 8th century BC.

As this example shows, when the subjects of a foreign ruler lived and worked in Assyria there was potential for conflict. People working under paid employment in Assyria were still considered subjects of the ruler of their country of origin, as a letter to Sargon by the distressed ruler of a northern vassal state, possibly Šubria, indicates. This ruler found himself the victim of Assyrian aggression directed against his people not only his own territories but also in Assyria. "They (*i.e.*, the Assyrians) attack my cities. They also capture my servants who work for hire in the countries (*i.e.*, in the provinces of the Assyrian Empire)!" (Lanfranchi and Parpola 1990: no. 46: 6′–8′).

People working for hire could move far from their place of origin, as is the case with some individuals mentioned in another letter from Sargon's reign. These were Assyrian subjects living in Assyria, but not in their original home region, which caused confusion regarding their status. What kind of work the people from Šadikanni (mod. Tell Ağağa) on the Habur were doing is left unclear in a letter from an official of that region to Sargon. But the author took care to leave no doubt that they were good tax-paying citizens who should be treated accordingly: "The king, my lord, knows that the men from Šadikanni are hired workers; they work in the countries of the king (*i.e.*, in the provinces of the Assyrian Empire). They are no fugitives. They perform their tax obligations and supply king's men (*i.e.*, conscripts for the Assyrian army) from their midst." (Parpola 1987: no. 223: 3–13). Hired workers, quite possibly the same group of people, are mentioned in a letter of another official from the Habur region to the king, too fragmentarily preserved to offer any further information (Parpola 1987: no. 207: 4–5).

A source from the time of Esarhaddon (r. 680–669 BC) shows that sailors worked for hire. This is clear from one of the stipulations found in the treaty with Ba'alu, king of Tyre, that grants the Tyrian ships access to the Mediterranean harbors under Assyrian control; it is specifically stated that the ships and their crew should not be harmed: "Nobody will [cause] injustice [to those] who are hired (as the ship's crew) nor impair their ships." (Parpola and Watanabe 1988: no. 5 iii 26′–28′). The treaty places the ships and their crews in a predominantly commercial context, but the sailors' duties are in many ways comparable to the tasks of the scouts and bodyguards attested in the above-referenced Sargon letters. Long-distance trade, whether overland or aboard a ship, was always a risky enterprise.

Turning to the available evidence for hired labor during the reign of Assurbanipal (r. 668–ca. 627 BC), we leave the world of mercenaries, scouts and sailors operating at the border zones of the Empire behind. Two letters of the king's correspondence with his scholarly advisors lead us instead into the world of the royal court and the cosmopolitan cities of the Assyrian heartland. That one could hire a tailor and pay him to sew one's clothes we may gather from the letter of an unhappy scholar, who eloquently pleads with his king to rescue him from dire straits. One of the more graphic examples for his increasingly troublesome financial situation is: "(I swear) that I can afford neither shoes nor the wages for a tailor!" (Parpola 1993: no. 294 rev. 27–28). If the writer of this letter is correctly identified with the exorcist Urdu-Gula, then we find another reference to his lack of proper clothing and, more importantly for our purposes, to wages paid to an exorcist's helper in a second letter of his correspondence. After listing various garments that a certain scholar had secured for himself as gifts from the king, Urdu-Gula contrasts these riches with his own poverty and that of his colleagues: "And we emerged with empty hands! How can we possibly mend our lack of clothing? When will we receive our wages, we who not even command wages as high as his assistant?" (Parpola 1993: no. 289 rev. 9′–13′).

The work of goldsmiths, too, was performed on a hired basis. A 7th century administrative text from Kalhu lists various expenses, mostly for foodstuffs such as bread, wine and meat; the last item listed, however, is of a different nature: "One shekel (of silver): wages of the goldsmith." (ND 2310: 22′; Postgate 1979: 100–101). This reference illustratoes our difficulty to distinguish full-time employment from occasional services provided for a fee. It is likely that the latter was the case here and that the goldsmith in question was a member of a palace or temple household. Nabû-balassu-iqbi from Assur was such a goldsmith. As one of the goldsmiths of the Aššur temple, he had to look for work elsewhere when he needed money to settle an outstanding debt. We learn this from a letter to Nabû-zeru-iddina, a high-ranking goldsmith of the Aššur temple during Assurbanipal's reign who is informed about Nabû-balassu-iqbi's activities by one of his subordinates: "I said to Nabû-balassu-iqbi: 'Where do you work for hire?' He answered: '[...]. I will pay off the old debts.'" (Radner 1999a: no. 52: 9–15). This last reference makes it clear that working for hire could be the result of financial difficulties and was then surely meant to supplement the basic income drawn from working one's own land or from the expected sustenance of other regular employment. Given the patchy documentation it would be rash to take this one reference as an indication for the emergence of an impoverished urban proletariat in the Assyrian centers of the 7th century. And yet, it is important to be aware of the fact that working for hire was seen a possible way of supplementing and even replacing one's income.

A legal text from the archive of Šamaš-šarru-uṣur of Kalhu documents another scenario for hired labor in the reign of Assurbanipal. This man was a royal eunuch with business activities that focused on poultry, raised presumably for their meat, eggs and feathers (ND 3433; Radner 2007a: no. 2). The city overseer of Kalhu (rev. 13–14: "Witnessed by Ribaya, the city overseer who has passed this verdict") settled a dispute with one Mannu-ki-Arbail by establishing a work relationship between the eunuch and an individual under the other man's authority. For his services, the man was to receive wages, payable to his superior: "Eight shekels of silver, being the wages of Ahu-edi which Šamaš-šarru-uṣur has given to Mannu-ki-Arbail on behalf of Ahu-edi, the apprentice (LÚ.TUR) under his authority. [*x months*] is the (agreed) term. He (*i.e.* Ahu-edi) will serve him (*i.e.* Šamaš-šarru-uṣur) during this term. As soon as his term has been completed he shall go and leave." These "wages", however, were a legal fiction that in reality constituted the contested sum.

After a certain predetermined period, the work relationship was to end and the man was free to leave. This illustrates the main difference between such an arrangement and the very common institution of pledge (Radner 2001: 269–271). A pledged person was placed with the creditor in order to cover the debtor's interest, and that person's discharge could only be brought about by paying back the debt sum. Nevertheless, the relationship between employer and employee can hardly be described as voluntary in this case.

3. The best known context: The hiring of caravan staff in late seventh-century Assur

The survey of sources from the reign of Tiglath-pileser III to Assurbanipal has given us an indication of the ubiquity of employment for hire in the Assyrian Empire. However, by far the most detailed documentation comes from the city of Assur during the two decades prior to the fall of Assyria, *i.e.* the reigns of Assurbanipal's successors, Aššur-etel-ilani and Sîn-šarru-iškun. Twenty-one legal contracts document the hiring of men—never women—for periods between one month and a year (designated by the term *ṭuppišu*, for which see Baker in press). The relevant sources have been collected and edited in an earlier version of this paper (Radner 2007a: nos. 3–23) and will not be repeated here.

These texts are the most informative source material presently available to us, as they provide us with data about both employers and employees, the length of the employment and the amount of the wages. The tables in the appendix provide an overview of the archival context (a), the length of employment (b), the monthly salary and any special circumstances that might explain the considerable variations (c), as well as the distribution of the contracts over the seasons (d) and the years (e).

Wages are paid in silver, for which it is currently impossible to establish a link with the value of grain in the late 7th century BC. The only reference to regular grain prices from the Neo-Assyrian period dates to the reign of Tiglath-pileser III (r. 744–725 BC) when the metal standard was copper rather than silver: "The land of the king is well. The royal sustenance fields have been harvested. The market rate is extremely favorable in the land. One homer of barley goes for one mina of copper in Nineveh, one homer and five seahs in Halahhu, two homers in the steppe." (NL 52 = Luukko 2012: no. 19). While this document does not indicate a price for Assur, the city's location requires us to take the price given for "the steppe" as the most likely approximation.

Some of the contracts indicate the nature of the work. One text (Radner 2007a: no. 4; Radner forthcoming: no. I.13) states explicitly that the hired worker was to bring in his employer's harvest. The contract is for only one month and was made in December, at a time when bringing in the crops was a good half year in the future; December was rather the season to think about planting the seed. As the text also explicitly mentions the unusual fact that the hired worker had already received his complete wages, the man in all probability had found himself short of cash and resolved this problem by pledging his labor for the busiest time of the agricultural year to somebody who was willing to help him out right now. According to the evidence of Neo-Assyrian debt notes, the debtor's obligation to provide harvesters during harvest time often replaces the provision of interest (Radner 2004: 68–69, 73), taking advantage of the debtor's financial situation to secure additional workers at harvest time. We can therefore safely assume that the hired worker's decision to pledge his labor months before the next harvest was to his employer's advantage. Indeed, the wage of one shekel of silver for a month's work is at the bottom scale of the wages attested in the Assur material (table c).

Four other Assur contracts contain the stipulation *alaktu ušēṣa ušērab* "He will make the caravan leave and enter", *alaktu ušērab ušēṣa* "He will make the caravan enter and leave" or *alaktu ušērab* "He will make the caravan enter" (Radner 2007a: nos. 12, 13, 15 and 22). *Alaktu* here certainly means "caravan; trading mission" as is clear from a group of private letters from a contemporary archive in Assur that deal with commercial activities conducted further up the Tigris in the "mountains" and feature a characteristic introduction formula. After the usual greeting formula the sender assures the addressee about the good state of their joint business: "The whole caravan (*alaktu*) is well. You may be happy!" (Radner forthcoming: nos. I.2, I.3, I.4). The point of reference for the clauses in our labor contracts is certainly the city of Assur. Whether we should take the variants as an indication of the specific itinerary of the employee, or whether these differences in phrasing should be disregarded, is difficult to decide at present. It is of course quite possible that staff members were hired at various stages of the trading mission, some when the trek was leaving Assur, others when setting out to return to the city. That all texts were found in Assur where they had in all likelihood been written makes it seem more likely, however, that they should be seen as variants of one and the same legal clause.

The men hired according to the four Assur contracts would seem to have been part of trade caravans leaving from Assur, and their duties can be easily compared with the bodyguards, scouts and sailors that we found attested in the Sargon letters and the Esarhaddon treaty. The men employed to go on long-distance trading missions would have been expected to find their way from Assur to their destination and back again and at all times guard merchandise and money with their lives. Their wages are among the top salaries of the Assur wage scale (table c), and it seems likely that the other contracts with similar arrangements for the length of the appointment (7–12 months) and its salary (2–3,25 shekels of silver per month) also deal with caravan staff members, the difference in payment probably reflecting the level of responsibility and experience. Traveling always meant putting one's life in danger, and the generally high wages attested in this group of documents indicate that the employees were thus compensated with payments that are at least twice the going rate for harvesting work.

The caravan contracts are all dated between late September/early October and late December/early January, *i.e.* the quiet season of the agricultural year when the fields had already been harvested but were not yet cultivated again. This would have allowed the employee to tend to his fields before accepting paid work. As evidence for the organization of trading missions is currently available only from Assur for the period in question, it is important to note that Assur's population was traditionally exempt from military service and corvee duty and hence had the option to use the part of the year normally reserved for state service for other activities. Assur's inhabitants were also exempt from taxation, and as trading enterprises were otherwise subject to heavy dues (Radner 2007b: 225–226; exact amounts unknown) the tax-exempt citizens of Assur may have been more likely than other inhabitants of the Assyrian Empire to engage in caravan trade.

All four contracts with the trading mission clause and eighteen of the twenty-one known labor contracts from Assur come from the same two archives, or rather one big archive that was stored in two parts. The archives N 9 and N 10 of the Hundureans (*Hundurāyê*) were found in the houses built in the so-called "Außenhaken" area in the northwest of the city of Assur (Pedersén 1986: 85–96). Hundur (also known as Hundir) is a region in Western Iran, the hinterland of the Median city of Kišessim that became the capital of a new Assyrian province founded by Sargon II in 716 (Radner 2003: 50, 57). In its primary meaning, the term *Hundurāyê* is the designation for the inhabitants of Hundur. They are attested in the city of Assur from the reign of Sargon onwards, and we can safely assume that the *Hundurāyê* of Assur were the deportees from the Hundur area, and later their offspring (Radner 2003: 62–63).

Additional evidence for the trading activities of the Hundureans is provided by a number of contracts found in their archive which serve to set up partnerships for financing a caravan (Radner 1999b: nos. 3, 6, 9, 20; nos. 21 and 22 can be linked to no. 6). But other than that, the archive of the Hundureans offers little information that would allow us to reconstruct the nature of their trading ventures. However, the contemporary archive of the wine importer Duri-Aššur allows us to provide some useful context to compare and contrast with, as it includes a number of letters and lists detailing the financing of individual missions (Radner in press).

Duri-Aššur organized trading ventures into the northern regions of Assyria together with three partners ("brothers") in the period of 651–614 BC, that is, until the Medes under Cyaxares conquered the city of Assur: some of his letters had not yet been opened when Duri-Aššur's house went up in flames. The ensuing wars certainly terminated the firm's activities—and we can of course assume that trade in general, on a large geographical scale, was badly affected during the next decade while the spoils of the Assyrian Empire were gradually divided up between the marauding Babylonian, Median and Egyptian armies. But while his business still flourished, Duri-Aššur seems to have stayed in the city of Assur while his partners did the traveling necessary to arrange and oversee their joint business activities. In addition to their own funds, the firm accepted investments from other inhabitants of Assur. Although some contributed substantial sums of money, most of the amounts invested were small, sometimes just a fraction of a shekel of silver. Duri-Aššur's firm had a loyal customer base and most investors invested in several trading missions.

Duri-Aššur and partners employed four agents as caravan leaders and these men each conducted three trips a year, leading a group of donkeys upstream along the Tigris with merchandise from Assur, including exclusive garments like hats and shoes, and textiles which also served as packing material for the supplies and the silver funds. One letter (Radner forthcoming: no. I.4) names Zamahu in the Jebel Sinjar as a destination, famous for its wines, and this may have been the usual goal of Duri-Aššur's caravans. Why vary the route if one had a reliable network of suppliers and business partners in one place? Once the caravan had reached its destination, everything was sold, including the donkeys. From the proceeds and the funds they had brought with them, Duri-Aššur's agents bought wine. The wine was filled into animal skins (mostly of sheep and goats, only exceptionally cattle hides) that were bound together with wooden beams in order to create rafts for the return journey to Assur on the Tigris. This was the best possible approach to the transport of wine: on the one hand, the river water kept the wine cool and prevented it from spoiling, on the other hand, all components of this means of transport constituted valuable merchandise back at Assur and could be sold off: the wineskins, of course, but also the logs which were much needed as building timber in forestless Assur.

At present, labor contracts for hiring caravan staff are exclusively found in the archive of the Hundureans. While Duri-Aššur's firm seems to have dispatched the same men as caravan leaders repeatedly (and, one assumes, employed them on a permanent basis), the Hundureans each time hired different people, none of whom is attested more than once. While it was the norm for Duri-Aššur's caravan leaders to set out from

Assur three times a year, the Hundureans' labor contracts are for periods of 7–12 months. This would seem to indicate that the traders had a more remote destination than those sent by Duri-Aššur.

But we can only speculate about the destination and nature of the trading missions organized by the Hundureans. Did their caravans go to Hundur, taking advantage of old family connections? While this would seem a likely destination we must bear in mind that we know next to nothing about Assyria's relationship with Western Iran in the second half of the 7th century. It is even unclear whether the provinces established there in the 8th century were still under Assyrian control. As soon as we assume regular trading contacts between private entrepreneurs from Assur with the Median heartland in the period immediately prior to the Median attack on Assur in 614 we must consider the role of these contacts in triggering Cyaxares' raid.

While our evidence for the organization of trade missions stems exclusively from the last two decades of the Assyrian Empire it is difficult to establish whether this is at all significant. We have to bear in mind that debt notes, labor contracts, partnership agreements and the like were, in contrast to purchase texts, not meant to be kept forever. Hence, the documentary record for these Neo-Assyrian types of documents typically date to the last decades before the destruction of the urban centers at the end of the 7th century BC. Due to the city's favorable tax status, it is far more likely that trading missions were dispatched from Assur also in the decades, and centuries, before. But the absence of relevant evidence from other Assyrian sites calls into question how common the organization of such trade enterprises may have been elsewhere.

Conclusions

Although relatively limited in number, the nature of the available sources for hired labor in the Assyrian Empire is diverse. We can make use of legal contracts, letters both private and royal, administrative notes and an international treaty dating to the period from 738 to 615 BC.

The wide range of sources elucidates a variety of different contexts and we find a range of occupations attested: the craftsmen (goldsmiths, tailors), specialized soldiers (bodyguards, scouts), scholars' assistants, sailors, caravan staff and harvesters represented in the available evidence indicate that hired labor was a widespread phenomenon that underpinned the Assyrian economy, albeit in a range of different circumstances. Some hirelings, such as sailors and mercenaries, were in full-time service while others, such as goldsmiths and tailors, were attached to a palace or temple household and hired out their work on the side, charging for their services.

To quantify the phenomenon of hired workers and salaried employment within the Neo-Assyrian labor marked is currently not viable. But all attempts to reconstruct the workings of the society and economy of Assyria Empire must accommodate the fact that there was labor available for hire.[2]

Appendix: 7th-century wages according to the Assur documentation

The numbers given in the first column of the following tables refers to the texts as edited in Radner 2007a.

a. Archival contexts:
N9 and N10 = archive of the Hundureans.

	Assur archive	Contract date	Length	Total salary (in shekels)	Monthly salary (in shekels)	Nature of employment
3	1979–80	ix. 616	12 months	10	0,833	
4	1990	iv. 631	1 month	1	1,000	To harvest
5	N2	vi. 620	12 months	15	1,250	
6	N9	viii. 631	9 months	20	2,250	
7	N9	viii. 629	10 months	17,5	1,750	
8	N9	viii. 625	8 months	30	3,750	
9	N9	ix. 625	9 months	[...]	[...]	
10	N9	vii. 624	10 months	12,5	1,250	
11	N9	viii. 623	10 months	not given	not given	
12	N9	vi. 623	7 months	14	2,000	To go on trading mission
13	N9	vii. 621	10 months	32,5	3,250	To go on trading mission
14	N9	vii. 621?	10 months	38,666	3,866	
15	N10	x. 628	7 months	14	2,000	To go on trading mission
16	N10	viii. 625	[...]	4	[...]	
17	N10	vii 624	8 months	15	1 7/8	
18	N10	vii. 621	10 months	35	3,500	
19	N10	viii. 621	[...]	15	[...]	
20	N10	vii. 619	10 months	11,666	1,166	
21	N10	viii. 619	10 months	35	3,500	
22	N10	ix. 616	12 months	>30	>2,500	To go on trading mission
23	N31	x. 622	2 months	4,666	2,333	

[2] Note that previous studies tended to ignore or actively reject the existence of labor for hire in the Assyrian Empire, see Radner 2007a: 186–188 for a discussion.

b. Length of work contract: mostly seven to twelve months.

	Length	Total salary (in shekels)	Monthly salary (in shekels)	Nature of employment	Contract date	Assur archive
4	1 month	1	1,000	To harvest	iv. 631	1990
23	2 months	4,666	2,333		x. 622	N31
12	7 months	14	2,000	To go on trading mission	vi. 623	N9
15	7 months	14	2,000	To go on trading mission	x. 628	N10
8	8 months	30	3,750		viii. 625	N9
17	8 months	15	1,875		vii. 624	N10
6	9 months	20	2,350		viii. 631	N9
9	9 months	[...]	[...]		ix. 625	N9
11	10 months	not given	not given		viii. 623	N9
20	10 months	11 2/3	1,166		vii. 619	N10
10	10 months	12 1/2	1,250		vii. 624	N9
7	10 months	17 1/2	1,750		viii. 629	N9
13	10 months	32 1/2	3,250	To go on trading mission	vii. 621	N9
18	10 months	35	3,500		vii. 621	N10
21	10 months	35	3,500		viii. 619	N10
14	10 months	38,666	3,866		vii. 621[?]	N9
3	12 months	10	0,833		ix. 616	1979/80
5	12 months	15	1,250		vi. 620	N2
22	12 months	>30	>2,500	To go on trading mission	ix. 616	N10

c. Wages per month: being paid in advance cuts the wages, and working abroad pays better.

	Monthly salary (in shekels)	Total salary (in shekels)	Length	Nature of employment and other special arrangements	Contract date	Assur archive
3	0,833	10	12 months	Third party (father) takes wages Wages already received	ix. 616	1979-80
4	1,000	1	1 month	To harvest Wages already received	iv. 631	1990
20	1,166	11,666	10 months	Third party takes wages	vii. 619	N10
5	1.250	15	12 months	Wages to pay off existing debt	vi. 620	N2
10	1,250	12,5	10 months	Third party (father) takes wages	vii. 624	N9
7	1,750	17,5	10 months	Guarantor appointed	viii. 629	N9
17	1,875	15	8 months		vii. 624	N10
12	2,000	14	7 months	To go on trading mission Guarantor appointed	vii. 624	N9
15	2,000	14	7 months	To go on trading mission Third party takes wages	x. 628	N10
6	2,222	20	9 months		viii. 631	N9
23	2,333	4,666	2 months		x. 622	N31
22	>2,500	>30	12 months	To go on trading mission	ix. 616	N10
13	3,250	32,5	10 months	To go on trading mission	vii. 621	N9
18	3,500	35	10 months		vii. 621	N10
21	3,500	35	10 months		viii. 619	N10
8	3,750	30	8 months		viii. 625	N9
14	3,866	38,666	10 months		vii. 621[?]	N9

d. Distribution of contracts over the seasons: mostly autumn and winter (September to January)

	Contract date	Length	Monthly salary (in shekels)	Nature of employment	Assur archive
4	iv. 631	1 month	1,000	To harvest	1990
12	vi. 623	7 months	2,000	To go on trading mission	N9
5	vi. 620	12 months	1,250		N2
17	vii. 624	8 months	1,875		N10
10	vii. 624	10 months	1,250		N9
13	vii. 621	10 months	3,250	To go on trading mission	N9
18	vii. 621	10 months	3,500		N10
14	vii. 621?	10 months	3,866		N9
20	vii. 619	10 months	1,166		N10
6	viii. 631	9 months	2,250		N9
7	viii. 629	10 months	1,750		N9
8	viii. 625	8 months	3,750		N9
21	viii. 619	10 months	3,500		N10
16	viii. 625	[...]	[...]		N10
11	viii. 623	10 months	not given		N9
19	viii. 621	[...]	[...]		N10
9	ix. 625	9 months	[...]		N9
3	ix. 616	12 months	0,833		1979-80
22	ix. 616	12 months	>2,500	To go on trading mission	N10
15	x. 628	7 months	2,000	To go on trading mission	N10
23	x. 622	2 months	2,333		N31

e. Distribution of contracts over the years (NB: Year sequence after 648 is uncertain!)

	Date	Length	Total salary (in shekels)	Monthly salary (in shekels)	Nature of employment	Assur archive
4	iv. 631	1 month	1	1	To harvest	1990
6	viii. 631	9 months	20	2,250		N9
7	viii. 629	10 months	17,5	1,750		N9
15	x. 628	7 months	14	2	To go on trading mission	N10
8	viii. 625	8 months	30	3,750		N9
16	viii. 625	[...]	4	[...]		N10
9	ix. 625	9 months	[...]	[...]		N9
17	vii. 624	8 months	15	1,875		N10
10	vii. 624	10 months	12,5	1,250		N9
12	vi. 623	7 months	14	2	To go on trading mission	N9
11	viii. 623	10 months	not given	not given		N9
23	x. 622	2 months	4,666	2,333		N31
13	vii. 621	10 months	32,5	3,250	To go on trading mission	N9
18	vii. 621	10 months	35	3,500		N10
14	vii. 621?	10 months	38,666	3,866		N9
19	viii. 621	[...]	15	[...]		N10
5	vi. 620	12 months	15	1,250		N2
20	vii. 619	10 months	11,666	1,166		N10
21	viii. 619	10 months	35	3,500		N10
3	ix. 616	12 months	10	0,833		1979-80
22	ix. 616	12 months	>30	>2,500	To go on trading mission	N10

BIBLIOGRAPHY

Baker, Heather D. (2010), "The meaning of *ṭuppi*." *Revue d'Assyriologie* 104: 131–162.

Fuchs, Andreas and Simo Parpola (2001), *The Correspondence of Sargon II, Part III: Letters from Babylonia and the Eastern Provinces* (State Archives of Assyria 15). Helsinki.

Jursa, Michael (2010), *Aspects of the Economic History of Babylonia in the First Millennium BC* (Alter Orient und Altest Testament 377). Münster.

Lanfranchi, Giovanni B. and Simo Parpola (1990), *The Correspondence of Sargon II, Part II: Letters from the Northern and Northeastern Provinces* (State Archives of Assyria 5). Helsinki.

Luukko, Mikko (2012), *The Correspondence of Tiglath-pileser III and Sargon II from Calah/Nimrud* (State Archives of Assyria 19). Helsinki.

Parpola, Simo (1987), *The Correspondence of Sargon II, Part I: Letters from Assyria and the West* (State Archives of Assyria 1). Helsinki.

— (1993), *Letters from Assyrian and Babylonian Scholars* (State Archives of Assyria 10). Helsinki.

Parpola, Simo and Kazuko Watanabe (1988), *Neo-Assyrian Treaties and Loyalty Oaths* (State Archives of Assyria 2). Helsinki.

Pedersén, Olof (1986), *Archives and Libraries in the City of Assur. A Survey of the Material from the German Excavations 2* (Studia Semitica Upsaliensia 8). Uppsala.

Postgate, J. Nicolas (1973), *The Governor's Archive* (Cuneiform Texts from Nimrud 2). London.

— (1979), "On Some Assyrian Ladies." *Iraq* 41: 89–103.

Radner, Karen (1999a), *Ein neuassyrisches Privatarchiv der Tempelgoldschmiede von Assur* (Studien zu den Assur-Texten 1). Saarbrücken.

— (1999b), "Traders in the Neo-Assyrian Period," in J. G. Dercksen (ed.), *Trade and Finance in Ancient Mesopotamia*: 101–126. Leiden.

— (2001), "The Neo-Assyrian Period," in R. Westbrook and R. Jasnow (eds.), *Security for Debt in Ancient Near Eastern Law*: 265–288. Leiden.

— (2003), "An Assyrian View on the Medes." in G. B. Lanfranchi, M. Roaf and R. Rollinger (eds.), *Continuity of Empire (?): Assyria, Media, Persia* (History of the Ancient Near East Monographs 5): 37–64. Padova.

— (2004), *Das mittelassyrische Tontafelarchiv von Giricano/Dunnu-ša-Uzibi* (Subartu 14). Turnhout.

— (2007a), "Hired labour in the Neo-Assyrian empire," *State Archives of Assyria Bulletin* 16: 185–226.

— (2007b), "Abgaben an den König von Assyrien aus dem In- und Ausland," In Himar Klinkott, Sabine Kubisch and Renate Müller-Wollermann (eds.), *Geschenke und Steuern, Zölle und Tribute. Antike Abgabenformen in Anspruch und Wirklichkeit*: 213–230. Leiden.

— (2011), "Between a Rock and a Hard Place: Musasir, Kumme, Ukku and Šubria—the Buffer States between Assyria and Urartu," in S. Kroll et al. (eds.), *Urartu-Bianili* (Acta Iranica 51). Leuven.

— (forthcoming), "Die beiden neuassyrischen Privatarchive," in Peter Miglus, Franciszek M. Stepniowski and Karen Radner, *Untersuchungen im Stadtgebiet von Assur: Wohnquartiere in der Weststadt, Teil 1* (Wissenschaftliche Veröffentlichungen der Deutschen Orient-Gesellschaft). Wiesbaden: Harrassowitz.

6.

Labor in Babylonia in the First Millennium BC

Michael Jursa
Universität Wien[1]

Introduction

The present paper attempts a synthesis on the issue of labor and labor relations in Babylonia in the first millennium BC. The bulk of the data comes from the "long sixth century" between the rise of the Neo-Babylonian empire (626 BC) and the Babylonian rebellions against Persian rule under Xerxes (484 BC); the main focus of this paper will therefore lie on this period.[2] Later data, *i.e.*, data from the later Achaemenid period of the fifth and fourth centuries and the subsequent Hellenistic period, can only be touched upon; they are overall far less informative than the sources of the long sixth century.

As in all other periods of Mesopotamian history, free and unfree labor coexisted in first millennium BC Babylonia. Free hirelings (*agru*) worked side by side with privately owned slaves (*ardu*, *qallu*) and with

1 This paper is based on research conducted under the auspices of two research projects funded by the Fonds zur Förderung der Wissenschaftlichen Forschung (Vienna): the research project "Economic History of Babylonia in the First Millennium BC" (2002–2009) and the research project "The Language of Power: Administrative Epistolography in First Millennium BC Babylonia" (2009–2015). Unpublished texts from the British Museum and the Yale Babylonian Collection are cited by permission of the Trustees of the British Museum and of the Curators of the Yale Babylonian Collection, B. R. Foster and U. Kasten, respectively.

2 Significant parts of the paper have been extracted from a recent extensive synthesis of the economic development of Babylonia in the period under discussion (Jursa 2010).

institutional dependants who, in the case of the temples, were called *širku*, *i.e.*, literally, "oblate." Finally, for public works, temple and palace construction, the digging of canals and generally the maintenance of irrigation installations, the authorities could levy manpower from the population on the basis of a complex system of labor obligations that were tied to certain types of rural and urban landownership, to patterns of residence, and to professional affiliation. The legal and economic framework within which each of these groups operated has been described adequately by prior research. Contractual labor was based on individual work contracts, laborers hired themselves out for a specific time or for the completion of a specific task, and were remunerated accordingly (Dandamaev 1987, 1988; Jursa 2010: 660ff.; Jursa 2014).

Privately owned slaves were never particularly numerous. They worked either in their owners' household or, as trained craftsmen especially in an urban context, independently, but still to the benefit of their owners; they could take out work contracts just as free men, but were required to pay part of the proceeds to their owners (Dandamaev 1984).

The status of oblates was not that of fully-fledged slaves or serfs, and they were allowed to live in families and enjoyed a certain degree of economic freedom of movement, but nevertheless they were subjected to the authority of their temple and were required to work for it according to the needs of the temple administrations. In return they were paid regular salaries, usually, but not exclusively, in kind, which allowed them and their families a minimum subsistence, probably not much above starvation level (Dandamaev 1984, Kleber 2011, Jursa 2008).

Corvée laborers were levied from free, but taxable households, as well as from larger entities, such as tax units, but also from temples, villages or cities, on a seasonal basis, or simply according to requirements. Inidivuals had to fulfil a limited period of service; the hiring of substitute labores recruited from the free population that did not own taxable properties was extremely common (Jursa and Waerzeggers 2009). While these several forms of labor are sufficiently well-understood on their own, their interplay, their respective role within the overall economy, and the relationship between money- and contract-based labor relations and other forms of labor extraction are in need of further clarification. It is here that some of the most distinctive characteristics of the Babylonian economy of the long sixth century come to the fore. The discussion will start with labor, especially with hired labor, in an institutional context, before moving to the private sector of the economy.

In general terms, the problem to be addressed is best defined by referring to the extraordinarily influential position of Moses Finley. In his *The Ancient Economy* he states that

> "[w]hen any [ancient, MJ] society we can trace attained a stage of sufficient accumulation of resources and power in some hands (whether king, temple, ruling tribe or aristocracy), so that a labor force was demanded greater than could be provided by the household or kinship group, for agriculture or mining or public works or arms manufacture, that labor was obtained not by hiring it but by compelling it, by force of arms or by force of law and custom."[3]

For Finley, labor in Antiquity was predominantly compulsory. Hired labor was, historically speaking, a latecomer which was never as important quantitatively as the different forms of compulsory labor.

All periods of ancient Mesopotamian history offer data which can be explained by reference to the Finleyan model. The texts contain an impressive amount of information on compulsory labor, especially corvée-style labor for agricultural work other than ploughing and seeding, for canal and irrigation works, brick making and large-scale construction work, and so forth.[4] Given the uniform appearance of these data, it has been queried whether hired labor had any role at all to play in this context and whether there were even significant numbers of institutionally unattached individuals who would have been available for hire—a question that imposes itself especially if one subscribes to the frequently argued understanding of the economy in southern Mesopotamia as largely, and in some periods (nearly) exclusively, dominated by the concerns of large public institutions, *i.e.*, temples and palaces (the "*oikos* model"). The institutional affiliation of a large part of the population and widespread reliance on a subsistence economy aiming at economic autarchy supposedly precluded modes of economic exchange other than redistribution and reciprocity from playing a significant role: there was little or no space for markets or market substitutes, and therefore also no significant role for labor and a labor market.[5]

3 Finley 1985: 66. Finley's paradigm is used here as a point of departure because of its continued influence and importance. This is not to deny the obvious fact that ancient economic history has moved on: Morris, Saller and Scheidel 2007: 1ff.

4 Ample evidence can be found, *e.g.*, in Powell (ed.) 1987, and in this volume.

5 There are of course many variants regarding the way this basic model is expressed and developed. See for the sake of convenience Renger 2003 and 2005.

As has been amply demonstrated elsewhere,[6] this traditional model, in whichever form it is cast, does not fit the evidence from our period. Of course all the traditional economic agents, including the institutions, *i.e.*, the palace or state sector of the economy and the temples, were still present, but their respective weight and the way they functioned economically both internally and in relation to the outside world differed from what would be expected on the basis of the *oikos* model. Principal factors characterising the institutional economy in Babylonia in the first millennium BC which cannot be accommodated by the model include an increasing monetisation of economic exchange and a considerable reliance on cash-crop agriculture (Jursa 2010: 469ff.). As a closer look at hired labor in the context of the institutional economy in the following pages will show, we have to add to these factors a chronic lack of manpower and the concomitant need to hire outside labor.

Hired mass labor and compulsory labor in the institutional economy

One of the most important issues in the present context is determining to what degree temples and the state made use of institutionally unattached individuals for their building projects in the cities and in the countryside. Given the number and the scale especially of the royally sponsored building activities of the sixth century, which greatly affected not only the urban environment in most of the old cities of the alluvium, but also parts of the rural hinterland through the massive reclamation work undertaken in the north and centre of the country (Da Riva 2008: 108ff.), this is a question which is essential for the understanding of the Neo-Babylonian economy as a whole.

The Neo-Babylonian archival documentation for "public" works, palace and temple building, earthworks and the like—the kind of undertakings for which, according to the usual understanding, corvée-style forced labor should have played a dominant role—has received a certain amount of attention in recent years.[7] Most of the information comes from the archives of Eanna and Ebabbar. Particularly informative dossiers from Uruk deal with the building of the North Palace in

6 For a critique of attempts to apply the model of *oikos*-type household economy, with its principal focus on redistribution, on the data from first millennium BC Babylonia, and for a description of the important role of commodity markets in this period, see, *e.g.*, Jursa 2010 passim, esp. 563ff.; Graslin-Tomé 2009: 148ff.; Pirngruber 2012.

7 Beaulieu 2005: 58f., 69, Zawadzki 2005a; Jursa 2005b: 173ff., Kleber 2008: 133ff.

Babylon (Beaulieu 2005), the *akītu* temple in Uruk (Jursa 2010: 668), and the city wall of Babylon (Kleber 2008: 164ff.). From the Ebabbar archive comes the dossier dealing with canal and dam building in the north of Sippar during the reign of Nabonidus (Zawadzki 2005a; Jursa 2010: 518ff.). Mention should also be made of a certain body of Eanna letters from the reign of Cambyses (and Cyrus; Stolper 2003). In all instances the evidence points unequivocally to the important role of hired labor. Whenever pertinent information is available, hired hands, *i.e.*, free laborers, outnumber the temples' dependants, *i.e.*, the compulsory labor force.

Urukean letters contain the most evocative anecdotal evidence. These letters were sent by temple officials overseeing building works in the countryside, who regularly had to contend with problems caused by the insufficient numbers of available temple personnel. The solution proposed by them consisted of hiring replacements, for which they however had to request additional funds from the central temple administration. We will cite just a few examples:

> "... The temple serfs dig only one thousand cubits of the lot of four thousand cubits that has been apportioned to us; hirelings have dug all (the rest) ..." (YOS 21, 72).

> " ... There are no workers here except two [...]; and when I said to the royal resident, 'hire some men,' (he) told (me): 'we don't have any silver.' Now, either send me a full complement of workers or have silver brought to the royal resident so that he might hire men and in this way assemble the necessary number of workers ..." (YOS 21, 156).

> "... Twenty-five workers (of a certain contingent) are going to leave on the first of Ulūlu because they are not paid: (my) lords should know that these are all hirelings and that a hireling only works for three shekels (per month). There is nothing I could give them. ..." (YOS 3, 133).

> "... Of the men you sent only eighty have arrived here, and they have no 'overseer of ten;' we have to employ 130 hirelings to make up for the(se) men ..." (Durand, EHE 601).

> " ... There are no hirelings left. They all went away for the month of Tašrītu [*i.e.*, for the month of the date harvest, MJ], and the temple serfs you send me don't have any provisions. They work five days and then run away; and the hirelings take each six shekels of silver as

their wages per man and month. I know that neither barley nor dates are left in Eanna; buy barley and dates with silver in the city centre, bring it (to the temple) and give thirty liters of barley for fifteen days to every man (available) and send me workers so that they will do the work. ..." (YOS 3, 69).

The last passage from YOS 3, 69 is particularly important: it shows that in the month of the date harvest it was difficult, if not impossible, to hire workers, certainly because they would go off harvesting their own gardens. This suggests that we are dealing with an independent, rural population, apparently without any institutional affiliation.

This point can be demonstrated even more clearly by reference to the workers' lists from the Ebabbar archive referring to the dam building project undertaken in the north of Sippar during the thirteenth and fourteenth year of Nabonidus.[8] Here is one example of a text, CT 56, 572 (Jursa 2010: 663 n. 3467).

"Temple personnel (*nišū bīti*), corvée workers (*urāšu*) and hirelings (*agru*) working on the dam at Gilūšu; 30.10.13 Nabonidus, king of Babylon:

thirty temple dependants, six of whom are cutting reeds;
nine corvée workers, one of whom is cutting reeds;
four men from Bīt-Dihummu;
three ploughmen;
two gardeners;
six [shepherds];
[(break)]
eleven [hirelings of ...];
eleven hirelings of Šamaš-ibni;
[n (hirelings)] of Šamaš-zēru-ibni;
... (there follow more damaged entries for hirelings of individuals and a summary)."

The texts typically concern just one day. The workers are listed according to category and origin: temple personnel—mostly ploughmen, gardeners, shepherds and craftsmen (*ummânu*, not mentioned in this text)—are distinguished from corvée workers—forced laborers, therefore—and hirelings. Among the latter, further distinctions are made. Many of the

[8] The then known texts are summarised in Jursa 1995a: 184ff.; additions can be found in Zawadzki 2005: 385 with notes 14f.

hirelings are said to be inhabitants of Gilūšu and Bīt-Dihummu.[9] These are settlements in the vicinity of the dam built by the temple. The terminology, with its carefully maintained distinctions between *agru* "hireling," *urāšu* "corvée worker" and *nišū bīti* "temple personnel," makes it clear that the men Ebabbar was recruiting locally were not formally under the jurisdiction of the temple: this was not compulsory labor, it was free wage labor provided by independent villagers.

At the end of the example translated above and of most of the other texts of this group, hirelings are listed who are attributed to certain individuals. These men are frequently identifiable. They are generally private contractors known to have a business relationship with the temple, temple officials from the middle echelons of the temple administration or owners of temple prebends. According to the rosters, they were obliged to hire workers and put them at the temple's disposal for the dam building project: these hirelings are substitutes employed by these men to fulfil their corvée obligations to the temple in the way described above (Jursa 2010: 649 with note 3412). The background of this obligation is never spelled out explicitly in the Sippar texts, but one can find an explanation in two (or three) Uruk letters.

In the context of complaining about the lack of workers and the prohibitive costs of hiring outside labor, and after stating the need to find additional resources, a temple official overseeing a building project in the countryside writes to his colleagues who are residing in Uruk: "open the writing board and see that you get a corvée worker (*urāšu*) from every single *mār banê* whose name appears in the list" (YOS 21, 72). In a parallel text, the same man writes as follows: "check the writing board listing the temple serfs; don't let any of them get away, send them all. The *mār banê* who are listed there should hire a man (each)" (YOS 3, 17 // TCL 9, 129).

These letters are important for the understanding of the implications of the term *mār banê*. The word is usually translated by "free citizen," but here, as probably in most cases when it is mentioned in temple archives, what is intended is rather "non-serf head of a household (loosely) affiliated to the temple." The *mār banê* intended here—certainly craftsmen not belonging to the group of the temple serfs, prebendaries and minor officials, clerks and the like—were obliged to supply the temple

[9] The word "hireling" is not used in line 8 of this text, but appears in analogous contexts in other tablets of this dossier, *e.g.*, in CT 56, 577: 5 ("twenty hirelings from Gilūšu").

upon demand with labor for communal building activities, maintenance work on the canal system and the like. They did not have to work physically for the temple at all times, as temple serfs had to do, but, according to YOS 21, 72, they could be called up for corvée. Originally this may have implied actual physical service, but in our case it simply meant paying someone who would do the work. The parallel letter YOS 3, 17 refers undoubtedly to the same obligation by demanding that the *mār banê* hire (*agāru*) wage-laborers (*agru*). The terminology here is more explicit regarding the economic mechanism lying behind the transaction, whereas the formulation in the former text, by using the technical term *urāšu*, "corvée worker," places greater weight on the grounds on which the obligation of the *mār banê* rested.

The inclusion of hirelings paid for by individuals linked to the Ebabbar temple in the Sippar lists of workers must result from analogous obligations incumbent on these Sipparean *mār banê*. Numerous additional examples for the hiring of substitutes for the fulfilment of service obligations can be found in other, private archives (van Driel 2002: 230ff.; Jursa and Waerzeggers 2009; Jursa 2011). This was particularly common when it came to strenuous service outside Babylonia, especially for military purposes. There are several contracts in which substitutes are hired by those liable for service. In part the relevant terminology reflects this practice: next to *ilku* "service obligation", *ṣāb šarri* "(service as) royal soldier", *dullu* "(corvée) service obligation" and the like one finds also *kutallūtu* "service as a substitute" among the terms for pertinent obligations. Such hirelings were sent off most often to corvée labor in Elam, but also to Northern Mesopotamia and to the Sealand in the far south of Babylonia. The relevant texts date from the mid-sixth century to the early fourth century, but the clearest evidence comes from late sixth century Borsippa and Sippar. In the latter city for instance, the urban population was divided into units of usually ten men for the purposes of military conscription. These divisions were made on the basis of either patterns of co-residence or professional affiliation—neighbours and/or professional colleagues were grouped together. Each of these groups had to make available one archer at any given time. Originally, this had been meant to be a rotating service obligation, the period of service being half a year, so that every member of the group would be called up every five years. In practice however, several documents prove that these men could simply raise the necessary money to hire an outsider to do the actual service. The wages of these men were high: they were paid up to ten shekels per month. While in a further step, the service obligation and the hiring of a substitute by the man or group burdened with the obligation could be replaced by a direct money payment to the crown, the fact remains that the availability of hired labor was transforming the corvée system by offering to those liable for service a convenient way to avoid irksome duties.

While the men hiring the substitutes are often well-known through their private archives, the substitutes themselves are not—frequently they are not even mentioned by name, and nothing can be said on their economic and social background. The most suggestive dossier comes from the Itti-Šamaš-balāṭu archive from Larsa (Jursa 2010: 651ff.). It concerns a father and his son who one after the other hired themselves out to the archive-owning family over a period of several years to fulfil the military service obligations of the male members of this family. Amurru-ibni, son of Ṣillāya, did military service for Itti-Šamaš-balāṭu in Northern Babylonia, probably in or near Sippar, at least from the fourth year of Nabonidus onwards and received equipment and payments at least until the ninth year of this king. The texts indicate that he served continuously throughout this period. His son Amurru-šarru-uṣur acted as the "king's soldier" (*ṣāb šarri*) of Itti-Šamaš-balāṭu's sons from the twelfth(?) year of Nabonidus onwards at least until the second year of Cyrus. This file clearly shows that working as a professional soldier for hire by the well-to-do Babylonians unwilling or unable to fulfil their military obligations themselves was a viable way of earning a living and maintaining a family and could even create a relationship between the businessman/employer and soldier/employee which was so stable that it could be continued by their respective sons in the same roles.

The importance of the rosters of workers from Sippar (there are about fifty of these texts) lies in the possibility of arriving at an approximate figure for the numbers of workers of each of the different categories of men employed over about half a year in the thirteenth and fourteenth year of Nabonidus (the period for which abundant information is available). Unfortunately the majority of the texts are fragmentary, but all the lists following the standard format of CT 56, 572 etc. that are sufficiently well preserved suggest that in general over two hundred men were working on the site and that most of them—perhaps on average two-thirds of the workforce, around 120–150 men—were hirelings (Jursa 2010: 665ff.). The subscript of BM 59671 mentions 603 workers, the best-preserved text of all, BM 79784, lists likewise over 600 workers, of which less then ten percent were temple personnel. Importantly, it can be also shown that these hirelings were paid silver wages of around three to four shekels per month (Jursa 2010: 519).

Gilūšu was just one of several building sites in the region of the Nār-šarri, and not only Ebabbar, but also other temples and the palace were engaged in the work. It is impossible to tell whether the composition of the workforce at Gilūšu was representative of that found in all the other building sites maintained by other institutions. However, given the high cost of hiring laborers, it is certain that Ebabbar would have done without wage labor had that been an option—which clearly was not the case. Taking into consideration the Eanna letters discussed above, it is clear that the case of Gilūšu was typical rather than exceptional, and that not only Ebabbar, but also other temples and the state itself had to hire a large part of the huge labor force required by their ambitious building projects.

One might think that mass labor could have been more easily raised by compulsion in an urban context than in the countryside where Ebabbar built its dam and where Eanna's administrators who wrote the letters mentioned above struggled with the chronic lack of manpower. Nevertheless, the available data suggest that also in the cities the institutions had to rely to a large extent on independent, hired labor. The richest source of information on these matters is a dossier of administrative texts from the Eanna archive dealing with this temple's contribution to the 'nation-wide' effort claimed by king Nebuchadnezzar for the construction of his North Palace in Babylon (Beaulieu 2005; Jursa 2010: 555f.). The temple sent its own personnel, temple serfs (*širku*), to Babylon, but since their numbers were insufficient, more workers had to be hired on site. These men were normally paid silver wages, as was common practice with institutional hirelings (Beaulieu 2005: 53f. and 69). While it is impossible to estimate with precision the relative numbers of the two groups of workers employed by Eanna in Babylon, it is certain that the local hirelings formed a sizeable part of the workforce and that, therefore, the royal building project resulted in much silver coming into the hands of the local population of Babylon.

This general conclusion is confirmed by other dossiers. As another example concerning Babylon, one can cite the still incomplete information available for the Ninmah archive, a fragment of a temple archive from Babylon dealing mostly with temple building activities. The archive contains, among other text groups, lists of hirelings as well as lists of small silver payments—certainly wage lists (Pedersén 2005a: 135ff.). So also in this case, a large-scale, state-sponsored building project (Beaulieu 1997) could not go ahead without a significant contribution from non-compulsory, hired labor paid in silver money. The same is true in principle for Eanna's rebuilding of the *akītu* temple in Uruk, even though the available record is somewhat more complex (Kleber 2008:

173ff.). The total number of hirelings employed was between eighty and one hundred. There is some evidence that wages were occasionally paid to these hirelings in kind, but overall the references to silver wages and generally the expenditure of silver for the purpose of the building project account for the larger part of the dossier (Jursa 2010: 668).

The evidence surveyed here (which comes from the north, the centre and the south of Babylonia) show that the hiring of mass labor predominantly for silver wages was a common phenomenon in the sixth century, both in the countryside and in the cities. It seems likely (and is certain in the case of the Gilūšu dossier) that the extent to which hired labor was used for public works undertaken by the kings and temples surpassed that of 'classical' compulsory labor. Given the scale of the building works in the Neo-Babylonian period, especially under Nebuchadnezzar, and their long duration, this must have had a considerable overall impact especially on urban society: a large workforce found (virtually) continuous employment, mostly earning and subsisting on money wages. A better understanding of the implications of this phenomenon requires a comparison of the costs of hired mass labor to those of a workforce of institutional dependants, *e.g.*, temple serfs.

The cost of labor in institutional contexts

Institutional personnel, temple serfs and other dependants of the institutional households, were normally remunerated by payments in kind (dates or barley), commonly designated as "rations." Other foodstuffs, oil, pulses and vegetables for instance, as well as beverages such as beer, were only issued infrequently and under certain circumstances; they were never a regular part of the monthly or yearly allowance of temple dependants. It may suffice here to summarise the evidence very briefly for the purpose of comparison (Jursa 2008). In Uruk, members of the temple household of the Eanna temple, *i.e.*, in the present context, compulsory laborers, were normally issued barley. The standards applied by the temple administration evolved over time, as follows:

Ration standard	Date
36–45 liters of barley (or occasionally dates)	reign of Nabopolassar
72 liters	early reign of Nebuchadnezzar
90 liters	mid-reign of Nebuchadnezzar to Cambyses
45 liters	mid-reign of Nebuchadnezzar to Nabonidus: half ration for sick men
180 liters	late reign of Nebuchadnezzar to Cambyses

Table 1: The most common standards for monthly "rations" attested at Uruk

In Sippar, in the Ebabbar archive, the evidence does not show a diachronic change within the system, but it does allow a reconstruction of internal distinctions mostly based on age: adult, fully trained workers received 180 liters per month, younger and untrained workers ninety liters, very young apprentices just sixty liters.

In essence the systems used in the two temples were the same from the reign of Nabonidus onwards. While there were differences in the size of rations owing to age, there were few and far less pronounced distinctions on the basis of profession and rank. Women and young children were not included in the redistributive ration system: families of temple dependants had to subsist on the rations paid to the working males (and on whatever the women might receive as compensation for their work, normally in textile production). The principal difference between Eanna and Ebabbar lay in the fact that in Uruk, where monthly rations increased over time, the "full" ration of 180 liters was not as common as it was in Sippar. In Uruk, many temple craftsmen and normally also unskilled laborers on detached duty had to content themselves with ninety liters per month. Furthermore, there were differences regarding the extent to which institutional personnel were paid in silver instead of in dates or barley. In Sippar this happened only under certain conditions, mostly when temple staff were sent overland and had to take part of their allowance with them. Travel funds were obviously far more convenient when issued in silver—if one could rely on the fact that the silver would be acceptable as a means of payment for food and other ordinary goods, which was obviously the case in this period. This practice was also followed in Uruk. In this city however, silver 'rations' were paid quite regularly also to city-based workers particularly during the second half of the reign of Nebuchadnezzar. The size of these silver rations was tied to the ration standard of ninety liters per month via the (volatile) barley price, as the close correlation between the attested barley prices (when converted into prices of ninety liters of barley) and the silver rations demonstrates.

The frequent substitution of rations in kind by money payments (which is mirrored by the increasing role money played in the prebendary sphere) is a peculiarity of the sixth-century temple archives (Jursa 2008; 2010: 522 and 553). It reflects not only the generally high degree of monetisation in this period, but also the particularly deep embeddedness of the temple economies of Ebabbar and Eanna in the money economy. In contrast, the palace personnel working in Nebuchadnezzar's South Palace were supplied through a "real" ration system, *i.e.*, a system intended to provide its dependants with the necessary variety of foodstuffs, rather than with just one commodity which could be used for exchange—at least, there is evidence for regular deliveries of oil, and probably also of beer, to palace dependants in addition to the common barley and date rations (Pedersén 2005a and b; Jursa 2008). The economic situation of the palace household was entirely different from that of the temples (structural similarities notwithstanding). The palace organisation benefited from a huge income in kind, partly coming from the royal estates, but also, and perhaps predominantly, resulting from the direct taxation of (only institutional?) harvests and from various indirect taxes (harbour dues etc.): it did not suffer from a shortage of commodities and had no need to issue silver instead.

From a diachronic perspective, the the divergent nature of the "ration systems" found in different archives in the sixth century is striking. A small institutional archive from the eighth century, the "Morgan archive" (Jursa 2010: 506ff.), includes no evidence for silver payments in the context of transactions within the institutional household. Also a letter archive from Nippur, likewise from the eighth century, suggests that the use of silver was restricted to a large extent to the "commercial" sphere in this period (Jursa 2010: 500ff.). The sixth-century temple records clearly reflect entirely different economic background conditions. From later centuries, we have mostly the Zababa archive from Kiš (from the late fifth and the fourth century), the Esangila archive (mostly from the fourth and third centuries), the brewers' archive from Borsippa (late fourth century) and the Rahimesu archive from Babylon (first century).[10] Interestingly, the ration system found in the Esangila archive and the Zababa archive were relatively "traditional" in comparison with those of the sixth-century temples:[11] rations of barley, dates and wool were issued to temple dependants, but generally in lesser amounts than in Uruk and Sippar under Nabonidus.[12] Women and children were included among the recipients, and silver rations were uncommon. The Borsippean brewers' archive is similar, but does not quite fit into this traditional scheme (Hackl 2013: 476ff.). The late Rahimesu archive on the other hand shows temple dependants being remunerated entirely by

[10] The ration system documented in the Rahimesu archive is studied by van der Spek 1998; the others are discussed in Jursa 2008: 415ff. and Hackl 2013: 380ff.

[11] If one disregards the innovation that in the Esangila archive there was no terminological difference between payments of prebendary income and rations of non-prebendary personnel: both were designated as *kurummatu*.

[12] Ninety litres per month was a common standard for dates or barley.

silver payments. Also the slightly older Astrologers' archive (late second century) mentions 'rations' of temple personnel which were paid in silver.[13] While the interpretation of these data is hampered by a lack of sources which for the time being preclude a better understanding of the degree of monetisation of the Babylonian economy in the final centuries of the first millennium BC (Pirngruber 2012), it is in any case clear that there was no straightforward, linear evolution towards ever higher degrees of monetisation of the institutional economy from the eighth through the sixth and on into the fourth and later centuries. The sixth century does stand out.

The *communis opinio* considers *kurummatu* "food rations" in the sixth century to have been just that, *i.e.*, primarily food meant for direct consumption by the recipients. However, this is demonstrably not the case for both large temple archives from the late reign of Nebuchadnezzar onwards. The early Urukean ration standard of thirty-six liters of barley per month could maintain an individual, provided he or she was able to obtain some supplementary foodstuffs, like vegetables and pulses, which were necessary in any case (it should be remembered that these things were not issued by the temples on a regular basis). There would, however, have been only a small margin, if there was one at all, to use some of the barley issued to obtain other commodities, and it can be excluded that whole families subsisted on such rations. The matter is different for the ninety-liter standard used in Uruk from the reign of Nebuchadnezzar onwards. This could support a man and leave a significant part for exchange, or it could be used, simply in terms of energy requirements, to feed also a woman and one or two smaller children. From this point onwards the practice of not including women and younger children in the ration system is reasonable from an administration's point of view. For families such rations were still not generous, but as far as nutritional needs are concerned, the system would seem viable. The 180-liter standard, frequent in Uruk during the reign of Nabonidus and generally used in Sippar, seems exaggerated for real food rations: a ration system which regularly provided one laborer, even a provider for a nuclear family, with food sufficient for four adult men is inconceivable. Nevertheless, the size of the rations undoubtedly reflects real demand. One must, therefore, conclude that by this time the supposed food

[13] On this archive see preliminarily Hackl 2013: 461ff. with further references. See, *e.g.*, CT 49, 144 and 186, McEwan 1981a: no. 4, BOR 4, 132 (van der Spek 1985: 549f.).

rations were used to a significant extent for the purpose of exchange. This is made clear by the frequent substitution of rations in kind by money payments (which were still designated as *kurummatu*), especially in Uruk (Jursa 2008: 404ff.). The temples always preferred to issue those commodities that they had a sufficient supply of and therefore frequently substituted one (comparatively scarce) commodity with another—but only if the substitute could fulfil the same purpose as the commodity it replaced. What receiving money rather than payments in kind meant for the temple personnel depends on the accuracy with which rations were converted into money payments. Even though, as can be demonstrated, the temples made an effort to adjust rations to price developments, the volatile nature in particular of the barley price is bound to have affected the temple serfs' living conditions very directly, and probably more often for the worse than the better.

For these reasons the traditional term "rations"—which has been used also here for the sake of convenience and tradition—is actually inaccurate and should best be rejected in favour of the more appropriate "salaries paid in kind." The value of these payments was not, or not exclusively, dependent on the nutritional requirements of the recipients, but more generally, on their cost of living—after all, the development of these comparatively "generous" basic rations went hand in hand with a near abolishment of the other traditional parts of a redistributive system: the distribution of flour, beer, oil and of other supplementary foodstuffs. Far from being supported by an essentially closed redistributive system catering to all their basic needs, the institutional personnel of Eanna and Ebabbar lived in an economic setting which forced them to obtain through economic exchange, *i.e.*, through purchase, much of what was needed for their livelihood.

For the purposes of the present paper, one main conclusion from the foregoing is that the cost of maintaining an institutional workforce of compulsory (unskilled) laborers recruited primarily from the ranks of the temple serfs can be gauged with great precision: in Uruk, ninety liters of barley per man and month were the norm (See Jursa 2008: 401ff. and Janković 2008: 458ff.). In Sippar, the cost was higher, 180 liters per man and month (normally paid in dates).

In Uruk, the comparatively frequent silver payments designated as "rations" change over time. Between 12 and 24 Nbk, the standard was 1.5 shekels; thereafter, monthly payments fell to between 0.75 and 1 shekel and remained roughly on this level until the end of the reign of Nabonidus (Jursa 2008: 407). Sipparean silver rations cannot easily be systematised. In the context of the issue of travel provisions, payments in kind and payments in silver were often mixed. One shekel of silver and one *kurru* of dates per month seem to have been the maximum, but other texts (dating to the reign of Nabonidus) use a simple standard of one shekel per month (Jursa 2010: 520ff.).

The "rations" or salaries in kind can be put into perspective by comparison with monthly wages paid to hired laborers. The range of attested wages (*idū*) is large, from fractions of a shekel to ten shekels per month. Wages obviously depended on the task, profession and/or qualification of the laborer. For the present purpose, one should only consider the wages paid for building work, either in the city or in the countryside, for corvée labor, military service and for harvest work in the steppe, *i.e.*, wages paid for work which presupposed full employment, heavy physical exertion and (mostly) involved travel to the place of work. The data are surveyed in Jursa 2010: 674ff. As a result, one can see that the often invoked "standard" (or "iconic") wage of one shekel per month (*e.g.*, Ries 1993–97: 181) has little economic reality. Wages lower than one shekel per month as a rule involve children and/or part-time employment—for instance for laundry work, which could be paid for on a yearly basis. Even the wage of one shekel per month is never paid for a full-time occupation involving heavy, or even just continuous labor (in contrast to guard or shepherding duties, for example). For activities of this kind, two shekels per month is the lower limit of what can be considered common, and even this is probably only true from the late years of Nebuchadnezzar to the middle of the reign of Nabonidus. Before and after this period, monthly wages paid for heavy labor were higher: three to five shekels: the cost of hiring a free laborer was much higher than that of maintaining an institutional dependant over the same period of time.[14]

The small number of wage attestations from the late sixth century notwithstanding, one does get the impression of a significant increase of wage levels roughly from the beginning of the Achaemenid period onwards and particularly during the reign of Darius. In the first decade of his reign, monthly wages of up to seven to ten shekels of silver were paid for corvée labor abroad and military service: much more than was paid for comparable service in preceding decades, and the single wage we have from the second decade, five shekels for private building work, is

[14] This is true for other periods of Mesopotamian history, too. See most recently Adams 2006: 160, where it is stated that this difference "argues quite persuasively for the existence of a labor market."

about double what was paid by private individuals for this purpose under Nabonidus. Unfortunately there is no information for the second half of Darius' reign, but the texts from the reign of Xerxes cited in the table above suggest that the high wage level reached under Darius persisted into the reign of his successor: wages of seven or nine shekels for building work are roughly twice as high as those paid for such work in the sixth century until the end of the reign of Nabonidus.

As data collected by Beaulieu (2005) show, a hired hand employed by Eanna in Babylon for work on the North Palace building project could be paid about five times as much barley (450–540 liters) as was issued to his unfree colleagues, the temple serfs (ninety liters). The silver wages paid to hirelings for building work likewise far exceeded the value of the average rations (or salaries) paid in kind or in silver, at least until the reign of Darius. This can best be shown by a comparison between the silver value of the Sipparean (and partly Urukean) standard salary in kind of one *kurru* (180 liters) of dates or barley on the one hand, and the attested monthly wages paid for strenuous full-time labor or service on the other. In the following graph, the price data are presented by moving ten-year averages. For the wage data such a rendering would be useless: they are too few.

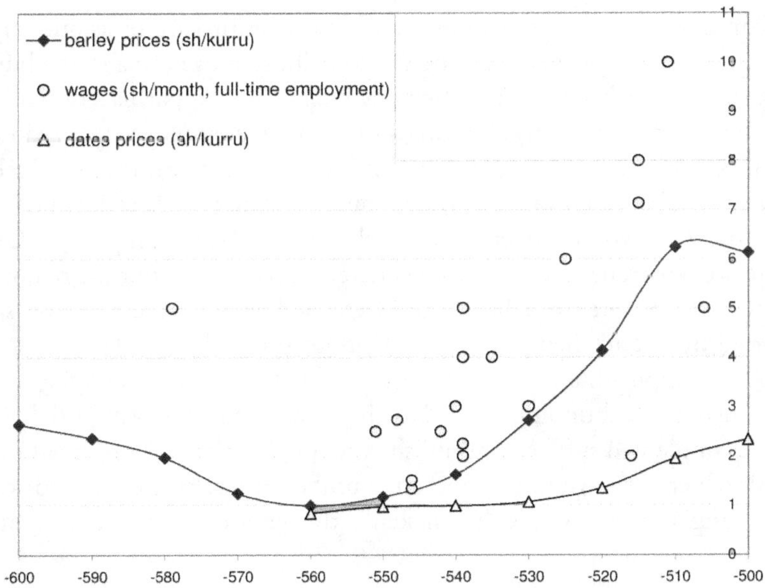

Fig. 2: Staple prices (moving ten-year averages) and wages (full employment)

As can be seen, the price of barley rose much earlier and more sharply than that of dates especially during the reign of Darius. Relatively speaking, this increase could have favoured the recipients of salaries in kind over recipients of silver wages, but this development was offset at least in part by a parallel rise of silver wages.

In any case, the wages paid to the hirelings working in the building "industry" from the very beginning of the sixth century onwards were considerable. Four shekels of silver per month equals forty-eight shekels of silver per year. Translated into staples this would correspond, in the reign of Nabonidus, to about forty to fifty *kurru* of dates, the yield of a substantial date garden—it was certainly possible to maintain a family with such wages, assuming employment was continuous, or nearly so. Even when one assumes just 7.5 months of employment, the resulting thirty shekels are above the level of the minimum household income of twenty-two to twenty-seven shekels (Jursa 2010: 296ff.).

The issue of continuity of employment is important. The difference between the monthly wages of hirelings and the hypothetical silver value of the salaries in kind paid to temple dependants is undeniable, but on the other hand a temple serf had, or should have had, one obvious advantage over a hireling: employment was theoretically secure, the temple could not choose not to pay for a *širku*, whereas a hireling could be out of work from one day to the next.[15] However, the employment of urban day-laborers was not necessarily always as precarious as one might imagine. The dossier concerning the contribution of Eanna to the building of the North Palace in Babylon as well as the Sippar lists of workers contain direct proof that hundreds of men were employed as obviously well-paid hirelings for months, and it is certain that, for instance, Nebuchadnezzar's vast building projects would have provided employment for thousands of workers over years, maybe decades. If the Sippar and Uruk data are representative, as is argued here, a large part, if not the majority, of these men were free laborers and were paid wages that could have supported them and their families throughout this time.

It is impossible to establish the size of the workforce employed for instance for the building of the North Palace or the city wall in Babylon. An example will suffice to establish very roughly the order of magnitude with which we have to reckon. The number of bricks necessary for constructing the city wall's "Osthaken", the part of Etemenanki's brick

[15] Note UET 4, 124, wherein hirelings are paid for just half a day (*a-hu* u_4*-mu*) of work.

structure that is demonstrably connected with Nebuchadnezzar and the western "Vorwerk" of the South Palace can be roughly calculated as 126 million.[16] If three men produce 11,000 bricks per month,[17] these bricks alone represent roughly the labor of 1,0310,000 man-days: 1,000 men working constantly for three years, just for brick making. It is certain that several thousand men were employed on these large building sites at any given time.

These people must then have formed a kind of urban working class with an at best limited background in agriculture and primary food production. The so-called "Mardonios texts" (Hackl 2013: 430ff., see below) form an archive that belonged to such workers—men who hired themselves out in small teams as brick-makers and perhaps builders. It is indicative of the importance of urban hired labor that members of this "humble" class of people appear, not as the object of written documentation owned by others, but as owners of an archive in their own right. A Sipparean temple weaver refers to such men when he is quoted as writing to his superior: "Let [my lord] give (me) money to hire laborers. I am beleaguered by men who are for hire, and my work cannot be done without the(se) hirelings."[18] This is an evocative anecdotal confirmation of the picture which can be drawn on the basis of the dossiers dealing with the temples' building activities. Clearly the cities were inhabited by significant numbers of people who were available for occasional or regular jobs in the institutional sphere without belonging to this sector of the society. For them, the economy would have been largely monetised, given the fact that their primary income was silver (and incidentally, large amounts of silver would have been brought into circulation in this way).

On the other hand, the living conditions of the *širkus* were not necessarily secure, even on the salary level granted to them by the temples, as anecdotal evidence especially from the Eanna archive shows.[19] The numerous attested attempts of these temple dependants to flee show clearly that they were aware of the existence of more desirable living conditions outside the temple households (Dandamaev 1984: 490ff.).

[16] Panitschek 1989: 258.

[17] BM 72139.

[18] CT 22, 133: [...] kù.babbar *a-na* ^{lú}hun.gá$^{\text{m[eš]}}$ *lid-din* ^{lú}hun.gá^{meš} *la-mu-ú-in-ni ù dul-la-a ina la* ^{lú}hun.gá^{meš} *baṭ-ṭil.*

[19] See, *e.g.*, Stolper 2003: 272ff. MM 504: "fifty of our workers are dead for lack of rations," or YOS 21, 98: "the workers desert me because they are famished (*ina bubūti*)".

Typically for this period, many of them chose to flee not into the steppe or the eastern mountains, according to the venerable Mesopotamian tradition, but to other cities: places where employment could be found.[20] Life as an independent day-laborer probably appeared attractive to them.

In conclusion, the evidence surveyed suggests first, that institutional building activities traditionally associated with compulsory mass labor in fact relied to a large extent on the employment of free hirelings, recruited from independent villages in the countryside or from the institutionally unaffiliated urban population; second, that the demand for hired labor of this kind was such that the wages paid far exceeded the salaries of the institutional personnel; and third, that the large-scale "prestige" building activities of the Neo-Babylonian kings may, by financing hired urban labor on a grand scale, (temporarily?) created something like an urban working class, *i.e.*, a stratum of society whose members were not (primarily) employed in agriculture and generally the production and processing of food, and who may also not have owned (significant amounts of) urban property, but who were embedded in a largely monetised economy. A necessary precondition for this partial substitution of the traditional compulsory labor by free labor is the clearly perceivable "weakness" of the institutional economy (as represented by the well-known temples Eanna and Ebabbar) in the sixth century: the contracting sphere of influence of the institutional households left much scope for other forms of economic and social interaction. The following sections of this paper investigate other evidence for city-based hired labor in the search for more information on the postulated urban 'working class,' including free craftsmen.

Slave craftsmen working in urban contexts

Since this topic is discussed in detail in Dandamaev's synthesis on Neo-Babylonian slavery (Dandamaev 1984: 279ff.), a brief summary will suffice (Jursa 2010: 235ff.). Numerous privately owned slaves were trained in a particular craft; investing in a slave's skill was an obvious attempt to raise the slave's value. The best evidence comes from the apprenticeship contracts (Hackl in Jursa 2010: 700ff.). Of the thirty-four known apprentices, seventeen are privately owned slaves (plus seven *širkus*; only eight

[20] Fugitives hiding in cities are mentioned, *e.g.*, in BIN 1, 93and GC 2, 395.

[21] This does not mean that most craftsmen were slaves, but only that most free craftsmen were trained by their fathers.

apprentices are free[21]). In nine cases the masters are slaves themselves.[22] From the fifth century come two texts in which all the parties, *i.e.*, also the person entrusting the apprentice to the master, are slaves.[23]

In general, baking is probably the most frequently attested profession for privately owned slaves.[24] Other professions include: barbers, weavers and other textile workers, leather workers and smiths. Training slaves and setting them up in their workshops, or hiring them out to third parties, was a lucrative way of making use of available resources, but there is nothing in the texts to suggest that the slave craftsmen outnumbered their free colleagues, at least as far as the trained "master-craftsmen" are concerned. This is suggested for instance by the apprenticeship contracts, where—in contrast to the apprentices—the majority of trained craftsmen is free, and by files like the comparatively rich dossier on craftsmen in the Bēlia'u archive: among the artisans employed by Šaddinnu//Bēlia'u, there are two temple serfs, but the rest are free men and women (Jursa 2010: 694ff. and see below).

The profitability for the owners of slaves working independently as artisans cannot be established in a general fashion. Many slaves paid a customary "quitrent," *mandattu*, of just six liters of dates or barley per day, *i.e.*, one *kurru* per month.[25] This is a figure based on traditional concepts of wages and prices in a non-monetary economy, one *kurru* = one shekel of silver being the most commonly cited 'ideal' monthly wage. Frequently however no information on the economic relationship between independently working slaves and their masters is available. Given the higher wages paid for instance in the building trade (see above), it seems certain that the *mandattu* cannot have been all a master was hoping to receive from his slave when the latter was working outside of the master's household. The solution for this apparent contradiction lies in the institution of the so-called peculium, *i.e.*, property the usufruct of which was the slaves', since the property in question was the fruit of their own, independent work, even though in the final reckoning the legal owner was the slave's master (Dandamaev 1984: 320ff., 384ff., 451ff.). A surplus over and above the customary *mandattu* therefore still

22 A slave can teach a free apprentice: ROMCT 2, 8.

23 BM 54558 (Jursa 2006: 203ff.); TSBA 4, 256 = Bellino E = Stolper 2004: 523.

24 See, *e.g.*, VS 5, 51, *Nbn*. 499, *Nbk*. 133, BM 54063.

25 See Dandamaev 1984: 379ff. But lower figures are also attested, *e.g.*, two litres per day for a trained baker (BM 82701), four litres for an (untrained?) slave (BM 94901).

benefited the owners. The *peculium,* when substantial, almost certainly consisted of silver money. However, while the profitability of slaves' independent labor must necessarily have exceeded the *mandattu* quitrent in many cases, it cannot be gauged reliably.

Free craftsmen and hirelings in urban contexts

A hired worker's remuneration defined by the time of service was designated as *idū,* "wage." Payment of hirelings "for the job," sometimes also designated as *idū,* is also found in the sources.[26] Silver predominated as the means of payment, but wages paid in kind and mixed payments are known too (see the survey of the data in Jursa 2010: 683ff.). For more taxing "piece work" involving the hire of whole parties of workers, YOS 6, 236 can serve as a model: three men are required to produce a certain number of bricks for Eanna. They receive ten shekels of silver and two *kurru* of barley—these are their actual wages—as well as some provisions in kind: beer, salt, cress and oil.

Only in a few specific contexts do payments in kind outnumber payments in silver. A case in point are the work contracts for the lower hierarchical levels of the Urukean prebendary economy (which was perhaps not as strongly monetised as the Sipparean equivalent): the slaves and free men working for the prebendary baker Bēl-supê-muhur most often were paid in kind.[27]

Specialists could also receive a 'gift,' *qīštu,* in return for services rendered: a stone carver for instance was granted two shekels of silver for work on a stela,[28] a prebendary baker received a gift in kind in return for undertaking to bake *takkasû*-cakes[29] and masters regularly were promised gifts (in money) for the successful teaching of apprentices. Probably also medical services were rewarded in this way (SBTU 2, 22: 113). Finally, craftsmen, who often received the raw materials from the customers who commissioned them to produce a certain item (at least this seems to be the case for smiths), could also be remunerated by a certain

[26] *E.g.*, GC 1, 268: silver is paid to hirelings for the digging of a stated section of a canal; CT 55, 693: silver is paid to a man as wages for caulking, *a-na i-di šá pe-hi-i.*

[27] See Kessler 1991, *e.g.*, nos. 20, 23, 30. No. 45 on the other hand stipulates a payment of silver wages.

[28] 2 gín *a-na* níg.ba *šá a-su-mit-ti a-na* PN lúkab.sar, TEBR 59: 41f.; see also VS 4, 39.

[29] Kessler 1991: 113f. no. 29; similarly Baker 2004: 37 on VS 4, 85 and BM 79293.

quantity of such raw material, which was then designated as *mandattu* (*EvM* 3). In this context, the word is best translated as "reward."

The evidence from private archives for hired labor, or more generally, for services and goods that were available for money, is quite rich. The most important source of information are work contracts and related documents referring to the 'sale' of labor by free men and by slaves (if they acted independently) or alternatively, by the owners of slaves. One hears of adolescents hired for just a few liters of barley, as well as of groups of able workers taken on for several years, and of soldiers and workers in general working abroad and earning salaries of up to ten shekels per month: a complete listing cannot be given here.[30]

The most vivid impression of the manifold forms of labor and craft production encountered in Babylonian cities is given by the *apprenticeship contracts* (Hackl in Jursa 2010: 700ff.). The masters in whose care the apprentices were placed were partly slaves, partly free, but they all pursued their profession independently, in their own workshops. The professions attested include, *i.a.*: baker, builder, carpenter, reed worker, sack maker, weaver, manufacturer of various distinct types of garments, fuller, dyer, leather worker, goldsmith, seal cutter, potter, barber, scribe, "rat" catcher, and entertainer (?, *kurgarrûtu, huppûtu*).

A particularly striking example for economic specialisation is found in the evidence for Babylonians working as professional soldiers or *mercenaries*, hiring themselves out to rich members of the upper class who in this way avoided military service as "royal soldier" themselves (see above). Such relationships could be quite stable and survive over some time (and could be continued by the sons of the original principals), thereby perhaps creating a kind of symbiotic relationship between the two families. The soldiers were paid in silver.

A different kind of labor specialisation is documented in the growing corpus of what one might call *laundry contracts* (Waerzeggers 2006). They document individuals, mostly free men, but occasionally also slaves and slave women, who undertook to wash their employers' clothes, normally for an indefinite period. The documents come from the archives of the employers, not the employees, whose situation in life remains largely unknown. The contracts concern part-time work, but occasionally a single household's laudry took up a substantial part of a laundryman's or laundrywoman's resources. This is suggested by the yearly wages quoted in the texts: they range from one shekel of silver to eight

30 See the surveys given by Dandamaev 1984: 121ff. and 1987.

shekels. The text attesting to the high wage of eight shekels comes from the Bēlia'u archive from Borsippa. The principal of the archive was not involved in textile manufacture, as one could have thought in light of this text, but he is known to have been the head of a large household which included numerous relatives and slaves, so we have to assume that this establishment produced enough dirty laundry to keep an employee busy for much of the year. It is remarkable that Šaddinnu//Bēlia'u found it convenient to contract out his laundry work even though he owned several domestic slaves.[31]

Mercenary service and the laundry business are perhaps the most striking examples of labor specialisation in our period. Among the more usual types of hired labor, one should mention first the considerable range of flexible work relationships which were generated by the complex system of cultic offices or *prebends*, particularly in the realm of the "purveying trades" (like prebendary brewers, bakers, oil pressers, etc.; Waerzeggers 2010, passim). To be able to fulfil their manifold duties related to the preparation of the regular food offerings, holders of such prebends routinely made business arrangements with their peers to share the necessary work, to swap service periods and specific obligations and to rent out prebends, all with the intention of facilitating the practical performance of the regular cultic duties. On a slightly lower level of the system, one frequently sees the prebend owners and occasionally also their slaves hire outsiders—both free and slave—for certain duties for whose performance no special cultic requirements existed: for the most part, these hirelings performed preparatory work for the food offerings, like brewing beer, grinding flour and baking bread.

Beer brewing for secular purposes is another well-known productive economic activity which was based on a reciprocal relationship between the parties, viz. the brewers and tavern keepers, on the one hand, and their employers and silent partners as well as their customers, on the other (Jursa 2010: 221ff.). Beer of dates was the preferred drink in Neo-Babylonian times; its production is the best-attested form of craftsmanship outside the institutional archives. Brewing workshops and retail outlets, or taverns, were often run by business companies (*harrānu*) set

[31] See Waerzeggers 2006: 95. She concludes that "[s]pecialist labor must have been either (relatively) cheap and efficient, or desirable among the rich" and suggests that "the emergence of a class of professionals specializing in domestic services could have been part of the general upwards economic trend in the mid-first millennium BC."

up by an investor and a brewer: typically, rich land-owning city dwellers developed the beer-brewing business as a sideline to profit from the surplus dates harvested on their own estates. They would also sometimes set up taverns run by slave women (Joannès 1992a and 1992b). Such companies could hire additional outside labor to help run the business. There are also work contracts in which independent brewers take on hired help or agree to work themselves as employees for others.

Finally, *wet-nursing* (Wunsch 2003/04: 211ff.) is a good example for a part-time occupation open to women (in very specific circumstances). Contracts most often call for a hiring period of two years (sometimes one or three), or simply state that the child is to be kept by the nurse until it has been weaned. A wet-nurse normally received significantly less than a shekel of silver per month, but was also allotted a standardised set of foodstuffs to allow her to support herself and the child. Furthermore, she was given a garment. Most wet-nurses attested in the contracts seem to have been free, but they normally did not come from an affluent stratum of society. In an age in which infant mortality naturally was high, there cannot have been a lack of women willing to hire themselves out under such conditions. The employers were men, not women, usually the fathers of the child put out to nurse: their wives most likely will have died in childbirth.

Surveys of individual archives can give an impression of the types of hired labor and the range of independent craftsmen well-to-do Babylonians had dealings with. The Borsippean Bēlia'u archive will serve as an example (Waerzeggers 2010: 475ff.). This is a group of roughly 350 tablets whose principal protagonist Šaddinnu//Bēlia'u is attested from the second year of Cyrus to the accession year of Šamaš-erība. The texts chiefly concern the cultivation of his date groves in the vicinity of Borsippa, his urban real estate and his activities in the sphere of the prebendary economy—he was the overseer (*šāpiru*) of the bakers of Nabû for several years and held baker's prebends in Ezida and other temples. Strictly commercial activities are documented through partnership contracts and texts dealing with the beer trade. In his archive, one sees Šaddinnu buy the products, and hire the services, of numerous craftsmen. The evidence is as follows.

He employs washermen; there are three laundry contracts (Waerzeggers 2006). He buys a door for seventeen shekels of silver from a free man who must be a carpenter (BM 96329), and clay pipes (*mušallû*) and other clay implements from a temple serf working as a potter (BM 96247). From a weaver, who also appears to be a temple serf, he orders two garments dyed in red.[32] Another free man, probably a builder, is to do repair work (*dulli bīti*) on one of his houses, and receives silver wages as well as provisions (BM 29111). Finally, one hears also of the hiring of a (free) brewer for the production of date beer—Šaddinnu is one of the landowners for whom the brewing and selling of date beer is a convenient sideline of their business (BM 28927). There is also one wet-nursing contract (BM 96259). There are also several instances in which Šaddinnu hires men without a profession being specified.[33]

While all this is purely anecdotal evidence that does not lend itself to any attempt at quantification, the documentation is dense enough to demonstrate that hired labor and independently working craftsmen were an important part of the economic environment in which Šaddinnu operated.

With a few exceptions, the men and women Šaddinnu hired received silver wages and were freeborn. The exceptions are *širkus*, temple serfs (the potter, the weaver). This information on independently working temple serfs is important, since such references are generally quite rare. It can be supplemented by only a few similar cases in other Borsippa archives: other *širkus* work as contractors for brick-making or are involved in the beer business (BM 17670, BM 26714), they rent houses and gardens from free men (BM 96303, BM 26524), but also appear as lessors (VS 4, 154), and a *širku*'s daughter worked as a wet-nurse (BM 27960). Also some data from the two large temple archives from Sippar and from Uruk can be added.[34] Temple serfs could act more or less like private slaves, working independently and paying a a quitrent to their master, the temple.

A picture similar to that sketched above on the basis of the Bēliaʾu archive emerges from the following brief survey of the evidence on free

[32] BM 96383. The precise dimensions of the garments are given in the texts: "two choice linen loincloths (made also) with wool dyed with 'beet root,' which are one cubit and eight fingers wide and eight cubits long (57 by 400 centimetres)": 2 níg.murub$_4$ gada *na-as-qu šá* sík *šu-mun-du šá* 1 kùš *ù* 8 šu.si *ra-ap-šú* 8 kùš *ar-ku*.

[33] BM 29195 (designation of profession lost in a break), BM 29790 (the hireling is a temple serf), BM 96233 (a free man from a well-known family is to do work for Šaddinnu and another man "with the (other) hirelings"), BM 28996 (the hireling seems to be a slave, *qallu*, and the rent(?) is paid to a temple serf, *širku*).

[34] For example, a linen weaver of Ebabbar (of Sippar) was active in Babylon (Pinches, *Peek* 2), as was a baker of Ebabbar, who is explicitly designated as a temple serf (BM 74390 and BM 67433 [= Zawadzki 1997: 229f.]).

and slave labor and on buying and selling of manufactured goods in the Egibi archive from Babylon.[35] The Egibis did not only have their slaves work in various trades and sell their products,[36] they also invested in the business of free craftsmen, as one text referring to a business partnership between an Egibi investor and a free tanner shows (*Cyr.* 148). On the other hand, the archive's protagonists can be seen buying a turban from a slave (*Nbk.* 307), sandals from another slave (*Nbn.* 566), jewellery from a free man[37] and bronze implements from two different free men.[38] From other free craftsmen the Egibis acquire beds (*Nbn.* 171, *Dar.* 189) and clay pipes.[39] Free hirelings doing unspecified work are mentioned in the archive, too (*Dar.* 215). In sum, free urban labor (whose products had to be paid for in silver in most cases) was a constant feature of the economic environment of the Egibis, too.

Archives of craftsmen

So far this paper has been concerned with evidence culled from institutional archives or from archives of rich, land-owning individuals or families, some of whom had strong entrepreneurial interests. None of these private archives belonged to craftsmen or free laborers: the texts deal with such men, but the documentation does not originate in their sphere. Yet archives of craftsmen are also known. There are of course numerous and large private archives of prebend-owning priestly families who specialised in various prebendary professions (prebendary brewers, bakers, etc.), but these rich and influential families can hardly be considered typical when it comes to describing the life of ordinary craftsmen outside the priestly sphere. There exist, however, several small archives that belonged to just such craftsmen.

35 See Wunsch 2000a etc. The following paragraph is based nearly entirely on the published material.

36 Examples of Egibi slaves working as craftsmen can be found, *e.g.*, in *Cyr.* 248 (baker), *Cyr.* 64 (weaver; apprenticeship contract) and *Dar.* 168 (beer brewing and probably tavern keeping); see Dandamaev 1984: 279ff.

37 *Nbn.* 216, *Nbn.* 267, *Nbn.* 501, TCL 12, 101.

38 BRM 1, 59, *Nbk.* 426. The seller in the latter text, certainly a bronze smith, bears the family name Nappāhu "smith". Also *Camb.* 153 records a sale of bronze implements by a free man to a member of the Egibi family.

39 *Dar.* 391 the potter manufacturing the pipes comes from the Pahhāru ("potter") family.

The first is the group of texts known as the *Dullupu archive* from Babylon (Jursa 2005: 62; Jursa 2010: 174, 229ff.). This is an archive of about forty tablets in the British Museum. The archive owners are two brothers, Bānûnu and Arad-Gula, of the Dullupu family, who were both working as blacksmiths. They were clearly not rich, but still comparatively well-to-do. One part of the archive deals with the two date groves the family owned in the hinterland of Babylon, the other part is mostly about blacksmithing. The steady income the gardens provided would have allowed the two brothers' families to subsist at a standard of living only moderately higher than that of the average family of temple dependants in Sippar (whose working males received one *kurru* of dates per month). Undoubtedly the smithing business provided a very welcome additional income. The two brothers manufactured and repaired iron and bronze tools for private customers; sometimes they also worked as silver smiths.[40] The pertinent tablets look like administrative texts originating in an institutional archive; only prosopography and the museum context reveals their origin in a private archive. In the following, we will discuss some of these tablets in greater detail to gain an understanding of the composition of the blacksmiths' archive and the nature of their business.

Text category

(**a**): the operative section states that working material, described as "such and such an amount of ... metal, the weight of such and such an object" is placed at the disposal of the Dullupu smith (BM 54108, BM 54109, etc.). This is the usual written form in which orders to manufacture small movable objects are phrased. As an example, a translation of *Nbk.* 371 is offered here.

> "One mina of silver, the weight of two ingots, for two *kandu* bowls; three minas, 54.5 shekels, the weight of two ingots, for two *kandu* bowls; three minas, 11.75 shekels, the weight of one ingot, for a

[40] The bronze objects attested in the archive include: *qabûtu* "bowl" (BM 54088), *mukarrišu* "brazier/incense burner" (?) (BM 54108), *kāsu* "cup" (BM 54108), *unqātu u daššātu ša erši ša saparri* "rings and hooks(?) for a (wooden) bed with a net (for the bottom)" (*Nbn.* 206), *urākē šá mu-šal-x* "chisels of ..." (*Nbn.* 206; see *AHw.* 1427b), *tārikātu ša magarri*? "(bronze) spokes of a (wooden) wheel?" (*Nbn.* 206, collated) and *šappatu* "container" (*EvM* 3). Silver is used for ⸢x⸣-*ru šá qa-bu-tu* (BM 54109), *kandu* and *mukarrišu* (*Nbk.* 371), iron for *šuk*[ik]-*ri ša se-er-pi* "... of shears" (*Nbk.* 324, collated).

> *mukarrišu* bowl, [three] minas, eight shekels, the weight of one ingot, for a *mukarrišu* bowl; altogether fourteen minas, 14.25 shekels, for six implements: this is at the disposal of Bānûnu, the smith. In the presence of ..." (witnesses and the date follow)[41]

(**b**) Inventories: this type is only represented by *Nbn.* 206, a witnessed note simply enumerating objects and weights.

(**c**) Receipts: finished objects are received from the smiths (BM 54149, *EvM* 3). *EvM* 3 is of particular importance as the text gives explicit information on how the smiths were remunerated for their services.

> "Nabû-ēreš and Niqūdu have received from Bānûnu one mina, twenty-six shekels of bronze, in the form of a complete (piece of work), viz., one *šappatu* container of the said weight. In the presence of (witnesses; date). Bānûnu has received forty-eight shekels (of bronze) from his reward" (Jursa 2010: 230 n. 1346).

The word translated here as "reward," *mandattu*, is more commonly attested as referring to the payment made for the service of a slave. Here it designates a payment made to the (free) smith consisting of an amount of bronze—probably he could simply keep part of the material given to him by the party commissioning the object.

(**d**) Evidence for sub-contracting: not all the work was done by the archive-owning smiths themselves. They delegated part of their tasks to third parties, certainly other independent (and apparently free) smiths. This can be seen from *Nbk.* 339, in which Bānûnu is owed bronze and silver which is to be returned in the form of a finished object (*dullu gamru*), and from BM 54088. This text concerns the whereabouts of bronze which was issued by a colleague (and subcontractor) of Bānûnu to yet another craftsman; here again, the bronze was intended for the manufacture of an object.

41 Transliteration (collated): (1) 1 ma.na kù.babbar ki.lá 2 *ku-uš-ru* (2) *a-na* 2 *kan-da-a-nu* (3) 3 ma.na 54½ gín ki.lá (4) 2 *ku-uš-ru a-na* 2 *kan-da-a-nu* (5) 3 ma.na 11 gín 3 *ri-bat* (6) ki.lá 1-*en ku-uš-ru a-na* (7) *mu-kar-ri-šú* (8) [3] ma.na 8 gín ki.lá (9) 1-*en ku-uš-ru a-na* (10) *mu-kar-ri-šú* (11) pab 14 ma.na 14 gín 4-*ut* (12) *a-na* 6 *ú-de-e ina* igi (13) ^{I}[*b*]*a*-⸢*nu*⸣-*nu* ^{lú}simug *ina* du (14) ... Date: 21.11.4[2] Nbk.

BM 54088 = Bertin 1642

ud.29.kam *šá* iti.šu ^{Id}a[g-numun-mu]
a-*šú šá* ^{I}ìr-^{d}nin.líl ^{Id}amar.utu-[su]
a-*šú šá* ^{Id}ag-numun-gál-*ši a-na* é
^{I}*ba-nu-nu* a-*šú šá* ^{I}*ki-rib-ti*(text: *ši*) *ib-bak-k*[*am-ma*]
ú-ka-na šá 2 ma.na zabar
GUR$^{?}$ *ṭa-ab-bu-*⌜*tu*⌝ *šá a-na qa-bu-tú*
l.e. [*i*]*n-*⌜*né-ep*⌝*-p*[*u-šu*]-⌜*u*'⌝ *a-na* ^{Id}ama[r.utu-s]u
⌜*it-ta*⌝-[*din*] ⌜x⌝
rev. [x x] ⌜x ki x x⌝ [x x x] ⌜x x x⌝
[x x x] ⌜*i-na*[*m-di*]*n* ⌜*ki*⌝-[*i*] ⌜*la*⌝
[*it-ta*]*n-*[*nu*] ⌜2⌝$^{?}$ ma.na [1$^{?}$]5$^{?}$ gín [zabar$^{?}$]
[x x x ma.n]a zabar *šá* ⌜x x x⌝
[x x x x *i*]*d*$^{?}$*-din-nu* 4 ma.na zab[ar]
[ ] ⌜x na x x x x x⌝
[ ] ⌜x⌝ [x]
u.e. [ ] ⌜iti.šu ud.10[+x.kam]
[mu.x.kam ^{Id}ag-níg.du]-⌜ùru⌝
⌜lugal tin.tir^{ki}⌝

"On the twenty-ninth day of Du'ūzu Na[bû-zēru-iddin[42]], the son of Arad-Mullissu, will bring Marduk-[erība], the son of Nabû-zēru-ušabši, to the house of Bānûnu, the son of Kiribtu, and he will (then) prove that he gave to Marduk-erība two minas of ... bronze which were to be made into a *qabûtu* bowl. (gap) He will deliver [the *qabûtu* bowl]. If he does not deliver (it), [he will return] two minas and fifteen shekels [of bronze] [...] bronze which [...] he had given, four minas of bronze [...] (continuation too broken for a translation).
10+.4.[±37 Nebu]chadnezzar, king of Babylon."

While not all the details can be reconstructed, the general sequence of events seems clear: bronze for a bowl had been given by Bānûnu to Nabû-zēru-iddin, the latter had passed it on to Marduk-erība, who was supposed to manufacture the bowl but failed to do so by the appointed time. Bānûnu put pressure on Nabû-zēru-iddin, who then promised to bring Marduk-erība and have the whole affair cleared up.

The need for partners and the pooling of resources felt by these craftsmen is also apparent from the one unfortunately damaged partner-

[42] The restoration is based on *Nbk.* 339.

ship (or *harrānu*) contract present in the archive. Here, Arad-Gula enters into a business relationship on equal terms with a certain Bulṭāya; the business capital of the partnership consists of fifty shekels of silver, not a small sum of money in the context of this archive.[43] As usual in such texts, the business this partnership was to engage in is not explicitly specified, but it is likely to have been smithing. This is also suggested by the archive to be discussed next.

The second archive, the *Arkât-ilī archive*, consists of only eight tablets at Yale and in the Free Library of Philadelphia. The archive holder is a goldsmith, Nabû-uballiṭ of the Arkât-ilī family, who was active in a place called Elammu, possibly a small settlement in the vicinity of Uruk (Dandamaev 1999; Jursa 2010: 231). These texts offer intriguing information on the organisation of Nabû-uballiṭ's goldsmithing business. He had a joint venture (*harrānu*) with two colleagues, Kalbāya of the Zērūtu family and Kî-Sîn, son of Ilī-aqabi.[44] Nabû-uballiṭ was the sole investor in this business when it was created in the seventh year of Nabonidus, but he also undertook to work for the company jointly with the other partners.[45] For an unknown reason, Nabû-uballiṭ soon dissolved this partnership: he discontinued his co-operation with Kalbāya at the end of the seventh year of Nabonidus and severed his business contacts with Kî-Sîn not long thereafter (in the second month of the eighth year of Nabonidus). The fact that Nabû-uballiṭ personally worked as a goldsmith and was not just a businessman/investor is also apparent from NBC 6236. In this text he accepts an apprentice whom he is to train as a goldsmith. The training period proper is to be five years; for three years thereafter half the earnings of the apprentice are to be given to Nabû-uballiṭ.

This small group of tablets obviously does not allow a full reconstruction of Nabû-uballiṭ's activities and their social and economic setting. There is, for instance, no information at all on whether or not Nabû-uballiṭ owned agricultural land of his own (it is certainly likely). In any case, the archive neatly confirms an impression given by the Dullupu archive regarding the business practices of free craftsmen without institutional backing. Working in trades like smithing, especially

43 BM 55321. The text is edited below in appendix 1.

44 Twice, the Aramaic name of the father appears in a variant form: ᴵdingir-*ma-a-da* (FLP 1582 and NBC 6162).

45 For this reason, he appears in two different roles in the text in question, NBC 6162, once as creditor and once as debtor. For this phenomenon see Jursa 2005c: 218ff. (where NBC 6162 should be added).

Text	Date	Contents
FLP 1574	1.9.7 Nbn	Nabû-uballiṭ s. of Nabû-iqbi of the Arkât-ilī family buys the Ionian slave (uru*i-ma-na-a-a*) Mušēzib-Nabû from Bibbanni s. of Raṣīpa and Marduk s. of Nabû-zēru-ukīn for 52 shekels of silver
NBC 6162 (edited below)	15.[9].7 Nbn	Promissory note: 1 mina, 12 shekels of silver is owed by Nabû-uballiṭ (the creditor!), Kî-Sîn s. of Ilī-māda and Kalbāya s. of Nabû-taqbi-līšir of the Zērūtu family to Nabû-uballiṭ s. of Nabû-iqbi of the Arkât-ilī family for a business venture; stipulations regarding the division of the proceeds of the partnership are added
FLP 1607	23.12.7 Nbn	Dissolution of a business partnership for goldsmithing run by Nabû-uballiṭ s. of Nabû-iqbi of the Arkât-ilī family and Kalbāya s. of Nabû-taqbi-līšir of the Zērūtu family
FLP 1578	9.2.8 Nbn	Promissory note: 50 shekels of silver are owed to Kî-Sîn s. of Ilī-aq[abi](?) by Nabû-uballiṭ s. of Nabû-iqbi of the Arkât-ilī family
Pfeiffer 1953 no.79 (edited below)[46]	9.2.8 Nbn	Dissolution of a business partnership for goldsmithing run by Nabû-uballiṭ s. of Nabû-iqbi of the Arkât-ilī family and Kî-Sîn s. of Ilī-aqabi; division of proceeds of the partnership
FLP 1582	16.7.8 Nbn	A promissory note for 1 mina, 7 shekels of silver owed to Šamaš-ir-na-gi-i s. of Šammiya by Nabû-uballiṭ s. of Nabû-iqbi of the Arkât-ilī family and Kî-Sîn s. of Ilī-māda is to be given to Kî-Sîn who is to hand it over to Nabû-uballiṭ
YOS 19, 25	1.8.8 Nbn	Promissory note: 1 mina of silver is owed by Ardiya s. of Bēl-ahu-iddin of the Rēʾû family and Nabû-uballiṭ s. of Nabû-iqbi of the Arkât-ilī family to Aplāya s. of Iqīšāya; interest of 1.5 shekels per mina per month (30 % p.a.)
NBC 6236 (Hackl 2011 no.5)	22+.2.[..] [Nbn]	Nabû-uballiṭ s. of Nabû-iqbi accepts Šamaš-pirʾu-uṣur as an apprentice goldsmith

Table 2: The Arkât-ilī archive

[46] The text should be in the FLP collection but is not included in Dillard's dissertation (Dillard 1975), where all the other FLP texts mentioned here can be found.

goldsmithing, which necessitated the possession of sufficient capital, such at best moderately well-to-do craftsmen tended to form small companies or partnerships with colleagues so as to be able to base their activities on a firmer capital foundation (Jursa 2010a). The principal interest of these texts however lies in their setting: the village/settlement Elammu cannot have been a major centre, yet it was possible for three free goldsmiths, craftsmen working by definition for elite consumption, to ply their trade there at the same time without any obvious institutional background. The amounts of money mentioned in the tablets show that the social stratum in which this group of tablets originated is approximately the same as that of the Dullupu archive, or possibly somewhat more elevated: it is not surprising at all that a craftsman like Nabû-uballiṭ kept an archive.

About ten tablets form the dossier dealing with the builder (*itinnu*)[47] *Bēl-ittannu, son of Nidintu* (Jursa 2010: 231f.; Hackl 2013: 434ff., second half of the fifth century). His professional activity can best be observed in BM 54205 (first published in Eilers 1934: 107ff.). In this text, he undertakes to build a house for a Persian official; the building site is adjacent to his own property and he has the right to use the new building for twenty years. Bēl-ittannu also appears elsewhere as a tenant of a house belonging to a Persian (BM 54557; Zawadzki 1995/96). The other texts show him as a creditor for the respectable amounts of silver and staples: in comparison to the other two craftsmen's archives discussed above, the dossier of Bēl-ittannu originated in a much more affluent stratum of society.

The last group to be mentioned here, the "Mardonios archive" (Jursa 2005a: 68; Hackl 2013: 430ff.) consists of ten tablets from Babylon which date to the third to the tenth year of Xerxes. Some of the texts have been studied by M. Stolper (1992) since they mention the estate of an Iranian aristocrat, Mardonios. They, however, do not originate in the administration of this estate. The chief protagonists of the archive are two manual laborers who seem to have made a living by hiring themselves out to different employers for brick making for one or two months at a time.[48] The pertinent data are as follows:

47 On the terminology of the building trades, see most recently Baker 2005: 7ff. Bēl-ittannu bears the title on BM 54205: 6.

48 These men may have prospered economically, however: in BM 64674 (Hackl 2013: No. 94), the son of one of the protagonists is able to invest 2 minas of silver in a business partnership: the equivalent of the value of two male slaves, a substantial sum of money.

Text	Date	Contents
BM 72136 (edited below)	23.12.3 Xer	Nabû-uṣuršu s. Nabû-mukku-elip hires himself out to Bēl-asûa s. Haddāya for three months and fifteen days. The wages (which are not indicated) have been prepaid.
BM 72139 (Stolper 1992: 212)	1.4.7 Xer	Nabû-uṣuršu s. Nabû-mukku-elip and Bēl-ana-mērehti s. Nabû-ina-Esangila-lūmur owe 11,000 bricks to Kî-Bēl, the steward of Mardonios. The bricks are to be delivered within a month's time, twenty-one shekels of silver have been paid for the work.
BM 72138 (edited below)	8 Xer	Nabû-uṣuršu s. Nabû-mukku-elip, Bēl-ittannu s. Rēmūt and Bēl-ana-mērehti s. Nabû-ina-Esangila-lūmur hire themselves out to Kî-Bēl, the steward of Mardonios, for brick-making, for twenty-one shekels of silver per month.
BM 64535 (Stolper 1992: 214)	20.3.8 Xer	Bēl-ana-mērehti s. Nabû-ina-Esangila-lūmur, Bēl-ittannu s. Rēmūt and Bēl-uballiṭ s. Nidintu owe 12,000 bricks to Kî-Bēl, the steward of Mardonios; they have been paid 21.25 shekels of silver.

Table 3: Labor in the "Mardonios archive"

In passing, it should be mentioned that these texts contain some of the best information available from the first millennium BC on the arithmetics of brick-making: the brick-makers were working in teams of three[49] and the standard monthly wage for a worker was seven shekels. This can be compared to a tablet from the Esangila archive, BM 95503, 17 Artaxerxes (II or III) (Hackl 2013: no. 20): 15,500 bricks are to be made by four hired workers who seem to have been paid 10 shekels each—this is probably a month's work (but the text does not say so explicitly). A team of three[50] is particularly appropriate for manufacturing bricks according to the observations made by K. Radner in Northern Syria (Radner 1997/98: 161). She observed three men making roughly 1,000 mud-bricks in three days (twelve hours of work).[51] Radner's workers got two rectangular bricks out of a single square mould (by dividing

[49] Although BM 72139 mentions only two men, three must have been involved, as the wages (twenty-one shekels) indicate.

[50] Also attested in BM 85578, BM 94602, YOS 6, 236, YOS 19, 214.

[51] "Ohne sich dabei einen Haxen auszureißen," *i.e.*, working at a leisurely pace: Karen Radner, personal communication.

the filling); hence the theoretical 10,000 bricks per month correspond nicely to the figures in our file if one assumes that our Babylonians worked eight rather than just four hours per day.

The other texts from the dossier give a few details on the workers' family relations; there is no information on real estate owned by the archive holders or any reference to an involvement in agricultural production in the available record. People such as these built the huge temples and palaces of Babylonia: they are representatives of the 'working class' embedded in the largely monetised sector of the economy which was created by the particular circumstances discussed above. It is a confirmation of the increasing importance of hired labor in the late period (at the expense of other forms of labor, in particular compulsory labor) that in this fifth century archive, for the first time at least in the first millennium, one finds common manual laborers not only as the subject matter of tablets of others, but as owners of written documentation in their own right.

Labor in the Late Achaemenid period

The preceding pages demonstrate the importance of hired labor and the existence of a relatively free labor market in the long sixth century.[52] Unfortunately, the pertinent evidence from later centuries is not nearly as abundant as that from the long sixth century. While it is clear that all forms of labor—slave, hired, constrained—continued to coexist as late as the Hellenistic period (*e.g.*, Hackl 2013: 256ff. for the late Achaemenid Esangila archive), it is uncertain whether their respective weight and importance had remained unchanged. Rather than catalogue the dispersed and scarce data on labor contracts etc. the following paragraphs will concentrate on the structural conditions that shaped labor relations in the late Achaemenid period.

The survival of the particular economic structures of the sixth century in the later centuries of the first millennium BC must have depended on three main factors:

(**a**) a continuing high degree of monetisation of the economy;
(**b**) the absence of significant social change in cities and in the countryside, *i.e.*, the continuing absence of wide-spread social restrictions on labor mobility and a concomitant revival of compulsory labor;

52 The Late Babylonian labor market is discussed in the wider context of factor markets in Jursa (2014), whence the following paragraphs have been taken.

(c) continuing high demand for hired labor in urban and rural contexts. These points will be discussed briefly in turn.

Ad (a): if the explanation for the increasing monetisation of exchange in the long sixth century that is advanced in Jursa 2010 is correct, viz., if much of the vast quantities of booty and tribute brought from the western parts of the Neo-Babylonian empire was spent by the Neo-Babylonian kings for their prestige building projects and thereby contributed to increased circulation of silver money and in the final count to the inflationary tendencies visible in the economy from the reign of Nabonidus onwards, then *a priori* a certain gradual contraction of the monetary base during the fifth and fourth centuries is to be expected. The Persians directed the spoils of empire mostly elsewhere, towards their heartland, thereby diminishing the influx of new precious metal. Also significant economic resources were withdrawn from Babylonia by the new rulers over time, mostly in the form of labor and in kind, but in part also in cash.[53]

Quantifiable data on prices and wage levels from the Late Achaemenid period have recently been summarised by Hackl and Pirngruber 2013. Interest rates in the later fifth, and even more so in the fourth century, tend to be higher than in the sixth century, and frequently go up to forty per cent per annum, i.a., to double the level common in the later part of the long sixth century (Hackl and Pirngruber 2013; Jursa 2010: 490–499): the cost of borrowing money had increased. The development of commodity prices can only be sketched in outlines. The barley prices that are known from the late fifth century are comparable to the high prices of the late sixth and early fifth century, but price levels in the fourth century were lower, while price volatility remained high. This is true for other commodities, such as dates, as well (Hackl and Pirngruber 2013). Wage data are largely absent for the fifth and fourth centuries (Jursa 2010: 676), but this can be compensated for by a comparison with the salaries in kind paid to institutional dependants. In the long sixth century, these salaries paid in kind ("rations") were demonstrably linked to wage levels and the cost of living (Jursa 2010: 296ff.; see above), a

[53] Contrary to what has often been claimed, the Persians did not directly and rapidly siphon off silver by extracting nearly exclusively cash taxes from the reign of Darius I onwards. See the survey of such and similar hypotheses in Stolper 1985: 143ff. The incorrect assumption that the Persians collected predominantly money taxes that were subsequently hoarded is owed mostly to Herodotus (Jursa 2010: 645f.; 2011: 174).

nexus which must have existed also in the later period. It is therefore significant that institutional salaries in Babylon in the late fifth and the fourth centuries tended to by paid out according to the ninety liter and the sixty-five liter standards for monthly payments (Hackl and Pirngruber 2013). This corresponds to the standard used in southern Babylonia in the mid-sixth century, but is significantly lower than the standard 180 liter salary paid in northern Babylonia towards the end of the sixth century and at the beginning of the fifth. This must mean that wages too had decreased in the intervening period.[54] Therefore, the available data are at least congruent with the assumption of a gradual contraction of the monetary base of the economy that follows from the interpretation of the data of the long sixth century, in particular with regard to the partly inflation-driven price and wage increase of the late sixth and early fifth centuries.

The second point (b) to be discussed concerns the question whether free labor continued to be available in large numbers in the absence of wide-spread social restrictions on mobility and contractual freedom, or whether the fifth and fourth century saw a ("relative") return of compulsory labor. Pertinent evidence is painfully scarce. There are however indications that background conditions in the countryside had undergone a transformation by the late fifth century: ownership patterns had changed. Much land was now held by the Great King himself as well as by members of his family and other Iranian nobles, and secondly by elite members of Babylonian society who owed their career and their families' fortunes to their cooperation with the Iranian conquerors.[55] Royal estates are known also earlier, both from the period of the Neo-Babylonian empire and from the Early Achaemenid period,[56] but in relation to the generally far less numerous sources from the fifth and fourth centuries the frequency of their appearance in this later period is surely significant and indicates an expansion of the king's domains. Even more

[54] Late Achaemenid slave prices on the other hand do not seem to fall significantly below the high levels reached in the Early Achaemenid period (Hackl and Pirngruber 2013), but as the data are very few it seems better to refrain from interpreting this fact.

[55] This aspect of landownership in Late Achaemenid Babylonia has mostly been studied with respect to the Murašû archive (locus classicus: Stolper 1985: 52ff.; van Driel 1989 and 2002: 194ff.; 230ff.); we will cite a few non-Murašû texts as examples to counterbalance this (understandable, given the richness of the archive) bias of scholarship.

[56] *E.g.*, BE 8, 118 (reign of Darius I), BE 8, 13 (Nebuchadnezzar II).

often one hears of royal land grants to officials of Iranian extraction. Land in the hand of Persian nobles and members of the royal family is likewise well attested, as is land held by royal officials of Babylonian origin.[57] This new group of landowners may have in part held newly reclaimed estates, especially in the geographically somewhat isolated Nippur region (Jursa 2010: 405ff.), but in general their rise implies a decline in the fortunes of other social groups.

The Babylonian urban elites suffered severely at the beginning of the fifth century, in the aftermath of the rebellions against Xerxes (Waerzeggers 2003/2004, Kessler 2004, Jursa 2013). Many important clans of northern Babylonia practically disappear from view. Their members were removed from their positions of power in provincial, city and temple administration: changes which are visible in the record and which demonstrably affected the core institutions of Babylonian society. We can take the case of Uruk as a model:[58] in the aftermath of the rebellion against Xerxes reprisals targeted those leading families of the city whose roots lay in Babylon. These northerners, who had dominated the socio-economic life in Uruk, were removed from their offices, the importance of the northern Babylonian gods Marduk and Nabû in the local cult was drastically reduced, and the local god Anu was promoted to chief deity in Uruk. The Urukean priesthood transferred their offices from Eanna to the Anu temple which experienced a steep ascendency at the time while the old Eanna temple was allowed to fall into ruin (Kessler 2004: 250f., Kose 1998: 9ff.). That much is evident from the available textual (and archaeological) record. What is less visible, but which must necessarily be inferred from the record, is the change in the countryside that the demise of the fortunes of the northern Babylonians entailed: since they lost their property in the city, houses and temple offices, they must also have lost their fields, and it is clear from the textual evidence discussed above who the beneficiaries must have been: the crown, Persian nobles, and Babylonian supporters of Persian rule, in the case of Uruk

[57] Royal estates: *e.g.*, Stolper 2007: no. 19; land grants to Iranian officials: *e.g.*, BE 9, 102, OECT 12 AB 243, OECT 10, 192; see Stolper 1995: 224; estates of Persian nobles and members of the royal family: *e.g.*, Stolper 2006 and Stolper 2007: nos. 6 and 15; estates of royal officials of Babylonian extraction: *e.g.*, OECT 10, 197; also much of the evidence from the Tattannu und Bābāya ('Kasr') archives belongs here (*e.g.*, Jursa 2005a: 61 and 94–97).

[58] The following is largely based on Kessler 2004, the importance of which has not been taken into account sufficiently in the discussion of the events of 484 BC.

mostly the local priestly families who must have resented the domination of the northerners over their local temple. Changes of this kind, in analogy to the well-documented case of Uruk, can be expected in all cities which are affected by the "end of archives" phenomenon—effectively, they must have occurred, *mutatis mutandis*, all over Babylonia, the capital city included. Thus, 484 BC entailed an upheaval of property rights and a shift of socio-economic power in the countryside. For the present purpose the main implication of these changes is that they favoured a type of landownership that was less strongly based on traditional and legally sanctioned property rights; rather, it had its roots in the political and military power of a new rent-seeking elite. For this elite, the relationship between landowners and tenants/laborers was largely dependent on patterns of socio-economic domination rather than contract-based: it is no accident of textual preservation that much of the evidence for unfree labor in the countryside, and nearly all of this evidence which does not come from a temple context, belongs to the fifth century (van Driel 2002: 203ff.).[59] Thus, at least in the countryside the fifth and fourth centuries experienced an expansion of compulsory labor at the expense of hired labor, and thus a contraction of the "factor market" for labor.

A final point on labor (c): as a corollary of the foregoing (b), it follows that not only was there a change in the "supply-side" of the labor market, owing to the fact that a larger part of the rural population was tied to the land, or to their landlords, in one way or another, there was also some reduction in the demand for hired labor in a rural setting. In the cities, the change from the Neo-Babylonian dynasty to Persian rule slowed the process by which the cities were transformed through massive royal investment in the construction of public buildings: temples, palaces and defensive structures (although some public construction

[59] Note that the new landowners also (and perhaps especially) made gains at the expense of the Babylonian temples, the bulwarks of compelled labor in Babylonian society: see below on the appropriation of temple lands (of Bēl) by Persian nobles and the integration of land farmed by temple personnel into the Persian system of military conscription as documented in the Murašû archive.—Among the documents that shed particularly clear anecdotal light on the socio-economic climate of the fifth century, BM 75222+ stands out (Hackl 2013: 172ff.): this is a contract establishing life-long self-indenture of one of its protagonists. The text implies a form of dependency that is unknown in the sixth century.

work occurred under Persian rule, too).[60] Labor and service obligations loom large in the record, and there was continuing demand for substitute laborers and soldiers and the like who served under the terms of contracts drawn with the individual, or tax unit, in whose name they were supposed to serve the authorities (*e.g.*, Jursa and Waerzeggers 2009). Nevertheless, we cannot assume the same level of activity as under Nebuchadnezzar, when large numbers of hirelings were employed more or less throughout the year on public building sites and had to live on their (comparatively high) money wages alone: in the cities, the labor market also contracted.

Conclusion

Contrary to the usual conception of Mesopotamian labor regimes, the richly-documented long sixth century in Babylonia is remarkable not for the preponderance of conscripted labor, but for the great importance, if not the dominance, of contractual labor relations in the city and the countryside, both in the institutional sphere, where forced dependent labor was always scarce, and in the private sector of the economy, where slave labor was an expensive resource that was unavailable to the majority of the population. This labor regime was based on the ubiquitous use of silver money; it is justified to speak of a "labor market"—obviously of limited reach and great volatility—where wages depended on supply and demand. In this economic setting, hired laborers and especially trained artisans could flourish in an urban setting and profit economically from the availability of salaried work—their presence in the archives of temples, rich city based land-owners, and especially the fact that some of these workers had their own tablet archives is ample evidence of this fact. It is probable that the outlines of this labor regime survived into the later centuries of the first millennium BC, but structural change in the socio-economic framework of labor relations is likely to have caused an increase in the importance of labor not based on contract, but on various forms of (political) dominance.

[60] Random examples: YOS 7, 120 and 143 from the reign of Cambyses refer to construction work done by Urukeans on the walls of Babylon; see Kleber 2008: 186ff. for this and other building projects.

Appendix 1: A partnership record from the Dullupu archive

BM 55321

[25 gín kù.babbar *šá* ^{I}ìr]-^{d}me.me a-*šú šá* ^{I}*ki-rib-tu*
[a ^{I}*dul-lu-pu* 25] gín kù.babbar *šá* ^{I}*bul-ṭa-a*
[a-*šú šá* PN a ^{I}]kal-^{d}im *it-ti a-ha-meš*
[*a-na* kaskal^{II} *iš-ku-u*]*n-nu-u*ʾ *mim-ma ma-la*
[*ina* uru *u* edin *ina m*]*uh-hi* kù.babbar *a*ʾ 50 gín «kù.babbar»
[*ip-pu-šu-u*ʾ *a-h*]*a*$^{\mathrm{⸢meš⸣}}$ *šú-nu* ^{I}ìr-$^{\mathrm{⸢d⸣}}$[me.me]
[ ]-⸢x⸣-*šú-nu* [ ]
(rest of obverse lost)

Rev. [ ]⸢x x⸣ [ ] ⸢x x⸣
[ ]⸢x⸣ *ma* GIŠ [*it*]-*ti-iq*
[ ]*muh-hi* ⸢x x⸣ [x x] $^{\mathrm{⸢lú⸣}}$*mu-kin-nu*
[^{Id}x$^{?}$-*ú*$^{?}$-*pa*$^{?}$]-*qu* a-*šú šá* ^{I}*sag-íl-lu*
[ ]-*ia* ^{I}*re-mut* a-*šú šá* ^{Id}ag-sur
[ ] ^{lú}umbisag ^{I}en-*šú-nu*
[a-*šú šá* ^{I}PN] a ^{Id}30-15
[tin.tir^{ki} it]i.zíz ud.25.<kam>
[mu.x.ka]m ^{d}ag-níg.du-ùru
[lugal tin.ti]r^{ki}

2 Bulṭāya is also attested in BM 54111.
6 *a-ha*^{meš}, if read correctly, must stand for the usual *ahātu*.
2′ This line contained a provision regarding expenses (*etēqu*).
6′ Possibly the name can be restored as Bēlšunu, son of Bēl-ahhē-iddin of the Sîn-imittī family: this man is known as a protagonist and witness from several roughly contemporary Egibi tablets (*Nbk.* 300 etc.; see Wunsch 2000a:199).

"[Twenty-five shekels of silver of Arad]-Gula, son of Kiribtu [of the Dullupu family; twenty-five] shekels of silver of Bulṭāya, [son of ...] of the Mudammiq-Adad family this they have invested [in a business partnership]. They shall have an equal share of whatever [they make of] these fifty shekels of silver [in the city or the countryside]. Arad-[Gula ...] (gap; the continuation of the operative section is too fragmentary for translation)

Witnesses: [GN-upā]qu, son of Saggilu of the [..]-ia family; Rēmūt, son of Nabû-ēṭer [of the ... family], (and) the scribe: Bēlšunu, [son of ...] of the Sîn-imittī family.

[Babylon], 25.11.[x] Nebuchadnezzar, [king of Babyl]on."

Appendix 2: One new tablet and one hitherto unedited text from the Arkât-ilī archive

Pfeiffer 1953: no. 79

kaskal^{II} *šá* ^{lú}kù.tim-*ú-tu šá* ^{Id}ag-⸢tin⸣-*i*[*ṭ*]
a-*šú šá* ^{Id}ag-e a ^{I}egir-dingir^{meš}
u ^{I}*ki-i*-^{d}30 a-*šú šá* ^{I}dingir^{meš}-*a-qa-bi*
ki *a-ha-meš il-li*-[*ku*]-*u*ʾ
*zu-za-a*ʾ kù$^{?}$.babbar$^{?}$ *gi-ni*
u ú-de-e šá ina é *gab-bi*
^{I}*ki-i*-^{d}30 *ki-i ú-ter-ru*
<*a-na*> ^{Id}ag-din-*iṭ it-ta-din*
Rs. <^{lú}>*mu*-[*kin*]-*nu* ^{I}*kal-ba-a* a-*šú šá*
<^{I}>^{d}ag-*taq-bi*-giš a ^{I}numun-*tú*
^{I}*ina*-sùh-sur a-*šú šá* ^{I}*na-din*
<a> ^{I}é.kur-*za-kir u* ^{lú}umbisag
^{I}níg.ba-^{d}šú a-*šú šá* ^{Id}ag-nunuz-ùru
a ^{lú}gír.lá ^{uru}*e-lam-mu*
iti.gu$_4$ ud.9.kam mu.8.kam
^{Id}ag-i lugal e^{ki}
[1-*e*]*n* ^{giš}*maš-šá-nu šá iz-zu-zu*
šá 3½ *qa i-ṣab-tu*$^{?}$ ^{I}*ki-i*-<^{d}30>
[*ki*]-*i* ^{giš}*maš*-⸢*šá*⸣-[*nu*] x x *šá*$^{?}$ <*a-na*>
4 gín kù.babbar sum-*in*
[*a-n*]*a* ^{Id}ag-tin-[*i*]*ṭ i-nam-din*

Since the tablet could not be collated, the transliteration must rely on the obviously inadequate and faulty cuneiform copy [I have not seen Pfeiffer's edition] and a certain amount of guesswork (based on FLP 1578 and FLP 1607).[61] The edition is presented here with all its shortcomings because Pfeiffer 1953 is not available easily outside the US. Only the less obvious and, therefore, more problematic emendations have been marked with a question-mark in the transliteration.

5 The copy has *zu za bu id gi ni*. BU is obviously a mistake for the Aleph sign, and the ID is copied in such a way that its division into kù.babbar appears not impossible. This would be the earliest attestation of the *ginnu* silver, but since the reading is far from certain, no conclusions can be based on it at the moment.

8–10 The copy does not indicate any damage at the beginning of these lines, but this must be a mistake since signs are clearly missing in every case.

[61] I am grateful to H. Baker, B. Janković and J. Hackl who participated in the attempt to interpret Pfeiffer's copy.

9ff. The first witness (a former *harrānu* partner of Nabû-uballiṭ) and the scribe also appear in FLP 1578, a document dealing with the same affair and written at the same day. The second witness appears in FLP 1607, the dissolution of a *harrānu* company of Nabû-uballiṭ and the first witness Kalbāya. The scribe appears as Iqīša-Marduk, son of Šamaš-pirʾu-uṣur in NBC 6162: maybe one should emend Pfeiffer's copy to ^{Id}utu$^{!}$-nunuz-ùru.

18f. Since the signs ^{d}30 are clearly missing at the end of line 18, probably owing to a break which is not marked in the copy, it seems warranted to restore *a-na* at the end of line 19. The signs in the copy at the end of this line—*lu id ni*$^{?}$—are unintelligible to me. The NI, as copied, might be the *šá* which is required by the syntax of this passage. The *maššānu* object, a household utensil according to CAD, cannot be identified with certainty.

"The goldsmithing business which Nabû-uballiṭ, son of Nabû-iqbi of the Arkât-ilī family, and Kî-Sîn, son of Ilī-aqabi, had run together has been divided among them. Kî-Sîn has returned to Nabû-uballiṭ the *ginnu*-silver(?) and all the tools which are in the house (workshop).

Witnesses: Kalbāya, son of Nabû-taqbi-līšir of the Zērūtu family; Ina-tēšî-ēṭer, son of Nādin of the Ekur-zākir family, and the scribe: Qīšti-Marduk, son of Nabû-pirʾu-uṣur of the Ṭābihu family. Elammu, 9.2.8 Nabonidus, king of Babylon.

Kî-Sîn will give to Nabû-uballiṭ one *maššānu* object which they have divided (?) and which holds 3.5 liters as a compensation for the *maššānu* object ..., which was sold for four shekels of silver."

NBC 6162

[1 ma.na 12 g]ín kù.babbar *šá*
[^{Id}ag-tin-*i*]*ṭ* ⸢a⸣-*šú šá* ^{Id}ag-*iq-bi*
[a ^{I}*ár*]-*kát*-⸢*ta*⸣-dingir^{meš} *ina* ugu
[^{Id}ag]-tin-*iṭ* ^{I}*ki-i*-^{d}30
[a-*šú šá* ^{I}]dingir^{meš}-*ma-a-da ù*
[^{I}*kal*]-*ba-a* a-*šú šá* ^{Id}ag-*taq-bi*-[giš]
⸢a⸣ ^{I}numun-*tú u*$_{4}$-*mu šá it-ti a-ha-meš*
ú-zu-za-ma-zu kù.babbar *a*$_{4}$
1 ma.na 12 [g]ín ^{Id}ag-tin-*iṭ*
e-lat ú-tur-šú ul-tu
Rev. [kaskal^{II}] *i-na-áš-ši* ^{I}*mu-še-zib*-^{d}ag
[*ù*] $^{⸢mí⸣ d!}$*na-na-a-si-lim*
[^{lú}*la-m*]*u-ta-nu šá* ^{Id}ag-tin-*iṭ*
[*šu-nu* ^{I}*k*]*al-ba-a ù* ^{I}*ki-i*-^{d}30

[*a-na* ug]u *ul i-šal-laṭ-ma a-na* kù.babbar-*šú*
[ta *ra*]*m-ni-šú* ^{Id}ag-tin-*iṭ*
in-da-⌈*na-šú*⌉*-nu-tu* ^{lú}*mu-kin-nu*
^{Id}utu-[di].kud-an-*e* a-*šú šá*
^{I}⌈*haš*⌉*-di* (text: *ki*)*-ia u* ^{lú}umbisag ^{I}ba-*šá*-^{d}šú
[a-*šú šá*] ^{Id}utu-nunuz-ùru ^{uru}*e-lam-mu*
[iti.gan u]d.15.kam mu.7.kam
[^{Id}ag-i] lugal tin.tir^{ki}

8 The verbal form stands for *uzawwazū*, a Aramaicizing 'strong' D stem of *zâzu*.

11ff. The purpose of this passage is to establish that the two slaves mentioned (who may have worked for the company) were bought by Nabû-uballiṭ from his own money and not from the company's funds and hence belonged to him alone and were not to be shared among the partners.

21 The month is restored on the basis of FLP 1574 (1.9.7 Nbn), the contract through which Nabû-uballiṭ acquired his Ionian slave, Mušēzib-Nabû.

"One mina, twelve shekels of silver are owed to [Nabû]-uballiṭ, son of Nabû-iqbi [of the Ar]kât-ilī family, by [Nabû]-uballiṭ, Kî-Sîn, [son of] Ilī-māda, and [Kal]bāya, son of Nabû-taqbi-[līšir] of the Zērūtu family. When they will make a division between themselves (of the proceeds of their association), Nabû-uballiṭ shall take this silver, one mina, twelve shekels, over and above his profit out of the [company (funds)]. Mušēzib-Nabû [and] Nanāya-silim are slaves of Nabû-uballiṭ. Kalbāya and Kî-Sîn have no claim on (them), Nabû-uballiṭ credited them to his own funds (having purchased them) [at] his own expense.

Witnesses: Šamaš-dayyān-šamê, son of Hašdiya, and the scribe: Iqīša-Marduk, son of Šamaš-pir'u-uṣur.

Elammu, 15.[9].7 [Nabonidus], king of Babylon."

Appendix 3: Two new texts from the "Mardonios dossier"

BM 72136 (82–9–18, 12140)

[^{I}]^{d}ag-ùru-*šú* a-*šú šá* ^{Id}ag-*muk-ku-e*-⸢*lip*⸣
a-na i-di-šú a-na 3 iti ⸢15 u_4-*mu*⸣^{meš}
ina igi ^{Id}en-*a-su-ú*-⸢*a*⸣ a-*šú šá* ^{I}*had-da-a*
u-šu-uz i-di-šú šá 3 it[i]$^{\mathrm{m[eš]}}$
15 u_4-*mu* ^{Id}ag-ùru-*šu ina* šu^{II}
^{Id}en-*a-su-ú-a ma-hi*[*r*]
ta ud.1.kam *šá* ⸢iti.šu⸣ [o]
[^{I}]^{d}ag-ùru-⸢*šú dul*⸣-[*lu*
Rev. *šá* ^{Id}en-[*a-s*]*u-ú-a* ⸢*ip*⸣-[*pu-uš*]
šuk.hi.a [*lib-bu*]-*ú* ^{lú}hun.g[á^{meš} *i-nam-daš-šú* (?)]
ki-i a-šar šá-nam-ma it-tal-ku ½ ma.na k[ù.babbar *i-nam-din*]
^{lú}*mu-kin*$_7$ ^{Id}en-kád a-*šú šá* ^{Id}ag-pab^{meš}-[x]
^{I}*ni-din-tu*$_4$-^{d}en a-*šú šá* ^{Id}en-tin-*i*[*ṭ*]
^{Id}en-*ana-mi*-⸢*re-eh*⸣-*tu*$_4$ lú-*ut-tu*$_4$ *u* ^{lú}umbisag
^{I}*la-a-ba-ši* <<[^{lú}]umbisag>> e^{ki}
iti.sig$_4$ ud.23.kam mu.3.kam
[^{I}]*hi-ši-ia-ar-šú* lugal kur.kur
l.e. [^{I}]^{d}en-*it-tan-nu* a-*šú šá* ^{I}⸢x⸣ [x x x]
[^{I}]^{d}en-*it-tan-nu* a ^{I}*re-m*[*ut*(-^{d}x)]

11f. The restored text at the end of the lines would have had to have been written over the (now damaged) right edge of the tablet.
14 The reading of the end of this line is uncertain.

"Nabû-uṣuršu, the son of Nabû-mukku-elip, will be at the disposal of Bēl-asû'a, the son of Haddāya, for his wages, for three months and fifteen days. Nabû-uṣuršu has received his wages of three months and fifteen days from Bēl-asû'a. Nabû-uṣuršu will work for Bēl-asû'a from the first day of the month of Du'ūzu onwards. He (Bēl-asû'a) [will give him] provisions like the (other) hirelings. Should he (Nabû-uṣuršu) go elsewhere, [he will pay] half a mina of silver.

Witnesses: Bēl-kāṣir, son of Nabû-ahhē-[..], Nidinti-Bēl, son of Bēl-uballiṭ, Bēl-ana-mērehti, the slave; and the scribe: Lâbâši, <<the scribe>>.

Babylon, 23.3.3 Xerxes, king of (all) the lands.

(Additional witnesses:) Bēl-ittannu, son of [..]; Bēl-ittannu, son of Rēm[ūt(-..)]."

BM 72138 (82–9–18, 12142)

^{Id}ag-ùru-*šú* dumu *šá* ^{Id}ag-*muk-e-lip* ^{Id}e[n-*it-tan-nu* dumu *šá*]
^{I}*re-mut* ^{Id}en-*ana-mi-re-eh-tu*$_4$ dum[u *šá*]
^{I}⸢é-sag-gil⸣-*lu-mur a-na i-di-šú-nu a*-⸢*na*⸣
le-bé-⸢*na* sig$_4$⸣$^{!}$.hi.a *a-na* iti ⅓ ma.na 1 gín kù.[babbar]
mun.hi.a [*šam-ni u sah*]-*lé-e* ⸢*ina* igi⸣ ^{I}*ki-i*-^{d}en [^{lú}gal é]
[*šá*] ⸢^{I}*mar*⸣(text: PI)-[*du-ni-ia ú-š*]*u*-⸢*uz*⸣-[*zu*]-*u*ʾ *ina* s[ah]ar.hi.a
[*šá* ^{I}*d*]*u*-[*uk-du*-(*uk*-)*ku* 2 *mar-ri*] ⸢an.bar 1-*et* ^{giš}⸣*na-al-bi*-⸢*it-tu*$_4$ *u*⸣
[1-*en ki-is-ki-ri* ^{I}*ki*]-*i*-^{d}en *a-na* ^{Id}ag-ùru-*šú*
[^{I}*re-mut u* ^{Id}en-*ana*]-⸢*mi*⸣-[*re*]-⸢*eh*⸣-*tu*$_4$ *i-nam-din-ma*
lo. e. [ ] ⸢*i*⸣-[*leb*]-⸢*bi*⸣-*nu-ma ina ki-is-si-šú*
[*a-na* ^{I}*du-u*]*k*-⸢*du-uk-ku*⸣ *i-nam-din-nu-u*ʾ
rev. [kù.babbar *a*ʾ ⅓ m]a.⸢na 1 gín⸣ *i-di-šú-nu ina* šu^{II}
[^{I}*du*]-⸢*uk-du-uk-ku ina na-áš*⸣-*par-tu*$_4$ *šá* ^{I}*ki-i*-^{d}en
⸢*e-eṭ-ri-i*ʾ x x mun$^{?}$⸣.hi.a ⸢*mar*⸣-*ri* an.bar-*šú*-[*nu*]
x ⸢*na*$^{?}$-*al*$^{?}$-*bi-tì*⸣ *u ki-is-ki-ri* ^{Id}ag-ùru-*šú ina* š[u^{II}-*šú* igi-*ir*]
pu-ut la pa-qa-ri šá sahar.hi.a ^{I}*d*[*u-u*]*k-du-uk-k*[*u na-ši*]
^{lú}*mu-kin-nu* ^{Id}en-*it-tan-nu* dumu *šá* ^{I}⸢x⸣ [x] ⸢x⸣ [ ]
^{I}⸢x x x dumu *šá*⸣ ^{I}*re-mut*-^{d}en ^{Id}en-⸢x⸣ [x]
dumu *šá* ^{I}*ni-din-tu*$_4$-^{d}en ^{Id}en-mu dumu *šá* ^{I}*am*-[x x x]
^{Id}en-*ik-ṣur* dub.sar dumu *šá* ^{Id}en-sur e^{ki} [iti.x ud.x.kam]
mu.8.kam ^{I}*ah-ši-ia-ar-šú* lugal *pa*[*r-sa u ma-da-a-a*]
[lug]al e^{ki} *u* kur.kur *me-e u* sahar.hi.ia *ina* [íd *šá* (?)]
pu-ra-du ^{I}*du-uk-du-uk-ku i-nam-din* ⸢x⸣[x x]
le. e. [x x x] dumu *šá* ^{Id}*iá*-[*a*]-*mu*-[x]

6 For sahar.hi.a in this text see Stolper 1993: 212f. on Evetts App. 4: "bricks" *ina i*-⸢*pi-ri*⸣ "with dirt of (*i.e.*, dug on the property of[?]) PN."

7 For Duk(u)dukku, son of Aplāya, see line 11 and BM 64535 = Stolper 1993: 214. There is no space here to restore a verb (something similar to *dullu ippušū* would have been expected).

22f. Presumably, we are dealing here with a topographic designation of some sort: *Carp Canal, for instance. At the end of line 23, one probably has to restore simply a suffix, *-šunūti*.

24 The restoration of the theophoric element as Jaw is, of course, uncertain. This line probably names an additional witness.

"Nabû-uṣuršu, son of Nabû-mukku-elip, B[ēl-ittannu, son of] Rēmūt, (and) Bēl-ana-mērehti, son of Esangila-lūmur, are at the disposal of Kî-Bēl, [the steward] of Mardonios, for their wages, for the making of bricks, for monthly one-third of a mina and one shekel of silver and (for) salt, [oil] and cress. (They shall work?) at the clay$^{?}$(-pit) of

[D]u[kdukku.] Kî-Bēl will give to Nabû-uṣuršu, [Rēmūt and Bēl-ana]-mērehti [two spades], one brick-mould and one *kiskirru*-board, and they shall mould [the bricks] (therewith) and shall deliver them to the brick-pile of Dukdukku. They have been paid [this silver, one-third of] a mina and one shekel, their wages, by Dukdukku, at the behest of Kî-Bēl. Nabû-uṣuršu [has received(?)] from [him] ... salt, their iron spades, the brick-mould and the *kiskirru*-board. Dukdukku guarantees for the fact that no one else will lay a claim to the clay(-pit).

Witnesses: Bēl-ittannu, son of [..], ..., son of Rēmūt-Bēl, Bēl-[..], son of Nidinti-Bēl, Bēl-iddin, son of Am-[..], Bēl-ikṣur, the scribe, son of Bēl-ēṭer.

Babylon, [x.].[y].8 Xerxes, king of P[ersia and the Medes], king of Babylon and of (all) the lands.

Dukdukku will give (them) water and clay at [the Canal of] Carps [..].

(Additional witness:) [...], son of J[a]w-[..]"

BIBLIOGRAPHY

For abbreviations of text editions and periodicals, see Jursa 2005a: 153ff.

Adams, Robert McC. (2006),"Shepherds at Umma in the Third Dynasty of Ur: Interlocutors With a World Beyond the Scribal Field of Ordered Vision," *JESHO* 49: 133–169.

Baker, Heather D. (2005), "The Property Portfolio of a Family of Builders from Hellenistic Uruk," in Baker and Jursa (eds.) 2005: 7–43.

Baker, Heather D. and Michael Jursa, eds. (2005), *Approaching the Babylonian Economy. Proceedings of the START Project Symposium Held in Vienna, 1–3 July 2004* (AOAT 330). Münster.

Beaulieu, Paul-Alain (1997), "A New Inscription of Nebuchadnezzar II Commemorating the Restoration of Emaḫ in Babylon," *Iraq* 59: 93–96.

— (2005), "Eanna's Contribution to the Construction of the North Palace at Babylon," in Baker and Jursa (eds.) 2005, 45–73.

Dandamaev, Muhammad A. (1984), *Slavery in Babylonia from Nabopolassar to Alexander the Great* (626–331 *B C*). DeKalb.

— (1987), "Free Hired Labor in Babylonia During the Sixth through Fourth Centuries BC," in M. A. Powell (ed.), *Labor in the Ancient Near East* (New Haven): 271–279.

— (1988), "Wages and Prices in Babylonia in the 6th and 5th Centuries B.C.," *AoF* 15: 53–58.

— (1999), "A Neo-Babylonian Colony in Transpotamia (?)," *ArOr* 67: 541–545.

Da Riva, Rocío (2008), *The Neo-Babylonian Royal Inscriptions.* (GMTR 4). Münster.

Dillard, Raymond B. (1975), *Neo-Babylonian Texts form the John Frederick Lewis Collection of the Free Library of Philadelphia.* Dissertation Dropsie College, Philadelphia.

van Driel, Govert, (1989), "The Murašûs in Context," *JESHO* 32: 203–229.

— (2002), *Elusive Silver. In Search of a Role for a Market in an Agrarian Environment. Aspects of Mesopotamia's Society.* Istanbul.

Eilers, Wilhelm (1934), *Iranische Beamtennamen in der keilschriftlichen Überlieferung, Teil I.* Abhandlungen für die Kunde des Morgenlandes 25/V. Leipzig.

Finley, Moses I. (1985), *The Ancient Economy.* Second edition. London and Berkeley.

Graslin-Thomé, Laetitia (2009), *Les échanges à longue distance en Mésopotamie au Ier millénaire. Una approche économique.* Paris.

Hackl, Johannes (2011), „Neu- und spätbabylonische Lehrverträge aus dem British Museum und der Yale Babylonian Collection," *AfO* 53: 77–97.

— (2013), *Materialien zur Urkundenlehre und Archivkunde der spätzeitlichen Texte aus Nordbabylonien.* PhD dissertation, University of Vienna.

Hackl, Johannes and Reinhard Pirngruber (2013), "Prices and Related Data from Northern Babylonia in the Late Achaemenid and Early Hellenistic Periods, ca. 480–300 BC," in R.J. van der Spek (ed.), *A History of Market Performance from Ancient Babylonia to the Modern World* (London: Routledge).

Janković, Bojana (2008), "Travel Provisions in Babylonia in the First Millennium BC," in P. Briant *et al.* (eds.), *L'archive des Fortifications de Persépolis. État des questions et perspectives de recherches* (Paris): 429–464.

Joannès, Francis (1982), *Textes économiques de la Babylonie récente.* Paris.

— (1992a), "Inventaire d'un cabaret," *Nouvelles Assyriologiques Brèves et Utilitaires* 1992 no. 64.

— (1992b), "Inventaire d'un cabaret (suite)," *Nouvelles Assyriologiques Brèves et Utilitaires* 1992 no. 89.

— (2001), "Rations d'entretien," in F. Joannès (ed.), *Dictionaire de la civilisation mésopotamienne* (Paris): 707–709.

— (2005), "L'argent des dieux babyloniens au VIe s. av. J.-C.," *Topoi* 12–13: 35–54.

Jursa, Michael (1995), *Die Landwirtschaft in Sippar in neubabylonischer Zeit* (Archiv für Orientforschung Beiheift 25). Wien.

— (2003–05), "Personenmiete. B. II. Neubabylonisch," RlA 10: 433–434.

— (2005a), *Neo-Babylonian Legal and Administrative Documents. Typology, Contents and Archives* (GMTR 1). Münster.

— (2005b), "Money-Based Exchange and Redistribution: The Transformation of the Institutional Economy in First Millennium Babylonia," in: Ph. Clancier *et al.* (eds.), *Autour de Polanyi: Vocabulaires, théories et modalités des échanges* (Nanterre): 171–186.

— (2005c), "Das Archiv von Bēl-eṭēri-Šamaš," in Baker and Jursa (eds.) 2005: 197–268.

— (2006), "Agricultural Management, Tax Farming and Banking: Aspects of Entrepreneurial Activity in Babylonia in the Late Achaemenid and Hellenistic Periods," in P. Briant and F. Joannès (eds.), *La transition entre l'Empire achéménide et les royaumes hellénistiques* (Paris): 137–222.

— (2008), "The Remuneration of Institutional Laborers in an Urban Context in Babylonia in the First Millennium BC," in P. Briant *et al.* (eds), *L'archive des Fortifications de Persépolis. État des questions et perspectives de recherches* (Paris): 387–427.

— (2010), *Aspects of the Economic History of Babylonia in the First Millennium BC: Economic Geography, Economic Mentalities, Agriculture, the Use of Money and the Problem of Economic Growth*. With contributions by J. Hackl, B. Janković, K. Kleber, E. E. Payne, C. Waerzeggers and M. Weszeli (AOAT 377). Münster.

— (2010a), "Business Companies in Babylonia in the First Millennium BC: Structure, Economic Strategies, Social Setting," in: M. Wissa (ed.), *The Knowledge Economy and Technological Capabilities: Egypt, the Near East and the Mediterranean 2nd millennium B.C.- 1st millennium A.D. Proceedings of a Conference Held at the Maison de la Chimie Paris, France 9–10 December 2005* (Aula Orientalis Supplementa 26), Barcelona: 53–68.

— (2011), "Steuer. D. Spätbabylonisch," RlA 13, 1/2: 168–175.

— (2013), "Epistolographic Evidence for the Trips to Susa by Borsippean Priests and for the Crisis in Borsippa at the Beginning of Xerxes' Reign," Arta 2013.003 (http://www.achemenet.com/document/ARTA_2013.003–Jursa.pdf)

— (2014), "Factor Markets in Babylonia from the Late Seventh to Fourth Century BC," *JESHO* 57: 173–202.

Jursa, Michael with contributions by Caroline Waerzeggers (2009), "On Aspects of Taxation in Achaemenid Babylonia: New Evidence from Borsippa," in P. Briant and M. Chaeuveau (eds.), *Organisation des pouvoirs et contacts culturels dans les pays de l'empire achéménide* Paris): 237–269.

Kessler, Karlheinz (1991), *Uruk. Urkunden aus Privathäusern. Die Wohnhäuser westlich des Eanna-Tempelbereichs. Teil 1: Die Archive der Söhne des Bēl-ušallim, des Nabû-ušallim und des Bēl-supê-muḫur.* (Ausgrabungen in Uruk-Warka, Endberichte 8). Mainz.

— (2004), „Urukäische Familien versus babylonische Familien. Die Namengebung in Uruk, die Degradierung der Kulte von Eanna und der Aufstieg des Gottes Anu," *AoF* 31: 237–262.

Kleber, Kristin (2008), *Tempel und Palast. Die Beziehungen zwischen dem König und dem Eanna-Tempel im spätbabylonischen Uruk* (AOAT 358). Münster.

— (2011), "Neither Slave nor Truly Free: The Status of the Dependants of Babylonian Temple Households," in L. Culbertson (ed.), *Slaves and Households in the Near East* (OIS 7; Chicago): 101–111.

Kose, Arno (1998), *Uruk. Architektur IV. Von der Seleukiden- bis zur Sasanidenzeit.* Mainz.

Morris, Ian, Richard P. Saller and Walter Scheidel (2007), "Introduction," in W. Scheidel, I. Morris and R. Saller (eds.), *The Cambridge Economic History of the Greco-Roman World* (Cambridge): 1–12.

Panitschek, Peter (1989), "Zur Möglichkeit der Entstehung von Vegetationsschäden durch forcierte Brandziegelerzeugung," in B. Scholz (ed.), *Der orientalische Mensch und seine Beziehungen zur Umwelt. Beiträge zum 2. Grazer Morgenländischen Symposion (2.–5. März 1989)* (Graz): 255–277.

Pedersén, Olof (2005a), *Archive und Bibliotheken in Babylon. Die Tontafeln der Grabung Robert Koldeweys 1899–1917* (Abhandlungen der Deutschen Orientgesellschaft 25). Saarbrücken.

— (2005b), "Foreign Professionals in Babylon: Evidence from the Archive in the Palace of Nebuchadnezzar II," in: W. van Soldt (ed.), *Ethnicity in Ancient Mesopotamia. Papers Read at the 48th Rencontre Assyriologique Internationale, Leiden, 1–4 July 2002* (Leiden): 267–272.

Pfeiffer, Charles F. (1953), *Neo-Babylonian Documents in the John Frederick Lewis Collection of the Free Library of Philadelphia.* Dissertation, Dropsie College, Philadelphia.

Pirngruber, Reinhard (2012), *The Impact of Empire on Market Prices in Babylon in the Late Achaemenid and Seleucid periods, ca. 400–140 B.C.* PhD Dissertation, VU Amsterdam.

Powell, Marvin A., ed. (1987), *Labor in the Ancient Near East.* New Haven.

Radner, Karen (1997/98), "Zur Bedeutung von *šaḫāṭu* im Neuassyrischen: "Ziegel herstellen" oder "Ziegel glasieren"?," *AfO* 44/45: 159–161.

Renger, Johannes (2003), "Oikos, Oikoswirtschaft," RlA 10, 1/2: 43–45.

— (2005), "K. Polanyi and the Economy of Ancient Mesopotamia," in Ph. Clancier *et al.* (eds.), *Autour de Polanyi: Vocabulaires, théories et modalités des échanges* (Nanterre), 45–65.

Ries, Gerhard (1993–1997), "Miete. B. II. Neubabylonisch," RlA 8: 174–181.

van der Spek, Robartus J. (1985), "The Babylonian Temple during the Macedonian and Parthian Domination," *BiOr* 42: 541–562.

Stolper, Matthew W. (1985), *Entrepreneurs and Empire. The Murašû Archive, the Murašû Firm, and Persian Rule in Babylonia* (PIHANS 54). Istanbul.

— (1992), "The Estate of Mardonius," *AuOr* 10: 211–221.

— (1993), *Late Achaemenid, Early Macedonian, and Early Seleucid Records of Deposit and Related Texts.* Napoli.

— (2003), "'No-one Has Exact Information Except for You': Communication between Babylon and Uruk in the First Achaemenid Reigns," in W. Henkelman and A. Kuhrt (eds.), *A Persian Perspective. Essays in Memory of Heleen Sancisi-Weerdenburg* (Leiden): 265–287.

— (2004), "The Kasr Texts, the Rich Collection, the Bellino Copies and the Grotefend Nachlass," in J.G. Dercksen (ed.), *Assyria and Beyond: Studies Presented to Mogens Trolle Larsen* (Istanbul 2004): 511–549.

— (2006), "Parysatis in Babylon," in A.K. Guinan *et al.* (eds.), *If a Man Builds a Joyful House: Assyriological Studies in Honor of Erle Verdun Leichty* (Leiden), 463–472.

— (2007), "Kasr Texts: Excavated—but not in Babylon," in M.T. Roth *et al.* (eds.), *Studies Presented to Robert D. Biggs, June 4, 2004* (Chicago): 243–283.

Waerzeggers, Caroline (2003/04), "The Babylonian Revolts Against Xerxes and the 'End of Archives'," *AfO* 50: 150–173.

— (2006), "Neo-Babylonian Laundry," *RA* 100: 83–96.

— (2010), *The Ezida Temple of Borsippa, Priesthood, Cult, Archives* (Achaemenid History 15). Leiden.

Westbrook, Raymond (2004), "The Quality of Freedom in Neo-Babylonian Manumissions," *RA* 98: 101–108.

Wunsch, Cornelia (2000), *Das Egibi-Archiv, I. Die Felder und Gärten.* (Cuneiform Monographs 20). Groningen.

— (2003–04), "Findelkinder und Adoption nach neubabylonischen Quellen," *AfO* 50: 174–244.

Zawadzki, Stefan (1995/96), "The Circumstances of Darius II's Accession in the Light of BM 54557 as Against Ctesias' Account," *JEOL* 34: 45–49.

— (1997), "A Contribution to the Understanding of *širkūtu* in the Light of a Text from the Ebabbar Archive," *AoF* 24, 226–230.

— (2005), "The Building Project North of Sippar in the Time of Nabonidus," in Baker and Jursa 2005: 381–392.

7.

Labor and the Pyramids
The Heit el-Ghurab "Workers Town" at Giza

Mark Lehner
University of Chicago and Ancient Egypt Research Associates

1. Introduction

In his appraisal in this volume of authority and compulsory or compensated labor, Ogden Goelet calls our attention to three decades that have passed since the publication of *Labor in the Ancient Near East,*[1] which included Eyre's[2] surveys of labor in the Old and New Kingdoms. Eyre began his treatment of Old Kingdom labor by listing all the limitations to what we could then know about the topic. Sources were limited to "the necropolis, the pyramids of the kings and the tombs of their officials…." On the point of dwellings and workshops, Eyre stated: "There are, indeed, no excavated remains of a permanent workmen's village from the Old Kingdom …."[3] Citing the *Lexikon der Ägyptologie* entry for Arbeitersiedlungen, he had in mind the New Kingdom segregated, walled settlements of Deir el-Medineh at Luxor, the Workers' Village at Amarna, and the Middle Kingdom settlement at el-Lahun.[4] Over the three decades

1 Powell 1987.
2 Eyre 1987a; 1987b.
3 Eyre 1987a: 7, 28.
4 Helck 1975b: 374–375, who authored the entry, stated that workers towns developed into the Pyramid Towns attached to pyramid complexes for officials and priests since the 4th Dynasty as attested by the titles of their leaders in tombs, a view he expressed earlier (Helck 1957). Eyre also cited the *Lexikon* entry for Pyramidenstadt, authored by Stadelmann (1984: 10–14) who did not believe that workers towns developed into Pyramid Towns, a view he expressed earlier (Stadelmann 1981a). He places el-Lahun into the latter

following Eyre's seminal contributions, Ancient Egypt Research Associates (AERA) salvaged between five and seven hectares of 4th Dynasty settlement at the southeastern base of the Giza Plateau, about 400 meters south of the Sphinx, a layout that has been called, loosely, "the Workers' Town" on the basis of our interpretation of a series of long galleries arranged in four large blocks as barracks for workers employed on the Giza pyramid projects.[5]

The 4th Dynasty pyramids on the high plateau to the northwest stand as the raison d'être for this settlement. The half dozen truly gigantic pyramids of the early Old Kingdom also stand as challenges to any notion of the society that built them, in terms of how that society mobilized labor. As Bernadette Menu expressed it:

> La pyramide transparaître donc en filigrane derrière cette étude... Toutes les lignes de la pyramide convergent vers le sommet, et c'est par l'haut qui j'ai choisi d'aborder le problème du travail dans l'Ancien Empire égyptien.[6]

I begin, in a sense, at the bottom, at the very lowest southeastern rim of the Pyramid Plateau where the outcrop of the Middle Eocene Moqqatam slopes into a broad wadi and low desert. Here we have recovered part of a footprint left by the Old Kingdom state, where it stepped down for two, possibly three generations, and then walked on. We call the site HeG, for *Heit el-Ghurab,* Arabic for "Wall of the Crow," after the most distinguishing feature, a 200-meter long stone wall, 10 m wide and 10 m tall, which forms the northwest boundary of a mudbrick and fieldstone settlement contemporary with the building of the pyramids of Khafre and Menkaure (fig. 1). An earlier phase possibly dates back to Khufu. So far, except for clay sealings, the site is textually mute, yet the patterns of walls, ways, and structures must have something to tell us about how authorities organized and mobilized labor and material resources. We must infer messages from architecture, material culture and spatial analysis against what we know about labor from texts. Many of the textual sources, which Goelet reprises in this volume, do indeed derive from the necropolis.

category. If Helck's view that pyramid towns developed out of a workers settlement is correct, we could place the town(s) attached to the Khentkawes monument at Giza and the adjacent settlement in the Menkaure Valley Temple as an exception to Eyre's statement. Stadelmann takes both these agglomerations together as the Pyramid Town of Menkaure. See Bußmann 2004; Lehner forthcoming.

5 Lehner 2002: 69–70, and so following suit, Kemp 2006: 188–191, "work camp."

6 Menu 1998: 209.

Michael Hudson cited the difficulty of focusing on labor organization per se, when "one can hardly define the mode of labor and its 'hiring' or 'employment' without describing the economy's overall fiscal and political structure"[7]—that is, the nature of a society as a whole. The Great Pyramid of Giza challenges any vision of Old Kingdom society, and how authorities at the top mobilized labor to build it. In relation to the laborers of the lowest status, "connections between the top and the bottom [have] remained obscure."[8]

However, over recent years a narrative has emerged, especially from secondary reports in the popular press[9], that our findings at the HeG site support a positive view of pyramid projects: workers who came in home-based fellowships were well treated, well-fed, perhaps in the contexts of feasts. The pyramid projects provided, intentionally or not,[10] an integrating force for the greater nation, creating a sense of unity and national identity. All worked with an enthusiasm and esprit de corps during a ritual suspension of taxes and a leveling of social status, not unlike Victor Turner's concept of *communitas* in his classic study, *The Ritual Process, Structure and Anti-Structure.*[11] This vision stands in contrast to a traditional, "negative view of the pyramid projects,"[12] where tyrannical authority coerced and compelled people to work against their will for royal or state

7 Hudson 2005: 1.

8 Toth 1999: 4.

9 For example, Morell 2001: 82–83 quoting Zahi Hawass; Shaw 2003: 99; Stille 2005: 64.

10 Baines 2009: 136.

11 Turner (1969) quoted Martin Buber (1961: 51): "Community is the being no longer side by side (and, one might add, above and below) but with one another of a multitude of persons. And this multitude, though it moves toward one goal, yet everywhere a turning to, a dynamic facing of, the others, a flowing of *I* to Thou." Specifically, this vision would be in accord with Turner's "normative communitas, where under the influence of time, the need to mobilize and organize resources, and the necessity for social control among the members of the group in pursuance of these goals, the existential communitas is organized into a perduring social system …" (Turner 1969: 132). Years of ritual studies have followed since Turner's book, as seen by perusing the journal, *Ritual Studies*. Cf. Moreno-García 1998b: 72, n. 7, invoking of Middle Kingdom texts where leaders claim to have judged both the *pꜥt* (patricians, the elite) and the *rḫjjt* (plebeians) and to have brought together the *rḫjjt* to build monuments of the king, though here the leaders maintain a superior, supervisory role.

12 Steinkeller, this volume, n. 59.

projects—unfree labor, bondage (with partial communal autonomy), and at worst slavery, without the right to move at will.[13]

This article surveys the so-called "Workers Town" at the *Heit el-Ghurab* in relation to information from Old Kingdom texts, art, and archaeology with the goal of learning more about the status of its inhabitants in the organization of labor for the building of the anomalously gigantic pyramids of the 4th Dynasty. In the first part I ask: Do indicators of an abundance of meat, the presence of hunted game, and Levantine "luxury" imports suggest good treatment of common workers, or does this material hint that the occupants enjoyed a higher status than common workers and that the HeG hosted functions other than a barracks for workers? In the second part I pivot to a related question: If, for building the Giza pyramids, central authorities required extremely large numbers of people of a lesser status than the HeG occupants, did they use foreign captives or native corvée?

Section 2 introduces the HeG settlement layout with its central feature, the Gallery Complex and the hypothesis that the galleries served as barracks. I review salient categories of material culture: animal bone and bakeries (bread and meat), hunted fauna, Levantine imports, and high-ranking scribal titles. Section 3 relates evidence from Old Kingdom art, texts, and archaeology to the findings from the HeG. The Gallery Complex begs us to guess at its message about the labor organization that built the colossal pyramids on the high plateau. Its long modular units suggest a match to units of labor organization known from builders' graffiti and other texts: crews or gangs (*ʿprw*), phyles (*zꜣw*) and divisions. Evidence for an abundance of meat and Levantine imports indicate either the generosity of central authorities in provisioning common workers, or that the inhabitants of the Gallery Complex enjoyed a higher status than we might expect for such workers. Possibilities for the occupants of the Gallery Complex include elite paramilitary, royal guard troops or "retainers" (*šmsw*), an early (4th Dynasty) formation of what became in the 5th Dynasty a special class of people attached to pyramids and pyramid towns, the *Ḫntjw-š*. In section 4 I suggest that Levantine imports and large quantities of granite from Aswan reinforce contextual evidence that the HeG served as part of a major Nile port, complicating the possibilities for the function of this site—as an entrepôt it could have served for storage—and for the status of its occupants, who could have included shipwrights, carpenters, and stevedores. In Part 2, section 5, I review the

13 Kolchin 1987.

conclusion that we have no evidence for a regular, out-of-district, national corvée and the alternative of captive foreigners as a labor source for pyramid building. In section 6 I relate the question of corvée to the idea that the 4th Dynasty was an exceptional time that saw pervasive intervention by central authorities, who may have sustained internal levies for longer periods than the normally episodic conscriptions for expeditions. Section 7, which concludes the survey, outlines a range of possibilities for the occupants and functions of the HeG and the Gallery Complex, defeating a simple dichotomy of elite and non-elite, or high and low status.

PART I

2. The *Heit el-Ghurab* Site (fig. 1)

Located at the low southeastern base of the Giza Plateau, 400 m south of the Great Sphinx, the *Heit el-Ghurab* site was one district of a larger series of settlement patches strung out north-south at the interface with the floodplain along the eastern base of the plateau. We know this from drill cores and trenches carried out in the late 1980s as part of the Greater Cairo Waste Water Project.[14] These settlement concentrations probably flanked the western side of a Nile channel that ran about 200 to 300 m east of the site at Giza.[15] And, like the sites of Tell El-Daba, Memphis, and Amarna more than a millennium later, the HeG must have served as part of a major inland port at the center of the Egyptian state.[16]

2.1. HeG Site Layout

Ancient Egypt Research Associates (AERA) began to excavate the HeG in 1988. Between 1999 and 2004 AERA carried out major operations to clear the site of an overburden of modern dumps and ancient sand. AERA teams mapped walls and other features that show in the underlying, undulating, very compact surface of the settlement ruins. This exposure amounts to a horizontal section through the settlement after people had abandoned and partially dismantled it at the end of the 4th Dynasty, and after remaining structures collapsed.[17] We were thus able to map the walls

14 El-Sanusi and Jones 1997.
15 Lutely and Bunbury 2008; Jeffreys 2008; Bunbury, Lutley, and Graham 2009; Lehner 2009.
16 Lehner 2013.
17 Lehner 2002: 30; 2007: 18–21.

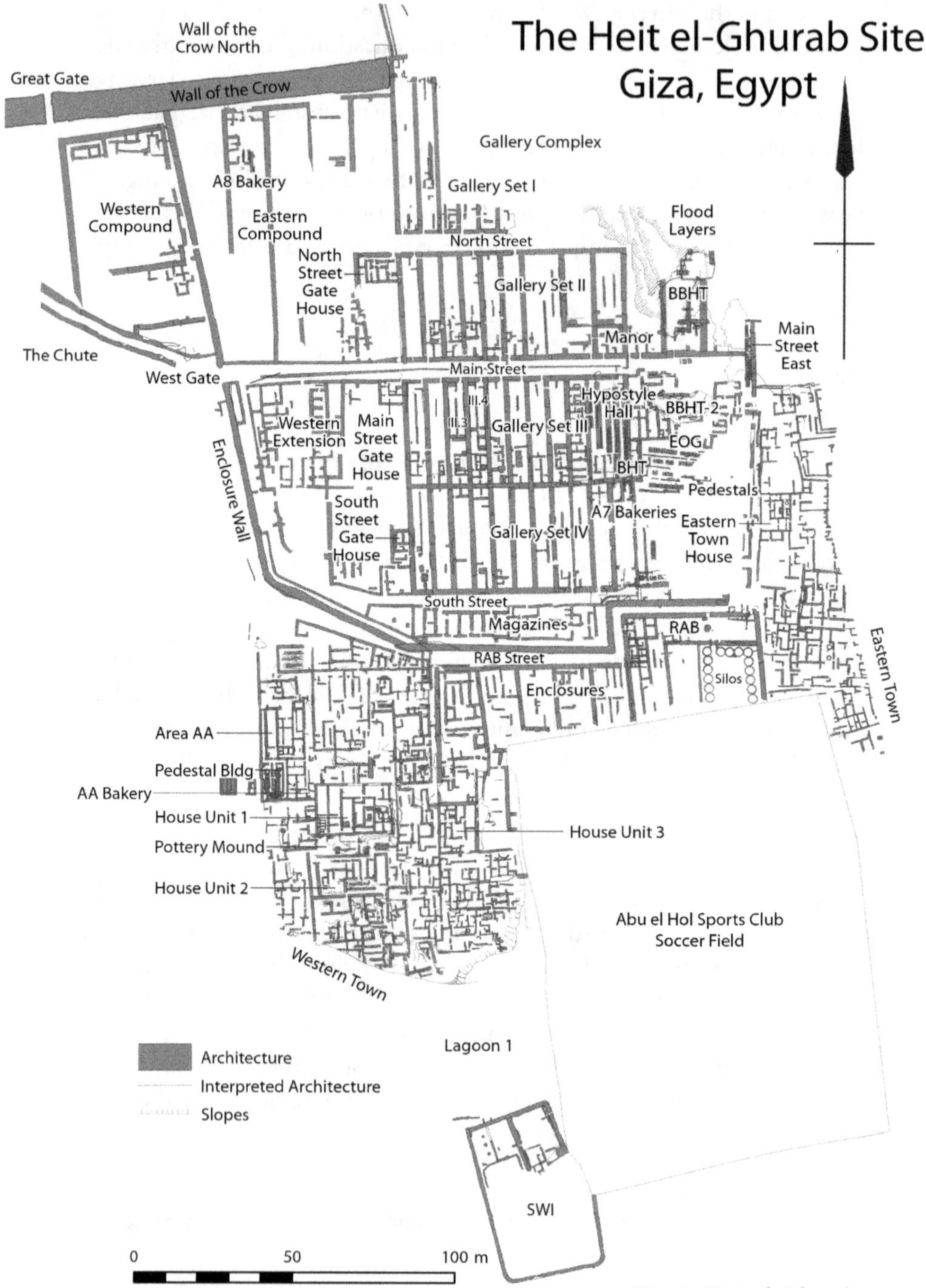

Fig. 1: Heit el-Ghurab

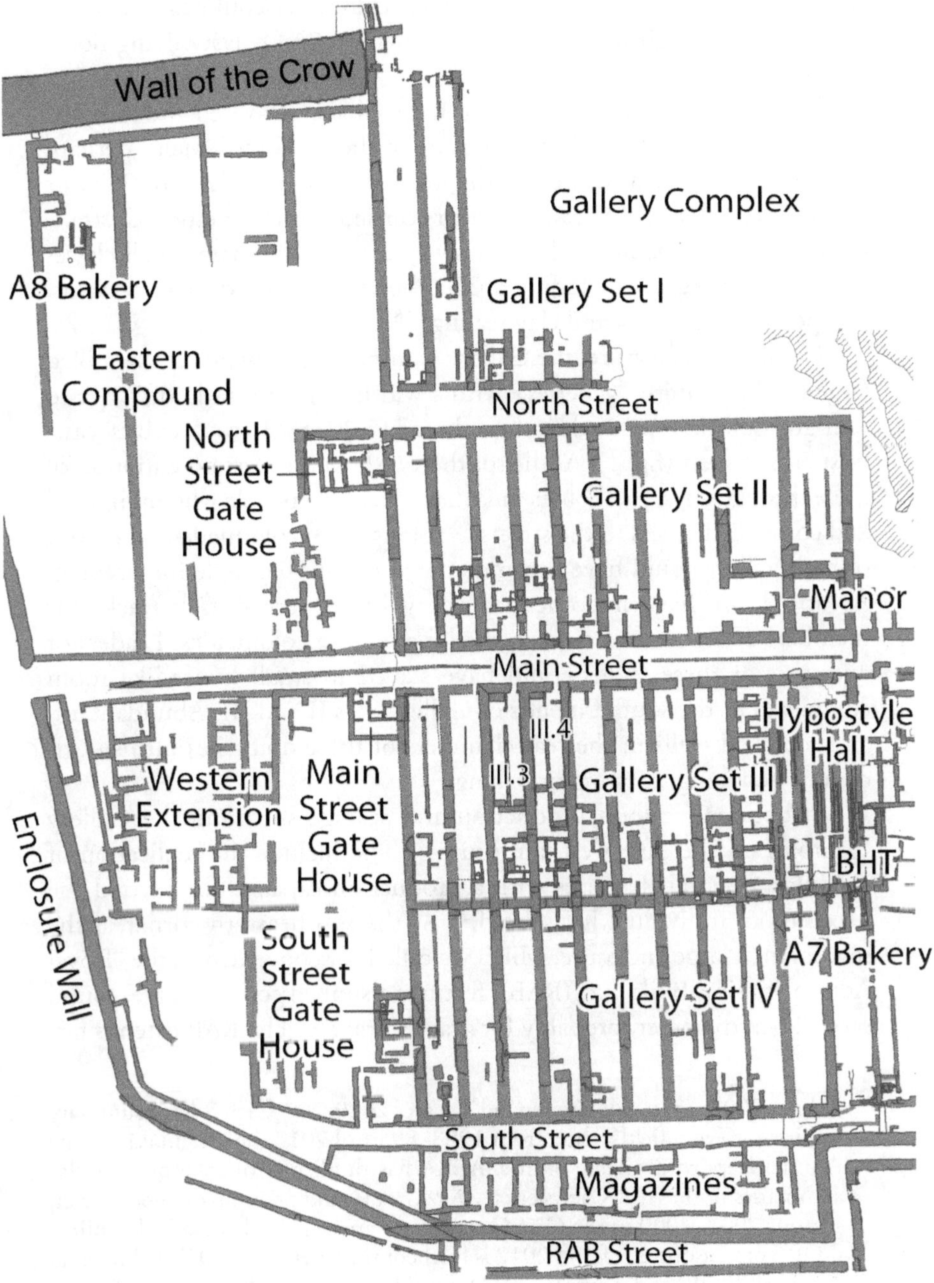

Fig. 2: Heit el-Ghurab, Detail: from the Wall of the Crow to RAB Street

and spatial structure over most of seven hectares. We could choose where to excavate through the "mud mass" down to 4th Dynasty living floors and other cultural deposits.

It is important to keep in mind that we have excavated and sampled only a small percentage of our exposure of the HeG settlement, perhaps 10% of the total area covered by the walls as mapped so far. For 25 years (1988–2012), as AERA team members carried out these targeted, stratigraphic excavations in the HeG, they systematically retrieved all classes of material culture—including animal bone, carbonized plant remains, chipped stone (lithics) and clay sealings.[18]

In the central feature, the Gallery Complex, state planners assembled large modular units, "galleries," with a width to length ratio of 7:1, into four great blocks separated by three, broad (5.20 m = 10 royal cubits) east-west cross streets (fig. 1). At the southern side of the western entrances of these throughways, gatehouses must have sheltered people who monitored and controlled access to the streets.[19] A long open colonnade at the front of each gallery could have accommodated 40 or 50 people for sleeping. As noted, we have hypothesized the galleries served as barracks for members of teams who slept in the long, empty colonnades. Leaders or overseers of these teams could have stayed in small house-like room complexes in the southern ends of Gallery Sets II and III. Abundant ash and scorched walls in the rear chambers of these domiciles furnish evidence of cooking, roasting or baking.[20]

Structures for food production and storage surround the Gallery Complex on the east, west and south. These include the replication of modular, open-air bakeries with a production capacity far beyond the needs of an individual household.[21] At the southeastern corner of the settlement a large enclosure, which we called for convenience, the "Royal Administration Building" (RAB), features a sunken court of large, round silos, 2.5 m diameter, probably for grain storage.[22] The RAB extends far-

[18] Lehner 2002: 73, n. 64; Lehner and Tavares 2010: 207–213. See for summary reports for every field season from 1988–89 until 2012 the Oriental Institute Annual Report, available online. AERA has published brief, more popular summaries in the AERA newsletter, *AERAGRAM,* and preliminary reports from seasons 2004–2009 in the Giza Occasional Papers 1–5, also available online. GOP 6 on seasons 2011 and 2012 is forthcoming. Lehner (2002), Lehner and Tavares (2010), and Tavares (2011) provide overviews of the site.

[19] Lehner 2002; Abd al-Aziz 2007a; 2007b; Kemp 2006:188–190; Tavares 2011.

[20] Lehner 2002: 68–72.

[21] Lehner 1992: 3–9; 1993: 60–67; Redding and Malleson forthcoming.

[22] Lehner and Sadarangani 2007.

ther south under the modern Abu Hol Sports Club and soccer field. We have found most of the bakeries in the industrial yard immediately north of RAB, the area we call EOG (East of the Galleries). We hypothesize that the RAB and EOG functioned together as storage and production unit.

On the far eastern limit of our exposure, we have recovered part of what we call the Eastern Town, a series of small chambers and courts that reflect more the self-organization or "organic" order that emerges from many individual choices characteristic of villages.[23] Here we find grinding stones that people used to produce flour for the bakeries that surround the Gallery Complex. The grain must have come from the central storage in the RAB. In spite of the proximity of these state storage facilities and bakeries, we find in the Eastern Town individual hearths and small household storage silos. This part of the settlement continues farther east under the modern road and urban sprawl of Kafr Gebel, beyond the limits of our salvage work.

In their assessments of the settlement as a work camp, Kemp and Bußmann[24] are missing the Western Town, a maze of walls between the RAB and the escarpment in which we can recognize thicker walls defining large "elite" houses.[25] Excavation of only half of "Pottery Mound," a large dump between two of the large houses, yielded thousands of sealings, some of which bore some of the highest-ranking scribal titles of the time of Khafre and Menkaure.[26] The dump fills and spills over a rectangular space between House Unit 1, at 400 m^2 the largest residence so far identified on the HeG site, and another large compound, House Unit 2, to the south. We infer that these houses, in particular House Unit 1 to the north,[27] probably served as administrative centers and scribal workshops. The sealings were mixed with quantities of beer jars, an abundance of cattle bone, and some leopard teeth, indicative of hunting, and perhaps of priestly leopard skin garments.[28] This material culture, in combination, furnishes as strong an indicator of elite status as we can expect in archaeology.

The Western Town and the Gallery Complex display orthogonal planning, a signature of top-down design. In spite of the evident elite status of the Western Town houses, they lie only 50 m north of a likely

23 Tavares 2011.
24 Kemp 2006: 189, fig. 66; Bußmann 2004: 29–30, fig. 6.
25 Lehner 2007:45–46.
26 Nolan and Pavlick 2008; Nolan 2010.
27 Kawae 2009; Sadarangani and Kawae 2011.
28 Redding 2007; 2011a.

corral and possible abattoir on the prominence of Standing Wall Island (area SWI), so-called because some of the fieldstone walls remained standing a meter or more in height. Here in 2004 we found two enclosures opening south into a larger enclosure that we cleared in 2011 in the depression we call Lagoon 2.[29] Redding interpreted the larger enclosure as a holding pen or corral.[30] Another deep depression, "Lagoon 1," filled with sand to depths below the water table, separates area SWI from the Western Town. We hypothesize the Lagoon 1 depression remains from an ancient feature of the topography, a possible put-in bay or southern service harbor for delivering protein (cattle) up into the SWI corral on the south, and carbohydrates (grain) up into the RAB compound on the north.

2.2. HeG Material Culture: Signs of Function and Status

Evidence of labor organization on the HeG site comes not in its architecture alone. We must take into account the material culture. When we excavate through the seal of decayed mud brick and other compact post-occupation deposits to the living floors, we systemically and intensively retrieve ancient objects, plant remains, animal bone, ceramics, sealings, lithics (chipped and ground stone), and charcoal. We count and weigh stone exotic to Giza, such as granite and alabaster. We take samples of archaeological deposits for the flotation process to recover charred plant remains. We dry sieve the sediments on site and wet sieve the finer material in the store to recover the smallest animal bone, chipped stone, pottery, and seal impressions. This material culture provides a great deal of additional evidence about life in the distinct parts of the HeG settlement.

Some caveats are in order. As with all distribution plots of material culture classes from AERA/GPMP excavations of the HeG, our plots of different classes of material across the site derive from a good but far from random sample of our exposure of this Old Kingdom settlement. According to my rough calculation, we have excavated less than 10% of this exposure. Most of the HeG map derives from our mapping of walls showing in the top of the ruin surface after removing an overburden of sand and modern material. Forces of erosion in effect cut an undulating horizontal section through the settlement ruins before the substantial accumulation of wind blown sand covered the ruins by the New Kingdom if not already by the late Old Kingdom. Also, ours is not a stratified

[29] GOP 1: 39–44.

[30] Redding 2011b; AERA 2011: 16–19.

random sample, that is, a random sample within different zones, like the Galley Complex. We have sampled the different zones on criteria other than obtaining a random sample. We must also take into account the depth, intensity and areal coverage of the excavation. For example, in the Eastern Town we have excavated and sampled only the "Eastern Town House"[31] whereas in the so-called Royal Administration Building we have spent several seasons of sustained excavation and retrieved floor deposits of an earlier phase.[32]

Nonetheless, after twenty-five years of excavation, certain patterns have persisted in our analysis of an increasing abundance of material culture.[33] At the same time we gained a finer focus of the distribution of different classes of material culture across distinct parts of the site. This sharper image prompts us to a reinterpret the site as more than, and more nuanced than, simply a workers settlement.

2.2.1. Abundance of Meat, Loaves, and Fishes

By 2002, after eleven seasons of excavation, we were impressed by the abundance of all classes of material culture, most notably bread molds, around the meta-household, industrial bakeries flanking the Galley Complex.[34] We have also been impressed by the quantities of animal bone, especially cattle, sheep and goat. And yet by 2002 we had identified less than twenty house-like room complexes inside and flanking the Gallery Complex, not counting the maze-like rooms of the Eastern Town, which we had only found that season. We had begun to wonder: "Where were all the consumers?" This question led us to excavate one complete unit, Gallery III.4.[35] To that point we had already seen repeating gallery features showing at the top of the settlement ruins, or in our 5×5 m excavation squares located variously throughout the Gallery Complex. In the extended front colonnade of Gallery III.4 we found low sloping platforms that resemble bed or sleeping platforms in other houses of the Old Kingdom and later periods. These structures solidified our barracks hypothesis. Although the G III.4 colonnade featured only five low plat-

[31] Lehner and Tavares 2010: 210; *Aeragram* 7.2: 6–7; *Aeragram* 8.1: 8–9;

[32] Sadarangani 2009; Lehner and Sadarangani 2007.

[33] For example, patterns noted already in Lehner 2003 and reiterated by Lehner and Tavares 2010: 208–214.

[34] Lehner 1992: 9; 1993: 56–67; 2002: 57–58; 2007: 24–28; *Aeragram* 1.1: 6–7. For more bakeries excavated after 2002, GOP 3: 44–49.

[35] Abd El-Aziz 2007.

forms, we hypothesized that this elongated space could comfortably sleep forty people, twenty stretched out to either side.[36] We estimated that the four blocks of galleries could accommodate around 1,600 people, more if the entire complex, standing some 7 m off the ground and stretching 150 m north to south, featured a loft-like second floor and a flat roof.[37]

It was at this point that the notion of well fed workers emerged, in large part from the fact that we were finding large quantities of cattle, sheep and goat bone, indicative of meat consumption on a large scale. We coupled this finding with the barracks hypothesis, leading us to envision well-fed workers rotating through the Gallery Complex during stints of obligatory service in the royal work projects to raise the pyramids on the high Giza Plateau to the northwest of the HeG.

All the fauna, flora and lithics suggested that authorities provisioned the people occupying the site. Flint implements (lithics) and grain, for example, appeared to have passed the most initial processing stages before coming into the site. Faunal analyst Richard Redding was finding enough cattle, sheep, and goat bone to feed large numbers of people. With some assumptions from our limited excavations, around 30 sheep and goat and 11 cattle per day could have provided meat for thousands of people.[38] I suggested we should look at this meat consumption and labor mobilization at Giza in terms of feasting and the concept of a work feast.[39]

Also, we had the rather neat inversion of a pattern established at the western Delta site of Kom el-Hisn a center for rearing pen-fed cattle attested by texts and evidenced by archaeobotanical and faunal evidence, possibly the locale known as the "Estate of the Cattle" as early as the First Dynasty.[40] In spite of this evidence, the excavators found low numbers of cattle bone and high numbers of pig bone, the inference being that people of Kom El-Hisn, raised cattle for export, while consuming pig for their own protein. Pig is more of a village animal that can be fed waste

[36] Lehner 2002: 69, fig. 20.

[37] Nolan and Heindl 2011 for reconstruction of loft-like second floors and contiguous vaulted roofs for the galleries. If builders filled the spring of the vaults, they could have made the roof into a continuous flat terrace.

[38] Lehner 2002: 68, n. 47, 72–73, based on Redding e-mail of March 11, 2003; assuming 50 kg of meat per sheep, 100 kg of meat per dressed bovine, a meat ration of 300 gm per day, and taking into account protein and calories from fish and other foods.

[39] Lehner 2002, 72, n. 61, citing Dietler and Hayden 2001, in which see Dietler and Herbich 2001.

[40] Moens and Wetterstrom 1988.

organics, produces numerous offspring, and yields high-calorie meat. Yet, with short legs, pigs cannot migrate long distances.[41] In 1992 Redding predicted that at "capital zone" centers like Giza he would find a "mirror," opposite ratio,[42] that is, high ratios of cattle to pig. Redding found such a ratio at the HeG site, a pattern sustained after 25 years of excavation.[43] As of 2010, the ratio of cattle to pig for the entire site *stands at 6:1, and for certain areas 16:1*. The pattern stands as a material culture correlate to the provisioning of the core by the provinces, such as we infer from texts and scenes of offering bearers bringing produce from villages and estates.[44]

In 2004 we cleared and mapped more of Eastern Town, the more normal settlement flanking the Gallery Complex and RAB enclosure on the east. That year we found the extensive Western Town of large house units surrounded by a maze of small chambers, flanking the RAB enclosure on the west. Unfortunately, a modern soccer field, covers most of the RAB. We salvaged and mapped what we could of the Western Town between the soccer field and the high desert escarpment. Aided by our Geographic Information System (GIS) and material culture data bases, with some classes numbering in the hundreds of thousands of iterations, we were beginning to see patterns of distribution.

Striking patterns for the overall site persist in faunal samples excavated up to 2005: cattle (*Bos taurus*) are the second most abundant mammal after sheep and goat. At the same time, bovines provide eight to ten times the amount of meat of sheep and goats. The cattle, sheep, and goat consumed on the site were predominately young (under two years old) and male,[45] suggesting that authorities were harvesting young male animals from herds in order to provision the site with high-quality meat.[46]

But areas began to differentiate in terms of the fauna.[47] In the Gallery Complex, mostly represented by Gallery III.4, we found fewer cattle bones than in the overall site, while numbers of sheep and goat bone were greater. Further, the ratio of goat to sheep was higher here than anywhere

[41] Redding 1991; Zeder 1991: 30–32. Being of local village life may be why attestations of pig are rare in Near Eastern economic texts.
[42] Redding 1992.
[43] Redding forthcoming; Lehner 2010: 91.
[44] Lehner 2010: 91.
[45] Male to female ratios are cattle 6:1, and sheep and goat 11:1.
[46] Redding 2007a: 266–269; 2010c: 68–69; 2011c: 106; forthcoming.
[47] Lehner and Tavares 2010: 208–214; Redding 2010c for summaries of material culture distribution patterns.

else on the site, and the ratio of meat bearing to non-meat bearing bone suggested the occupants slaughtered and butchered the animals nearby,[48] perhaps in the broad cross streets such as "Main Street," which featured a channel running down the middle.[49] Goat is lower in body fat and calories than sheep, and therefore less desirable. Fish served as an important supplement. In the Gallery complex catfish bones, a "cheaper" catch because people could trap catfish in catchment basins as the flood water receded, were more numerous than Nile perch, a more "expensive" fish as it was mostly caught one at a time by line and hook in the deep Nile channel.[50] Redding writes of a "cattle perch" complex where high numbers of cattle and perch are found together,[51] such as in North Street Gate House, one of the residential units at the entrance of the street between Gallery Sets I and II. These gatehouses served as interfaces between the gallery occupants and the evidently more elite occupants of the Western Town.[52] The Eastern Town, a more "normal" village-like component of the site,[53] yielded pig bone at numbers higher than site average. Pig bone was also more frequent in later deposits from the RAB enclosure, where people from the Eastern Town may have worked to grind flour from grain stored in the RAB silo granaries. The ratio for sheep-goat to pig in the Eastern Town is almost identical to that at Kom el-Hisn, the Old Kingdom village and "Estate of Cattle" in the western Delta, *while contrasting markedly with the Gallery Complex where the ratio of sheep and goat to pig is 41.6 to 1.*[54] At the other extreme of the HeG faunal spectrum, "Pottery Mound," a dump between two of the large House Units (1 and 2) in the Western Town, yielded extraordinary large amounts of cattle bone. For the most part, the cattle bone derived from animals under 8–10 months at the time of slaughter, with ratios of cattle to sheep-goat 13.6 to 1.[55] Zeder stated "animal economy has left witnesses in two major components of the archaeological record in the Near East—texts and bones..."[56] Texts and bones came together in Pottery Mound. The texts, from some 1,190 sealings, bore witness not to meat provisions, but to some of the highest

[48] Redding 2007b for Gallery III.4.

[49] Abd el-Aziz 2007a; Redding 2007a states that the fauna from the street, while more fragmented, was similar to that from the galleries.

[50] Redding 2007b; *Aeragram* 6.2: 1, 4–5.

[51] Redding 2010c: 73.

[52] Lehner and Tavares 2010: 194–202.

[53] Tavares 2011: 271.

[54] Redding, forthcoming.

[55] Redding 2007c; Redding 2010c: 73.

[56] Zeder 1991: 24.

ranking scribal titles of the time (Menkaure to Khafre), such as Scribe of the Royal Documents and *Scribe of the Royal Works*.[57] Much of this trash emanated from House Unit 1 to the north, which must have housed administrators of high status, as well as a scribal workshop.[58] Redding concluded: "The residents (of the Western Town) had preferential access to cattle at levels not found on any other area of the site … they also had preferential access to wild fauna."[59]

2.2.2. HeG and the Hunt: Wild Taxa

As team specialists in different materials continued to explore the HeG site through painstaking, often microscopic, analysis in the AERA field lab, we began to see materials that did not quite fit a barracks of common pyramid workers. We were forced to consider whether the material suggests very good treatment of common people, a *communitas* leveling of status for pyramid building, or simply a higher status for the occupants of these barracks-like structures.

Wild fauna is relatively rare on the HeG site. However the distribution and kinds of animals represented are noteworthy. Redding identified only 6 iterations of wild fauna from the Gallery Complex and the adjacent eastern industrial zone, and 44 from the Eastern Town, RAB compound, and Western Town combined. More than half (24) of the total of wild fauna came from the Western Town,[60] where we have found the largest houses on the HeG site along with high numbers of cattle bone, and sealings bearing high ranking scribal titles. The largest sample of wild fauna came from the Pottery Mound dump between two of the large compounds, from which Redding identified 7 Dorcas gazelle bones.[61] He noted:

> This was a hunted resource and its occurrence in the Pottery Mound, another SFW [Soccer Field West = the Western Town] sample, reinforces the pattern noted to date of a concentration of hunted resources in the [RAB] and SFW areas. People in these areas had preferential access to hunted resources; either only *they had the time to hunt or they received the hunted resources from specialized hunters*.[62]

[57] Nolan 2010; Nolan and Pavlick 2008.
[58] Redding 2007b; 2011a.
[59] Redding 2010: 74; 2007a; 2011b; Kawae 2009; Sadarangani and Kawae 2011.
[60] Redding 2010c, 70, fig. 5.2.
[61] Redding 2010a: 233; 2010b: 239.
[62] Redding 2010a: 233, emphasis mine.

We might consider certain birds in the category of hunted or captured wild fauna, or semi-wild fauna brought into captivity in aviaries and poultry yards. Redding finds for the Western Town relatively high numbers of pintai (*Anas acuta*), Teal (*Anas crecca*), and Wigeon (*Anas Penelope*), calling the latter two, "semi-domesticates."[63]

Inferences about status and diet based on the distribution of animal bone do face serious challenges.[64] Redding infers that wild taxa were hunted, either by or for elites. At the HeG he is able to relate this inference to the other indicators of high status in the Western Town.[65] Redding reported two leopard teeth from all Pottery Mound strata.[66] From continued excavations in House Unit 1 in the Western Town, Redding and Rasha Nasr Abd el-Mageed found two more leopard teeth during the 2011 field season. Overall the faunal remains from House Unit 1 are very similar to Pottery Mound, lending support to the inference that this dumped material derived from the high status occupants of House 1.[67] Leopard teeth could serve as another signal of high status, perhaps deriving from a leopard tooth garment worn by Sem-Priests. A further reference to ritual may come in a significant preponderance of hind to forelimb elements from the cattle bone, which Redding relates to the common scenes of slaughter in elite tombs where the cattle are trussed with the hind limbs tied as butchers take off the forelimb for a traditional offering.

The discovery in 2012 of a complete hippopotamus hip in the back of Gallery III.3, the second gallery that we excavated completely, along with the pit of a tree fruit, possibly olive, drew our attention to the potential significance of wild fauna and Levantine imports for understanding the role and status of gallery occupants, even if these two particular pieces are singular or rare finds.[68]

AERA archaeologists retrieved the hippo hip along with limestone fragments, mudbricks, and silt filling a niche in the eastern wall of the eastern of two back chambers of Gallery III.3. Included in this fill was a complete, upturned example of one of the large bell-shaped bread-baking

[63] Redding 2010c 68, Table 5.1, "It is unclear when these birds were domesticated in Egypt, but it is at least likely that the pintail may have been domesticated as early as the Old Kingdom as pintails are readily domesticated" (citing Houlihan and Goodman 1986).

[64] deFrance 2010.

[65] Redding 2007c; 2010c: 69.

[66] Redding 2007b: 7.

[67] AERA 2011: 26; Redding 2011a.

[68] AERA 2012: 22–23.

pots so ubiquitous across the HeG site, accounting for 70% of industrial zones east of the Gallery Complex, where we have identified multiple bakeries. The niche probably served as one of the hearths we have found in the back chambers of the galleries, which appear to have been reserved for cooking.

This hip is not the only hippopotamus bone we have excavated from Pyramid Age settlements at Giza. Redding reported: "Hippo (*Hippopotamus amphibius*) is represented by 21 fragments at our sites. These are mostly tusk fragments, the ivory of which would have been used for decoration. Two tusk fragments that are clearly worked from the small Eastern Town House may be the 'waste' from ivory craftwork,"[69] suggesting that this little urban estate[70] in the village-like component of the site may have housed some skilled crafts people. "Other hippo parts range from a metapodial (foot bone) from the South Street Gate House (square 4.ZZ6–7, excavated in 1998), and a patella (kneecap) from the Khentkawes Valley Complex (KKTE+), in addition to the pelvis in G III.3."[71]

The importance of wild, hunted taxa for understanding the HeG site emerges when we look at those who hunted wild game for ancient Egyptian estates, expeditions, and those who accompanied the royal hunt (see section 3.6).

2.2.3. Levantine Imports at HeG

Evidence of olive, foreign pottery and charcoal of coniferous woods testify that HeG occupants handled and distributed Levantine products obtained in the well-documented Old Kingdom trade with the eastern Mediterranean. Abundant and ubiquitous granite fragments scattered across the HeG site, in addition to the bulk granite used in the Giza pyramid complexes, show the HeG occupants trafficked in trade with Aswan, which was itself an entrepôt for trade with lands farther south.

The first signals of Levantine traffic came when botanist Rainer Gersich identified scattered bits of olive wood in his analysis of thousands of charcoal fragments that we retrieved from excavations of the HeG settlement up to 2008.[72] *This is the oldest attestation of olive in Egypt.*[73] Olive trees might have been raised in Egypt by the time of the 18th Dy-

[69] Redding, personal communication, e-mail July 9, 2012.
[70] *Aeragram* 7.2: 6–8.
[71] Redding, personal communication, e-mail July 9, 2012.
[72] Gerisch 2008.
[73] Gerisch, Wetterstrom, and Murray 2008.

nasty, but more likely not until the Roman period. In eastern shore lands of the Mediterranean people grew and harvested olive trees for oil since the Chalcolithic.[74] It has been a matter of debate just when the Egyptians began to import olive or its products from the Levant.[75] The olive charcoal from HeG derived from small pieces or twigs. Just how the wood of the olive tree, as opposed to its fruit or oil, came into the site is a matter to question. Perhaps after production and decanting of olive oil into export jars, and during loading for transport, some of the olive branches and twigs might have been introduced as packing between jars full of oil. During season 2012, Claire Malleson possibly added to this evidence when she identified an olive pit, which would be Egypt's oldest, from an ashy deposit on the floor of a cooking chamber in the back end of Gallery III.3 next to the chamber where we found the hippopotamus hip bone.[76] If imported olive products, chiefly oil, remained a luxury and perk of high status for most ancient Egyptians during the Pyramid Age (see section 3.7), why would we find olive on the site of a town or camp for common workers?

We must ask the same of 18 fragments (sherds) of Early Bronze III metallic combed ware pottery vessels, so-named because the makers etched or dimpled the surface, as though by a comb, before they fired the clay so hard as to make a metallic sound when struck against a hard surface. During the Old Kingdom (EB III in the Levant), potters made combed ware throughout the Levant, but not in Egypt. Levantine vessels of other forms and surface treatments had been finding their way into Egyptian tombs since the Early Dynastic Period.[77] During the Old Kingdom

[74] Ancient olive pits and wood have been taken as confirmation of olive cultivation "far outside the natural range of olives" in the Chalocolithic Period at Teleilat Ghassul, north of the Dead Sea (Serpico and White 2000: 399, citing Zohary and Hopf 1993: 141), and olive wood was taken as evidence of olive cultivation in the Upper Jordan Valley (Serpico and White 2000: 399, citing Neef 1990: 300–301), though perhaps in both cases the evidence was more abundant than the single olive pit and 15 pieces of olive wood charcoal recovered from the HeG.

[75] Stager 1985; Amnon Ben-Tor 1991; Ward 1991. The dispute has focused on whether the Egyptian word *bꜣq* stood for olive or moringa oil.

[76] *Aeragram* 13.2: 24. During Season 2013, Malleson 2013: 24 considered the possibility that the pit derives from the walnut-sized fruit of the Egyptian plum. The pit, charred and split in half, could be either. Whether this pit is olive or plum, Gerisch's olive wood charcoal stands as evidence for the presence of olive during the 4th Dynasty HeG occupation.

[77] Kantor 1992.

Levantine potters made such vessels in combed ware. We find only sherds, but they stand as some of the oldest known combed ware from a settlement site. Anna Wodzińska and Mary Ownby plotted the find spots of the combed ware sherds across the HeG site.[78] Pieces of these ceramic imports turned up in the Gallery Complex, in the bakeries of the industrial zones to the northwest and southeast (Area EOG), and in the so-called Royal Administrative Building (RAB), where the inhabitants stored grain in round silos and probably ground it into flour.

Returning to Gerisch's charcoal analysis, although 93.3% of the wood charcoal from the HeG proved to be local Nile Acacia,[79] Gerisch found other wood that can only have come from outside Egypt: Cyprus, Pine, Oak, and the Cedars of Lebanon.[80] To reiterate, we have excavated down to "living floors" and into ancient trash deposits inless than 10% of the total area represented by our map of the HeG. When we plot the occurrence of charcoal from wood that grew in the Levant but not in Egypt, the distribution is nearly the same as where we have excavated down to 4th Dynasty living floors or into contemporary dumps. Cedar is relatively abundant in the galleries, occurring in the entire length and every part of Gallery III.4. As we have excavated only a small percentage of the living floors and occupation deposits elsewhere, we might take the relative frequency and distribution of Levantine wood charcoal to reflect an overall abundance of imported wood at the site. The historical context of the HeG makes this inference reasonable.

3. Old Kingdom-HeG Correspondences: Text, Art, and Archaeology

In trying to understand what the HeG site means for labor organization we look for correspondences between its architectural, spatial, and material culture aspects with what is known from ancient Egyptian and specifically Old Kingdom texts, art, and archaeology.

Even before we turned a trowel of dirt on our site at Giza, we wondered what any architectural footprint would tell us about how the ancient Egyptians organized their society and mobilized their labor for building the Sphinx and Pyramids. How would the ground plan relate to what we know from ancient texts and the stone monuments themselves? One set of clues comes from graffiti that workers left on stone walls never meant to be seen.

[78] Wodzińska and Ownby (2011: 291, fig. 8).
[79] Gerisch, Wetterstrom, and Murray 2008.
[80] Gerisch 2008.

3.1. Gangs, Graffiti and Phyles

In looking for correspondences between the spatial structure of the HeG and labor organization as known from texts, I begin with builders' graffiti on the masonry of five chambers, each only about three feet high, stacked one over the other, the whole series above the granite-lined King's Chamber of the Khufu Pyramid. These rectilinear spaces, about the same floor dimensions as the King's Chamber, were never meant to be seen, although builders left a crawl space, a small tunnel, from the top eastern side of the Grand Gallery to the lowest chamber, which a man named Davison entered in 1760. In 1832 Howard Vyse, armed with gunpowder and a rather liberal permission to explore the Giza Pyramids, confirmed his suspicions of more chambers higher up when he blasted a vertical passage that breached four more chambers. The chambers were separated one from another by huge granite beams, weighing up to 40 or 50 tons, with smooth under sides that formed the ceiling of the chamber below, but left undressed in the floor of the chamber above. Gabled limestone beams roof the top chamber, so that the weight of the pyramid above is displaced down the beams to either side, rather than directly onto a flat ceiling. Thought to have been the 4th Dynasty builders' attempt to relieve the stress on the King's Chamber, these dead spaces are called the Relieving Chambers.

Now these chambers are covered with the back-soot graffiti of visitors who managed to enter them since the early 19th century. But when Howard Vyse went into the upper four he saw the bright red-painted marks of the ancient builders: leveling lines, axis markers, cubit notations, and *the names of work gangs compounded with the name of the king.* Workers or scribes applied those graffiti that name work gangs on the stone blocks before fitting them into the monument. So unlike setting lines and measurements, these texts concern the block itself—mostly probably its transport—rather than the overall structure.

Looking at the record that Howard Vyse[81] and his collaborator, J. S. Perring[82] made of the masons' graffiti, Ann Roth noted that ten blocks on the northern side of the combined construction bore graffiti of gang (*ʿpr*) names compounded with the *nswt-bjtj* name of the king, Khnum-Khuf ("The God Khnum Protects"), while seven blocks on the southern walls bear gang names compounded with the king's Horus name, *Ḥr-*

[81] Howard Vyse 1840: 279–285.

[82] Perring 1839: pls. 5–7.

Mḏdw (something like, "The Striker Horus").[83] Roth notes that the end walls are divided in half, with the gang name on each half matching that on the nearest sidewall. The division suggests that two gangs competed, and cooperated, in this unusual construction, probably mostly during the transport of the stones.[84] Vassil Dobrev translates the northern name, "The Followers of the Powerful White Crown of Khufu," and the southern as "The (Two Lands) Purifiers of Horus-Medjedu."[85] A third gang name occurs twice, showing clearly on one of the southern ceiling beams, *śmrw Ḫwfw*, "The Friends, or Companions, of Khufu."[86]

Between 1906 and 1907 George Reisner found similar builders' graffiti on the large limestone core blocks of the Menkaure Pyramid Temple.[87] The information conveyed is so important for our understanding of the HeG site *because these builders' graffiti are exactly contemporary with the main phase of occupation that we have found at the HeG, and because they attest to a gang, phyle, and division structure of labor, which we should think about it terms of our barracks hypothesis for function of the Gallery Complex.*

Menkaure's workers set the large, locally-quarried limestone blocks, weighing up to 200 tons, to form the cores of the temple walls (hence the term, core blocks). Like the Khufu relieving chambers, the annotated faces of these blocks were never meant to be seen. The builders had begun a casing of hard granite to cover the core blocks, but they stopped work, apparently when Menkaure died. Under his successor, Shepseskaf, masons finished the wall casings quickly in plastered mud brick. When Reisner peeled off this mudbrick casing he saw the brightly painted leveling lines, cubit notations, and graffiti, 30 cm high, giving the names of work gangs (*ʿprw*) including one called "The Friends (*śmrw*) of Menkaure." Roth

83 Roth 1991: 125–127, fig. 7.2.

84 But see Verner 2003: 450 where three different gang names were found in a restricted part of the unfinished Raneferef pyramid at Aubusir.

85 Dobrev 2003: 30–31.

86 Reisner 1931: 275, saw in the Khufu relieving chamber graffiti four gang names. However, *ʿprw Ḥr-mḏdw-wʿb-tꜣwy* ("Horus Medjeduw is the Purifier of the Two Lands"), which Reisner translated "Horus Mededuw is Pure," is probably the same name as that without the *tꜣwy*. He translated the gang name, *ʿprw Ḫwfw-śmrw* as "Cheops [=Khufu] Excites Love," and the third gang name, *ʿprw ḥdt-Ḫnm-ḫwfw-sḫm(t)* "The gang, The White Crown of Khufu is Powerful." Dobrev 2003: 31 reads "The Two Lands, Purifiers of Horus Medjedu" and "Purifiers of Horus Medjedu." Verner 1991: 76 sees in this graffiti three gang names.

87 Reisner 1931, pls. XI–XII.

noticed from Reisner's records[88] that he found the two graffiti naming this gang on the southern side of the temple, while thirteen names of another gang, *tḫw Mn-kꜣw-Re*, "The Drunkards of Menkaure," were found on the northern side of the temple.[89]

The name of a unit called *zꜣ* (plural *zꜣw*) followed the gang names in the Menkaure Pyramid Temple builders' graffiti. The *zꜣ* hieroglyph depicts a rope tied in a series of loops, that is, a cattle hobble such as bound the legs of animals so that they moved together, and could therefore be controlled. *Zꜣ* can mean "protection," but the term also designates groups of people rotating through periods of labor on building projects and in temple service.[90] In the bilingual (Greek and Egyptian) Canopus Decree honoring Pharaoh Ptolemy III Euergetes and his queen Berenice, dated 238 BC, Egyptian priests translated *zꜣ* with the Greek word, φυλή, *phyle*, "clan" or "tribe."[91] Hence Egyptologists translate *zꜣ* as "phyle."

We know of five phyle names in the Old Kingdom. One of these names could follow *ꜥprw* gang names in builders' graffiti. The names bear some kind of relationship to the parts of a boat.[92] From the Abusir archives of royal mortuary service, as well as inscribed phyle names in so-called "private" tombs, we know that when listed together these names follow a particular "canonical" order,[93] presented below with rough translations and nautical equivalents that have been suggested:

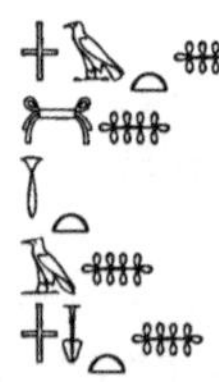

"Great" (*wr*): , or (*ỉmj-wrt*): - starboard
"Port" (*tꜣ-wr*) or "Asiatic" (*sṯ*): - port, larboard
"Green" or "Fresh" (*wꜣḏt*): - bow
"Little" (*nḏs*, or *ỉmj nḏs*): - stern
"Last" (*ỉmj-nfrt*): - no certain equivalent

The graffiti from the Menkaure Pyramid Temple show only two phyle names, *wꜣḏt* and *nḏs*, occurring on both the north and south sides of the western temple, that is, both phyles are found with either of the two *ꜥpr*-gangs, illustrating that the same phyle names are used across different

[88] Reisner 1931: 274–277.
[89] Roth 1991: 127–130, fig. 7.3; Dobrev 2003: 30–31 would read the word *tḫw* as "Laborers of Menkaure" rather than "drunkards."
[90] Goelet 1982: 444; Hannig 2003: 1052–1054.
[91] Budge 1904; Sethe 1904: 134–36; Roth 1991: 2–3.
[92] For references and discussion of an old idea that the phyle names derive from ships watches (Reisner 1931: 276) and the relationship between phyles names and nautical terms, *ỉmi-wrt* ("starboard," or "western half") and *tꜣ-wr* (larboard) see Roth 1991: 41–59.
[93] Posener-Kriéger 1976: 565–574; Roth 1991: 9–40.

gangs. The builders put these marks on the blocks prior to setting them in place, witnessed by the fact that when a block bearing such a graffito was set on end, as indicated by the geological strata running through it, the graffito is also on end.[94] The texts therefore document the labor of transporting the heavy stones to the temple wall from the nearby quarry, probably the quarry southeast of the pyramid. It appears that two phyles worked together, here transporting different blocks, but in mastabas of the Giza Cemetery GIS, two phyles worked together on the same large block.[95]

The phyles were composed of smaller groups or divisions designated with single hieroglyphs that could convey positive ideas, such as "strong, first, noble, rising," which can be taken as qualities and praise of the workers and their work.[96] There appear to have been at least four divisions in each *zꜣ* of the Menkaure Temple builders.[97] Many representations of the cattle hobble have ten loops. It is possible that divisions numbered 10 individuals, as reflected in the Old Kingdom title, "Overseer of Ten." Or, it is possible that this title meant "Overseer of One-Tenth" of a gang, with 2 divisions per *zꜣ* times five *zꜣ*.[98] In the Menkaure Pyramid Temple, one division, marked by the hieroglyph of an ibis, occurs on three different blocks, in each case with the *nḏs*-phyle, reflecting that the division names are specific to a given phyle and gang.

3.2. Division Signs, the Delta and Middle Egypt: The Question of Local Recruitment

We have no generic term (an equivalent to *zꜣ*) for "division."[99] Some of the signs for divisions are the same as certain district or nome emblems, which could indicate home regions whence workers were levied.[100] The main reference for this inference from Old Kingdom builders' graffiti is this corpus of builders' graffiti from the Menkaure temple. As examples, Verner cites graffiti signs for Nomes 10 and 17. Carrying on this infer-

94 Reisner 1931: 273; Roth 1991: 128.
95 Roth 1991: 130–131.
96 Verner 1991: 74.
97 Roth 1991: 142.
98 Roth 1991, 120–121; Jones 2000: 145–146, nos. 566–567 for overseers of tens of various crews.
99 Roth 1991: 120. Andrássy 2009a: 2–3 n. 10, cited a late 6th Dynasty letter that indicates *ṯst* as a subdivision of *ꜥpr* (Gardiner 1927: 75–78). But see section 3.3 for *ṯst* as superordinate to two or more *gśw*, "sides" of craftsmen or specialized stone workers.
100 Verner 1991: 74; Andrássy 2009a: 3–4.

ence, Andrássy excerpts from Reisner's record the graffito of the jackal-with feather standard of Upper Egyptian Nome 17, *Jnpwt*,[101] which marked a division of the *wꜣḏt* phyle and the gang, "Drunkards of Menkaure," on a large limestone core block from the northwest corner of the temple.[102] Conceivably, the antelope marking another division of the same gang and phyle[103] could stand for the Gazelle Nome (*mꜣ-ḥḏ*), Upper Egyptian Nome 16.[104]

Andrássy also finds in the Menkaure temple corpus the district emblems of Lower Egyptian Nomes 3 and 15. Reisner found these graffiti on the granite casing blocks in corridor 13. Andrássy took a bird that Reisner saw as an ibis (graffito Sa1) as the ibis emblem of Lower Egyptian Nome 15. If so, perhaps the ibis signs on three other blocks, these of limestone, in the temple northwest corner also signify this nome, making the division from this nome very busy in this area. Andrássy takes a very sketchy hieratic sign of a standard, which Reisner read *jmn* (graffiti Sa3 and Sb1), as the falcon on a plumed standard emblem of Lower Egyptian Nome 3, named *jmntt*, "The West."[105]

[101] Helck 1977: 391.

[102] Andrássy 2009a: 4, fig. 2; Reisner 1931: 274, no. 6viii, pl. XI.

[103] Andrássy 2009a: 4 n. 16; Reisner 1931: 274, no. 1i-ii, pl. XI.

[104] Helck 1977: 392.

[105] Andrássy 2009a: 4, n. 16, citing Reisner 1931: pl. XII, nos. Sa1, Sa3, Sb1. See, for the nomes, Helck 1977: 394–395. The Sa3 and Sb1 graffiti occur on the granite blocks in Corridor 13. These graffiti are thought to reflect the organization of specialized craftsmen or stoneworkers into "sides" (*gśw*) and "troops" (*ṯswt*); see section 3.3. Haeny (1969: 31), looking at the term *gśw* in graffiti from the Userkaf Sun Temple, and Menkaure and Sahure pyramids, believed that the organization of the craftsmen corresponded to the cardinal directions (not unlike Roth's observation about the *ꜥpr*-gang names on either side of a structure), so that *gś ỉmntj* would be "the west workers section," *gś rśj* "the south workers section." Perhaps we should yet ask if the term *jmn* in these graffiti did not refer to the placement of the granite blocks on one side of the corridor. The graffiti include the term *gś*, literally, "side" but also "administrative sector," as in *gś-pr*, "administration" (Hannig 2003: 1377), or "gang," for specialized craftsmen (Andrássy 2009a: 4). The graffiti on all four blocks on the northern side of Corridor 13 begin *gś ỉmj-wrt*, literally "starboard side." However *ỉmj-wrt* can also mean "west" or "western" (Hannig 2003: 78–79), specifically the western part of a building or temple (Roth 1991: 12) or nome (Fischer 1959b: 136), or "right hand side" (Jones 2000: 50, no. 250). It is therefore ironic that Helck (1975b: 371–374, n. 24) suggested the workers used *ỉmj-wrt* here in place of "east," because "east" conveyed bad mythological associations. Only the graffiti on blocks on the southern side of the corridor bear the term *jmn* (Reisner 1931: 277), which also means "west"

The attestation of Nome 3, if this is the correct reading in the Menkaure temple graffiiti, adds to the significance of the Old Kingdom settlement at Kom el-Hisn for the HeG. Kom el-Hisn as the "Estate of the Cattle" (*Ḥwt-jḥjt*)[106] might have been a center whence cattle were dispatched to the HeG.[107]

If those in control of work used division signs as district emblems in graffiti on blocks, this would suggest that workers for transporting blocks and other tasks of building pyramids came some distance from the provinces of Middle Egypt and the Delta. Given the hints of this provincial conscription as early as the late 4th Dynasty in the Menkaure builders' graffiti, it is worth looking at builders' graffiti from the later Old Kingdom, and also at the more elaborate "control notes," as Felix Arnold termed builders' graffiti from Middle Kingdom pyramid complexes.

In the 5th Dynasty builders' began to apply graffiti on stone blocks that convey the names of work crews formed with the names of prominent persons and officials who dispatched labor to build both royal tombs and the tombs of high officials. This practice was common by the time of Pepi I.[108] Graffiti with names and titles did not totally replace the *ʿpr* gang names formed with the name of a king and qualified by a phyle name. Gang and phyle names have also been found in builders' graffiti from the 6th Dynasty Pepi I Pyramid.[109] In fact we begin to see here in building, as in temple service, two facets of the same system: *"a whole range of dignitaries of different social levels" contribute labor of their people to phyle*

or "right side" (Hannig 2003: 142–143). Given the Egyptians' orientation upriver to the south, west equaled right hand (*jmn*). However three of the southern graffiti (Sa7, Sb2, Sb3) also bear the sign *tr* or *rnpt* ("time," "year" or "occasion") and *rsj*, "south." The corridor runs east-west. If one turned to the west, "right" becomes north. If these terms are directional, why would the graffiti writers use another term for "right" and/or "west" on the southern blocks? These texts are not linear like the gang, phyle, and division graffiti. It is possible that *jmn* on the southern blocks qualified another term in these graffiti, the "western" *ḥmwt smjt*, desert workshop, or *ḥmwt ḫ3st*, "foreign craftsmen," see section 3.3.

106 Helck 1977: 395; also possibly the latter place-name *Im3w*.

107 Old Kingdom settlement so far excavated at Kom el-Hisn dates to the 5th and 6th Dynasties, with some settlement extending into the Middle Kingdom (Wenke *et al.* 1988:13), but it is very likely, given the possible link with the "Estate of the Cattle," that the settlement was occupied through the early Old Kingdom and since the Early Dynastic.

108 Dobrev 1996; 1998; Andrassy 2009a.

109 Vymazalova 2013: 182, n. 21 citing personal communication with V. Dobrev.

formations subordinated to their authority as holders of certain rank and office.[110] Now, from the 5th Dynasty, builders' graffiti designate groups of workers by the name of the prominent householder or estate owner who donates their labor.

So, for example, on blocks of the large and elaborate mastaba tomb of Ptahshepses at Abusir, graffiti include his name as well as other officials. Names and titles of King's wives and daughters appear on blocks in the mastabas of their relatives, husbands and fathers, for example the "King's Wife Khentkawes" appears on a stone from the pyramid of her husband, Neferirkare. Names of officials or large householders can be found in graffiti on the blocks of their own mastabas, or in the monuments of other officials. *Andrássy has shown that the graffiti with such names mark not the donations of the stone as such, rather the labor of their transport, and possibly of cutting and trimming, before setting in place.* For example the label "Khnumhotep" on a block within the mastaba of Ptahshepses would indicate that Khnumhotep donated the labor for moving this block to the project of building Ptahshepses's tomb memorial.[111]

Donations of labor to royal monuments from districts and communities becomes more explicit in Middle Kingdom builders' graffiti, which Felix Arnold aptly called control notes.[112] We find two kinds of notes. For the literate supervisors, scribes painted notes on stones that document the date of transport, the workmen in charge of the stone, and stages reached from quarry to pyramid (although quarrymen are never referred to in the control notes). "Brought from" or "removal from" the quarry are the most common control notes. Transport ships are mentioned, and we read of stone delivered at the *mereyt*, "harbor" or "embankment;" for example, "removed from the quarry to the pyramid <by> *Hewet-ankh* <and> the ships of Heliopolis in the fourth month of the inundation, day 25." Stones are noted as "brought from the embankment" and delivered to "storage enclosures." Stones are also noted as "brought" or "dragged" to the pyramid or "delivered to the ramp": for example, "[Year] 12, first month of Winter, day 17. Brought [from] the storage [enclosure];" "delivered to the ramp <by> the overseer of the work, Mek." Cowherds, who may have driven oxen for pulling stones, are mentioned: "First month of Summer, day 12. Dragged <by> the cowherds [of the southern district]. Delivered at the workshop of ..."

[110] Andrassy 2009a; Verner 2003: 450.
[111] Andrássy 2009a: 7.
[112] Arnold 1990.

The second kind of note takes form as oversized signs that sometimes overlap the smaller, more meticulous text. These are team marks that must have been written and "read" by the illiterate workmen. Some are known hieroglyphs while others are invented geometric signs, pitchforks, crossed sticks, and the like. Arnold believes the team marks may have identified the hometowns and villages of corvée workers, while the made-up hieroglyphs represented smaller villages,[113] a suggestion that Andrássy confirmed.[114] The team marks either present a stage between illiterate (and therefore anonymous) pre-formal symbols,[115] or abbreviations of places, in contrast to the formal hieratic script applied by literate controllers.[116] It is still possible that the team marks represent, as well as home-based groups, the subdivision of work gangs, like 20-member phyle divisions or the 10-member subdivisions of Old Kingdom work gangs (see below). In the Middle Kingdom the divisions were termed *ṯst*, "troop." A controller and scribal assistants kept the control notes for six such divisions. So the large team marks may have represented both toponyms and troop divisions at the same time.

The more literate texts specify places that range in geographic scale: estates (*rmnjt*) and households of officials; towns, such as Hermopolis (*Wnwt*) in Nome 15 of Middle Egypt, Sais (*Sꜣw*) in Nome 5 of Lower Egypt, and the pyramid town *Sḫm-Jmn-m-ḥꜣt ʿnḫ ḏt r-nḥḥ* "Amenemhet is Powerful, May He Live Forever," the name of the pyramid town of king Amenemhet II;[117] the Ptah Temple in the central quarter of Memphis; and administrative districts of large towns, such as "the second district of Heliopolis" and "the provisioning quarter of the divine offering of Heliopolis." Andrássy concludes:

[113] Arnold 1990: 22–23.

[114] Andrássy 2009a; 2009b.

[115] Andrássy, Budka and Kammerzell 2009.

[116] Andrássy (2009b: 120) notes that similar signs outside the repertoire of the hieroglyphic script, or from that repertoire but inversed with respect to the rest of the entry, occur in the Papyrus Reisner accounts of copper donated to a dockside workshop. Literate scribes certainly compiled these accounts, in which case the signs in question must be taken as abbreviations or copies of marks engraved onto the copper tools being accounted.

[117] This is the pyramid town where, according to the Mit Rahina inscription (see section 5.2) Amenemhet II settled his Asiatic captives (see section 5.2). The control note mentioning this place comes from the pyramid of his successor, Senwosret II (Arnold 1990: 25, 168).

> The context makes it clear that, of course, not places, estates, households, domains and so on transported the stones, but the people coming from there, who were sent by the local authorities for corvée at the pyramid building sites. A place name can therefore be considered as an abbreviation for "men of town, estate, household, domain ... X."[118]

Arnold plotted on a map of Egypt the home districts of the workers mentioned in the control notes of Middle Kingdom pyramid complexes. The area around the old "capital" zone—Memphis to Heliopolis—plus the Delta, and the area of Nomes 12–15 of Middle Egypt predominate.[119] Often the Lower Egyptians are designated without specifying a particular town, but using the term *bjtyw*, "Lower Egyptians."[120] Could this *nisbe* have been a counterpart to *nìswtjw*, a term for colonizers on royal land, with both terms stemming from the designation of the royal prenomen, *nswt-bjtì*, literally, "he of the sedge and bee", emblems of south and north respectively?[121]

Arnold's plot of the distribution of locales supplying labor from the Delta and Middle Egypt *bears resemblance to the distribution of Old Kingdom estates*, a product of the internal colonization of these same broader floodplains.[122] The Middle Kingdom control notes also show that labor came from the Memphite area, and the "capital zone" (Heliopolis, Memphis, the Ptah Temple, and the Amenemhet II pyramid town). The distribution bears comparison to a pattern that Moreno García points to repeatedly where the Delta and Middle Egypt, under relatively direct administration from the center, served as hinterland extensions of the Memphite capital zone.[123]

The possible references in the Menkaure builders' graffiti to Upper Egyptian Nomes 16–17 (in Middle Egypt, north of the Qena Bend[124]), while tenuous, are intriguing considering many associations of the 4th Dynasty kings and their outposts in these and other districts of Middle Egypt. Recent excavations at Shaykh Said in Nome 15 by the Leuven

[118] Andrássy 2009a: 8–9.
[119] Arnold 1990: 24, fig. 1.
[120] Arnold 1990: 25.
[121] Gardiner 1969: 74; Allen 2000: 65.
[122] Jacquet-Gordon 1962: 104–121; Kemp 1983: 91, fig. 2.2.
[123] Moreno García 2013: 99, 112, 114–119, 123–125, 131.
[124] Lehner 2000: 298–300, figs. 5–6; Qena Bend refers to the large bend where the Nile and its valley turn east, then bend to the west at Qena, before opening out into the broad valley of Middle Egypt at Hiw, Nome 7.

University mission revealed the remains of a royal domain of the 4th Dynasty, installed during the reign of Khufu for the purpose of quarrying calcite alabaster from the Maghara (quarry) Abu Aziz to the east up the Wadi Zabayda from the excavation site SS/WZ. Willems *et al.* suggest that just as the royal domain at Elephantine produced granite, which the builders used in large quantities at the Memphite Pyramid cemeteries, especially Giza, Shaykh Said produced calcite alabaster (or travertine)[125] and limestone.[126]

Not unlike HeG, the site SS/WZ flanks an embayment from the floodplain into the low desert at the mouth of a wadi delivery tract. The team has recorded in this embayment geophysical and stratigraphic evidence of a harbor, recalling that HeG must have flanked a delivery zone and harbor north of the Wall of the Crow, a difference being, that HeG lies south while SS/WZ lies to the north of the hypothesized harbor.[127]

Willems *et al.* (2009) cite multiple correspondences between the material culture at Shaykh Said and HeG at Giza.[128] The "massive amounts of flat and deep bread molds" suggests the kind of intensified production and provisioning evidenced at HeG in the areas surrounding the Gallery Complex.[129] One similarity between Shaykh Said and the HeG, cited by the SS/WZ investigators, is high numbers of cattle, sheep, and goat bone, and deep-channel Nile Perch, suggesting protein provisioning. The Shaykh Said mission members suggest the cattle probably came from herds nearby.[130] Also like HeG, the presence of formal, institutional sealings suggest the presence of, or a connection to elite state administrators,[131] although, apart from remains of an apparent bakery,[132] the

[125] Here, I use the crude term "alabaster" and forgo the discussion of calcite, calcite alabaster, travertine, or gypsum; see Willems *et al.* 2009: 295, n. 9. Saleh 1974: 138 characterized the stone in the industrial settlement southeast of the Menkaure Pyramid as "yellow-red calcite (or crystalline calcium) stones which resemble alabaster."

[126] Willems *et al.* 2009: 325.

[127] Willems *et al.* 2009: 321–322, Pl. I.

[128] The Leuven University team dates the stone working site, SS/WZ, to the time of Khufu on the basis of ceramics, and one sealing fragment bearing the bottom of a serkeh, with *mḏdw*, which must be part of Khufu's Horus name, *Ḥr-mḏdw*.

[129] Lehner 2002: 71; Lehner 2007b: 279–283; Lehner and Tavares 2010: 207–214.

[130] Willems *et al.* 2009: 323.

[131] Nolan 2010.

[132] Willems *et al.* 2009: 303–307, figs. 6–7.

absence at SS/WZ of formal architecture, so far, suggests more of a camp. The investigators suggest the settlement may lie elsewhere, but nearby.

The investigators count the site as one of a network of royal domains (*ḥwwt*).[133] Willems *et al.* point to the similarities in layout between the quarry Maghara Abu Aziz at Shaykh Said and the well-know calcite alabaster quarries at Hatnub, southeast of Shaykh Said, where the earliest royal inscriptions start with Khufu. They hypothesize a royal domain founded near Hatnub.[134] The pyramid builders certainly used much calcite alabaster for statues and paving in the temples. At Giza they installed alabaster pavements in the Khafre pyramid temple and valley temple. In the early 1970s Abd El-Aziz Saleh excavated a settlement southeast of the Menkaure Pyramid that served as a kind of depot, perhaps at the end of the Shaykh Said/Hatnub run, for large, raw alabaster pieces and a working area for shaping them as well as other industries.[135]

In regional survey, the Deir el-Bersha Project has identified cemetery evidence of other possible nodes of the 4th Dynasty network: the Old Kingdom cemeteries of rock cut tombs at Nuwayrat in Nome 16 and stone circle tombs with burials in pottery coffins and large ceramic vats at both Nuwayrat and Deir el Bersha. They date these cemeteries from the late 3rd to the early 4th Dynasty[136] and suggest that the cemeteries imply nearby communities of people who buried their leaders—or minor elites of a royal domain—in the upper rock cut tombs, some with false doors and decoration.

At Zawiyet el Meiyitin, north of Nuwayrat, a king built a small step pyramid, one of a series of small provincial step pyramids that includes one at Elephantine probably built by Huni at the beginning of the 4th Dynasty. A few hundred meters southwest of the Zawiyet el Meiyitin pyramid, an Old Kingdom cemetery and settlement near Zawiyet el-Sultan may mark the ancient place named Hebenu.[137] All these sites could once have belonged to a network of royal outposts in Middle Egypt.

De Meyer et al. point out that the series of estates in the so-called Valley Temple of Sneferu list five in Nome 16 of Middle Egypt.[138] The place names Menat Sneferu ("Nurse of Sneferu") and Menat Khufu,

[133] Willems *et al.* 2009; de Meyer *et al.* 2011.
[134] Willems *et al.* 2009: 325.
[135] Saleh 1974.
[136] de Meyer *et al.* 2011.
[137] Moeller 2001.
[138] De Meyer *et al.* 2011: 692.

possibly referring to the same estate, may have been located in this nome at a wadi mouth south of Beni Hassan.[139] De Meyer *et al.* point to Old Kingdom mastaba tombs modeled after the large mastabas at Giza near Deir Abu Hinnis and between Tihna el-Gebel and Zawiyet el-Meiyitin. The mastaba tomb at Zawiyet el-Meiyitin belonged to a man named Ny-ka-ankh. The authors date his tomb to the early 5th Dynasty. His father and grandfather can be linked to other large tombs at the site, which would place these tombs, and the careers of these men, into the 4th Dynasty. They continue to investigate the hypothesis that in this region of Middle Egypt "more or less regularly spaced sites that were probably (linked to) royal domains existed."[140]

The formal sealings from HeG show links to this area of Middle Egypt. John Nolan's reconstruction of 12 seal patterns from the Pottery Mound corpus includes one with the name of the god "Khnum-Foremost of Hermopolis."[141] Hermopolis was located in Nome 15, on the bank opposite Shyakh Said. Nolan relates this reference to the fully-written name of Khufu, Khnum-khuf, "it is Khnum who Protects me," and we can add these associations to the names, Menat-Khufu ("Nurse of Khufu") and Menat-Sneferu, of places near Beni Hassan, just northeast of Hermopolis. Seal 2, reconstructed from the Pottery Mound corpus, names "Seshat, Foremost of the House of the Book Roll," and the king as Horus, "[brother] of Min and Amun."[142] Sehsat, the female goddess of writing associated at Hermopolis with Thoth, the male god of records and writing, was called "Lady of the Eight-town." Amun was a member of the Ogdoad worshipped at Hermopolis, and if Nolan's identification of one of two ithyphallic figures as Amun is correct, it would be the oldest representation of this deity.

These Middle Egypt districts must have sent labor, as indicated by division signs for Nomes 16–17, and possibly 15, and materiel — calcite alabaster, produce, and cattle — to Giza and the HeG site.

139 Kessler 1981:197–198.

140 De Meyer *et al.*, 2011:693, n. 61.

141 Nolan 2010:81–85, Seal 1, of Khafre. The name of Hermopolis is literally "Eight-town" *Ḫmnw*, a reference to the Ogdoad, eight deities worshipped at Hermopolis in the Old Kingdom. This may be the oldest known reference to *Ḫmnw*.

142 Nolan 2010:86–124, Seal 2; the same two facing figures, ithyphallic and crowned with the double plume, appear on Seal 6, and partially on Seal 8.

3.3. Granite Graffiti, Links to Elephantine, and Hints of Foreign Labor

Reisner noted that the graffiti on the granite blocks in the Menkaure Pyramid Temple differed from those on the limestone core blocks.[143] This difference has been taken as indicating a special department of the workforce for skilled craftsmen permanently settled near the building site.[144] Verner and Andrássy convey the idea that the granite graffiti manifests a difference between levies of Egyptians for the *ʿpr*-gangs, as indicated by graffiti on the limestone blocks that include division signs for home districts, and foreigners who were specialized craftsmen, in this case, the granite workers.[145]

The graffiti written in red on the granite blocks of the unfinished granite casing of corridor 13 are less linear than those mentioning gangs, phyles, and divisions on the limestone blocks. Reisner saw four elements to the most complete graffiti on granite: (1) the word *gś*; "side"; (2) either *ỉmj-wrt* (northern blocks) or *rmn* plus *tr* or *rnpt* ("time, year" or "occasion") and *rsj* (only on the southern blocks); (3) a "variable element," which Reisner took as a "distinguishing mark" like the division signs on the limestone core blocks; and (4) *ḥmwt smjt,* "desert workshop,"[146] according to Reisner's translation. Stadelmann maintained that *ḥmwt smjt* referred to the industrial settlement and alabaster depot at the far, southeastern rim of the quarry that furnished much of the core stone for the Menkaure Pyramid.[147] Abd el-Aziz Saleh excavated this settlement in the early 1970s, and found much evidence for working calcite alabaster, but not granite.[148] Others understand the term *ḥmwwt smjt* as "craftsmen of the desert."[149]

Looking at the attestations of the term *gś* in the graffiti of the pyramid complexes of Menkaure and Sahure as well as the Userkaf Sun Temple, scholars believe that the term designates an organization of specialized craftsmen separate from that of the *ʿpr*-gangs and phyles. The *gś* organiza-

[143] Reisner 1931: 267–277, pl. XII.
[144] Helck 1975b: 372–373; Verner 1991: 77–79.
[145] Andrássy 2009a: 4–5.
[146] Reisner 1931: 277. Reisner noted that the sign *ḏʿm* occurs twice on the granite blocks in corridor 13 and also in room 24, and we have noted that the ibis division marker, conceivably the sign for Lower Egyptian Nome 15, is also found on both these granite blocks and the limestone core blocks, so it could be the same division worked on both, and this would go against the idea that *ḥmwt smjt* indicates a separate guild of specialist craftsmen.
[147] Stadelmann 1981: 67.
[148] Saleh 1974.
[149] See Andrássy 2009a: 5, n. 24 for references.

tion was divided into "sides" (*gś*), each side led by an overseer (*ỉmj-r gś*).[150] These craftsmen lived permanently near the worksite. As made explicit in the title "Scribes of the Troops (comprised of) Four Sides of Craftsmen" (*sš ṯst (nt) gś 4 ḥmwt*), a larger unit, the *ṯst,* ("troop"), could be divided into four "sides." Helck thought the craftsmen were so divided on the basis of their living quarters.[151] Verner suggested those so organized could have served in the quarries for longer terms than the members of *ʿpr*-gangs, as they were specialized in the extraction and procurement of more valuable stone.[152] Could they have come from the locales where such costly stone was quarried?

Recently Andrássy also argued that the granite graffiti attest "a special kind of craftsmen." Instead of *ḥmwt smjt,* Andrássy reads *ḥmwwt ḫꜣst,* "foreign craftsmen", citing a text from the Abusir mastaba of Ptahshepses[153] where the term is spelled out and includes determinatives of seated Asiatics as part of a line of text following *stp-zꜣ,* literally, "the Chosen Phyle."[154] Andrássy noted that the term *ḥmwwt ḫꜣst* has not been found in builders' graffiti later than Menkaure, but states "the role of foreign craftsmen in the building of pyramids and temples must not be underestimated later on."[155]

The marks on the granite blocks could relate, like the graffiti on limestone core blocks, to the labor of their transport, or, as Verner suggested, workers who specialized in such stone, from quarrying to transport, shaping and setting.[156] Unlike the colossal limestone core blocks, which were dragged from the nearby quarries,[157] the granite blocks came from

150 Haeny 1969: 31; Helck 19759; Verner 1991: 77–79; Andrássy 2009a: 4–6.

151 Helck 1975a; but see Verner 1991: 78: "die Beziehung zwischen *ḥmwt smjt* und *ṯst* ist in den Baugraffiti nicht belegt."

152 Verner 1991: 78.

153 Andrássy 2009a: 5 citing Vachala 2004: 171.

154 Goelet 1986: 86. Look for the term as designating the group of 200 men bringing fine limestone from the eastern quarries at Turah to the pyramid of Khufu documented in the recently discovered journal of the Inspector (*śḥḏ*) Merer, part of the 4th Dynasty papyri records of building the Khufu Pyramid recently found at Wadi el-Jarf; Tallet, personal communication; and see Tallet and Marouard 2014; Tallet, forthcoming.

155 Andrássy 2009a: 6.

156 Reisner noted that graffito Sa3, on one of the southern blocks, crossed the plaster of the joint with the adjacent block, in which case the graffito was applied after the setting of the blocks.

157 Lehner 1985a: 132, fig. 16; 154. The quarries immediately below and southeast of the Menkaure Pyramid show channels and wedge-sockets that quarrymen used to separate from the bedrock just such large core blocks like those in the Menkaure temple.

Aswan at the first cataract. If Andrássy's reading and inference of foreign labor are correct, we should not be surprised to find "foreign craftsmen" or the like associated with granite blocks. A whole infrastructure must have existed at Aswan and the fortified island settlement of Elephantine for procuring, shaping, loading, and shipping granite. However, we must consider Andrássy's inference about skilled, higher status craftsmen who specialized in stone like granite with other evidence that the 4th Dynasty Egyptians might have taken captives from Nubia for labor (see section 5.2). The determinatives in the Ptahshepses scene of *ḥmwwt ḫ3st* are Asiatic, not Nubian, but given the quantities of granite that had to have been shipped the 600 km downstream from Aswan to Giza, could we expect Asiatic (Syrian) crews as well as craftsmen? Perhaps not for domestic Nile barges as opposed to sea-faring ships at such an early period, though by later times in the Old Kingdom Syrian sailors, shipwrights and carpenters had become routine for expeditions to the Levant (see section 3.7).[158] In any case, we can be practically certain that Elephantine served as another important node, like those in Middle Egypt, in an inter-regional network with Giza as its center during three generations of 4th Dynasty pyramid building, and therefore we should not be surprised at the idea that foreigners might have been among the occupants of HeG.

Indeed, Reisner estimated it would have taken 1,200 to1,500 granite blocks to clad the walls of the Menkaure Temple, had the workers finished it.[159] A similar order of magnitude of granite casing blocks was probably already set in place in the lower 16 courses of the pyramid, albeit left mostly untrimmed. All this granite must have been imported from Aswan, nearly equal in distance on a straight line from Giza (685 km = 426 miles) as Byblos (625 km = 388 miles), but located upstream on Egypt's southern border. The Old Kingdom Egyptians removed as much as 45,000 cubic meters (1.5 million cubic feet) of granite from the Aswan quarries.[160] They brought most of this granite to the capital zone just above the apex of the Nile Delta. Generally across the Giza Pyramids Plateau, and on the HeG site, one finds granite fragments everywhere.

Much of the granite was off-loaded from barges on the margins of the HeG site, evidenced by two concentrations of waste from working this heavy, hard stone. Certainly the 4th Dynasty builders could move very heavy loads overland, including up steep slopes to the pyramid itself; witness the granite blocks and beams in the King's Chamber of the Khufu

[158] Bietak 1988.
[159] Reisner 1931: 277.
[160] Röder 1965: 472; Arnold 1991: 36.

Pyramid. Nonetheless, the labor saved in getting heavy items as close as possible to their destination before offloading is why the desert-edge cultivation zone, that is to say, the flood season waterfront, is so important. This is the setting of the HeG. Near the eastern end of the Wall of the Crow we found a massive bank of "granite dust."

Late in the 4th Dynasty sequence, the inhabitants used this waste from intensive, large-scale granite works to fill and close a large cut, possibly caused by desert wadi flooding, through the northern enclosure wall of Gallery Set I.[161] The Menkaure Pyramid and the Khentkawes I monument[162] were the last major granite works at Giza. The larger fragments included red and black granite and diorite. From what survived of the Menkaure temple casing, the builders were favoring black granite but also used red.[163]

We found the second concentration of granite at the far southeastern corner of the site where, again, late in the occupation sequence, builders had used large fragments of granite in the fieldstone wall around the sunken court of silos. The sharp breaks indicated these fragments came from the initial stages of dressing, and some of the pieces featured rounded faces like the "handling bosses" on the unfinished Menkaure pyramid casing.[164] The two concentrations of granite may reflect two offloading and deliver zones, a landing or harbor north of the Wall of the Crow,[165] and possibly a smaller "put-in bay" at the south, where we found a deep, sand-filled depression ("Lagoon 1") between the main HeG settlement and an "island" of settlement further south where the 4th structures ("Standing Wall Island"—SWI) may comprise a corral and abattoir (fig. 1).[166] If foreigners—Nubians or Asiatics—were involved in granite procurement, delivery, and working, we must consider them as possibly among the inhabitants of the HeG.

161 Lehner 2002: 48–53;

162 Khentkawes I's builders used granite to make the doorjambs of her chapel, her colossal false doors, and the lining of her burial passage.

163 Reisner 1931: 70–72.

164 Lehner 2002: 63–64.

165 Lehner 2013. We recently discovered a basin east of the Khentkawes Town and about 300 meters farther west of the east end of Wall of the Crow. While this basin was cut down to the estimated level of the 4th Dynasty floodplain, it is questionable that it served as a harbor for major deliveries of food, fuel, and building materials during the main pyramid construction. The Khentkawes basin is more likely a harbor that served symbolic functions and deliveries for the maintenance of the cults of Khentkawes I and Menkaure.

166 GOP 4: 39–44; Redding 2011.

The kind of connections we infer from builders' graffiti and material culture between the HeG and Elephantine/Aswan for granite, and between HeG and the Middle Egyptian nomes for calcite alabaster or travertine, were summed by Weni in regard to his procurements of these very materials for the pyramid of Merenre, in the 6th Dynasty, some two hundred years after Menkaure. The king sent Weni to granite quarries around Elephantine to get granite for his pyramid capstone, sarcophagus, symbolic false door, real doors, lintels and other elements, as well as to the Middle Egypt alabaster quarries of Hatnub (Nome 15) for a "great offering table of alabaster." On one of his expeditions to Nubia, the rulers of Irtjet, Wawat, Iam and Medja cut down local acacia trees to make barges to carry the granite, and these local rulers may have levied their people for the work Weni mentioned of cutting canals for the transfer north of the heavy stone accouterments for Merenre's pyramid at South Saqqara.[167] We must think of Weni's expedition to Aswan multiplied many times over during the three generations of 4th Dynasty pyramid building at Giza.

In addition to a source for granite, Aswan served as an entrepôt and gateway for mining and quarrying expeditions for other hard stones and copper, and for trading expeditions for products from farther south, including the southern land of Punt.

3.4. Gangs, Phyles and the HeG: Correspondence of Overall Structure?

In this section I look at a possible correspondence between the gang/crew and phyle organization and the spatial structure of the HeG Gallery Complex. For this review we need to look at the numbers of people per unit.

To summarize, the builders' graffiti from Giza suggests a system in which the royal house assigned a crew of two competing *ʿpr*-gangs to some area or part of the pyramid complex. Four or five phyles, always with the same set of names, comprised an *ʿpr*-gang. Only the first four phyles are so far attested from the 4th Dynasty,[168] so it is possible the *ỉmj-nfrt* phyle

[167] *Urk*. I: 98–110; Strudwick 2005: 352–357, no. 256

[168] Roth 1991: 35–36, 142, 120, 202–203, 211, points out that the inscriptions on shallow bowls or plates from the Djoser Step Pyramid register a 5th phyle, with a hieratic sign, possibly a baboon, that might have been an Archaic writing of *imj-nfrt*. And now look for the attestations of the five phyles in the recently discovered Wadi el-Jarf papyri documents relating to the building of the Khufu Pyramid, Tallet, personal communication. For the papyri see Tallet and Marouard 2014, Tallet forcoming.

was not used until later.[169] The phyles were composed of smaller groups or divisions. In temple service texts later than Dynasty 4 each phyle includes two divisions.[170] There appear to have been at least four divisions in each phyle of the Menkaure Temple.[171] Many representations of the cattle hobble, the *zꜣ*-hieroglyph, feature ten loops, possibly signifying that divisions numbered 10 individuals, as reflected in the Old Kingdom title, "Overseer of Ten." It is possible that this title meant "Overseer of One-Tenth" of a gang, with 2 divisions per phyle times five phyle.[172]

The general picture is a numerical-size hierarchy of people in crews, gangs, phyles, and divisions. For the 4th Dynasty, Ann Roth saw royal work crews composed of two gangs of 4 or 5 phyles, each phyle with 4 or more divisions. Obviously, large pyramids like those of Khufu and Khafre might have required many crews.[173]

Vassil Dobrev recently suggested that rather than the phyles being a subdivision of larger crews and *ꜥpr*-gangs, these gangs were, in effect, temporary enlistments of the phyles.[174] The idea is the *ꜥpr*-gangs were temporary, whereas the four or five phyles could have been broader, more permanent affiliations. In this case we might think of the phyles along the lines of our college sororities and fraternities to which we might belong no matter what school, dormitory, or year we attended college. Phyles, like the natural or artificial Greek "tribes"[175] whence our translation of the Egyptian *zꜣ* derives, may have cut across family and lineage, or even across regional boundaries. In traditional societies leaders have drawn upon such non-kin associations and broad sodalities that crosscut household, tribe and lineage to form special purpose groups that make war, form expeditions, and carry out so-called "public works."[176] If the phyles were the larger associations (along the lines of a fraternity), from which work gangs were recruited, the *ꜥpr*-gangs are listed first, Dobrev remarks, because they were compounded with the name of a pharaoh,

169 Verner 1991: 72.

170 Posner-Kriéger, Verner, and Vymazalová 2006: 264–266 for the phyle divisions in the Neferirkare and Raneferef temples.

171 Roth 1991: 142.

172 Roth 1991: 120–121.

173 Roth 1991: 120, 210–211; Andrássy 2009a: 2–4; Verner 1991.

174 Dobrev 2003: 30.

175 Trail 1975.

176 Harris and Johnson 2007:165–166. An issue to be explored further concerns the unnamed phyles of the provinces, against the attestation of the five named phyles (*wr*, *st*, *wꜣḏt*, *nḏs*, and *imyt-nfr*) only in the Memphite cemeteries, Roth 1991: 210–211.

and so honorific transposition moves the gang name forward, whereas it was actually the *zꜣ* that has first place as the broader, more lasting association.[177] The nature of phyle membership is still not entirely understood.[178]

For understanding the labor organization of building pyramids, Dobrev pointed to the limitations of the Abusir Papyri, which account for 200–250 people at most, organized into phyles for the memorial service of a king.[179] But we know that authorities did organize the workforce for building the truly gigantic pyramids of the early Old Kingdom by phyle and division. While the evidence shows a certain development of the phyle system from the Early Dynastic through the Old Kingdom,[180] by the time of Menkaure and later phyles were widely used in both royal and so-called "private" memorial foundations (pyramid temples and tomb chapels).[181]

As for estimates of the numbers of people per labor unit, a full phyle enlistment most probably numbered about forty persons.[182] A key text comes on a 4th Dynasty graffito on a limestone flake from "the debris of mastaba G5110 in the Western Cemetery," "therefore of uncertain date."[183] Under the sign for "West" appear the signs for "*sṯ*-phyle." Below this a vertical line divides the words, *wꜣḏt* and *sṯ*, probably two division names, followed underneath by the title, "Overseer of Ten" (*ỉmj-rꜣ* 10). Under this title we find the names of two men, Per-neb and Iwfy, each apparently an "Overseer of Ten." Here a division, in what Verner took as a 4th Dynasty context,[184] would number 10.

177 Dobrev 2003: 30.

178 Roth 1991: 61–75 on the nature of phyle membership.

179 Dobrev 2003: 31.

180 Roth 1991: 197–216; Verner 1991: 72.

181 Roth 1991: 119–143.

182 See Verner 1991: 76 for the range of estimates of numbers in a phyle from Reisner's (1931: 276) 200 to 250 to Helck's (1975: 129) 20 per phyle. All estimators so far assume that a phyle is a separate discrete body of men specific to a particular foundation or building project, as opposed to a wider sodality or association whence authorities levied people for special purpose labor and temple service. If the latter, any number of persons belonging to a given phyle could be enlisted for a period of service. See now, Spalinger 2013: 65, 177–178 who would like to see a phyle as numbering 30. I thank Miroslav Bárta for this reference.

183 Smith 1952: 126, fig. 8.

184 Verner 1991: 75.

On the other hand, three of four limestone tablets from the Userkaf Sun Temple at Abusir might give the numbers of persons in divisions as 22, 23, and 20 (tablet D gives 20 each for the two divisions *nfr* and *rśỉ*).[185] It is not clear if these numbers, which qualify a term, ꜥ, written with the sign of a human arm,[186] give members of a division, which could include overseers, but if these are division members the numbers are evidently not constant in this early 5th Dynasty context. However, the numbers are close to 20, and this abetted Posener-Kriéger's conclusion that around, but not exactly, 20 people made up the half-phyles in the late 5th Dynasty papyrus archives of the Neferirkare temple.[187] Yet another source, the Raneferef pyramid temple archives, gives numbers of people serving per phyle that are half or less those of the roughly contemporary Neferirkare archive.[188] However, we cannot be certain that the total number of phyle members, or the total number of members of a particular phyle assigned to one institution, were on duty at any given time.

The number of labor units would not have stayed constant over the course of a building project. Ann Roth pointed out that labor units could be added, subtracted, and overlapped or not to increase or decrease the numbers:

> If the size of a division remained constant, the number of workers available at a given time could be reduced eight-fold by halving the number of divisions, abandoning the overlapping rotation [of phyles], and rotating the divisions as well as the phyles. If the organization of two gangs was also abandoned, the reduction becomes sixteen fold.[189]

[185] Edel 1969; Verner 1991: 75–76.

[186] We might understand the term ꜥ, literally "arm, hand," as persons, as in English "hired hand," but with *mḥtỉ* ("north") or *rsj* ("south") the term could mean "area, section," or "district." Alone, the sign could also mean "piece" or "length of fabric" (Hannig 2003: 247–251). Roth (1991: 133–143) disagrees with reading this term as members of a phyle division, and took ꜥ as referring to a unit of work. She also understood the *ỉmj-wrt* on tablet B as a direction, not a phyle, and *rsj* on tablet D as a direction, not a divison. Here again we have less than complete clarity of whether we are dealing with worker or work units, or directions. See note 105. Also, see Verner's 1991: 449 comments on Roth's conclusion, drawn from these tablets, that phyles took over the function of ꜥ*pr*-gangs in assignments to parts of buildings. The sign of an arm, ꜥ, followed by a number is used in the Abusir papyri for units of cloth distributed to phyles (Posener-Kriéger, Verner and Vymazalová 2006: 225; pl.13A).

[187] Posener-Krieger 1976: 573; Posener-Kriéger, Verner, and Vymazalová 2006: 365.

[188] See Posener-Kriéger, Verner, and Vymazalová 2006: 367–368, for this difference and other irregularities for the model of a system of regular rotation in a 10-month cycle.

[189] Roth 1991: 143.

The wrinkle presented by the low numbers per phyle, such as seven in one instance in the Raneferef archive, is that we cannot conclude that the numbers of a phyle or division remained constant.

Given these caveats, and for heuristics, if we accept for the large pyramid-building projects of the 4th Dynasty that the "Overseer of Ten" indicates the smallest division of ten people—which is the most that can efficiently work on an average-sized pyramid block, and if we assume at least four divisions per phyle, we end up with a phyle of 40 persons, times four or five phyles, results in 160 to 200 per gang and 320 to 400 per crew. If we accept a very low estimate of around 2,000 total workers for building the large 4th Dynasty pyramids,[190] five or six such crews would be needed (not counting quarrying and distant transport).

It is reasonable to ask if the great Gallery Complex we have mapped across five hectares of our site reflects this 4th Dynasty labor organization known from texts. The phylo-like modularity and combining form of the galleries, and the evidence that they functioned as barracks, now begs this question.

The forty persons in the estimate of members of a phyle corresponds to the number that could comfortably stretch out on either side of the 20-meter long front colonnade of Gallery III.4, as our team members demonstrated during our 2002 season.[191] Each side could accommodate easily twenty people, the estimate for a half-phyle in the Neferirkare temple. Together the two sides of Gallery III.4, separated formally by the low stylobate-like wall in which were embedded the bases for the columns of the colonnade, could easily accommodate 40 to 50 people. Perhaps here in a gallery we see the architectural counterpart to a phyle, each side a half phyle, or two divisions of 10.

We found eight galleries in each of Sets II and III to the west of the Manor compound and Hypostyle Hall respectively (fig. 1). Each of Gallery Sets II and III could have housed two *ʿpr*-gangs at four phyles per gang, or one complete crew. Just as a gallery served as the architectural base of a phyle, we could see Gallery Sets II and III as the housing of a complete crew. Perhaps this fits with the lack of evidence for the fifth, *ỉmj-nfrt* phyle in Dynasty 4.[192] With modifications, we might hypothesize each of the four blocks of galleries as the architecture of a crew.

190 Lehner 1997: 224–225.

191 Lehner 2002: 69–70, fig. 20

192 Although we look to future publications of the Wadi el-Jarf Papyri for attestations of all five phyles in the reign of Khufu; Tallet and Marouard 2014; Tallet, personal communication.

As we excavate more of the Gallery Complex we can test our very rough estimates of 1,600 to 2,000 occupants, based on 40 to 50 persons per gallery. When we excavated Gallery III.3 in 2012, we found again the low, linear molding, like a stylobate, divided the rather empty front colonnade roughly down the middle. We found column bases embedded within the stylobate. The colonnade was not as long as that of Gallery III.4, excavated ten years earlier. But Gallery III.3 featured a square open space or court between the colonnade and the rear, southern domicile, where more people could have slept.[193] We see enough signs of variability in the galleries that we probably cannot assume a standard number of persons per gallery, but we keep to this number for the sake of an estimate at ground level. Below I revisit the estimate for the numbers of occupants.

Gallery Sets II and III show eight galleries west of a space given over to the Manor compound and to the Hypostyle Hall complex (fig. 1). We might think that nine of the galleries in Set IV possibly accommodated people. The tenth and, certainly the eleventh gallery on the east of Set IV were given over to baking and seem unsuitable for sleeping. Most of Gallery Set I, which was 55 m long as opposed to 35 m like the southern sets, was eroded away, leaving us the southwestern corner. We might assume the eight western galleries of Set I functioned in part as dormitories, leaving the width of three galleries on the east given over to some other pattern/function, and that the longer Set I galleries accommodated 55 persons. On these assumptions, we can revisit the estimate of people under the barracks hypothesis:

Gallery Set I:	8×55	=	440
Gallery Set II:	8×40	=	320
Gallery Set III:	8×40	=	320
Gallery Set IV:	9×40	=	360
Total			1,440

As Kemp observed[194] this is still only a fraction of the labor required to build the Giza pyramids (though it would suffice to build the later, smaller pyramids). We have only part of the total HeG settlement, which continues farther east. Boreholes in the modern floodplain indicate other settlement concentrations to the north and northeast. Also, if the galleries featured a second loft-like level that would support people, or if an entire gallery set featured one, continuous, terrace-like roof, the numbers who

[193] AERA 2012: 16–17.
[194] Kemp 2006: 189.

could be accommodated increase.[195] On the other hand, to the extent that storage of materials took gallery space, the numbers of occupants would have to decrease.

Yet, the impression is that the Gallery Complex, a substantial investment in mudbrick construction, was intended for something more than common workers.[196] And here we should note the idea that authorities did not use the *ꜥpr*-gangs and phyles to organize the unqualified broad masses of workers, if masses were required.[197] Rather, special people comprised these sodalities.

According to Verner, the members of the *ꜥpr*-gangs were not seasonally employed, unlike an unqualified mass ("unqualifizierten Massen") who could be taken from the agricultural infrastructure during the flood season. Recruitment of *ꜥpr*-gangs depended upon the scope and character of the building project. Authority called upon the *ꜥpr*-gangs as needed, especially for the procurement of building materials, which had to flow without delay. Their use as specialized expeditionary crews is why phyle names have been found on tools in far-flung places like Nubia and Lebanon.[198] The "Einsatz der Phylen" was also a call to service from the broad *zꜣw*-associations for assignment to gangs working particular critical parts of buildings, as shown in the stack-construction of relieving chambers above Khufu's burial chamber, the western Menkaure temple, or the Userkaf Sun Temple.

These gang and crew assemblages carried the same or similar names between different reigns, compounding epithets like "noblemen" (*špsw*), "friends" (*śmrw*), "acquaintances" (*rḫw*), or "beloved ones" (*mrw*), with the name of the reigning king.[199] Andrássy concluded: "This kind of name

[195] Heindl forthcoming reconstructed a vaulted roof over each gallery. If the builders filled in the springing of the vaults to create a continuous upper terrace, as illustrated in Nolan and Heindl 2010, many could have slept on roof.

[196] Heindl (forthcoming: 31) estimated it took 185,000 bricks to make Gallery III.4; 1,182,080 for Gallery Set II; and 5,088,000 bricks for the whole Gallery Complex.

[197] As just stated, 6 crews or 12 *ꜥpr*-gangs would, on the estimates cited, make up a force of around 2,000, corresponding to a low estimate for the numbers need to build the largest Giza Pyramids.

[198] Verner 1991: 76–77, citing Engelbach 1938: fig. 59; also Rowe 1936: fig. 36 and Rowe 1938: 393.

[199] Verner 2003: 450, n. 33. In this article Verner listed such crew or gang names from the reign of Sahure through that of Niuserre.

rather points to elite troops of young recruits for whom a lasting service has to be presumed than to ordinary workmen."[200]

3.5. Meat and Elite: What Status the Consumers?

The idea that young recruits of the *ꜥpr*-gangs stayed in the galleries, rather than "unqualified mass" of laborers, nuances the narrative of well-fed workers. Egyptologists suggest these troops were chosen and therefore somewhat "elite."[201] At the same time, if the *ꜥpr*-gangs dragged Menkaure's multi-ton core blocks, we would certainly class them as workers. Yet, as members of royal expeditionary forces, they may have enjoyed a certain privileged status. We may see in the Gallery Complex the footprint of an expeditionary force, one more formal and longer-term than those expeditions that went abroad to procure valued raw materials. Or, here in the HeG site, we see a home base of those expeditions. This sheds a different light on the evidence for abundant meat provisions.

Meat allocations, whether "rations," "pay," or *Arbeiterversorgung*, are known from ancient Egypt. From the Wadi Hammamat a stele of the 20th Dynasty reign of Ramses IV lists a daily allowance of 10 units of bread, 3 jars of beer, 2 cakes and 2 units of meat (*iwf*) for members of an expedition.[202] A stela of the the 19th Dynasty reign of Seti I at Gebel Silsileh records as a daily allocation to stone workers 20 units *wdnt* bread, 3 bundles (*ḫrš*) of vegetables, and 1 unit of *ꜣšrt* (grilled) meat, as well as two sacks of grain per month.[203] An inscription of Ramses II from Manshiyet el-Sadr records that the king allocated to his stonemasons bread, cakes, ointment and meat for all ten days of their monthly service, as well as wheat, salt and beans.[204] The residents of Deir el-Medina, the builders of the royal tombs in the Valley of the Kings, received fish, and were assigned fishermen. From time to time they received meat with other special allowances.[205] And now we learn from the newly discovered Wadi el-Jarf papyri that those who delivered fine limestone from the eastern quarries to Khufu's pyramid project were provisioned with roasted

[200] Andrássy 2009a: 3.

[201] A word used perhaps too facilely in archaeology and Egyptology: "An elite in political and sociological theory is a small group of people whop control a disproportionate amount of wealth or political power," http://en.wikipedia.org/wiki/Elite, Dec. 2, 2013.

[202] Helck 1975c: 375; Goyon 1957: 103–106, no. 89.

[203] Helck 1975c: 375–376; Sander-Hansen 1933: 3.

[204] Helck 1975c: 375–376; Hamada 1938: 217ff.

[205] Helck 1975c: 376.

meat,[206] among other provisions from various areas, including the Delta.[207]

Loprieno cites as an example of obligatory corvée labor what he called "the first dated graffito at Wadi Hammamat," by a man named Djati on an expedition for an unknown king, perhaps near the end of the Old Kingdom. The royal house provisioned this expedition with live animals, apparently for meat.

> Mission carried out by the eldest son of the king, the treasurer of the god, the general of the expedition (*mšʿ*, "army"), Djati, known as Kanofer, who had care of his men on the day of battle, who knew how to foresee the coming of the day of obligatory recruitment.[208] I distinguished myself among the multitude, and I carried out this task for Imhotep, with 1,000 men of the royal palace, 100 men of the necropolis, 1,200 pioneers, and 50 engineers. His Majesty ordered all these people to come from the Residence, and I organized this task in exchange for provisions of barley of all kinds, while his Majesty placed at my disposal 50 oxen and 200 goats for the daily victuals.[209]

While Loprieno quoted the passage as an example of corvée, Goelet, in his study of the Old Kingdom palace, cites this inscription as evidence that, "all the men came from the *ẖnw* (Residence) and were probably considered to be attached to this place."[210] The numbers amount to an ox and a dozen goats for every forty-seven people. However, the text does specify the number of days. Expedition members must have herded 50 oxen plus 200 goats into the Wadi Hammamat, exemplifying that: "The use of the living animal as a meat locker solves the storage problem for

[206] Tallet, personal communication.

[207] Tallet and Marouard 2014: 8.

[208] Loprieno reads as "obligatory recruitment" *sṯp qd*(*w*) *ḥwỉ m nḏwt-r3* (*Urk*. I 149.2–3); *sṯp*, "recruitment" (Hannig 2003: 1269); *qd*, "building," "building work" (Hannig 2003: 1342) or *qdw* ("mason"); *ḥwỉ* (literally "to beat"), and *m nḏwt-r3*, "counsel" (Hannig 2003: 685).

[209] Loprieno 1990: 192; *Urk.* I (= Sethe 1933), 148.16–149.10. John Nolan pointed out to me that Goelet 1982: 26–27 translates: "I performed this work of Imhotep with: 1,000 men of the *pr-ʿ3*, 100 quarrymen, 1,200 workers (?) 50 *bwt*(?)-workers. His Majesty caused that these numerous troops should come from the *ẖnw*..." I thank John Nolan for this reference. The term *bwt* (Loprieno's "engineers"), possibly with a determinative of a casting mold (or a ladel?) for molten metal, might refer to metal workers or blacksmiths, Jones 2000: 413, no. 1523.

[210] Goelet 1982: 27.

this otherwise highly perishable animal product (meat), making meat a suitable commodity for regulated distribution."[211]

Throughout his publications, Moreno García portrays an Old Kingdom landscape of state-supported and state-supporting special-purpose settlements (*grgt*), household estates (*pr*), control towers (*swnw*), production centers (*pr šnʿw*), and, above all, plantations (*ḥwwt*) and great plantations (*ḥwwt ʿ3t*).[212] A *ḥwt*, also called an estate or domain,[213] was "a kind of royal farm, warehouse, processing and administrative center and defensive building,"[214] or a center similar to an *ezba* of more recent times. Among other functions, one purpose was to furnish cattle to the royal center, as we have already suggested for Kom el-Hisn in Lower Egyptian Nome 3, possibly the *ḥwt jḥjt*, "Estate of the Cattle."

Moreno García points to an emphasis of the stewards of Upper Egypt and nomarchs in the late Old Kingdom and Middle Kingdom on raising and increasing cattle herds and filling stables with birthed calves for local wealth and prestige and for meeting the fiscal needs of the royal house.[215] He discusses evidence for a number of *ḥwwt*, estates or "plantations," strategically located in the Edfu region to supply expeditions passing on the river and through nearby wadis to the Red Sea.[216] A man named Qar, who became nomarch and the head of Upper Egypt in the 6th Dynasty, boasted in his tomb biography that the bulls of this nome were more numerous than the bulls in the stable of the head of all Upper Egypt.

Who were the meat-eaters on these expeditions? Titles from a number of tombs from the early 5th Dynasty relate to the supervision and control of troops of young men assembled into armies and expeditionary forces. A man named Kaaper recorded in his tomb at Abusir[217] a long list of

211 Zeder 1991: 34.

212 Moreno García 1996; 1997; 1998; 1999; 2010; 2013.

213 Jacquet-Gordon 1962.

214 Moreno García 2013: 88.

215 Moreno García 1998; although see Eyre's 2004: 183 n. 167 objection to Moreno García's claim that meeting fiscal needs of the state included corvée to such an extent that it led to crisis in the late Old Kingdom.

216 Moreno García 1998: 152.

217 The information on this Kaaper comes to us from relief scenes and texts from his tomb, which he had built in the 5th Dynasty in south Abusir. Fischer (1959) wrote about this man's career from relief fragments in museums; the location of the tomb, thought to be Saqqara, was unknown. Members of the Saqqara Inspectorate of the Ministry of Antiquities located the tomb at south Abusir in 1989. The Czech team excavated and surveyed the tomb in 1991. Miroslav Bárta (2001: 143–191) published it in *Abusir V*.

titles, many of which relate to expeditions. He rose, apparently, from the lowest and most basic title, *nfr*, "Recruit" or in this case, "Cadet,"[218] to the highest, "Overseer of All Works of the King."[219] In between, his sequence of twenty-six titles includes others related to the organization of labor, including *ỉmy-r mšʿ*, "Overseer of the Army" or "Overseer of the Expedition,"[220] and *sš mšʿ*, "Scribe of the Army," a title concerned with foreign lands, expeditions, and works.

In regards to considerations of meat allocations for "elite" gangs of workers and expedition members, Kaaper's title sequence begins with "Herdsman of the Dappled Cattle" and "Scribe of the Pasture Lands of the Dappled Cattle."[221] With due consideration that the second of these titles makes Kaaper already a scribe, we might ask: is it possible that in his youth Kaaper worked as a herdsmen and that his titles reflect a practice of allocating cattle to royal military/expeditionary forces? Kaaper's father may have been a man named ʿIy who was "Overseer of Royal Works," and whose father, in turn, may have been "Overseer of the Army," Tjenti. Kaaper's titles may then reflect a tradition of provisioning cattle to labor organized for military campaigns, expeditions and royal building projects.[222]

Scenes in Sahure's upper temple show a special class of young men, labeled *ḫntjw-š*, bringing cattle and fowl, sources of meat.[223] The *ḫntjw-š* (literally "those Foremost of the Basin") are also labeled, *šmsw pr ʿ3*, "Retainers-" or "Followers of the Great House," that is, the palace. These young troops (*nfrw*) formed an elite guard for the palace. We meet them again in scenes of expeditions and the royal hunt.

[218] Fischer 1959: 259.

[219] Strudwick 1985: 145, no. 139.

[220] Literally "of a multitude;" or per Spalinger 2013: 466, of a "host."

[221] Fischer 1959a: 257–258. Fischer's sequence relies to some extent on his reconstruction of the west wall of Kaaper's chapel from loose blocks and photographs. Bárta (2001: 173–177, fig. 4.24 followed Fischer's reconstruction, with some caveats.

[222] Fischer 1959a: 255; see Bárta's (2001: 184; 1999: 17–20) reservations on Kaaper's filiations in light of features that may indicate Tjenti's tomb (Saqqara Tomb B1) dates to the late 5th Dynasty. Strudwick (1985: 145, no. 139) sees the filiation between Kaaper and *Ỉy* as particularly problematic. He dates *Ỉy* to the second half of the 5th Dynasty.

[223] Borchardt 1913, pl. 55. The last part of the term, *ḫntjw-š*, the *š* plus the mountain determinative, show in one of six fragments that Borchardt (1913, pl. 55) displays with other fragments of a scene of leading cattle and fowl.

As well as being provisioned with meat, expeditions and raids into foreign countries served also to procure cattle, sheep and goats. So royal inscriptions attest, if we can take these as historical, although the numbers are most probably exaggerated. The Palermo Stone annals relate for one year (PS r.VI.2) in the reign of Sneferu, the import of 7,000 captives and 200,000 sheep and goats. The same entry mentions building some kind of great wall:

> … building a 100-cubit "Adoring the Two Lands" boat and 60 "sixteener" royal boats (of) cedar (*mr*(*w*)); smiting Nubia, bringing (in tribute) 7,000 male and female live captives (*sḳr*(*w*) *ꜥnḫ*), 200,000 sheep and goats; building of the wall of the south and north-land (called) "The Mansions of Sneferu"; bringing 40 ships laden? (with) pine-wood (*ꜥš*)…[224]

We do not know if the captive people and animals were connected to the mentioned building operations, but the juxtaposition of the events suggests so. Helck believed the royal house settled these captives on the newly created estates and cattle ranches mentioned in the next year-register (PS r. VI.3), the seventh year of counting:[225]

> … creating 35 estates with people? (and) 122 cattle-farms; building a 100 cubit "Adoring of the Two Lands" boat (of) pine, and two 100-cubits boats (of) cedar; seventh occasion of the census …[226]

Then there is the well-known scene in the Sahure upper pyramid temple of the accounting goddess Seshat, "Foremost of the House of the Book Roll," "writing down the number of captives of all the foreign lands." Seshat faces subjugated Libyan tribesmen. Lower registers show, and specify numbers for cattle (123,440), donkeys (223,400), goats (223,413), and sheep (243,688).[227] These numbers are most probably far too large even if representing the entire holdings of the Libyan tribes. In the bottom register, the wife and children of a Libyan ruler raise a hand to beg for mercy. This composition was once part of a larger scene; to the left, the king slayed the Libyan chief. As with all such scenes in the pyramid temples, this was iconic.[228]

224 Wilkinson 2000: 141.
225 Helck 1974.
226 Wilkinson 2000: 143.
227 Borchardt 1913, 13, Bl. 1; Strudwick 2005: 84, no. 10; Roccati 1982: 58–60.
228 That such scenes were repeated on pyramid temples as ritual, not (only) historical signifiers, is shown by the fact that more than two hundred years later, Pepi II's artists repeated the scene of king slaying the Libyan chieftain as his wife and son look on, labeled with the same names. Stadelmann (1985:

The juxtaposition in compressed year compartments of the Palermo Stone Annals of events relating to Levantine wood and ships and the capture of cattle and people bears a certain resemblance to the association of high numbers of cattle, evidence of Levantine imports and wood, and the compressed modular spaces of the Gallery Complex on the HeG site. It is also coincident with Sahure's scene of Seshat and cattle accounting that we find texts on seal impressions invoking Seshat, "Foremost of the House of the Book Roll"—the very title of Seshat title in the Sahure scene, in the same deposit that yielded an abundance of cattle bone in Pottery Mound in the Western Town of the HeG (fig. 1). People discarded this waste from their occupation of House I, which served as scribal workshop. Here, meat consumption [229] and scribal activity came together.[230]

3.6. Who Were the Hunters?

When we think about presence of bones of hunted fauna on the HeG site, especially from the largest mammal in the Egyptian Nile Valley, the hippopotamus, we should consider that hunters are listed among other specialists in expeditions and estates (*ḥwwt*).

An inscription recording an expedition of 18,660 persons into the Wadi Hammamat during the 38th year of the 12th Dynasty king Senwosret I lists 30 hunters as one of thirteen groups of skilled and unskilled workers, along with 60 sandal makers, 100 stone cutters, 100 quarrymen, 200 rowers, 1,000 guardsmen (300 Theban naval soldiers and 700 infantrymen), soldiers, millers, brewers and bakers, and butlers.[231] A whole bureaucracy marched along, comprised of officials also divided into thirteen groups, including seal bearers and 20 mayors (*ḥ3tyw-ʿ*) of towns "presumably because it was their responsibility to supply most of the

199) doubts that this takes away from the historicity of the Sahure relief, were it the prototype. Because they are so stereotypical, Vachala (1991: 96, n. 22 for refs.) rejects such scenes from royal temples for establishing historical events.

229 Note that only 50 m to the south, in the area we designated "Standing Wall Island" (SWI), we found a large enclosure that appears to have been a corral, with chambers that might have served as abattoirs (Redding 2011). Between SWI and the Western Town, the depression, Lagoon 1, might remain from a put-in bay for the delivery of cattle on hoof or by boat (fig. 1). Carbohydrates went to the north into the court of large silos in the Royal Administration Building (RAB), protein (on hoof) went to the south into the SWI corral. Scribes in the Western Town, at the head of the bay, may have accounted both kinds of delivery.

230 Nolan 2010: 86–89, Seal 2, 98–100, Seal 5; Redding 2010: 229–240.

231 Goyon 1957: 17–20, 81–85, no. 61; Mueller 1975: 256.

drafted or conscripted labour."[232] A critical point for questions of status and rations, compensation, or provisioning in the Middle Kingdom expeditions is that quantities differed according to specialty and rank. Stonecutters were given more than common laborers, who received 10 bread units and one-third of a unit of beer. Hunters ranked with stonecutters and quarrymen and received 15 bread loaves and one-half a unit of beer, whereas a craftsman got 20 loaves and one-half a unit of beer.[233] We might see this expedition as a Middle Kingdom version of the HeG site on the move.

The Gebelein Papyri list hunters as a class of specialists among some 300 people from two villages (determined with the *nỉwt* "town" sign) that comprised an estate near the site of Gebelein in Upper Egypt.[234] These documents date possibly to the reign of Menkaure,[235] that is, the exact period of our main exposure of the HeG site and of the *ˁpr*-gang and phyle graffiti in the unfinished Menkaure Pyramid Temple. The papyri list personnel in categories, like a stationery version of the Senwosret I expedition, or perhaps authorities registered people from these two villages for an expedition or labor mobilization away from home.[236] The fact that in one list (Roll IV) they are sorted by locality reminds us of the graffiti or control notes from the Middle Kingdom pyramid complexes.

It is remarkable that a class of specialized hunters, comprising "un nombre assez important," feature among other specialists in this small number of people from two provincial villages at this early period. Posener-Kriéger notes that the accounted people must have been of modest or low status. The titles show several of the same occupations we see in painted scenes carved in relief on the chapel walls of tombs of large estate holders: bakers, brewers, craftsmen, boat makers, sailors and rowers, masons, metal workers, stockmen, grain measurers, a "sealer of the granary," as well as the hunters and two "nomads" (*ḥrj-š*).[237] These are the basic specialists we would find in any large farm, ranch, or plantation, here, in an Old Kingdom estate. Some scribes are also included, as well as employees of the archive and the spouses, children and parents who generally go unnamed.[238]

232 Kemp 2006: 181.
233 Mueller 1975: 251 n. 9, 253, 256.
234 What we could call an estate, or domain, is here termed a *pr ḏt* (literally, "house of eternity"). This term is used for a household estate as opposed to a *ḥwt*.
235 Posener-Kriéger 1975: 216–217.
236 Posener-Kriéger 1975: 212.
237 Hannig 2003: 874.
238 Posener-Kriéger 1975: 219.

Roll I of the Gebelein Papryi lists a group of persons with the title *nfrw*.[239] This is the basic, early title, "Cadet" or "Recruit," that Kaaper held, probably long before he rose to become "Scribe of the King's Army" and "Overseer of All Works of the King" (see section 3.5). The same term, *nfrw*, could be used for the "elite troops of young recruits" that Andrássy sees as making up the *ʿpr*-gangs and phyles in the Menkaure graffiti.[240] On the other hand, Eyre stated that *nfrw* were "typically young men of low status engaged on large projects." They were "probably levies of a certain age, called up for mass labour."[241] The *nfrw*, "recruits", and titles reflecting the direction of *nfrw*, figure prominently in the titles concerned with the organization of both military and building forces over the long-term of the Old Kingdom.[242]

Nfrw served on land expeditions to very distant mines and quarries, on the royal hunt, and on ships and boats.[243] The title, "Overseer of a 'Detachment' (or 'Expedition') of Recruits" is widely attested in the Old Kingdom.[244] An expedition to Hatnub was comprised of 1,600 *nfrw* in three roughly equal groups from three different places.[245] The *nfrw* could form army troops, serving, in local militia,[246] under command of local notables, which we may take as attested by *ḥqꜣ* ("ruler," "chief") signs above the village lists in the Gebelein, or *nfrw* could be conscripted for military, expeditionary, or building service for the royal house.

It is such young troops of estates who hunted the largest animal of the ancient Egyptian Nile Valley. The inhabitants of HeG hunted, or interacted with those who hunted hippopotami, which inhabited the river and its banks along with fish, waterfowl, and crocodiles.[247] Given the wide spatial distribution of hippo parts from our excavations of the Giza

[239] Related to the word, *nfr*, generally, "good, beautiful, perfect," but also possibly *nfryt* "end, bottom," and *nfrw*, "ground level, base" (Faulkner 131–132: 1962/1996; Hannig 2003: 624–628).

[240] Andrassy 2009a: 3, and see Fischer 1960: 5 and Jones 2000: 705–706, no. 2575 for the "Director of the *ʿpr*-gangs of Young Recruits."

[241] Eyre 1987a: 19.

[242] Faulkner 1953: 34–35.

[243] Fischer 1959a: 260–261, n. 65; Fischer 1960.

[244] Jones 2000: 142–143, no. 551, 552.

[245] Anthes 1928, Gr. 6; Eyre 1987: 19.

[246] Faulkner 1953: 35–36.

[247] Linseele and Van Neer 2009: 49. Hippos may have remained more abundant for a longer time in the quiet waters of the marshy Delta, the preferred hippo niche. The hippo was reportedly last seen in Upper Egypt in the 20th century (Krzyszkowska 1990: 20, citing Sidney 1965: 99; Manlius 2000: 62, fig. 1).

settlements—both the Heit el-Ghurab and Khentkawes Town sites, it is highly unlikely that all these elements came from one individual. The diversity of parts suggests that whole animals were brought to the site.

Scenes from the tombs of officials and estate owners depict coteries of young men as the estate's harpooners.[248] Altenmüller suggested it was the job of such harpooners to secure the work and passage through the papyrus thickets of fishermen and cattle ranchers belonging to the estate.[249] He emphasized the occurrence of scenes of hippo harpooners in association with cattle fording water. Troops of young men formed a kind of vanguard clearing the way of hippos for estate workers, herders, and for the estate owner in marginal wet zones and on the edges of papyrus thickets.[250]

A scene in the entrance vestibule of the upper pyramid temple of Pepi II showed the king larger than life harpooning a hippopotamus while standing on a stylized reed boat, his right hand raised and gripping the end of a long harpoon, his left hand grasping the end of double ropes sunk in the yawning mouth of a wounded hippopotamus, who turns menacingly toward the king in a threatening roar.[251] The scene is iconic, repeated in its basic elements at least since the First Dynasty, and throughout Pharaonic history.[252] As a Pharaonic version of St. George spearing the dragon, the hippo hunt is only one reflection of the theme, ever-repeated in ancient Egyptian art, monarchical order over chaos.[253] In the Pepi II scene the king is the corporeal composite of his troops, or, hero-

[248] Harpur 1987: 355–67, feature 7, fig. 189.

[249] Altenmüller 1989: 15–16.

[250] Behrmann (1995:15–16) objected that Altenmüller's idea of a vanguard clearing the way of hippos for fording cattle and estate workers misunderstands the behavior and disposition of hippopotami, which are not predators and whose instinct would be to flee at the approach of noisy cattle and humans on boats. This may be true to some extent, but Lydekker (1902: 1037–1038) relates anecdotes of surprised hippos attacking boats and seizing cattle in their gaping jaws.

[251] Jéquier 1940: 20–22, pl. 32, pls. 33–35.

[252] Behrmann 1989; 1995; 1996.

[253] Other kings may have included the hippopotamus harpooning scenes in their pyramid temples. Fragments hint of such a scene in the pyramid temple of Userkaf at Saqqara (Labrousse and Lauer 2000: 110–111, fig. 224; Harpur 1987: 184–185). Borchardt (1913: 29–30, 180, pls. 15–16) assigned a scene of hippopotami to the left side of the portico entrance to the Valley Temple of the Sahure pyramid complex, and saw in small fragments, evidence of a harpooning scene.

like, singly performs the feat of many. But here, too, the scenes probably signify an apotropaic function, order against chaos.[254]

Rainer Stadelmann suggested that the Egyptians might have actually *enacted the archetype*, that is, performed the age-old ritual of harpooning the hippo with a real, live animal in a canal or basin at the base of the pyramid complex.[255] The Pepi II hippo-harpooning scene includes a unique addition to the more standard aspects of the composition. Behind the king, six men (in pairs, two abreast) pull what seems to be a live hippo tied firmly to a sled. Jéquier refers to this as a second hippo,[256] but we can interpret this as an event prior to the thrust of the royal harpoon: the king's troops first arrive with the same hippo, captured and brought to the site for the ritual enactment.

It may seem far-fetched that young men of the royal entourage would capture a hippo, deliver it to the pyramid zone and hold it for a performance (wherein, surely, they, not the king himself, delivered the killing blows, his thrusting arm simply a manifestation of his troops). But Egyptologists, archaeologists, art historians, and zoologists who have looked at rock art, tomb scenes, images on artifacts and pottery, and skeletal remains of animals in Early Dynastic and Old Kingdom contexts see compelling evidence that in these times and in later periods Egyptians did indeed capture and contain wild animals. In fact, most of the commentators who have remarked on the evidence of bones, tomb and temple images, and texts believe that the Egyptians hunted, captured, transported, and kept wild animals of both the swamp and desert.

> … the study of the so-called decorations in the Egyptian tombs and temples of the Pyramid Ages…led to a highly surprising result…In ancient Egypt there was a complex system of 'gathering', hunting, transporting and keeping desert animals, establishing an economic section of its own alongside other important ones, i.e. a swamp-economy, cattle breeding and agriculture.[257]

Hunting and capturing wild animals, which first peaked in the Old Kingdom, during the 5th and 6th dynasties,[258] was a team effort.[259] Scenes, myths and ethnographic accounts show that hippopotamus hunting was

[254] Staehelin 1978.
[255] Stadelmann 1985: 198.
[256] Jéquier 1940: 21.
[257] Herb and Föster 2009: 17–18.
[258] Linseele and Van Neer 2009: 47–48; citing Boessneck 1953: 28; 1988: 35.
[259] Säve-Söderbergh 1953: 12.

a group activity, involving teams or troops (men of the estate, gods, royal followers). In the Pepi II hippopotamus scene the six men who pull the sled to which the recumbent hippo is firmly lashed must represent the royal troops of the moment. Many more figures of the royal entourage likely filled the empty spaces. Next to the king's forward striding leg appears the label *m śtp zꜣ*, "in the *Śtp-zꜣ*." To reiterate, the compound *śtp zꜣ*, means literally "to select-" or "to choose a protection" or to choose a phyle, *zꜣ*.[260] In some uses we could see the body of men so formed as a most elite or chosen phyle, selected to escort or accompany the king.

In the Old Kingdom *śtp zꜣ* is related closely to the palace while not yet written with the *pr*-sign, the building or house determinative. In times later than the Old Kingdom, *śtp zꜣ* became one of the five major terms for the palace. As a verbal noun the term can mean "escort," "body guard," making it a synonym with *šmś*, "to follow."[261] Verbs in clauses containing *m śtp zꜣ* have to do with decision-making processes where the subject is often craftwork, building or construction. *Śtp-zꜣ* is then used as a context in which such decisions are made in consultation.[262]

Goelet quotes from the famous biography of the 6th Dynasty official, Weni: "I acted so that his majesty praised me, by performing *śtp-zꜣ* (*m ỉrt śtp-zꜣ*), in preparing (*ỉrt*: lit. "making") the way of the king, and performing (*ỉrt*) attendance (*ʿhʿw*)."[263] Goelet concludes that Weni's expressions reflect watching, attending and escorting for the king and members of the king's household. Altogether, attestations of *Śtp-zꜣ* as verbal expressions in non-religious texts indicate "a type of protection service offered to a human (indirect) object who was in transit … the notion of escorting or acting as a body-guard."[264] In the Pepi II scene, appears also the term, writ large, *Per Weru*, literally "house of the Great Ones," indicating something like an honor guard according to Posener-Kriéger.[265] *Per Weru* juxtaposed with the label *m śtp-zꜣ* shows that the *Per Weru* comprised part of the *śtp-zꜣ*; "the people closest to the king were treated as a collective body."[266]

260 Goelet 1982: 444, n. 4, 445–451.
261 Goelet 1986: 85–86.
262 Goelet 1986: 90. See above, section 3.4, the association of the *hmwtt hꜣst*, "foreign craftsmen" with the *śtp zꜣ*. Andrassy 2009a: 5, fig. 4.
263 Goelet 1982:446–448; 1986: 87.
264 Goelet 1982: 450; 1986: 88.
265 Posener-Kriéger 1976: 498.
266 Goelet 1982: 459.

In addition to high-status equerries, the *Setep-Za* appears to have included people of lesser rank and file, as shown in the use of the term as a label for men guarding and serving in team-based delivery of animals and material for prominent, so-called "private" individuals, and for the hunting and capture of wild animals. We find this expression of *śtp-zꜣ* in the tomb chapel of a Vizier named Ptah-hotep at Saqqara, much visited by modern tourists. A procession delivers the contributions of huntsmen, including a caged lion and leopard, gazelles, oryx, ibex, hedgehogs and hares.[267] Standing at the head of a register of men leading antelopes, gazelles, and other livestock, a man named Ptah-nefer-khu is labeled "Foremost of Those in the *Setep-Za*," (*ḥꜣty imyw śtp-zꜣ*), as well as "Director of Those Who are in the Following" (*ḫrp imyw šmꜥw*), and "Overseer of Those Who Are in the Crews" (*imy-rꜣ imyw isw*). Goelet concludes: "The term *śtp-zꜣ* thus effectively stands in parallel with the words *šmśw* 'following', and *isw,* 'crews',"[268] and serves as a virtual synonym for *šmś,* to follow." It is the crews of the *śtp-zꜣ,* or a *śtp-zꜣ*—a select enlistment, a set of recruits—who hunt and deliver the exotic animals of the desert economy for the estate of Ptah-hotep,[269]

This example from the tomb of Vizier Ptah-hotep associates the term *śtp-zꜣ* with troops, crews, and a suite of men who capture and deliver wild animals, a practice so abundantly represented in tomb chapels of the pyramid age that Herb and Förster conclude it amounted to a desert- and swamp-economy, alongside cattle breeding and agriculture.[270]

In the left upper register of the Ptah-hotep scene, young men wrestle, and on the right six naked males with the side locks of youth march behind another youth with his hand tied behind his back, possibly a prisoner (in a game?). Griffiths stated: "This row evidently represents the military section of Ptah-hetep's people."[271]. In other words, Ptah-hotep's domain was large enough for its own para-military troops, in all probability formed from the young men of his estate. As in many cultures, these troops consisted of "cohorts of younger sons, young unmarried males, and 'noble youths' who yet remained dependent, and so something

267 Paget, Pirie and Griffiths 1898: pl. XXXIII.

268 For other attestations of this or similar combination of titles, see Jones 2000: 57.

269 Goelet 1982: 465. Ptahhotep was the Overseer of the Pyramid Towns of the 5th Dynasty kings Izezi, Niuserre, and Menkauhor.

270 Herb and Förster 2009: 17–18.

271 Paget, Pirie and Griffiths 1898: 29, pl. XXXIII.

like servants in status."[272] Such troops, the referents of the terms *nfrw, šmśw,* and *ỉsw,* and who comprised the *ʿprw*-gangs and the *śtp-zꜣ,* may have inhabited the Gallery Complex.

If the HeG settlement and the Gallery Complex accommodated such elite troops, the context of this settlement in the larger spatial arrangement at Giza might have provided the social, administrative and geographic impetus for yet another group of people especially attached to pyramids and their settlements, the *Khentiu-she* (*ḫntjw-š*),[273] a title first attested and probably first formalized in the reign of Sahure, not long following the HeG occupation. I bring this up here because in the elaborate scenery from the Sahure pyramid temples, it is *Ḫntjw-š* who carry on the royal hunt.

Much has been published on the *ḫntjw-š*. The literal, denotative meaning of *š* is "basin,"[274] which in early Egypt could be either a tract of land or a body of water for the reason that the Egyptians organized their irrigation and agriculture into great and small basins that retained the annual flood water long enough for it to deposit rich silt on the fields. So the original, detonative meaning of *ḫntjw-š* might have been, "those foremost of the basin," possibly a large basin excavated or modified at the valley-low desert interface in front of pyramid complexes.[275] For the pyramid complexes of Khafre and Menkaure at Giza, such a large basin and general delivery area existed north of the Wall of the Crow (*Heit el-Ghurab*) and extended north as far as the front of the Sphinx Temple and Khafre Valley Temple, as far west as the front of the Menkaure Valley Temple and Khentkawes Town, where between 2009 and 2012 we exca-

[272] Stager 1985b: 25–27. While noting that troops of youths are common in many cultures, Stager (1985) wrote about the *naʿar,* "lad, youth, servant" in ancient Israel, but also cites the crack troops (*naʿaruna*) that Ramses II sent ahead to lead the charge against the Syrians at Kadesh.

[273] Hannig 2003: 959, who, in his dictionary entry for *ḫntj-š*, gives "Siedler, Pächter (*in* der Pyramidenstadt, viell. ursprünglich bezogen auf das Bassin des Giza Zentralfeldes."

[274] Spalinger 2013: 201 finds a translation of *š* as "basin" as "far from the mark." He cites Brovarski 2001: 98 who concluded that the term *š n pr-ʿꜣ* "seems to form the setting for a number of royal activities not particularly appropriate to a body of water, but rather to an administrative area of the palace grounds where the king conducted public business." However, "basin," whether dry or watered (seasonally or perennially), has to remain the fundamental, denotative meaning, similar to the Arabic word *ḥod,* "basin," also a basic unit in land administration, whether the land was flooded or not. See below on the *š* and *rꜣ-š* of Khufu as a water body, port, and as an institution near Giza in recently found Wadi el-Jarf Papyri.

[275] Berlandini 1979: 14; Schott 1965: 10.

vated the westernmost reach of this artificial basin system.[276] This general zone comprised the *rꜣ-š*, the "entrance to the basin," which was the valley access to the pyramid complex and its settlement.[277]

Now we have multiple attestations to the *rꜣ-š* of Khufu and, perhaps as an abbreviation, the *š* of Khufu, in the Wadi el-Jarf Papyri, found in the last two years at a Red Sea port of Khufu. These documents, as so far studied and published, have nothing to do with Red Sea faring.[278] The papyri all relate to building the Khufu pyramid at Giza and include the journal of an Inspector (*śḥḏ*) named Merer and his 200 men who bring limestone blocks on boats from the eastern quarries at Tura to the pyramid, *Akhet Khufu*, "the Horizon of Khufu," which is mentioned repeatedly. Before arriving at the pyramid, Merer and his men overnight in the *rꜣ-š* of Khufu, which makes Pierre Tallet believe it must be some distance from Giza, near Abusir about 12–14 km south of Giza. With a major Nile channel on the west, pressing its high western levee against the low desert of the pyramid zone, it might have been necessary to begin to draw water for filling a large harbor basin via a canal that began some considerable distance south, higher on the longitudinal slope of the river levees and general valley floor. Access to flood basins was never perpendicular to the Nile channel,[279] in which water stood 7 m below the levee tops during later Spring/early Summer low water. So access would have to begin some distance south of any actual basin at Giza, and the slope of the levees makes a beginning 12–14 km south sensible, putting the canal entrance, *rꜣ*, of the harbor basin, *š* near Abusir.[280] In any case, Tallet relates how Merer's journal, involving more than one round trip, shows clearly that the *rꜣ-š* of Khufu, and the *š* of Khufu were place(s) of delivery by water, a harbor basin lined by stone dikes, and a place or places of administration, not surprising given that the Wadi el-Jarf Papyri show the same meticulous accounting mindset as expressed in the Old Kingdom papyri from Gebelein and Abusir.[281] We also have to keep in mind the many kinds of materials and people that would have been coming

[276] GOP 5: 15–52; *Aeragram* 12.1: 10–13.

[277] Stadelmann 1981: 163–164; Lehner 1997: 230–231.

[278] Tallet and Marouard 2014.

[279] Goyon 1971: 146.

[280] Willcocks 1889: 39 wrote: "Since the slope of the basin canals is 1/20,000, while that of the Nile is 1/12,900 and that of the country 1/10,800, it takes 36½ kilometres for the basin canal to gain 1 metre on the Nile, and some 23½ kilometres to gain 1 metre on the country."

[281] Tallet forthcoming.

through, and being accounted for, in the *š* of Khufu: building stone, wood, gypsum, grain, cattle, and imports from the Levant, Sinai (via Wadi el-Jarf), Elephantine and points further south. The *R3-Š* of Khufu would have been a kind of early port authority, a government authority for a special district that operates a port.[282] Basin, royal domain, administrative precinct, and economic institution—the Wadi el-Jarf Papyri confirm that the *š* of Khufu was all of these, administered by an Overseer of the *R3-Š* of Khufu, who was none other than Ankhaf, half-brother of Khufu and owner of the gigantic mastaba tomb G7510 where Reisner found his famous bust and secured it for the Museum of Fine Arts in Boston.

Whether or not, as Stadelmann suggested, the *š*, as in *š n pr-ꜥ3* ("the *š* of Pharaoh") could stand for an entire royal precinct,[283] or mainly the valley port district flanking the basin, including its levees, dikes, terraces, service buildings, and possible royal residence, the inhabitants of the HeG site were literally *ḫntj*, "at the head of," or "foremost of" or "south of" (another meaning of *ḫntj*[284]) the *š* ("basin" or delivery precinct).

Long after the royal house moved away from pyramid building sites, residents of pyramid towns included *ḫntjw-š* who shared with *ḥmw nṯr* the ritual service in the pyramid temples for the memorialized dead kings.[285] Whatever the original, denotative meaning, the title *ḫntjw-š* attained a status of "palace attendant," both the palace of the living king and the funerary estate.[286]

While expressing the view that the title *ḫntjw-š* originated in land fronting the pyramid complex, Schott pointed to *ḫntjw-š* involvement with the royal escort, guard force, and leadership of expeditions with responsibilities for enforcing discipline.[287] Weni prefaced his oft-quoted statement that he performed *śtp-z3*, "in preparing the way of the king," by stating that the king (Pepi I) appointed him Overseer of the *Ḫntjw-š*.[288] Kanawati suggested that *ḫntj*, literally, "one who is in front of," connotes "watcher," "escort," or "guard."[289] He builds on Schott's delin-

[282] http://en.wikipedia.org/wiki/Port_authotity; accessed July 5, 2014.
[283] Stadelmann 1981: 157–161.
[284] Hannig 2003: 957–958.
[285] Posener-Kriéger 1976: 577–581; Posener-Kriéger, Verner and Vymazalová 2006: 372–373.
[286] Roth 1995.
[287] Schott 1965: 11–12.
[288] *Urk.* I: 100, 8–10; Goelet 1986: 86–87, n. 6.
[289] Kanawati 2003: 14–24.

eation of the *ḫntjw-š* as royal escorts in military campaigns, celebrations, transportation, and hunts to suggest the that "guard" should be the essential translation and understanding of the title, *ḫntj-š*, while noting they also served in temple ritual and as musicians. Overall, their concern was the security and well being the king, alive and in the Afterlife.

The Sahure pyramid temples showed the *ḫntjw-š* on the royal hunt. The original placement of the hunt scene in the eastern end of the southern ambulatory corridor around the court,[290] which functioned thematically to establish order near the front part of the temple, belies the symbolic, apotropaic function of the scene. It complemented scenes of the king fishing and fowling in the opposite, northern corridor.[291] From the southern corridor we see in a bottom register *Khentiu-she* of the palace (*ḫntjw-š pr ꜥꜣ*) below two upper registers showing the hunt and capture of wild animals.

As with the Pepi II scene of the hippopotamus hunt, the king on the far left of the whole scene is shown larger than life. It is he who hunts. The king shoots arrows, no doubt manifesting the entire hunting party. As with the Pepi II scene, representatives of the highest officials filled the registers behind the king, including, with some ancient emendation, his successor, Neferirkare, with royal cartouche and uraeus on his forehead. On the right, members of the royal party have erected a desert corral, consisting of thick rope and a wooden frame.[292] The royal party hunts and traps oryx, antelope, wild cattle, hyena, and other wild animals.

In the bottom register a row of young men who bow and hold staves lowered to the ground are labeled *ḫntj-š pr ꜥꜣ* ("*Khentiu-she* of the Palace") and *šmś* "Following ..." or "Escort," and farther right, *rꜣ-šmś n nfr-*[*ꜥprw*], "Escort (*rꜣ-šmś*) of Gangs (*ꜥprw*) of Young Recruits (*nfrw*)."[293] We see the same compounded label in front of troops running below the ship of state from the Sahure Valley Temple. [294] The inscription above the valley temple group also gives the name of an *ꜥpr*-gang compounded with the cartouche name of the king, something like "The Gang, Sahure is Noble." A Sahure cartouche in the far left of the upper temple hunt season must also belong to the name of an *ꜥpr*-gang.

[290] Borchardt1913: pls.17, 55.
[291] Borchardt 1913, Bl. 16.
[292] See also Herb and Förster 2009: 28, fig. 10.
[293] Goedicke (1971: 71) citing Junker (1941) who read *rꜣ-šmś* as a compound word for "escort."
[294] Borchardt 1913, Bl. 9. This label appears again with a similar group, bowing with lowered staves down in Borchardt 1913: Bl. 52.

The Sahure reliefs bring together these terms: *ʿpr*-gang names, the *nfrw* youth, the *šmśw* (followings"), and the *ḫntjw-š*, all in the context of the hunt. From the same source, we find these terms together in the nautical scenes that depict expeditions such as must have brought Levantine products to the HeG.

3.7. Who Were the Handlers? Levantine Imports and the Byblos Run

In the Sahure hunt scene we see *ḫntjw-š* associated with wild animals from the Levant, such as the deer among the animals native to the Egyptian deserts.[295] Sahure's artists might have seen deer in Syria. Borchardt suggested the Egyptian hunters in Syria spared a deer and brought it back to Egypt for the royal luxury hunt, like Prussians did with elk in his day.[296] Scene fragments found near the northern side of the columned court and ambulatory show tall-necked red-painted Syrian jars with handles and bears—Asiatic booty.[297] Two of the bears are collared and tethered. Traces of the signs for *ḫntjw-š pr ʿꜣ* remain from the label for the register below, which featured a row of bowed men—the head of one remains. Borchardt suggested they must have had something to do with the presentation of the booty. These scenes have received much comment.[298]

Relief scenes from the southern end of the eastern wall of the Sahure upper temple ambulatory showed a sea-going fleet returning to Egypt with Asiatics on board.[299] Bietak argued that rather than captives, these Asiatics served Egyptian maritime trade with the Levant, and not only as ships crews. Over time they were also employed as shipwrights, carpenters, and stevedores.[300]

Of the EB III combed ware, imported from the Levant, we find only sherds from the HeG site, but they stand as some of the oldest known combed ware from a settlement site. We could too easily assume that the contents of the combed ware jars were "luxurious," and that only the wealthy or people of high status received these vessels with their contents. Most combed ware vessels have been found in the large mastaba tombs

295 Borchardt 1913: Bl. 17.

296 Borchardt 1913/1981: 33; Bietak 1988: 35, suggests these animals and products originated in Lebanon or north Syria.

297 Borchardt 1913, pl. 3. The fragment showing the tethered bears ended up in the Getty Museum (http://www.gettyimages.com/detail/news-photo/fragment-of-a-relief-from-the-cult-temple-of-sahure-it-news-photo/152196675).

298 Borchardt 1913/1981: 16. See for recent discussion, Sowada 2009: 158–160.

299 Bietak 1988; Borchardt 1913: Bl. 12, 13.

300 Bietak 1988.

of high officials in the royal cemeteries around the pyramids at Meidum, Dahshur, and Giza.[301] The importation of these vessels appears to have reached a peak in the 4th Dynasty, indicated by thirty-six out of fifty-four complete jars.[302] It should not be surprising that we find combed ware in the HeG site, for Giza was the "bulls eye" of the state in the 4th Dynasty. The attributes of combed or metallic ware jars suggest they served as the specialized "commercial maritime container" of their time, the equivalent of the Classical amphora, developed by Early Bronze Age Levantine potters "for the rigors of transport" and "long periods of time at sea."[303] The combed ware jars probably arrived filled. Resin, wine, olive oil, or olives are the most likely contents.[304] In the Levant, the association of these jars with olive production equipment—limestone basins, presses, hearths and large combed ware vats, favors olive oil as the prime content.[305]

By petrographic analysis of the clay, Mary Ownby traced the origin of eighteen combed ware sherds from HeG to the region around Byblos. Variability of the clay "may suggest several sites in the area were participating in trade with Egypt."[306] "Byblos ... was a major centre for the trade in the commodity contained inside the [combed ware] jars."[307]

Byblos served as a major entrepôt during the Old Kingdom. People at Byblos gathered goods from smaller sites upland and inland, making Byblos the main port power on the Eastern Mediterranean, linked with

301 Helck 1971: 28–37. After reviewing evidence for trade between the Eastern Mediterranean and Old Kingdom Egypt, Sowada (2009: 165) concluded, "This suggests that the [combed ware] jars and their contents did not filter beyond the court during the early Old Kingdom." However, Kantor (1992: 20) made the point twenty years ago that while most of the Syro-Palestinian pottery imported in the Old Kingdom derives from the large mastaba tombs at Giza (Reisner and Smith 1955: 62–65, 73–76, figs. 80, 95–98), these vessels and presumably their contents "were not limited to the nobility." Kantor cited the occurrence of combed ware vessels in modest graves at Saqqara (Jéquier, Youssef and Lauer 1929: 26, fig. 25) and Matmar. Wodzińska (2007: 311) gives references for additional combed ware found at Saqqara, Abusir, Abydos, Ballas and Edfu. Forstner-Müller and Raue (2008: 139) report on imported Levantine ware found in late 5th and 6th Dynasty contexts at Elephantine, of which two fragments showed a combed surface.

302 Helck 1971: 33.

303 Marcus 2002: 410–411; Sowada 2009: 180.

304 Sowada 2009: 160–161; Ownby 2012: 23, 27; Serpico *et al.* 2003.

305 Esse 1991; 119–125; Stager 1985: 176–177.

306 Ownby 2012: 24.

307 Sowada 2009: 181.

Egypt since the beginning of the dynastic era.[308] So much evidence exists for trade between Egypt and Byblos in the Old Kingdom that scholars who focus on the Levant have coined the term, "the Byblos Run."[309] They suggest that corresponding homeports must have existed somewhere on the Nile.[310]

Timber, primarily the fabled, towering cedars of Lebanon, was the Byblos resource most useful for the pyramid builders to fetch for their wood-challenged country. They could also harvest Cypress, Pine, and Oak, none of which grew in Egypt. Gerisch identified all these woods in the charcoal from HeG. But Cedar is the most the abundant imported wood in the charcoal we have sampled at HeG. Cedar occurred with a high relative frequency in the Gallery Complex,[311] for example, in every part down the entire length of Gallery III.4, which we excavated in 2002.[312]

We know that the Old Kingdom Egyptians used Cedar for ship hulls, masts, and palace doors. An oft-cited entry in the Palermo Stone annals for one year (perhaps the 13th) in the reign of Khufu's father, Sneferu, states that the Egyptians built "a 100 cubit 'Adoring the Two Lands' boat and 60 'sixteener' royal boats of Cedar" (*mr*[*w*]), and that they brought 40 ships of *ash* (*ʿš*) wood.[313] The 4th Dynasty builders used Cedar in pyramid building. A cedar-beam frame remains in the upper, western chamber of Sneferu's Bent Pyramid at Dahshur.[314] Gerisch identified Cedar among wood fragments from excavations through the builders' dumps to the northwest of the Khufu Pyramid.[315]

In recent years archaeologists have excavated galleries and settlements at proven ports on the western Red Sea and Suez Gulf coasts. These ports served as nodes on a greater, interregional network, like Elephantine and the Middle Egyptian and Delta sites, that supported the 4th Dynasty state and its colossal pyramid building projects.[316] These ports include galleries

[308] Stager 2001.

[309] Fragments of Egyptian stone vessels at Byblos include the names of the Old Kingdom rulers Khufu, Khafre, Sahure, Neferirkare, Niuserre, Isesi, Unis, Teti, Pepi I, Merenre I and Pepi II (Kantor 1992: 21).

[310] Marcus 2002: 409.

[311] Gerisch 2008.

[312] Aeragram 6.1: 4–5.

[313] Wilkinson 2000: 140–143. Some understand *ʿš* to be Cedar, others Fir or Juniper or coniferous wood in general.

[314] Fakhry 1959: 52–59, figs. 20–24, pls.11–14; Lehner 1998: 109, fig. 3.

[315] Gerisch 2012: 50, tb. 3.1. The so-called Rowad Trench after the name of the contracting firm that excavated this trench in which the tourist entrance complex was built in 2003–2004.

[316] Moreno García 2013: 87–105.

and other major attributes similar to the HeG site and its Gallery Complex.[317] Two of the Red Sea port settlements, Ayn Sukhna[318] and Wadi el-Jarf,[319] date back to the Old Kingdom. The Wadi el-Jarf port dates to the early 4th Dynasty, so it is nearly contemporary with the HeG. The most recent discoveries show it to have been active in the reign of Khufu. In the middle of the sandy plain of Wadi el-Jarf the French team found "the largest Pharaonic building discovered to date along the Red Sea coast."[320] This building, 30×60 m, resembles the blocks of galleries at HeG and it is of comparable size. Also, the "13 elongated rooms" of this building resemble in their proportions the individual Giza galleries, except they are formed of dry stone rather than mudbrick. The French-Egyptian team is also said to have excavated workers houses. They have begun to publish details about papyri documents relating to building operations of the Khufu pyramid during the 27th year of that king's reign (see above, section 3.16).[321]

When he analyzed charcoal from the Middle Kingdom, 12th Dynasty, port at Wadi Gawasis,[322] Gerisch found, as at Giza, most of it was native Egyptian wood: Acacia, Sycamore, Tamarisk and Mangrove (the latter two probably local to Wadi Gawasis). But Cedar, which here too must have originated in Lebanon, was the second or third most abundant.[323]

A big difference between Gawasis and Giza is that the Gawasis environment allowed wood itself to be preserved. The team recovered thousands of wood fragments, over 40 wooden cargo boxes and disassembled ship timbers, including more than 100 hull components,[324] as well as coils of rope stored in a gallery.[325] Some of the wood pieces had also been left for storage in the galleries. In addition, the Gawasis excavators found many wood chips and fragments, left "when ancient workers disassembled ships whose shipworm-riddled timbers suggest substantial sea journeys."[326] Shipwrights had trimmed and cleaned the

[317] Manzo 2010.
[318] Tallet 2012.
[319] Tallet and Marouard 2012: 41; Tallet, Marouard and Laisney 2012; Tallet 2013.
[320] Tallet and Marouard 2012: 40 plan, 43.
[321] First announced, *Ahram Online* (http://english.ahram.org.eg/) April 12, 2013. Now see Tallet and Marouard 2014; Tallet forthcoming.
[322] Bard and Fattovich 2007; 2010; 2011; Bard, Fattovich and Ward 2011.
[323] Gerisch 2007: 170–175; 2011.
[324] Ward 2012: 222; Ward and Zazzaro 2009.
[325] Veldmeijer *et al.* 2008; Borojevic and Mountain 2011.
[326] Ward 2012: 221.

parts. Ancient expedition members then used scrap wood to fuel hearths, converting it to charcoal, sometimes for warmth or for cooking inside the galleries. It is clear that the Gawasis gallery occupants, in addition to scrap wood trimmings, also burnt ship timbers in hearths within the galleries,[327] perhaps after they had been used as gallery flooring, and then deteriorated irreparably.

The cedar charcoal at HeG might similarly result from inhabitants trimming and reworking ships parts, and reusing the scrap as fuel in hearths. They might have also incorporated, as at Gawasis, wooden planks into the thresholds, floors, or upper reaches of the galleries and other buildings in the HeG. This may be why we find cedar residues in the charcoal almost everywhere we have excavated down to gallery floors.

4. HeG as a Port Settlement: Implications for Labor Organization

Marcus reasoned that Levantine ports, especially Byblos as the "principal partner port of Egypt in the Old Kingdom," would have counterparts in "sophisticated ports and anchorages, such as the Old Kingdom basins at Giza and Saqqara."[328] For two, possibly three generations, the HeG site must have flanked *the* major Egyptian home port of the Byblos and Aswan runs, perhaps comparable for its time to the known Nile ports of the Second Intermediate Period and New Kingdom at Tell el-Daba and Memphis.[329]

Instead of a "city of the workers" only, we should see the HeG site and the Gallery Complex as a major part of a larger port city to which goods were brought for import and distribution, the receiving end of Levantine trade, as well as the receiving end for calcite alabaster from Middle Egypt, granite from Aswan, and products from farther south including from the land of Punt. On this hypothesis, is it possible the inhabitants of the various parts of the site occasionally enjoyed some of the spoils?

Wodzińska suggested that the combed ware came into HeG because the site served for temporary storage and transfer.[330] In other words, the HeG was an *entrepôt*. Traces of this and other Levantine products at the

[327] Bard and Fattovich 2010: 7.

[328] Marcus 2002: 409.

[329] Jeffreys 1996: 292–294. Bietak (2005) and Jeffreys (2006) weigh the evidence as to whether Avaris/Piramesse (Tell el-Daba-Qantir) or Memphis hosted the New Kingdom river port, naval stronghold, and harbor town named Perunefer ("the Good Going Forth").

[330] Wodzińska 2007: 313.

HeG suggest these products were delivered and stored here, with some ultimately going into elite Giza tombs. Structures where shipments can be immediately and temporarily stored before distribution are a standard feature of ports. The long galleries could well have served in part as warehouses for some of these goods.

4.1. Expeditionary Template: Parallels with Proven Ports

Comparable features at the ancient Red Sea ports of Mersa Gawasis, Ayn Sukhna and Wadi el-Jarf[331] reveal, in spite of differences of date, setting and material, a *transpatial* template of infrastructure for an expeditionary force[332] like that of an army making camp after a march. No matter what the location or topography, the army sets up camp with "a clear set of instructions" so that "the army camp model means a highly structured organization which will be reduplicated in other army camps."[333] As part of a major Nile port, we should consider the HeG as the footprint of a formal and long-term expeditionary force. Troop members may have resided at HeG for long-term, in rotation, or semi-permanently over some thirty-five to fifty years, whereas full occupation at the Red Sea ports may have been episodic.[334] Still, certain similarities and common components must reflect standard practices when the royal house mounted expeditions or mobilized labor for special purposes.

Seeing the HeG as an expeditionary template requires that we also reconsider the categories and status of people who lived and worked here. Men, perhaps many young recruits (*nfrw*), who traveled abroad for wood and other products comprised expeditionary forces.[335] They and their goods must have traveled and stayed together until they had reached their final destination. Thus we can imagine that the galleries also housed crews along with wood, pottery, and olive oil, and other products they had procured. To the extent that the Gallery Complex served as barracks, we should consider that this substantial investment in mudbrick architecture sheltered members of nautical crews, or the royal guard of such crews, *"des Haupttruppenhafen*."[336]

[331] Manzo 2010; Lehner 2013: 5.
[332] Eichler 1993: 157–258.
[333] Hillier and Hanson 1984: 38–40.
[334] Eichler 1993: 149–151.
[335] Eyre 1987: 19; Eichler 1993: 81, 85, Nos. 154, 168–169, 181–184.
[336] Bietak 1988: 39.

4.2. HeG and the Sahure Scenes: Bringing All Together

We could take heuristically many of the scenes in the Sahure pyramid temples and causeway as a pictorial of principal activities in the HeG site, in the basin and delivery zone to the north of the Wall of the Crow, and on the riverbank and inlet some 250 m to the east of the site. Scenes from the Sahure pyramid complex show nautical crews of ships of state and escort boats bearing the same gang names as found in workers graffiti on the monuments. In these scenes crews, apparently nautical, and workers compete in rowing, wrestling, and archery.[337]

Again we must acknowledge that a narrative of specific events is not the sole or even the primary purpose of tomb chapel and temple scenes, but such scenes must contain information on actual experience.[338] In order to emerge and function as symbols and icons, the attributes of such scenes must have appeared at some point in everyday life, that is, "although highly symbolic, they must on some level refer to reality."[339] As an overarching, granted bold, hypothesis—again for the sake of heuristics, we consider that relief scenes from the Sahure complex present formal, pictorial and textual expressions of groups and their activities that 4th Dynasty regimes organized at the base of the Giza Plateau, in particular, alongside and south of the central Giza basin and south and east of the Wall of the Crow.

What are the putative larger events of the recently published Sahure causeway scenes? It is the completion of the king's pyramid by the dragging and setting of the capstone (pyramidion) with a celebration of

337 The inner walls of Sahure's pyramid temples and causeway are thought to have originally displayed 10,000 m² of scenes in fine, painted raised relief carving. We knew some broad strokes of that program from Borchardt's (1913, 1913/1981) publications. More relief scenes from the causeway came to light during excavations of the Supreme Council of Antiquities between 1994 and 2004 (El-Awady 2009: 121–130; Hawass and Verner 1996).

338 There is a sizeable bibliography on the issue of the "objective reality" of ancient Egyptian scenes and representations for a number of themes. See, for example, Arnold 2005: 46–48; Adams 2007; Samuel 1993.

339 Graf, Eyckerman, and Hendrickx 2011: 455. El Awady (2009: 43–85), grapples with the issue of narrative in the Sahure scenes and the distinction between oft-repeated leitmotifs comprising "program" and scenes that represent unique historical events, or between tradition and narrative, which need not be mutually exclusive in that Egyptian artists could fit actual events into archetypical themes. Baines (2009: 138–139), while expressing caution against "any simple reading of the decoration" in tomb and temple scenes, does note the correspondence between ceramic vessels depicted in tomb scenes and the actual vessels found in settlement and cemetery sites.

feasting, singing, and dancing as well as (concomitant with?) the arrival at homeport of an expedition to the southern land of Punt with incense trees (Frankincense or Myrrh) to be received by the king and his family.

4.2.1. Royal Escort and Guard Forces: *Šmsw* and *Ḫntjw-š*

The recently found Sahure reliefs convey more scenes of young men in formations, like those of the royal guard in the scenes of the royal hunt (see section 3.6). One scene depicts royal sailing boats.[340] In the register below, and in two upper sub-registers between the two royal ships, rows of men run to greet the boats at the moment of arrival. They are labeled *šmsw pr-njswt,* Retainers, or Followers of the Royal House," and *šmsw ḏbꜣt,* "Followers of the Changing (or Robing) Room." Here, too, appear the *Ḫntjw-š* of the royal house (*pr-ꜥꜣ*). El-Awady notes that these "running sailors" are similar to those shown in other scenes of Sahure and in Old Kingdom non-royal tombs, except here they wear kilts and hold batons instead of loin cloths and coiled rope, and they lack the "gang" or "crew" determinative, *ꜥpr*. These are "troops of soldiers of the royal escort,"[341] and we note again, as in Sahure's royal hunt, this guard force includes the *Ḫntjw-š*.[342]

Scenes of young men in gangs, crews, and troops in rank and file belonging to the escort, bodyguard, and the military section of the royal suite were much pictured in pyramid complexes perhaps as early as Khufu. We know this, in part, from fragments of relief decoration from Old Kingdom pyramid temples that 12th Dynasty builders incorporated into the pyramid superstructure of Amenemhet I. Hans Goedicke brought together a number of these fragments under the heading, "royal suite."[343]

[340] El-Awady 2009: 140, n. 906 pl. 1, translates "Retainers of the Divine Mansion." The somewhat problematic title, *šmsw ḏbꜣt* was known previously from scene fragments of the Niuserre pyramid temple (Goelet 182: 589; Jones 2000, 993, nos. 3669, 3678),

[341] El-Awady 2009: 141, n. 909, n. 911. The troops cited in section 3.6 belonging to a scene from the Sahure Valley Temple are labeled "Escort (*rꜣ-šmś*) of Gangs of Young Recruits *nfrw*)." They march in a register just below the great ship of state; Borchardt 1913, Bl. 9.

[342] To reiterate, Kanawati 2003: 14–24 comes to the conclusion the *Khentiu-she* of the living king served him as palace guards.

[343] Goedicke 1971. The troops in these scenes are not labeled *Setep-Za,* but from other contexts, titles like *ỉmy-*[*rꜣ wỉꜣ*] *nb-śtp-zꜣ*, "Overseer of the Bark, Lord of Protection," or "Overseer of all Barks of the *Setep-Za,*" and *ỉmy-rꜣ wꜥb*(*w*) *n tpw wỉꜣ nbw m Nb-śtp-zꜣ* "Overseer of the Wab-Priests of the foremost barks of the *Setep-Za*," attest the association of ships and their crews with the *Setep Za* (Jones 2000: 83–86).

4.2.2. Arriving at the Pyramid: Expeditionary Forces

The recently discovered Sahure causeway blocks include parts of a scene depicting the return of an expedition from Punt on the southern Red Sea coast,[344] an event documented in the Palermo Stone for the last year of Sahure's reign.[345] The arrival of such expeditions can be added to the mix of activities that might have taken place in the HeG at the low southeastern access to the Giza Plateau some thirty years, one generation, before Sahure.

We see four sea going cargo ships, and the rear end of a fifth. Two men on the prow of one ship are labeled "Overseer of the Prospectors," (*jmỉ-rꜣ smntjw*)[346] Menia, and "Overseer of the Quarry Work," (*ỉmj-rꜣ mr*),[347] Kaaper.[348] These titles suggest that Sahure's Punt expedition sought not only the incense trees and people shown in these scenes, but also stones and minerals.[349] El-Awady identifies this Kaaper with the man who held the

[344] El-Awady 2009: 155–161, pl. 5.

[345] Wilkinson 2000: 169–170.

[346] Jones 2000: 228–229, no. 846.

[347] Jones 2000: 139, no. 541, 243, no. 889 (*jmj-rꜣ š*);

[348] El Awady 2009: 157, pl. 5.

[349] The newly found scenes show Sahure receiving Frankincense trees brought by this Punt expedition, perhaps the most prized cargo (El-Awady 2009: 155–163, pl. 5). Given this and other evidence that the Old Kingdom Egyptians took pains to "capture" and deliver exotic trees, just as they did wild animals, we should at least consider whether the presence of olive wood on the HeG reflects an attempted transplantation. A scene in the 5th Dynasty tomb of *Ni-ankh-khnum* and *Khnum-hotep* depicts men picking fruit from non-native trees alongside the harvest of a fig tree, which was native to Egypt. On the right, the label reads *wḥꜣ prt-šnỉ*, "picking *šnỉ* fruit," otherwise unknown from Old Kingdom tombs (Moussa and Altenmüller 1977: 111, fig. 15). Papyrus Ebers indicates *prt-šnỉ*, with medicinal qualities, derives from Byblos. Sowada (2009: 197) suggested "the species in the relief may have been imported as a tree from Byblos or grown in Egypt from seeds or cuttings that were sourced from that city." Already in the early 4th Dynasty, Sneferu was shown in the reliefs of his lower pyramid temple inspecting his fresh pine (ꜥš) and myrrh (ꜥ(*n*)*tjw*) trees growing or producing fruit (Edel 1996: 199–203, fig. 1). Herb and Förster (2009: 20–22, fig. 3–A/B) note that this composition compliments a scene of Sneferu "Inspecting the corrals of the living antelopes" (Edel 1996: 206–208, fig. 4). The complimentary scenes represent floral and faunal exotic to the Nile Valley floor, transplanted for Sneferu. Hatshepsut's importation of non-native incense trees from her expedition to Punt is well known (Naville 1898: Pls. LXIX–LXXVI), but also the subject of much debate as to whether the incense trees are frankincense or myrrh (Serpico 2000: 438). It may have been easier to import, transplant, and possibly cultivate resinous trees than to import and cultivate olive trees. Olive seeds are low in germination rates and are very slow to grow (Serpico and White: 2000: 399 citing Zohary and Hopf 1993: 135–138). Olive trees may take 10 to 20 years to fruit (Serpico and White, 399–400 with references).

title, "Overseer of the Expedition" or "Overseer of the Army" (*ỉmj-rȝ mšʿ*), as well as titles connected with boats, and who was buried at Giza south of the Khafre pyramid causeway.[350] The Giza Kaaper may also be the son of the Kaaper buried at Abusir, who rose from Cadet, *nfr*, to "Overseer of the Expedition" (or army) and "Overseer of All Works of the King" (see section 3.5).[351] With his tomb dated to the early 5th Dynasty, the Abusir Kaaper (senior) may have very well walked the HeG, because he must have begun his career decades before he had his titles inscribed in his memorial chapel.

The cargo on two of the vessels returning from Punt incudes 24 people: men, women, and children with distinctive features from Punt, as well as Egyptians who stand above the Puntites and in six cases place a hand or fist on the heads of the foreigners to force them to bow. The ship's crews definitely act as police and guards over Puntites. Dogs and baboons, both of which may have been used to guard or police,[352] are tethered to the lowered masts of the ships. Egyptians and Puntites alike raise one or both arms up to the direction of the king, shown large in the upper register using an adze to scrape the branches of an imported incense tree to let out the resin.

We will consider these Puntites with other evidence that the Old Kingdom Egyptians captured people and cattle, as well as trees and wild animals, in terms of the overall labor for building pyramids (section 5.2).

4.2.3. Finishing the Pyramid: *ʿpr*-Gangs and Workers

An important point for labor organization is that we find the same *ʿpr*-gang names on relief-decorated blocks, such as those from Sahure causeway and temples, and in builders' graffiti.[353] Ships and their crews comprise a dominant theme. Remains of one Sahure causeway scene show two royal ships accompanied by a fleet of more than nine smaller boats.

[350] El-Awady (2009: 157); Hassan 1936: 155–158. The Giza Kaaper was probably the man of the same name who was "Overseer of the Expedition" in a graffito in the Wadi Hamammat (Fischer 1959a: 254–255).

[351] Fischer 1959; Bárta 2001: 143–191.

[352] Baboons and a monkey on leashes appear in the market scene from the tomb of Niankhkhnum and Khnumhotep at Saqqara (Moussa and Altenmüller 1977: 81–82; Tf. 27, Abb. 10, n. 362 for further references).

[353] Verner 2003: 446. Andrássy 2009: 3 cites Reisner 1931: plan XI, no. ix for the sign of a ship (*wiȝ*) following the *ʿpr* sign in the gang name, "Dunkards of Menkaure." Andrássy reads *ʿpr wiȝ*, "Ship's Crew" or "Crew of the Fleet." This graffito was among those on the large limestone core blocks of the Menkaure Pyramid Temple.

Labels name each boat, such as "Sahure's Palace" (*ʿḥ S3hw-R3*) for one of the escort boats with another name for each crew. The crew names are what I have been calling *ʿpr*-gangs, with the gang-sign as determinative. For example, the crew *ʿpr Śmr(w) S3hw-[R3]*, "Crew (or Gang) of the Companions of Sahure," appears above the deck of one of the royal ships for which the king himself maneuvers the sail. El-Awady points out that the boat crews (= *ʿpr*-gangs) included personnel on the ground, apparently receiving the boat.[354] In one case five men who run behind an escort boat, two of whom carry coils of rope, are named after the Horus-name of the king, "Crew (*jst*) of the Gang (*ʿpr*) of Horus, Neb-kha'u."[355]

Here the same *ʿpr*-gangs known from building works are most explicitly nautical, as Egyptologists have thought about the phyles. Yet we do not see in these scenes any breakdown into phyles.[356]

Seeing the possibilities that inhabitants of the Gallery Complex included members of royal guard forces, expeditionary troops, and/or nautical crews does not negate the additional possibility that many of them labored in the most basic skills and exertions to build pyramids and temples. Studies of Nile navigation through time show that it involved much punting, pushing, and towing from the banks, the same basic exercise needed to drag stone blocks for building pyramids, tombs, and temples.[357]

In fact, one of the Sahure scenes shows nautical crews dragging the very capstone to finish off Sahure's pyramid. Three blocks preserve part of this larger scene, which was divided into five horizontal registers. The second register from the top shows the dragging of the pyramidion capstone to crown and complete Sahure's pyramid with an accompanying feast and celebration.[358] Here is the culmination of very same kind of mission—obtaining an apex stone, that Weni accomplished generations later when he went south to quarry and obtain a pyramidion for Merenre (see section 3.3). Twenty-six men of a nautical crew pull on the rope to drag the pyramidion. Although we are missing the pyramidion on its sledge, the label makes explicit the object of the scene: "(Bringing) the white gold pyramidion of the pyramid 'Sahure's Soul Shines' by the two crews (*ʿprwj*) of the two boats (*wj3(wj)*)."[359] Facing the load, high-ranking

[354] El-Awady 2009: 206, n. 1171.
[355] El-Awady 2009: 146, pl. 2.
[356] El-Awady 2009: 206, n. 1171.
[357] Cooper 2012: 26–27.
[358] El-Awady 2009: 186–205, pls. 9–11; Hawass and Verner 1996: 181–186.
[359] El-Awady 2009: 192.

individuals stand between the pullers and the pyramidion, beside a man pouring water to slicken the way of the load, which must have been conveyed on a wooden sledge. One of the men is labeled Ptahshepses, perhaps the famous Ptahshepses, owner of one of the largest non-royal tombs at Abusir, who rose to become Vizier.[360] It is possible that the complete scene showed the king himself present. The identity of the pullers as a ship's crew is determined, among other things, by the pair who do "the dance of pulling the rope" (*ṯrf jṯt*) as they hold the lead-end of the rope. El-Awady cites an inscription in the Saqqara tomb of Akhethotep where the dance refers to the sledge as a boat: "Behold the dance of pulling the boat" (*wjꜣ*).[361] Also, between the pullers and the pyramidion, four men clap, probably to keep the rhythm of the pull. They are labeled "Singers of the Boat."[362]

Dancers and bowing men labeled *šms*(*w*) *nfrw* and *šmsw* (*njw*) *pr ꜥꜣ* ("a following of young recruits," or "young retainers" and "retainers of the Great House")—again, a royal guard, preceed the train pulling the pyramidion. The *šmsw* also form a vanguard for those of the royal household (*pr*(*ỉw*) *ꜥꜣ*) who are carrying the funerary furniture in the third register down. At the head of this guard, we see more dancers. At the head of men carrying fowl and bread in the fourth register, we find again the ships crews, the *ꜥpr*-gangs, named after the king. A long row of bowing men on the right of the lowest register are labeled as another of the *ꜥpr*-gangs, or ships crews, "Sahure's Noblemen." This group is also labeled *šmsw pr-ꜥꜣ*, "Retainers of the Great House." A third label identifies this group as *ḫntjw-š pr-ꜥꜣ*, the *Khentiu-she* of the Great House." As with Sahure's hunt scenes, all these terms, royal guard, *ꜥpr*-gang, and *ḫntjw-š*, designate the same company of men.[363]

Another of the newly discovered blocks from the Sahure causeway bears a scene of young men receiving lessons in archery, fighting with sticks, wrestling, and rowing boats.[364] Such scenes of military activity must have been common in Old Kingdom pyramid temples judging from the fragments reused in the core of the Amenemhet I pyramid.[365] These are

[360] El-Awady 2009: 193, n. 1127. Of the name, only the last part, *Špss*, remains. Krejcí 2009: 40; 2010: 194.

[361] El-Awady 2009: 191, n. 1120; Ziegler 1993: 114; 2007: 89, fig. 34.

[362] All who work in Egypt are familiar with the chanting and singing of workers as they pull or maneuver heavy loads, or carry baskets of sand and soil.

[363] El-Awady 2009: 204–205.

[364] El-Awady 2009: 206–214, pl. 12.

[365] Goedicke 1971: 62–63 (nos. 34–36), 66–67 (no. 41), 74–77 (no. 43) for archers.

the royal versions of young men of the estate shown in officials tombs wrestling and playing games, like the scene in the Saqqara tomb of Ptahhotep (section 3.6). El-Awady sees the wrestling and rowing scenes from the Sahure causeway as a competition between the *ʿpr*-gang, "Companions (*śmrw*) of Sahure," and another group designated as *m jrjww ἰḫt,* which El-Awady translates as "workers." If this is the correct understanding, we would have workers so-designated competing with the (higher status?) members of an *ʿpr*-gang and ship's crew.[366]

The very bottom register of this block shows a procession of named minor officials, followed by another *ʿpr*-gang, named *ʿpr ἰst S3ḥw-Rʿ*, ("The Crew of Sahure"). At the front of this group we see again the label, *r3-šmsw nfrw,* ("Escort," literally, "a following of youth" or "of young recruits") as also found in front of running men below the ship of state on a scene from the Sahure Valley Temple. The same compound term labels young men who receive rewards in a scene from the upper temple (see section 3.6).[367]

In his early assessment of these scenes, Verner affirmed: *"The inscriptions accompanying the scenes leave no doubt that in the ceremonies and games were engaged the same men from work crews who had previously been engaged on building the pyramid,"*[368] and "… the scenes from Sahura's mortuary temple and, especially those on the recently discovered blocks from the king's causeway indicate how broad and versatile was the function of the crews; they could have worked on the building site, brought the pyramidion from a distant quarry in the desert, operated a sea going ship, taken part in the ceremonies and games following the conclusion of the pyramid's construction, etc."[369]

The fact that the same gang-name or epithet, like *śmrw,* "Friends," or "Companions," can be compounded with the name of a number of kings, from Khufu to Menkaure to Niuserre and Raneferef, indicates for Verner that the gangs were permanent in the Memphite area. The *ʿpr*-gang formations, like modern military units, remained from one administration to another, while succeeding generations of recruits passed through in periods of service.

[366] But the signs transcribed *m jrjww ḫt* are damaged and unclear. El-Awady 2009: 210, n. 1178 cites Edel 1955: 100 §230 for *jrjww ἰḫt* as "workers." Hannig 2003: 163 translates *jrj-ἰḫt* "Aufseher, Verwalter, Sachverwalter."

[367] Goedicke 1971: 71; Junker 1941. In the valley temple, the label reads *r3 šmś n nfr-ʿprw* (Borchardt 1913: pls. 9, 52), literally, "A Following of Gangs of Young Recruits."

[368] Verner 2003: 446, emphasis mine.

[369] Verner 2003: 449; and see Verner 2006: 201.

4.2.4. Of Feast and Famine: Starving Foreigners

The scene of dragging the pyramidion depicts a celebratory feast that ensues,[370] perhaps a special feast out of the many regular feasts that we know so well from tomb and temple texts, a kind of work feast.[371] We see racks of hanging meat, to be shared and consumed for the occasion. We might think of such feasting in terms of our evidence for an abundance of cattle, sheep, and goat consumed at the Lost City, and consider that "workers' town" and "port city" of the pyramids may not have been mutually exclusive.

The uppermost register depicts an abundance of processed food of all kinds, mats and baskets piled high with fruits and vegetables, caged and trussed poultry, carinated bowls (casseroles) of (stewed?) meat, and racks of hanging meat. In the fourth register down from the top, men slaughter and butcher oxen.

The feasting scene provides one very striking contrast that leads our thoughts in the direction of the final the topic of this paper, captive labor (part 2). At the bottom right of the scene of celebration and feasting on the occasion of the pyramid's completion we find eleven starving foreigners, of which two are women. These famished people occupy two subregisters in the far right of what is preserved of the lowest register, so that the whole of the ritual act of dragging the pyramidion, the celebration, the feast and the abundance of food rises above them.[372]

The Sahure scene of famished foreigners is similar to a scene from the causeway of the Unas pyramid at Saqqara,[373] which depicts emaciated men and women, including one family and a child. It had been suggested that the Unas scene reflects royal generosity toward marginal, nomadic people during a time of ecological stress. Schott looked closely at the details of the scene, and made much of the titles preserved in what remains of the top of the register immediately under the stressed, starving figures: *šmsw pr ꜥꜣ* ("Followers of the Palace"), *ḫntjw-š pr ꜥꜣ* ("Foremost of the

[370] El-Awady 2009: 187–189, pls. 9–11.

[371] Dietler and Herbich 2001. Another of the newly found Sahure scenes shows a banquet in the king's presence at which overseers of sculptors and craftsmen eat poultry, fruits and vegetables and drink beer, El-Awady 2009: 174–177, pl. 6.

[372] El-Awady 2009: 202–204, fig. 93, pl. 9; Hawass and Verner 1996: 185, fig. 22a.

[373] Hassan 1955; Drioton 1942–43; Labrouse and Moussa 2002: 85–86, figs. 117–118.

Basin or Precinct"), and *iry mḏ3t pr* ꜥ*3* ("Archivist of the Palace").[374] Schott points out that these titles must have labeled a row of men directly below.

As we have seen, guard troops, with variations on the title *šmsw* (followers) + *pr* ꜥ*3* (literally, Great House—the palace) were much represented in scenes of the royal suite in pyramid temples and causeways.[375] While noting the origin of the title *ḫntj-š* as people occupying land fronting the pyramid complex, Schott lays out the involvement of the *ḫntjw-š* with the royal escort, guard, and, drawing on the biography of 6th Dynasty Weni, who became Overseer of the *Ḫntjw-š* under Pepi I, leadership of expeditions with responsibilities for enforcing discipline.[376] He sees the titles *šmsw pr* ꜥ*3* and *ḫntjw-š* in the Unas "famine scene" as the forces sent on order of the palace, documented by the palace archivist, to help a tribe on Egypt's borders. This royal force then reported back on their commission.

Once again I invoke Kanawati's suggestion that *ḫntj*, literally, "one who is in front of," connotes "watcher," "escort," or "guard (see section 3.6)."[377] He built on Schott's delineation of the *ḫntjw-š* as royal escorts in military campaigns, celebrations, transportation, and hunts to suggest the that "guard" should be the essential translation and understanding of the title, *ḫntj-š*.

Hawass and Verner point out that the caption above the emaciated foreigners in the Sahure scene, which mentions the pyramidion (*bnbnt*) and so probably the celebration of its placement, puts the interpretation of the king feeding starving Bedouins in doubt—as should the overall context of foreigners starving in the midst of Egyptians feasting:[378] The caption reads: "… pyramidion in the Three Great Halls very much" (*[bnb]nt m ḥwwt wrt* ꜥ*3 wrt*).[379] The *ḥwwt wrt*, literally something like "great mansions" or "great administrative districts" or "great estates," served as courts of law and justice or ministries.[380] Behind the emaciated foreigners in the Sahure scene stand six named men who bow. They bear the title, *z3b*, which means essentially, "bailiff."[381] Their full titles read:

374 Schott 1965.
375 Goedicke 171: 56–77
376 Schott 1965: 11–12.
377 Kanawati 2003: 14–24.
378 Hawass and Verner 1996: 184.
379 El-Awady 2009: 202, pl. 9.
380 Hannig 2003: 783–784; Faulkner 1962/1996: 165.
381 Goedicke 1971: 72–73.

smsw hꜣjt (n) zꜣb, "Elder of the Hall of the Judiciary."[382] Like the later scene from the Unas causeway, the artists put the emaciated foreigners next to titles related to guarding and judging.

Hawass and Verner suggested that the emaciated Bedouin served as some referent to hardships the Egyptians faced in the mountainous desert zone whence they extracted the suitable hard stone for the pyramidion.[383] El-Awady noted that these famished Bedouin come before depictions of the judicial officials (the bowing men in the lower register to the left).[384] In the east to west sequence of the northern causeway wall the Bedouin and judicial officials follow troops of soldiers and guards who are labeled—as in the Unas Bedouin scene—*šmsw pr-ꜥꜣ* and *ẖntjw-š*. El-Awady suggested that the emaciated foreigners were being punished, "that the Bedouins were captured when they tried to attack the king's expedition sent to find the stone of the pyramidion …" and that "they were denied food as a form of punishment while they were being escorted to the royal residence," and, we might ask, in the midst of food abundance and feasting as the pyramid triumphantly reached its apex with the setting of the capstone that they themselves might have been pressed to quarry? Note that Weni, when he was sent to Ibhat (Elephantine and perhaps Toshka) to obtain granite for the royal sarcophagus, false door, jambs and lintels, as well as a pyramidion for the pyramid of Merenre, employed the service of "the rulers of those foreign lands of Irtjet, Wawat, Iam and Medja" to excavate canals, cut wood, construct barges,[385] and possibly to quarry the granite, though the later task is not specifically stated.

If a royal guard (*šmsw pr ꜥꜣ*), elite *ꜥpr*-gangs, or the *ẖntjw-š* occupied the HeG, it might make more sense of the exotic materials like Olive, Cedar or other Levantine wood, oil jars, the relative abundance of cattle, sheep and goat, and hunted game, especially the hippopotamus, as well as making sense of the colossal investment in mudbrick structures across five hectares, than if the occupants were common workers and the site was only a "workers camp."

This brings us to the question, if it was the *ꜥprw*-crews as elite troops who occupied the HeG and its Gallery Complex,[386] and if they were separate from more numerous masses of pyramid builders,[387] what people

[382] Jones 2000: 904 no. 3317.
[383] Hawass and Verner 1996: 184.
[384] El-Awady 2009: 204.
[385] Strudwick 2005: 356–357, n. 256.
[386] Andrássy 2009a: 3.
[387] Verner 1991: 69–72.

comprised those masses, and where were they accommodated at the construction site? This also brings up alternative answers to the first of these questions: foreign captives or native corvée. Egyptologists find the first option fairly explicit in textual sources, while evidence for systemic corvée of native Egyptians remains indirect and vague.

PART II

5. Corvée vs. Captives

In his review of labor on early, large Old Kingdom construction sites, Verner delineates three basic groups. I have touched on two in relation to the HeG site, the *ꜥpr*-gangs (or crews) and the specialists in hard stone quarrying and craftwork. Verner distinguishes these from the "beschäftigten Massen."[388] If the first two groups worked fulltime and enjoyed a better-than average status, we are then still left to ask about the greater numbers of workers, their recruitment, rotation, and accommodation at the building sites.

Verner wrote that organization for the broad mass of workers on large building projects is unknown. A set organizational structure may not have obtained, given the idea that the numbers of workers must have changed as the character and amount of work changed over the course of a building project like the pyramids. Verner suggested: "Ein Organisationssystem und eine genaue Kontrolle der Arbeitsleistung dieser Massen wäre für die Bauorganisatoren wohl eine administrativ zu große Belastung und in der Praxis kaum durchführbar gewesen."[389] These thoughts might pertain to the gigantic 4th Dynasty pyramids, where *ꜥpr*-gangs and craftsmen crews may not have sufficed. But consider that on a low estimate of 2,000 total workers required,[390] even for the gigantic pyramids, 12 to 13 *ꜥpr*-gangs of 160 would suffice.

Verner accepts the estimate of Borchardt and Croon for the total numbers required to build the early large 4th Dynasty pyramids, from 10,000 (Meidum) to 36,000 (Khufu).[391] If so, more people than in a

[388] Verner 1991: 72–79, and following suite, Andrássy 2009a: 2–6.

[389] Verner 1991: 71–72, n. 21. Verner 1991: 69–70 gives references for a range of estimates for total numbers of pyramid workers.

[390] Lehner 1997: 224–225.

[391] Borchardt and Croon 1937. Stadelmann 1985: 228 and Arnold 1983: 1 tend toward such numbers.

dozen ꜥpr-gangs would be needed. Even on the low estimate, many more workers were required for carrying gypsum and water (to make mortar), wood for sledges and levers, as well as wood fuel for making mortar. People would be needed to carry and dump debris for raising ramps and for clearing stone cutting waste, as well as support industries like baking, brewing butchering.

5.1. No Regular Corvée?

It is sometimes simply assumed that to make up broad masses for pyramid building the state commandeered Egyptians in a national, out-of-home-district corvée, an enlistment that utilized customary, obligatory labor,[392] along the lines of military service.[393]

Other scholars who survey Egyptian labor conclude we have no evidence of a regular, systemic corvée in ancient Egypt. Some see Pharaonic administration as largely ad-hoc,[394] precluding a regular-timed, cyclical draft of the entire population. No set Old Kingdom administrative structure is apparent below the title Overseer of Works or its variants; certainly none for agriculture,[395] probably because agricultural and irrigation works were largely under local management.[396] The lack of a structured works "department" may be due to the "absence of an independent military corporation," and the fact that authorities mounted expeditions and military campaigns on an ad hoc basis.[397] The same lack of a clear Old Kingdom administrative hierarchy or pattern is true for other "offices" indicated by titles.[398] Kemp noted the absence of an abstract concept of administration and observed:

> The workings of Egyptian administration are another example of self-organization, of a system evolving its coherence through innumerable

[392] For example, see general statements by Assmann 1996/2002: 53–54; Redford 1993: 51; Loprieno 1997: 192. In his earlier review of labor organization, Eyre 1987a: 18 stated, "the mass of people needed on any project can only have been provided by corvée, compulsory conscription or national service, but information is sparse and mostly indirect."

[393] Goelet, this volume, for characterizations of the idea of a national corvée.

[394] Moreno García 2013a: 111, 118–120, 142; Moreno García 2013b.

[395] Strudwick 1985: 247–248.

[396] Eyre 1987: 18; Lehner 2000: 310–314.

[397] Spalinger 2013: 462–463.

[398] Moreno García 2013a: 111, 120, 142; Moreno García 2013b.

> local adjustments to circumstances, the 'checks and balances' process which prevents societies, for most of the time, from straying far from a common path.[399]

When they write of corvée in the Old Kingdom, Egyptologists invoke royal decrees that exempt certain temple and pyramid town personnel from labor and property tax.[400] They also refer to the texts on shabtis, which were funerary servant statuettes that took the form of mummies (to indicate transposition to the world beyond death). Shabtis came inscribed with a spell that referred to obligatory agricultural work and to labor to control the inundation, which the shabti servant would carry out as deputy of the deceased.[401] These sources provide evidence for corvée in the negative sense that obligatory labor is avoided through exemption or substitution.[402]

The shabti and its spell begin to appear only in the 12th Dynasty, Middle Kingdom, but Roth developed the idea that the shabtis replaced the function of servants and workers depicted in Old Kingdom tomb scenes, wooden models, and limestone "serving statuettes."[403] People began to place serving statuettes in the serdabs (inaccessible statue

399 Kemp 2006: 305, 308. The idea of *self-organization* in complex systems, which has gained prominence in many fields and disciplines over the last three decades, is too broad to give but a few general references: Cowan, Pines and Meltzer 1994; Waldrop 1992; Lewin 1992; Holland 1998; Mitchell 2009, and recently, Lineweaver, Davies and Ruse 2013. For applications to archaeology, see Kohler and Gumerman 2000; Blanton and Fargher 2008, and the contributions in Carballo 2013. For application to ancient Egypt, see Lehner 2000. For reactions to this point of view of ancient Egyptian bureaucracy, and counter arguments for rational Middle and New Kingdom bureaucracies mixed with patrimonialism, see Wegner 2010: 135, 139, Baines 2009: 133 ff.; Eyre 2004: 158ff.; Shirley 2013: 573–574, and Warden 2014: 16–20.

400 Goedicke 1967; Hafemann 2009: 102–111.

401 Scheinder1977; Stewart 1995. The implication of shabtis for obligatory labor and for a national or local corvée has received much comment (Goelet this volume; Loprieno 1997: 204; Eyre 1987b: 207–208; 2004: Eyre 182; Roth 2002: 119).

402 That is to say that corvée is revealed "largely by implication" (Goelet, this volume).

403 Roth 2002. Roth's choice of "serving" rather than "servant" statues underscores her point that we cannot assume the identity and status of the persons represented.

chambers) and burial chambers of tombs of their deceased in the late 4th Dynasty. They did so with increasing frequency starting in the mid-5th Dynasty.[404] Counter to a clear and simple dichotomy between "elite" and "non-elite,"[405] Roth lays out compelling evidence from several burial assemblages that the serving statues represent the children, wife, or dependents of the proprietor, and in the case of seated scribal statues, the head of the estate himself. Like the New Kingdom shabtis that could carry the owner's name, it is not entirely certain that the serving statues represent the person himself, or a servant figure belonging to his estate.[406] A servant-lord relationship—"the idea of labor as a means of association with a high-status person"—was played out at successive stages of the hierarchy; "... people depicted in the serving statues are demonstrating their service to tomb owner, just as the tomb owner demonstrates his service to the king, and the king demonstrates his service to the gods."[407]

While the shabtis and Old Kingdom serving statuettes reveal obligatory labor as a fact of life, it is a further leap of inference that they signal a regular national corvée as opposed to service for one of "many lords and numerous masters"[408] in the household/estate hierarchy of Egyptian society.[409]

The royal decrees likewise hint of obligatory labor but they exempt very specific local communities from calls on their work and properties by members of the royal house, by officials, by nome- and village leaders,

404 Breasted 1948.

405 If we take *a priori* a dichotomy "elite and non-elite" and then approach evidence of ancient Egyptian society, such facts as serving statuettes labeled as the estate proprietor or his family become problematic. A possible solution is to see the serving statuettes so labeled as "role playing" for an idealized afterworld. For an adjusted, nuanced treatment of the theme of elites, see Baines 2009, where allusion is made to the king, an "inner elite" (royal family members?), a "lower elite," "provincial elite," "local elite," "minor officials," and then "non-elite subordinates" as well as "complex hierarchies" (expressed in dress). Altogether these terms suggest considerable fractionation of the dichotomy.

406 Stewart 1995: 9; Schneider 1977: 22–24.

407 Roth 2002: 121.

408 Goelet (this volume, citing Caminos 1954: 51) quotes a passage from the didactic *Late Egyptian Miscellanies* advising the young to become a scribe so as avoid working with hoe and mattock, carrying a basket and plying the oar. Becoming a scribe "spares you torment, as you are not under many lords and numerous masters."

409 Eyre 1994, 123; 2010: 304; Moreno García 2012; Lehner 2000: 308–309; Schloen 2001.

and by estate rulers. This falls in line with Old Kingdom and Middle Kingdom builders' graffiti that show contributions of labor for dragging blocks from households and estates of ranking individuals.[410] The king issued these decrees to reserve the service, work and products of the stated communities for their special raison d'être, serving in memorial foundations of gods, kings, or high-ranking officials. Also, we might ask what the "mechanics of recruitment" as revealed in these decrees[411] tell us about mobilization of labor on the scale we think must have been required for building the gigantic early 4th Dynasty pyramids. Most of the known decrees date to the late Old Kingdom and concern comparatively small-scale work that is local as opposed to out-of-home-district.[412]

In an essay, "Who Built the Temples of Ancient Egypt?," Eyre emphasizes local involvement at all periods and concludes: "There is no satisfactory evidence from Pharaonic Egypt for the existence of a corvée, in the classic sense of a formalized, regular and quantified work duty imposed on the rural population as a whole."[413] He too cites the Old Kingdom temple decrees, which bar officials from laying claim to temple produce and people, but notes: "there is little information about the nature or more critically the regularity of labour demands." Similarly, after his review of the sources, Goelet concludes: "One thing is clear, nonetheless—in all the evidence discussed above there is little evidence for a regular—in the sense of well scheduled—corvée existing in Egypt. State compulsion seems to have occurred on an *ad rem* basis."[414]

If, during the four or five generations of the early 4th Dynasty, central authorities would not, or could not, impose a "formalized, regular and quantified work duty ... on the rural population,"[415] which would have extracted people from productive agricultural work, to build the gigantic pyramids, they were left with the alternative of captive foreign labor.

410 Andrássy 2009a; see section 3.2.

411 Eyre 1987a: 18–19 pointing to the Koptos B decree of Pepi II.

412 For example Koptos G relates to work on 30 arouras (about 8.27 ha) of land (Strudwick 2005: 114; Goedicke 1967: 128, fig. 10). Moreno García (1998b: 76) relates that the Vizier's bureau, which he alleged directed the *mr.t* corvée, emerged well after the 4th Dynasty, in the mid 5th Dynasty, to be replaced by other departments by the time of the Koptos decrees in the 6th Dynasty.

413 Eyre 2010: 136.

414 Goelet, this volume.

415 Eyre 2010: 136.

5.2. Captive Labor

An overarching question stands behind the theme of labor mobilization on the scale needed for the building the early gigantic pyramids: Did the royal house override the existing social order, or work with it? In the latter case, they would have requisitioned from the heads of villages, estates and households labor on the scale needed for the early pyramids. In a kind of bucket brigade up the hierarchy, labor would have come from many estates (*ḥww.t*) and villages (*nἰww.t*) throughout the country. On the other hand, captive labor provided an option to by-pass the standing social order, while setting up substantial influence upon society long-term.

It has been said, in general, that large-scale slavery emerges concomitant with agricultural expansion.[416] Egyptologists see evidence during the early Old Kingdom that authorities undertook major agricultural expansion, and recruited and mobilized labor for this expansion. It is thought that during this period the Egyptian state formalized the nomes[417] and began to regularize the great basins, the natural infrastructure of flood recession agriculture, in an internal colonization by founding new estates and villages[418] in the broader floodplains of Middle Egypt and the Delta.[419] These broadest areas of the Egyptian Nile Valley provided frontiers more open and less densely populated than the Qena Bend in the south, whence the early state emerged, and the so-called "capital zone" (lined on the west by the pyramid fields) in the north, where the valley is narrowest from the Fayum entrance to the apex.[420] State bureaucracy was emerging from direct patrimonial rule by the royal house.[421] Bureaucracy crossed a threshold toward greater complexity and professionalism during the reign of Menkaure—just about the time of the second major phase of occupation on the HeG site[422]—and into the early 5th Dynasty.[423] During this formative period and its efflorescence as the high Old

[416] Kolchin 1987 for agricultural expansion leading to Russia serfdom as unfree labor and to slavery lasting into the second half of the 19th century in the American south.

[417] Helck 1974b; 1977. For nome formations already in the Early Dynastic Period, see Engel 2006.

[418] Badawy 1967; Eyre 2004: 86–88.

[419] Kemp 1983: 90–91, fig. 2.2; Jacquet-Gordon 1962.

[420] Butzer 1976; Lehner 2010: 86–88.

[421] Helck 1954; Baer 1960; Schmitz 1976; Strudwick 1985; Baud 1999: 307–332; Bárta 2013.

[422] Nolan 2010.

[423] Bárta 2013.

Kingdom, land was plentiful and cheap, while labor was of higher value. This remained the case until the New Kingdom and into the Late Period.[424] Eyre stated:

> At most periods … the emphasis lay on shortages of people rather than land, and focused on managerial concern for the retention of agricultural workers.[425]

Therefore, in addition to capturing wild animals, exotic plants and cattle, Old Kingdom Egyptians also captured people and settled them in the peripheral zones of agricultural expansion. Did they use captive foreigners to build pyramids? In his influential publications, Wolfgang Helck made explicit his idea of a link between captive labor, agricultural expansion, and the building of the early gigantic pyramids beginning with Djoser and Sneferu in the 3rd and 4th Dynasties.[426]

Of course, Egyptologists have to evaluate the historicity of textual evidence for this point against the leitmotif, expressed variously and repeatedly over the duration of the ancient Egyptian monarchy, of the nomadic people on or just beyond Egypt's borders representing social and cosmic chaos and disorder, subdued and controlled by the divine force of the king. We see statues of bound foreigners in the pyramid temples, and representations of bound prisoners along the bases of numerous statues, on pivot sockets and ships rudder abutments (so that the heel of the door or edge of the rudder turns on them), on footstools and palace floors.[427]

On lexical grounds, Helck dates to the early 4th Dynasty two rock inscriptions left by governors of Upper Egyptian nomes 14 and 17 at Khor el-Aquiba in Nubia, north of Abu Simbel, published by J. Lopez.[428] One of the inscriptions documents an expedition by the governor of Upper Egyptian Nome 17 named Khabaubat with 20,000 men "to hack up Wawat." The other inscription alleges the capture of 17,000 Nubians by Zauib, governor of "the northern part of the Eastern [Delta] Nome." Helck related these inscriptions to the record in the Palermo Stone annals for one year in the reign of Sneferu, cited above (see section 3.5), when the Egyptians are alleged to have captured 7,000 Nubians and 200,000 of their sheep

[424] Baer 1962; Eyre 1987b: 208.
[425] Eyre 2004: 177.
[426] Helck 1974; Helck 1975: 98–99; Helck 1977; 1980.
[427] Helck 1980: 786; Bresciani 1997: 221; Schneider 2010.
[428] Helck 1974a; Lopez 1966: n.27–28; 1967; Roccati 1982: 269; Strudwick 2005: 150, n. 76.

and goats.[429] Helck believed the royal house settled these captives on the 35 estates and 122 cattle-farms mentioned in the next year register.[430]

Immediately thereafter follows the Palermo Stone entry of Sneferu's eighth year of counting.[431] The entry refers again to a royal construction project:

> ... erecting (the building) 'Sneferu, High of the White Crown' (at) the base? (*tp-r*) of the southern gateway, (and the building) 'Sneferu, High of the Red Crown' (at) the base? (*tp-r*) of the northern gateway; making doors for the royal palace of pine; eighth occasion of the census ...[432]

Because of the assumption of a regular, biennial "cattle count"—a supposed nation-wide assessment of holdings for taxation purposes—scholars have given much discussion to the two consecutive years of counting.[433] Stadelmann related the Palermo Stone statements of the 7th and 8th counting years to the extraordinary scale of Sneferu's pyramid building––three of the six gigantic stone-block pyramids, one at Medium and two at Dahshur.[434] Specifically, Stadelmann believed that the back-to-back cattle counts corresponded to a hiatus in building the Meidum pyramid (7th count), the transfer of the royal residence to Dahshur, and the first building phase of the Bent Pyramid (8th count).

Two consecutive entries for the year after the first count of the 5th Dynasty king Userkaf mention this king's pyramid, *Wʿb-jswt-Wsr-kꜣf*, "Pure are the Places of Userkaf," in connection with captive foreigners.[435] Poor preservation obscures the beginning of the preserved text of the four vertical columns on the far right,[436] but the text seems to relate to people being brought to the pyramid in the year after the first counting:

> ... (and) 303 prisoners? ... were brought for (the pyramid) 'Userkaf is Pure(st) of Places' (together with?) 70 women?..of the hill country? ... year after the first occasion of the cattle census.[437]

[429] PS r. VI.2; Wilkinson 2000: 141.
[430] PS r. VI.3.
[431] PS r. VI.4.
[432] Wilkinson 2000: 144.
[433] Wilkinson 2000: 145 summarizes the discussion about these consecutive counting years.
[434] Stadelmann 1985: 87; 1987: 236.
[435] The Userkaf entries are on Cairo Fragment 1-verso (CF1 v.II.1), probably once part of the same annals as the Palermo Stone, Wilkinson 2000: 217–218, fig. 6.
[436] Wilkinson (2000: 181) quotes Breasted (1931: 710), any reading "is an epigraphic task of peculiar difficulty."
[437] Wilkinson 2000: 217.

Possibly a chief and some number of people (perhaps 303) regarded as prisoners(?), and 70 women of foreign- or hill country (*ḫ3st*), were brought to Userkaf's pyramid at Saqqara. Wilkinson quotes Daressy's translation of the entry: "1 chef, 303 prisonniers du Khenti et 70 femmes du désert, des bédouines, ont été amenés à la pyramide du roi, évidemment pour les travaux de sa construction."[438] As with the Palermo Stone entry (PS r.VI.2) for Sneferu, Userkaf's importation of people is entered with the same text as the building of a named, probably monumental, wall. Sethe's understanding of the sequence in the far left column starts with *r ḳd ỉnb*, "building the wall."[439]

It is remarkable that, to the extent we can rely on the Palermo Stone and its related fragments as annals of historic events, we have numbers of foreign people brought to pyramid sites. The mention of Hathor and other associated records suggest these people may have been settled on a tract of land allocated to the pyramid in the valley floor and alongside a basin, *š*, as a harbor. In this interface between the low desert and floodplain, which is the setting of the HeG, developed those special purpose settlements that Egyptologists know as pyramid towns.[440] This is also the locale of those special class of people attached to pyramids, the *ḫntjw-š*, who served as guards and royal followers (*šmsw*) for the living king, bringing livestock and poultry offerings (section 3.5), leading his hunt (section 3.6), and guarding his captured and emaciated foreign prisoners (section 4.2.4).

As with many Egyptian royal inscriptions, we cannot be certain to what extent events are historical or formulaic, but Helck and scholars who followed believed the Nubian campaigns happened. Jaromir Malek suggested that the high number of captives signals this as the primary aim of the campaigns. Nubia "was regarded as a source of manpower, wood and minerals at a time when Egypt's economy was stretched to the limit because of monumental building projects," and Egyptians taking captives contributed to the "almost complete depopulation of Nubia, which lasted until the beginning of the Sixth Dynasty."[441]

438 Wilkinson 2000: 217; Daressy 1916: 171.

439 Sethe 1933: 240 = *Urk.* I, p. 240 lines 16–17. A lacuna follows the possible mention of a wall, and then *nt* ("of") and, possibly, *Ḥwt-ḥr*, "Hathor", based upon the left side of a damaged, tall, rectangular sign. The *ḫnt* sign comes next, followed by another lacuna and then the name of Userkaf's pyramid.

440 Helck 1957; Stadelmann 1981a; 1983; Bussmann 2004.

441 Malek and Foreman 1986: 98.

To the extent that we can establish the HeG site as flanking a harbor and delivery area, perhaps the major Nile port of it time,[442] we should expect that captives and other cargo entered the site, if, as in later times, captives and cargo were kept at ports before being distributed to other places and works.[443] At all periods, shipping, expeditions, and captives must have come together in the major Nile ports.

We find a version of the same specific theme, the import and the settlement of foreigners in proximity to a pyramid town, in the annals of the 12th Dynasty king Amenemhet II, which were etched into granite on a slab reused in Ramesside times near the southern entrance of the Ptah Temple at Mit Rahina (Memphis). Probably dating to the end of co-regency with Senwosret I, and to the first year of the sole reign of Amenemhet II, [444] this is an expanded, more elaborate form of the same kind of annals represented by Palermo Stone and Cairo fragments.[445] Much of the text conveys a "cargo manifest" that includes foreign goods and people.

The text lists captives from the Levant: 1002 Asiatics (*ʿ3mw*) from *Sṯt* (M13);[446] 1,554 Asiatics from places called *Iw3i* and *Iʿsi* (M16); and 65 Asiatics from Lebanon (M21), which is referred to as *Ḫnty-š*.[447] Then, in columns M25–26, under the heading that Altenmüller and Moussa entitle, "Belohnung der Soldaten und der Beamtenschaft für ihre Dienste," (Rewards of soldiers and civil servants for their service) we find listed:

"...slaves, fields, gold (of honor), cloth and all exceedingly fine things for the Head of the Fighting Force (*jmy-r mnf3t*), Leader of the Recruits (*ḫrp nfrw*), and for the recruits (*nfrw*), who returned from hacking the [fortresses of] *J3wj* and *I3sjj*, [for a supply of] labor (*msṯt*)[448] [for] the pyramid town, "Powerful is Amenemhet" with captives (*ʿnḫw*)."[449]

[442] Lehner 2013.

[443] Menu 2004: 192–193.

[444] Altenmüller and Moussa 1991: 38; Marcus 2007: 143.

[445] Malek and Quirke 1992.

[446] "M" followed by a number indicates Altenmüller and Moussa's 1991 column numbers.

[447] Malek and Quirke 1992: 14; Altenmüller and Moussa 1991: 10–17; Marcus 2007: 139–141.

[448] Altenmüller and Moussa (1991: 18 M25) render the text, "und Nachschub (an Arbeitskräften) besorgt haben (*msṯt*)."

[449] Malek and Quirke (1992: 16–17) for the latest epigraphic record; Altenmüller and Moussa (1991: 18) for German translation; Marcus (2007: 142) for English version of this and the rest of the text relating to maritime cargo.

The expedition delivers these people to Amenemhet II's pyramid town for *msṯt*-labor. *Msṯt,* with the determinative of the seated man holding a basket on his head, stands for "transport workers, charges, obligations."[450]

As understood and translated, this is a remarkably direct statement that the Egyptian 12th Dynasty royal house captured foreigners for work on the royal pyramid, or at least for work in the service of the pyramid town, and it strengthens the inference that the statements in the Palermo Stone about foreign captives in the early years of kings' reigns during the Old Kingdom relate to their pyramid projects. Marcus calculated that the prisoners accounted for most of the total cargo weight of this shipment.[451]

The (M26) text continues, with some restoration through a lacuna: "[the spoils were brought of the] cities of these two foreign countries and the Asian food of the prisoners was eaten, for the king's children (*msw njswt*), for the King's nobles (*špsjw njswt*), and for the head of the King's bird catchers (*ḥ3tjw ꜥḥ ḏsf njswt*)."[452] If the restoration and translation of this text is near true, we have another rather remarkable statement, to wit, that the food of the prisoners was eaten by members of the Egyptian court. If we can take this passage as historic,[453] could the "food of the prisoners" simply refer to the imports from the Levant so prized and imported by Egyptians since the late Predynastic: wine, olive oil and perhaps other Levantine foodstuff? Or, the passage might relate to "the need of sailors away from home to have food prepared for them."[454] Perhaps it would

450 Hannig 2003: 565; 2006: 387 defines *msṯt* as "Transportarbeiterschaft, Lasten, Verpflichtungen."

451 Marcus 2007: 150.

452 Altenmüller and Moussa (1991: 18): "[die Beute gebracht haben aus den] Städten dieser beiden Fremdländer und gegessen haben die asiatischen Gerichte der Gefangenen für die Königskinder (*msw njswt*), für die Königsedlen (*špsjw njswt*), für die Leiter des Vogelfangs des Königs (*ḥ3tjw ꜥḥ ḏsf njswt*)."

453 The taking of food between the Asiatics and Egyptians goes the other way in the Prophecy of Neferti, who foretells "All good things have passed away, the land being cast away through trouble by means of that food of the Asiatics who pervade the land" and who "approach thought want." Faulkner (1973: 234) characterized the text as a "blatant political pamphlet to support the new regime" [of Amenemhet I], a generation or less prior to Amenemhet II. Hungry nomads vs. well fed Egyptians fit another leitmotif. We could, however, take the Annals of Amenemhet II not as a literary, rather as an administrative text: "In the administrative texts ... attention is focused exclusively on single episodes" (Loprieno 1997: 190). Being etched in granite, perhaps for temple display, we might not be able to do so.

454 Eyre 1998: 176.

be a much further reach to believe that the Egyptian elites and their militia purposefully deprived captives of their food. But we might at least consider this Middle Kingdom text next to those presentations of starving foreigners in the newly published reliefs from the causeway of the Sahure Pyramid at Abusir, as well as the scene of emaciated foreigners from the Unas causeway (see above, section 4.2.4).

To the extent that the relief-carved and painted scenes of this or any pyramid complex reflect historical events, we can further add to the attestations of foreigners imported to Egypt the newly found and published scenes of bringing Puntites in the expedition portrayed on the south side of the Sahure causeway (see section 4.2.4).[455] We consider these in addition to the longer-known scenes from Sahure's pyramid temple of the arrival of ships with Asiatics and their children, as well as pottery and bears,[456] albeit these Asiatics do not appear to be so guarded and controlled by Egyptians as do the Puntites.

5.3 Coerced Labor

How effective is captive, coerced, or forced labor? Quarrying and working stone is exceedingly hard work, harder for granite than limestone. Until the development of iron, which could be used to split granite with wedges, workers shaped obelisks, lintels, and statues by hand-pounding and pulverizing trenches that formed the general outlines, and then they pounded underneath to free the monuments from bedrock.[457] Unfinished examples in the Aswan granite quarries testify to the excruciating labor.

On the one hand we have the view that members of the *ʿpr*-gangs (crews) and foreign craftsmen (*ḥmwwt ḫ3st*) who joined expeditions to procure granite and other exotic stones, and who specialized in working such hard materials, enjoyed a higher status than common workers (see sections 3.1–3.3).[458] On the other hand, we think that workers who pounded and pulverized granite "were certainly prisoners of war or people condemned to 'be sent to the granite,' apparently thought of as a severe punishment."[459]

455 Hawass and Verner 1996; El-Awady 2009: 119–128.

456 Borchardt 1913: pls. 3, 12–13; Bietak 1988.

457 Röder 1965.

458 Andrássy 2009a; Verner 1991.

459 Arnold 1991: 39, 55, n. 62. Goelet, this volume, observes of ancient and Roman Egypt: "Oaths and other sources inform us that miscreants could be sent on quarrying and mining expeditions. This was certainly true much later during the Roman era when assignment to the Nubian mines was tantamount to a death sentence."

As a modern example of extreme, coerced work of exactly this kind—quarrying granite—we might consider the granite quarry concentration camps of the Deutche Erd- und Steinwerke (DEST; the German Earth and Stone Works), created in 1938 by the paramilitary organization, *Schutzstaffel* (SS) of the Nazi regime. The DEST created forced labor camps near clay deposits and good granite outcrops (including Flossenbürg, Mauthausen, Gusen, and Groß-Rosen) expressly to make bricks and to quarry stone for the *Führerbauten*, monumental buildings of the ruler (Adolf Hitler), planned by his overseer of works (Albert Speer).[460] In his book, *The Architecture of Oppression*, Paul Jaskot points to the contradiction inherent in the combination of severe punishment and architectural production; "the emphasis on punishment denied the efficient maximization of labor."[461]

As for stone output, DEST laborers worked at first with primitive tools; by 1940 authorities brought in cranes and machines, raising production from the granite quarries of Flossenbürg and Mauthausen to 12,000 m^3 between 1940–42 when authorities undertook some training to make stonemasons of inmates.[462] Jaskot notes that 12,000 m^3 was "a comparatively huge amount of stone … the major commission of the New Reich Chancellery used 5,000 m^3."[463] Even with the "primitive" tools, this labor had the advantage over ancient Egyptian quarrymen of iron and steel. Still, we might note that the 2-year output is nearly one-fourth the estimate of 45,000 cubic meters (1.5 million cubic feet) of granite that the Old Kingdom Egyptians removed from the Aswan quarries.[464]

460 Jaskot 2000: 140 ff. Populations of Nazi forced labor camps were comparable to the numbers of ancient Egyptian sea-faring and mining expeditions known from texts; for example, 4,004 at Flossenbürg by 1943; 14,838 at Mauthausen by 1943 (Jaskot 2000: 40). Ancient Egyptian expeditions numbered from 300 to 17,000 (Eichler 1993: 155–156) and 18,660 in the Wadi Hammamat during the reign of Senwosret I (Goyon 1957: 17–20, 81–85, no. 61). Depending on the terms, the extremely high numbers may indicate units of man-days rather than men (Eichler 1993: 155–156; Müller 1967: 351–364), for example, 18,660 in the Wadi Hammamat mission during the reign of Senwosret I (Kemp 2006: 181; Goyon 1957: 17–20, 81–85, no. 61; Mueller 1975: 256). Expeditions of around 1,400, 1,600 to 2,300 members—about the estimate for total occupants in the Gallery Complex—were not unusual (Eyre 1987a: 14). A Red Sea mission totaled 3,756 (Sayed 1977; Bard and Fattovich 2010: 3–4).

461 Jaskot 2000: 37–38.

462 Jaskot 2000: 41–43.

463 Jaskot 2000: 42.

464 Röder 1965:472; Arnold 1991: 36.

Forced labor camps were able to produce as much as they did because those in control simply expended foreigners, who were ideological adversaries,[465] by working them to death.[466] "Production was, of course, successful in these years for DEST because it was based on the exploitation of a camp labor that, at this stage in the war, seemed unlimited to the SS administrators."[467]

Did the 4th Dynasty Egyptians create and maintain the symbolic importance of the early, gigantic Old Kingdom pyramids at the expense of people they captured and pressed into quarrying and transport of stone? Pyramid Age texts leave us fairly compelling evidence that central authorities comprised at least some of the pyramid workforce from people captured in campaigns on Egypt's periphery.

5.4. Integrated Labor: Settling Captives

If, like the National Socialists for the *Führerbau*, 4th Dynasty central authorities used captive foreign labor for pharaoh's building, there is a major difference in that the Egyptian central authorities settled captive foreigners into agricultural estates and integrated them into the Egyptian economy and society.

Helck saw the settling of captive foreigners into Egyptian farms and ranches as intrinsic and necessary to the core idea that motivated pyramid building, agricultural expansion, and reorganization of the countryside in a kind of feedback loop.[468] The core motivation, for Helck: the belief that resurrection and survival of the community through its leading patrons depended on the resurrection and survival of the king in the Afterlife, which depended on the "nourishment" of his funerary endowment, and

[465] Egypt's traditional enemies, especially in early periods, were the nomadic peoples along the border, caricatured repeatedly as bound tribesmen, or the nine bows, under Pharaoh's feet, so decorating footstools, floors, and the base of thrones, or, in the pyramid age depicted as bound captives in limestone statues in pyramid temples (Helck 1980: 786).

[466] For example, of 5,000 Soviet prisoners in early 1942, only 80 were alive by March (Jaskot 2000: 40).

[467] Jaskot 2000: 41. As the war against the Allied powers waged, the SS curtailed stone production to put more labor on armaments. The first granite quarries closed in 1943 (Jaskot 2000: 41). Cf., on a much longer timescale, the numbers of captives-turned-slaves also decreasing with a decline in imperial power after the New Kingdom (Loprieno 1997: 212).

[468] Helck 1974a; 1975: 98–100; 1977a; 1980. "Der Zwang zum Pyramidenbau liegt aber wie jede tiefgreifendere Veränderung in diesen Epoche nicht in wirtschaftlichen, sondern in geistesgeschichtlichen Gründen" (Helck 1974a: 220).

so too the endowments of his subordinates. But agricultural expansion and reorganization of the country required an expansion of bureaucracy, and so more officials, who themselves became lords and patrons, resulting in an expansion of larger estates and "pious foundations"—and so the feedback loop. The 5th Dynasty saw further increase of endowed land and produce for gods.

The Egyptians needed people to work new estates and herds, in particular to consolidate and integrate the Delta margins, especially on the east, but with major cattle pastures on the west. According to Helck, they also needed people to work on pyramids, so as not to remove Egyptians from the fabric and cycle of agricultural year. Helck surmised that for this program Nubians would have proven useful, given their experience with cattle herding and farming.

Settled captives and prisoners of war were integrated rapidly into the social economic fabric, according to Helck.[469] Egyptologists agree on this point,[470] and on the point that that even those persons designated by certain words as "slaves"—such as *ḥm* (used for "slave" for the most part after the late Old Kingdom), enjoyed many of juridical capacities of other dependent people.[471] Particularly in the New Kingdom, "slaves" could be promoted upward in social rank.[472] Menu presented a very clear delineation and a strong statement of this aspect of slavery in ancient Egypt, again from a focus on captive foreigners in the New Kingdom, when the conversion of captives into *ḥmw/ḥmw.t* ("slaves") represented a step to attaining the full legal capacity and rights as autochthonous workers:[473]

> D'ailleurs, l'existence d'un système de réquisition forcée et de travail obligatoire pendant des périodes détermines au service de l'État

[469] Helck 1974a: 224.
[470] Goelet, this volume; Eyre 1987a: 37; 1987b: 188.
[417] Bakir 1952: 29–34; Helck 1984; Allam 2001: 294.
[472] Loprieno 1997: 208.
[473] Menu 2004. Cf. Loprieno 1997: 208, who writes of the term *wꜥb*, "pure," used in the Middle Kingdom as a condition of temple service that exempted a heretofore dependent commoner from state service. In the New Kingdom the term "came to mean promotion from the status of slave to that of paid temple servant." This included foreign slaves in a kind of "democratization." "From this viewpoint, the presence of slavery should not automatically be regarded as the sign of a politically despotic structure, compared to that of a society without slavery. In New Kingdom Egypt, slavery paradoxically became one of the signs that the social structure was evolving toward 'democracy'" (Loprieno 1997: 208).

> pharaonique, autrement dit le système de la corvée, applicable à toute le population et bien attesté dès les hautes époques, rend bien inutile le recours à l'institution de l'esclavage.[474]

These are New Kingdom practices. We cannot be certain that the Old Kingdom Egyptians pressed foreign captives into building pyramids—the textual evidence adduced above for captive labor does not make an explicit link—as opposed to working the land that supported such projects and their subsequent economic functioning. In his 1987 overview of work and its organization in the Old Kingdom Eyre noted the "considerable evidence for the influx of captives and herds, throughout the Old Kingdom, taken as booty from the surrounding countries."[475] He cited Helck,[476] but suggested "the numbers recorded consistently seem unrealistically high." Eyre agreed that the Old Kingdom authorities probably settled foreign captives and their flocks in new settlements, in a program of internal colonization, but he concluded "there is no evidence for their use in clearly defined groups on work projects in Egypt."[477]

On the other hand, New Kingdom Egyptians pressed Libyan and Nubian prisoners into labor for building certain temples, and these builders then became the temple staff and cultivators on that temple's land. Ironically, prisoners pressed into building works on these temples became the very people exempt from wider calls on their labor. New Kingdom captives were also incorporated into the army.[478]

Granting Eyre's point that we have no direct evidence for this practice in the Old Kingdom, we do see hints of foreigners in builders' graffiti, in royal decrees, and in certain texts associated with the *ḫntjw-š* and the pyramid towns. These hints might suggest that Old Kingdom authorities had already applied the New Kingdom practice of using captives both for building temples, in his case pyramid complexes, and then bound them to the pyramid temples as service staff and cultivators of temple land. Authorities may have also called on their service for expeditions and quasi-military roles.

The decree of Pepi I for the double pyramid town, or two pyramid towns, of Sneferu's two Dahshur pyramids is of special relevance.[479] The meanings of some technical terms are not certain, but it is clear that the

474 Menu 2004 : 205.
475 Eyre 1987: 36–37.
476 Helck 1974a; 1975: 98–99.
477 Eyre 1987: 37.
478 Eyre 1987b: 189; and so Menu 2004.
479 Borchardt 1905; Goedicke 1967: 55–77.

decree protects the material assets set in reserve for the residents: fields, cattle, canals, flood basins, wells, watering places and trees. It prohibits the dependents (*mr.t*) of any royal wife, king's son, royal companion, or official to cultivate the fields assigned to the residents. Taking first place before these property protections, the decree declares the two pyramid towns exempt from work (*kꜣt*) for the royal house and from tax or impost (*mḏd*)[480] by the Residence.

We see a distinct foreign, in this case Nubian, aspect to those who would monitor and enforce the imposed labor or use of resources that the decree sought to annul. The chain of command in carrying out the edict proceeds from the Vizier to the Overseer of Works, then to a title something like "Charmed of Arm,"[481] thence to the Overseer of the *Khentiu-she* (named Weni, quite possibly the same Weni, Overseer of the *Khentiu-she,* as the subject of the oft-cited tomb biography from Abydos), to the Overseer of the House of Reversionary Offerings, and then to a "Sole Companion" (*smr wʿtj*). Next come the names of individuals who bear titles connected with foreigners, particularly the Nubian lands where, according to texts from the early Old Kingdom and time of Sneferu, the Egyptians captured people in order to, as Helck inferred, put them to work on pyramids or to settle them on estates that supported the building and expansion of pyramid cemeteries: the "Inspector (*sḥḏ*) of the (*ʿw*) Foreigners,"[482] or, for the word (*ʿw*), of "interpreters, translators," or "dragomen."[483] Goedicke takes this title together with the following names of Nubian places as "Vorsteher der Hilfstruppen," that is to say, director of auxiliary troops, from the three Nubian territories, Medja, Yam, and Irtjet known from Old Kingdom texts.[484] In his catalogue of Egyptian titles, Jones gives for the title *sḥḏ ʿw*, "Inspector of Egyptianised Nubians."[485]

If the Pepi I Dahshur decree, like other royal exemption decrees, implies corvée, it also suggests that in this particular vicinity the "pacified" (*sḥtp*) Nubians were enforcers, not, according to Goedicke as a standing professional police force or army,[486] but as paramilitary auxiliaries

480 Eyre 1987a: 18.
481 Strudwick 2005: 103, no. 20; see Goedicke 1967: 55, 58 (5), n. 11.
482 Strudwick 2005: 103.
483 Hannig 2003: 260; Bresciani 1997: 228.
484 Goedicke 1967: 55. Strudwick 2005: 103 translates: "the inspector of foreigners and overseer of Medja, Iam, and Iertjet."
485 Jones 2000: 916: no. 3367, with references.
486 Goedicke 1967: 62–63, n. 24.

(*Hilfstruppen*) to enforce requisitioning of people and property. The decree mentions the pacified Nubians four times, three times in regards to those who might requisition the cultivation of fields for a king's wife, son, companion (*smr*) or official. The text also forbids any man "beholden to these pacified Nubians" to enter the *wʿb*-priesthood.

At one point the text sates "that it is forbidden that any *ḫntj-š* of these two pyramid towns, who has been or will be on their register, be taken away by any man, or by any pacified Nubian (just) because they were with them before. They have no legal right thereto."[487] Goedicke translated *ḫntj-š* here as "Ausländer," noting that, as opposed to 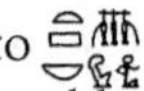 elsewhere in this text, here the writing is , determined by the hill sign (N25) used in words like *ḫȝst,* foreign land" (but not infrequently used in the writing of *ḫntj-š* in other texts).[488] According to Goedicke, unless we accept this understanding, the provision would be stating that some *ḫntjw-š* individuals might have been in a dependent relationship with other individuals, maybe even with peaceful Nubians, before being incorporated into the pyramid town, and he sees a prior dependency of the *ḫntjw-š* on Nubians as difficult to reconcile with the role of *ḫntjw-š* in the royal mortuary cult. He suggests we could understand *ḫntj-š* in this instance as "Südbewohner," or we might read *ḫntj-ḫȝst* as a term for foreigners or Bedouin, which he deems unlikely. Goedicke opts for "Ausländer" as servants or even slaves of foreign origin who had worked for "private" persons. He does affirm that the text suggests some members of the pyramid town might have come into its cadaster from a prior dependency on other persons.[489]

However, *ḫntj-š* written with the foreign-land determinative (N25) is typical for the Old Kingdom. Fettel, after his cataloging and review of various writings of *ḫntj-š*, found the foreign-land sign in more than half of the attestations, pointing out that this sign is unknown from the writings of this word in later periods.[490] He discounted the idea, expressed by Kanawati,[491] that the foreign-land sign should be read as a separate

[487] Strudwick 2005: 104; Goedicke 1967, fig. 5; VIII; *Urk. I:* 211, 5–11.

[488] Goedicke (1967: 56) translated: "Die Majestät befahl, daß man nicht wegführen soll irgendeinen "Ausländer" dieser beiden Pyramidenstädte, der gekommen ist zum Platz ihres Katasters, oder der kommen wird, durch irgendeinen Ägypter oder irgendeinen Nubier, (nämlich) die, die (früher) bei ihnen gewesen sind."

[489] Goedicke 1967: 64, n. 26.

[490] Fettel 2010: 37–38.

[491] Kanawati 2003: 16.

word: *ḫntj-š h3st,* since this sign, unlike the *š,* lacks the determinative stroke. Fettel thought it unlikely that *š* in *ḫntj-š* carried a literal reference to "basin," but referred to a zone attached to the palace or pyramid.[492]

Berlandini suggested large basins must have fronted each of the pyramid complexes.[493] Such basins would lie at the interface between the high desert and floodplain. This is just the zone where we should expect to find pyramid towns, and the exact setting of the HeG site. The hieroglyphic writing, "those foremost of the basin" would have fittingly included either the "basin" sign or the "highland" determinative. At the same time, given other indications, we are left to wonder if the hill-land determinative might not have also carried a sense of the *ḫntjw-š* as of foreign origin.[494]

Overall, the Pepi I Dahshur decree does suggest that people of Nubian extraction were much on the minds of its composers. Nubians were part of the local geography, and in the midst of the pyramid town, if not of it.[495] Is it possible that some "peaceful Nubians" descended from those people that Sneferu's forces transferred from Nubia some 320 years earlier?

The suggestion that Libyans, Nubians and Asiatics could have been present on the HeG site derives from texts of later periods indicating that Egyptians put captives to work on building projects, or on land that supplied the construction of pyramid complexes and its functioning temples with grain and meat; foreigners as members of expeditions, whether ships crews or specialists in hard stone quarrying and shaping (the *ḥmwt ḫ3st,* see section 3.3); titles connected with foreigners and attestations of "pacified Nubians" in the pyramid towns of Sneferu (many generations after work stopped on Sneferu's pyramids); and the explicit transfer of captives from the Levant to the pyramid town of Amenemhet II. These sources, later than the 4th Dynasty, suggest that non-Egyptians could be integrated, assimilated, and assume in their own right the role of enforcers, or that they could (in the New Kingdom) rise to the status and privilege of exemption from tax and calls to duty other than to the

492 Fettel 2010: 117.

493 Berlandini 1979.

494 Yoyotte 1959: 31. See the discussion in section 3.6 to the point that the most basic, denotative meaning of *š* is "basin" in the sense of the great and small irrigation basins of premodern Egypt, which were both tracts of cultivated land and, during the six to eight weeks of the inundation, bodies of water. The Wadi el-Jarf Papyri confirm the *Š* of Khufu was a water port as well as an royal institution.

special foundations and estates in which they were settled, marked by monumental structures they may have worked to create.

The idea that captive foreigners worked on the early pyramids has been cited in terms of evidence lacking for a systemic, out-of-district corvée of the native population. A review, and evidence already cited in section 3.2, suggests both captive and conscripted labor built the pyramids.

6. Conscripted Labor and 4th Dynasty Exceptionalism

By their sheer size, the five or six pyramids of the 4th Dynasty stand as hallmarks of an exceptional time that lasted three or four generations, from Sneferu to Menkaure. Following suit, the HeG site with its elaborate 5-ha Gallery Complex may be an exceptional footprint.

In an essay on temple building Eyre refers to the HeG site at Giza: "How the workforces were recruited for a project the size of the Great Pyramid is a matter of guesswork. The archaeological record of their labour camp does, however, look more appropriate to a model of migrant labour gangs, rather than that of an established and permanent population."[496] He defaults to: the "easiest model for actual organization of workers… is quasi military."

The issue of how the Egyptians organized labor to build the gigantic pyramids of the 4th Dynasty lies outside the comfort zone of textual sources,[497] which otherwise support the vision of local labor, that is, local corvée, and local materiel for building temples. Eyre noted: "The pyramids of the 4th Dynasty evidently required massive and *regular* labour input, but *these are exceptional monuments*."[498]

Being more specific about the term "corvée," Eyre stated: "The application of a heavy, thorough and systematic corvée in Egypt—the use of extensive conscription out of district, provoking major peasant

[495] Vachala (1991: 97) suggests a Nubian military colony in the Memphis area near the Residence in Dynasty 6.

[496] Eyre 2010: 127–128, citing Lehner 2004.

[497] Although now the Wadi el-Jarf Papyri document specifically the construction of the Khufu Pyramid, including accounts and the journal of an Inspector Merer and his team of men who deliver limestone from the eastern quarries at Turah. We await more information. As of this writing, see Tallet and Marouard 2014; Tallet forthcoming.

[498] Eyre 2010: 128, emphasis mine.

resistance and revolt—was an innovation of Mohamed Ali necessary to his military and development projects, and reflecting his policy of centralization...the projection of Nineteenth Century practice back to Antiquity would be a serious anachronism."[499]

With much respect, I beg to disagree. In rejecting a comparison because it deals with social-economic systems widely separated in time may "throw out the baby with the bath water." That is to say, we loose the possibility of seeing broad patterns, the very purpose of comparative studies of civilization over the long duration. Especially here in the same ecological zone, we should look at similarities of how social systems unfold, even with major changes in complexity, crops and technologies.

Eyre cites Cuno's treatment of corvée in Mohamed Ali's reign.[500] Cuno stated: "The use of corvée labor to maintain the irrigation system was nothing new, but the grand corvées ordered by Muhammed Ali were unprecedented in the peasants' experience, since they were taken to work on large projects often distant from their own villages and not of direct benefit to themselves."[501] Similarly, Marsot wrote that, even if unpopular, corvée was not new for local, large-scale irrigation works, having been carried on "from time immemorial."[502] Corvée had been a fact of life in the Nile Valley for a very long time, but the scale and invasive central direction of Mohammed Ali's grand corvées appear to have been anomalous. And so we might think for the 4th Dynasty.

Mohammed Ali attempted to impose a highly centralized, absolutist, monopolist state system with "an unprecedented degree of control established by the central government in the countryside."[503] Mohammed Ali's programs involved an "unprecedented penetration of ... new methods of power."[504] We suspect a similar burst of central authority for 4th Dynasty Egypt, while in its own unique and relatively simpler circumstances. Both periods involve "order bursts" generated from the top down, sending the overall country with its self organized coherence, resulting from "innumerable local adjustments to circumstances,"[505] in new directions like spin on a gyroscope.

[499] Eyre 2004: 183.
[500] Cuno 1992: 121–123.
[501] Cuno 1992: 122.
[502] Marsot 1984/1996: 150.
[503] Cuno 1992: 201.
[504] Mitchell 1991: 43.
[505] Kemp 2006: 305. See note 399.

As in the 4th Dynasty, Mohammed Ali's administration formed armies and allowed or forced nomads to become sedentary. Like Sneferu, Mohammed Ali settled Bedouin nomads from Egypt's marginal zones on land for cultivation. "The government, which needed manpower to till the soil, treated the Bedouin differently from the other fellahin, for instance they did not have to perform corvée duties ... Conscription did not bother the Bedouin either because from time immemorial they had been irregulars in the armies and continued to perform the same tasks under Muhammed Ali."[506] Settled nomads were, as well, shepherds and livestock breeders. Because of the reforms, smaller farmers lost land to large estates and their holders,[507] a process discernable from the 4th to the 5th Dynasty. Villages were organized and incorporated into personal estates, placed in the custody of officials and members of the ruling family.[508] More extensive public works (summer canals) required more stringent corvée.[509] Government had to learn how to ramp up to these large-scale corvée projects from a disorganized start with the Mahmudiyya Canal.[510] All this[511] bears some similarity to state interventions that we infer from evidence for the early Old Kingdom.

Can we discount "grand corvées" for building the gigantic 4th Dynasty pyramids as anachronistic? Given that expeditions to distant places in ancient Egypt certainly involved "conscription out of district," I think not. At least, such a rejection begs the question at hand. The question is the degree to which the 4th Dynasty was as exceptional for what had preceded and what followed as was the reign of Mohammed Ali. A related question for the HeG, as an expression of that dynasty, is the degree to which the

506 Marsot 1984/1996: 123- 124.

507 Marsot 1984/1996: 121–125.

508 Mitchell 1991: 43.

509 Marsot 1984/1996: 121, "The benefits to be derived from these large-scale works were obvious to the pasha and to his entourage, but they were not at all apparent to the fellah, who saw little advantage to his work on these ditches, especially if they were dug far away from his home village and benefited no one in his *zimam*" [village territory]. We might ask the same for a 4th Dynasty Pyramid, or did the high symbolism of the pyramids ring true to the conscript's instincts as much as, or more so than, the imagination of the court architect?

510 Marsot 1984/1996: 151.

511 Except for the summer canals, but it may be useful to observe how out-of-district corvée imposed by a highly centralized state for the summer canals worked, in terms of our thinking about expeditions and pyramid building.

Gallery Complex was anomalous.[512] Was the HeG an expression of a very short order burst, a moment of experimentation during "an exceptional situation,"[513] designed by high officials (individuals in the royal household) of unusual generations who also gave us the ultimate gigantism in the Great Pyramid and, carved from living rock, the uniqueness of the Great Sphinx?

A crucial question about corvée in the reign of Mohammed Ali concerns its regularity and predictability for large scale "public works" vs. the capriciousness of conscription ad hoc for episodic expeditions and military campaigns. One takes the impression that, while local corvée for irrigation and agricultural works might have been regular and (seasonally) recurring from "time immemorial," Mohammed Ali's "grand corvées" were not.

Accomplishing the Great Pyramid required a minimum of confusion, keeping to what modern contractors for large projects call the critical path.[514] The planned, orthogonal organization of the HeG and its central feature, the Gallery Complex, express a keeping of confusion to a minimum. If the hypothesis is correct that the HeG Gallery Complex served as a barracks for workers of labor gangs conscripted out-of-home-district, the massive investment in this mudbrick architecture, its regularity, orthogonal layout, and signatures of control[515] suggest an order and regularity that held for the two or three generations that people occupied the site, rather than ad hoc and episodic mobilizations. Was the HeG an exception to more normal times, when the centralized state imposed no "formalized, regular and quantified work duty … on the rural population,"[516] leaving responsibility for such duty to local heads of households, estates, and villages?

Expeditions to remote places like Punt, Wadi Hammamat, Sinai, and the Levant certainly involved work and service out of district, though perhaps not on a regular basis. If already in the 4th Dynasty, as well as in later pyramid complexes, we see marks in builders' graffiti that signify provincial nomes and districts in the broad expanses of Nile Valley land in Middle Egypt and the Delta (see sections 3.2, 3.3), these then are signs that authorities conscripted people for labor away from home base.

[512] Or was the Gallery Complex an innovation that, as with certain technology, emerges some time before its integration into the technical system (Gille 1978)?

[513] Foucault 1977/1995: 2005.

[514] Smith 2006, applied to pyramid building.

[515] Lehner and Tavares 2010.

[516] Eyre 2010: 136.

The idea that the state mobilized labor from the provinces for building pyramids is not necessarily inconsistent with the idea that the state used captive labor. Builders graffiti from Old and Middle Kingdom pyramid complexes indicate authorities conscripted workers from Middle Egypt and the Delta, and these were just the zones of internal colonization where Old Kingdom authorities created new estates, cattle farms, and royal plantations to which foreigners could be assigned and soon integrated into Egyptian institutions and foundations.

In the Middle and New Kingdoms, captives were brought with other cargo into ports, as Giza must have been in the 4th Dynasty, and registered.[517] The royal decrees have been cited to support the idea that the Old Kingdom state registered Egyptians and most everyone in the land for the purpose of corvée. Specifically, the Pepi I Dahshur decree refers to any *ḫntj-š* of the two pyramid towns "who has been or will be in the register."[518] But some scholars doubt the state could have registered people throughout the country. The lack of evidence for a bureaucratic structure below the title Overseer of Works makes this this office seem less systemic than what we might think was required for such a nation-wide census and cadaster (see section 5.1).

On the other hand, we see in the Gebelein Papyri just such a register, very possibly compiled during the reign of Menkaure.[519] We see in these provincial papyri the same accounting mindset and capability as indicated by the Pepi I decree for a pyramid town at the core "capital zone." At Gebelein scribes registered some 300 people working for an estate comprised of two small villages in Upper Egypt. The inhabitants of these two villages included persons with the title *nfrw*,[520] "recruits." Men designated by this term made up military, building, and ships crews over the long-term of the Old Kingdom. The term *nfrw* indicates not so much "elite" troops per se,[521] as youths anywhere in the country whom authorities could conscript for expeditions, shipping, or labor crews, at core or periphery, elite or otherwise. Posener-Kriéger suggested that scribes accounted for people in the Gebelein Papyri on the occasion of an inspection by central authorities. The close similarity in spread-sheet organization of the Gebelein and the Abusir Papyri accounting for the

[517] Marcus 2007: 142 where captives were brought to the pyramid town of Amenemhet II; Menu 2004: 192 for a New Kingdom example.

[518] Strudwick 2005: 104; Goedicke 1967, fig. 5, VIII; *Urk.* I: 211, 5–11.

[519] Posener-Kriéger 1975.

[520] Posener-Kriéger 1975: 212.

[521] Andrássy 2009a: 3.

pyramid temple of Neferirkare, dating to the late 5th and early 6th Dynasty, suggests a pan-regional, long-term, bureaucratic mind-set, a state-wide meme for ordering people and products.[522] And now we see the same accounting mindset in the Wadi el-Jarf Papyri accounts related to building the Khufu Pyramid itself.[523]

The royal decrees concern obligatory labor only at the very local level, and for labor and product allocations miniscule compared to what was required for the 4th Dynasty pyramids. However, these decrees do show, ostensibly, the penetration of central authority down to this scale as indicated, for example, by the addressees of the Koptos B decree of Pepi II, which Eyre pointed to as showing "the mechanics of recruitment."[524] The list of pertinent officials begin with the Overseer of the Pyramid Town,[525] the Vizier, the Overseer of Scribes and Royal Documents, the Overseer of Upper Egypt, the Overseer of Priests, the Inspector of Priests, "and all the chiefs of the Koptite nome."[526] The text next specifies the Overseer of Upper Egypt "who shall make a levy on them,"[527] "the local governor" (*ḥrj-tp*),[528] Great One of the Tens of Upper Egypt, Overseer of the Phyles (*zꜣw*) of Upper Egypt, Overseer of Commissions, Royal Acquaintance (*śmr*), Overseer of Crews, and Overseer of *Nswtjw* (a category of people thought to enjoy freehold tenure or usufruct, also thought to have been colonizers).[529] Moreno Garcia points to Koptos decree K, where the king orders "soul priests" (*ḥmw kꜣ*) to be assigned to the tomb chapel of the Overseer of Upper Egypt, Shemai, from the *mr.t* of Shemai's estate (*ḏt*), in association with, or from, "families (*ꜣbwt*) of the nome of Koptos … of your estate (*ḏt*). Afterwards it is to be placed in the registry."[530]

Such references in the Koptos decrees and other texts that cite town rulers or village chiefs suggest that if the central authorities had imposed out-of-district corvée for some time during the 4th Dynasty, the mechanics of mobilization of labor came down through the hierarchy to the nome, village, estate, and possibly household/family level of a national network

522 Kemp 2006: 163–171.
523 Tallet and Maroaurd 2014: 8.
524 Eyre 1987a: 18–19.
525 Goedicke 1967: 87 gives "the Residence."
526 Strudwick 2005: 106, no. 24.
527 Strudwick 2005: 108.
528 Eyre 1987a:18.
529 Hannig 2003: 661; Jones 2000: 489, no. 1828.

that Moreno-García argues was well in place by the end of the 3rd Dynasty.[531] While the orders came down from central authority, it would have been the provincial village chiefs who drew labor from their constituents and sent conscripts to the core area.[532] We imagine this transfer of labor out of district through a bucket-brigade-like chain of command that we see in the decrees. As during the Islamic periods and through the modernizing time of Mohammed Ali, *village rulers acted as the interface between the state and their people.*[533] The absence in this "mechanics of recruitment" of the Overseer of Works, and the absence of a clear hierarchy below that particular title, might indicate the Overseer of Works bore direct responsibility for order essential to staying on the critical path at the construction site itself.

On this point, the newly discovered Wadi el-Jarf Papyri inform us that late in the Khufu Pyramid project the half-brother of Khufu and Overseer of All the King's Works (*jmj-r kꜣt nbt nt njswt*), Ankh-haf,[534] was also Overseer of the *Rꜣ-Š* of Khufu,[535] a kind of port authority, that is, an administrative center that received incoming materials and labor recruits, which the papyri show were carefully accounted and allocated so as to keep the whole complex project on its critical path to completion.

7. Conclusion: Labor Complexity and Multi-ethnicity at the HeG

Just as the Ur III "governmentally sponsored" national building projects received provincial support, Egyptologists imagine that building the gigantic pyramids of the 4th Dynasty must have "involved the participation of the entire kingdom" and a far-flung interregional network. However, as

[530] Moreno Garcia 1998b: 81; Strudwick 2005: 120; Goedicke 1967: 206–213.
[531] Moreno-García 2013: 87–107.
[532] Moreno García 2013: 129, 141–150.
[533] Cuno 1992: 121–124, 157. As was the case through much of Egypt's history: "Historically, the delegation of fiscal responsibility to the richest local residents has been normal in Egypt. At the local level of land [and labor] management we should visualize considerable continuity in the role of persons referred to as *ḥqꜣ ḥwt* in the Old Kingdom, as *rwḏw* in the New Kingdom, as holders of liturgies in the Ptolemaic period, or as village headmen (*shaykh/umda*) in later periods. They were personally responsible for the flow of revenues to the 'lords of the land'." Also, "the delegation of labor took place at a level below the scribal functionaries and so is poorly documented" (Eyre 1994: 125, 127).
[534] Strudwick 1985: 77–78, no. 34. Ankh-khaf, who also became Vizier, is famous for his life-like bust, which Reisner found in mastaba G7510, the largest east of the Khufu Pyramid.
[535] Tallet and Marouard 2014: 10.

with the Ur III projects, provincial support appears not to have been sufficient and so "additional workers had to be brought from the outside."[536] Most probably people of all of the known classes, Egyptians and foreigners, elite gangs of young men, ships crews, craftsmen and common workers, took part in the pyramid construction projects, the expeditions that supplied them, and the estates and villages that supported them and their endowments.

In thinking about such matters we often return to the biography of Weni, quite possibly the same Weni addressed in the decree of Pepi I for the double Sneferu pyramid town. Five times,[537] when he was Overseer of the *Ḫntjw-š*, he led against Asiatic Bedouin an "army," *mšʿ*, the same term for expedition forces sent afar for raw materials.[538] Weni specifies that his force numbered "many tens of thousands" and included people from all of Upper Egypt, from Elephantine in the south to Medenyt in the north, from Lower Egypt, including "both sides of the Delta,"[539] as well as two places called Sedjer and Khensedjer. His force included Irtjet-Nubians, Medja-Nubians, Yam-Nubians, Kau-Nubians and people from the Tjemehu (Libyans).

Sneferu is alleged to have raided Nubia for thousands of cattle and captives. The Nubian chiefs of Weni's expedition are those he pressed into service cutting timber to build barges to float large granite blocks for the pyramid of Merenre. But Weni's military also included Egyptians (and settled foreigners?) levied from Upper and Lower Egypt, led by high officials as well as leaders of villages, towns, and estates:

> … nobles (*ḥ3ty-ʿ*), royal seal bearers, sole companions who were great estate chiefs (*ḥwt ʿ3ty*), [local] chiefs (*ḥry-tp*), and town rulers (*ḥo3 ḥwt*) of Upper and Lower Egypt, companions, overseers of foreigners, chief priests of Upper and Lower Egypt, and chiefs of *gs-pr* at the head of the troops of Upper and Lower Egypt from the manors (*ḥwt*) and towns (*njwt*) that they governed (*ḥq3*) and from the Nubians of those foreign lands.[540]

[536] Quotes from Steinkeller, this volume.

[537] Spaced evenly through a 35-year reign of Pepi I, this would amount to an expedition every seven years. For the frequency of expeditions in the Old Kingdom, see Eichler 1993: 151.

[538] *Urk.* I, 101–102, 9–16, 102, 3–8; Strudwick 2005: 256, no. 354; Lichtheim 1975: 19–20.

[539] *gswj pr*, literally, "Two Sides of the House."

[540] *Urk.* I 102–3–8; translated by Eyre 1999:38.

Although Weni wrote his biography more than two centuries after the reign of Menkaure, evidence suggests that any and all of such people could have contributed to building the Giza Pyramids.

As for who occupied the HeG and the Gallery Complex, their status, ethnicity, and labor were probably much more nuanced and complex than simple notions of an elite overseeing a board mass of common workers, because the site was most probably part of a major Nile port as well as a gigantic "public works."

The Gallery Complex, with its planned, orthogonal layout, modular galleries, controlled access, high ratio of empty space to house-like units, and with its material culture strongly signaling a provisioned population, begs us to guess at its message about labor organization for building the colossal pyramids on the high plateau to the northwest.

After reviewing Old Kingdom correspondences to the HeG site and its material culture, I believe that those who occupied the galleries enjoyed a status above that of the most common workers in the home provinces. However, authorities might have chosen those who occupied the galleries from young men (*nfrw*) of the provinces and core population zones, as hinted by district signs for divisions, the subunit unit of the phyle and *ʿpr*-gang formations. The fact that the same gang names have been found in builders' graffiti and on scenes of royal flotillas, suggest that very hard work and higher status came together in the *ʿpr*-gang formations. The newly discovered Wadi el-Jarf Papyri confirm that the same *ʿpr*-gangs (or crews) that transported stone served on expeditions and ships.[541] The crew-gang-phyle-half phyle labor organization is attested in the Menkaure temple, contemporary with the HeG final occupation. While hypothetical, the fit with the blocks, galleries, and half-colonnades of the Gallery Complex reinforces the inference that such gangs ensconced in the galleries, to the extent these modular spaces served as barracks,

Traces of Levantine imports in the HeG, and parallels between this site and proven ports on the Red Sea at Wadi Gewasis, Ayn Sukhna, and Wadi el-Jarf, reinforce an interpretation of the HeG as the template of an expeditionary force. The HeG must have served a major, if not the main, Nile port of its time.

[541] As indicated by the presence of these papyrus documents relating to Khufu's pyramid building at his Red Sea port, which was probably used for expeditions to and from Sinai for copper and other minerals; by the very fact that the journal of Inspector Merer and his men relates days spent delivering limestone from the eastern quarries at Turah to Khufu's pyramid; and by the several new *ʿpr*-gang names found on pottery and stone blockings of the Wadi el-Jarf galleries; Tallet and Marouard 2014: 11–12.

As such we can imagine the gangs (or crews) sharing functions with, intermingling with, or combining with formations of young men serving in the royal guard and escort. The Sahure nautical scenes label these formations *šmśw,* "followers," or *rꜣ-šmś nfrw,* "escort of young recruits," and *ḫntjw-š,* literally, "foremost of the basin," of the royal house. The labels establish an equivalence between these troops. The term, *ḫntjw-š,* and the social class it designates, which became so important for Old Kingdom pyramid towns and temples, appears frequently for the first time in the Sahure scenes of the royal hunt, of imported animals and products, of nautical events and of juridical/guarding duty. Artists and craftsmen created these scenes some twenty-five years after the royal house abandoned the HeG site. I ask if the massive, sustained social and topographical organization at Giza, with the HeG stretching south of the major delivery zone, might not have been the origin of the term and the social class, *ḫntjw-š*. As royal guards, some *ḫntjw-š* may have derived from foreign captives settled in proximity to the pyramids.

Whether or not the *ḫntjw-š* emerged from initial conditions at Giza, we should envision nautical and expeditionary events of the kind portrayed in the Sahure causeway as taking place in the HeG and the basin delivery zone to the north. Altogether, the HeG occupants enjoyed a higher status than "common workers." The HeG may even provide a vestigial, archaeological footprint of the *Śtp-zꜣ,* or at least part of the referent of this term for the collective royal entourage.

I hypothesize three main groups occupied the HeG: high ranking scribes and support personnel in the Western Town; *ꜥpr*-gangs, phyles and divsions, whose members could serve as ship crews, in the Gallery Complex; and service personnel who processed foodstuffs in the Eastern Town, where we might also look for further evidence of more permanently settled craftsmen, foreign (*ḥmwt ḫꜣst*) or Egyptian.

While the HeG was a place of hard work, and a place that accommodated those who worked hard on the pyramids (such as moving megaliths), it was also, on the evidence and correlations I have tried to make, a rather elite place, if we have to invoke that implicit dichotomy. Authorities must have recruited some of those *chosen* for "elite" service in royal gangs and crews from provincial nomes, on the evidence of district signs for the divisions of *ꜥpr*-gang and phyles. The HeG was a place of high-status royal service and possibly higher-quality recompense than recruits might have known in their home districts.

To the extent that the pyramid-building authorities needed "mass labor" (Massenbeschäftigung) organized other than in the *ꜥpr*-gangs to transport stone, they probably obtained it direct from households and estates of prominent people, as suggested by builders' graffiti of the mid to late Old Kingdom and Middle Kingdom, or through a relay of labor from households, estates, villages and nome and temple towns in both core and peripheral areas, as suggested by the late Old Kingdom royal decrees and by the make-up of expeditions. I do not, as yet, see a part of the HeG site that would accommodate large masses of common workers.

A review of Old Kingdom texts and scenes that correlate with the archaeology of the HeG makes it certain that a simple label like "workers camp," or the simple dichotomy of elite vs. non-elite, obfuscates the range of possibilities for people and goods that inhabited or moved through the HeG site. Labor at the pyramids, and the people of the HeG, were certainly diverse. Status was more nuanced than "high" and "low." We should envision young recruits (*nfrw*) in gangs and crews, specialized quarrymen and craftsmen, scribes and administrators, bakers and probably brewers, shipwrights, carpenters, and stevedores, either foreign (Asiatic) or Egyptian; dependents (*mrw*.t) of households, estates, and villages; and captives from Nubia, Libya, or the Levant.

Further evidence from the ancient Egyptian texts, from the HeG and from contemporary sites elsewhere in Egypt, Nubia, on the Red Sea coast, and in the Levant will help focus our view of this exceptional time and place.

BIBLIOGRAPHY

Abbreviations

AERA	Ancient Egypt Research Associates
ASAÉ	*Annales du Service des Antiquités de l'Égypte*
ÄuL	*Ägypten und Levante: Internationale Zeitschrift für ägyptische Archäologie und deren Nachbargebiete—Egypt and the Levant: International Journal for Egyptian Archaeology and Related Disciplines*
BÄBA	Beiträge zur ägyptischen Bauforschung und Altertumskunde
BASOR	*Bulletin of the American Schools of Oriental Research*
BdÉ	Bibliothèque d'Étude (Cairo: IFAO)
BIFAO	*Bulletin de l'Institut français d'archéologie orientale*
BMSAES	*British Museum Studies in Ancient Egypt and Sudan*
CRIPEL	Cahiers de Recherches de l'Institut de Papyrologie et d'Égyptologie de Lille (Lille: Université Charles-de-Gaulle)
EA	*Egyptian Archaeology*

GOP1	Giza Occasional Papers = Lehner, Mark, Mohsen Kamel, and Ana Tavares (2009a), *Giza Plateau Mapping Project Season 2004 Preliminary Report* (Boston: Ancient Egypt Research Associates).
GOP2	Giza Occasional Papers = Lehner, Mark, Mohsen Kamel, and Ana Tavares (2006), *Giza Plateau Mapping Project Season 2005 Preliminary Report* (Boston: Ancient Egypt Research Associates).
GOP3	Giza Occasional Papers 3 = Lehner, Mark, Mohsen Kamel, and Ana Tavares (2009b), *Giza Plateau Mapping Project Season 2005 Preliminary Report* (Boston: Ancient Egypt Research Associates).
GOP4	Giza Occasional Papers 4 = Lehner, Mark, Mohsen Kamel, and Ana Tavares (2009c), *Giza Plateau Mapping Project Season 2006–2007 Preliminary Report* (Boston: Ancient Egypt Research Associates).
GOP5	Giza Occasional Papers 5 = Mark Lehner (ed.) (2011), *Giza Plateau Mapping Project Season 2009 Preliminary Report* (Boston: Ancient Egypt Research Associates).
IFAO	Institut français d'archéologie orientale
JAEI	*Journal of Ancient Egyptian Interconnections*
JARCE	*Journal of the American Research Center in Egypt*
JEA	*Journal of Egyptian Archaeology*
JESHO	*Journal of the Economic and Social History of the Orient*
JNES	*Journal of Near Eastern Studies*
MDAIK	*Mitteilungen des Deutschen Archäologischen Instituts, Kairo*
LÄ	*Lexikon der Ägyptologie* [Vol. I: W. Helck and E. Otto, eds., Vol. II & V: W. Helck and W. Westendorf, eds.]
OLA	Orientalia Lovaniensia Analecta
RdÉ	*Revue d'Égyptologie*
SAOC	Studies in Ancient Oriental Civilization
ZÄS	*Zeitschrift für Ägyptische Sprache und Altertumskunde*

References

Abd el-Aziz, Ashraf (2007a), "Gallery III.4 Excavations," in Lehner and Wetterstrom 2007: 109–140.

— (2007b), "Main Street Excavations," in Lehner and Wetterstrom 2007: 193–229.

Adams, Matthew D. (2007), "Household Silos, Granary Models, and Domestic Economy in Ancient Egypt," in Hawass and Richards 2007: 1–23.

AERA (2011), "The OK Corral," in *Working Through Change: Annual Report 2010–2011,* (Boston: Ancient Egypt Research Associates): 16–19.

AERA (2012), "Archaeological Science: Hippo Hip and Olive Pit," *New Light on Transitions, Annual Report 2010–2011* (Boston: Ancient Egypt Research Associates): 22–23.

Aeragram 1.1 (1996), "Pyramid Age Bakery Reconstructed," *Aeragram 1.1:* 6–7.

Aeragram 6.1 (2002), "A Gallery Revealed," *Aeragram* 6.1: 4–5.

Aeragram 6.2 (2003), "Life Stories of the Pyramid City Unfold," *Aeragram* 6.2: 1, 4–5.

Aeragram 7.2 (2004), "Behind Mudbrick Walls: Life in an Eastern Town House," *Aeragram* 7.2: 8–7.

Aeragram 8.1 (2006), "Conservation Pilot Project: A Humber Compound Reborn," *Aeragram* 8.1: 8–9.

Aeragram 13.2 (20), "Egypt's Oldest Olive Pit at the Lost City of the Pyramids," *Aeragram* 13.2: 24.

Allam, Shafik (2001), "Slaves," in D. B. Redford (ed.), *The Oxford Encyclopedia of Ancient Egypt Vol. 3* (Oxford: Oxford University Press): 393–396.

Allen, James P. (2000), *Middle Egyptian* (Cambridge: Cambridge University Press).

Altenmüller, Hartwig (1989), "Nilpferd und Papyrusdickicht in den Gräbern des alten Reiches," *Bulletin de la Société d'Égyptologie, Genève* 13: 9–21.

Altenmüller, H. and A. M. Moussa (1991), "Die Inschrift Amenemhets II. aus dem Ptah-Tempel von Memphis," *Studien zur altägyptischen Kultur* 18: 1–48.

Andrássy, Petra (2009a), "Builders' Graffiti and Administrative Aspects of Pyramid and Temple Building in Ancient Egypt," in R. Preys (ed.), *7. Ägyptologische Tempeltagung: Structuring Religion, Leuven 28. September – 1. Oktober 2005* (Wiesbaden: Harrassowitz): 1–16.

— (2009b), "Symbols in the Reisner Papyri," in Andrássy, Budka and Kammerzell 2009: 113–122.

Andrássy, Petra, Julia Budka and Frank Kammerzell, eds. (2009), *Non-Textual Marking Systems, Writing and Pseudo Script from Prehistory to Modern Times,* Lingua Aegyptia Studia Monographica 8 (Göttingen: Seminar für Ägyptologie und Koptologie).

Anthes, Rudolf, (1928), *Die Felsinschriften von Hatnub nach den Aufnahmen Georg Möllers.* Untersuchungen zur Geschichte und Altertumskunde Aegyptens 9 (Leipzig: Hinrichs).

Arnold, Dieter (1983), "Pyramidenbau," in *LÄ*, Band V: 1–4.

— (1991), *Building in Egypt* (Oxford: Oxford University Press).

Arnold, Dorothea (2005), "The Architecture of Meketre's Slaughterhouse and Other Early Twelfth Dynasty Wooden Models," in P. Jánosi (ed.), *Structure and Significance: Thoughts on Ancient Egyptian Architecture* (Vienna: Österreichische Akademie der Wissenschaften), 1–75.

Arnold, Felix (1990), *The Control Notes and Team Marks,* The South Cemeteries of Lisht Volume II (New York: The Metropolitan Museum of Art).

Assmann, Jan; Andrew Jenkins (trans.) (1996/2002), *The Mind of Egypt* (New York: Metropolitan Books).

Badawy, Alexander (1967), "The Civic Sense of Pharaoh and Urban Development in Ancient Egypt," *JARCE* 6: 103–109.

Baer, Klaus (1960), *Rank and Title in the Old Kingdom: The Structure of the Egyptian Administration in the Fifth and Sixth Dynasties* (Chicago: University of Chicago Press).

— (1962), "The Low Price of Land in Ancient Egypt," *JARCE* 1: 25–45.

Baines, John (2009–2010), "Modelling the Integration of Elite and Other Social Groups in Old Kingdom Egypt," in J. C. Moreno García (ed.), *Élites et pouvoir en Égypte Ancienne.* CRIPEL 28: 117–143.

Bakir, Abd el-Mohsen (1952), *Slavery in Pharaonic Egypt.* Supplément aux ASAÉ 18 (Cairo: IFAO).

Bard, Kathryn A. and Rudolfo Fattovich, eds. (2007), *Harbor of the Pharaohs to the Land of Punt: Archaeological Investigations of at Mersa/Wadi Gawasis, Egypt, 2001–2005* (Naples: Università degli Studi di Napoli "L'Orientale").

— (2010), "Spatial Use of the Twelfth Dynasty Harbor at Mersa/Wadi Gawasis for the Seafaring Expeditions to Punt," *JAEI* 2.3: 1–13.

— (2011), "The Middle Kingdom Red Sea Harbor at Mersa/Wadi Gawasis," *JARCE* 47: 105–129.

Bard, Kathryn A., Rudolfo Fattovich, and Cheryl Ward (2011), "Mersa/Wadi Gewasis 2010–2011" (Online report: www.archaeogate.org).

Bárta, Miroslav (2001), *The Cemeteries at Abusir South I,* Abusir V (Prague: Czech Institute of Egyptology).

— (2013), "Kings, Vizier and Courtiers, Executive Power in the Third Millennium BC," in Moreno García 2013: 153–175.

Baud, Michel (1999), *Famille royale et pouvoir sous l'Ancien Empire égyptien,* 2 vols. Bibliothèque d'Étude 126 (Cairo: IFAO).

Ben-Tor, Amon (1991), "New Light on the Relations Between Egypt and Southern Palestine During the Early Bronze Age," *BASOR* 281: 3–10.

Behrmann, Almuth (1989), *Das Nilpferd in der Vorstellungswelt der alten Ägypter, Teil I, Catalogue,* Europäische Hochschulschriften, Reihe 38, Archäologie, Bd. 22 (Frankfurt am Main: Peter Lang).

— (1995), Überlegungen zur Darstellung von Nilpferden im Papyrusdickicht in den Gräben des alten Reiches, *Göttinger Miszellen* 147: 15–18.

— (1996) *Das Nilpferd in der Vorstellungswelt der alten Ägypter, Teil II, Textband.* Europäische Hochschulschriften, Reihe 38, Bd. 62 (Frankfurt am Main: Peter Lang).

Berlandini, Jocelyne, (1979), "La pyramide 'ruinée' de Sakkara-Nord et le roi Ikauohor-Menkaouhor," *RdÉ* 31: 3–28.

Bietak, Manfred (1988), "Zur Marine des Alten Reiches," in J. Baines, T. G. H. James, A. Leahy, and A. F. Shore (eds.), *Pyramid Studies and Other Essays Presented to I.E.S. Edwards* (London: The Egypt Exploration Society): 35–39.

— (2005), "The Tuthmoside Stronghold of Perunefer," *EA* 26 (Spring): 13–17.

Blanton, Richard and Lane Fargher (2008), *Collective Action in the Formation of Pre-Modern States* (New York: Springer).

Boessneck, Joachim (1953), *Die Haustiere in Altägypten*, Veröffentlichungen der Zoologischen Staatssammlung 3 (München: Pfeiffer).

Borchardt, Ludwig (1905), "Ein Königserlaß aus Dahschur," *ZÄS* 42: 1–11.

Borchardt, Ludwig (1913), *Das Grabdenkmal des Königs S'a³ḥu-Reᶜ, Band II: Die Wandbilder*, Wissenschaftliche Veröffentlichungen der Deutschen Orient-Gesellschaft 26 (Leipzig: Hinrichs).

Borchardt, Ludwig and L. Croon (1938), *Die Entstehung der Pyramide an der Baugeschichte der Pyramide bei Meidum nachgewiesen. Mit einem Beitrag über Lastentransport und Bauzeit von L. Croon.* BÄBA 1,2 (Berlin: Springer).

Borojevic, Ksenija and Rebecca Mountain (2011), "The Ropes of Pharaohs: The Source of Cordage from 'Rope Cave' at Mersa/Wadi Gawasis Revisited, *JARCE* 47: 131–141.

Breasted, James Henry (1931), "The Predynastic Union of Egypt," *BIFAO* 30: 709–724.

— (1948), *Egyptian Servant Statues,* Bollingen Series 13. (Washington, D.C.: Pantheon Books).

Bresciani, Edda (1997), "Foreigners," in Sergio Donadoni (ed.), *The Egyptians* (Chicago: Chicago University Press): 221–253.

Brovarski, Edward, (2001), *The Senedjemib Complex, Part I.* Giza Mastabas Vol. 7 (Boston: Museum of Fine Arts).

Bunbury, Judith M., Lutley, Katy and Graham, Angus (2009), "Giza Geomorphological Report," in Lehner, Kamel and Tavares 2009b: 97–151.

Bußmann, Richard (2004), "Siedlungen im Kontext der Pyramiden des alten Reiches," *MDAIK* 60: 18–39.

Buber, Martin, R.G. Smithm trans. (1961), *Between Man and Man* (London: Fontana Library).

Budge, E. A.Wallis (1904), *The Decrees of Memphis and Canopus. Vol. 3: The Decree of Canopus* (London: Kegan Paul, Trench, Trübner & Co.)

Butzer, Karl (1976), *Early Hydraulic Civilization in Egypt: A Study in Cultural Ecology* (Chicago: University of Chicago Press).

Caminos, Ricardo (1954), *Late-Egyptian Miscellanies*, Brown Egyptological Studies 1. (London: Oxford University Press).

Campana, D., Pam Crabtree, Susan D. deFrance, J. Lev-Tov and A. Choyke, eds. (2010), *Anthropological Approaches to Archaeology: Complexity, Colonialism, and Animal Transformations* (London: Oxbow)

Carballo, David, ed., (2013), *Cooperation and Collective Action* (Boulder: University of Colorado Press).

Cooper, John P. (2012), "Nile Navigation 'Towing All Day, Punting for Hours,'" *EA* 41 (Autumn): 25–27.

Cowan, George A., David Pines, and David Meltzer, eds. (1994), *Complexity: Metaphors, Models, and Reality,* Santa Fe Institute Studies in the Science of Complexity, Proceedings Vol. XIX (Reading, MA: Addison-Wesley).

Cuno, Kenneth M. (1992), *The Pasha's Peasants: Land, Society, and Economy in Lower Egypt, 1740–1858* (Cambridge: Cambridge University Press).

Daressy, Georges (1916), "La pierre de Palerme et la chronologie de l'Ancien Empire," *BIFAO* 12: 161–214.

deFrance, Susan D. (2009), "Zooarchaeology in Complex Societies: Political Economy, Status, and Ideology," *Journal of Archaeological Research* 17: 105–168.

— (2010), "Chiefly Fare or Whose Feeding the Cacique? Equality in Animal Use at the Tibes Ceremonial Center, Puerto Rico," in Campana, Crabtree, deFrance, Lev-Tov, and Choyke 2010: 76–89.

De Meyer, M. and S. Vereecken, B. Vanthuyne, S. Hendrickx, L. Op de Beeck, and H. Willems (2011), "The Early Old Kingdom at Nuwayrāt in the 16th Upper Egyptian Nome," in D. Aston B. Bader, C. Glorini, P. Nicholson, and S. Buckingham (eds.), *Under the Potter's Tree: Studies on Ancient Egypt Presented to Janine Bourriau on the Occasion of her 70th Birthday*. OLA 204 (Leuven: Peeters): 679–701.

Dietler, Michael and Brian Hayden, eds. (2001), *Feasts: Archaeological and Ethnographic Perspectives on Food, Politics, and Power*, (Washington/London: Smithsonian Institution Press).

Dietler, Michael and Ingrid Herbich (2001), "Feasts and Labor Mobilization: Dissecting a Fundamental Economic Practice," in Dietler and Hayden 2001: 240.

Dobrev, Vassil (1996), "Les marques sur pierres de construction de la nécropole de Pépi Ier. Étude prosopographique," *BIFAO* 96: 103–142.

— (1998), "Les marques de la pyramide de Pépy Ier. Notes complémentaires," *BIFAO* 98: 151–170.

— (2003), "The Administration of the Pyramid," in Z. Hawass (ed.) *Treasures of the Pyramids* (New York/Vercelli: Barnes and Noble/White Star): 28–31.

Drioton, Étienne (1942–43),"Une representation de la famine sur un bas-relief égyptien de la Ve Dynastie," *Bulletin de l'Institut d'Egypte* 25: 44–45.

Edel, Elmar (1955), *Altägyptische Grammatic, I.* Analecta Orientalia 34 (Rome: Pontificium Institutum Biblicum).

— (1969), "Die Kalksteintäfelchen," in Ricke 1969: 2–22.

— (1996): "Studien zu den Relieffragmenten aus dem Taltempel des Königs Snofru," in Peter Der Manuelian (ed.), *Studies in Honor of William Kelly Simpson, Vol. 1* (Boston: Museum of Fine Arts): 199–208.

Eichler, Eckhard (1993), *Untersuchungen zum Expeditionswesen des ägyptischen Alten Reiches,* Göttinger Orientforschungen IV: Reihe Ägypten, Band 26 (Wiesbaden: Harrassowitz).

El-Awady, Tarek (2009), *Sahure—The Pyramid Causeway: History and Decoration Program in the Old Kingdom,* Abusir XVI (Prague: Charles University).

El-Sanusi, Ashraf and Michael Jones (1997), "A Site of Maadi Culture Near the Pyramids," *MDAIK* 53: 241–253.

Endesfelder, Erika, ed. (1991), *Probleme der frühen Gesellschaftsentwicklung im alten Ägypten* (Berlin: Humboldt-Universität zu Berlin, Institut für Sudanarchäologie und Ägyptologie).

Engel, Eva-Maria (2006), "Die Entwicklung des Systems der ägyptischen Nomoi in der Frühzeit," *MDAIK* 62: 151–160.

Engelbach, R. (1938), "The Quarries of the Western Nubian Desert and the Ancient Road to Tushka," *ASAÉ* 38: 369–390.

Esse, Douglas L. (1991), *Subsistence, Trade, and Social Change in Early Bronze Age Palestine.* SAOC 50 (Chicago: The Oriental Institute).

Eyre, Christopher. J. (1987a), "Work and the Organization of Work in the Old Kingdom," in Powell 1987: 5–47.

— (1987b), "Work and the Organization of Work in the New Kingdom," in Powell 1987: 167–221.

— (1994), "Feudal Tenure and Absentee Landlords," in Schafik Allam (ed.), *Grund und Boden in Altägypten,* Untersuchungen zum Rechtsleben im alten Ägypten II (Tübingen: Schafik Allam): 107–133.

— (1998), "The Market Women of Pharaonic Egypt," in Nichlas Grimal and Bernadette Menu (eds.), *Le commerce en Égypte ancienne* (Cairo: IFAO): 171–191.

— (1999), "The Village Economy in Pharaonic Egypt," in A. K. Bowman and E. Rogan (eds.), *Agriculture in Egypt from Pharaonic to Modern Times* (Oxford: Oxford University Press): 31–60.

— (2004), "How Relevant Was Personal Status to the Functioning of the Rural Economy in Pharaonic Egypt?" in Menu 2004: 157–186.

— (2010), "Who Built the Temples of Egypt?" in Bernadette Menu (ed.), *L'organisation du travail en Égypte ancienne et en Mésopotamie.* BdE 151 (Cairo: IFAO): 117–138.

Fakhry, Ahmed (1959), *The Monuments of Sneferu at Dahshur, Vol. I: The Bent Pyramid* (Cairo: Government Printing Office).

Faulkner, Raymond O. (1953), "Egyptian Military Organization," *JEA* 39: 32–47.

— (1962/1996), *A Concise Dictionary of Middle Egyptian* (Oxford: Griffith Institute).

— (1973), "The Prophecies of Neferti," in W. K. Simpson (ed.), *The Literature of Ancient Egypt. An Anthology of Stories, Instructions, and Poetry* (New Haven: Yale University Press): 234–240.

Fettel, Jens (2010), Die Chentiu-schi des alten Reiches. Ph.D. dissertation, University of Heidelberg (http://archiv.ub.uniheidelberg.de/volltextserver/11390/1/Dissertation_J._Fettel_Die_Chentiu_schi_des_Alten_Reiches.pdf).

Fischer, Henry G. (1959a), "A Scribe of the Army in a Saqqara Mastaba of the Early Fifth Dynasty," *JNES* 18: 233–272.

— (1959b) "Some Notes on the Easternmost Nomes of the Delta in the Old and Middle Kingdoms," *JNES* 18: 129–142.

— (1960), "The Inspector of the Youths, *Nfr-n-Ḫwfw*," *Oudheidkundige Mededelingen uit het Rijksmuseum van Oudheden te Leiden* 41: 1–13.

Forstner-Müller, Irene and Dietrich Raue (2008), "Elephantine and the Levant," in E.-M. Engel, V. Müller, and U. Hartung (eds.), *Zeichen aus dem Sand: Streiflichter aus Ägyptens Geschichte zu Ehren von Günter Dreyer* (Wiesbaden: Harrossowitz): 125–148.

Foucault, Michel; A. Sheridan (trans.) (1977/1995), *Discipline & Punish: The Birth of the Prison* / (1975) *Surveiller et punir: Naissance de la prison* (New York: Vintage Books / Paris: Éditions Gallimard).

Gardiner, Alan H. (1927), "An Administrative Letter of Protest," *JEA* 13: 75-78.

— (1927/1969), *Egyptian Grammar* (3rd ed.). (London: Oxford University Press).

Gerisch, Rainer, (2007), "Identification of Wood and Charcoal," in Bard and Fattovich 2007: 170–188.

— (2008), "Charcoal_Oct08." Excel document on file, Ancient Egypt Research Associates, Inc.

— (2011), "Wood Anatomical Identification and Vegetation Studies," in K. A. Bard, R. Fattovich, and C. Ward, Mersa/Wadi Gewasis 2010–2011. *Archaeogate* 2011 (Online report: wwwe.archaeogate.org: 19–23).

— (2012), "The Stone Village Wood and Charcoal," in A. Stevens, *Akhenaten's Workers" The Amarna Stone Village Survey, 2005–9* (London and Cambridge: The Egypt Exploration Society and The Amarna Trust): 47–74.

Gerisch, Rainer, Wilma Wetterstrom and Mary Anne Murray (2009), "Egypt's Oldest Olive," *Aeragram* 9.2 (Fall): 3.

Gille, Bertrand; J. Brainch, trans. (1986), *The History of Techniques I* (1978 *Histoire des techniques), Vol. 1: Techniques and Civilizations* (New York/ Paris: Gordan Breach Science Publishers/Encyclopeaedie de la Pléiade).

Goedicke, Hans (1971), *Re-used Blocks from the Pyramid of Amenemhet I at Lisht* (New York: The Metropolitan Museum of Art).

Goelet, Ogden (1982), *Two Aspects of the Palace in the Egyptian Old Kingdom.* Ph.D. dissertation, Columbia University. Ann Arbor: UMI.

— (1986), "The Term *Śtp-sꜣ* in the Old Kingdom and Its Later Development," *JARCE* 23: 85–98.

— (forthcoming), "Problems of Authority, Compulsion, and Compensation in Ancient Egypt."

Goyon, G. (1957), *Nouvelles inscriptions rupestres du Wadi Hammamat* (Paris: Nationale Librairie d'Amérique et d'Orient Adrien-Maisonneuve).

— (1971), "Les ports des pyramides et le Grand Canal de Memphis," *RE* 23: 137–153.

Graff, Gwenola, Merel Eyckerman and Stan Hendrickx (2011), "Architectural Elements on Decorated Pottery and Ritual Presentation of Desert Animals," in R. F. Friedman and P. N. Fiske (eds.), *Egypt at Its Origins 3. Proceedings of the Third International Conference "Origin of the State. Predynastic and Early Dynastic Egypt, London 27th July–1st August 2008,"* OLA 205 (Leuven: Peeters): 437–465.

Haeny, G. (1969), "Die Steinbruch- und Baumarken," in Ricke 1969: 23–48.

Hafemann, Ingelore (2009), *Dienstverpflichtung im alten Ägypten während des Alten und Mittleren Reiches.* Internet-Beiträge zur Ägyptologie und Sudanarchäologie 12 (Berlin/London: Golden House Publications).

Hamada, Abd el-Hadfi (1938), "A Stela from Manshiyet es-Sadr," *ASAÉ* 38: 217–230.

Hannig, Rainer (2003), *Ägyptisches Wörterbuch I: Altes Reich und Erste Zwischenzeit,* Hannig Lexica 4, Kulturgeschichte der Antiken Welt, Band 98 (Mainz: Philipp von Zabern).

— (2006), *Großes Handwörterbuch Ägyptisch-Deutsch* (2800–950 v. Chr.) (Mainz: Philipp von Zabern).

Harpur, Yvonne (1987), *Decoration in Egyptian Tombs of the Old Kingdom, Studies in Orientation and Scene Content* (London: KPI).

Harris, Marvin and Orna Johnson, (2007), *Cultural Anthropology.* 7th edition. (Boston: Pearson).

Hassan, Selim (1936), *Excavations at Giza Vol. II, 1930–1931* (Cairo: Government Press).

— (1955), "The Causeway of Wnis at Sakkara, *ZÄS* 80/2: 136–139.

Hawass, Zahi (1996), "The Workmen's Community at Giza," in M. Bietak, (ed.), *Haus und Palast im alten Ägypten / House and Palace in Ancient Egypt. International Sympsosium in Cairo, April 8. to 11. 1992.* Vienna, 53–67.

Hawass, Zahi and Miroslav Verner (1996), "Newly Discovered Blocks from the Causeway of Sahure," *MDAIK* 52: 177–186.

Hawass, Zahi and J. Richards, eds. (2007), *The Archaeology and Art of Ancient Egypt: Essays in Honor of David B. O'Connor* (Cairo: Supreme Counsel of Antiquities).

Heindl, Günter (2008), *Wege zur Rekonstruktion der Arbeiterunterkunft "Gallery III.4" in der Arbeitersiedlung südlich der Krähenmauer in Giza.* Unpublished report on file, Boston: AERA.

Helck, Wolfgang (1954), *Untersuchungen zu den Beamtentiteln des ägyptischen alten Reiches,* Ägyptologische Forschungen 18 (Glückstadt/Hamburg/ New York: J.J. Augustin).

— (1957) "Bemerkungen zu den Pyramidenstädten im alten Reich," *MDAIK* 15: 91–111.

— (1971), *Die Beziehungen Ägyptens zu Vorderasien im 3. und 2. Jahrtausend v. Chr.*, 2nd ed. Ägyptologische Abhandlungen 5 (Wiesbaden: Harrassowitz).

— (1974a), "Die Bedeutung der Felsinschriften," in J. Lopez, *Inscripciones Rupestres Nr. 27 und 28.* Studien zur Altägyptischen Kultur 1: 215–225.

— (1974b), *Die altägyptischen Gaue.* Beihefte zum Tübinger Atlas des Vorderen Orients, Reihe B (Geisteswissenschaften) Nr. 5 (Wiesbaden: Reichert).

— (1975), *Wirtschaftsgeschichte des alten Ägypten im 3. und 2. Jahrtausend vor Chr.* (Leiden/Köln: Brill).

— (1975a), Arbeiterabteilungen und -organisation," *LÄ* I: 371–373.

— (1975b) "Arbeitersiedlung," *LÄ* I: 374–375.

— (1975c), "Arbeiterversorgung und -entlohnung," *LÄ* I: 375–378.

— (1975d), "Abgaben und Steuern," *LÄ* I: 3–11.

— (1977), "Gaue," *LÄ* II: 385–426.

— (1977a), "Fremdarbeit," *LÄ* II: 304–306.

— (1977b), "Frondienst," *LÄ* II: 333–334.

— (1980), "Kriegsgefangene," *LÄ* III: 786–787.

— (1984) "Sklaven," *LÄ* V: 982–988.

Herb, Michael and Frank Förster (2009), "From Desert to Town: The Economic Role of Desert Game in the Pyramid Ages of Ancient Egypt as Inferred from Historical Sources (c. 2600 – 1800 BC): An Outline of the Workshop's Inspiration and Objectives," in Riemer *et al.* 2009: 17–44.

Hillier, Bill and Julienne Hanson (1984), *The Social Logic of Space* (Cambridge: Cambridge University Press).

Holland, John H. (1998), *Emergence, From Chaos to Order* (Reading, MA: Addison Wesley).

Houlihan, Patrick F. and Steven M. Goodman (1986), *The Birds of Egypt* (Warminster: Aris and Phillips).

Howard Vyse, Richard (1840), *Operations Carried Out at the Pyramids of Gizeh in 1837*, Vol. 1, 3 vols. (London: James Fraser).

Hudson, Michael (2005), "My notes on the Labor Colloquium."

Jacquet-Gordon, Helen K. (1962), *Les noms des domaines funéraires sous l'Ancien Empire Égyptien* (Cairo: IFAO).

Jaskot, Paul .B. (2000), *The Architecture of Oppression: The SS, Forced Labor, and the Nazi Monumental Building Economy* (London: Routledge).

Jeffreys, David (1996), "House, Palace and Islands at Memphis," in M. Bietak (ed.), *Haus und Palast im alten Ägypten* (Vienna: Österreichische Akademie der Wissenschaften): 287–294.

— (2006), "Perunefer: at Memphis of Avaris?" *EA* 28 (Spring): 36-37.

— (2008), "Archaeological Implications of the Moving Nile," *EA* 32 (Spring): 6–7.

Jéquier, Gustave (1940), *Le monument funéraire de Pepi II, Tome III: Les approches de temple* (Cairo: IFAO).

Jéquier, Gustave, Ahmed E. Youssef, and Jean Philippe Lauer (1929), *Tombeaux de particuliers contemporaines de Pepi II* (Cairo: IFAO).

Jones, Dilwyn (2000), *An Index of Ancient Egyptian Titles, Epithets and Phrases, of the Old Kingdom.* 2 vols. BAR International Series 866 (Oxford: Archeopress).

Junker, Hermann (1941), "𓂋 [*rꜣ*] 'Handlung' als Präfix in Zusammensetzungen," *ZÄS* 77: 3–7.

Kanawati, Naguib (1980), *Governmental Reforms in Old Kingdom Egypt* (Warminster: Aris & Phillips).

— (2003), *Conspiracies in the Egyptian Palace* (London: Routledge).

Kantor, Helene (1992), "Egypt," in R. W. Ehrich (ed.), *Chronologies in Old World Archaeology* (3rd ed.), 2 vols. (Chicago: University of Chicago Press): vol. 1, 3–21;Vol. 2, 2–16.

Kawae, Yukinori (2009), "House Unit 1," in Lehner, Kamel, and Tavares 2009b: 87–91.

Kemp, Barry J. (1983), "Old Kingdom, Middle Kingdom, and Second Intermediate Period," in B. Trigger, B. J. Kemp, D. O'Connor, and A. Lloyd (eds.), *Ancient Egypt, A Social History* (Cambridge UK: Cambridge University Press: 71–182.

— (2006), *Ancient Egypt, Anatomy of a Civilization* (2nd ed.) (London: Routledge).

Kessler, Dieter (1981), *Historische Topographie der Region zwischen Mallawai und Samalut.* Tübinger Atlas des Vorderen Orients, Beiheft 30 (Wiesbaden: Reichert).

Kohler, Timothy and George J. Gumerman, eds. (2000), *Dynamics in Human and Primate Societies: Agent-Based Modeling of Social and Spatial Processes* (New York: Oxford University Press).

Kolchin, Peter (1987), *Unfree Labor: American Slavery and Russian Serfdom* (Cambridge, MA: Harvard University Press).

Krejcí, Jaromír (2009), *The Architecture of the Mastaba of Ptahshepses,* Abusir XI (Prague: Charles University).

— (2010), *The Royal Necropolis in Abusir,* Abusir XVIII (Prague: Charles University).

Krzyszkowska, Olga (1990), *Ivory and Related Materials: An Illustrated Guide.* Classical Handbook 3. Bulletin Supplement 59 (London: Institute of Classical Studies).

Labrousse, Audran and Jean Philippe Lauer (2000), *Les complexes funéraires d'Ouserkaf et de Néferhétepés.* 2 vols. Bd 130/1 (Cairo: IFAO).

— (2002), *La chaussée du complexe funéraire du roi Ounas*, Bd 134 (Cairo: IFAO).

Lehner, Mark (1985), "The Development of the Giza Necropolis: The Khufu Project," *MDAIK* 41: 109–143.

— (1992), "Excavations at Giza: 1988–1991," in W. M. Sumner (ed.), *The Oriental Institute News and Notes* 135 (Fall): 1–9.

— (1993), "Giza," in W. M. Sumner (ed.), *The Oriental Institute 1991–1992 Annual Report* (Chicago: The Oriental Institute): 56–67.

— (1997), *The Complete Pyramids* (London: Thames and Hudson).

— (1998), "Niches, Slots, Grooves and Stains: Internal Frameworks in the Khufu Pyramid?" in H. Guksch and D. Ploz (eds.), *Stationen: Beiträge zur Kulturgeschichte Ägyptens, Rainer Stadelmann gewidmet* (Mainz: Philipp von Zabern).

— (2000), "The Fractal House of Pharoah: Ancient Egypt as a Complex Adaptive System, a Trial Formulation," in T. Kohler and G. J. Gumerman (eds.), *Dynamics in Human and Primate Societies: Agent-Based Modeling of Social and Spatial Processes* (New York: Oxford University Press): 275–353.

— (2002), "The Pyramid Age Settlement of the Southern Mount at Giza," *JARCE* 39: 27–74.

— (2003), "Life Stories of the Pyramid City Unfold," *Aeragram*: 6.2: 1, 4–5.

— (2004), "Zau of What? The Royal Guard?" *Aeragram* 7.1: 14–15.

— (2007), "Introduction," in Lehner and Wetterstrom 2007: 3–47.

— (2009), "Capital Zone Walk-About 2006: Spot Heights on the Third Millennium Landscape," in Lehner, Kamel and Tavares 2009b: 97–151.

— (2010), "Villages and the Old Kingdom," in Wendrich 2010: 85–101.

— (2013) "The Heit el-Ghurab Site Reveals a New Face: The Lost Port City of the Pyramids," *Aeragram* 14.1: 2–7.

— (forthcoming), "The Menkaure Valley Temple Occupation in Context," *Towards a New History for the Old Kingdom: Perspectives on the Pyramid Age,* Symposium at Harvard University April 26, 2012.

Lehner, Mark, ed. (2011), *Giza Plateau Mapping Project, Season 2009, Preliminary Report*, Giza Occasional Papers 5 (Boston: AERA).

Lehner, Mark, and Ana Tavares (2010), "Walls, Ways, and Stratigraphy: Signs of Social Control in an Urban Footprint at Giza," in M. Bietak, E. Czerny, and I. Forstner-Müller (eds.), *Cities and Urbanism in Ancient Egypt* (Vienna: Österreichische Akademie der Wissenschaften): 171–216.

Lehner, Mark, Mohsen Kamel and Ana Tavares, eds. (2009), *Giza Plateau Mapping Project Seasons 2006–07 Preliminary Report,* Giza Occasional Papers 3 (Boston: Ancient Egypt Research Associates).

Lehner, Mark and Freya Sadarangani (2007), "Beds for Bowabs in a Pyramid City," in Hawass and Richards 2007: 73–96.

Lehner, Mark and Wilma Wetterstrom, eds. (2007), *Giza Reports. The Giza Plateau Mapping Project, Vol. 1: Project History, Survey, Ceramics and Main Street and Gallery III.4 Operations* (Boston: AERA.)

Lewin, Roger (1992), *Complexity: Life and the Edge of Chaos* (New York: Macmillan).

Lichtheim, Miriam (1975), *Ancient Egyptian Literature, Vol. I: The Old and Middle Kingdoms* (Los Angeles: University of California Press).

Linseele, Veerle and Wim Van Neer (2009), "Exploitation of Desert and Other Wild Game in Ancient Egypt: The Archaeozoological Evidence from the Nile Valley," in Riemer *et al.* 2009: 47–78.

Lineweaver, Paul, C.W. Davies and Michael Ruse (2013), *Complexity and the Arrow of Time* (Cambrige: Cambridge University Press).

Lopez, Jesus (1966), "Las inscripciones rupestres faraónicas entre Korosko y Kasr Ibrim," Inst. Español de Prehistoria—C.S.I.C.Madrid.

— (1967) "Inscriptions de l'Ancien Empire à Khor el-Aquiba," *RdÉ* 19: 51–66.

Loprieno, Antonio (1997), "Slaves," in S. Donadoni (ed.), *The Egyptians* (Chicago: The University of Chicago Press): 185–219.

Lutley, Katy and Judith Bunbury, (2008), "The Nile on the Move," *EA* 32 (Spring): 3–5.

Lydekker, Richard (1902), *Library of Natural History*, Vol. II (New York: Saalfield).

Malek, J. (1992), "The Annals of Amenemhet II," *EA* 2: 16.

Malek, Jaromir and Werner Foreman (1986), *In the Shadow of the Pyramids: Egypt During the Old Kingdom*, Echoes of the Ancient World (London: Golden Press).

Malek, Jaromir and Stephen Quirke (1992), "Memphis, 1991: Epigraphy," *JEA* 78: 13–18.

Malleson, Claire (2013), "Egypt Earliest Olive Pit Reconsidered: A Case of Mistaken Identity?" *Aeragram* 14.1(Spring): 24.

Manlius, Nicolas (2000), "Biogéographie et Ecologie historique de l'hippopotame en Egypte," *Belgian Journal of Zoology* 130 (1): 59–66.

Manzo, Andrea (2010), "Typological and Functional Remarks on Some Structures at Mersa Gewasis (Red Sea, Egypt), in F. Raffaele, M. Nuzzolo, and I. Incordina (eds.), *Recent Discoveries and Latest Researches in Egyptology* (Wiesbaden: Harrassowitz): 157–175.

Marcus, Ezra S. (2002), "Early Seafaring and Maritime Activity in the Southern Levant from Prehistory through the Third Millennium BCE," in E.C.M. van den Brick and T. E. Levy (eds.), *Egypt and the Levant: Interrelations from the 4th through the Early 3rd Millennium BCE* (London: Leicester University Press): 403–417.

— (2007), "Amenemhet II and the Sea: Maritime Aspects of the Mit Rahina (Memphis) Inscription," *ÄuL* 17: 137–190.

Marsot, A.L. al-Sayyid (1984/1996), *Egypt in the Reign of Muhammed Ali* (Cambridge: Cambridge University Press).

Menu, Bernadette (1998), *Recherches sur l'histoire juridique, économique et sociale de l'ancienne Égypte*, 2 vols. (Bibliothèque d'Étude 122. Cairo: Institut français d'archéologie orientale).

— (2004), "Captifs de guerre et dépendance rurale dans l'Égypte du Nouvel Empire," in Menu 2004: 187–209.

Menu, Bernadette, ed. (2004), *La dépendance rurale dans l'Antiquité égyptienne et proche-orientale.* BdÉ 140 (Cairo: IFAO).

Mitchell, Melanie (2009), *Complexity, A Guided Tour* (Oxford: Oxford University Press.

Mitchell, Timothy (1991), *Colonising Egypt* (Berkeley: University of California Press).

Moens, Marie-Francine and Wilma Wetterstrom (1988), "The Agricultural Economy of an Old Kingdom Town in Egypt's West Delta: Insights from the Plant Remains," *JNES* 47: 159–173.

Morell, Virginia (2001), "The Pyramid Builders," *National Geographic* (November): 79–99.

Moreno García, Juan Carlos (1996), "Administration territoriale et organisation de l'espace en Egypte au troisième millénaire avant J.-C.: *grgt* et le titre *ꜥ(n)ḏ-mr grgt*," *ZÄS* 123: 116–138.

— (1997), "Administration territoriale et organisation de l'espace en Egypte au troisième millénaire avant J.C. (II): *swnw*," *ZÄS* 124: 116–130.

— (1998a), "Administration territoriale et organisation de l'espace en Egypte au troisième millénaire avant J.C. (II): *niwt, mꜣwt* et *ḥwt-ꜥꜣt*," *ZÄS* 125: 38–55.

— (1998b), "La population *mrt*, une approche du problème de la servitude dans l'Egypte du IIIe millénaire (I), *JEA*: 84: 71–83.

— (1999), *Ḥwt et le milieu rural égyptien du IIIe millénaire: économie, administration et organisation territoriale* (Bibliothèque de l'Ecole des Hautes Etudes – Sciences Historiques et Philologiques 337. Paris: Honoré Champion).

— (2008), "La dépendance rurale en Égypte ancienne," (review article), *JESHO* 51: 99–150.

— (2012), "Households," in E. Frood and W. Wendrich (eds.), *UCLA Encyclopedia of Egyptology*, Los Angeles (http://digital2.library.ucla.edu/viewItem.do?ark=21198/zz002czx07).

— (2013a), "The Territorial Administration of the Kingdom in the 3rd Millennium," in Moreno García 2013: 85–151.

— (2013b), "The 'Other' Administration: Patronage, Factions and Informal Networks of Power in Ancient Egypt," in Moreno García 2013: 1029–1065.

Moreno García, Juan Carlos, ed. (2013), *Ancient Egyptian Administration.* Handbook of Oriental Studies, Section 1, Ancient Near East (Leiden: Brill).

Moeller, Nadine (2005), "An Old Kingdom Town at Zawiet Sultan (Zawiet Meitin) in Middle Egypt: A Preliminary Report," in A. Cooke and F. Simpson (eds.), *Current Research in Egyptology II January 2001*, BAR International Series 1380 (Oxford: Archeopress): 29–38.

Moussa, A. M. and H. Altenmüller (1977), *Das Grab des Nianchchnum und Chnumhotep*, Archäologische Veröffentlichungen 21 (Mainz: Philipp von Zabern).

Mueller, Dieter (1967), "Neue Urkunden zur Verwaltung im Mittleren Reich," *Orientalia* 36: 351–364.

— (1975), "Some Remarks on Wage Rates in the Middle Kingdom," *JNES* 34.4 (Oct.): 249–263.

Naville, Édouard (1989), *The Temple of Deir el-Bahri III.* (London: Egypt Exploration Society).

Neef, Reinder (1990), "Introduction, Development, and Environmental Implications of Olive Culture: The Evidence from Jordan," in S. Bottema, G. Ents-Nieborg and W. van Zeist (eds.), *Man's Role in the Shaping of the Eastern Mediterranean Landscape* (Rotterdam: Balkema): 295–306.

Nicholson, Paul T. and Ian Shaw (eds.) (2000), *Ancient Egyptian Materials and Technology* (Cambridge: Cambridge University Press).

Nieboer, H.J. (1900), *Slavery as an Industrial System: Ethnological Researches* (The Hague: Martinus Nijhoff).

Nolan, John (2003), "The Original Lunar Calendar and Cattle Counts in Old Kingdom Egypt," in S. Bickel and A. Loprieno (eds.), *Basel Egyptology Prize 1* (Basel: Schwabe & Co. AG): 75–97.

— (2010), *Mud Sealings and Fourth Dynasty Administration at Giza.* Ph.D. dissertation, Dept. of Near Eastern Languages and Civilizations, University of Chicago.

Nolan, J. and A. Pavlick (2008), "Impressions of the Past: Seals and Sealings from Pottery Mound," *Aeragram* 9.1: 2–4.

Nolan, J. and G. Heindl (2010), "Double-Decker Dorm? Reconstructing the Galleries," *Aeragram* 11.2: 7–9.

Ownby, Mary F. (2012), "The Importance of Imports: Petrographic Analysis of Levantine Pottery Jars in Egypt," *JAEI* 4.3: 23–29.

Paget, R.F.E., A.A. Pirie and F.Ll. Griffith (1898), *The Tomb of Ptah-hetep.* Bound with J.E. Quibell and W. Spiegelberg, *The Ramesseum.* (British School of Archaeology in Egypt). Egyptian Research Account 1896 (London: Bernard Quaritch).

Perring, John Shea (1839–1842), *The Pyramids of Gizeh, From Actual Survey and Measurement*, 3 fascicles (London: J. Fraser).

Posener-Kriéger, Paule (1975), "Les Papyrus de Gébélein. Remarques préliminaires," *RdÉ* 27: 211–221.

— (1976), *Les archives du temple funéraire de Néferirkarê-kakaï (les papyrus d'Abousir)*, 2 vols. (Cairo: IFAO).

Posener-Kriéger, Paule, Miroslav Verner, and Hana Vymazalová (2006), *The Pyramid Complex of Raneferef, The Papyrus Archive.* Abusir X (Prague: Czech Institute of Egyptology).

Powell, Marvin A., ed. (1987), *Labor in the Ancient Near East.* American Oriental Series 68 (New Haven: American Oriental Society)

Redding, Richard (1991), "The Role of the Pig in the Subsistence System of Ancient Egypt: A Parable on the Potential of Faunal Data," in P. J. Crabtree and K. Ryan (eds.), *Animal Use and Culture Change*, MASCA Research Papers in Science and Archaeology, Supplement to Vol. 8 (Philadelphia: University of Pennsylvania Museum of Archaeology and Anthropology): 20–30.

— (1992), "Egyptian Old Kingdom Patterns of Animal Use and the Value of Faunal Data in Modeling Socioeconomic Systems," *Paléorient* 18: 99–107.

— (2007a), "Main Street Faunal Remains," in Lehner and Wetterstrom 2007: 171–178.

— (2007b), "Gallery III.4 Faunal Remains," in Lehner and Wetterstrom 2007: 263–269.

— (2007c), "Treasures from a High-Class Dump," *Aeragram* 8.2: 6–7.

— (2010a), "Appendix A. Preliminary Report on the Faunal Remains Recovered from Feature 21,577 (SFW.PM)," in Nolan 2010: 408–417.

— (2010b), "Appendix B. Preliminary Report on the Faunal Remains Recovered from Feature 24,462 (SFW.PM)," in Nolan 2010: 418–427.

— (2010c), "Status and Diet at the Workers' Town, Giza, Egypt," in Campana *et al.* 2010: 65–75.

— (2011a), "The Telltale Tooth," *Aeragram* 12.1: 14.

— (2011b), "The OK Corral: Standing Wall Island Mystery, Solved," *Aeragram* 12.1: 2–5.

— (2011c), "Why We Excavate Where We Do," in Lehner 2011: 105–109.

— (forthcoming), "A Tale of Two Sites", in B. De Cupere, V. Linseele, and S. Hamilton-Dyer (eds.), *Proceedings of the 10th Meeting of the ICAZ Working Group 'Archaeozoology of Southwest Asia and Adjacent Areas'.* Ancient Near Eastern Studies Supplement Series (Leuven: Peeters): 307–322.

Redding, Richard, and Claire Malleson (forthcoming), "Modeling Old Kingdom Food Production: What is the Limiting Factor?"

Redford, Donald (1993), *Egypt, Canaan, and Israel in Ancient Times* (Princeton: Princeton University Press).

Reisner, George Andrew (1931), *Mycerinus, The Temples of the Third Pyramid at Giza* (Cambridge, MA: Harvard University Press).

Reisner, George Andrew and William Stevenson Smith (1955), *A History of the Giza Necropolis Vol. 2. The Tomb of Hetep-heres, The Mother of Cheops: A Study of Egyptian Civilization in the Old Kingdom.* (Cambridge, MA: Harvard University Press).

Ricke, Herbert (1969), *Das Sonnenheiligtum des Königs Userkaf II*. BÄBA 8 (Wiesbaden: Schweizerisches Institut für ägyptische Bauforschung und Altertumskunde).

Riemer, H., F. Förster, M. Herb, and N. Pöllath, eds. (2009), *Desert Animals in the Eastern Sahara: Status, Economic Significance, and Cultural Reflection in Antiquity*, Proceedings of an Interdisciplinary ACACIA workshop held at the University of Cologne, December 14–15, 2007. Colloquium Africanum 4 (Cologne: Heinrich-Barth-Institut).

Roccati, Alessandro (1982), *La littérature historique sous l'ancien empire Égyptien.* (Paris: Les Éditions du Cerf).

Röder, Josef (1965), "Zur Steinbruchgeschichte des Rosengranits von Assuan," *Archäologischer Anzeiger* 3. Beiblatt zum Jahrbuch des Deutschen Archäologischen Instituts 80 (Berlin: Walter de Gruyter & Co.): 476–552.

Roth, Ann (1991), *Egyptian Phyles in the Old Kingdom,* SAOC 48 (Chicago: University of Chicago Press).

— (1995), *A Cemetery of Palace Attendants, Including G2084–2099, G2230+2231 and G2240* (Boston: Museum of Fine Arts).

— (2002), "The Meaning of Menial Labor 'Servant Statues' in Old Kingdom Serdabs," *JARCE* 39: 103–121.

Rowe, Alan (1936), *A Catalogue of Egyptian Scarabs, Scaraboids, Seals and Amulets in the Palestine Archaeological Museum* (Cairo: IFAO).

— (1938), "Provisional Notes on the Old Kingdom Inscriptions from the Diorite Quarries," *ASAÉ* 38: 391–296.

Sadarangani, Freya (2009), "BB: The Royal Administrative Building (a.k.a. RAB)," in Lehner, Kamel, and Tavares 2009: 59–65.

Sadarangani, Freya and Yukinori Kawae (2011), "Soccer Field West, House Unit 1, 2009," in Lehner 2011: 135–145.

Saleh, Abd el-Aziz (1974), "Excavations Around the Mycerinus Pyramid Complex." *MDAIK* 30: 131–154.

Samuel, Delwen, (1993), "Ancient Egyptian Cereal Processing: Beyond the Artistic Record, *Cambridge Archaeological Journal* 3.2: 276–283.

Sander-Hansen, C. E. (1933), *Historische Inschriften der 19. Dynastie, Teil I* (Bruxelles: Fondation Égyptologie Reine Élisabeth).

Säve-Soderbergh, Torgny (1953), *On Egyptian Representations of Hippopotamus Hunting as a Religious Motif.* Horae Soderblomianae 3 (Uppsala: C.W.K. Gleerup Lund).

Sayed, Abdel Monem A.H. (1977), "Discovery of the Site of the 12th Dynasty Port at Wadi Gawasis on the Red Sea Shore, *RdÉ* 29:150–173.

Schloen, David (2001), *The House of the Father as Fact and Symbol* (Winona Lake: Eisenbrauns).

Schmitz, Bettina (1976), *Untersuchungen zum Titel S3-NJSWT "Königssohn"* (Bonn: Rudolf Habelt).

Schneider, Hans D. (1977), *Shabtis: An Introduction to the History of Ancient Egyptian Funerary Statuettes, Vol. 1* (Leiden: Rijksmuseum van Oudheden).

Schneider, Thomas (2010), "Foreigners in Egypt," in Wendrich, ed. (2010): 143–163.

Schott, Siegfried (1965), "Aufnahmen vom Hungersnotrelief aus dem Aufweg der Unaspyramide," *RdÉ* 17: 7–13.

Scott, J. C. (1998), *Seeing Like a State.* (New Haven: Yale University Press).

Seidlmayer, Stefan (1996), "Town and State in the Early Old Kingdom: A View from Elephantine," in J. Spence (ed.), *Aspects of Early Egypt* (London: British Museum Press): 108–127.

Serpico, Margaret (2000), "Resins, Amber, and Bitumen," in Nicholson and Shaw 2000: 430–474.

Serpico, Margaret and Raymond White (2000), "Oil, Fat, and Wax," in Nicholson and Shaw 2000: 390–429.

Serpico, Margaret, Janine Bourriau, L.M.V. Smith, Y. Goren, B. Stern, and C. Heron, (2003), "Commodities and Containers: A Project to Study Canaanite Amphorae Imported into Egypt During the New Kingdom," in M. Bietak (ed.), *The Synchronization of Civilizations in the Second Millennium B.C. II* (Vienna: Österreichische Akademie der Wissenschaften): 365–376.

Sethe, Kurt (1904), *Hieroglyphische Urkunden der Griechisch-Römischen Zeit II* (Leipzig: Hinrichs).

— (1933), *Urkunden des alten Reiches I* (Leipzig: Hinrichs).

Shaw, Jonathan (2003), "Who Built the Pyramids?" *Harvard Magazine* 105.6 (July-August): 42–49, 99.

Shirley, JJ (2013), "Crisis and Restructuring of the State: From the Second Intermediate Period to the Advent of the Ramesses," in Moreno García 2013: 521–606.

Sidney, Jasmine (1965), "The Past and Present Distribution of Some African Ungulates," *Transactions of the Zoological Society of London* 30: 1–399.

Smith, Craig (2006), *How the Great Pyramid Was Built.* (New York: HarperCollins).

Smith, William Stevenson (1952), "Inscriptional Evidence for the History of the Fourth Dynasty," *JNES* 11: 113–128.

Sowada, Karin N. (2009), *Egypt in the Eastern Mediterranean during the Old Kingdom: An Archaeological Perspective,* Orbis Biblicus et Orientalis 237 (Fribourg: Academic Press).

Spalinger, Anthony (2013a), "The Organisation of the Pharaonic Army (Old to New Kingdom)," in Moreno García 2013: 393–478.

— (2013b) "Further Remarks on the Old Kingdom Phyle System," *Orientalia* 83(3): 157–177–206.

Staehelin, Elisabeth (1978), "Zur Bedeutung der Jag im alten Ägypten.," in M. Triet (ed.), *Spiel und Sport im alten Ägypten. Beiträge und Notizen zur Ausstellung im Schweizerischen Sportmuseum Basel, 1.9–30.10* (Basel: Schweizerisches Sportmuseum): 23–35.

Stadelmann, Rainer (1981a) "La ville de pyramide à l'ancien empire," *RdÉ* 33: 67–77.

— (1981b), "Die *ḪNTJW-Š*, der Königsbezirk *Š N PR ʿ3* und die Namen der Grabanlagen der Frühzeit. *BIFAO* 81: 155–164.

— (1984) "Pyramidenstadt," *LÄ* V: 10–14.

— (1985), *Die ägyptischen Pyramiden: vom Ziegelbau zum Weltwunder* (Mainz: Philipp von Zabern).

— (1987), "Beiträge zur Geschichte des Alten Reiches: Die Länge der Regierung des Snofru," *MDAIK* 43: 229–240.

Stager, Lawrence. E. (1985a), "The First Fruits of Civilization," in J.N. Tubb (ed.), *Palestine in the Bronze and Iron Ages: Papers in Honour of Olga Tufnell.* (London: Institute of Archaeology): 172–188.

— (1985b), "The Archaeology of the Family in Ancient Israel. *BASOR* 260 (Fall, November): 1–35.

Steinkeller, Piotr (forthcoming), "The Employment of Labor on National Building Projects in the Ur III Period."

Stewart, Harry M. (1995), *Egyptian Shabtis.* Shire Egyptology (Buckinghamshire: Shire Publications).

Stille, Alexander (2005), "Mark Lehner," *Smithsonian* (November): 62–64.

Strudwick, Nigel (1985), *The Administration of Egypt in the Old Kingdom: the Highest Titles and Their Holders* (Boston: KPI).

— (2005), *Texts from the Pyramid Age* (Leiden: Brill).

Tallet, Pierre (2012), "Ayn Sukhna and Wadi el-Jarf: Two Newly Discovered Pharaonic Harbours on the Suez Gulf," *BMSAES* 18: 147–168.

— (2013), "The Wadi el-Jarf Site: A Harbor of Khufu on the Red Sea," *JAEI* 5(1): 76–84.

— (forthcoming), "Un aperçu de la région Memphite à la fin du règne de Chéops selon le 'journal de Merer' (P. Jarf I-III), in S. Dhennin and Cl. Somaglino (eds.). *Toponymie et perception de l'espace en Egypte de l'Antiquité au Moyen Age* (Cairo: IFAO).

Tallet, Pierre and Grégory Marouard (2012), "An Early Pharaonic Harbour on the Red Sea Coast," *EA* 40: 40–43.

— (2014), "The Harbor of Khufu on the Red Sea Coast at Wadi al-Jarf, Egypt," *Near Eastern Archaeology* 77:1: 4–14.

Tallet, Pierre, Grégory Marouard and Damien Laisney (2012), "Un port de la IVe dynastie au Ouadi el-Jarf (mer Rouge)," *BIFAO* 112: 399–426.

Tavares, Ana (2011), "Village, Town, and Barracks: A Fourth Dynasty Settlement at Heit-el-Ghurab, Giza," in N. Strudwick and H. Strudwick (eds.) *Old Kingdom New Perspectives: Egyptian Art and Archaeology 2750–2150 BC* (Oxford: Oxbow Books): 271–277.

Toth, James (1993), "Manufacturing Consent and Resistance in Peripheral Production: The Labor Process among Egyptian Migrant Workers and Egyptian National Development," *Dialectical Anthropology* 18: 291–335.

Trail, John S. (1975), *The Political Organization of Attica: A Study of the Demes, Trittyes, and Phylai and Their Representations in the Athenian Council*, (Princeton: American School of Classical Studies at Athens).

Turner, Victor (1969) *The Ritual Process: Structure and Anti-Structure* (New York: Aldine).

Vachala, Bretislav (1991), "Zur Frage der Kriegsgefangenen in Ägypten. Überlegungen anhand der schriftlichen Quellen des Alten Reiches," in Endesfelder 1991: 93–99.

— (2004), *Die Relieffragmente aus der Mastaba des Ptahschepses in Abusir*, Abusir VIII (Prague: Czech Institute of Egyptology).

Veldmeijer, A.J., C. Zazzaro, A. J. Clapham, C.R. Cartwright, and F. Hagen (2008), "The 'Rope Cave' at Mersa/Wadi Gewasis," *JARCE* 44: 9–39.

Verner, Miroslav (1991), "Zur Organisierung der Arbeitskräfte auf den Großbaustellen der Alten Reichs-Nekropolen," in Endesfelder 1991: 61–91.

— (2003), "The Abusir Builders' Crews," in N. Kloth, K. Martin, E. Pardey (eds.), *Festschrift für Hartwig Altenmüller*, Studien zur Altägyptischen Kultur, Beiheft 9 (Hamburg : Helmut Buske Verlag): 445–451.

Vymazalová, Hana (2013), "The Administration of the Royal Funerary Complexes," in Moreno García 2013: 177–195.

Waldrop, M. Mitchell (1992), *Complexity: The Emerging Science at the Edge of Order and Chaos* (New York: Simon and Schuster).

Ward, Cheryl (2012), "Building Pharaoh's Ships: Cedar, Incense, and Sailing the Great Green," *BMSAES* 18: 217–232.

Ward, Cheryl and Chiara Zazzaro (2009), "Evidence for Pharaonic Seagoing Ships at Mersa/Wadi Gawasis, Egypt," *The International Journal of Nautical Archaeology* 39: 1–17.

Ward, W.A. (1991), "Early Contacts Between Egypt, Canaan and Sinai: Remarks on the Paper by Amnon Ben-Tor," *BASOR* 281: 11–26.

Warden, Leslie Anne (2014), *Pottery and Economy in Old Kingdom Egypt* (Leiden: Brill).

Wegner, Josef (2010), "Tradition and Innovation: The Middle Kingdom," in Wendrich 2010: 119–142.

Wendrich, ed. (2010), *Egyptian Archaeology* (Malden/Oxford: Wiley-Blackwell.

Wenke, Robert J., Paul E. Buck, Hany A. Hamroush, Michal Kobusiewicz, Karla Kroeper, and Richard Redding (1988), "Kom el-Hisn: Excavation of an Old Kingdom Settlement in the Egyptian Delta," *JARCE* 25: 5–34.

Wodzińska, Anna (2007), "Preliminary Report on the Ceramics," in Lehner and Wetterstrom 2007: 279–324.

Wodzińska, Anna, and Mary Ownby (2011), "Tentative Remarks on Levantine Combed Ware from Heit el-Ghurab, Giza," in J. Mynářová (ed.), *Egypt and the Near East—The Crossroads* (Prague: Czech Institute of Egyptology): 285–295.

Willcocks, William (1889), *Egyptian Irrigation* (London: Spon Ltd.).

Wilkinson, Toby A. H. (2000), *The Royal Annals of Ancient Egypt: The Palermo Stone and its Associated Fragments* (London: Kegan Paul International).

Willems, H., S. Vereecken, L. Kuijper, B. Vanthuyne, E. Marinova, V. Linseele, G. Verstraeten, S. Hendrickx, M. Eykerman, A. Van den Broeck, W. Van Neer, J. Bourriau, P. French, C. Peeters, V. De Laet, S. Mortier, and Z. De Kooning (2009), "An Industrial Site at Al-Shaykh Saʿid/Wadi Zabayda," *ÄuL* 19: 293–331.

Yoyotte, Jean (1959), "Le bassin de Djâroukha," *Kêmi: Revue de Philologie et d'Achéologie* 15: 23–33.

Zeder, Melinda A. (1991), *Feeding Cities; Specialized Animal Economy in the Ancient Near East* (Washington: Smithsonian Institution Press).

Ziegler, Christiane (1993), *Le Mastaba d'Akhethetep: Une Chapelle Funéraire de l'Ancien Empire* (Paris: Editions de la Réunion des Musées Nationaux).

— (2007), *Le Mastaba d'Akhethetep*, Fouilles du Louvre à Saqqara I (Leuven/Paris: Peeters/Musée du Louvre).

Zohary, Daniel and Maria Hopf (1993), *Domestication of Plants in the Old World* (Oxford: Clarendon Press).

8.

Problems of Authority, Compulsion, and Compensation in Ancient Egyptian Labor Practices

Ogden Goelet, Jr.
New York University

I. Introduction: Fundamental Problems in the Study of Egyptian Labor

Although nearly three decades have passed since the publication of the *Labor in the Ancient Near East*, itself the outgrowth of a section of a conference held about a decade earlier,[1] the purpose of this paper is not to offer a full-scale reexamination of the question of labor in ancient Egypt. Such an endeavor would be far beyond the intent (and scope!) of the present collection of essays—one need only consider that in the 1987 conference volume the Egyptian aspects alone had three separate papers, which covered 2100 years of history and comprised nearly 210 pages of discussion.[2] Among other major contributions to the study of labor practices in Egypt in the interim, one also should consider a more recent volume of conference papers edited by Bernadette Menu[3] as one example among many. In addition there have been recent comprehensive studies on aspects of Egyptian administration and administrative documents.[4] Instead, I intend to focus primarily on two interrelated questions, probably unanswerable, that lie at the foundation of all work—what was the relationship between employer and laborer, how should one weigh the

1 Powell 1987. For the history of the collection, see also Powell's introductory remarks, *op. cit.* vi-vii.

2 The three essays on Egypt in Powell's collection were: Berlev 1987, "A Social Experiment in Nubia during the Years 9–17 of Sesostris I"; Eyre 1987a, "Work and Organisation of Work in the New Kingdom"; and Eyre 1987b, "Work and Organisation of Work in the Old Kingdom."

3 Menu 2010.

influence of class and status, and what induced an individual to work? Implicit in these questions is a range of motivations ranging from an individual worker's profit incentive to the compulsory labor of corvée and slavery.

Any study of labor in Egypt in the period from the New Kingdom up to the start of the Hellenistic era must overcome some considerable technical obstacles from the beginning, if for no other reason than the intrinsic difficulty of examining a major sector of the unmonetized economy in isolation of other factors.[5] As we shall see repeatedly in the discussions below, the question of Egyptian labor is necessarily intertwined, perhaps inextricably, with such issues as the structure of the state, the nature of private landowning, the definition of slavery, among other subjects. In fact, it would be fair to say that the study of labor in ancient Egypt often leads into a definitional and lexicographical morass. Additional problems arise because the available evidence on the economic and social life tends to be heavily skewed towards the upper class and the vast institutions that the elite managed. As far as documentation of labor practices is concerned, a very high proportion of what survived derives from official, rather than private sources. At the same time, remarkably enough, institutional records seldom provide much insight on how labor was recruited, managed, and recompensed on specific projects. For example, records of work projects such as quarrying and mining expeditions or a building project at the beginning of the Twelfth Dynasty often consist mainly of work rosters.[6] Occasionally the titles of the individuals mentioned can give one an idea of what the status of expedition or project members might have been—at least on the upper echelons of the work force. One of the few exceptions to these generalizations comes from that most unusual of Egyptian communities,

4 Moreno García 2013 and Eyre 2013.

5 The question of 'money' in Egypt is more complicated than it appears on the surface and should not be linked solely to the use of precious metals as standards of exchange. Menu has raised the question as to whether some of the numerous records of private transactions recorded at Deir el-Medina might not have functioned as more than proof in the event of legal disputes, but may have also served as a local form of "monnaie scripturale," see Menu 1979. On the question of money and monetization, see also Römer 1998: 136–142.

6 Perhaps the best documented of all Egyptian work projects date to the early part of Dynasty Twelve and are recorded on the Reisner Papyri, see Simpson 1963, 1965, 1969, and 1986.

Ramesside Deir el-Medina, a government-subsidized village where the highly skilled artisans who built and decorated the royal tombs dwelled. Much of the evidence on labor from this site was produced by the inhabitants of this cloistered community for the records of the official institution to which they were attached. Considering that their work required access to the royal tombs in the Valley of the Kings and involved creating highly valuable items for the king's burial—the extraordinary wealth from the tomb of Tutankhamun comes immediately to mind—these men and their families seem to have enjoyed a comfortable, but sequestered existence. To what extent they were free is debatable.[7] We should avoid the temptation to assume that conditions at Deir el-Medina can be applied equally to the vast agricultural economy, where we are forced to examine the management of labor almost entirely from the institutional, official viewpoint.

Unlike the other essays in this volume, the present study must focus heavily on agricultural labor—otherwise there would be insufficient documentation for a real discussion. We are hindered too by our lack of understanding of the fiscal regime that funded the nationwide temple and royal organizations.[8] Only scattered bits of documentation concerning the skilled labor of artisans and their recompense has survived, even when these men were employed by institutions. This imbalance in the nature of the available evidence certainly reflects the character of most labor

7 On this question, see Burkard 2003a; *idem* 2003b; and Dorn 2009; for a contrary opinion, see Ventura 1986: 120–144. The "walls" (*inbw*) around the settlement mentioned in some texts appear to have been watch stations that restricted access (or egress) from the settlement. Demarée (2010: 186–187) notes that prior to the end of the Eighteenth Dynasty, the workforce that operated in the Valley of the Kings may not have been gathered into a single, unified and long-standing workforce or community until the establishment of the Deir el-Medina community during the reign of Horemheb. For the Deir el-Medina community during the Eighteenth Dynasty, see also Valbelle 1985: 1–26, esp. p. 10; Megally 1974; Haring 2006: 107–109. Prior to that time, crews of specialized workers from Thebes and the neighboring region apparently were gathered for the tasks at hand. Perhaps the wave of tomb robberies that occurred during the Amarna Period and its immediate aftermath awakened the Theban authorities to the need of greater control over those working in the Valley.

8 For discussion of the construction of the pyramids of the Old Kingdom, see Lehner in this volume. Kings initiated the building and the funding of the great divine temples of the New Kingdom, including the various cults within them, see Andrássy 2007, but occasionally private persons also contributed to the maintenance of temples and cults, see Eyre 2010.

arrangements between private individuals—these would overwhelmingly be connected with farming. Since a predominantly pre-literate environment prevailed in the countryside, most business arrangements were concluded on the basis of long-standing local arrangements and were normally made orally and informally—'off the grid,' to use a modern American expression. Under these conditions, the dearth of private documentation on agriculture and its associated labor is only to be expected.[9] We should not conclude that private hire was rare—on the contrary, it likely was overwhelmingly the normal state of affairs in countryside—but it would rarely leave any trace in the written record. As it is often said, the absence of evidence is not evidence of absence.

The Efficacy of Lexicographical Approaches to Egyptian Labor and Labor Practices

This overview of labor and command shall discuss the relevant Egyptian terminology, but without the usual amount of emphasis on the lexicographical issues, even though nearly all our information on labor practices must inevitably be filtered through textual sources.[10] Usually one of the most fruitful methods of examining cultural or economic aspects of ancient societies is to examine the pertinent vocabulary, then show how these terms were used in the evidence. In the case of the Egyptian

[9] On this point, see Eyre 1999: 50–51. Other than the Hekanakhte letters, almost no documentation of agricultural arrangements between private individuals has survived and even in this case no actual record of a lease has survived. Even in this instance, Hekanakhte requests that arrangements be made, but we are never given the wording or the form of these agreements. A rare written reference to an agricultural arrangement between private individuals is provided by an Eighteenth Dynasty 18 letter (Pap. Louvre 3230a) that is strongly reminiscent of some themes in the Hekanakhte correspondence, from a man who identifies the addressee as his 'brother,' which could possibly be a term for 'colleague.' He informs the recipient that "I sowed much barley for you, and now it has grown for you [...] into your(?) barley which is in a corner of arable land along with your flax...," see Wente 1990 no. 116, pp. 91–92 and Peet 1926: 70–74, but note also the remarks of Eyre 1994: 48–50 with n. 93.

For the Hekanakhte letters, see primarily Allen 2004. For other some discussions of the leasing practices, see James 1962; Goedicke 1984; and Baer 1963.

[10] A skeptical view of efficacy of such lexically-based approaches to problems in ancient Egyptian history—quite correct in my opinion—has been put forth by Eyre 2004: 157–159.

economy, unfortunately, such lexicographical studies have been far less fruitful than one might expect. One obvious reason for this failure lies in the great chronological sweep of Egypt's political and economic history. For example, some economic terms that occur prominently in Old Kingdom decrees largely disappeared from the record in subsequent periods, underwent considerable changes in their meaning, or were replaced by other terms, presumably synonyms.[11] Similarly, there could be a major reorganization of the basic administrative structure, even within a single dynasty, like the one that occurred during the reigns of Senwosret III and his successor.[12] Although economic and administrative practices were in a constant state of flux, the Egyptians had a tendency to reuse or slightly modify the same words to describe realities that had changed considerably in the interim.

Additional problems arise because of the great disparity between today's world and Ancient Egypt. In the Western world, doubtlessly because of the enduring influence of the Roman state, there has always been a close connection between the law and most economic transactions, leading to the expectation that Egyptian economic terminology had an equivalent degree of exactitude that actually seldom existed in pharaonic times. The remarkable lack of terminological precision in Egyptian economic transactions, combined with a similar vagueness in defining the relative social status of the individuals involved have often led studies with a lexicographical focus scholars to a common methodological pitfall. This is the temptation to match (or translate) Egyptian vocabulary with modern economic and social concepts, a misstep that is often compounded by a desire to find a unitary rendering of a given word. However, as Janssen once warned in a discussion of several attempts to define such key words

11 For examples, the words *wpt*, *ḥ3*, and *st-ḥ3* all indicate finely differentiated types of impositions in the form of work that play an important role in the royal exemption decrees of the Old Kingdom, yet some of these disappeared from later texts or else were used elsewhere with considerably changed meanings, see Goedicke 1967: 60 (*st-ḥ3*); 119–120 (*ḥ3*); 47, 61, 132, 167–168 (*wpt*). On this point, see also Eyre, 1999: 52–53 and especially his overview of the problematic interpretation of the relevant vocabulary, Eyre 1987b: 18–19. Quirke (2004: 12–13), notes that *ḥ3w* continued as an uncommon word for corvée. He is uncertain as to the regularity of such impositions, which were likely to be *ad rem*.

12 Gesterman 1995. For a more specific treatment of the changes in the administrative structure over the course of the Twelfth Dynasty, see Grajetzki 2013: 215–225.

as *ỉnw* and *bꜣkw*, "...[a]gain, it seems to me that the author presents what *ỉnw* could mean according to *our* economic concepts, but that is not what the Egyptians had in mind when they used the word."[13] In the same article, Janssen additionally pointed out the dangers of seeking just one rendering of these fundamental economic words, noting as an example the evolution of the term *bꜣkw* over the course of time, during which he observed, "...the development from 'work' to 'product', and then to the 'value of the product' (hire charge). This is a well-known semantic process, not unlike a similar transformation once pointed out by Davies, by which a word for container came to denote the thing contained."[14]

Similar problems arise when we attempt to understand the distinction between two other common (and occasionally contrasted) words for labor: *kꜣt*, whose determinative (Sign-list A9) significantly depicts a man holding a common worker's basket on his head and , var. *bꜣk*, whose determinatives (Sign-list D40 and A24) simply denote vigorous action. The verb *bꜣk* is obviously related to the noun *bꜣk* "servant," leading one to the obvious assumption that *bꜣk* as a verb might denote some degree of involuntary labor, whereas *kꜣt* would apply to agricultural activity, royal projects including temple construction, as well as work of a more voluntary nature.[15] However, attempts to apply this supposition to actual texts in which these words appear quickly reveal that the situation was far more complicated than this simple proposition. The term *bꜣk* does not appear with the sense of "work" until the First Intermediate Period and can mean "product," "transform (raw materials)

13 Janssen 1993: 91. On the frequent methodological errors involved in such comparative exercises, see also Eyre 2004: 157–158. Among other difficulties, comparative approaches often fail to consider the extent to which the irrigation patterns and ecology of the country have changed since—and even during—pharaonic times,

14 Janssen 1993: 91, with n. 60–61. Similarly, the Egyptians did not distinguish between the part of the harvest paid out as tax or rent and the harvest itself; both were called *šmw*, see Eyre 1994: 127.

15 Kóthay 2010: 155–165, esp. 156–157. In light of the later development of the term *bꜣk* as described by Janssen and others, it might be better to distinguish between the terms more generally by adopting Eyre's suggestion (2013) that *kꜣt* is work "in the sense of '(physical) labor', as against *bꜣk* as 'work' in the sense of production." Perhaps more to the point on the term's variability is Eyre's observation (*ibid.* 208), "Economic power and political authority were direct reflections of control over production: *bꜣkw*, 'work', that *in context* [emphasis supplied] translates as 'production', 'revenues', 'taxes'.

by work," and "tax / imposition (in the form of labor)" as well,[16] a development that in itself indicates how the meaning of a fundamental term can change in the course of a few hundred years. Whatever the case might be, the advantage of being an administrator, manager, or a mere scribe is well stated in an oft-quoted passage from a Ramessside didactic text (Pap. Sallier I 6,10-6,11):[17]

> "Be a scribe. It saves you from toil (*kꜣt*) and protects you from all manner of work (*bꜣk*). It sunders you from plying the oar. You do not carry a basket nor are you under many lords and various masters."

Herein lies one of the central challenges of any economic history of ancient Egypt. Janssen's observations about changes in the concept of *bꜣkw* should be extended to the economy as a whole and to the terminology of labor in particular. There is a fundamental mismatch between the categories of labor in Egypt and the way in which their apparent equivalents have come to be defined in the contemporary world. For example, if we examine an important phenomenon such as slavery, it is rather difficult to define that concept in the Egyptian context with any precision from a modern perspective, with the result that the underlying problem only becomes greater when attempting to apply our conceptual framework to Egyptian practices. In all these efforts, we should also realize that we are, unconsciously or not, greatly influenced by the institution as it existed among the Romans.[18] Especially because of the Roman model, we might seek a legal exactitude that never existed in the practices of Egypt's great bureau-

16 Kóthay (2010: 162–163) stresses the transformative nature of *bꜣk*, but also notes some exceptions to her proposed distinction on pp. 164–165. It seems doubtful, however, that the Egyptians necessarily considered *bꜣk* as an inferior kind of labor in comparison with *kꜣt*. Even by the Middle Kingdom, one can already see the changes in the term according to the development that Janssen (1993) envisioned. Since raw materials were certainly transformed into finished products during the Old Kingdom, there may have been another terms for craft production or exploitation of natural resources at that time.

17 As noted by Eyre 2013: 9. For the text, see Gardiner 1937: 84; for the translation, see Caminos 1954: 317, with Egyptian transliteration supplied in parentheses.

18 Bernadette Menu has commented on the manner in which studies of slavery under Roman law have overly influenced our views on labor in the ancient world, see Menu 1998: 193–194. For another study on the inapplicability of other culturally based concepts of slavery to the Egyptian context, see Cruz-Uribe 1986.

cratic organizations. Finally, we must acknowledge that terminological consistency and precision would be unnecessary for the mundane, oral transactions between private individuals.

II. Authority, Compulsion, Compensation, and Labor

The basis of all authority in the monarchial state would presumably reside with the king. The king could initiate important projects by means of a royal command or decree (*wḏ-nswt*), a word that appears prominently at the beginning of Egyptian decrees.[19] Eyre has raised the possibility that there was also a more general term ʿ "authority, authorization (document), writ," whose fuller writings are supplied with (Sign-list Y3) significantly determined by the image of a rolled papyrus tied with a seal.[20]

An essential step towards grasping the nature of labor in the Egyptian economy is to understand the basis of *delegated* authority. Who besides the king could command and why? As the quote from Pap. Sallier I above shows, this question was closely entwined with another issue—who was exempt from compulsory labor? What gave some people the authority to command or contract labor? Understanding the nature of authority in the Egyptian context would allow us better to evaluate a wide variety of relationships implied by such key terms as leases, commissions, contracts, requests, and commands, especially when delegation of royal authority was probably implied. The latter two words—requests and commands—are of particular significance because they form part of a fluid scale that runs roughly from mutual bargaining to outright compulsion. The relationship between labor and command according to the degree of compulsion or obligation necessary thus effectively defined the nature of the work being performed. The balance of power, so to speak, between employer and laborer obviously varied from a negotiated payment for a skilled, free artisan to the uncompensated, involuntary labor that characterizes slavery. A problematic intermediary position arose, of course, when someone sold or leased out the labor of a third person, an arrangement that may not have required the consent of the worker

19 For a comprehensive examination of the *wḏ-nswt* in Egypt, see Vernus 2013; see also the study by Hays 2000, which looks at the situation from the perspective of the Old Kingdom practices.

20 Eyre 2013: 79–80, with references, "The term ʿ probably derives from the ordinary word for 'hand' or 'arm', in the extended meanings of 'assistance', 'authority', 'control'." Eyre believes, probably rightly, that the related term ʿ "document" is a secondary derivation. For another related term *nt-*ʿ "habit, routine, duty, ritual," see also Goelet-Levine : 262–264.

involved.[21] Somewhere along this fluid scale lay the obligatory labor that we call corvée, which might be conveniently defined as unpaid, unskilled manual labor exacted in lieu of taxation in the form of money or goods. A characteristic of corvée was that it generally entailed involuntary service and normally involved a great mass of people from a given locality. Normally, the impressment was temporary and may have been based on a quota that local officials had to meet. It is unclear whether corvée was practiced on a set schedule, since the only evidence for its regularity apparently occurs in the text on *shabtis*, those model workers provided for the afterlife.[22] It is also unclear whether corvée always required royal authorization, but it seems unlikely that it did. For Egyptologists such nuances in the various forms of compulsion are particularly important due to the popular misconception of Egypt as a society that relied heavily on slavery. The shades of obligation between the extremes of free labor and slavery provide us with some loosely defined, yet useful, categories for studying Egyptian labor. As Bernadette Menu has shown, the Egyptians could make some rather subtle distinctions between types of compensation and labor and, furthermore, differentiated between a finished product and the cost of the labor needed to produce it.[23] Of course, questions of recompense can readily lead to a temptation to drift into the broader subject of commodity prices, but I shall try not to investigate that aspect of the topic insofar as it is feasible to avoid it.

The Enigmas of Class, Obligation, and Compulsion in Ancient Egypt

In order to create a model of labor in any given economy is essential first to arrive at an understanding of who manages and who labors; who can command labor in its various forms; and the nature of specific types of labor and the recompense for performing it. Accordingly, a few words on the subjects of class, status, and governance seem appropriate at this juncture; for some people were normally considered exempt from manual

21 For a detailed examination of such transactions, see Menu 1998b. Many of these arrangements, even those that seem at first glance to be connected with apparent self-enslavement, actually may have involved temporary contracts and provided a means of discharging debt.

22 See Eyre 2004: 182. For more on the significance of the *shabiti* and the associated texts, see below n. 000 and 000. Eyre (2010: 156), "There is no satisfactory evidence from pharaonic Egypt for the existence of a corvée, in the classic sense of a formalized, regular and quantified work duty imposed on the rural population as a whole."

23 On this point, see Menu 1998b: 196.

labor, yet were expected to manage it. To use a time-worn expression about labor—who and for whom?

Over its long history, Egyptian society and its attendant administrative structure changed frequently—the "eternal Egypt" of the popular imagination is but a mirage. Despite a constantly changing answer to the question of command authority in pharaonic society, literacy was always a fundamental feature of the governing class, as the ever popular scribe statues of high officials and reliefs depicting the tomb owner receiving documents attest. Ancient Egypt could be justly described as a "literocracy."[24] If there was to be any degree of efficiency and uniformity of governance, the long, narrow geography of Egypt virtually imposed the need for written documents as the elite's basic means and perhaps even its fundamental rationale for control over those who labored. As can be expected, the vocabulary describing the composition of Egyptian society changed with the times, particularly in respect to the peasantry and the lower orders, but the terminology for the elite as a whole remained remarkably stable. The most frequent collective terms for the elite were:[25] *pʿt*, roughly "elite, patricians";[26] , var. *sʿḥw* "nobles," a word that included a visually punning determinative (E 31), depicting a goat wearing an official stamp-seal as a collar;[27] *wrw* "great ones," a term often accompanied by a determinative depicting a standing man wearing a wig and holding such status markers as a walking stick and a handkerchief (Sign-list A21);[28] *srw* "officials,"[29] which employs the same determinative as *wrw*, but in two isolated examples in an Old Kingdom royal decree (*wḏ-nswt*), the term *srw* has a variant of (Sign-list D40) for a determinative in which the

24 Assmann 2002: 48. Eyre 2013: 9–11 describes how writing was the chief means of social control in Egypt and other ancient societies.

25 For a classification and terminology of the elite and lower orders of Egyptian society, see Kóthay 2012: esp. 484–510.

26 The term can have a more general meaning as "humanity," but it was more frequently a designation for the elite, see Gardiner 1947, I 98*–110* and Faulkner 1962: 88, in contrast to *Wb.* I, 503, 2–11, which prefers the more general "die Menschen." In the very common ranking title *ỉry-pʿt / rpʿt* "(hereditary) noble," the term clearly refers to the upper levels of the elite.

27 *Wb.* IV, 51, 1–11; Fischer 1979: 22. The pun (or "sportive writing") derives from the fact that the word for "goat" and "noble" apparently were homophones (*sʿḥ*).

28 *Wb.* I, 328, 24 – 329, 20. The term can be applied to the ruler of a foreign country as well.

29 *Wb.* IV, 188, 3 – 189, 9.

hand appears to be holding a writing brush or a papyrus roll rather than a stick;[30] *ḳnbt* "council, court";[31] and *ḏꜣḏꜣt* "magistrates, assessors."[32] There are other terms that could be added to this short list of collective terms for the elite, particularly on the individual level, if one should include the enormous repertoire of official titles,[33] the overwhelming majority of which would presumably imply that the title bearers were managers with sufficient rank to exempt them from corvée.[34] However, even high ranking officials could be called upon to recruit and to supervise corvée labor, tasks that could expose them to rather arduous and unpleasant conditions, especially on quarrying expeditions. Ironically, scribes were often men of low status,[35] yet indispensable for labor management and therefore presumably exempt. As the quote above from Pap. Sallier I asserts, scribes were exempted from impressment and menial

30 Koptos Decree B of Pepi II, see Goedicke 1967: 99–100, n. 22 with Eyre's observations (*idem* 2013: 92). It is unclear whether the term in these instances might be used as a denominative verb "to act as a *sr*."

31 *Wb.* V, 53, 9–54, 11. We might also include here the related *nisbe*-formation *ḳnbty* "(person) belonging to the court," *Wb.* V, 54, 12–15. For a non-elite, local *ḳnbt* that consisted mostly of the senior members of the Deir el-Medina community, see McDowell 1990: 143–186.

32 *Wb.* V, 528, 1 – 529, 20.

33 If we consider the situation in the Old Kingdom alone, Müller-Wollermann (1987/88: 31) estimates that there were approximately 1,000 titles, roughly half of which were attested only once. For a comprehensive listing of Old Kingdom titles in two large-format volumes, see Jones 2000. Jones lists over 3,765 titles, but how many of these were truly distinct is uncertain.

34 Moreno García (1998: 83) has introduced a useful descriptive term—"corvéable." The distinction between the presumably literate title bearers and those liable for corvée may appear rather simple in theory, but determining status confronts scholars with many subjective judgments in the case of minor figures. For example, when an individual is identified as a "merchant" (*šwty*) in a ration-list such as Turin Necropolis Journal, *KRI* VI 560–598, should we assume that the nature of that occupation would require a certain degree of literacy, or not? In some rare instances, low-level workers, on the basis of whose titles we would normally consign to the ranks of the illiterate, learned to write, see Dorn 2006.

35 Cruz-Uribe (1994: 45 with Fig. 3.1) quotes the late Klaus Baer's observation that throughout its history ancient Egypt was ultimately ruled by a group of fifty or so families. He also presents a diagram of a frequent, but common over-simplification of Egyptian governmental structure—the Pyramid Model—that significantly has scribes at the base of the entire administrative structure, then later (p. 47) demonstrates the inadequacy of such a blanket estimation of scribes' powers which varied according to the rank of the officials they served.

labor. It can be fairly said that exemption from impressment and the manual labor of corvée marked the great dividing line of class in Egyptian society.[36] Those people who could claim the status of *wab*, literally "pure one," and often "*wab*-priest," might be able to claim exemption as members of a temple staff, in which case perhaps the term might have an extended meaning as "free from compulsory labor," but it is uncertain whether this would always be the case.[37]

It is virtually impossible to collect a corresponding descriptive vocabulary for the lower classes, since their legal and administrative status varied constantly according to time period, the changing legal nature of the agricultural regime, and where the people were located.[38] The terminology in the royal decrees that is used to describe the people who were subjected to corvée or arbitrary compulsion seems to be particularly sensitive to the type of work that was apt to be required in a particular region. The exemption of low-level gold workers, for example, plays a prominent role in the Nauri decree that was concerned with the Nubian territories during the Ramesside Period, but these men are entirely unmentioned in the Old Kingdom royal decrees exempting people attached to pyramid cities.

The degrees of compulsion and obligation between the actors in Egyptian society might seem at first glance far removed from the subject of labor, but in fact these points lay at the very core of the nature of labor in the economy overall. Since labor in Egyptian society normally meant agricultural labor, the arrangements between institutions or individuals and the farmer are of particular interest for the present study, even if the

36 Kóthay 2013: 486, "The focus is on the normative character of the distinction, that is, on setting a moral boundary between those who hold control over the natural, economic and human resources of the country and administer, and those who are subject to produce (*bꜥk*) and liable to taxes and conscription."

37 Kóthay 2013: 490–492.

38 For a description of the group terms for the peasantry and other members of the lower levels of Egyptian society, see Kóthay 2013 and Katary 2013. Kóthay (2013: 484–487) notes that the distinction is between dominant and the dominated, a dualism that is terminologically vague, especially in defining the lower end of the social scale. There are marked differences between the vocabulary and the legal status of certain groups that prevailed in the Middle Kingdom and the New Kingdom. There is a fairly large number of terms employed for people in slave or near-slave status, see below, p. 000.

juridical status of low-level farmers in Ancient Egypt remains unresolved.[39] These arrangements may possibly have a bearing on how skilled labor and manufacturing was handled as well. Since the elite did not personally till the land, real estate would be pretty much worthless unless someone could be found to cultivate it.[40] The same was true for even the mightiest of Egyptian institutional foundations such as the divine temples and memorial temples, all of which were ultimately dependent on the agricultural economy. For the moment, however, I shall delay a discussion of craft labor—skilled labor engaged in the manufacture of specialized goods, such those a metal worker might produce, for example—and concentrate on the production of agricultural goods. How, then, did some individuals become effectively the landowners in Egyptian society?

It has always been quite difficult to get past what one might call the ideological presentation of Egyptian society as it appears on royal and private elite monuments in order to grasp the true relationship between the classes, especially on the local agricultural level. The question always remains, how were authority and social status constructed? Were official positions necessarily endowed with land? When an individual or an institution either hired or conscripted another person to farm, what might be the expectations of both parties? The official explanations, such as they were, are puzzling and contradictory; above all, the justification underlying these arrangements was never explicitly stated. In its simplest formulation, the official ideology of the Egyptian state was that the government was virtually the personal property, a creature, so to speak, of the king who in turn appointed all the functionaries of the state. There was some truth to this presentation, but the reality naturally was far more complex and subtle.

Ultimately, it was the regional authorities who were charged with the execution of royal commands, initiating the first step in a chain of local command. The head of the local elite was normally styled as a *ḥ3ty-ʿ*,[41]

39 Quirke 2004: 11, "There is a widespread but unproven assumption in Egyptology that Egypt was a redistributive economy. In reality we do not have reliable information on the juridicial status of farmworkers – in other words, on whether they were closer to the tenants, the serfs, or the landowners perhaps more familiar to us from European history."

40 Eyre 1999: 46, makes a seemingly obvious, but very important, observation about land-holding in Egypt by noting that there always seems to have been enough land available for cultivation, but "[l]and was valueless without people." The same opinion appears as well in Eyre 2004: 159.

41 The title *ḥ3ty-ʿ* translates literally as "the foremost of the ʿ," but sense of the key component ʿ is elusive. The word can mean a "piece" of land or a "docu-

but how certain men achieved recognition as the local headman is unclear. Depending on the political conditions of an historical period, a *ḥ3ty-ʿ* could be roughly the equivalent of a nomarch or just a local mayor. Judging from the inscriptions of the nomarchs of the First Intermediate Period and the Early Middle Kingdom, the nomarchial rank passed from father to son. At the same time, there is evidence showing that it may have been necessary for the king to confirm their right of succession.[42] In fact, the most plausible explanation for the decline of the institution of a powerful normarchy is that the kings of later part of Dynasty Twelve simply ceased reappointing nomarchs except in the exceptional case of the strategic First Upper Egyptian Nome of Elephantine that stood at the border between Egypt and Nubia. Perhaps a century and a half later, the so-called Stèle Juridique describes the transfer of the office of a similar kind of heritable local governorship at El-Kab, apparently in order to discharge debts.[43] The stela of Queen Ahmose Nefertari of the early Eighteenth Dynasty records the settlement of the office of Second Priest of Amun upon the Queen with the clear implication that the office was both hereditary ("from son to son, heir to heir"), but at the same time transferable to an unrelated person.[44] In both instances the official transfer of the positions was done in the presence of the king, thus implying that his consent was required, and the details were recorded on stelae that most likely were erected in plain sight along a processional way in the Karnak temple with the expectation that the arrangement would be virtually permanently heritable. Lengthy genealogies, both real and fictive, are common on private monuments, to be sure, but the intention often seems more to stress a stela owner's deeply rooted ties to a locality and its elite rather than his right to an office or his connection to land holdings.[45]

Accounts papyri and other official documents give the impression of a highly structured, efficient government in operation, but this is almost certainly misleading.[46] Among other things, a well-run administration

ment," among other things. In a number of Old Kingdom tomb inscriptions, Eyre (2014: 81–83) proposes the translation "authority" in the sense of the ability to act in connection with an inheritance or an endowment.

42 Franke 1991 and Lloyd 1992.

43 Eyre 2014: 149–153.

44 Eyre 2013: 147–148 with extensive references; Trapani 2002.

45 For a collection of essays on various aspects of genealogy in Egyptian texts, see Fitzenreiter, ed. 2005.

46 As Eyre (2013: 9), so pungently puts it, "... it is impossible to credit the Egyptian bureaucracy with a significant level of impersonal efficiency. The real impression is that of a rather ramshackle and highly personalized administration."

would need an efficient and centralized system of record keeping, something that hardly existed even on the local level.[47] Significantly, these texts never specifically describe the legal foundations underlying the authority of the institutions or the officials managing them beyond the purported will of the monarch; legal or administrative decrees were nearly always styled as royal commands.[48] Occasionally one might encounter references to such vague concepts as *hp*, which means 'law.'[49] Indeed, unlike the Roman Empire, the Egyptian state apparently relied more on long-established customs and oral tradition instead of a system based on written legal codes. An exception to this generalization might be an otherwise unspecified "forty scrolls of the law," on which the vizier was supposedly required to base his decisions.[50] In light of the rarity of references to specific laws, the absence in the Egypt of any legal text comparable to the Code of Hammurapi or the Laws of Eshnunna may not be due simply to accidents of preservation.[51]

On what one might describe as the executive level, our translations of the Egyptians' official titles and epithets are styled so that a causal outside observer might believe that the Egyptians lived in a world much like European medieval society, yet these renderings are necessarily mere approximations of the underlying administration. Similarly, the elaborate organizational charts delineating a highly compartmentalized governmental structure that one finds in history books are equally misleading, as even their authors would readily admit. These well-defined presen-

47 On this point, see Eyre 2009.

48 The *wḏ-nswt* "royal command" is discussed extensively by Vernus 2013.

49 Although one might be tempted to render the word *hp* as "custom," it is important to note that the word derives from a term for a leather roll which was used as a writing surface, and therefore had an immediate connection with written law as opposed to oral tradition. For a discussion of *hp* and the function of written law in Egypt, see Kruchten 1981: 214–220; Nims 1948; Otto 1956; Wilson 1954; van den Boorn 1988: 166–169, with additional references in n. 105–114; and Vernus 2013: 271–272, with n. 60. Most references to *hp* connect the law or regulation with a regulating institution or the high official administering it; references to *hp* apparently imply the existence of a 'king's law.'

50 Urk. IV 1104, 7; the Horemheb decree, however, does make several references to existing *hp* 'law' in the text. These are summarized and discussed by Kruchten 1981: 214–220; Vernus 2013: 266.

51 This lack of references to law codes does not seem to be entirely due to accidents of preservation, but lies at the heart of the role of written law in Egyptian society, see the references listed in n. 000 above. For two overviews of a complicated situation, see Lorton 1995 and Kruchten 2001.

tations tend to disguise the highly fluid and cooperative nature of the relationship between the administrative segments of the Egyptian state.

Although these are certainly vexing problems, there is an even greater problem in understanding the nature of wealth and status in Egypt—namely, why and how did people achieve elite status that would allow an individual to command or hire labor? Despite some analogies with European medieval society that Egyptologists employ in their translations of ancient titles and institutions, Egyptian society apparently never developed an enduring institution of 'blood nobility,' nor did the upper class derive its status from long-held land-holdings, unlike the situation in Europe. Even without these characteristic features, Eyre has convincingly pointed out several instructive parallels between pharaonic Egypt and the classical manifestations of European feudalism.[52] These parallels have their basis in the relationship between the Egyptian elite, the land, and the peasantry. In both Egyptian and European feudal societies, a sense of mutual obligations informed the relationship between the classes. Both styles of feudalism were alike in that their elites certainly did not personally farm their land holdings or plots to which they had title or else may have leased. In the case of Egypt, this interplay of obligations could easily mislead observers into believing that its economy followed a classical redistributive model, pure and simple.[53] Where the analogies between medieval European society and Egypt diverge most dramatically, however, is on the fundamental issues of landownership and tenancy.

According to the almost impenetrable ideological façade presented in royal decrees and private tomb texts, the pharaoh appointed his administrators on the basis of their abilities and their loyalty.[54] Such high

52 Eyre 1994: 107–108, with references. Eyre is careful to point out that there was an extensive array of styles of European feudalism that varied from country to country and from period to period.

53 For a presentation of the redistributive features of the Egyptian economy in the manner of Polyani, see Warburton 1997. This book and Warburton's previous articles on the Egyptian economy have been criticized, sometimes rather sharply, *e.g.*, Eyre 1999; Eichler 1992; Wilkinson 1997.

54 Interestingly enough, in the self-presentations of high-status individuals that one encounters in their "biographical" texts in tombs or on funerary stelae, the quality of their loyalty was stressed more in the *epithets*, rather than in the official titles themselves. For a study of such phraseology in the Middle Kingdom, see Doxey 1998. The reality, of course, was otherwise. The meritocratic veneer often concealed the fact that the highest levels of administrative ranks and titles frequently stayed within well-connected families and tended to pass from father to eldest son, see Eyre 1994: 113–114; Cruz-Uribe 1994: 45.

ideals were almost never strictly maintained. Looking closely at the self-presentations ("biographical inscriptions") of many high officials, we can see that either a family connection or some manner of personal relationship with the king frequently played a role.[55] The king also insured that the members of this supposed meritocracy were given land grants in *usufruct* in recognition of their faithful service. In principle all the land of Egypt belonged to the king,[56] a theoretical position probably related to his role as the guarantor of life and the one who dispensed divine gifts to this subjects. He retained the right of real ownership to whatever land grants he made, be it to individuals or to institutions.[57] Although the connection between office and land endowment played an important role in the establishment or transfer of an office, due to the principle of usufruct, the weakened sense of ownership that would otherwise link an official and his endowment might imply that the elite needed to be reconstituted by royal appointment with the passing of each generation. At least in theory, this would also imply that all the land that the elite held in usufruct would never be truly considered as the unencumbered property of the grantee.[58] There is evidence throughout Egyptian history that either the king could effectively enfranchise or disenfranchise officials by means of his power of appointment. Such arrangements might further imply that land holdings of the elite would not be reliably alienable through the normal means of sale or inheritance.

55 Perdu 1995; Gnirs 1996; and Cruz-Uribe 1994.

56 Römer 2000: 257, notes that the ultimate owners of all Egyptian land were the gods and further observes that "the king of the New Kingdom does not seem to have been the sole possessor of all land, but he was—alongside the gods—*one* of the possessors, being godlike himself ..." Römer's brief study confirms the rather questionable status of private land ownership in Egypt, although he notes that there were periods when purchase was possible. Land leases, where they are attested, seem to have lasted only for short terms, see *op. cit.* 258 and Baer (1962). For another opinion that also views the theoretical royal ownership of all land as a basic "legal fiction" underpinning the Egyptian state, see Grandet (2013) 894–899.

57 Admittedly, there never was any official text that explicitly stated the fundamental ideological principle that the king and the gods owned all the land, but this principle is strongly implied by the frequent representation of the important royal ritual called 'the donation of the field,' among other sources. For the question of the king position as Egypt's effective 'owner' on behalf of the gods, see Römer's statement in the previous note as well as Warburton 1997: 61, n.118; and Menu 1997: 247.

58 Menu 1994: 136, notes that only the king had a direct tenure on property. For everyone else, a large number of possible encumbrances would probably apply.

In reality, however, a few surviving private legal texts such as the Inscription of Mose[59] indicate that land grants, especially if they were large, had a tendency to remain, albeit divided and sub-divided, for many generations within an extended family and thus became heritable to a certain degree.[60] However, in this respect, we are talking about custom rather than law. Klaus Baer made an important observation when he stated that, at most junctures in Egyptian history, the country was probably in the hands of a small number of interrelated families.[61] When one looks carefully beneath high officials' self-presentation of their careers, their genealogies usually reveal that rank and status frequently passed from father to son, a situation that seems impossible if wealth in the form of landholdings was not also transferable in some manner. The heritability of office appears to have been the normal case even at Amarna, despite the protestations that Akhenaten's appointees were 'new men.'[62] Nonetheless, usufruct restrictions on the quality of ownership meant that a large segment of elite theoretically did not actually own the land on which a major part of their wealth and status were supposedly based.

Slavery as a Concept and an Institution in Egyptian Society

Perhaps I should expand generally my remarks above on compulsion, labor, and compensation by considering first the extreme case of slavery as an example of how Egyptian conceptual metaphors and an imperfect understanding of the underlying vocabulary can affect our understanding of societal institutions. The problem of slavery is critical to the question

59 For a detailed discussion of this text from an administrative and legal point of view, see Eyre 2013: 155–162.

60 For a discussion of the limited rights to private ownership of land, heritability, alienation of property, and the divisibility of holdings, see Eyre 1999: 47–53 and his discussion of entail and tenure along similar lines, Eyre 1994: 112–127.

61 Klaus Baer, quoted in Eugene Cruz-Uribe 1994: 45.

62 It is unclear how many of the old high officials of the realm chose (or were chosen) to accompany the so-called 'heretic pharaoh' Akhenaten when he decided to establish his new capital at Tell el-Amarna, see Aldred 1975: 50, with n. 5 and Manuelian 1999: 145–147. In this respect, it is quite significant that Tutankhamun's 'Restoration Stela' states that the king had refurbished the priesthoods that his father had vacated by deliberately seeking out members of the former elite: 'he [Tutankhamun] installed lay priests and higher clergy from among the children of the officials of their cites, each one being the 'son-of-a-man' whose name was known," see Murnane 1995: 213.

of labor because we must evaluate the impact that the many degrees of compulsion had upon labor as a whole, including whatever might be put under the vague, yet significant rubric of 'conscription.' The image of Egypt as a 'slave society' has always played an important role in the popular imagination, most likely due to the description of Egypt in the Bible.[63] Even so, slavery, even at the peak of the New Kingdom, does not seem to have existed as a significant part of the agricultural sector of the economy.[64] From our modern viewpoint, slavery can be usefully defined as a permanent social status in which an individual is compelled to work unwillingly for no little or no compensation. Furthermore, according to most definitions of slavery, a slave will have no right to his own physical being ('freedom') or to what wealth his labor might produce. It is fitting that the term 'human bondage' often appears as a synonym for slavery, for the slave finds himself in a prison-like state in which he is effectively a piece of property, sometimes to the extent that an enslaved person could be branded with the name of the owning institution.[65] Slaves normally represented the lowest stratum of any society because they were effectively 'owned' by an individual or an institution; they could be leased, sold, or otherwise transferred like other types of property.[66] Even so, people designated as slaves could apparently be land-holders.[67] At the same time, ancient and more recent societies have had many other lesser degrees of servitude and/or compulsory labor—serfdom, helotry, and corvée, for example—that might meet some, if not all, the definitions of slavery just offered. Significantly, these other terms all defined the varying degrees to

63 Loprieno (1997: 185) remarks that Egypt appears in the Hebrew Bible as *bet abadim* "the house of slavery." Menu (2004: 337) has made similar observations about the influence of biblical image on Egypt.

64 Such is the assertion of Janssen 1975b: 171–173. This is roughly the same conclusion of Eyre 1987a: 209–213. It is striking that in the Old Kingdom, precisely the political and economic environment where one might most reasonably expect that some form of large-scale 'industrial' slavery would have prevailed, the term *ḥm* is hardly attested, see Helck 1994: 983.

65 Menu 1998b: 194 and 196.

66 However, Janssen (1975b: 171) has made the interesting observation that when a slave was sold under certain conditions, one is not sure what was sold: the slave him/herself or (part of) the slave's labor.

67 Pap. Wilbour 51, 45–51, as quoted by Eyre 2013: 184.

which a theoretically immobile peasantry was essentially bound to the land it cultivated and could be obliged to produce labor. Egyptian agriculture and the people who did the actual farming seem to have been much more mobile due to the work cycle that the annual inundation imposed.[68] There would be times of intense activity followed by lengthy periods of under-employment after the crops had been planted. In fact, both Menu and Eyre believe that there was a considerable supply of mobile or even migrant labor in Egypt. It might be fairly said that under some circumstances a contrast between slavery and serfdom that is bound to the land might be a distinction without a difference. On the other hand, if corvée tended to be imposed only occasionally and on an *ad hoc* basis, the practice would make whole-scale, *i.e.*, industrial, slavery largely unnecessary. We might think, rather, in terms of work quotas.

The Egyptians could distinguish between labor, the product of that labor, and the value added to an object or commodity through labor.[69] In this light, someone else's labor could be treated as commodity in Egypt, especially in connection with the work of a slave. One could rent out or assign the labor of a slave to another individual; several people could even share in the income derived from such rentals.[70] Slavery is a particularly thorny subject in the study of ancient societies and their economies because, as noted above, our conceptual framework on the subject has been so heavily influenced by the institution as it existed in the Roman world. However, as Menu has pointed out, our view of slavery (and that of the Romans) is anachronistic when applied to the realities of ancient Egypt where the practical borders between categories of labor were readily broached.[71] Indeed, she describes the situation as being notably variable in respect to both the terminology and the social status of the personnel. Nevertheless, Menu did believe that it was quite probable that institutional slavery, namely, slavery connected with state-run organizations, existed in Egypt.[72] More to the point, however, is Allam's insight that everyone in Egyptian society acknowledged some "lord," who might be a king, official, or deity.[73] For the Egyptians, the

68 For a discussion of migrant and seasonal labor in Egypt, see Eyre 2010: 137–138, especially the quote from Menu in n. 110.

69 Menu 1998b: 194.

70 Allam 2001.

71 On this point, see Menu 1998b: 130. Helck (1984: 982–983) has made much the same observation.

72 Menu 1998b: 193.

concept of an autonomous individual in the sense that we today or even the Romans, might conceive that fundamental state of being, did not exist. Yet, this sort of 'unfreedom' is by no means the same as outright slavery.[74]

To this simplified overview of the problems inherent in defining slavery, we must inject yet another strong note of caution—the Egyptians never used the related terminology consistently. To begin with, the basic vocabulary of (involuntary) servitude—*ḥm* "servant, body"; *ḥmw-nswt* "royal servants"; *bꜥk* "worker, servant"; *ḏt* "serf, personnel,"; *ḥsbw* "forced laborers,"; *mrt* "dependent"; *sqr-ꜥnḫ*, "prisoner of war (perhaps literally "smitten (while) alive)"; *ꜥꜣm* "Asiatic"—to list the more common terms[75] —was seldom employed with much precision, certainly not by comparison with their counterparts in Roman law. Most of the words on this list do not imply a permanent state of servitude, nor do they all translate directly as "slave," but rather they characterize more broadly defined groups of individuals who have been reduced to slave-like circumstances. This is particularly true of foreigners, prisoners of war, who were brought back to Egypt in the aftermath of military expeditions and attached primarily to temple and state institutions,[76] and occasionally valid for native agri-

73 Shafik Allam 2001: 394. This sentiment is expressed in a well-known passage from Pap. Anastasi II in the *Late Egyptian Miscellanies*, quoted below p. 000.

74 For a discussion of both the general notion of and the degree of freedom in Ancient Egypt, see Théodoridès 1998: 297–304. This, too, is an area in which the modern and ancient mentalities differed greatly.

75 This list is derived from a brief catalog of the most common terms for "slave" by Loprieno 1998: [155]. Similar list of terms have been developed by Menu 1995: 220 and Menu 2004: 344–346; Menu has concluded that none of these terms necessarily entails slavery in the period of pharaonic rule. One might note here that most of this vocabulary could refer not so much to slaves *per se* as to classes of individuals who had been reduced to slave-like status. I have supplemented Loprieno's translations of the basic vocabulary with a few alternatives of my own.

76 For the relationship between slavery and prisoners of war during Dynasty 18, see Janssen 1963 and Badawi 1943; Eyre 1987a: 188–190; Helck (1980): 787; Menu 2004. Similar practices existed earlier, as shown by the status of Asiatics who appear in documents during the Middle Kingdom, see Menu 1998: 197–198. Not all foreigners, however, were prisoners of war or types of other involuntary laborers. Also present in New Kingdom Egypt were numbers of voluntary Asiatic migrants from Syria-Palestine, such as the *Apiru*-Asisatics, some of whom were skilled laborers entered Egypt during the Middle Kingdom and later. Included in this category were the Amorites and the people later given the designation "Hyksos."

cultural labor as well.[77] Not surprisingly, since a great many prisoners of war and immigrants came from the Syria-Palestinian region, the term *ʿ3m* became important in this context. In all instances, we must bear in mind an important observation by Bernadette Menu that an individual might be treated one way judicially, but in quite a different manner economically.[78]

The Egyptian words that most consistently meant "slave" in our sense of the word were *b3k* and *ḥm*, both of which have a wide range of meanings. These two terms were frequently used interchangeably, but occurred as well in many instances where 'slave' would be an inappropriate translation.[79] For instance, the word for the higher grade of priest was *ḥm-nṯr*, which, if taken literally, means "the slave of the god," but in practice as well as by virtue of their normally high social status, an official bearing this title would be more aptly considered "the god's servant," a rendering with much less of a servile connotation. The words *ḥm* or *b3k* in religious contexts implied a metaphorical dependency, simply indicating the full measure of a person's devotion to his or her deity.[80] However, with lower status individuals—the great preponderance of examples of both terms—the words generally implied an 'unfree' status. The Horemheb Decree, a text that I shall discuss in some detail below, seems to make a distinction between *ḥmw* as servants or slaves of private individuals and *sḏmw*(-*ʿš*), literally "those who hear (the voice)," who appear to serve government organizations, including those working in an official

77 Bernadette Menu has collected and examined the status of prisoners of war who were impressed as agricultural workers during the New Kingdom, see Menu 2004.

78 Menu 1998b: 194.

79 Menu 1998b: 130 [check this reference !].

80 Joseph Manning, "Land and Status in Ptolemaic Egypt," has noted that in Hellenistic Egypt the term *nmḥ* , whose agricultural and legal meaning was probably close to "unhindered," apparently developed into the antonym of *b3k*. [page reference needed] According to Eyre 1994: 000, the term *nmḥ* originally meant something akin to "orphan," and had been applied to types of freehold plots (*3ḥt nmḥw*) as early as the Old Kingdom. It might not be too far a stretch to see the Egyptian elite's paternalistic attitude towards their agricultural workers in their use of a word for orphan to denote freeholders and their land holdings. For similar observations about the use of these two words in earlier periods of Egyptian history, see Menu 1998b: 193–194.

81 Reference to stela lines and Kruchten commentary; self-reference to discussion below.

capacity.[81] The word *ḥm* fundamentally means something akin to "body," and focuses on the physical being of a person, without any bearing on rank. Thus, the frequent designation of the king as *ḥm.f*, which has been so frequently rendered as "his Majesty," should be more accurately translated as "his Presence," "his Person," or "his Incarnation," since the term refers to the actual presence of the monarch in some activity in addition to the king's role as the physical, earthly presence of the deity.[82] What both king and slave had in common was the idea that the occupation and the individual were so characteristic as to be inseparable. The same observations can be applied to the word *bꜣk* "worker, servant," who thus was also a person completely identified with his work.

In their more servile sense, *ḥm* and *bꜣk* normally referred to people employed in small scale, domestic contexts, exactly the environments in which most definitions of 'non-industrial' slavery would apply; neither term had a particularly strong association with agricultural labor. One major exception to this generalization might be foreign prisoners of war who were apparently impressed into involuntary agricultural labor as *ḥmw*, yet could claim legal rights akin to those held by native Egyptian farmers.[83] Another term on the list above that seems to occur under similarly limited circumstances was *mrt* "dependent," which we shall treat shortly below. Since my aim is primarily to examine the topic of compulsion in labor relations on a broader scale, I will not describe Egyptian slavery in great detail. Much evidence could be marshaled to prove that in many ways the Egyptian institution of slavery conformed to what we know of the institution from other societies, *i.e.*, that slaves worked involuntarily and without compensation; that slaves could be sold or inherited; that voluntary self-enslavement for reasons of debt existed;

82 Menu 1998b: 194, would translate the expression *ḥm.f* as meaning "son (propre) serviteur," indicating that the king was a servant to himself alone. There was a sentiment among Egyptians that every lower class person was in some manner subject to a master or lord, see below in the comments to a passage from the *Late Egyptian Miscellanies* (Pap. Anastasi II, 6,7 – 7,5) 000 (self ref.).

83 The prisoners of war in this category have been discussed at length by Menu 2004: 187–205. She concluded foreigners placed into this regime had been originally classed among the *sḳrw-ꜥnḫ* and that the transition to the status of *ḥmw* actually marked a step not only towards Egyptianization, but also towards greater status and the legal protections that the monarch afforded all his subjects. In Menu's opinion, these foreign *ḥmw* had a number of rights that would hardly fit into our concept of slavery, see esp. *ibid.* 204.

that slavery could become a heritable condition for children of a slave mother, *etc.* On the other hand, unlike slavery among the Romans, for example, Egyptian slaves on occasion could own property and enjoyed a surprising degree of status in comparison with other low-ranking individuals. Slaves, furthermore, were not necessarily always viewed as the lowest members of society. Domestic slavery of this sort does not appear to have been wide-spread among the elite, nor does it appear to have existed in large enough numbers to have significantly impacted labor or the economy overall.[84] Furthermore, the ambiguity of the underlying vocabulary leaves observers uncertain as to whether in a given instance we are dealing with servants or slaves outright.

People bearing the designations *ḥm* / *ḥmt* and *bꜣk* / *bꜣkt* occur in a large number of interesting documents coming from Deir el-Medina during the Ramesside Period.[85] According to these sources, the government apparently supplied the workmen's community with some manner of regular domestic services on a rotational schedule, presumably because the work on the royal tombs required the men of the households to be absent from the homes for long stretches of time. The female holders of both these titles considerably outnumbered their male counterparts. Following a practice well attested with slaves, there is evidence to show that it was possible a crew member to trade or rent out the services to other community members for a fee. From terminological and functional points of view it is quite difficult to distinguish between the roles of the *bꜣk* and *ḥm* in this situation. Yet, despite their status not only as domestic workers, but also as arguably the lowest-ranking individuals in the social structure of Deir el-Medina, there is nothing in the records to show that these

84 In his overview of the New Kingdom economy (Janssen 1975b: 171–173) he comes to the conclusion that "the economic importance of slavery during the NK seems to be rather small," but "[f]or a more reliable result one should also take into consideration questions such as the legal obligations of the entire population," which is more or less the view of this current essay. For a different viewpoint that considers lack of physical and social mobility in the labor sector as perhaps lending itself to a form of 'state' slavery, see Menu 1998b: 193–194. She believes that sometimes the *ḥmw* and *bꜣkw* were "traitées comme un capital mobile" and could be attached to institutions. The chief unknown in this question is the degree and manner of internal colonization.

85 See Černý 1973: 175–181. The function of these people—particularly as to whether they were servants or slaves—has been reexamined more recently by Hofmann 2006: 113–118.

ḥmw and *b3kw* were owned in any real sense either by members of the workmen's community or by the governmental institutions that supplied these servants to work in the village—they were servants, not slaves.[86] In this instance, as in many other cases, the circumstances of the labor, not the terminology applied to the laborer, was the determining factor.

Another category of laborers who are often viewed as similar to slaves were those people bearing the designation *mrt*, a term that is usually rendered as "serf," or more broadly, "dependent."[87] Although the broader translation may be preferable, the hieroglyphic writing of the term— deliberately connected these people with the *mrt*-hoe and stressed their agricultural background.[88] Most definitions of serfdom, as opposed to slavery, similarly associate it with farming and focus on a hereditary and involuntary nature of the serf's link both to the plot he cultivates and to the landowner, his presumed overlord. The serf may not be owned as chattel in the manner that a slave might be, but as far as his individual autonomy is measured, this might be a distinction without much difference.[89] In most societies where serfdom has occurred, the in-

86 Hofmann 2006: 115.

87 This is the rendering adopted in the most recent study of the *mrt* people by Allam 2004: esp. 123–124, a study that deals extensively with the New Kingdom. Allam wrote in partial response to two thorough studies of *mrt* status in earlier times by Moreno García 1998 and 2000. Both Allam's study and the two latter articles contain extensive bibliographical references to previous scholarship on the subject, but focus largely on the periods prior to the New Kingdom. "Serf" is also Eyre's translation of the term *mrt*, see "Feudal Tenure," 112.

88 *Wb.* II 106, 11–20. Allam 2004: 123, limited his study to writings that employed the hoe-sign (Sign-list U 6 and variants), but looks elsewhere for the root meaning of the word, see *op. cit.* 124, n. 10. Nevertheless, he recognized that there often was a lack of terminological rigor in Egyptian texts which could lead to the substitution of such words as *rmṯ*, an observation that Moreno García makes as well. The hoe-sign is significantly also a key element in a common term for Egypt, *i.e.* , and variants, *t3-mrỉ* lit. "hoe-land," Faulkner 1962: 293.

89 Allam 2004: 124, n. 10. Loprieno 1997: 193, makes a distinction between the *servitude* of a slave and the *service* of the *mrt*-personnel, the former term presumably implying a more permanent and involuntary situation. A complication in the analysis of the *mrt*-personnel is that they should be distinguished from another group of workers who are also called *mrt*. The initial bilitteral (Sign-list M 36) that forms the second word may have the same transliteration as (Sign-list U 6), but according to Allam, "[c]e vocable est à distinguer absolument d'un terme quasi homophone ," see further *idem* 2010: 41–44.

stitution has normally been linked with agriculture, whereas slavery often had no such connection to fixed plots of land; the Egyptian evidence on the *mrt* seems to reflect much same circumstances. The fact that *mrt*-people are occasionally included along with royal gifts of land certainly implies that such transfers could be done without their consent, a state of affairs that Third Intermediate inscriptions apparently confirm.[90] However, as we can see from the difficult questions raised above concerning the degree to which someone could be said to "own" a plot of land at any given moment in Egyptian history, it becomes equally difficult to decide where a person farming that plot sits along a scale running from freeholder to tenant farmer to serf. In this respect, one of the more striking features of the *mrt*, particularly during the Old Kingdom, is how often they appear as large groups of workers who apparently have been forcibly conscripted for work on various projects that are mostly, but not always, agricultural in nature and connected to the 'state,' broadly construed. Particularly because many citations of *mrt* arise in royal exception decrees, the words "serf" and "corvée" suggest themselves as natural translations in the relevant passages. Additionally, *mrt*-people could be assigned to members of the elite as part of an endowment in return for service on behalf of the monarch. Yet, Moreno García appears to have concluded that, as the status of these *mrt*-people evolved during the Old Kingdom, eventually the *mrt* "semble correspondre à des corvéables et non à des serfs permanents." This formulation is quite important since it implies that *mrt-status* was not permanent and at the same time raises the question of under whose authority low-status individuals could become "corvéables." Moreno García has also shown that the nature of authority in the long period between the Old Kingdom and the end of the First Intermediate Period was constantly changing and thus the status of the *mrt*-people was in constant flux as well. Further developments reveal just how contextual and time-sensitive our view of any such social group must be.

According to Moreno García, the changing political landscape that marked the transition from the Old Kingdom to the First Intermediate Period, when decentralized and sometimes autonomous local government prevailed, seems to have resulted in an impoverishment of the peasantry in many instances. These developments had a particularly negative impact on the *mrt*-class because the increasingly arbitrary and powerful local elites no longer provided these laborers with the protections that had for-

[90] Allam 2004: 123, n. 4 and see below, p. 000.
[91] Moreno García 2000.

merly existed under royal authority.[91] It is significant that wealthy and powerful individuals in this era seem to have been able to purchase or otherwise acquire those they called *b3kw* "workers," *tpw* "heads," or, more generally, *rmṯ* "people." The number of people involved in such transactions could occasionally be quite sizeable, yet, oddly enough, the terms that were more normally connected with servitude or serfdom—*ḥmw*(-*nswt*), *nsywtyw* "royal (people)," and *mrt*—were relatively uncommon in such texts.[92] High ranking men of the First Intermediate Period also frequently boasted about acquiring or purchasing land, themes that had been relatively absent from comparable 'biographical' inscriptions of the Old Kingdom,[93] a remarkable sign of the decline in the king's theoretical role as Egypt's only true landowner during this period. Indeed, most political histories of the First Intermediate Period would describe the era as one in which the power of the local elites apparently outweighed that of the monarch. The end result was that the status of *mrt*-laborers and other lower class individuals generally had declined from being serfs bound to the land to becoming purchasable chattel, the characteristic that most clearly marks slavery, despite any imprecision in terminology. Although it is difficult to gauge whether conditions mentioned in any given text were applicable only for a limited area or for all of Egypt, this evidence lends support to the notion that the degree of proprietorship over land and people, *i.e.*, the ability to command labor, particularly in the absence of central government authority, must have always been closely linked in Egypt.

This balance between state control and the power of local authorities is reflected in the Hekanakhte Papers, a small archive of private documents written as the First Intermediate Period came to a close and central power was being reestablished under the new Twelfth Dynasty. Hekanakhte, a minor local official during the early reign of Senwosret I, apparently did not own land, but he could lease certain plots, and thus had to hire peasant farmers to work his fields, rather than simply command them to do so. We can see in these letters how labor conditions had changed from the rather bleak state of affairs prevailing during the First Intermediate Period as Moreno García described them.

92 Moreno García 2000 : 129–132.
93 Moreno García 2000 : 127–128.

Contracting out the Labor of a Third Party and Labor Contracts between free Individuals

In the Third Intermediate Period there is evidence of land transfers that specifically mention the names of the individual tenants on the plots. Since it seems on its face value that control over the tenants' labor was transferred along with the title to the land, arrangements of this sort would fit some definitions of serfdom. Two individuals had arrived at an exchange that ultimately involved the labor of third parties, apparently without their consent. Presumably, contemporary political conditions had allowed the peasantry to revert to a status reminiscent of the First Intermediate Period, a period of similar weak governmental control. Unfortunately, we do not have any continuity in terminology in these documents, some of which had been confirmed through oracular procedures and recorded on stelae, particularly emphatic forms of public affirmation of their legitimacy—divine assent, significantly, having become the best form of official confirmation in a period of weak government.

Menu has examined many of the documents of this era with the intention of discerning, among other things, the degree of compulsion involved in such contracts.[94] After all, when a high status individual rented out a peasant's labor or effectively sold both a field and the farmer working it to a third person, what then would be the legal and social status of the laborer and how voluntary could that worker's labor be? In some instances, arrangements of this sort were based on the involuntary labor of a slave, but these were rather special cases and not quite as common as one might assume. More frequently, individuals worked off debts by temporarily entering into a state of temporary servitude. In my discussion of the term *ḥm* above, I already mentioned more informal arrangements that apparently did not involve slavery, but rather the work of a free individual, so presumably there was some form of recompense due to the laborer, even if this was not mentioned. According to Menu's study of similar documents, these arrangements exhibit a wide variety of social rank among the parties. Interestingly enough, parallels can be drawn between the hiring of workers to third parties and the rental of draft animals such as donkeys, where the animal was rented out explicitly for its labor (*r b3k.f*).[95]

94 Menu 1998b: 206.

95 Since there are examples in which a female donkey was hired for her labor (*r b3k.s*), Janssen (1993): 81–94, was able to demonstrate a fundamental misinterpretation of a critical passage in the standard *shabti*-spell that had been proposed by Warburton (1984–1985): 345–355.

The two most informative documents on this difficult topic are the Stela of Prince Sheshonq and the so-called Apanage Stela. In the case of the land transfers recorded on the Sheshonq Stela,[96] the tenants on the plots were mentioned specifically by name and thus apparently considered to be legally attached to the property or to the institutions that owned the property. Furthermore, these people hardly fit the description of peasantry, but rather included individuals of a somewhat higher status, agricultural specialists such as beekeepers, butchers, and weavers. In some instances the men listed were followed by the epithet *mꜣꜥ ḫrw*, perhaps indicating that they had died and had not yet been replaced. This situation could indicate that their labor or, more likely, the position that they held within the institution was held in perpetuity by whoever might succeed them as tenants. Yet, the most logical explanation of all for the presence of all these names on the stela because this was the simplest and most efficient means of identifying the plots involved. In any event, Menu points out that in a situation such as this, it was not really the person who was placed at the disposition of the institution, but rather some part of his (obligatory) services that devolved from his tenancy, *i.e.*, labor, not individuals, were being transferred from one party to another.[97] At least technically, the underlying arrangement would not be a form of serfdom since the transaction had little bearing on the tenant's personal status—only the ultimate recipient of any obligatory payments has been changed, not the amounts themselves.[98]

The Apanage Stela was made in the favor of a certain Khaemwaset who was the grandson of Osorkon I, the second king of Dynasty 22.[99] The circumstances behind this donation are rather complex. Simply put, the intent of the document was to provide Khaemwaset with an *apanage*, or endowment for his office. In this case, however, the compensation paid to the previous owners of the land seems rather poor, so that the transfer of the properties virtually amounted to expropriation. The tenants or

96 Stela Cairo JE 66285, an oracular land transfer made in favor of the future Sheshonq I of Dynasty 22, see Menu 1997: 250–252.

97 Menu 1997: 251–252.

98 As Menu (1997: 252), "La nature de ces 'prix' paraît évidente au résultat de l'analyse: il s'agit d'un *droit de mutation*, payé par le roi au temple d'Osiris pour la dotation d'une nouvelle institution culturelle."

99 Stela Cairo JE 809, now Cairo JE 31882, likewise in the form of an oracular transfer, for which see Menu 1997: 252–255, with references and Eyre 2013: 168–171. For a recent translation with further references, see Ritner 2009: 271–278.

land-owners on the stela are mentioned by name, their holdings briefly described, then each plot suspiciously declared to be 'exhausted' or otherwise undesirable land. The transaction's validity was confirmed by an oracular pronouncement made by the god Amun himself that additionally threatened the god's wrath against anyone objecting to his affirmation of the transfer. Once again, we should not assume that because the tenants were specifically named that they were transferred along with the land, nor that they were in some manner permanently attached to the plots. However, if they were to stay on those parcels of land, their obligations in the form of labor would now be involuntarily transferred to the new landowner, and the new landowner, in turn, would be ultimately responsible to the state or the king for whatever taxes were due.[100] This does not mean that, by extension, the tenants were in any real sense owned by the landowner. We are ultimately left with the thought about whether some of the sales of *mrt*-people and other low-status individuals during the First Intermediate Period that Moreno García studied might not also have been actually merely transfers of their obligations rather than their personal beings.

Conscription and Serfdom

The discussions of slavery and serfdom above demonstrated that terminology alone was a rather unreliable indicator of a worker's actual status and the degree of his or her freedom, especially when we take into consideration the 'middle ground' implicit in the less permanent condition of conscription.

If the strength of central authority was a determining factor in the ability of non-governmental forces to command labor, then we can examine the role of compulsion in labor along the same lines. The very word corvée is ideally connected to a demand for labor made on behalf of the state in pursuance of a limited objective such as the digging of canals, the construction of roads, or quarrying expeditions that might be quite distant from the workers' home territory.[101] Corvée in this sense would involve a substantial temporary workforce and perhaps was the earliest form of taxation to appear in ancient societies. Corvée, further-

[100] As Eyre (2004: 174) accurately remarks, "The man responsible for the tax was the 'owner' as far as the state was concerned." This may be the situation in an instance in the Wilbour Papyrus where a slave appears as the person in charge of a plot of land.

[101] For an overview of the question of corvée in Egyptian economy and law, see Helck 1975: 3–12 and *idem* 1977: 333–334.

more, normally entailed temporary compulsory labor without necessarily implying a permanent condition; this and a diminished connection with agricultural labor might distinguish corvée labor from serfdom. Officials charged with raising the workforce for corvée apparently were charged with filling a quota and could seize a substitute if a person who was considered liable for service was unavailable. In a short letter from Lahun dating to the reign of Amenemhat III, a local "mayor" (*ḥꜣty-ꜥ*) in charge of a temple informs the temple scribe that the temple's doorkeeper had approached him saying, "… I was seized as a substitute for my son (*ỉwꜣ.kw ḥr zꜣ.ỉ*), the porter of the temple there, [by] my district officers (*ꜣṯw.ỉ*) who said that he is in deficit for (lit. of) the corvée force (*m nhw hꜣw*) …"[102]

Under these conditions, we may understand the rationale for Moreno García's distinction between those who were merely 'corvéable' and 'serfs permanents.' Those who were 'corvéable,' as we have seen above, might be subject to the arbitrary control of some powerful local official acting on his own interests without state sanction. This was by no means a minor problem since the unauthorized removal of personnel appears as a central concern for the institutions to which they were attached in several of the royal decrees that have survived.[103] A further difficulty in defining corvée in its Egyptian context is posed by the New Kingdom practice of employing military units on work projects such as the construction of monuments, stone transportation and even agricultural labor—all tasks that one would normally characterize as civil or public works.[104]

102 Pap. Berlin 10023A; translation, Wente 1990: 74 (no. 88); text, Scharff 1924: Pl. 2. The basic meaning of the verb 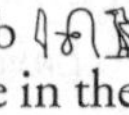 *ỉwꜣ* is unclear. Wb. I 49,16 suggests "fortnehmen?," but a passage in the Coffin Texts (Spell 472; CT VI 1f.), which is strongly reminiscent of the *shabti* spell, indicates that "substitute" might be more appropriate. For the practice of assigning "substitutes" in compulsory labor during the Middle Kingdom, see Kóthay 2010: 168–169; Gardiner 1951: 111; and Quirke 1990: 162–163.

103 Eyre 1994: 110, n.12, raises this point particularly in connection with the Nauri Decree.

104 Gnirs 2013: 667–675; Murnane 1998: 198. Especially where quarry work was concerned a major problem for the historian is that the Egyptians used the same word—*mšꜥ*—to indicate a military unit or a non-military expedition. In any case, quarrying expeditions tended to be organized according to the expeditionary model, partly due to the nature of the work and the general militarization of the regime during the course of the New Kingdom, see Eyre 2010: 130–132.

Although it is hard to define what might constitute corvée with any precision, it is striking that the Egyptians transferred the concept of obligatory and compulsory work for the greater good, so to speak, to the world beyond the grave. A veritably ubiquitous item in nearly every elite burial assemblage during the New Kingdom and later was the funerary figurine known as the *shabti* or *ushebti*, which represented a standing worker with arms crossed at the breast and holding agricultural tools such as a basket and a hoe. According to a spell written on the figurine, if the deceased owner were to be "accounted" (*ỉp*) for work (*kꜣt*) in the God's Domain, the *shabti* would spring to life and perform that obligatory duty on its owner's behalf.[105] Significantly, the tasks that it might be called upon to perform consisted of hard manual labor needed to do the sort of work that was required to maintain canals and dykes or other agriculturally-related corvée around the time of the annual inundation or its aftermath. Since kings as well as commoners were supplied with these magical figurines, there were no status-related exemptions from corvée in the next world. At times the *shabti* will be inappropriately dressed in fine clothes and when a tomb owner has vast numbers of *shabti*s available, a few of the figurines would be designated as "overseers." As tantalizing as this evidence is, it is highly questionable that these model workers can provide reliable evidence about circumstances in this world.

Conscription for Royal Institutions, Corvée, and Military Labor—The Nauri Decree, the Horemheb Decree, and other Sources

From the Dashur Decree of Pepi I, a protective decree on behalf of the two pyramids cities of Snofru at that site, to similar decrees of the New Kingdom such as those promulgated by Horemhab and Seti I, the need to prohibit a wide range of officials from conscripting personnel from royal establishments appears to have been a central administrative and legal issue. On its face, such a need was remarkable, since it underscored a recurring problem in enforcing royal commands and maintaining institutional integrity over the long term. Although there seems to have always been sufficient cultivable land to support various royal and temple endowments throughout pharaonic history,[106] it was quite another matter for a king

[105] Due to its popularity and wide variation, the description given here is a rather broad one, for there are many variations in the form of the *shabti* and the implements it carries as well as the costume. For two general discussions of the *shabti* with references, see Spanel 2001: 567–570 and Schlögl 1985: 896–899.

[106] Eyre 1986a: 208.

to insure that a royal establishment would have sufficient agricultural and other workers on institutional fields and that these and other laborers would be shielded from the arbitrary actions of outside officials. There are, additionally, some important questions as to the initial status of the workforce mentioned in the Nauri decree—had these workers been recently conscripted and moved onto land in Nubia or, more likely, did these people simply represent the reorganized remnants of previous royal establishments that had since fallen into desuetude? As we know from several sources, monarchs would occasionally be forced to resort to various forms of internal colonization, employing such means as military colonists or forcibly settling prisoners of war on institutional lands.[107]

Conscription, which we associate today primarily with compulsory military service on state command, implies a much longer period of service ("for the duration ..."), perhaps even a permanent condition. We can add to this another gradation of servitude, what might be considered a problematic middle ground—how free is a person when his or her labor can be contracted out to another period, presumably without the worker's prior agreement? A fairly large number of royal decrees have survived from the New Kingdom, but only a handful are long enough and adequately preserved to provide information on the subject of conscription in its various aspects.[108] In fact, there are but few official texts surviving that offer any detailed discussion of the categories of labor conscription.

A. The Nauri Decree—*iṯꜣ*, *kfꜥ*, *bḥ*, *bryt*, and Corvée

Of two New Kingdom decrees mentioned above, the Nauri Decree of Seti I,[109] a protective decree on behalf of the Nubian lands, property, and personnel attached to his famous Osiris temple at Abydos, provides the

107 A valuable summary of the persistent problem of internal colonization to meet institutional needs appears in Eyre 2004: 165–170. During the New Kingdom especially, prisoners of war and foreign captives were used extensively for internal colonization and were settled on temple and other state land. They were frequently termed *ḥmw* "slaves," in such contexts, see Menu 2004. This is the closest to slavery as an industrial system in Egypt, but in the rural, agricultural context they were not slaves, see *ibid.* 185–195.

108 For a partial list of similar monumental royal decrees of the New Kingdom, see Kitchen 1993b: 49.

109 This text is perhaps the most extensively studied of all Nineteenth Dynasty legal inscriptions, so only a partial bibliography follows here: Griffith 1927; Edgerton 1947; Gardiner 1952; Kitchen 1993a: 45–58; Kitchen, 1993a: 38–50; Kitchen, 1993b: 48–55; Davies 1997: 278–308.

Are these quotes correct or do you prefer a different format?

more informative insights into the state's role both in conscription and its opposite counterpart—the exception of labor from arbitrary compulsion. This royal decree represents a command of a monarch in the fullness of his powers, yet the localities it protected—Nauri is located not far from the Third Cataract—were at a great enough distance from the borders of Egypt proper that it would have been precisely sort of place where one might expect the force of law to have been weaker than usual and where local authorities might be more apt to abuse their powers. Of course, since the text of this decree was "published" high up on a desert butte where it was virtually unreadable, there are immediate questions as to how realistic any expectations of the enforceability of its provisions might be.[110]

Since this was a protective decree, the people who were enjoined from acting injuriously against the temple property and its personnel are somewhat predictable—the viceroy, his staff, and several ranks of the military, *i.e.*, the institutional management, broadly speaking, or people just passing through on missions to the Nubian territories. The temple was engaged in farming, stock and wild-fowl raising, transport, and all aspects of gold-mining operations, so the laborers who fell under protection of the edict are equally predictable—a wide range of agricultural occupations, gold-washers, fowler-fishermen, *etc.* It is unclear, however, whether these people, both management and staff alike, represented a newly-arrived population who had been recently settled in the region, or, more likely, whether the decree reflected a reorganization of the people who had already been living and working in the region, perhaps as part of previously established state institutions that had since fallen into desuetude.[111]

An especially informative passage in the text threatens a variety of punishments against: "(42) … any people who shall take away (*iṯꜣ*) any people" attached to the temple foundation, "by seizure (*m kfꜥ*), (or) from

[110] As Eyre (2013: 58) so pungently puts it, "[h]ere the sanctions are specific and ferocious, but they carry an air of unreality about them, designed to serve as exemplary, sometimes even poetic justice."

[111] It is far more likely that a reorganization of pre-existing arrangements was at hand here, especially given the early date in Seti's reign (Year 4). Although the Egyptians were known to have resettled large numbers of Asiatic or Libyans prisoners of war within Egypt, there is no indication that any large groups of people were ever similarly relocated in the distant reaches of Nubia, see 000. Had this been the case with the Seti Abydos temple, one would expect some reference to this event either in the lengthy poetical prolog or in the body of the main text.

one district to another district, (or) by contract (*m brt*) or by corvée (*m bḥ*) for plowing (scil. planting) or by (43) corvée for harvesting …"[112] The main thrust of the prohibition is directed against the general activity designated by *iṯꜣ*, further specified by a string of additional qualifications. In this case, the entire phrase makes the most sense when one construes *m brt* and *m bḥ* functioning as further modifications of the action of *m kfꜥ* rather than as the final two of four adverbial clauses introduced by the preposition *m* and modifying the verb *iṯꜣ*.[113] The apparent distinction between removal for contract labor and removal for corvée indicates that, without royal protection, the institutional staff might have been 'corvéable' or otherwise subject to arbitrary removal, as the term *bḥ* might imply. However, at the same time, it seems that the decree prevented these workers from entering into non-coercive labor contracts on their own, as the term *brt* might imply. Since the decree forbade the temple personnel from hiring themselves out to work for others, their labor had become virtually limited to the temple foundation's interests. One might say that the institutional staff had now effectively become protected serfs under the aegis of Seti's Abydos temple

The terminology is nuanced and striking. Since this passage reveals much about labor compulsion and freedom during the New Kingdom, it merits close examination. The main thrust of the prohibition was to prevent removal (*iṯꜣ*) beyond the temple lands, a transgression that could take several forms: *kfꜣ* "seize", *brt* "contract, pact," and *bḥ(w)* "corvée."[114]

112 The precise wording is: (43) … *rmṯ nb nty iw.f r iṯꜣ rmṯ nb n tꜣ ḥwt Mn-Mꜣꜥt-Rꜥ ib hrw m ꜣbḏw m kfꜥ m w r w m brt m bḥ n skꜣ m* (44) *bḥ n ꜥwꜣyw*, see *KRI* I 52, 14–15.

113 As David 2006: 43, aptly describes this chain of legal terms, it is, "… a typical case of multinominal sequence enumerating contiguous terms for precision and all-inclusiveness as in modern legalese." The chief interpretive difficulty with this passage how one should handle the four parallel phrases, each introduced is by the same preposition *m*, see Kitchen 1979: 454–458, among others.

114 This passage and its terminology has been extensively studied, but the most comprehensive examination to date from the both the legal and lexicographical point of view (and with which I find myself in substantial agreement) appears in David 2006: 56, where the passage in question is rendered, "(45) … who will seize anybody …(46) from a distinct to (another) district, by (submission?) contract, by/as a forced labor (corvée) of ploughing (or) by/as a forced labor of harvesting …"

Eyre has also remarked on the implications of this passage for our knowledge of compulsory labor practices in Egypt, but hesitates rendering *bḥ* as 'corvée' noting "the tendency to use the term rather loosely for any mobili-

Since words for plowing and harvesting further define the act of removal here, the primary objective of this section of the decree seems to have been insuring the stability of the agricultural labor force, but the exemptions were additionally extended to cover the entire temple personnel. Contrary to what one might expect, even though the term *bꜣkw*, whose base meaning is "work, service," is one of the most important—and controversial—of all Egyptian administrative terms in New Kingdom legal and economic texts, this concept does not appear to have a direct connection with corvée or other forms of compulsory labor.[115]

Of the three words in this key excerpt—*kfꜥ*, *brt*, and *bḥ*(*w*)—*kfꜥ* "seizure" is the most common, occurring in campaign inscriptions beginning with the Old Kingdom where it was originally used to describe capture of foreign prisoners of war and their forcible removal to Egypt.[116] During the New Kingdom and Ramesside period regular campaigning became an important aspect of royal prestige and power, so that military expeditions under various pretenses were quite frequent. Captives were most often put to work on temple and state institutions, obviously involuntarily; some were assigned as "attendants" (*šmsw*) to members of the military. As a mark, literally speaking, of their servile status, captives were occasionally branded like cattle with the name of the organization to which they had been assigned, in that case surely an indication of a permanent slave status.[117] Eventually, the sense of *kfꜥ* was extended to

sation of labour, without clear definition of administrative, legal or economic context," see Eyre 2004: 152 in relation to an example of the term *bḥ* in a private letter, Pap. Mallet III, where it seems to refer to an obligation that could be imposed on an individual by an official for his own concerns, perhaps the onerous labor of land-clearing. For the relevant passage, see Pap. Mallet III, 6–7, K*RI* VI 66 (text) and Wente 1990: 127–128 (translation).

115 The literature on the term *bꜣkw* is considerable; only a selection of studies shall be listed here: Bleiberg 1988: 157–168; Boochs 1987: Helck 1975: 8; Janssen 1993: 81–94; Warburton 1987: 237–257. In fact, *bꜣkw* seem to designate something that must be obligatorily produced rather than the work involved.

116 *Wb.* V 121, 6 "Beute machen im Kriege, etw. erbeuten, auch in der Verbindung: Kriegsgefangene Leute"; Lesko 2004, vol. II: 173 "to plunder, take captive, take booty, to capture"; Hasel 1998: 74–75; Kruchten 1981: 62–63 "travail forcé," and similarly in other studies of New Kingdom decrees. The word appears in Coptic as kba[S], yba[B], see Crum 1939: 99B "compulsion, forced labour."

117 For discussions of the branding of prisoners of war and others, see Caminos 1954: 230–231, commenting on a passage in Pap. Anastasi V 7, 6.

include the forcible removal or assignment of native Egyptians as well.[118] This seems to have been the case with the Nauri Decree where both *iṯꜣ* and *kfꜥ* were connected with removal "from (one) district to (another) district" (*m w r w*).[119] In this instance, it should be noted, there was no indication of a foreign origin for any of the Abydos Temple's personnel who were being protected from *kfꜥ*. Even if a seizure had the force of law behind it, the interests of the institution affected would suffer. Whether foreigners or Egyptians were involved, this motif's frequency demonstrates that government planning frequently put unreasonable demands on inadequate labor resources. It is easy to see how arbitrary seizures would have been a common official abuse whenever revenue was needed to meet official or personal needs.

For evaluating the forms of conscription and compulsion, the key words in this passage are the parallel terms *brt* "contract, pact," and *bḥ(w)* "corvée,"[120] which function almost like antonyms. They explain further the manners in which *kfꜥ* "removal" could happen. The term *bḥ(w)* occurs in several texts of an official character, where it clearly refers to a form of obligatory labor. In fact, *bḥ(w)* appears to have been the primary New Kingdom word for the compulsory state-enforced labor that we call corvée. As such, *bḥ(w)* apparently replaced older terms for commissioned or compulsory labor such as *wpt*, *hꜣ*, and *st-hꜣ* that had occurred in comparable contexts in the exemption decrees of the Old Kingdom[121] The latter two activities from the Old Kingdom repertoire—*hꜣ*, and *st-hꜣ*—seem to have been concerned chiefly with non-agricultural tasks, particularly dragging stone. Other rare New Kingdom words —*hꜣyt* and the related *rmṯ-hꜣy*—have also been proposed as expressions for corvée and compulsory labor. These resemble the Old Kingdom *hꜣ* (and *st-hꜣ*) and appear in similar contexts, but their relationship with

118 This extended legal sense of *kfꜥ* to include Egyptians and the term's semantic background are well explained in David 2006: 48–49. In the case of the Nauri Decree, Kitchen (1979: 456) would render *kfꜥ* as 'press-ganged.'

119 One should not be too hasty in assuming that *m w r w* "from (one) district) to (another) district" modifies only *kfꜥ* here and not *iṯꜣ* because of another passage in the decree (line 68) in which the disjunctive element *m r-pw* "or" intercedes between *m kfꜥ* and *m w r w*, see Kitchen 1979: 456 and David 2006: 82–83.

120 The necessity of the terminal *-w* is uncertain; the word is written both with and without it.

121 See above, note 000.

these older counterparts is uncertain.[122] An terminological puzzle remains—since high status individuals could apparently force peasants or other laborers to work on personal, non-state sanctioned projects and describe that work as *bḥ(w)*,[123] should an imposition of that nature also fall under the rubric of corvée?

More controversial is the meaning of the term *brt* / *brṯ*, a word of Semitic origin that occurs in this passage and as well as in similar contexts in at least two additional lines of this decree.[124] Francis Griffith, the original publisher and translator of the Nauri decree, translated *brt* as "impressed."[125] William Edgerton similarly believed it to be a word for "compulsory labor," but was uncertain as how *brt* was to be distinguished from *bḥ(w)*.[126] Alan Gardiner offered the suggestion that *brt* was related to an ancient West Semitic term for an agreement between two individuals and should be considered as a word for some type of contract, presumably of a voluntary nature and in contrast to the following *bḥw* 'corvée,'[127] an explanation with which Kenneth Kitchen essentially concurred.[128] On

122 The word *ḥꜣyt* and the related term *rmṯ-ḥꜣyt* "corvée(?)-people (*Wb.* II 475, 7–8) occur only in didactic texts where they appear to be connected with stone-dragging, see Caminos 1954: 351 and 457; Goedicke 1967: 119–120; Lesko, *DLE* I 272 and 284.

123 The term *bḥ* also occurs in a private agricultural context (Pap. Mallet III) where it refers to work that local farmers are being compelled to do on behalf of a local official, see above n. 00.

124 David (2006: 45) has remarked that this is the earliest example of the loan word in Egyptian texts. For the word, see Lesko 2004, vol. 1: 138 (s.v. *bryt*) and 137 (s.v. *brṯ*); Hoch 1994: 108–109, n. 135. In the Nauri Decree *brt* appears in Lines 32, 43, 46, and possibly in a now destroyed portion of Line 101 as well.

125 Griffith 1927: 201 hesitantly rendered the entire phrase: "by capture from (one) district for (another) district, by corvée (?) as impressed (?) for plowing (44) (or) impressed for harvesting."

126 Edgerton (1947: 221 with n.12) indicated that *brt* should translate roughly as 'corvée.'

127 Gardiner (1952: 28–29) identified *brt* with the Hebrew *berit* 'covenant, contract' and asserted further that, "… *brt* in our decree cannot mean 'corvée', since that is the meaning of *bḥw* that follows."

128 Kitchen (1979: 457) summarizes his discussion by suggesting different translations according to the text register in which *brt* appears, "But 'hire/contract' (Nauri) and 'hired/contract labour' (Pap. Anastasi) in the economic sphere and 'compact/covenant' and 'vassal-treaty/covenant' in the political realm are entirely more accurate and precise renderings in the context concerned." By these renderings, Kitchen apparently does not believe that the term necessarily implied a coercive agreement.

the whole, it seems more plausible that the intent of the critical passage in the decree was to present a contrasting parallelism between *brt* and *bḥ(w)*, respectively as voluntary and involuntary labor arrangements. An explanation along these lines, however, has not found universal acceptance and has been disputed recently by James Hoch[129] and José Galán,[130] in the latter instance, specifically in connection with the Nauri decree passage. Both authors have asserted that *brt* was also a type of involuntary or at least an unbalanced labor agreement between two parties, as Hoch's suggestions "obligatory service, treaty of submission" convey.

B. The Horemheb Decree—*Ḥtr* and other Forms of "Obligation"

The other major New Kingdom source that can provide information on how compulsory labor was treated on the official level is the Horemhab Decree.[131] This edict, dated to the eighth year of the last king of the Eighteenth Dynasty, belongs to a period a few decades earlier than the Nauri Decree when the royal house was still in the process of reestablishing the *status quo ante* in the wake of disruptions following the reign of the so-called "Heretic King," Akhenaten. Like Seti I's decree, Horemheb's was a protective measure, but instead was concern primarily with shielding individuals on a nationwide basis rather than exempting the people and property of a particular royal establishment. Significantly, a major portion of Horemheb text set forth the regulations of lawcourts and protocols for these courts vis-à-vis state employees as a means of regulating governmental operations. One similarity with the Seti I edict, however, was that the abuses which Horemheb Decree sought to prevent were being committed by governmental representatives, often military officers, as they went about the country on official business. Although it is hard to make a definitive assessment, the infractions appear to have been done under the color of official business and not in pursuit of private interests. The language may not be clear, but the intent of the edict was to prevent unauthorized exercises of the power to conscript (or impress) and to (mis-)appropriate—*i.e.*, abuse of power while on mission. The economic misdeeds envisaged were generally small-scale and, on the

129 Hoch 1994: 108–109, n. 135.

130 Galán 2000: 259–260 with n. 34.

131 Text conveniently presented in *Urk.* IV 2140–2161 with additional textual remarks in Helck 1955. The most comprehensive study of this text to date remains Kruchten 1981. For a recent English translation of the edict, see Murnane 1995: 235–240.

whole, far more specific than those enjoined in the Nauri Decree: seizure of small private boats, the misappropriation of hides, illegally seizing servants (or slaves), and various other impediments to the collection of regular royal imposts. As a rule, crimes against private property and regular government functions rather than offenses against people appear to have been the main concerns. In comparison with the Nauri Decree, the geographical scope of Horemheb Decree seems larger, covering both Upper and Lower Egypt. Given the more generalized, non-institutional perspective of the Horemheb Decree, it is not surprising that it shares little of the same terminology with the Nauri Decree when it comes to the critical subject of labor compulsion.

In the Horemheb Decree, those people most directly affected by the abuses appear to have been the independent individuals typical of rural life such as fishermen, herdsmen, or the agricultural workers called *nḥmw*, who might be comparable to our notion of freemen. Unlike the government agents, these low-status people were not primarily identified with state or temple institutions. By arbitrarily interfering with the activities of the peasantry, the offending officials would be hindering the rural population from fulfilling their normal obligations—*ḥtr*(*i*) and the less important term *pss*[132]—to the pharaoh. It is remarkable that the decree additionally forbade state agents from interfering with officials who would ostensibly outrank them, such as local mayors (*ḥꜣty-ꜥ*), who were apparently being unlawfully forced to provide goods and services in support of the royal progress throughout the land.

Much hinges on the nature of the term *ḥtr* here and in other New Kingdom texts, because of a tendency to consider this word a term for taxation. Although *ḥtr* appears only a few times in the edict, its use here has considerable implications for its meaning elsewhere, particularly as it pertains to compulsory labor as a form of taxation in Egypt. During the New Kingdom one of the most common terms used to describe state im-

[132] Although the word *pss* occurs as frequently as *ḥtr* in the edict, it is not as common in New Kingdom texts overall. *pss* can mean either some form of hard labor or simply normal work performed by individuals as an obligation to the king, but it does not seem to entail the large-scale undertakings that one associates with the concept of corvée, see Kruchten 1981:40. Significantly, Kruchten believes that *pss* is at least administrative equivalent to the type of service called *bꜣk*(*w*), on which see *op. cit.* 64, 65, 73, and 223. In discussing the appearance of *pss* in a passage likewise describing preparations for a royal visit (Pap. Anastasi IV 14, 10), Caminos 1954:208 rendered the word simply as "undertaking."

positions, be they in the form of goods or labor, was *ḥtr(ỉ)*, which is derived from a root with a formidably broad range of meanings. The word *ḥtr(ỉ)* was used both as noun and as a verb in the edict. Semantically, *ḥtr(ỉ)* appears to be related to the concepts of pairs and of binding two things or beings together, thus leading to such translations in the economic/legal sphere as "tax, impost, levy, dues, assessment,"[133] in the sense of linking an individual to an obligation or an assessment. Even these suggestions may be misleading, for they can imply that New Kingdom Egypt had a regular fiscal and taxation regime comparable to that of the Romans.[134] We should be cautious, moreover, in assuming that *ḥtr* necessarily operated from lower to higher social strata. At Deir el-Medina, for instance, the word *ḥtr(ỉ)* came to mean the deliveries of foodstuffs to the community.[135] Since the person under obligation in this instance was the Pharaoh, rather than the workmen, one can see why it would be wise to adopt the more neutral "obligation, responsibility" when rendering *ḥtr* elsewhere. The picture that emerges is reminiscent of the network of mutual obligations that theoretically underlay feudal society of the European during the Middle Ages. For the sake of the current discussion, of course, we are concerned only with cases in which the obligation was explicitly connected with labor *per se* rather than the product of that labor.

In order to sense what *ḥtr* means in the Horemheb Decree, it would be helpful as well to examine the general problem of abusive conscription and seizures that the edict addresses. Obviously, if corvée had been a long existing practice in Egypt, the state or the royal house must have had the occasional need to impress people on a more limited scale as well. It seems clear from the preamble that Horemheb intended the decree to suppress "... instances/crimes of plunder (*spw n ꜥwn*) in the land,"[136] that might be usefully be summarized as arbitrary seizures by those acting on official business, or those purporting to be doing so. Where impositions

133 For a survey of major studies that have been done on the word *ḥtr(ỉ)*, see Helck 1975:7–8; Warburton 1997:275–276; and Kruchten 1981:41. Perhaps most important of all is the extensive discussion by Kruchten 1980. In addition to the sense of an obligatory payment or quota, Janssen (1975b: 176) has also suggested that the term signified "deliveries" in the context of Deir el-Medina.

134 On this point, see the remarks on the tendency to translate *ḥtr* by the overly specific term "tax" in Spalinger 1996:355–357.

135 Significant to this point is that the payee was the Pharaoh and that the *ḥtrỉ* were always rendered in grain, see Janssen 1975a:455–457.

136 Stela, line 13, see Kruchten 1981:21.

against the rural population were discussed in the Horemheb Decree, the word *bḥ(w)* did not appear, nor most of the terminology of compulsory labor that was so critical later in the Nauri Decree.

The sole exception is *kfꜥ* which appears three times in the Horemheb decree each time in connection with people,[137] but not with property; *ḥtr*, by contrast, seems to apply here to things rather than people. In one typical passage, *kfꜥ* meant something like "requisition for work" for saffron gathering,[138] a rather limited task that would last a few days at most, hardly the extended seasonal labor for which people might be seized in the Nauri Decree. The impressed workers in this instance happened to be the slaves and servants of private people who would be deprived of their services not only for an indeterminate, if short, period of time, but also without recompense to their masters.[139] Thus, in passing, the text provides an example where the labor of a third party was treated as a commodity. In a similar manner, another passage implied that seizures of boats deprived the owners of their ability to perform obligatory (labor) service—*i.e.*, *ḥtr*—on behalf of the king.[140] Yet, at the same time, this passage makes it clear that the offenders were performing a task on behalf of the king too. The more common term *iṯꜣ* unexpectedly was not employed in the Horemheb Decree, although the roughly similar verb *sṯꜣ* "drag, haul, present" does appear instead, but not in connection with labor.[141]

Returning now to a passage just mentioned, perhaps the most informative instance of *ḥtr* occurs shortly after an unfortunately damaged section of the text containing the same word, most likely in a closely similar or parallel passage. This better preserved example concerns the requisition of privately owned boats (line 15): *ir imw*(?) *nty ḥtr*(*.w*) *r Wꜥbwt n Pr-ꜥꜣ*

137 Kruchten 1981: 62–63.

138 Stela line 23, see Kruchten 1981: 62–63.

139 According to Murnane (1995: 236), the pertinent phrase says, "...and these servants [seize the male and female slaves of an] individual: and these servants send [them on the job of gathering the saffron] for six or seven days, without its being known whether they (=the state employees) are free to dispose of them (=the slaves)." Stela lines 21–22, see Kruchten 1981: 62–63, where other examples of this verb are discussed.

140 Stela line 15, see Kruchten 1981: 30, with commentary on pp. 38 and 41.

141 Stela line 20, see Kruchten 1981: 54–55. The verb *ḥtr* with the preposition *r* is employed elsewhere in connection with a direct object denoting the payment of imposts or tribute. The verb also appears without any object, in which instances it pertains to the regular payment of some assessment, but is not used to denote imposts in the form of labor.

ʿ*.w.s* "As to any boat which is put to work (*ḥtr.w*) for the benefit of the Offering Halls of Pharaoh, l.p.h. ..."[142] Shortly following this quote, there is the section discussed above that forbade government agents from seizing (*kf*ʿ) boats, an indication that the offense ultimately was that the original owner had been deprived of his normal means of performing obligatory labor on behalf of the king. Similarly, few lines later in the stela, the Deputies of the Army were enjoined against confiscating goods that other individuals would have otherwise contributed (*sṯꜣ*) to the king's Private Quarters. This diversion of an obligation is described in the following fashion (Line 20): *m-mitt r nꜣ n Wdnw n Nṯrw nbw iw.w ḥtr*(*.w*) *ḥr pꜣ idnw* 2 *n pꜣ mšʿ* "... and likewise [those who contribute] to the Sacrifices to all the Gods which are put to work on behalf of the two Deputies of the Army..." In both the latter two examples, it is clear that the offending officials were actually acting on behalf of the Pharaoh, so that the nature of their offenses lay not so much in the seizures themselves, but rather that the seizures prevented others from performing their normal obligations to the king—in essence, "robbing Peter to pay Paul."

Both the Horemheb Decree and the Nauri Decree exhibit a similar attitude towards conscription from the state's perspective. In fact, one might say that some aspects of these royal protective measures had not changed significantly since their counterparts in the Old Kingdom. All such edicts aimed to shelter people who were deemed to be working on the king's behalf, especially if they were on institutional lands. Furthermore, it is not hard to draw some rough parallels with a different subject altogether, namely the varying situation of the *mrt* population as described by Moreno García. By comparing the status of the rural population in both cases, it seems that the peasantry was often vulnerable to compulsion or even long-term subjugation by powerful individuals. This is hardly surprising, yet these edits show that occasionally this vulnerability extended even to the wealthier stratum, including the administrative class, in the countryside.

Whatever general information about the normal operation of corvée that we can derive from these two edicts comes largely by implication—these documents, after all, were aimed against abuses of power, not its le-

142 Murnane (1995: 236) rendered the word *ḥtr* here in the more traditional manner, "[a]s for every boat which is taxable for the offering halls of Pharaoh ..." The word for 'boat' is written ideographically with the general P1 determinative that could be transliterated as ʿ*ḥa*(*w*), *imw*, or *dpt*, but the only vessel type spelled out fully in the text is ʿ*ḥ*ʿ(*w*) "masted boat."

gitimate exercise. Although we might be approaching an argument from silence by doing so, perhaps we should assume that there were otherwise no restrictions on corvée and that functionaries working on behalf of temple, state, or royal institutions could force the peasantry and other low-ranking individuals to work on officially commissioned tasks. In this respect it is significant that throughout Egyptian history, monarchs found themselves constrained to issue protection and exemption decrees. The essential question of whether high-ranking individuals were allowed to conscript labor at will remains largely unanswered. What is clear, however, is that abusive practices could result in humiliating punishments, most of which resulted in a loss of social status, in particular being reduced to a mere cultivator (*iḥwty*).

Large-scale Conscription in other Sources

Concrete evidence of massive works on behalf of the state can still be found today everywhere one looks in the Egyptian landscape, from the great temples and tombs to quarry inscriptions in the desert.[143] Yet, the few textual sources describing these are ironically vague as to the nature of the work force composition; perhaps it was obvious to the Egyptians that large-scale projects on behalf of the king or, more generally, the state, would employ conscript labor, including foreign captives. The army was an equally significant source of manual labor when a great number of workers were required.[144] Needless to say, a military task force by its very nature would have a high proportion of conscripts. Actually, the lack of details concerning the laborers themselves should not surprise us, since nearly all descriptions of the great projects of the New Kingdom derive either from royal inscriptions lauding the kings who commissioned the projects or from the tomb biographies of the high officials managing the work. For the reign of Amenhotep III, for example, we have brief descriptions the excavation of the vast lake at his Malkata palace, his expansion of the Karnak and Luxor temples, and the construction of his large mortuary temple on the Theban west bank. Some, if not all, of these under-

143 Most such projects required only a small percentage of skilled labor—the bulk of the remaining force was engaged in the more labor-intensive tasks of dragging stone or earth removal. For a useful overview of this more basic type of work and how it was managed, see Eyre 1987a: 186–193.

144 In this respect it is significant that *mšꜥ*, the Egyptian word for "army," had a more basic meaning "expeditionary force," military or otherwise, see Lichtheim 1988, 139, note 3q. For further information on the army as a public works force, see Eyre 1987a: 187–188.

takings must have required some degree of conscription and even the importation of a considerable number of laborers from outside of the Theban nome, but such details go largely unmentioned in the textual evidence.

The other type of large scale projects about which we have a fair amount of information are gold mining and stone quarrying. As much as we know about the often appalling conditions under which these expeditions were conducted and the occupational divisions composing the workforces, there is a regrettable dearth of information on how and where those laborers were gathered beforehand. The high death tolls during mining expeditions in the Nubian regions are strong evidence for conscription and that labor or prisoners of war were a major component of these forces. Oaths and other sources inform us that miscreants could be sent to work on quarrying and mining expeditions. This was certainly true much later during the Roman era when assignment to the Nubian mines was tantamount to a death sentence.

In the inscriptions describing royal commissions—temple building, quarrying expeditions, and the like—the various words for corvée encountered in the royal edicts discussed above are remarkably uncommon, being replaced by such uninformative, common terms as *k3t* "work" or *b3k* "work, service, production." The vizier or other high officials presumably in charge of such ventures bore titles like *imy-r k3t* (*nt nswt*) "Overseer of Work (of the King)," but the underlying terms here do not seem to have been necessarily associated with conscript labor. Even the rather broad term *b3k* played a small role in such contexts, eventually becoming primarily a word for a type of imposition or payment in kind to the monarch. Thus, the inscriptions describing the massive New Kingdom expeditions provide virtually no solid *terminological* evidence to show that the workers consisted largely of conscript or convict labor. Our sense of the circumstances tells us that this was the case, but the texts themselves and their wording provide little support. We are left with no objective criteria by which we can designate a project as corvée.

Craft specialists may have been attached to royal or temple workshops, but they were not considered impressed labor, as the case of crew at Deir el-Medina shows. These royal tomb-builders certainly produced some of the larger constructions of the New Kingdom, not only in the Valley of the Kings, but elsewhere at Thebes as well. The permanence of this community, some of whose inhabitants had dwelt there for generations, alone speaks strongly against conscript status, even if they may not have been entirely "free."[145] It was a privilege, in fact, to be a member of

[145] On this point, see above n. 000 (self ref. to Burkard articles)

the crew, since it guaranteed housing, sustenance, and a steady occupation. Indeed, not every male child of the community was guaranteed entrance into the crew. Once a member of the crew, that state (or royal) affiliation does not seem to have prevented the village's craftsmen from occasional work on their own behalf, even leading to an "informal workshop" for which they could produce funerary goods for other private individuals, separately from their regular activities on behalf of the state.[146] Attendance rosters also frequently note that workmen were absent while attending to personal matters or engaged in work for a superior—presumably some private affair of that official. In both circumstances, the individuals involved appeared to be working voluntarily and for their own benefit, rather than for the tomb-building administration. Naturally, Deir el Medina is certainly not the only source for voluntary labor contracts, as we shall see in the discussion in the section following. If we recall the wording of the Nauri Decree, these were the sort of voluntary contracts that the members of Seti I's institution were apparently proscribed from entering. Unlike the largely rural population mentioned in Seti I's edict, many of the men in the workmen's village had unusual skills that must have been in demand elsewhere in the funerary industry of the Theban West Bank. In sum, Deir el-Medina, which yields many insights on the management of labor during the New Kingdom, thus offers little direct information on the focus of this essay: corvée, conscription, and compulsion. However, since the material from the workmen's village do not mention arbitrary seizures for labor that was not related to the normal work there, this unique site indirectly offers an example of what life could be like when a place or an institution was under strong royal protection.

To what extent the conditions and practices of the specialized, government-supported community at Deir el-Medina can be compared with the rest of the country, natural, is problematic. One thing is clear, nonetheless—in all the evidence discussed above there is little clear evidence for a regular—in the sense of well-scheduled—corvée existing in Egypt. State compulsion seems to have occurred on an *ad rem* basis.

146 See Cooney 2006: 43–55. However, as Cooney emphasizes, the degree of freedom from the intervention of superiors is hard to measure. In Hellenistic era and later there is evidence of cult guilds associated with temples, a practice that may have its roots in pharaonic times but does not imply the existence of craft guilds, see Eyre 2004: 123–124.

Labor and Conscription in Literary and Other Non-official Sources

Non-official sources such as literary works and the letters of private people provide some interesting views on labor conscription. The reason for this lies largely in the character of the sources, especially in the case of Wisdom Literature, a genre which is probably more accurately called didactic literature, since a large proportion of such texts can actually be tied to scribal training by the tone of the material, references to students and instructors, and occasionally even specific colophons inserted into the texts.[147]

Didactic texts had a two-fold nature; today we often classify them as literary works, yet their nature rooted them strongly in the practical world. These texts were surely based on reality, but frequently exaggerated in order to make their case. Didactic literature may not quite represent an official viewpoint in the sense that we have been dealing with thus far, but these texts conform well to the facts about labor and compulsion as these topics appear in royal decrees and other sources. The most important didactic texts were styled as "instructions"—*sbꜣyt* in Egyptian. These were such works as "*The Instruction of Ptahhotep*" or "*The Instruction of Dua-Kheti*," that gathered together 'life lessons' and other advice for the students. The compositional date of *Dua-Kheti*, often called "*The Satire on the Trades*" (pSallier II), has long been a much debated point. Although the text was written in the Middle Egyptian dialect, all exemplars date to the New Kingdom and may thus reflect the attitudes of a later time. Whatever the case may be, *The Satire on the Trades* was used extensively to train students during the Ramesside era at Deir el-Medina, probably because it presented a grim description of all manual occupations, comparing each trade invidiously with the scribal profession. The central theme was that all non-scribal occupations reduced men to the level of animals and, most importantly, exposed workers to arbitrary conscription. In addition to the good career and a chance for social advancement and wealth that the scribal trade might bring, two remarks from *The Satire of the Trades* stressed a particular advantage of the profession. The first of these statements appeared near the beginning of the instruction—"I have seen beatings (*mꜣꜣ.n.i ḳnḳn zp-sn*)! Set your mind upon writing, (for) I have looked at one seized for his labor (*dgꜣ.n.i nḥmw ḥr bꜣkw.f*)."[148] The *topos* is reminiscent of the royal decrees discussed above, although the vocabulary is not the same

[147] For the significance of colophons in didactic texts, see Quirke 1996: 380; Lenzo-Marchese 2004; and Hagen 2006: 88–92.

[148] Pap. Sallier II 4,2; Helck 1970: 19–20.

and more generalized. Here the admonition to learn writing is bracketed by two appeals to the narrator's experience—he has seen people beaten and seized. The implication is clear even if not explicitly stated—the scribal profession sheltered one from the arbitrary seizures and rough treatment that characterized corvée and other types of conscription. The same theme appears again in the middle of the teaching, but here the phrasing was even less specific—"Look, there is no profession free of administrators—except for the scribe, he is the administrator (*m.k nn i͗ꜣt šw(t) m ḫrpw wp-ḥr zh ꜣw ntf pw ḫrp*)."[149] Although the ultimate source of the orders and the reasons for seizures remained undefined, the message was unambiguous—only administrators and scribes were immune from labor conscription.

Even with the passage of several centuries, several themes and the lessons of didactic literature remained much the same in the *Late Egyptian Miscellanies*. These were Ramesside compilations of assorted, shorter didactic pieces and practice letters. Although they date several hundred years after the earlier group of texts, the Miscellanies maintained the tradition of reminding student scribes about the special status that their chosen occupation held, using much the same tone as *The Satire of the Trades*. One of the most famous of these admonitions appears in several variations, the most vivid of which occurred in Pap. Anastasi II, 6,7–7,5 (with omissions):[150]

"Be a scribe. It saves you (7, 1) from toil (*bꜣk*) and protects you from all manner of work (*kꜣt*). It spares you from bearing hoe and mattock, so that you do not carry a basket.[151] (7, 2) It sunders you from plying the oar and spares you torment, as you are not under many lords (7, 3) and numerous masters. (A) man comes forth from his mother's womb and runs to his master: the child is in the service of (7, 4) a soldier, the stripling is a skirmisher. The old man is put to be a cultivator ...... (8, 5) But the scribe, he is ahead of all manner of work in this world."

This portrait of Egyptian society is remarkable and somewhat bleak, even allowing for palpable exaggerations. According to this exercise, which was repeated in pretty much the same words in other versions

149 Pap. Sallier II 9,1–2; Helck 1970: 118.

150 For the text, see Gardiner, 1937: 17. We follow essentially the translation by Caminos 1954: 51, with parenthetical insertions of relevant Egyptian vocabulary in transliteration. This passage has a close parallel in the citation from Pap. Sallier I quoted at . 000 above.

151 The determinative for both the noun and verb *kꜣt* "work" significantly is a squatting man with a work basket on his head 𓀉 (Sign-list A 9).

within the *Miscellanies*, the entire working class of Egyptian society—effectively 95% of the population—was effectively unfree and bound to the orders of some superior from childhood right through old age. The image of the child immediately running from the womb to a master is particularly compelling and chilling.

For the purposes of this study, however, the *Miscellanies* exercises most profitable for our purposes are not similar admonitions about the superiority of the scribe's profession and inferiority of all other lines of work. The exercises with the greatest verisimilitude were essentially model letters. Despite the obvious scribal bias that always ran close to the surface, exercises of this type were based on situations that could realistically arise in contemporary life of the Ramesside Period. It is likely that some pieces were actual letters that had been edited for instructional purposes. What rings true about a number of examples is that they mention specific instances of conscription instead of emphasizing the invidious nature of manual labor, the constant *Leitmotiv* of the *Satire on the Trades*. The theme of this later type of exercise letter is that the writer (the student scribe) is supposedly informing someone (his scribal master or some other official) that an unfortunate individual has been conscripted and this event has caused problems that need to be solved either by a superior's intervention or by a letter that the scribe should write to a superior. Several letters of this nature involve detailed questions and protestations as to the validity of the seizure, a central problem in several of the royal decrees that have been discussed here. Tellingly, none of these model letters involve complaints that the scribe himself or one of his colleagues has been wrongfully impressed, but that might be in keeping with a desire to idealize the social status of scribes.

Wrongful Avoidance of Corvée and Impressment

Corvée and rightful impressment did exist in Egypt. It was a universal obligation that the untitled and unlettered agricultural lower classes of Egypt had to satisfy from time to time as the need arose. Local and governmental officials, however they might be defined, were charged with fulfilling a quota of a given number of people for the tasks at hand. On occasion, officials may have had lists of specifically named people who would be recruited, willingly or unwillingly. For a moment, I would like to put aside the question of how the validity of an impressment might be determined and look instead at a situation that goes almost unmentioned in the royal decrees and other documents examined here—what might happen when an able-bodied individual who could claim no right to exemption attempted to avoid his or her obligations.

Most of our information about this situation derives from a Late Middle Kingdom papyrus which contains a lengthy register of people who are apparently in custody under the authority of the *ḫnrt ꜥꜣt*, a puzzling term that has often been translated as "the Great Prison," but may mean something less ominous like "the Great Enclosure."[152] The papyrus is badly damaged, which considerably increases the problems of interpretation that merely begin with the meaning of the term *ḫnrt*. It is unclear whether the papyrus might have been used and re-used over a long period and thus contains various unconnected records or whether it might represent a summary copy of a group of related documents. What does seem clear is that it contains, among other things, a long list of people some of whom are identified as *tš* "deserter" or *wꜥr* "fugitive." Several of these individuals appear to have been Asiatic domestic slaves who had been given Egyptian names. The papyrus also mentions an institution named *ḫꜣ n dd rmṯ* (*n wꜥrt rst*) "the office of providing (lit. giving/placing) people (of the Southern district)," strongly suggesting that the individuals listed had been captured after absconding from households to which they had been attached or else may have been people who had run away to avoid their assigned corvée duties. It is also important to note that papyrus states that the people listed would be dealt with according to the law (*hp*) pertaining to those who desert or run off, but the punishment is unspecified. The presence of Asiatics on these lists comports well with the known practice of putting foreign prisoners of war or abductees as workers on institutional lands.

Some Brief Concluding Observations

The focus of this study has been on compulsion rather than on labor generally. I make no claim that this is the central question in the study of Egyptian labor practices, but it cannot be denied that our perceptions of the degree and nature of compulsion in any labor transaction affects deeply our understanding how the Egyptian economy functioned. In this and many other aspects of economic thinking, we and the Egyptians proceed from entirely different conceptual frameworks. Among other things, a fundamental economic motivation such as profit-making appears to have been absent from their economy thinking for much of their history. Record keeping likewise frequently proceeded from a different point of view as to what should be accounted and how.

[152] Pap. Brooklyn 35.1445. See Hayes 1955; Quirke 1988; Quirke 1990: 127–186; Eyre 2013: 261–263; Grajetzki 2013: 233–234.

The imprecision in Egyptians' use of terminology poses an enormous obstacle, of course. This vagueness is not simply due to a careless attitude among the Egyptians, but we should realize the effects of the enormous time span from which our evidence derives. In the case of the investigation of the role that corvée may have played in the economy, the lack of a sound terminological basis meant that one is frequently left with subjective notion based on the size of a project instead of any solid criteria.

The question of compulsion in labor necessarily touches upon social relations and particularly how and when a free labor market may have risen in Egypt. Regrettably, we have information most from only the agricultural sector. The craft sector and the work of other specialties are very sparsely documented when it comes to compensation, but it seem fairly certain that for the period covered in this study that any highly trained artisan would have been primarily a state employee who occasionally might have an opportunity to contract out some of his skilled labor for other individuals—an 'informal workplace' at best and, for the time span studied in this paper, not a significant element in the economy.

BIBLIOGRAPHY

Allam, Shafik, ed. (1994), *Grund und Boden in Altägypten (Rechtliche und sozio-ökonomische Verhältnisse). Untersuchungen zum Rechtsleben im Alten Ägypten 2. Akten des internationalen Symposions Tübingen 18.–20. Juni 1990.* Tübingen.

— (2001a), "Ein Erbstreit um Sklaven (Papyrus BM 10568)," *ZÄS* 128: 89–96.

— (2001b), "Slavery," in Redford, ed. 2001: vol. 3, 393–396.

— (2004), "Une classe ouvrière: les *merit* 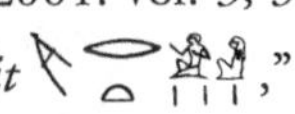," in Menu, ed. (2004b): 123–155.

— (2010), "Les équipes dites *meret* 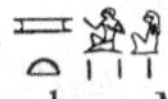 spécialisées dans le filage tissage en Égypte pharaonique," in Bernadette Menu, ed. (2010): 41–64.

Aldred, Cyril (1975), "Egypt: The Amarna Period and the End of the Eighteenth Dynasty," in CAH, II, Part 2, 3rd ed. Cambridge: 49–97.

Allen, James P. (2004), *The Heqanakht Papyri* (Publications of the Metropolitan Museum of Art Egyptian Expedition 27). New Haven.

Andrássy, P. (2007), "Zur Organisation und Finanzierung von Tempelbauten im Alten Ägypten," in Martin Fitzenreiter, (ed.), *Das Heilige und die Ware. Zum Spannungsfeld von Religion und Ökonomie* (IBAES 7). London: 143–164.

Assmann, Jan (2002), *The Mind of Egypt; history and its meaning in the time of the Pharaohs*, Andrew Jenkins, trans. Cambridge, MA.

Badawi, Alexandre (1943), "Die neue historische Stele Amenophis' II.," *ASAE* 42: 1–23.

Baer, Klaus (1962), "The Low Price of Land in Ancient Egypt," *JARCE* 1 (1962) 25–45.

— (1963), "An Eleventh Dynasty Farmer's Letters to his Family," *JAOS* 83: 1–19.

Berlev, Oleg D. (1987), "A Social Experiment in Nubia during the Years 9–17 of Sesostris I," in Powell 1987: 143–157.

Boochs, Wolfgang (1987), "Zur Bedeutung der *b3kw(t)* Leistungen," *VA* 3: 207–214.

Burkard, Günter (2003a), "'…die im Dunkeln sieht man nicht': Waren die Arbeiter im Tal der Könige privilegierte Gefangene?," in H. Guksch, E. Hofmann, and M. Bommas, (eds.), *Grab und Totenkult im Alten Ägypten*. Munich: 128–146.

— (2003b), "'Oh, diese Mauern Pharaos!' Zur Bewegungsfreiheit der Einwohner von Deir el Medine," *MDAIK* 59: 11–39.

Caminos, Ricardo A. (1954), *Late-Egyptian Miscellanies* (Brown Egyptological Studies 1). London.

Černý, Jaroslav (1973), *A Community of Workmen at Thebes in the Ramesside Period* (BdÉ 50). Cairo.

Cooney, Kathlyn M. (2006), in Dorn and Hofmann, eds. (2006): 43–55.

Crum, Walter E. (1939), *A Coptic Dictionary*. Oxford.

Cruz-Uribe, Eugene (1986), "[Review of] Orlando Patterson, *Slavery and Social Death: A Comparative Study*," *JNES* 45: 308–311.

— (1994), "A Model for the Political Structure of Ancient Egypt," in David Silverman, (ed.), *For his Ka. Essays Offered in Memory of Klaus Baer* (SAOC 55). Chicago: 45–53.

David, Arlette (2006), *Syntactic and Lexico-Semantic Aspects of the Legal Register in Ramesside Royal Decrees*. Classification and Categorisation in Ancient Egypt 5 (GOF 38). Wiesbaden.

Davies, Benedict G. (1997), *Egyptian Historical Inscriptions of the Nineteenth Dynasty* (Documenti Mundi. Aegyptiaca 2). Jonsered.

Demarée, Robert J. (2010), "The Organization of Labour among the Royal Necropolis Workmen of Deir el-Medina. A Preliminary Update," in Menu, ed. (2010): PAGES.

Dorn, Andreas (2006), "*M33-nḫt.w=f*, ein(?) einfacher Arbeiter, schreibt Briefe," in Dorn and Hofmann, eds. (2006): 67–85.

—— (2009), "Die Lokalisation der '5 Mauern' / Wachposten (*tꜣ 5 jnb.t / nꜣ jnb.wt / tꜣ jnb*," *JEA* 95: 263–268.

Dorn, Andreas and Tobias Hofmann, eds. (2006), *Living and Writing in Deir el-Medine. Socio-historical Embodiment of Deir el-Medine Texts* (AH 9). Basel.

Doxey, Denise M. (1998), *Egyptian Non-royal Epithets in the Middle Kingdom. A Social and Historical Analysis* (PÄ 12). Leiden.

Edgerton, William F. (1947), The Nauri Decree of Seti I: a Translation and Analysis of the Legal Portion," *JNES* 6: 19–30.

Eichler, Eckhard. (1992), "Polyani – Keynes – Warburton: Zur Rekonstruktion der altägyptischen Wirtschaftssystems," *GM* 131: 25–31.

Eyre, Christopher J. (1987a), "Work in the New Kingdom," in Powell (1987): 167–221.

—— (1987b), "Work in the Old Kingdom," in Powell (1987): 5–47.

—— (1994), "Feudal Tenure and absentee Landlords," in Allam, ed. (1994): 107–133.

—— (1998), "The Market Women of Pharaonic Egypt," in Nicolas Grimal and Bernadette Menu, eds., *Le commerce en Égypte ancienne.* (BdÉ 121). Cairo: 173–191.

—— (1999), Village Economy in Pharaonic Egypt," in A.K. Bowman and E. Rogan, (eds.), *Agriculture in Egypt from Pharaonic to Modern Times* (Proceedings of the British Academy 96). Oxford: 33–60.

—— (1999), "[Review of] David A. Warburton, *State and Economy in Ancient Egypt: Fiscal Vocabulary of the New Kingdom.* OBO 151 (Fribourg and Göttingen 1997)," *JESHO* 42 (1999) 575–577.

- (2004), "How Relevant was Personal Status to the Functioning of the Rural Economy in Pharaonic Egypt?" in Menu, ed. (2004): 157–186.

—— (2009), "On the Inefficiency of Bureaucracy," in C. Orsinego and P. Piacentini, (eds.), *Egyptian Archives: Procedings of the First Session of the International Congress, Egyptian Archives/Egyptological Archives, Milano, September 9–10, 2008.* Milan: 15–30.

—— (2010), "Who Built the Great Temples of Egypt?," in Menu, ed. (2010): 117–138.

—— (2013), *The Use of Documents in Pharaonic Egypt* (Oxford Studies in Ancient Documents 1). Oxford.

Faulkner, Raymond O. (1962), *A Concise Dictionary of Middle Egyptian.* Oxford.

Fischer, Henry G. (1979), *Ancient Egyptian Calligraphy. A Beginner's Guide to Writing Hieroglyphs.* New York.

Fitzenreiter, M., ed., *Genealogie – Realität und Fiktion von Identität*. IBAES 5 (London 2005).

Franke, Detlev (1991), "The career of Khnumhotep III of Beni Hasan and the so-called 'decline of the nomarchs'," in Stephen G. Quirke, ed., *Middle Kingdom Studies*. London: 51–68.

Galán, José M. (2000), "The Ancient Egyptian *Sed*-Festival and the Exemption from Corvée," *JNES* 59: 255–264.

Gardiner, Alan H. (1937), *Late-Egyptian Miscellanies* (BiAe 7). Brussels.

— (1947), *Ancient Egyptian Onomastica*, 3 vols. Oxford.

— (1952), "Some Reflections on the Nauri Decree," *JEA* 38: 24–33.

Gesterman, Louise (1995), "Der politische und kulturelle Wandel unter Sesostris III.," in L. Gestermann and H. Sternberg-El Hotabi, (eds.), *Per Aspera ad Astra, Wolfgang Schenkel zum neunundfünfzigsten Geburtstag. Ein Entwurf*. Kassel: 31–50.

Goedicke, Hans (1967), *Königliche Dokumente aus dem Alten Reich* (ÄA 14). Wiesbaden.

— (1984), *Studies in the Hekanakhte Papers*. Baltimore.

Goelet, Ogden, and Baruch Levine (1998), "Making Peace in Heaven and on Earth: Religious and Legal Aspects of the Treaty between Ramesses II and Hattušili III," in Meir Lubetsky, *et al.*, eds., *Boundaries of the Ancient Near Eastern World. A Tribute to Cyrus H. Gordon*. Sheffield: 252–299.

Gnirs, Andrea M. (1996), "Die ägyptische Autobiographie," in Antonio Loprieno, (ed.), *Ancient Egyptian Literature. History and Forms* (PÄ 10). Leiden: 191–241.

— (2013), "Coping with the Army: The Military and the State in the New Kingdom," in Moreno García, ed. (2013): 639–717.

Grandet, Pierre (2013), "The Ramesside State," in Moreno García, (ed.) (2013): 831–899.

Grajetzki, Wolfram (2013), "Setting a State Anew: The Central Administration from the End of the Old Kingdom to the End of the Middle Kingdom," in Moreno García, ed. (2013): 215–258.

Griffith, F. Ll. (1927), "The Abydos Decree of Seti I at Nauri," *JEA* 13: 193–208.

Grimal, Nicolas and Bernadette Menu, eds. (1998), *Le commerce en Égypte ancienne* (BdÉ 121). Cairo.

Hafemann, Ingelore (1985), "Zum Problem der staatlichen Arbeitspflicht im Alten Ägypten II. Auswertung der Expeditionsinschriften des Mittleren Reiches," *Altorientalische Forschungen* 12: 179–215.

— (2009), *Dienstverpflichtung im alten Ägypten während des Alten und Mittleren Reiches* (*IBAES* 12). Berlin and London.

Hagen, Fredrik (2006), "Literature, Transmission, and the Late Egyptian Miscellanies," in Rachael J. Dann, (ed.), *Current Research in Egyptology 2004. Proceedings of the Fifth Annual Symposium. University of Durham 2004.* (Oxford 2006) 84–99.

Haring, Ben J.J. (2006), "Scribes and Scribal Activity at Deir el-Medina," in Dorn and Hofmann, eds. (2006): 107–112.

Hasel, Michael G. (1998), *Domination and Resistance. Egyptian Military Activity in the Southern Levant, 1300–1185* BC (PÄ 11). Leiden.

Hays, Harold M., "*wḏ*: the context of command in the Old Kingdom," *GM* 176: 63–76.

Hayes, William C. (1955), *A Papyrus of the Late Middle Kingdom in the Brooklyn Museum* [*Papyrus Brooklyn 35.1446*]. Brooklyn.

Helck, Wolfgang (1955), "Das Dekret des Königs Haremheb," *ZÄS* 80: 109–136 and plates X-XI.

— (1970), *Die Lehre des Ḏwꜣ-Ḫtjj* (KÄT). Wiesbaden.

— (1975), "Abgaben und Steuern," in *LÄ* I: 3–12.

— (1977), "Frondienst," in *LÄ* II: 333–334.

— (1980), "Kriegesgefangene," in *LÄ* III: 785–788.

— (1984), "Sklaven," in *LÄ* V: 982–987.

Hoch, James E. (1994), *Semitic Words in Egyptian Texts of the New Kingdom and Third Intermediate Period*. Princeton.

Hofmann, Tobias (2006), "Arbeitseinsätze und Löhne der sogenannten Sklavinnen von Deir el-Medine," in Dorn and Hofmann, eds. (2006): 113–118.

James, Thomas G.H. (1962), *The Hekanakhte Papers and other Early Middle Kingdom Documents* (Metropolitan Museum of Art Egyptian Expedition Publications 14). New York.

Janssen, Jacobus J. (1963), "Eine Beuteliste von Amenophis II. und das Problem der Sklaverei im Alten Ägypten," *JEOL* 17: 141–147.

— (1975a), *Commodity Prices from the Ramessid Period. An Economic Study of the Village of Necropolis Workmen at Thebes*. Leiden.

— (1975b), "Prolegomena to the Study of Egypt's Economic History during the New Kingdom," *SAK* 3: 127–185.

— (1993), "*Bꜣkw*: From Work to Product," *SAK* 20: 81–94.

Jones, Dilwyn (2000), *An Index of Ancient Egyptian Titles, Epithets and Phrases of the Old Kingdom*, 2 vols. (BAR International Series 866, I and 866, II). Oxford.

Katary, Sally L.D. (2013), "The Administration of Institutional Agriculture in the New Kingdom," in Moreno García, ed. (2013): 719–783.

Kitchen, Kenneth A. (1979), "Egypt, Ugarit, Qatna and Covenant," *UF* 11: 453–464.

Kitchen, Kenneth A. (1970–1990), *Ramesside Inscriptions: Historical and Biographical*. Oxford.

— (1993a), *Ramesside Inscriptions Translated & Annotated: Translations* I. *Ramesses I, Ramesses I, Sethos I and Contemporaries.* Oxford.

— (1993b), *Ramesside Inscriptions Translated & Annotated. Notes and Comments* II. *Ramesses I, Ramesses I, Sethos I and Contemporaries.* Oxford.

Kóthay, Katalin A. (2010), "La notion de travail au Moyen Empire. Implications sociales," in Menu, ed. (2010): 155–170.

— (2013), "Categorisation, Classification, and Social Reality: Population Control and Interaction with the Population," in Moreno García, ed. (2013): 479–520.

Kruchten, Jean-Marie (1980), "Le verbe *ḥtr* et ses derivés jusqu'à la fin du Nouvel Empire. Sens et traduction," *Annuaire de l'Institut de Philologie et d'Histoire Orientales et Slaves* 24 (1980) 39–51.

— (1981), *Le décret d'Horemheb. Traduction, commentaire épigraphique, philologique et institutionnel.* Université Libre de Bruxelles, Faculté de Philosophie et Lettres 82. Brussels.

— (2001), "Law" in Redford, ed. (2001): vol. 2, 277–282.

Lesko, Leonard H. (2004), *A Dictionary of Late Egyptian*, 2 vols., 2nd ed. Providence.

Lichtheim, Miriam (1988), *Ancient Egyptian Autobiographies Chiefly of the Middle Kingdom. A Study and an Anthology* (OBO 84). Freiburg and Göttingen.

Lloyd, Alan B. (1992), "The Great Inscription of Khnumhotpe II at Beni Hasan," in Alan B. Lloyd, ed., *Studies in Pharaonic Religion and Society in Honour of J. Gwyn Griffiths* (The Egypt Exploration Society, Occasional Publications 8). London: 21–36.

Loprieno, Antonio (1997), "Slaves," in Sergio Donadoni, (ed.), *The Egyptians.* Chicago and London: 185–219.

Lenzo-Marchese, Guiseppina (2004), "Les colophons dans la littérature égyptienne," *BIFAO* 104: 359–376.

Lorton, David (1995), "Legal and Social Institutions of Pharaonic Egypt," (*CANE* I). New York: 345–362.

Manning, Joseph G. (1994), "Land and Status in Ptolemaic Egypt: the Status Designation 'Occupation Title + *b3k* + Divine Name'," in Allam, ed. (1994): 147–175.

Manuelian, Peter D. (1999), "Administering Akhenaten's Egypt," in Rita E. Fried, *et al.*, (eds.), *Pharaohs of the Sun. Akenaten-Nefertiti-Tutankhamen*. Boston: 145–147.

McDowell, Andrea G. (1990), *Jurisdiction in the Workmen's Community of Deir el-Medîna*. (Egyptologische Uitgaven 5). Leiden.

Megally, M. (1974), "À propos de l'organisation administrative des ouvriers à la XVIIIe dynastie," *Festschrift Wessetsky. Studia Aegyptiaca* 1: 297–311.

Menu, Bernadette (1979), "[Review of] Jac J. Janssen, *Commodity Prices from the Ramesside Period*," *CdÉ* 54: 255–260.

— (1979), "La fondation culturelle accordée à Sheshonq," *CRIPEL* 5: 183–189.

— (1994), "Questions relatives à la détention des terres au prèmier millenaire av. JC," in Shafik Allam, ed. (1994): 135–145.

— (1997), "Le prix de l'utile en Égypte au 1er millénarie avant notre ère," in Jean Andrieu, Pierre Briant, and Raymond Descat, (eds.), *Prix et formation des prix dans les economies antiques* (Entretiens d'archéologie et d'histoire 3). Saint-Bernard-des-Comminges: 245–275.

— (1998a), "Cessions de services et engagements pour dette sous les rois kouchites et saïtes," in Bernadette Menu, *Recherches sur l'histoire juridique économique et sociale de l'ancienne Égypte* II (BdÉ 122). Cairo: 369–383.

— (1998b), "Les échanges portent sur le travail d'autrui," in Grimal and Menu, eds. (1998): 193–206.

— (2004a), "Captifs de guerre et dépendence rurale dans l'Égypte du Nouvelle Empire," in Menu, ed., (2004): 187–209.

— (2004b), "La question de l'esclavage dans l'Égypte pharaonique," *Égypte pharaonique. Nouvelles recherches sur l'histoire juridique, économique et sociale de l'ancienne Égypte* (Collection Droits et Cultures 4). Paris: 337–359.

— (2005), "Une approche de la notion de travail dans l'Ancien Empire égyptien," in Bernadette Menu, *Recherches sur l'histoire juridique économique et sociale de l'ancienne Égypte* II (BdÉ 122). Cairo: 209–223.

Menu, Bernadette, ed. (2004), *La dépendence rurale dans l'Antiquité égyptienne et proche-orientale* (BdÉ 140). Cairo

Moreno García, Juan Carlos (1998), "La population *mrt*: une approche du problème de la servitude dans l'Egypte du IIIe millénaire (I)," *JEA* 84: 71–83.

— (2000), "Acquisition de serfs durant la Première Période Intermédiaire: une étude d'histoire sociale dans l'Égypte du IIIe millénaire," *RdÉ* 51: 123–139.

Moreno García, Juan Carlos, ed. (2013), *Ancient Egyptian Administration* (HdO 104). Leiden and Boston.

Müller-Wollermann, Renate (1987/88), "Das ägyptische Alte Reich als Beispiel einer Weberschen Patrimonialbürokratie," *BES* 9: 25–40.

Murnane, William J. (1995), *Texts from the Amarna Period in Egypt* (SBL Writings from the Ancient World 5). Atlanta.

— (1998), "The Organization of Government under Amenhotep III," in David O'Connor and Eric H. Cline, (eds.), *Amenhotep III. Perspectives on His Reign*. Ann Arbor: 173–221.

Nims, Charles F. (1948), "The Term *hp*, "law, right" in demotic," *JNES* 7: 243–260.

Otto, Eberhard (1956), "Prolegomena zur Frage der Gesetzgebung und Rechtsprechung in Ägypten," *MDAIK* 14: 150–159.

Peet, Eric (1926), "Two Eighteenth Dynasty Letters: Papyrus Louvre 3230," *JEA* 12: 70–74.

Perdu, Olivier (1995), "Ancient Egyptian Autobiographies," in Jack Sasson, (ed.), *Civilizations of the Ancient Near East* IV. New York: 2243–2254.

Powell, Marvin A., ed. (1987), *Labor in the Ancient Near East* (American Oriental Series 68). New Haven.

Quirke, Stephen G. (1988), "State and Labor in the Middle Kingdom. A Reconsideration of the Term *ḫnrt*," *RdÉ* 39: 83–108.

— (1990), *The Administration of Egypt in the Late Middle Kingdom: the hieratic documents* (New Malden 1990).

— (1996), "Archive," in Antonio Loprieno, (ed.), *Ancient Egyptian Literature. History and Forms*. (PÄ 10). Leiden: 379–401.

— (2004), *Titles and bureaux of Egypt 1850–1700 BC*. London.

Redford, Donald B., ed. (2001), *The Oxford Encyclopedia of Ancient Egypt*. 3 vols. Oxford.

Ritner, Robert K. (2009), *The Libyan Anarchy: Inscriptions from Egypt's Third Intermediate Period*. (SBL Writings from the Ancient World 21) Atlanta.

Römer, Malte (2000), "Landholding," in Redford, ed. (2000): vol. 2, 255–258.

Scharff, Alexander (1924), "Briefe aus Illahun," *ZÄS* 59: 20–51, with 12 pls.

Schlögl, Hermann A. (1985), "Uschebti," in *LÄ* VI: 896–899.

Simpson, William K. (1963), *Papyrus Reisner I. Transcription and Commentary. The Records of a Building Project in the Reign of Sesostris I.* Boston.

— (1965), *Papyrus Reisner II. Transcription and Commentary. Accounts of the Dockyard Workshop at This in the Reign of Sesostris I.* Boston.

— (1969), *Papyrus Reisner III. Transcription and Commentary. Records of a Building Project in the Early Twelfth Dynasty.* Boston.

— (1986), *Papyrus Reisner IV. Transcription and Commentary. Personnel Accounts of the Early Twelfth Dynasty.* Boston.

Spanel, Donald B. (2001), "Funerary Figurines," in Redford, ed. (2001): vol. 1, 567–570.

Spalinger, Anthony (1996), "From Local to Global: The Extension of an Egyptian Bureaucratic Term to the Empire," *SAK* 23: 353–376.

Théodoridès, Aristide (1997), "Freiheit," in *LÄ* II: 297–304.

Trapani, Marcella (2002), "Une nouvelle enquête sur la stèle d'Ahmès-Néfertari," *ZÄS* 129: 152–165, with Pls. XXXII–XXXIV.

Valbelle, Dominique (1985), *"Les ouvriers de la tombe." Deir el-Médineh à l'époque ramesside* (BdÉ 96). Cairo.

van den Boorn, Guido P.F. (1988), *The Duties of the Vizier. Civil Administration in the Early New Kingdom.* London and New York.

Ventura, Ralph (1986), *Living in a City of the Dead. A Selection of Topographical and Administrative Terms in the Documents of the Theban Necropolis* (OBO 69). Göttingen.

Vernus, Pascal (2013), "The Royal Command (*wḏ-nsw*): A Basic Deed of Executive Power," in Garcia Moreno, (ed.) 2013: 259–340.

Warburton, David A. (1984–1985), "Some Remarks on the Manufacture and Sale of Shabtis," *BSEG* 9–10: 345–355.

— (1997), *State and Economy in Ancient Egypt. Fiscal Vocabulary of the New Kingdom* (OBO 151). Freiburg and Göttingen.

Wente, Edward (1990), *Letters from Ancient Egypt* (SBL Writings from the Ancient World 1). Atlanta.

Wilkinson, Toby A.H. (1997), "[Review of] D.A. Warburton, *State and economy in ancient Egypt.* OBO 151 (Fribourg and Göttingen 1997)," *DE* 39: 149–151.

Wilson, John A. (1954), "Authority and Law in Ancient Egypt," *JAOS* 17: 1–7.

Abbreviations

ÄA	Ägyptologische Abhandlungen
AH	Aegyptiaca Helvetica
ASAE	*Annales du Service des Antiquités de l'Égypte*
BdÉ	Bibliothèque d'Étude (IFAO)
BES	*Bulletin of the Egyptological Seminar*
BiAe	Bibliotheca Aegyptiaca.
BIFAO	*Bulletin de l'Institut franqais d'archéologie orientale*
BSEG	*Bulletin de la Société d'égyptologie de Genève*
CAH	Cambridge Ancient History
CANE	J. Sasson, ed., *Civilizations of the Ancient Near East*
CdÉ	*Chronique d'Égypte*
CRIPEL	*Cahier de recherches de l'Institut de papyrologie et égyptologie de Lille*
CT	Adriaan de Buck, *The Egyptian Coffin Texts*, 7 vols., OIP 34, 49, 64, 67, 73, 81, 87.
DLE	L. Lesko, *Dictionary of Late Egyptian*
DE	*Discussions in Egyptology*
IBAES	Internet-Beiträge zur Ägyptologie und Sudanarchäologie
IFAO	Institut français d'archéologie orientale
JAOS	*Journal of the American Oriental Society*
JEA	*Journal of Egyptian Archaeology*
JEOL	*Jaarbericht 'Ex Oriente Lux'*
JNES	*Journal of Near Eastern Studies*
KÄT	Kleine Ägyptische Texte
K*RI*	K. A. Kitchen, *Ramesside Inscriptions. Historical and Biographical* See above, Kitchen 1969–1990.
LÄ	*Lexikon der Ägyptologie*
MDAIK	*Mitteilungen der Deutschen Archäologischen Instituts, Abteilung Kairo*
OBO	Orbis biblicus et orientalis
OIP	Oriental Institute Publications
PÄ	Probleme der Ägyptologie
RdÉ	*Revue d'égyptologie*
RITA	K. A. Kitchen, *Ramesside Inscriptions Translated & Annotated*
RITANC	K. A. Kitchen, *Ramesside Inscriptions Translated & Annotated. Notes and Commentary*
SBL	Society of Biblical Literature
SAK	*Studien zur Altägyptischen Kultur*
SAOC	*Studies in Ancient Oriental Civilisation*
UF	*Ugarit-Forschungen: Internationales Jarhbuch für die Altertumskunde Syrien-Palästinas*
Urk. I/IV	K. Sethe, *Urkunden des aegyptischen Altertums* I/IV
VA	*Varia Aegyptiaca*
Wb.	A. Erman, and H. Grapow, eds., *Wörterbuch der ägyptischen Sprache*
ZÄS	*Zeitschrift für Ägyptische Sprache und Altertumskunde*

9.

Labor and Individuals in Late Bronze Age Pylos

Dimitri Nakassis
University of Toronto

Most studies of economy and labor in the Mycenaean world focus on the overall structure and organization: that is, they consider the designations used to describe classes of laborers, the technical terms for the conditions or obligations involved in work, and the organization of systems of remuneration.[1] Recent studies have greatly improved our understanding of specialized economic terminology and its relevance to the organization of Mycenaean palatial economies.[2] Yet in seeking to understand the use of specific terms, laborers within a given sphere of production tend to be treated as a homogeneous group. For example, the Mycenaean term *ta-ra-si-ja* (*talasiā*) is associated with a system of production in which raw materials are weighed out and allocated to workers, probably on an annual basis.[3] The workers are required in exchange to render manufactured goods to the palace. The term is thus best translated as "an amount [of raw material] weighed out and issued for processing."[4] The *ta-ra-si-ja* system organized the production of textiles, bronze products, and chariot wheels. In his recent review, John Killen tentatively concludes that *ta-ra-*

1 This paper has benefited enormously from the comments of the participants at the workshop in 2005 and later from the written comments of Michael Hudson and Piotr Steinkeller.

2 For example, Duhoux 1976; Hutton 1990–91; Killen 1999, 2001a, 2008; Palaima 2000, 2001. Cf. Bernabé and Luján 2008.

3 Killen 2001a; Nosch 2006.

4 Ventris and Chadwick 1973: 583; Killen 2001a: 161.

si-ja production is characteristically spatially decentralized and involves many workers of relatively low status.[5]

Such approaches operate under the assumption that laborers can and do constitute a homogeneous group. An alternative approach might focus instead on individual laborers. Indeed, my prosopographical research on named individuals at Pylos shows that one class of *ta-ra-si-ja* workers, namely smiths (Linear B *ka-ke-u*, *k^h^alkeus*; plural *ka-ke-we*, *k^h^alkēwes*), was a heterogeneous group that included members of the elite.[6] This conclusion suggests that despite the important scholarly gains made by general studies of the Mycenaean economy, the focus on the overall structure of the economy and general categories of laborers needs to be refined by an assessment of the diverse contributions of individuals. I argue in this paper that the labor of the men and women identified by name in the Linear B texts is crucial to our understanding of the economy of the Mycenaean state centered on the site of Pylos in southwestern Greece circa 1200 BC.

The identity of named individuals

The data for this study are compiled from a prosopography of all personal names attested in ca. 1000 Linear B texts from Pylos.[7] There are 1,683 occurrences of 964 personal names, of which 700 are completely preserved and certainly identified as names. To put this quantitative data into a broader perspective, the territory of the Pylian kingdom, with a territory of 2,000 square kilometers (see Figure 1), carried an estimated Late Bronze Age population of 50,000.[8] Stefan Hiller calculates that

5 Killen 2001a: 175; cf. Killen 1984a: 61; Nosch 2006: 163–164. Duhoux (1976: 115; cf. 2008: 268), on the other hand, considers *ta-ra-si-ja* workers "artisans libres et indépendants."

6 Nakassis 2013: 74–102, 153–186. See too Nakassis 2006: 267–319 and Nakassis 2008.

7 Nakassis 2013. This new prosopographical study substantially revises the pioneering work of Lindgren 1973.

8 For the population of the Pylian state, see most recently, Whitelaw 2001: 64. Earlier estimates tend to be higher (*e.g.*, McDonald and Hope Simpson 1972: 141; Carothers and McDonald 1979). For the area of the Pylian polity, see Bennet 1995: 587. Of the total population, adult males are likely to constitute about one quarter (Nakassis 2013: 34 n. 24). This is significant since almost all of the individuals mentioned by name in the tablets are males, and all are presumably adults.

minimally 4,100 people are monitored in the tablets from Pylos, whether identified individually or as part of a group.[9]

In most cases, individuals are simply identified by a single personal name. Where additional information is provided, the most common modifiers are patronymics, professional designations or ethnics. Almost 80 per cent of the individual personal names come from five major subject groupings of texts:

1. **An series:** a diverse set of texts characterized by the presence of the ideogram for men (VIR), it consists largely of personnel registers, including the *o-ka* set, which records individuals and groups of men watching the coast in a military context;
2. **Cn series:** texts that primarily record the location and composition of flocks of sheep, goats and pigs, as well as the named individuals responsible for them;
3. **Fn series:** texts characterized by the ideogram for barley (HORD); they primarily record the payment of grain and occasionally olives or figs to specific individuals and groups;[10]
4. **E-series:** texts that record the land holdings of individuals in various locales, and
5. **Jn series:** texts that relate to bronze (AES); the largest subset of this series records allocations of metal to smiths for production under the *ta-ra-si-ja* system.[11]

About two thirds of the personal names appear only once in the Pylos texts (469 of 700 complete names, or 67%), leaving us with 231 names that recur (*i.e.*, that appear in more than one text). The earliest studies argued that in most cases these recurring names simply indicated different, homonymous, individuals.[12] These studies pointed out that many recurring names appeared listed against different toponyms, suggesting that different individuals must have been meant. This hypothesis is not without its problems, since in some cases it is not known where a toponym was located, or whether a toponymic designation indicated a dis-

9 Hiller 1988: 60.

10 The identity of the ideograms for wheat and barley is contested (Palmer 1989; the traditional identifications are defended by Halstead 1995 and Killen 2004). In this paper I use the traditional values of the HORD and GRA ideograms as barley and wheat, respectively.

11 The ideogram AES and the Linear B *ka-ko* (Greek *k^h^alkos*) might represent copper, bronze, or both; for a discussion of this issue and the Jn series generally, see Smith 1992–93. For simplicity, I refer to AES as bronze.

12 Ventris and Chadwick 1973: 352; Lejeune 1971: 187–188; Lindgren 1973, I: 14.

trict within a larger town or regional unit.[13] In many cases it is also possible to show that different toponyms at which a single name is listed are fairly proximate to each other.[14] More important, however, is the fact that these arguments are based on the tacit belief that these people were of low-status and were therefore incapable of managing multiple tasks at different sites. The two largest groups of names, smiths and herders, are commonly thought to be menial laborers. The crucial role played by assumed social status in early studies is revealed by the fact that the identity of recurring names of clearly high-status individuals is routinely accepted, no matter how extreme the variation in the toponyms associated with these individuals.[15]

By examining sets of names that cluster together in more than one text, I have been able to establish that in most cases recurring names can be shown to represent a single individual with a high degree of confidence.[16] This procedure is possible because the texts at Pylos are highly concentrated in time, space and function. All of the preserved texts were temporary clay documents, almost all of which were baked by the fire that attended the final destruction of the palace. They can consequently be dated to a small temporal window of about one year, although most texts probably represent a considerably shorter span of time.[17] All of the tablets were also found in the palace proper, and were composed solely for the administration of the palatial economy.[18] The end result of my contextual analysis of recurring names is that in 67 per cent of all possible cases, we can make at least one prosopographical match (*i.e.*, at least two occurrences of the same name represent a single person) with cer-

[13] Lang 1988.

[14] Nakassis 2013: 42–44.

[15] See, *e.g.*, Sutton 1970: 105 n. 10, 128, 540; Lindgren 1973, II: 135–136, 153–155.

[16] Nakassis 2013: 29–72 provides a fuller discussion of these prosopographical methods.

[17] On the timespan represented in the texts from Pylos, see Palaima 1995; Bennet 2001; Driessen 2008. A handful of texts are probably earlier in date, perhaps LH IIIA, ca. 1390–1340/1330 BC. (Palaima 1983; 1988: 111–113, 133, 162–169, 172; Melena 1996–97a: 166; 2000–01a: 367; Skelton 2008: 171–172; Skelton 2010). The chronology of these tablets does not significantly affect my prosopography, however, since these fragmentary texts contain only three personal names.

[18] The palace is under one hectare in size. More than 80% of all texts were found in a small two-roomed Archives Complex (Palaima 1988: 172; see too Pluta 1996–97).

tainty; this figure increases to 79 per cent if we include matches classed as probable. Of names attested in more than one series (i.e., more than one administrative set of texts), 45 per cent have a certain prosopographical match, and 69 per cent have a probable or certain match. These should be considered minimum figures, since the fragmentary nature of the epigraphical record tends to impede identification.

These prosopographical identifications significantly change the way we understand the identities and roles of named individuals. The people whose names recur in multiple texts are involved in several economic and administrative activities under palatial purview, sometimes in parts of the kingdom that are distant from each other. For example, a man with the name *Plouteus* (Linear B *po-ro-u-te-u*) is responsible for working 1.5 kg of bronze (Jn 310.5), herding 90 male sheep (Cn 131.5), and gathering 20 goats (Vn 493.4). Each of these activities is located in different parts of the Pylian kingdom: he works metal in the southwest near the palace (at the toponym *a-ke-re-wa*), herds sheep in the northwest (at *pi-*82*), and gathers goats in the northeast (at *e-ra-te-re-wa*) (see Figure 1). Since we can identify with certainty that the same man is responsible for multiple activities, he and other multi-tasking individuals like him must be important people, probably members of the elite, since only they would be capable of managing multiple administrative tasks in different parts of the kingdom. The conclusion that recurring names represent members of the elite runs against the scholarly consensus that most of the people identified on the tablets by name, particularly smiths and herders, were low-status menial laborers.[19] This consensus is based on assumptions about the organization of labor in the Mycenaean economy. For example, most assume that all the individuals named in herding texts (Cn series) were actually herders in the field, and that all individuals in texts recording allocations of metal (Jn series) were actually smiths. However, it is equally likely that these individuals are agents responsible for ensuring that palatial flocks remained at full strength or that the requisite amount of bronze goods was manufactured, either by doing it themselves or by arranging for others to do it.

There is no reason to think that this was not the case, at least in some instances, since there is a good Mycenaean analogue: a significant portion of the palatial economy was allocated to men known in modern scholarship as "collectors." It is important to note that there is no Mycenaean

[19] Baumbach 1983; Chadwick 1976: 64; Killen 1979, 2001a: 173; Ventris and Chadwick 1973:122–123.

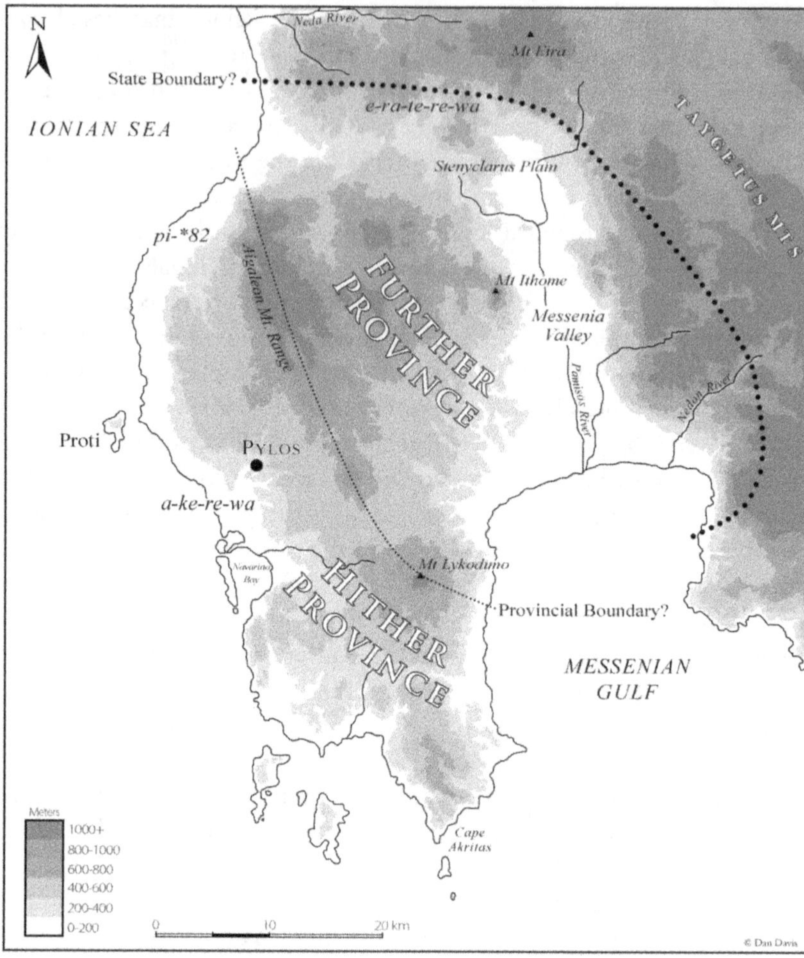

Figure 1: A topographic map of Messenia, with places mentioned in the text. The locations of Linear B toponyms are approximate. Map drawn by Dan Davis.

term, so far as we know, used to describe these men. They are listed only by personal name, and appear to be responsible for the organization of large parts of the textile industry, including the herding of palatial livestock; they also have interests in a variety of other economic activities monitored by the palace.[20] One of the four collectors at Pylos, *Alksoitās*

[20] There is an extensive bibliography on the "collectors." Recent contributions include Bennet 1992; Carlier 1992; Godart 1992; Killen 1995; Rougemont 2001; Rougemont 2009: 249–524.

(Linear B *a-ko-so-ta*), appears 15 times in shepherding texts, supervises a land inspection, and acts as an agent that gives, receives and distributes various goods.[21] It would be difficult to argue—and no one has done so—that this is not one and the same man, an important member of the elite, to whom economic activities were allocated or even contracted out.[22] It is therefore likely that other named individuals, certainly less prominent than the "collectors" yet important people in their own right, might assume multiple responsibilities for the palace.

Near Eastern administrative records also provide a number of parallels to multi-tasking Mycenaeans: for example, at Ugarit there is an individual, Attanu-purli-anni, who is a high priest and "chief of the shepherds,"[23] in the Ur III state a man named Babati is an archivist, royal accountant, military and civilian governor.[24] The occasional spatial dispersion of the Mycenaean elites is also matched elsewhere: Kathryn Keith has shown that in the Old Babylonian period wealthy individuals owned city houses in addition to country estates.[25]

It may be fruitful to think of the Mycenaean "collectors" not as a coherent group of administrators, as most have done, but as members of a wider group, namely supervisors identified by personal name.[26] The lack of a Mycenaean technical term to designate "collectors" also encourages us to compare them to other individuals who were likewise identified simply by personal name. We should perhaps conceive of named individuals as located at various points along a continuum of administrative importance: at the top are the "collectors," who are typically involved in a wide variety of significant activities, while further down are multi-tasking administrators such as *Plouteus*, whose responsibilities are somewhat more mundane and less wide-ranging than those of the "collectors" (see Figure 2).[27]

21 Nakassis 2006: 385–186; Nightingale 2008.

22 Killen 1995: 213–114.

23 Lipiński 1988: 131–133.

24 Postgate 1992: 151.

25 Keith 1999, 2003. Historical Greek elites were also typically active in a variety of religious, economic and political pursuits, and their holdings were often spatially dispersed.

26 Rougemont 2001; 2009: 251–309 critically reviews definitions of "collectors" in modern scholarship. Bennet 1992: 96 notes the difficulty in distinguishing "collectors" from other named palatial agents.

27 Nakassis 2013: 161

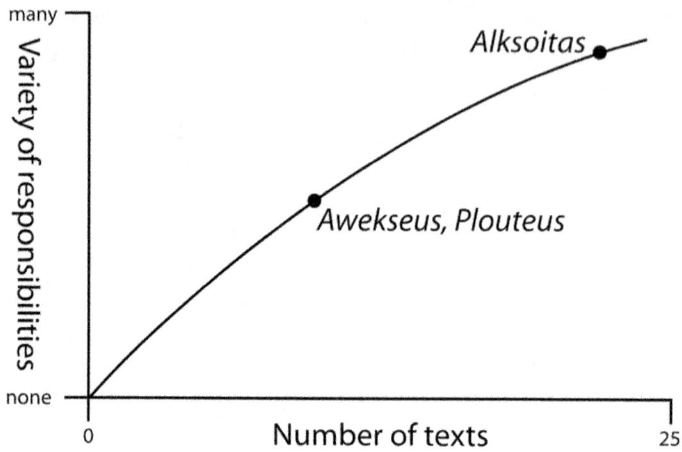

Figure 2: A schematic representation of the relationship between administrative importance of named individuals and the variety of their responsibilities.

Contributions of named individuals to the palatial economy

Now that I have sketched out the roles and identities of named individuals, it remains to be determined what their contribution was to the palace economy. From the discussion above, it is clear that named individuals were responsible for a wide variety of activities. In the following, I examine the contribution of four groups of individuals to the palatial economy: smiths, herders, military officers and supervisors of work groups.

Smiths

As mentioned above, there are a large number of smiths recorded individually by personal name in the Pylos texts (at least 225). The Jn series of tablets records precisely how much bronze was allocated from palatial stores to smiths in the *ta-ra-si-ja* system, whereby the palace provided weighed-out raw materials to craft specialists in return for finished products (see Text 1). Bronze allotments are individual, implying that the individual smith (or perhaps his household) is the basic unit of production.[28] If we were dealing with large, state-run workshops or factories,

[28] This is not universally true; for example, one smith named *a-mu-ta-wo* is allocated 31 workers on Jn 431.26.

then we might expect a simpler method of disbursement for administrative purposes.[29] Not all smiths are allocated bronze; about 30% are designated as not having an allotment (*a-ta-ra-si-jo*). Even those Pylian smiths to whom bronze was allocated did not work full-time for the palace: the amounts of bronze allocated tend to be rather small (allotments range from 1.5 to 12 kg, with an average of 3.5 kg), and unless the Jn series represents a short administrative period, there is not enough bronze allocated to justify full-time production. What evidence we do have suggests that *ta-ra-si-ja* allocations were annual.[30]

The allocation texts of the Jn series do not specify what products are to be made.[31] One collection text (Jn 829) records a levy of temple bronze from each district of the Pylian kingdom to make javelin- and spear-points, but the amount of metal collected is relatively small (less than 50 kg total) compared to the metal from the Jn series as a whole (from 594 to 1046 kg).[32] It is most likely that different smiths produced different types of goods, depending on their specialty, which was presumably known to Pylian administrators. Chadwick deduced from the large number of smiths that the palace produced bronze goods for export, and from the presence of out-of-work smiths that there was a temporary bronze shortage. Another possibility is that the situation reflected in the Jn texts is the normal result of the desire among a number of individuals to engage in smithing work for the palace. The excess labor would have allowed the palace to increase production easily depending on changes in the supply of metal and the demand for metal products.[34]

[29] For example, Ugaritic texts apparently list large disbursements (250 kg) of bronze to a single individual, probably a chief smith who then divided up the metal among subordinate smiths (Heltzer 1979: 491–493).

[30] The Knossos text So(2) 4442 refers to a deficit in last year's (*pe-ru-si-nwa*) *ta-ra-si-ja*.

[31] One possible exception is that smiths on Jn 750 are designated as *pa-ra-ke-te-e-we*, which might be translated as "helmet-makers," although this translation is not without its problems and its critics. For a review, see Aura Jorro (1993: 81–82 *s.v. pa-ra-ke-te-e-u*).

[32] 594 kg represents the minimum amount of bronze distributed in the Jn series without duplicating amounts from "working tablets" as defined by Smith 1992–93. 1046 kg is the amount of bronze recorded on the totaling tablet Ja 749. For Ja 749 as the totaling tablet of the Jn series, see Lejeune 1971: 194–195; Ventris and Chadwick 1973: 356, 508–509.

[33] Ventris and Chadwick 1973: 509–510; Chadwick 1976: 141. Michel Lejeune (1971: 178) thought that the tablets represented a time of crisis when smiths were asked to work *more* bronze than usual.

[34] For similar production arrangements designed to maximize flexibility in output, see Costin 1996: 212.

I estimate that 54 smiths—about one fifth—can be certainly or probably identified with other occurrences of the same name. Why do some smiths recur while others do not? Other than the fragmentary nature of our evidence, one explanation may be that the smiths were not a homogeneous group. Smiths who were involved in producing relatively ordinary goods might not be involved in the palatial economy to the extent that they would appear elsewhere by name. On the other extreme are smiths identified as royal craftsmen such as *Atuk^h^os* (Linear B *a-tu-ko*), who appears to have had a direct relationship with the king that enabled him to hold multiple plots of land near the palace (En 609.5). Smiths appear to have operated at different scales as well—several smiths are recorded as having dependent labor at their disposal. Thus, palatial bronze production is managed through the agency of many individuals of varying statuses, probably of different abilities, specializations and scales.

Herders

In the Linear B texts from Pylos there are at least 154 individuals who are listed as responsible for flocks ranging in size from 10 to 230 animals, primarily sheep, but also goats and pigs (see Text 2). In total, some 12,000 livestock are recorded.[35] It is common for the same personal name to be listed against more than one flock, and in nearly all of these cases it is clear that a single individual herds multiple flocks.[36] It is almost certain that the flocks themselves are the property of the palace, although Killen has modified this by demonstrating that the palace did not own particular animals but rather enjoyed the use of a specific number of animals and their products, especially wool.[37] Halstead has also convincingly shown on the basis of the records at Knossos that shepherds replaced sheep that died in the field with sheep from their own personal flocks, and that shepherds could freely move animals from their personal flocks into palatial flocks and *vice versa*. He suggests that shepherds could benefit from this arrangement by swapping their own sheep for fat palatial wethers for consumption or palatial ewe lambs for rapid expansion of their personal flocks.[38] Consequently, all shepherds were probably individuals with substantial personal holdings of sheep. Moreover, prosopo-

[35] Ventris and Chadwick 1973: 198 count the following numbers: 10,157 sheep (8,217 of which are male), 1825 goats (1004 male), and 540 pigs.

[36] Kyriakidis 2008.

[37] Killen 1993.

[38] Halstead 2001: 43.

graphical matches with other texts suggest that many of these herders had other responsibilities and therefore could not have been actual herders in the field, as is commonly assumed. I conclude that the individuals named in herding texts were not herders, but the agents responsible for maintaining palatial flocks. In Pylos, as in Old Babylonian Ur, the actual herders in the field are absent from our documentation; instead, the palace records herding supervisors.[39]

There are a number of similarities between the palatial management of bronze production and of animal husbandry, and indeed at least 27 individuals are both smiths and herders (or rather, herding supervisors). In both economic fields, the palace directly allocated palatial resources of significant value to a large number of specific individuals, identified in the texts only by personal name and location. These named smiths and herding supervisors were arguably the most important agents for the palace's administration of these economic fields.[40]

Military officers

Most names from the An series at Pylos appear in simple lists of men. However, a significant subset (about one third) appears attached to what are plausibly interpreted as groups of men organized into military units that guard the coastline (see Text 3).[41] The units are called *o-ka* in Linear B and the texts are accordingly called the *o-ka* set. Units are made up of

[39] Cf. Kyriakidis 2008. For Old Babylonian parallels, see van de Mieroop 1992: 86–97, Postgate 2001: 188–90.

[40] Some limited vertical hierarchy of administration is evidenced in animal husbandry by the presence of four "collectors," and in bronze production by three individuals identified as *g^w^asilēwes* (Linear B singular *qa-si-re-u*, plural *qa-si-re-we*); both of these higher-level administrators are simply identified by personal name. Nevertheless, the "collectors" are only responsible for some 30% of the total number of flocks monitored by the palace, and their interests seem to focus on particular aspects of shepherding (Bennet 1992: 83–86; Godart 1992). The three *g^w^asilēwes* in the Jn series were evidently involved in the management of bronze distribution (or perhaps production), but their presence in the Jn series is sparse: only three appear on the 18 allocation tablets. In any case, as the names of "collectors" and *g^w^asilēwes* are listed *in addition to* the names of herders and smiths respectively, they do not simplify the written administration, although they may represent a hierarchy of personal responsibility. Since the presence of "collectors" and *g^w^asilēwes* appears to be optional, it seems that the individually named smiths and herders (or rather, herding supervisors) were the critical element in the palace's administration of these economic fields.

[41] Ventris and Chadwick 1973: 184–194, 427–430.

individuals identified by name, who are listed along with groups of 10 to 110 men identified by toponymics and ethnics. The named individuals appear to act as unit commanders, officers, and a select dozen are called *e-qe-ta* (singular *^{h}ek^{w}etās*), a title normally translated as "follower [of the king]." These followers are high-ranking officials who are almost always identified by name and patronymic. Their role is unclear but they are plausibly representatives of the central administration.[42] In some cases, they may also be responsible for furnishing groups of fighting men.[43]

Supervisors of work groups

Mycenaean work groups are typically recorded as being under the supervision of named individuals. At Pylos, work groups called *qa-si-re-wi-ja* (*g^{w}asilēwiā*) and *ke-ro-si-ja* (*geronsiā*) are always accompanied by a personal name in the genitive, almost certainly indicating the supervisor of the group.[44] The text An 340 records at least 13 named individuals who are managed by a man named *a-ta-o*, almost certainly in the context of craft production.[45] These work groups appear in three types of texts:

(1) records of the composition of the work group in question, *i.e.* personnel lists;
(2) records of incoming deliveries of finished products, and
(3) records of outgoing payments of staple goods to support the workmen.

In some cases, scribes may omit reference to the work group, and simply record payment to named administrators. For example, a woman with the name *Kessandrā* (Linear B *ke-sa-da-ra*) is listed against unusually large amounts of grain and figs on the texts Fg 368 (480 liters of wheat and an equal amount of figs) and Fg 828 (480 liters of wheat). On An 435, she appears to be the recipient of men identified by personal name, who have been allocated to her by the "collector" Alksoitās.[46] It is likely that these records are related to each other. Nine ideograms indicating men

[42] Deger-Jalkotzy 1978.

[43] Nakassis 2012: 272–273.

[44] On these groups, see Palmer 1963: 228–29, Ventris and Chadwick 1973: 171–172. Likewise in the *o-ka* set, unit commanders are named in the genitive immediately after the word *o-ka*.

[45] Nakassis 2013: 93–94.

[46] On this interpretation of An 435, see Nakassis 2012: 279–282 (*pace* Palmer 1994: 79, Melena 1994–95a: 97). For recent improvements to the text of An 435, see Melena 1992–93: 314, 321; Melena 1994–95a: 97, 99–100; Melena 1994–95b: 278; Melena 2000–01b: 373.

(VIR) are preserved on An 435, but a close inspection of this fragmentary text reveals that the tablet had a minimum of 19 entries. If 20 men were allocated to *Kessandrā*, 480 liters of grain would divide evenly into 24 liters for each man. This could either represent rations sufficient to support the laborers for 20 days at 1.2 liters per day, the standard male daily ration,[47] or a single lump payment of staples at levels above subsistence.[48] Wheat and figs are regularly allocated together in equal amounts as rations for dependent textile workers (Ab series) and in other contexts (Fg 253, Fg 374, Fn 187).[49] Thus, *Kessandrā* might have been a prominent woman to whom laborers and the grain to support them were allocated by the palace through the agency of the "collector" Alksoitās.

A similar text, Fn 7 (see Text 4), records payments of foodstuffs to support a group of craftsmen in an architectural project.[50] There is a clear hierarchy reflected in the amounts of the payments. The wall-builders (*to-ko-do-mo*) and sawyers (*pi-ri-je-te-re*) receive 1.2 liters of grain per day, the standard male ration, while the all-builder (*pa-te-ko-to*), perhaps a highly skilled foreman, receives more than twice that amount (3.2 liters per day). The individuals named *qa-ra*$_2$ and *pa-ka* receive even greater amounts of foodstuffs, which, as Melena has noted, are too great to represent rations.[51] They may represent instead payment of salaries, in which case the larger amounts of staples would reflect the higher social status of the recipients.[52] It is however very rare to find so many foodstuffs allocated to individuals over an extended period of time.[53] It is possible that *qa-ra*$_2$ and *pa-ka* were architects, but this function was

47 Ventris and Chadwick 1973: 393, 420; Chadwick 1976: 118–119; Palmer 1989: 96–97.

48 This amount of barley is allocated, for example, to the man named *e-ti-me-de* on Fn 324.1. Killen (2001b: 411) argues that Fn 324 represents a single day's allocation.

49 Killen 2004: 161–163. Other relevant texts include Pylos An 128.11–12, Un 1322 and Mycenae Fu 711.8.

50 Melena 1996–97b: 171–76; Nakassis 2013: 275–279.

51 Melena 1996–97b: 175.

52 Palmer 1992: 481 distinguishes between "rations" and "handouts." The former constitute subsistence for dependent labor, while the latter are "given to people because of their status, or affiliation with a religious groups" and are "probably a minor source of food." On status distinctions reflected in the size of these "handouts," see Palmer 1989: 90, 117–118; Palmer 1992; Melena 1996–97: 175–176; James 2002–03: 411.

53 The best parallel is Fn 79, which seems to record allocations over a five day period (Chadwick 1976: 118–19), with several individuals receiving 19.2 liters of olives per day. But Fn 7 records the allocation of rations for an entire month.

probably filled by the all-builder, and normally teams of builders are supervised by a single foreman who is also a master craftsman. More plausibly, therefore, these staples might have been allocated to *qa-ra*$_2$ and *pa-ka*, at least in part, to support what is evidently missing from the text: the gangs of unskilled labor required to complement the skilled labor of the wall-builders, sawyers and the all-builder.[54] These unskilled laborers would have been necessary to haul materials, excavate foundations, tear down unwanted constructions, and so on. The staples allocated to *qa-ra*$_2$ and *pa-ka* in Fn 7 may be like those allocated to *Kessandrā* in Fg 368 and 828, but without the personnel record corresponding to An 435. It may be that the palace simply allocated them staples with the expectation that they would make the necessary arrangements to mobilize labor.

In some cases, then, it seems that named individuals were agents responsible for raising and supervising groups of men. In some cases the palace would supply the staples required to support their labor, although only rarely do we know both the purpose of the task in addition to the duration of its activity. It is difficult to determine how this labor was raised. There is evidence that suggests that military service was due to the palace in respect of landholdings, and that this rule applied to groups of small-scale landholders as well as important aristocrats. Mühlestein long ago pointed out a number of correspondences between the numerical values in the Na series at Pylos, which records taxes to be paid in flax, and the numbers of military men recorded in the *o-ka* set and related rower texts.[55] Chadwick showed through an analysis of the terminology in the Na series that the flax impost was directly related to landholdings.[56] It therefore seems plausible that holding land in the Na series incurred two obligations: payment in flax and military service. These obligations seem to have applied to groups of anonymous individuals as well as named members of the elite. The high-ranking "collector" named **we-da-ne-u* is responsible for furnishing twenty rowers (An 610.14), and his landholdings in the Na series correspond to a total of twenty units of flax (Na 856, Na 1041). It seems likely that in this case, **we-da-ne-u* provided the twenty rowers he owed in respect of his landholding

[54] Nakassis 2012, with parallels to the records from Ur III Garšana (Heimpel 2009) and early modern Greek architectural guilds. On gang labor in Mycenaean palatial building, see Wright 1980: 82–83.

[55] Mühlestein 1956: 15–18.

[56] Ventris and Chadwick 1973: 469–471. See further de Fidio 1987: 132, Killen 2008: 170.

with personal dependents, perhaps the men who were actively involved in working the land. This system of raising labor directly in respect to landholdings may have been supplemented with another system in which laborers were "hired" indirectly by named individuals acting as administrative intermediaries. As mentioned above, it is plausible that the supervisors from Fn 7 (*qa-ra*$_2$ and *pa-ka*) hired unskilled laborers using the foodstuffs which the palace provided to them. Perhaps individual Pylians could be hired when not engaged in fulfilling their corvée requirements to the palace.[57]

Rewards to named individuals for their service

Named individuals stood to gain from their service to the palace. Several texts record tax exemptions for smiths, presumably in exchange for their labor.[58] With regard to herders in the Cn series, Paul Halstead has suggested that because the palace was not interested in individual sheep but rather in maintaining the total number of the flock, shepherds could have manipulated the composition of palatial and personal flocks to their advantage.[59] This could potentially make shepherding palatial flocks quite valuable to those individuals who already had substantial personal holdings of sheep.

The allotment of land was one of the main ways that the palace could directly reward individuals for their service.[60] In the E-series texts, the palace records the precise land-holdings of named individuals in particular districts; individual records include the landholder's personal name and additional information indicating the reason for which he or she holds the land. For example, a man named *Atuk*^{h}*os* (*a-tu-ko*) holds two plots of land near the palace and is identified as the royal armorer (En 609.5/Eo 211.2, Ep 301.5). All in all, 36 land-holders identified by name appear outside of landholding texts, and most of them (20, or 55.5%) are smiths or herders. These are encouraging results, and they have persuaded some scholars to posit a remunerative system whereby land or payment in kind was regularly granted to individuals in return

57 Cf. Postgate 1992: 237.

58 Ma texts with smiths are Ma 90.2, 120.2, 123.3, 124.2, 193.3, 221.2, 225.2, 365.2, 378.2, and 397.3. Na texts with smiths are Na 106.B, 252.B, 425, 529.B, 923.B, 941.B, and 1357.3.

59 Halstead 2001: 42–43.

60 This is suggested by the fact that a land lease is called *o-na-to*, which literally means "benefit" (Aura Jorro 1993: 26–27).

for their labor.[61] However, the evidence does not allow us to argue that the palace always—or even often—gave land to those who gave their service to the palace, since of the 225 complete names of smiths preserved, only 16 (7%) appear in our landholding texts.[62] Those individuals who appear as smiths or herders *and* land-holders tend to be high-ranking officials, however, and it is therefore likely that these men represent a privileged group of individuals who, based on their high status, are allocated land by the palace. That is, rather than being the norm, they are the exception.

On the other hand, it is also possible that the palace did award land to individuals, but that records of this do not survive. After all, the extant landholding texts refer to an area constituting a small percentage of the total amount of land in Messenia, although how much of that land was directly controlled and administered by the palace is difficult to estimate. There may be indirect evidence in some texts for palatial grants of land. For example, taxes given to the palace in the form of flax, as recorded in the Na series, appear to be paid by landholders, including smiths, in respect to specific landholdings.[63] Smiths in these texts are always exempt from taxation, but the fact that these exemptions are recorded in the first place implies that as landholders, smiths were tax-eligible.[64] The landholdings in the Na series are not the same as those allocated to individuals, however, and it is possible that they represent ancestral landholdings of local groups from which the palace extracted taxes. In any case, it is clear that the evidence cannot support systematic remuneration of all palatial laborers via allocations of land. Despite the fact that landholding and taxation texts are precisely those mostly likely to be kept by the scribal administration for future reference, there are simply not enough records of landholdings to account for all the individuals under palatial supervision.[65]

[61] Gregersen 1997.

[62] Of course, the landholding texts we possess are not a complete register of landholders in the kingdom, but rather relate to specific districts, especially those located near the palace (Killen 2008: 165–173), but on the other hand, it is likely that only two thirds of the Jn series is preserved (Lejeune 1971: 194–195).

[63] Ventris and Chadwick 1973: 368–373; Killen 1979: 133; Foster 1981: 76, 83; Halstead 2001: 44.

[64] See too Killen 1992–93a.

[65] See, *e.g.*, Killen 1984b, Pluta 2006.

As I have discussed above, a number of individuals and groups receive allocations of staple goods from the palace.[66] While these texts often give little information about the organizing principle of the allocations and how often these amounts are paid out, the surviving texts largely seem to be short-term payments made on an *ad hoc* basis.[67] Some of these texts seem to have a craft context, as certain individuals named as recipients are possible prosopographical matches with smiths.[68] Thus, smiths as a group are heterogeneous in the benefits they receive (land or foodstuffs), although no individual smith is both a landholder *and* a recipient of staple goods, suggesting that these are on the whole distinct spheres of remuneration.[69]

Conclusions

The named individuals at Pylos do not constitute a homogeneous group.[70] Some are very important individuals in the state, while most individuals appear to have had more limited contact with the palace. A significant portion of individuals who are recorded by name and occur in multiple texts must be members of the elite.[71] Many of these individuals participate in two of the most important industries managed by the state, both of which are characterized by spatial decentralization, namely the production of bronze goods and animal husbandry.[72] Bronze and textile production are two fields where long-distance exchange or trade may have been part of the motivation for production, since the scale of production for both is probably beyond the needs of local consumption. Indeed, the few texts we have that may attest to exchanges

66 Palmer 1992: 481.

67 Killen 2001b: 439–441. It is likely that these "ration" texts have a relatively short life-cycle. That is, they were probably pulped shortly after the foodstuffs had been paid out. See Bennet 2001: 27–30.

68 Nakassis 2013: 95–98.

69 It is rare to find individuals who are both recipients of staples and landowners; the only examples are *du-ni-jo* (prosopographical identification possible) and **34-ke-ja* (prosopographical identification certain).

70 Nakassis 2013: 156–162.

71 Nakassis 2013: 162–173.

72 The third major productive field of the Pylian state was the production of perfumed olive oil (Shelmerdine 1985).

between polities involve textiles,[73] whereas metal trade is amply attested in the archaeological record.[74]

It is striking that the palace chose to record the precise activities of these individuals rather than introducing vertical managerial hierarchies in the documentary process. Perhaps this is attributable to the fact that these named individuals were of interest to the administration, or were important people, in their own right. It also seems that the individuals responsible for managing flocks and bronze production may have changed from year to year, so the palace had an interest in knowing which particular individuals were responsible for production in any particular year.[75] Moreover, a few documents show that the palace was also concerned to identify how much named individuals were to pay in taxes.[76] As we have seen above, service to the state may have led to exemptions for certain individuals and groups, so it might have been necessary for palatial administrators to track the services of named individuals in order to correctly assess their contributions in any given year.

Just as the contribution of individuals was variable, so too was their remuneration. The evidence suggests that land-grants were only awarded to a fraction of the named individuals involved in the management of the palatial economy, and those who appear as recipients of plots of land tend to be high-status individuals. Staple goods, on the other hand, are allocated to work-groups and to named individuals, including those who act in a managerial capacity for specific tasks, such as architectural projects, and those who are part of a group of skilled laborers put together on an *ad hoc* and temporary basis. While the amount of staple goods awarded to highly dependent laborers appears to be stable across the Mycenaean world,[77] there is much variability in the amount of material awarded to named individuals, presumably reflecting the fact that payment was made with different combinations of goods for different types of services which were differently valued by the palace. This may have

[73] The relevant texts are Mycenae X 508, which records the delivery to textiles to Thebes, and the Knossos Ld series texts that refer to cloth for guests, which might refer to export (Aura Jorro 1985: 353–354). Chadwick (1976: 141) argues that the large number of smiths recorded in the tablets suggests that the Pylian kingdom produced bronze goods for export.

[74] See, *e.g.*, Sherratt 2000.

[75] Killen 1993.

[76] Pylos Nn 831, discussed by Killen 2008: 168–169.

[77] Palmer 1989.

hindered the development of set rates of remuneration above the level of highly dependent labor.

Named individuals could constitute dependent labor, in a sense: smiths received metal from palatial stores, herders managed palatially-owned flocks, and so on. On the other hand, it appears that these individuals possessed considerable personal holdings. Many of the arrangements implied by the texts presumably existed prior to the emergence of the palaces. For instance, wealthy individuals must have possessed extensive flocks, which in all likelihood they did not herd themselves, but assigned to junior members of their households or members of dependent households. Thus, the palace seems to have successfully yoked the personal holdings of the local elites to serve its needs by offering these individuals opportunities to manage aspects of the state's economy in areas where they were already active.[78]

It is unclear whether or not these duties were onerous to those who performed them. The fact that there seems to be excess labor in both shepherding and smithing has been taken to mean that these duties were avoided by individuals,[79] though it might equally suggest the opposite, that many individuals were willing to participate in palatial economies. Given that the individuals undertaking these responsibilities appear to come from an elite class, and that similar arrangements in Near Eastern palatial economies seem to have been potentially profitable for individuals,[80] it seems unlikely that they were onerous except perhaps in bad years. Some arrangements, as we have seen, may have provided opportunities for enrichment.

Named individuals allowed the palace to manage extensive and decentralized economic activities in an administratively simple arrangement. For example, the personal holdings of individuals allowed the palace to entrust the maintenance of a fixed number of animals to specific agents, because they could recoup losses due to accidental death in palatial flocks with their own animals. This system represents a significantly simpler administrative arrangement than the alternative, which would require the authentication of each accidental death to prevent

78 Nakassis 2013: 180–181.
79 Killen 1993: 215.
80 *E.g.*, Postgate 1992: 159–161; Postgate 2001: 188–189.

fraudulent reports.[81] Thus, the palace both relied upon the private holdings of herders to maintain the palatial sheep rearing system, and benefited from the administrative simplicity of assigning tasks to individuals capable of executing them.

This description bears some resemblance to the economic system reconstructed for the Old Babylonian state, referred to as a "Palastgeschäft."[82] While the Old Babylonian system is largely reconstructed on the basis of written contracts between agents and the palace that specify the obligations involved, the highly restricted uses of writing in the Mycenaean world mean that such agreements are not preserved for us, but must be inferred from the palatial records that we do have. The advantage of such systems is their administrative simplicity, not to mention the fact that some risk was absorbed by the elite instead of the state. There are certainly a number of important differences between the Mycenaean and Old Babylonian palatial economies, such as scale, but they are comparable insofar as they represent examples of one type of administrative strategy with particular strengths and weaknesses. From this perspective, the relevant issue is how the conditions attending the ongoing formation of the Mycenaean state at Pylos made this administrative strategy possible and desirable.

The Pylian state did not materialize *ex nihilo*, but emerged through complex processes of competition and cooption whereby the center at Pylos established authority over other settlements in Messenia and their elite families over time.[83] John Bennet has argued that the expansion of Pylos' political authority began circa 1600 BC, and its rule gradually expanded to include the western "Hither Province" circa 1380 BC, and

[81] Authentication of individual animals to prevent fraud is a palatial concern in select areas: Killen (1992–93b: 102) has persuasively argued that palatial plow oxen were given descriptive names in the Knossos Ch tablets to prevent fraud by the individuals who loaned them from the palace, and the Thebes Wu sealings, which record the collection of animals for sacrificial consumption, appear to reflect such concerns as well (Piteros *et al.* 1990: 156–157; cf. Palaima 2004: 107–108 on the administrative process by which the obligation of delivering these sacrificial animals was monitored).

[82] van de Mieroop 1992: 241–250; Postgate 2001: 187–190; Renger 2000; 2001; Stol 2004: 919–944. My model of the Mycenaean economy was not influenced by work on the Old Babylonian palatial economy; I thank Piotr Steinkeller for pointing out the similarities to me.

[83] Nakassis 2013: 179–183.

the eastern "Further Province" circa 1330 BC (Figure 1).[84] Thus, at the time of the tablets (circa 1200 BC), the Pylian polity had only controlled all of its territory for four or five generations, and its dominance over the more immediate western half of Messenia (the "Hither Province") was perhaps six to seven generations old (200 years). As the center at Pylos gained ascendancy over an increasingly large territory, the elite residing at Pylos became dominant over the members of regional elites who were the leaders of their own local communities, whose families were probably buried in the sometimes massive and conspicuous tombs in Messenia.[85] These local elites could present a problem to the ruling households at Pylos, as their cooperation was crucial to the integration of the state.[86] Moreover, they and their families likely controlled resources locally that were of interest to the palace: land, livestock, and so on.

One strategy open to the palatial elite was to integrate the traditional activities of the local elites into the palatial economy. Instead of imposing this system onto unwilling individuals, the palace may have offered powerful incentives for members of regional elites to participate. The nature of the Mycenaean palatial economy may therefore be seen as the historical product of the emergence of the Pylian state, namely the fact that the expansion of the Pylian polity involved interacting with and incorporating, and perhaps excluding, elite families living within its territory.

[84] Bennet 1995, 1999a, 1999b; Shelmerdine 2001. For Mycenaean palatial chronology, see Shelmerdine 1998: 539–541.

[85] On early Mycenaean burial practices in Messenia, see Boyd 2002.

[86] Cf. Brumfiel 1992: 557–558.

Appendix: Texts

Note on the translations: Names have been rendered in Greek where interpretation is relatively clear. Where it is not, I have simply transcribed them.

Text 1: Pylos Jn 601

Transcribed text

.1 po-wi-te-ja , ka-ke-we , ta-ra-si-ja , e-ko-te

.2 wo-di-jo , AES M 6 to-ro-wi AES M 8 e-u-po-ro-wo AES M 8

.3 o-qa AES M 4 te-u-to AES M 5 pu$_2$-ti-ja AES M 6

.4 po-to-re-ma-ta AES M 8 wa-pa-no AES M 8

.5 po-so-ro AES M 8 mo-da AES M 8 pe-po-ro AES M 4

.6 o-na-se-u AES M 12[ ] AES M 8̣[ ]

.7 ko-to-wa-[ ] AES M 8 ṭọ[-so-]d.e. , e-p̣ị-da-to AES M 7

.8 qa-si-re-u , pa-qo-ṣị[-jo]1

.9 to-so-pa , ka-ko [ ] AES L 3 M 14[

.10 *vacat*

.11 to-so-de , a[-ta-ra-]ṣị-jo[ka-ke-we]ti-na-jo 1

.12 po-so-ri-j.o.[ ]ne-wo 1 i-pe-ra-ta 1

.13 sa-nu-[ ] 1[ ]*vacat* [ ] *vacat*

.14 *vacat*

.15 *vacat*

.16 *vacat*

Translation

.1 At *po-wi-te-ja*, smiths having a *ta-ra-si-ja*:

.2 *Wordios* BRONZE 6 kg *to-ro-wo* BRONZE 8 kg *E*$^{(h)}$*uplowos* BRONZE 8 kg

.3 *o-qa* BRONZE 4 kg *Teut*^{h}*os* BRONZE 5 kg *P*^{h}*ut*^{h}*iās* BRONZE 6 kg

.4 *Ptolemātās* BRONZE 8 kg *wa-pa-no* BRONZE 8 kg

.5 *Psolōn* BRONZE 8 kg *mo-da* BRONZE 8 kg *Peplos* BRONZE 4 kg

.6 *Onaseus* BRONZE 12 kg [ ] BRONZE 8 kg

.7 *ko-to-wa-*[ ] BRONZE 8 kg and so much distributed extra: BRONZE 7 kg

.8 The *g*^{w}*asileus Pagg*^{w}*ōsios*: 1

.9 Sum total bronze: BRONZE 114 kg

.10

.11 So many [smiths] without a *ta-ra-si-ja*: [ ]*ti-na-jo* 1

.12 *Psoliōn* [1] *ne-wo* 1 *i-pe-ra-ta* 1

.13 *sa-nu-*[1

.14

.15

.16

Text 2: Pylos Cn 599

Transcribed text

.a	pa-ro	
.1	wa-no-jo , wo-wo , ne-ti-ja-no a-ke-o-jo	CAP^{m} 100
.2	a_2-ne-u-te , pa-ro , ka-so , a-ko-so-ta-o	CAP^{m} 45
.3	a_2-pa-tu-wo-te , pa-ro , a-ke-ra-wo , a-ke-o-jo	CAP^{m} 90
.4	a_2-pa-tu-wo-te , pa-ro , ru-we-ta , a-ke-o-jo	CAP^{f} 40
.5	a_2-pa-tu-wo-te , pa-ro , a-wo-i-jo ,	CAP^{f} 50
.6	wa-no-jo , wo-wo , pa-ro , ke-re-no , a-ke-o-jo	CAP^{f} 80
.7	a_2-pa-tu-wo-te , pa-ro , e-zo-wo	SUS^{f} 30
.8	e-ko-me-no , pa-ro , ti-ri-po-di-ko	SUS^{f} 57

Formula: PLACE-NAME + *pa-ro* ("with") SHEPHERD'S NAME in dative + [optional COLLECTOR'S NAME in genitive], TYPE OF ANIMAL + NUMBER OF ANIMALS

Translation

.1	At *wa-no-jo wo-wo*, with *Nestianōr*, of *a-ke-o*:	male GOAT 100
.2	At *a_2-ne-u-te*, with *ka-so*, of *Alksoitās*:	male GOAT 45
.3	At *a_2-pa-tu-wo-te*, with *Ark^{h}elāwos*, of *a-ke-o*:	male GOAT 90
.4	At *a_2-pa-tu-wo-te*, with *ru-we-ta*, of *a-ke-o*:	female GOAT 40
.5	At *a_2-pa-tu-wo-te*, with *Āw$^{(h)}$o^{h}ios*:	female GOAT 50
.6	At *wa-no-jo wo-wo*, with *Gerēnos*, of *a-ke-o*:	female GOAT 80
.7	At *a_2-pa-tu-wo-te*, with *e-zo-wo*:	female PIG 30
.8	At *Erk^{h}omenos*, with *Tripodiskos*:	female PIG 57

Text 3: Pylos An 657

Transcribed text

.1 o-u-ru-to , o-pi-a_2-ra , e-pi-ko-wo,
.2 ma-re-wo , o-ka , o-wi-to-no,
.3 a-pe-ri-ta-wo , o-re-ta , e-te-wa , ko-ki-jo,
.4 su-we-ro-wi-jo , o-wi-ti-ni-jo , o-ka-ra_3 VIR 50
.5 *vacat*
.6 ne-da-wa-ta-o , o-ka , e-ke-me-de ,
.7 a-pi-je-ta , ma-ra-te-u , ta-ni-ko ,
.8 a_2-ru-wo-te , ke-ki-de , ku-pa-ri-si-jo VIR 20
.9 *vacat*
.10 a_3-ta-re-u-si , ku-pa-ri-si-jo , ke-ki-de VIR 10
.11 me-ta-qe , pe-i , e-qe-ta , ke-ki-jo
.12 a-e-ri-qo-ta , e-ra-po , ri-me-ne ,
.a o-wi-

.13 o-ka-ra , -to-no VIR 30 ke-ki-de-qe , a-pu$_2$-ka-ne ,
.14.A VIR 20 me-ta-qe , pe-i , a$_3$-ko-ta , e-qe-ta ,

Translation

.1 Thus the watchers are guarding the coastal regions:
.2 The unit of *Māleus* at *o-wi-to-no*:
.3 *Ampelitāwōn, Orestās, ^{h}Etew(w)ās, ko-ki-jo*
.4 *Suwerrowiyos*. Of *o-wi-to-no, o-ka-ra$_3$* MAN 50
.5
.6 The unit of *Nedwātās*: *Ek^{h}emēdēs*
.7 *Amp^{h}iertās, Marat^{h}eus, Tainiskos.*
.8 At *a$_2$-ru-wo-te, ke-ki-de* Kyparissians MAN 20
.9
.10 At *Ait^{h}aleus*, Kyparissians *ke-ki-de* MAN 10
.11 and with them the follower, the son of *Kerkos*
.12 *A^{h}erik^{wh}oitās*,[87] at Deer Harbor.
.13 *o-ka-ra* at *o-wi-to-no* MAN 30 and *ke-ki-de* from *a-pu$_2$-ka*
.14 MAN 20, and with them *Aigortās* the follower.

Or *A^{h}erik^{wh}ontās* (see García Ramón 2011: 222 n. 19).

Text 4: Pylos Fn 7

Transcribed text

.1 qa-ra$_2$]2 OLIV T 2
.2 pa-ka] OLIV T 1̣
.3 to-]ḳọ-ḍọ-mo ḤỌṚḌ [] Z 3 VIR 20[
.4 pi-ri-e-te-re HORD [] Z 3 VIR 5
.5 pa-te-ko-to[ ] ḤỌṚḌ [ ]Ṿ2 [
.6 *vacat*
.7 qa-ra$_2$-te , o[-pi-me-]ṇẹ[ ]OLIV 6̣
.8 pa-ka , o-pi-ṃẹ-ṇẹ , [OLIV
.9 pa-te-ko-to , o-pi-me-ṇẹ [ ] ḤỌṚḌ 1 [
.10 pi-ri-e-te-si , o-p̣ị-ṃẹ-ne-]ḤỌṚḌ 1̣ T 4̣[
.11 to-ko-do-mo , o-p̣ị-me-ne[ ]ḤỌṚḌ 7̣ [T] 5

Translation

.1 [*K^{w}allans*: BARLEY? x liters], OLIVES 19.2 liters
.2 [*pa-ka*: BARLEY? x liters], OLIVES 9.6 liters
.3 wall-builders: BARLEY 1.2 liters MEN 20
.4 sawyers: BARLEY 1.2 liters MEN 5
.5 all-builder: BARLEY 3.2 liters

87 Or *A^{h}erik^{wh}ontās* (see García Ramón 2011: 222 n. 19).

To *K^{w}allans*, per month [BARLEY$^{?}$ x liters], OLIVES 576 liters
To *pa-ka*, per month [BARLEY$^{?}$ x liters, OLIVES 288 liters][88]
To the all-builder, per month, BARLEY 96 liters
To the sawyers, per month, BARLEY 134.4+ liters
To the wall-builders, per month, BARLEY 720 liters

88 Based on the number of sawyers and the amount of their daily ration, there should be 180 liters of barley, which would be written (transcribed) as HORD 1 T 8 V 4 Z 2.

BIBLIOGRAPHY

Aura Jorro, Francisco (1985), *Diccionario micénico* 1 (Madrid: Instituto de Filología).

— (1993), *Diccionario micénico* 2 (Madrid: Instituto de Filología).

Baumbach, Lydia (1983), "An Examination of the Personal Names in the Knossos Tablets as Evidence for the Social Structure of Crete in the Late Minoan II Period," in O. Krzyszkowska and L. Nixon (eds.), *Minoan Society: Proceedings of the Cambridge Colloquium 1981* (Bristol: Bristol Classical Press): 3–10.

Bennet, John (1992), "'Collectors' or 'owners'? An examination of their possible functions within the palatial economy of LM III Crete," in J.-P. Olivier (ed.), *Mykenaïka. Actes du IXe Colloque international sur les textes mycéniens et égéens* (BCH Supplement 25): 65–101.

— (1995), "Space Through Time: Diachronic Perspectives on the Spatial Organization of the Pylian State," in R. Laffineur and W.-D. Niemeier (eds.), *Politeia: Society and State in the Aegean Bronze Age* (*Aegaeum* 12): 587–602.

— (1999a), "The Mycenaean Conceptualization of Space or Pylian Geography (...Yet Again!)," in S. Deger-Jalkotzy, S. Hiller and O. Panagl (eds.), *Floreant Studia Mycenaea. Akten des X. Internationalen Mykenologischen Colloquiums in Salzburg von 1.-5. Mai 1995* (Österreichische Akademie der Wissenschaften, Philophisch-Historische Klasse. Denkschriften 274). Vienna: 131–157.

— (1999b), "Pylos: The Expansion of a Mycenaean Palatial Center," in M. L. Galaty and W. Parkinson (eds.), *Rethinking Mycenaean Palaces: New Interpretations of an Old Idea* (Los Angeles: Cotsen Institute of Archaeology): 9–18.

— (2001), "Agency and Bureaucracy: Thoughts on the Nature and Extent of Administration in Bronze Age Pylos," in S. Voutsaki and J. Killen (eds.), *Economy and Politics in the Mycenaean Palace States* (Cambridge Philological Society Supplementary Volume no. 27). Cambridge: 25–37.

Bernabé, Alberto and Eugenio R. Luján (2008), "Mycenaean Technology," in Y. Duhoux and A. Morpurgo Davies (eds.), *A Companion to Linear B: Mycenaean Greek Texts and Their World. Volume 1* (Bibliothèque des cahiers de l'Institut de Linguistique de Louvain 120). Louvain-la-Neuve: 201–233.

Boyd, Michael J. (2002), *Middle Helladic and Early Mycenaean Mortuary Practices in the Southern and Western Peloponnese* (BAR International Series S1009). Oxford.

Brumfiel, Elizabeth M. (1992), "Distinguished Lecture in Archaeology: Breaking and Entering the Ecosystem — Gender, Class and Faction Steal the Show," *American Anthropologist* 94: 551–567.

Carlier, Pierre (1992), "Les collecteurs sont-ils des fermiers?," in J.-P. Olivier (ed.), *Mykenaïka. Actes du IXe Colloque international sur les textes mycéniens et égéens* (BCH Supplement 25). Athens: 159–166.

Carothers, Joan and William A. McDonald (1979), "Size and Distribution of the Population in Late Bronze Age Messenia: Some Statistical Approaches," *Journal of Field Archaeology* 6: 433–454.

Chadwick, John (1976), *The Mycenaean World* (Cambridge: Cambridge University Press).

— (1987), "The Muster of the Pylian Fleet," in P. Ilievski and L. Crepajac (eds.), *Tractata Mycenaea. Proceedings of the Eight International Colloquium on Mycenaean Studies* (Skopje: Macedonian Academy of Sciences and Arts): 75–84.

Costin, Cathy L. (1996), "Craft Production and Mobilization Strategies in the Inka Empire," in B. Wailes (ed.), *Craft Specialization and Social Evolution: In Memory of V. Gordon Childe* (University Museum Monograph 93). Philadelphia: 211–225.

de Fidio, Pia (1989), "L'artigianato del bronze nei testi micenei di Pylos," *Klio* 71: 7–27.

— (1987), "Palais et communautés de village dans le royaume mycénien de Pylos," in P. Ilievski and L. Crepajac (eds.), *Tractata Mycenaea. Proceedings of the Eight International Colloquium on Mycenaean Studies* (Skopje: Macedonian Academy of Sciences and Arts): 129–149.

Deger-Jalkotzy, Sigrid (1978), *E-QE-TA. Zur Rolle des Gefolgschaftswesens in der Sozialstruktur mykenischer Reiche* (Vienna: Österreichische Akademie der Wissenschaften).

Driessen, Jan (2008), "Chronology of the Linear B Texts," in Y. Duhoux and A. Morpurgo Davies (eds.), *A Companion to Linear B: Mycenaean Greek Texts and Their World. Volume 1* (Bibliothèque des cahiers de l'Institut de Linguistique de Louvain 120). Louvain-la-Neuve: 69–79.

Duhoux, Yves (1976), *Aspects du vocabulaire économique mycénien: cadastre, artisanat, fiscalité* (Amsterdam: A.M. Hakkert).

— (2008), "Mycenaean Anthology," in Y. Duhoux and A. Morpurgo Davies (eds.), *A Companion to Linear B: Mycenaean Greek Texts and Their World. Volume 1* (Bibliothèque des cahiers de l'Institut de Linguistique de Louvain 120). Louvain-la-Neuve: 243–393.

Foster, Ellen D. (1981), "The Flax Impost at Pylos and Mycenaean Landholding," *Minos* 17: 67–121.

García Ramón, José Luis (2011), "Mycenaean Onomastics," in Y. Duhoux and A. Morpurgo Davies (eds.), *A Companion to Linear B: Mycenaean Greek Texts and Their World. Volume 2* (Bibliothèque des cahiers de l'Institut de Linguistique de Louvain 127). Louvain-la-Neuve: 213–251.

Godart, Louis (1992), "Les collecteurs dans le monde égéen," in J.-P. Olivier (ed.), *Mykenaïka. Actes du IXe Colloque international sur les textes mycéniens et égéens* (BCH Supplement 25): 257–283.

Gregersen, Marie Louise (1997), "Pylian Craftsmen: Payment in Kind/Rations or Land?," in R. Laffineur and P.P. Betancourt (eds.), *TEXNH: Craftsmen, Craftswomen and Craftsmanship in the Aegean Bronze Age* (*Aegaeum* 16): 397–405.

Halstead, Paul (1995), "Late Bronze Age Grain Crops and Linear B Ideograms *65, *120, and *121," *Annual of the British School at Athens* 90: 229–234.

— (2001), "Mycenaean Wheat, Flax and Sheep: Palatial Intervention in Farming and its Implications for Rural Society," in S. Voutsaki and J. Killen (eds.), *Economy and Politics in the Mycenaean Palace States* (Cambridge Philological Society Supplementary Volume no. 27). Cambridge: 38–50.

Heimpel, Wolfgang (2009), *Workers and Construction Work at Garšana* (Bethesda, Md.: Cornell University Studies in Assyriology and Sumerology 5).

Heltzer, Michael (1979), "Royal Economy in Ancient Ugarit," in E. Lipiński (ed.), *State and Temple Economy in the Ancient Near East* (Orientalia Lovaniensia Analecta 5-6). Leuven: 459–496.

Hiller, Stefan (1988), "Dependent Personnel in Mycenaean Texts," in M. Heltzer and E. Lipiński (eds.), *Society and Economy in the Eastern Mediterranean* (Orientalia Lovaniensia Analecta 23). Leuven: 53–68.

Hutton, William F. (1990-91 [1993]), "The Meaning of the Word qe-te-o in Linear B," *Minos* 25-26: 105–131.

James, Sarah A. (2002-03 [2006]), "The Thebes Tablets and the Fq Series: A Contextual Analysis," *Minos* 37-38: 397–417.

Keith, Kathryn (1999), *Cities, Neighborhoods and Houses: Urban Spatial Organization in Old Babylonian Mesopotamia* (Ph.D. dissertation, The University of Michigan).

— (2003), "The Spatial Patterns of Everyday Life in Old Babylonian Neighborhoods," in M. Smith (ed.), *The Social Construction of Ancient Cities* (Washington, DC: Smithsonian Institution Press): 56–80.

Killen, John T. (1979), "The Linear B tablets and economic history: some problems," *BICS* 26: 133–134.

— (1983), "PY An 1," *Minos* 18: 71–79.

— (1984a), "The Textile Industries at Pylos and Knossos," in C.W. Shelmerdine and T. G. Palaima (eds.), *Pylos Comes Alive: Industry and Administration in a Mycenaean Palace*, (New York: Fordham University): 49–63.

— (1984b), "Last Year's Debts on the Pylos Ma Tablets," *Studi micenei ed egeo-anatolici* 25: 173–188.

— (1992-93a [1995]), "*ke-u-po-da e-sa-re-u* and the Exemptions on the Pylos Na Tablets," *Minos* 27–28: 109–123.

— (1992-93b [1995]), "The Oxen's Names on the Knossos Ch Tablets," *Minos* 27–28: 101–107.

— (1993), "Records of Sheep and Goats at Mycenaean Knossos and Pylos," *Bulletin of Sumerian Agriculture* 7: 209–218.

— (1995), "Some Further Thoughts on 'Collectors,'" in R. Laffineur and W.-D. Niemeier (eds.), *Politeia: Society and State in the Aegean Bronze Age* (*Aegaeum* 12): 213–226.

— (1999), "Mycenaean o-pa," in S. Deger-Jalkotzy, S. Hiller and O. Panagl (eds.), *Floreant Studia Mycenaea. Akten des X. Internationalen Mykenologischen Colloquiums in Salzburg von 1.-5. Mai 1995* (Österreichische Akademie der Wissenschaften, Philophisch-Historische Klasse. Denkschriften 274). Vienna: 325–341.

— (2001a), "Some Thoughts on ta-ra-si-ja," in S. Voutsaki and J. Killen (eds.), *Economy and Politics in the Mycenaean Palace States* (Cambridge Philological Society Supplementary Volume no. 27). Cambridge: 161–180.

— (2001b), "Religion at Pylos: The Evidence of the Fn Tablets," in R. Laffineur and R. Hägg (eds.), *Potnia: Deities and Religion in the Aegean Bronze Age* (*Aegaeum* 22): 435–443.

— (2004), "Wheat, Barley, Flour, Olives and Figs on Linear B Tablets," in P. Halstead and J.C. Barrett (eds.), *Food, Cuisine and Society in Prehistoric Greece* (Sheffield Studies in Aegean Archaeology 5). Oxford: 155–173.

— (2008), "Mycenaean Economy," in Y. Duhoux and A. Morpurgo Davies (eds.), *Companion to Linear B: Mycenaean Greek Texts and Their World, Volume 1* (Bibliothèque des cahiers de l'Institut de Linguistique de Louvain 120). Louvain-la-Neuve: 159–200.

Kyriakidis, E. (2008), "Who's Who: The Shepherds in the Cn Series at Pylos," in L. Godart, A. Sacconi and M. Negri (eds.) *Atti del XII Colloquio Internazionale di Micenologia, Roma, 20-25 febbraio 2006* (Pisa-Rome: Istituti Editoriali e Poligrafici Internazionali): 449–459.

Lang, Mabel (1988), "Pylian Place-Names," in J.-P. Olivier and T.G. Palaima (eds.), *Texts, Tablets and Scribes: Studies in Mycenaean Epigraphy and Economy Offered to Emmett L. Bennett, Jr.* (Minos Supplement 10): 185–212.

Lejeune, Michel (1971), *Mémoires de philologie mycénienne: deuxième série (1958–1963)* (Incunabula Graeca 42) Rome.

Lindgren, Margareta (1973), *The People of Pylos. Prosopographical and Methodological Studies in the Pylos Archives* (Uppsala Studies in Ancient Mediterranean and Near Eastern Civilizations 3). Uppsala: *Boreas*.

Lipiński, Edward (1988), "The Socio-Economic Condition of the Clergy in the Kingdom of Ugarit," in M. Heltzer and E. Lipiński (eds.), *Society and Economy in the Eastern Mediterranean* (Orientalia Lovaniensia Analecta 23). Leuven: 125–150.

McDonald, William A., and Richard Hope Simpson (1972), "Archaeological Exploration," in W.A. McDonald and G.R. Rapp, Jr. (eds.), *The Minnesota Messenia Expedition. Reconstructing a Bronze Age Regional Environment* (Minneapolis: University of Minnesota Press): 117–146.

Melena, José Luís (1992-93 [1995]), "244 Joins and Quasi-Joins of Fragments in the Linear B Tablets from Pylos," *Minos* 27–28: 307–324.

— (1994–95a [1997]), "28 Joins and Quasi-joins of Fragments in the Linear B Tablets from Pylos," *Minos* 29–30: 95–100.

— (1994–95b [1997]), "133 Joins and Quasi-joins of Fragments in the Linear B Tablets from Pylos," *Minos* 29–30: 271–288.

— (1996–97a [1998]), "40 Joins and Quasi-Joins of Fragments in the Linear B Tablets from Pylos," *Minos* 31–32: 159–170.

— (1996–97b [1998]), "13 Joins and Quasi-joins of Fragments in the Linear B Tablets from Pylos," *Minos* 31–32: 171–178.

— (2000–01a [2002]), "24 Joins and Quasi-Joins of Fragments in the Linear B Tablets from Pylos," *Minos* 35–36: 357–369.

— (2000–01b [2002]), "63 Joins and Quasi-joins of Fragments in the Linear B Tablets from Pylos," *Minos* 35–36: 371–384.

Mühlestein, Hugo (1956), *Die* oka-*Tafeln von Pylos. Ein mykenischer Schiffskatalog?* (Basel: Self-published).

Nakassis, Dimitri (2006), *The Individual and the Mycenaean State: Agency and Prosopography in the Linear B Texts from Pylos* (Ph.D. dissertation, The University of Texas at Austin).

— (2008), "Named Individuals and the Mycenaean State at Pylos," in L. Godart, A. Sacconi and M. Negri (eds.) *Atti del XII Colloquio Internazionale di Micenologia, Roma, 20–25 febbraio 2006* (Pisa-Rome: Istituti Editoriali e Poligrafici Internazionali): 549–561.

— (2012), "Labor Mobilization in Mycenaean Pylos," in P. Carlier, C. De Lamberterie, M. Egetmeyer, N. Guilleux, F. Rougemont and J. Zurbach (eds.) *Études mycéniennes 2010. Actes du XIIIe colloque international sur les textes égéens.* (Biblioteca di Pasiphae 10). Pisa-Rome: Fabrizio Serra: 269–283.

— (2013), *Individuals and Society in Mycenaean Pylos.* (Mnemosyne Supplements, History and Archaeology of Classical Antiquity 358). Leiden/ Boston: Brill.

Nightingale, G. (2008), "A-ko-so-ta and the Economy of Pylos," in L. Godart, A. Sacconi and M. Negri (eds.) *Atti del XII Colloquio Internazionale di Micenologia, Roma, 20–25 febbraio 2006* (Pisa-Rome: Istituti Editoriali e Poligrafici Internazionali): 569–586.

Nosch, Marie-Louise (2006), "More Thoughts on the Mycenaean *ta-ra-si-ja* System," in M. Perna (ed.), *Fiscality in Mycenaean and Near Eastern Archives. Proceedings of the Conference held at Soprintendenza Archivistica per la Campania, Nampes, 21–23 October 2004* (Paris: de Boccard): 161–182.

Palaima, Thomas G. (1983), "Evidence for the Influence of the Knossian Graphic Tradition at Pylos," in O. Pavel and A. Frolíková (eds.) *Concilium Eirene XVI, Proceedings of the 16th International Eirene Congress* (Prague: Kabinet pro studia řecká, římská a latinskáČSAV): 80–84, plates I–II.

— (1988), *The Scribes of Pylos* (Incunabula Graeca 87) Rome.

— (1995), "The Last Days of the Pylos Polity," in R. Laffineur and W.-D. Niemeier (eds.), *Politeia: Society and State in the Aegean Bronze Age* (*Aegaeum* 12): 623–633.

— (2000), "The Transactional Vocabulary of Mycenaean Sealings and the Mycenaean Administrative Process," in M. Perna (ed.), *Administrative Documents in the Aegean and their Near Eastern Counterparts* (Torino: Paravia scriptorium): 261–276.

— (2001), "The Modalities of Economic Control at Pylos," *Ktèma* 26: 151–159.

— (2004), "Sacrificial Feasting in the Linear B Documents," in J. C. Wright (ed.), *The Mycenaean Feast* (=*Hesperia* 73.2): 97–126.

Palmer, Leonard R. (1963), *The Interpretation of Mycenaean Greek Texts* (Oxford: Oxford University Press).

Palmer, Ruth (1989), "Subsistence Rations at Pylos and Knossos," *Minos* 24: 89–124.

— (1992), "Wheat and Barley in Mycenaean Society," in J.-P. Olivier (ed.), *Mykenaïka. Actes du IXe Colloque international sur les textes mycéniens et égéens* (BCH Supplement 25). Athens: 475–497.

— (1994), *Wine in the Mycenaean Palace Economy* (*Aegaeum* 10). Leuven: Peeters.

Piteros, Christos, Jean-Pierre Olivier and José Luís Melena (1990), "Les inscriptions en linéaire B des nodules de Thèbes (1982): La fouille, les documents, les possibilities d'interprétation," *Bulletin de correspondance hellénique* 104: 103–184.

Pluta, Kevin (1996-97 [1998]), "A Reconstruction of the Archives Complex at Pylos: A Preliminary Report," *Minos* 31–32: 231–250.

— (2006), "Mycenaean Literate Administration," unpublished paper, XII Colloquio Internazionale di Micenologia, Rome.

Postgate, J. Nicholas (1992), *Early Mesopotamia: Society and Economy at the Dawn of History* (London: Routledge).

— (2001), "System and Style in Three Near Eastern Bureaucracies," in S. Voutsaki and J. Killen (eds.), *Economy and Politics in the Mycenaean Palace States* (Cambridge Philological Society Supplementary Volume no. 27). Cambridge: 181–194.

Renger, Johannes (2000), "Das Palastgeschäft in der altbabylonischen Zeit," in A.C.V.M. Bongenaar (ed.), *Interdependency of Institutions and Private Entrepreneurs* (Istanbul: Nederlands Historisch-Archaeologisch Instituut te Istanbul): 153–183.

— (2001), "When Tablets Talk Business: Reflections on Mesopotamian Economic History and Its Contribution to a General History of Mesopotamia," in T. Abusch, P.-A. Beaulieu, J. Huehnergard, P. Machinist and P. Steinkeller (eds.), *Proceedings of the XLVe Rencontre Assyriologique Internationale. Part I, Harvard University. Historiography in the Cuneiform World* (Bethesda, MD: CDL Press): 409–415.

Rougemont, Françoise (2001), "Some Thoughts on the Identification of the 'Collectors' in the Linear B Tablets," in S. Voutsaki and J. Killen (eds.), *Economy and Politics in the Mycenaean Palace States* (Cambridge Philological Society Supplementary Volume no. 27). Cambridge: 129–138.

— (2009), *Contrôle économique et administration à l'époque des palais mycéniens (fin du IIe millénaire av. J.-C.)* (Athens: Ecole française d'Athènes).

Shelmerdine, Cynthia W. (1985), *The Perfume Industry of Mycenaean Pylos* (Göteborg: Paul Åströms Förlag).

— (1998), "Review of Aegean Prehistory VI: The Palatial Bronze Age of the Southern and Central Greek Mainland," *American Journal of Archaeology* 101: 537–585.

— (2001), "The Evolution of Administration at Pylos," in S. Voutsaki and J. Killen (eds.), *Economy and Politics in the Mycenaean Palace States* (Cambridge Philological Society Supplementary Volume no. 27). Cambridge: 113–128.

Sherratt, Susan (2000), "Circulation of Metals and the End of the Bronze Age in the Eastern Mediterranean," in C. F. E. Pare (ed.), *Metals Make the World Go Round: The Supply and Circulation of Metals in Bronze Age Europe* (Oxford: Oxbow Books): 82–98.

Skelton, Christina (2008), "Methods of Using Phylogenetic Systematics to Reconstruct the History of the Linear B Script," *Archaeometry* 50: 158–176.

— (2010), "Re-Examining the Pylos Megaron Tablets," *Kadmos* 48: 107–123.

Smith, Joanna S. (1992-93 [1995]), "The Pylos Jn Series," *Minos* 27–28: 167–259.

Stol, Marten (2004), "Wirtschaft und Gesellschaft in altbabylonischer Zeit," in D. Charpin, D.O. Edzard and M. Stol (eds.), *Mesopotamien: Die altbabylonische Zeit* (Göttingen: Vandenhoeck & Ruprecht): 643–975.

Sutton, Dana F. (1970), *An Analytic Prosopography and Statistical Guide to the Land Tenure Tablets from Pylos* (Ph.D. dissertation: University of Wisconsin).

Van de Mieroop, Marc (1992), *Society and Enterprise in Old Babylonian Ur* (Berlin: D. Reimer).

Ventris, Michael and John Chadwick (1973), *Documents in Mycenaean Greek*, second edition (Cambridge: Cambridge University Press).

Whitelaw, Todd (2001), "Reading between the Tablets: Assessing Mycenaean Palatial Involvement in Ceramic Production and Consumption," in S. Voutsaki and J. Killen (eds.), *Economy and Politics in the Mycenaean Palace States* (Cambridge Philological Society Supplementary Volume no. 27). Cambridge: 51–79.

Wright, James C. (1980), "Mycenaean Palatial Terraces," *Archäologische Mitteilungen* 95: 59–86.

10.

The Mycenaean Mobilization of Labor in Agriculture and Building Projects: Institutions, Individuals, Compensation and Status in the Linear B Tablets

Tom Palaima
University of Texas, Austin

In the many regions of mainland Greece and the island of Crete that are best suited to sustaining sizable human populations, during what is known as the full Mycenaean palatial period (approximately 1400–1200 BC with a ramping up 1600–1400 BC), complex systems of social, economic and political organization developed and functioned efficiently by successfully adjusting to local conditions and producing special forms of local products that became desirable in the international trade networks of the period. Chief among these were varieties of perfumed olive oil (archaeologically visible through the widespread finds of distinctive clay transport vessels of varying sizes known as stirrup jars *and* attested in clay tablet records that monitored transactions and other features of the production and distribution of the perfumed oil and associated pottery) and high-quality fabrics and garments made of locally produced high-grade linen and wool and making use of "royal" purple murex dye among other coloring agents (all archaeologically invisible, except in images of fabrics, garments and other items of cloth in contemporary fresco representations *and* attested in the texts of clay tablets and a variety of related clay writing forms that record aspects of the overall production, *e.g.*, [a] the providing of raw materials; [b] the doling out of what Mycenologists call rations, but following Steinkeller and Jursa in this volume we will more properly call food allotments, to specialist workers; and [c] the reckoning of the numbers and sometimes the provenience of such workers, their work specializations and their physical locations in workshops administered by the bureaucratic apparatuses of the palatial complexes; [d] the destinations for shipments of finished products, and so on).

These regional industries and others like them (there are at least eleven work-specialists identified, usually collectively, by compound noun formations using as a second element *-wo-ko* = -ϝοργος 'worker', *e.g.*, *ku-wa-no-wo-ko* = "a specialist working with κύανος = a lapis-lazuli-colored material") required careful organization of material and human resources and making sure that specialist workers involved in all facets of the operation of such industries were in place and as efficiently and continuously at work as possible. This organization is reflected in the clay tablet records in what is known as the Linear B script that have been recovered almost exclusively from palatial centers.[1]

Piotr Steinkeller's starting points or thematic guidelines regarding labor and its mobilization from an early Mesopotamian perspective raise questions that are interesting to consider in the Mycenaean palatial period. To borrow a term from the classical period, the *politeia* (or the general ethos and organized system of life that prevailed in the territories under the control of palatial centers) of each region was sustained by intensive and careful economic exploitation reinforced by equally carefully promoted ideological systems.[2] How labor was organized, directed, sustained and controlled and how the labor of individuals or collective groups was apportioned among or exacted from varying interest groups

[1] For the most up-to-date and concise overviews of the Linear B tablet evidence, its nature, the methods and resources for studying the texts, the chronology and nature of the individual archives and deposits of tablets, and the general historical picture into which the tablets fit and for which they provide their peculiar evidence, see Palmer 2008, Driessen 2008, de Fidio 2008 and Shelmerdine 1998. For a concise discussion of Mycenaean "industries" within a larger context of economic organization, see Shelmerdine and Bennet 2008, especially 303–306. It should be assumed throughout, unless otherwise specified, that interpretations, etymologies and semantic specifications of Mycenaean and historical Greek words rely on entries in Aura Jorro 1985 and 1993 (with indices now on-line at http://www.cervantesvirtual.com/bib/portal/diccionariomicenico/pcuartonivelf9e1.html?conten=presentacion); Beekes 2010 (now on-line at http://iedo.brillonline.nl/dictionaries/content/greek/index.html); and Chantraine 2009.

[2] For the importance of the ideology of "abundance," "satisfying," "benefiting" and "securing" promoted by the palatial centers in nomenclature, feasting rituals and even personal naming practices, see Palaima 2012a, 2008 (especially p. 385), 2007 and 2004a.

(in the interests of the individual themselves and the families, clans, towns and larger or more powerful interest groups to which they belonged, with which they identified, and by which they could be influenced or compelled) are important questions that I shall now try to answer at least partially in the paper that follows.

I will focus on three main points: (1) the different types of obligation, requirement, reward and benefit attached to the labor and production of individuals and groups; (2) the stake that the palatial centers had in work activities, especially larger scale *corvée*-type projects, recorded on the tablets; and (3) how the methods used by the palatial centers to see that their interests were met developed through time. I am trying as much as possible to avoid a handbook-style overview. I deal with particulars in the texts that I believe offer insights into both the complexities of the socioeconomic palatial systems and the problems Mycenologists face when trying to interpret how the inhabitants of Mycenaean palatial territories went about their work and how the elites at various levels in the socio-political and economic hierarchies went about seeing that work in their own interests was undertaken and completed.

I stress again from the start the peculiar nature of the Linear B documentation.[3] The clay tablets are bare-boned economic records focused on palatial concerns and written by still "anonymous" individuals trained in the skill and practice of writing and somehow involved with keeping track of how resources are being used, and where, when, why, and by and for whom.[4] The records and the information-gathering, -retrieving, -preserving, -checking and -dispensing activities that they reflect are focused almost exclusively on the "needs" of the palatial centers and the elites who were located at palatial centers or regional centers linked to them.[5] The records are written by individuals trained in the Linear B script and in the mechanics of recordkeeping on clay tablets and other forms of clay documents (in the Mycenaean period mainly labels and counter-inscribed sealings). These tablet-writers would themselves have

[3] See Palaima 2004b and 2003 and Duhoux 2011.

[4] On the nature of Aegean literacy and on Mycenaean writing and the role of writing and those who used writing in the Mycenaean palatial period, see Pluta 2011 and Palaima 2011a: 95–124.

[5] These needs include the need to fulfill obligations, specific and general, to regional elites and the general populations of the territories in which the palatial centers were situated and the need to live up to the ideological identities that the palatial centers and their elites created and promoted. See Palaima 2012a.

been the primary users of the clay records *per se* and for purposes that seem to be in some way "mnemonic."

Killen describes the Linear B clay records, from an economic perspective, as "merely *temporary* records: aides-mémoire, often of an extremely laconic character, which relate, with a few possible exceptions, only to the single, last year before the destruction of the particular palace [*i.e.*, palatial center] that contained the [particular] archive."[6] Thus the texts generally contain the categories of data the tablet-writers anticipated needing within a given administrative year. The broad and narrow contexts for these data were known to the Linear B tablet-writers. They themselves were likely the very readers consulting the tablets later. Consequently they often forego writing down information that they know, and that we do not know, but would like to know. Therefore, we have to ferret out answers to questions about features of Mycenaean economic practices that are readily available in Near Eastern economic records. But the exercise is salutary for Mycenologists, and we hope for Near and Middle Eastern scholarly specialists looking on, like spectators at a Greek tragedy, with a mixture of pity and fear.

The paper by Dimitri Nakassis in this volume looks at the records from the perspective of prosopography and agency theory, with a focus on the best documented, archaeologically and textually, palatial territory, the region of Messenia in southwestern Greece, and the persons recorded individually or collectively, with titles and work specialties or responsibilities designated or not, in the surviving Linear B clay-tablet records from the main controlling center in late Bronze Age Messenia, the so-called Palace of Nestor at Pylos.[7] His work represents a significant break-

[6] For a standard synthetic view of the Mycenaean economy and the contents of the Linear B tablets, see Killen 2008. The description of the nature of the tablet evidence comes from p. 162. Our emphasis (*e.g.*, Palaima 2007 and 2012a) on how the palatial centers necessarily used ideology to maintain fine balances within what we might call the political power structures in the territories over which they presided and the emphasis of Nakassis 2006 and 2013 (and this volume) on agency theory both make the "control" of the Mycenaean palatial center seem much less all-encompassing and forcefully and restrictively imposed.

[7] On the geography of the regions connected with the three palatial centers (Knossos in north central Crete, Pylos in Messenia in the southwestern Greek mainland and Thebes in Boeotia in central Greece north of Athens) that have yielded major collections of tablets, see Bennet 2011: especially 148–157; and Palaima 2011b. For a two-stage scholarly assessment, in 1999 and 2007, of the Palace of Nestor as an engineer of the palatial economy of Messenia, see Galaty and Parkinson (2007).

through in helping us see that the Mycenaean palatial centers and the elites who held power at them made use of preexisting and still functioning systems of organization and existing relationships among individuals at various levels in the socio-political and economic power hierarchies in the territory of Messenia and in well-defined provinces, districts and settlements within it.[8]

Some of the structures and methods of mobilizing and controlling labor that we can detect in the Linear B records must have pre-existed the imposition or insertion of the palatial system and then been adapted to new conditions and ways of operating. Others continued to operate at local and regional levels fairly independently of the palatial centers even in the period we are discussing. The palatial centers made use of these in partial, sometimes seemingly *ad hoc*, ways using *do ut des* and *quid pro quo* strategies with entities and individuals in towns, clan groups and natural geographical areas. We would also stress that economic, political, military and social security were main concerns for all inhabitants of a palatial territory, no matter on what terms they performed their labor.[9] We are looking here at major questions and problems regarding the mobilization of labor and issues surrounding remuneration, compensation and other methods of mobilizing workers and gathering resources and materials so that the work the palatial centers viewed as within their sphere of interest got done.

Mobilization of Labor in Agriculture

Given the intensive focus of Linear B clay records, at every site where they are found, upon the here and now of single administrative periods (mostly annual, with rare references to next year and last year), we do not have a historical perspective that would document how systems and practices came into being and evolved over time. Where there are different approaches to labor mobilization within our surviving records and where the terminology reflects, etymologically or otherwise, concerns that we might consider on the one hand primary or original and on the other hand secondary or later, we can make conjectures and suggestions about how the procedures seen in our texts, dating mainly from the mid to late 13th century BCE, evolved from earlier stages.

In the records of land use—and again we emphasize that these occasion-specific records are kept for the purposes of the palatial centers and reflect their perspectives, we see what looks like a system of landholding,

[8] Nakassis 2013.

[9] Palaima 2012a and 2007.

rather than landowning. The system attested in the Linear B records likely developed as social, economic and political networks evolved from single smaller localities into districts with settlements of different populations, different natural resources and different geographical strategic advantages or disadvantages. These districts, in turn, would then have been configured into natural and mutually beneficial combinations of districts, followed by the formation of regions and provinces, within what we see finally as holistic palatial territories.[10] In the end, what Killen has to say is suitably cautious and represents, we believe, something like the *opinio communis*:[11] "[I]t is still not possible to say for certain who ultimately owned the land in Mycenaean kingdoms; but there is a good deal of evidence to suggest that, just as palaces and temples in the Near East were often significant owners of land, so the central institutions in the Mycenaean world had an effective control over—even if they did not technically own—substantial tracts of the arable [land]."

Just as there exists at the end of the full palatial period a hierarchy of interdependent individuals of varying power, authority and influence—and corresponding duties and obligations, there are also indications of how collective groups operated at varying levels from the local settlements and towns to regional centers and upward to provincial capitals.

Top down, the personal power hierarchy[12] descends from the *wanax* ("king") and *lāwāgetās* ("leader or collector of the *lāwos* = adult males capable of and responsible for bearing arms") through palatially appoint-

[10] See Hope Simpson 2014: 45–70, for a full picture of the political and economic geography of Messenia during the late Mycenaean palatial period, with attention paid to the texts and the archaeological remains. See Nakassis 2013: 181–183, for a capsule summary of the gradual formation of the whole of Messenia into a coherent, unified palatial territory between 1700/1675–1420/1410 BCE and 1330/15–1200/1190 BCE.

[11] Killen 2008: 162. On the almost sacred aspect of "earth" (γῆ) as the concept nearest to what we call "nature" and on belief in its "eternal" quality as the conceptual underpinning for human beings "occupying," "partitioning," "improving upon" and "making use of" portions of land in the daily lives of human societies, see Palaima 2014: 93–96. It is this concept that ultimately gives rise to the notion that land is not "owned" by individual persons or human social groups, but simply occupied and temporarily possessed.

[12] For somewhat differing, but still mainstream, comprehensive overviews of palatial officials, other officials, the *dāmos* and collective bodies of control, influence and mobilization, see Shelmerdine 2008: 127–135 and Nakassis 2013: 6–19. These views differ from mine presented here mainly in determining from whom various officials derive their powers and authority and whose interests they are primarily obligated to serve.

ed officials known as the *dāmokoroi* (literally "satisfiers of the *dāmos*")[13] and the *korestēres* and *prokorestēres* (literally "agents and vice-agents of satisfaction," *i.e.*, again, palatially appointed head administrators and vice-administrators[14] of major districts within provinces), to longstanding heads of village settlements known as *g^w^asilēwes* (in historical times "kings", but in the late Mycenaean palatial period local "big men" or village chieftains who interact with palatial officials and interests, but derive

[13] The *dāmos*, often translated as the "people" as a whole or even as a local community or village, is in fact in the Mycenaean palatial period in all cases, so far as I can tell, the body or group of collective (at any level of community organization) land-holders who manage land allotments and use. We have evidence that the persons who make up the *dāmos* are known as *telestai*. It is easy to understand how this group eventually over time came to stand for both the territory made up of the land they controlled and dispensed and also the people who lived on that land, physically and in terms of dependence upon it for their own survival.

The *dāmokoroi* are effectively palatially appointed or palatially sanctioned and ratified "governors" of major provinces. They would have functioned much like satraps, singular *xšaθrapāvan*, literally "protectors of the province," the Median/Persian king's eyes and ears, in the satrapies into which the Median and then Persian empire was organized from the mid–7th century BC onward. In Pylos tablet Ta 711, we have recorded as the time phrase marking the ceremonial occasion for compiling a written inventory of ritual vessels, implements and furniture: "when the *wanax* appointed *au-ke-wa* as *dāmokoros*." The nature of the items inventoried mark the occasion as an important ritual event (Palaima 2004: 234). This indicates that the palatial ruler made the appointment of the "governor" (at least as an overseer of palatial interests) of each province. Ideologically, however, the emphasis is on what this personage can do to bring satisfaction to the inhabitants of the region he oversees.

[14] The standard translation of these terms as "mayor" and "vice-mayor" gives a false sense of the source or basis of their power—the *korestēres* and *prokorestēres* are palatially appointed, not locally selected or elected—and of the range of their power. The term "mayor" implies a very defined geographical area of concern and a perspective limited to the population, resources and concerns of that relatively small area. A "mayor" is quite literally the "bigger" man in the local scheme of things, the top who looks down upon a small geographical area. As a term, "mayor" does not make significant the groups and interests that lie above figures so designated in the power hierarchy of the whole palatial territory. The officials known as *korestēres* and *prokorestēres*, however, seem to look to affairs in what we call districts or in modern terms "counties" and look "top-down" from, and in the interests of, the real top, *i.e.*, the palatial center.

their status and authority locally).[15] There are also individuals designated as *e-qe-ta* = *hekʷetai*, traditionally in Mycenaean studies translated as "followers." In my view the *hekʷetai* are "agents of making others follow or attend," *i.e.*, very close in meaning to "mobilizers" of personnel, often for military service.[16]

Within this structure we find that land is parceled out basically for "holding" as a "benefit." The exact term used for such a landholding parcel is an *onāton*.[17] We may compare the equivalent Carolingian land-parcel allotment, a *beneficium*. The Mycenaean term *onāton* shares with the Latin term an underlying sense of *usufruct*, namely that by holding and using the land, the holder gains a "fruit" of his or her labor (*usufruct*), "is done well or does well," *i.e.*, he benefits, by so doing (*beneficium*), and

15 Palaima 2006a. Given the etymological and ideological links among *dāmokoros*, *korestēr* and *prokorestēr*, and the fact that all three terms disappear with the demise of the palatial centers, I am persuaded that all three terms and offices are linked to the administrative apparatus of the palatial centers and that holders of these offices managed economic, political and other matters in the interests of the palatial centers, interfacing with figures like the *gʷasilēwes* and perhaps the regional elites known in modern parlance as "collectors," who derive their power and authority from political, economic and social groups and longstanding social ranking at the town or district levels.

16 Ruijgh 2011: 285, points out that the active form **sekʷō* of the verb that in the middle means "to follow" has causative use ("make X to follow") in the stage of Greek represented by the Linear B tablets. See in Duhoux 2008: 386–387, the fuller discussion of the form *a-pi-e-qe* (Thebes tablet Fq 254) = *amphi-he-skʷ-e*, as a reduplicated aorist (without augment) in causative sense = "he made people to follow/be around him" (although the word is subject to alternative reconstructions and semantic interpretations, *e.g.*, Melena 2014: 39, 118, interpreting it from *sekʷ-/skʷ-* "to say"). See also Nakassis 2012: 272–273. Nakassis 2013: 7 and 89, stresses the military sphere in which the 13 men designated as *hekʷetai* at Pylos mostly operate as a clue to their primary function. He views their involvement in the religious sphere as perhaps a "by product of their high standing among palatial officials." He rightly emphasizes that since contingents of mobilized men in the *o-ka* tablets have each only one *hekʷetās*, these figures may "act as a liaison between the palace and the troops." I argue further that the causative force of the verb suggests that the liaison service provided by these figures was as actual mobilizers of the forces under their control.

17 In the historical period, the term that is used for a parcel of land within a community (*klāros*) has a proposed etymology as a piece of stone or wood that is drawn in an allotment procedure (Beekes 2010: 715; Chantraine 2009: 522). To be ἄκληρος signifies being landless, poor, detached from the community defined by ownership of land within it. The term disassociates the conferring of land from any kind of power transaction or relationship.

finds so doing "useful and helpful and advantageous"—this is the root meaning of *onāton* as seen in the historical Greek verb ὀνίνημι.

The records frequently stipulate that land is "held" (Myc. Gk. *e-ke* = ἔχει) by specified parties under the oversight or through the authorization of the *dāmos*, which, as we noted above (n. 13), in origin means, and in the late Mycenaean period still functions as, the "collective group of individuals who see to the parceling out of landholdings under different terms and conditions."[18] Since the pertinent sets of tablets relate to land, or to contributions expected from parcels of land held by individuals or collective groups, in specific locales, a reasonable assumption is made that each *dāmos* reference is particular to the area in question on the text in which it occurs. Other terms and conditions for landholding are still not fully understood and are mainly interpreted by how they stand in contrast to the basic land parcel, *i.e.*, the *onāton* that someone "occupies and uses" or "holds" (*e-ke* = ἔχει).

What we can put together from the texts we have is as follows.[19] Allotments of larger or smaller plots of land are made to individuals for their use according to the status they acquire through their work within the palatial systems and related components of social organization. That is to say, the allotments are made in return for work or service performed or provided. Holding the allotments then was contingent upon such work or service continuing to be performed or provided. Access to plots of land for raising crops and maintaining livestock would have been a great benefit to individuals, their families and clan groups and consequently a great carrot to encourage a high level of performance of work and fulfillment of service obligations and a great stick to see that satisfactory work continued to be done and obligations continued to be met. It was a reward for work that far exceeded either the food allotments apportioned to groups of captive women working within the Pylian cloth industry (Aa, Ab and Ad series at Pylos)[20] or the quantities given out as daily food allotments in return for work to about 67 names or occupational titles (and even animals where the allocation stands for the person-

18 The word is analyzable as **deh$_2$-mo-s* and is connected with the notions of "dividing," "parceling," "partitioning."

19 See now Nakassis 2013: 124–135 for a succinct analysis of individual landholders in the Pylos corpus.

20 Chadwick 1988; Palaima 2011b: 64–65; for specific calculations of quantities see Palaima 2006b: 145. These dependent worker women each get about 0.64 liters of grain (on whether this is wheat or barley, see below n. 27) and a like amount of figs daily.

nel associated with their care, maintenance or use) as more than basic food maintenance in the Thebes Fq series, *e.g.* Fq 254[+]255.[21] For the individual plot-holders, the system seems to have had built into it ways to encourage a high level of productivity and to discourage complacency and potential fall-offs in productivity over time. For the elites in the palatial centers, the system had the potential to bring more resources within palatial territories into use through time.[22]

The basic parcel of land assignable was called a *ko-to-na* = *ktoinā*, a term that seems to signify in the late palatial period simply a parcel of land or ground-plot.[23] Del Freo has put forward the most sensible and ingenious explanation of the chief ways of distinguishing such plots of land within the Linear B records: [24]

> From the point of view of the Mycenaean palatial administrative systems, the land parcels were classified according to demographic kinds of criteria. One was making then a distinction between parcels that were "inhabited" and those that were "uninhabited". In the first group ("inhabited" land) were those parcels that are called *ki-ti-me-na* and *pu-te-ri-ja*; in the second group, those that are called *ke-ke-me-na*. All of these parcels of land were probably distributed by the palatial centers according to the principle of *conditional tenure*, even if it is possible that the obligations varied as a function of the conditions of fundamental land occupancy. In particular, it seems probable that the parcels termed *pu-te-ri-ja* had been subjected to a system of allotments at two levels, in this sense that the parcels which had already been allocated to the "planters" in order to make sure of their exploitation could eventually also be ceded in turn to other individuals.

The simplest way to view the rather complex terminology applied to land plots and landholders is through imaginative use of etymology. With regard to landholdings, the term *ke-ke-me-na* is contrasted with the term

[21] Palaima 2006b: 144–146. On the Fq series, allotments of 0.8 liters of grain (barley? or wheat?; see below n. 27) are common and some quantities reach 3.2, 4.8, 5.6 liters.

[22] See Palaima 2014: 98–99, for fuller discussion on how deserted (even perhaps once occupied, but now no longer agriculturally active) land (Mycenaean *e-re-mo* = *erēmos* or *erēmon*, cf. modern English "hermit") and wild (*i.e.*, never before put into any kind of agricultural use) land (Mycenaean *a-ko-ro* = *agros* or plural *agroi*) were brought into productive use.

[23] Del Freo 2001: 31; Duhoux 2008: 299, with historical (Rhodian) parallel.

[24] Del Freo 2001: 42. Translation mine.

ki-ti-me-na. These are basically descriptive terms. *ke-ke-me-na*, from the root *$*g^heh_1$-* "to be empty, void", is uncultivated, undeveloped land. *ki-ti-me-na* refers to a plot of land that is "built upon" or "cultivated," *i.e.*, taken out of a "wild" or "natural" state through what we might call farming (sowed grain crops) or planting (fruit and vine crops) activities. The Indo-European form **tḱei-*, to which *ki-ti-me*-na is related, seems to continue an older present form of the root **teḱ-* "to procreate".[25] Conceptually then the Mycenaeans viewed agriculture, arboriculture and viticulture literally as processes that cause the land to be productive, hence the extended related meanings of "cultivate" or "found" or "build upon" or "inhabit." An individual who does this can be termed a *ki-ti-ta* = *κτίτης* or *κτίστης*. A second way to bring land "to fruition" or "an inhabited state" is by assigning it for a time to a *pu-te* = *φυτήρ* or "planter" of vine and tree crops. This kind of land is known specifically and literally as *pu-te-ri-ja* "plantation" land. There are instances where a *pu-te* is allotted *ke-ke-me-na*, i.e., "uninhabited" or "empty" land, which is then understood as land that he is bringing into cultivation. *ke-ke-me-na* land is listed in the Pylos E-series as *pa-ro da-mo*, *i.e.*, somehow in control of the local *dāmos* organization.[26]

Also operating, it seems at the level of the *dāmos*, are individuals known as *te-re-ta* = *telestai* = "men of service," derived from the word *telos* meaning, *inter alia*, a "service commitment." 14 *telestai* are recorded in the Pylos En/Eo landholding texts and 45 *telestai* are recorded at the western Cretan site of *a-pa-ta-wa* on Knossos tablet Am 826.1. We also have recorded a case (Pylos Eb 149.1) where the *te-re-ta* is specifically noted to have to live up to his title, namely he is obliged to perform a service "*telos*" (the infinitival form of the denominative verb is *te-re-ja-e*). But we also learn there that he is not doing so.

Other landholders known as *ka-ma-e-we* (literally those having to do with plots of land known as *ka-ma*) are listed as holding collectively plots of land of the *ke-ke-me-na* type on an *o-na-to* basis and "working" (*wo-zo-te*) these plots (Pylos tablet Ed 236.2). There is an oft cited correspondence in Pylos tablets Un 718 and Er 312. The *dāmos* group is responsible for foodstuff contributions to a feast in quantities recorded on tablet Un 718. These amounts of foodstuffs seem to be based on the amount of land that the *dāmos* in the district of *sa-ra-pe-da* controls,

[25] Beekes 2010:791.
[26] Nakassis 2006:75–76.

namely 30 GRA[27] units as recorded on tablet Er 312 as the seed grain quantity of land (see below). On Er 312, three *telestai* stand in for the *dāmos*. We do not know if these three stand in for a larger number of *telestai* in this *dāmos* or are themselves the full group.

For a sense of scale, we should note that land is measured in terms of seed grain. We now fortunately, because of the indefatigable ingenuity of José Melena, can calculate rough equivalents in actual land measure.[28] The three *telestai* on tablet Er 312 hold 30 GRA units worth of land. This equals ca. 45 acres of wheat land or 22.5 acres of barley land. 14 *telestai* at the site of *pa-ki-ja-ne* hold 44 GRA units. This would equal about 66 acres of land sown with wheat or 33 acres of land sown with barley. The unspecified number of *ka-ma-e-we* on Pylos Ed 236.2 are responsible for working 30.25 GRA units, *i.e.*, 45.375 acres of wheat land or 22.6875 of barley land.

A sense of scale of how important land is as an incentive and reward for labor and service is indicated by the case of an individual named *e-*65-to.*[29] *e-*65-to* is a "servant" (*do-e-ro*)[30] of the deity. He "holds" an *onāton* plot of *ki-ti-me-na* land and is classed explicitly thereby as an

[27] There are two main types of grain listed in the Linear B texts, barley and wheat. There is now still some controversy as to whether the original identifications of sign **120* GRA(num) as wheat and sign **121* HORD(eum) as barley are correct. See Palmer 1989, 1992, 1999. Melena 2014: 137, follows the traditional designations. Arguments are based on caloric values and on what classes of individuals receive barley (a coarser grain) and wheat (a finer grain). There is no entirely clear solution, since GRA, as we have seen, is allocated to women, some of them likely spear-captives or at least foreign slaves, working in the Pylos cloth industry (Ab series). But it is also offered to the god Poseidon (Es series) and contributed as a main grain to important communal and palatially sponsored feasts. HORD meanwhile is also given to a variety of deities and religious officials and sanctuaries (*e.g.*, Fn 187), to individuals identified by personal name or occupational titles (Thebes Fq series), and to laborers listed collectively on tablets dealing with *corvée* type projects (Fn 7). We shall here skirt the issue mainly by speaking of grain generically when discussing texts that use the ideograms GRA and HORD.

[28] Melena 2014: 159–160. 1 hectare is 100 ares or 10,000 square meters or 2.471 acres in US and British imperial land measurement. Melena has calculated on the basis of seeding quotients of 1:6 that 1 GRA unit (= 96 liters) of seed grain would produce 576 liters of wheat. Using modern equivalencies for Messenia of 10 hectoliters per hectare for wheat and 18 hectoliters per hectare for barley, Melena proposes that 1 GRA unit of seed grain would sow ca. 60 ares (ca. 1.5 acres) of land in wheat and 33 ares (ca. 0.83 acres) of land in barley.

o-na-te (*ὀνατήρ), *i.e.*, a possessor of an *o-na-to* (literally an agent of benefit or, in this case, an active recipient of the reward of landholding, in Spanish a "beneficiario"). He is one of seven individuals who is recorded as holding an *o-na-to* plot from one of the 14 *telestai* in the district of *pa-ki-ja-na*, who is named *ru-*83*. The size of *e-*65-to*'s land allotment here is measured as 1⁄60 of a GRA unit, *i.e.*, 0.025 acres equaling 1,089 square feet of wheat land, or 0.0125 acres equaling 545 square feet of barley land. On tablet En 609, the same individual holds 1⁄5 of a GRA unit as an *onāton* parcel (0.3 acres of wheat land or 0.15 acres of barley land). By contrast *pe-ki-ta*, the royal fuller, holds a like *onāton* plot of *ki-ti-me-na* land in the quantity of 1⁄10 of a GRA unit (0.15 acres of wheat land or 0.075 acres of barley land). According to these levels of land usage rewards, *e-*65-to*, the "servant" of the deity, holds one plot of land that at most is about 30 feet by 36 feet in area, a kind of garden plot. His other plot is at most ca. 13,000 square feet or 130 feet by 100 feet. The royal fuller holds a plot that is roughly 65 by 67 feet.

It is clear that rewards in terms of assignments of landholding plots in return for work and service performance were to this extent micro-managed, but also no doubt appreciated by the recipients.

Large-Scale Work Projects: Tools and Raw Materials

Unfortunately, the Linear B documents do not give us information about distributing tools and equipment to laborers involved in building projects, agricultural work or specialized crafts and industries. This is best seen by surveying the full ideographical repertory found in the corpus of Linear B inscriptions as we now know it.[31]

Only two items in this large repertory, roughly ninety of which are manufactured items (including vases, furniture, garments, work materials like ingots, hides and cloth bundles, and implements, all with some form of practical non-military use) are the kinds of work tools we would associate with *corvée* labor projects (road work, bridges, dams, major irrigation projects) and connected with the extraction and hauling of quarried stone and felled wood to building sites and handling stone and

29 Nakassis 2013: 265

30 *do-e-ro* (later Greek *doulos* "slave") seems here to be an honorific term, much as Roman Catholic altar boys were known as "servers" at the ritual known as Mass. On records of bronze allotment (Jn series) the term seems to denote the condition of actual, non-ritual servitude.

31 Melena 2014: 134–152.

wood during building projects (including palatial structures, workshops, fortification walls, and monumental burials in what are called *tholoi* and chamber tombs).[32] We leave out here ideograms for different kinds of crops and trees, foodstuffs, animals, human beings and all sorts of weaponry.[33]

The two tools that could be given out for major labor operations are:

> (1) **74*, which also occurs as a phonetic abbreviation associated with other ideograms with the meaning *zeugos* or "pair." But **74* is used independently twice on tablets at Knossos in textual contexts that make clear that the ideographic use of the sign on those two tablets is meant to stand for "saw" (Mycenaean Greek *pi-ri-je* = *prīēn*). Sign **74* resembles a saw schematically in shape.

and

> (2) **182*, which, judging from its form, may specify large tongs or pincers used to hold and move building stones.[34]

That the only two work implements recorded ideographically seem by their form to be connected with construction activities in stone makes large-scale building projects stand out within the corpus of Linear B texts relating to the mobilization of labor, despite the rarity of the references.[35]

Knossos K 740.1–.5

tablet damaged above
.1]traces of writing[
.2 *dipas* BRONZE **214*^{VAS}+*DI* 30[
.3 *qe-ro*$_2$ "BRONZE" **255* 16
.4 *ku-ru-su-*56* **207*^{VAS} 1
.5 *prīēn* *ZE* 1 Translation: saw SAW 1

The items are: on line .2 sizable bronze vases; on line .3 bronze platelets to be riveted together in the construction of larger-scale bronze vessels;[36]

[32] On the scale and practical manpower, man-hour and equipment aspects of major public works projects during the Mycenaean palatial period, see Loader 1998: 96–122 and appendix 4; Santillo Frizell 1998; Zangger 1994 and 2008.

[33] Melena 2014: 150–151, itemizes 23 ideograms designating spears, javelins, arrows, bows, helmets, body armor, and chariots and their component parts.

[34] Melena 2014: 151–152.

[35] For large-scale bronze saws on Minoan Crete, see Wells 1974 (for a brief, well-illustrated overview), and Shaw 2009: 44–51. For the Mycenaean evidence for saws themselves and for cutting marks from different kinds of saws, see Blackwell 2014.

[36] Palaima 2004c: 276–278.

on line .4 a three-legged vase with a neck and handles perhaps with a Minoan name and perhaps used for placement over fires;[37] and finally on line .5 a single saw with its material unspecified, but most likely, too, of bronze.

Knossos R 1562

pri]ēnes ZE 12 Translation: saws SAW 12

Knossos U 876

**182* 8 *amphithe[tērsi*[38] Translation: PINCER? 8 for the stone-clampers?

Since we have a text at Pylos (Fn 7) that lists on consecutive lines in two sections daily and monthly allotments of grain to *toikhodomoi* (wall-builders), *prīētēres* (sawyers) and a *pantektōn* (something like a general building project director or contractor) and because of the association on K 740 of the ideogram ZE with vases made of metal, there is less to question here about the idea that we are dealing with large-scale bronze saws used in the cutting of timber and perhaps even stone blocks in the course of building projects.[39] We should also repeat that it is unusual that the

[37] Melena 2014: 147, remarks that the form of the vase and new tablet evidence from the Laconian site of Hagios Vasileios cast doubt on interpreting the beginning of the name of the vessel *ku-ru-su-* as connected with the Greek word for "gold" *khrusos*, itself a loan word.

[38] This reading of the lexical unit is conjectural on my part. The noun would be a formation in *–tēr* parallel to *pi-ri-je-te-re*, dative plural *pi-ri-je-te-si*, and indicate, after the entry of the 8 stone-pincer devices that they are for the people who literally are the "set-on-both-siders," *i.e.*, "the stone clampers." J. L. Melena (personal communication 06/16/2014) notes that my reconstructed form is sound, but it is a new word unattested in historical Greek, so that he prefers to restore (also so far unattested in the Linear B texts) */amphithe[toi/* or */amphithe[tai/*, either as a noun gloss on or as an adjective describing ideogram **182*. But the same objection as to the placement of the term relative to the ideogram would apply, and even more forcefully. Jörg Welhartner, who is doing a full study of Linear B ideograms, adjuncts and ligatures, writes (personal communication 06/17/2014): "I know of no case where the word identifying the logogram comes after logogram and quantity." Moreover, the *-tēr* suffix is productive in Mycenaean Greek (cf. *ko-re-te* and *po-ro-ko-re-te*), and in historical Greek we do get an agent noun in the form *pristēr* = "sawyer".

[39] On building techniques and tools and workers using them Shaw 2009: 53–54, 145–146, 166–169; and 46–51 for stone-cutting with saws. For how saws and other tools like hammers, adzes, chisels and wedges might have been used in Mycenaean palatial quarrying and building work, see Loader 1998: 46–49. Most recently, Nicholas Blackwell's meticulous study of the Lion Gate relief at Mycenae offers solid evidence that straight-edge, convex and pendulum saws were in use on major stone construction projects (including evidence from masonry at Tiryns and on tholoi in the Mycenae area) in the late Mycenaean palatial period, 13th century BC (Blackwell 2014: 459–464, 466, 470 and fig. 18).

"stone pincer tongs" on Knossos U 876 are being distributed to the "stone-clampers" since the recipients of distributions on Linear B texts in all cases I can think of precede the ideogram and number entries. That is, we would expect: *amphithe[tērsi *182* 8. But the contextual association on a single short tablet reinforces our identification and interpretation of the ideogram and the fragmentary word-entry. And it would be an even more unusual positioning if the word-unit to be restored here were the name of the item itself, *i.e.*, the stone pincer tongs.

We get some sense occasionally and, as usual in Linear B texts, indirectly that distributions of work tools were made regularly and that some claim to "ownership" of this equipment, in its used condition, stayed with the distributing authorities, as represented by overseers of work "in the field," as it were. For example, on Pylos tablet Jn 829, the administration in the palatial center calculates the quantities of "recycled" bronze that the palatial *korestēres* and *prokorestēres* in each of the 16 districts of its two provinces will provide by collections they undertake through interactions, respectively, with functionaries known as *du-ma-te* (superintendents, perhaps of sanctuaries; singular *du-ma*)[40] and with "religious" and "agricultural" functionaries known as "key-bearers" (likely temple treasurers) and "fig-supervisors" (tree-fruit overseers) and "overseers of digging" (likely supervisors of grapevine tenders and irrigators). The tablet reads as follows:

Jn 829

.01 thus will give the *ko-re-te-re*, and *du-ma-te*,
.02 and *po-ro-ko-re-te-re*, and "key-bearers", and "fig-supervisors", and "digging supervisors"
.03 temple bronze as points for light javelins and spears

.04 at pi-*82 ,	*ko-re-te* , BRONZE 2 kg.		*po-ro-ko-re-te*	BRONZE 0.75 kg.
.05 at me-ta-pa ,	*ko-re-te*	BRONZE 2 kg.	*po-ro-ko-re-te*	BRONZE 0.75 kg
.06 at pe-to-no ,	*ko-re-te*	BRONZE 2 kg.	*po-ro-ko-re-te*	BRONZE 0.75 kg.
.07 at pa-ki-ja-ne ,	*ko-re-te*	BRONZE 2 kg.	*po-ro-ko-re-te*	BRONZE 0.75 kg.
.08 at a-pu$_2$,	*ko-re-te*	BRONZE 2 kg.	*po-ro-ko-re-te*	BRONZE 0.75 kg.
.09 at a-ke-re-wa ,	*ko-re-te*	BRONZE 2 kg.	*po-ro-ko-re-te*	BRONZE 0.75 kg.
.10 at ro-u-so ,	*ko-re-te*	BRONZE 2 kg.	*po-ro-ko-re-te*	BRONZE 0.75 kg.
.11 at ka-ra-do-ro ,	*ko-re-te*	BRONZE 2 kg.	*po-ro-ko-re-te*	BRONZE 0.75 kg.

[40] Aura Jorro 1985: 195 *s.v. du-ma* §8 and §9. The *du-ma* is reasonably connected with later Greek δάμαρ, -αρτος "wife." Its etymology is opaque, *i.e.*, unknown, but links with Indo-European roots and Greek words for "house" (literally "a building constructed in layers") and "fasten" or "join" have been proposed, as well as a connection with the later Greek ταμία that argues for *du-ma* being a pre-Greek term (Beekes 2010: 301, *s.v.* δάμαρ).

.12 at ri-]jo , *ko-re-te* BRONZE 2 kg. *po-ro-ko-re-te* BRONZE 0.75 kg.
.13 at ti-mi-to-a-ko *ko-re-te* BRONZE 2 kg. *po-ro-ko-re-te* BRONZE 0.75 kg.
.14 at ra-]wa-ra-ta_2 , *ko-re-te* BRONZE 2.75 kg. *po-ro-ko-re-te* BRONZE 0.75 kg.
.15 at sa-]ma-ra , *ko-re-te* BRONZE 3.75 kg. *po-ro-ko-re-te* 0.75 kg.
.16 at a-si-ja-ti-ja *ko-re-te* BRONZE 2 kg. *po-ro-ko-re-te* 0.75 kg.
.17 at e-ra-te-re-wa *ko-re-te* BRONZE 2 kg. *po-ro-ko-re-te* 0.75 kg.
.18 at za-ma-e-wi-ja *ko-re-te* BRONZE 3.75? kg. *po-ro-ko-re-te* 0.75 kg.
.19 at e-ro , *ko-re-te* BRONZE 3.75? kg. *po-ro-ko-re-te* 0.75 kg.

In this operation, the two palatial agents (*korestēres* and *prokorestēres*) looking to the interests of the palatial center in each of the sixteen districts have an authorized claim to what appears to be the scrap-metal bronze that comes from worn tools used in agriculture and from cult implements that are in disposable condition. They interact with power figures appropriate to their own two levels—it would seem that the lower-ranking *prokorestēres* see to the actual process of gathering the recyclable bronze objects and pieces in cooperation with the Mycenaean versions of temple treasurers and the overseers of work teams who do the planting and tending of fig trees and vines.

Following this transaction in reverse, we might posit reasonably that the palatial center could lay claim to these objects because they had been responsible for their distribution or donation in the first place. But again this is a view from the palatial center. The record is concerned with these activities at a higher administrative level than one that would let us see the gritty details of how the bronze tools for arboriculture and viticulture or the bronze cultic implements were given out in the first place and even how they later were retrieved in a worn-out state from persons and localities within the provincial districts.

In livestock tablets (C- series) from Knossos, oxen specified as *we-ka-ta* (ϝεργάτᾱς = a "worker" in the singular), *i.e.*, "worker" oxen are given out in one case in paired teams (C 5734 *we-]ka-ta* BOS *ZE* 20, where *ZE* here is used, as we noted above, as an acrophonic abbreviation for the word *zeugos*, a pair, here literally a "yoked pair") and in other cases (*e.g.*, Ce 59) in multiples of 2 located at different sites in Crete, among them, *da-wo*[41]

[41] The site of *da-wo* is a major agricultural center located somewhere in the Mesara plain in south central Crete. The plain is a major bread basket on the island. *da-wo* may be the site now known now as Hagia Triada (or Holy Trinity), named in modern times after a nearby abandoned medieval village and located three kilometers northwest of the Minoan palatial center of Phaistos. *da-wo* is the site of a large "harvest" *a-ma* record KN F(2) 852 that records roughly a million liters of grain and large quantities of olives and *cyperus*. The

in south central Crete, Tylissos in north central Crete relatively near Knossos and Kydonia, the major center on the northern coast in the far west of the island. On Ce 59, for each of the entries dealing with the sites of *ku-ta-to*, *da-*22-to* and Tylissos, in the upper space above the designation *we-ka-ta*, there are annotations: for the site *ku-ta-to* a probable man's name (*ta-ra-me-to*) is written, and for the other two sites a two-sign word which in early scholarship was interpreted as *da-mo* = *dāmos*. In the most recent edition, the reading of the first sign of what was read as *da-mo* is now considered uncertain.[42]

Still, the traditional reading on Ce 59 is not definitively ruled out and the occurrence of the *dāmos* in two entries in an allocation of worker oxen that could be put to agricultural use would make good sense. Moreover, the written stipulation of the "person in charge" at *ku-ta-to* and of the *dāmos* as the responsible entity at *da-*22-to* and Tylissos might be linked to the fact that these three sites are geographically in the orbit of the palatial center at Knossos, while *da-wo* and *ku-do-ni-ja* are remote and in other natural territories (the northwestern or eastern Mesara and far western Crete, respectively).

It appears that the palatial center had a concern with managing these major animate tools of traction and hauling and in three nearby sites entrusted an individual (perhaps a minor "collector")[43] and the *dāmos* or-

grain alone would require 1,000 hectares of in-use agricultural land and most likely 1,000 additional hectares lying fallow (Bennet 1985: 237 and n. 18). For the general administrative map of Mycenaean Knossos, see Bennet 1985: 236, Ill. 4 and table 1 on page 239. Tylissos = TURISO. *da-*22-to* has a west central location. Privitera 2014: 436, 440 and n. 88, argues that Hagia Triada took on the name of *pa-i-to* (Phaistos) in the post-LM I B Mycenaean phase on the island of Crete and suggests that perhaps *da-wo* should be located in the eastern Mesara.

42 Chadwick *et al.* 1986: 34 now read in the entry for *da-*22-to*: [.]-*ṃọ*; and for Tylissos [.]-*mo*. For the Tylissos entry they consider a reading "*ḍạ-mo* virtually impossible; perhaps *ṛẹ-mo*." We should note that the whole of line .3 is over an erasure, making the reading particularly difficult. Since the editors' apparatus remark and the accompanying photograph do not completely rule out the original reading, we might have here a reference to the involvement of the *dāmos*, as opposed to two occurrences of the same otherwise unattested personal name.

43 At Pylos, one of the four major "collectors," *we-(u-)da-ne-u*, is listed frequently with livestock, in fact nearly twenty times, including with *a-ko-ra* (literally a "collection") of sheep. On Cn 418, he is in charge of fatted bulls whose color markings are described, an indication that they are being prepared for a sacrificial feasting event. See Olivier 2001: 141; Palaima 1989: 104–108.

ganization to see to their care and use. We do not know in specific what projects these animals were being used for, or on what basis the animals were located at these sites. But in other texts, *e.g.*, Pylos tablets An 18 and An 852, ox-tenders (*qo-u-ko-ro*) are listed along with wall-builders (*toikhodomoi*), men of service (*telestai*), and *tektones* (carpenters or construction workers), suggesting that the worker oxen they tended were to be put to use at least part of the time in building operations. On another tablet An 830, four groups of ox-tenders (18 to 66 in number) are recorded in a context having to do with *ke-ke-me-na* "uninhabited" land, perhaps in the process of converting it to agricultural production.[44]

Because the palatial center at Knossos is here on Ce 59 noting the placement of the animals in different localities, we can assume they have an interest in seeing to the work services to which the worker animals are put. Knossos tablet Ce 50 is a peculiar case. On both the front and the back of the tablet are recorded four entries of the same sequence of personal names and associated classes of livestock. The individuals and their associated kinds and numbers of livestock, respectively front and back, are:

a-qi-ru (male sheep, front 134 and back 190);
qa-ra$_2$*-wo* (female sheep, front 43 and back 144);
a-nu-ko (female sheep, front 51 and back 133); and
ro-ru (female sheep, front 32 and back 150).

The *recto* text is annotated with small-scale interspersed signs referring to what seems to be the site of *te-pa-ra* and the interests of an individual known as *pe-re-qo-ta*. The *verso* specifies in the same way that the animals are *o-pa* or "finishing" work. When the term *o-pa* is used with animals, it mostly has to do with fattening and bringing them into a proper state for use, generally for sacrifice and consumption at feasts, and generally in the palatial interest.[45] On the top side of the leaf-shaped tablet, the scribe has inscribed an entry of 6 male *we-ka-ta* oxen. Extrapolating from Ce 59, we might conclude that here at the site of *te-pa-ra*, the figure *pe-re-qo-ta* is responsible from the central administration's point of view (as are *ta-ra-me-to* and the two possible *dāmos* groups on Ce 59) for the worker oxen specified as located here. This would be consistent with groups of workers who are listed en masse in other tablets, especially the Pylos tablets to which we have just referred.

44 Palaima 1989: 101.
45 Palaima 2004a: 227; Killen 1999.

Public Projects: Mobilization and Participation

We have already mentioned above the harvest labor that underlies the large harvests recorded on the Knossos texts, *e.g.*, F 852 with its massive harvest of grain at the site of *da-wo*. On a smaller scale, the palatial center at Knossos is interested in a "harvest" (*a-ma*) recorded in the brief text of an unfortunately fragmentary tablet (F 845) that lacks its place entry. The text of F 845 does note the involvement of the *dāmos* (see above on Ce 59) with recorded amounts of 8 (and perhaps more, given that the area on the tablet surface where units for signs for "ten" would occur is damaged) GRA units (= 768 liters of grain), and 12 units of wild olives (equaling perhaps 1,152 liters).

We have also already mentioned, too, that Pylos tablet Fn 7 specifies both daily and monthly allotments of foodstuffs made to a group of 20 *toikhodomoi* (wall builders), 5 *priētēres* (sawyers) and a single *pantektōn* (general building project manager). The wall builders and sawyers receive each 1.2 liters of grain daily. The *pantektōn* 3.2 liters. Two other individuals (*qa-ra*$_2$ and *pa-ka*) are also listed there, apparently by personal name, as receiving grain and olives. How the operation was managed, who was responsible for having the supplies of grain on hand and for conveying and distributing them to the working parties, whether this text referred to a specific project being undertaken and where, and whether the central administration knew or cared to know the identity of the *pantektōn*, are all unknown to us. We can say minimally that these two groups of specialist workers and the *pantektōn* were capable of working collaboratively on a project and that they either had been or were about to be mobilized for such a project.[46] The palatial center clearly has an interest in maintaining these workers for a period of a month.

A similar association among wall builders, ox-tenders and most likely either *telestai* ("service men") or *tektones* ("carpenters" or "construction workers") is found on Pylos tablet An 18.[47] Its heading seems to have to do with the occupation or office known as an *ereutēr* "inspector or examiner," but there is no sure way of knowing the precise significance of the fragmentary word and heading. Of the conjectures made by eminent Mycenologists C.J. Ruijgh and M. Lejeune,[48] it strikes me that, if, as is likely, the heading refers to the contents of the entire tablet, we should

46 Like reasoning applies to Pylos tablet An 18.

47 I have used here the abbreviation *top* = *toponym* to indicate that the word in a particular position is a place name designation. The most likely restoration in line .11 is either *telestai* or *tektones*.

48 See Aura Jorro 1985: 243 *s.v.*

read *e-re-u-te-ri-jo*, *i.e.*, a reference that the entries on the tablets concern "persons in the sphere of interest of the *ereutēr* or inspector."

A figure by the name of *di-wi-je-u*, a personal name that seems to be derived from a theonym and to mean literally something like the man having to do with the goddess *di-wi-ja*,[49] holds the title of *ereutēr* on tablet Cn 3. On Cn 3.2, he is recipient of oxen destined for sacrifice. He is attested again in the *o-ka* "coastal guard contingents" series as a *hek^{w}etās* or "mobilizer" (see below).

The two toponyms specified in lines .9 and .11 of tablet An 18 have important associations: the area of *ti-no* with the *lāwagetās* (see below) and the area of *pa-ki-ja-ne* as the main religious district associated with the palatial center. The tablet as a whole then looks to be a report of single men of some importance in place at these different locations—and in one case missing—and somehow all viewed as under the oversight of an *ereutēr*.

In line .12 of An 18, the number 256 interpreted either as the number of "carpenters" or as the number of "men of service" in the sanctuary district of *pa-ki-ja-ne* would seem to be a high figure.[50] Given the detailed list of landholdings that we have for the district of *pa-ki-ja-ne* (also designated as *pa-ki-ja-na* and *pa-ki-ja-ni-ja*) close to the palatial center proper, a case can be made that the district and its many sanctuaries could accommodate that many "men of service" in its agricultural activities or that the word *tektōn* might still not have a specific designation as "carpenter", *i.e.*, woodworker, per se, but would mean something more general, and appropriate to its root meaning, like "construction worker" or "builder," as we have been glossing it and for precisely this reason.

An 18

.1	e-re-u-te-ri-[		
.2	te-ko-to-na-pe	VIR [	
.3	i-na-ni-ja	VIR 1[	jạ VIR [
.4	ṛẹ-ṣị-we-i	ṾỊṚ [] 1 a se-e	VIR 1
.5	*vacat*		
.6	te-re-ne we , to-ko-do-mo a-pe-o		VIR 1
.7	i-na-ne	VIR 1	te-ko-to-na-pe 1
.8	*vacat*		
.9	qo-u-ko-ro ti-no	VIR 90	
.10	*vacat*		
.11	pa-ki-ja-si , to-so , te-[ ]		
.12		VIR 256̣[ ] *vacat*	

[49] See Aura Jorro 1985: 182 *s.v.* § 8.

[50] But see below Knossos tablet Am 826.

An 18

at *top* MAN			
at *top*	MAN 1	at *top* ?	MAN [
at *top*	MAN 1	at *top*	MAN 1
	blank line		
at *top*, wall builder absent			MAN 1
at *top*	MAN 1	at *top*	1
	blank line		
	ox-tenders	at *ti-no*^{top}	MAN 90
	blank line		
at *pa-ki-ja-ne*^{top} , so many , *te*-[ ]			
	MAN 256?		

One of the other ways, beside through "inspectors," that the palatial centers managed their own interests is through individuals of high status who do not fill any official position or hold any title in the bureaucratic hierarchy that kept track of, and integrated itself into, all activities in their palatial territories. These individuals are known as "collectors."[51]

Citing Mesopotamian parallels, Nakassis argues, in my view convincingly, that the "collectors" were Mesopotamian-style entrepreneurs, but not palatial administrators per se:[52]

> It is equally possible to compare the Mycenaean "collectors" to these Mesopotamian entrepreneurs, individuals who could hold important positions as administrators but also had various interests of their own. This might explain why "collectors" are referred to by personal name rather than by official title, why their activities are so diverse, and why it is difficult to separate out the "collectors" from other named individuals. So, although the activities of "collectors" were tracked by the palatial documents, their high standing makes it difficult to imagine they were merely employees of the palace.

51 Nakassis 2013: 7–8 (with further references there in notes 41–47); 168–169; and especially 174–175. Only two of the individuals identifiable as collectors are associated with official titles, and those indirectly. As Nakassis 2018: 18, n. 98, explains, in one case the individual *Alksoitās* may be *hek*^{w}*etās*, but there is a preferable interpretation of the syntax where his name and the term co-occur; in the other case, the individual *Amphimēdēs* has "personal servants" who are described adjectivally as *hek*^{w}*esioi*. However, it is possible that they are so described because they have connections with another individual or other individuals classed as *hek*^{w}*etai*.

52 Nakassis 2013: 174–175.

I myself have argued that these elite individuals, who appear as important economic agents and facilitators, could have served the same functions in the relatively newly formed palatial regions as the Carolingian *Reichsaristokratie*.[53] On Knossos tablet E 847 a collector known as *a-no-qo-ta,* whose name appears in eleven texts having diverse purposes,[54] is listed, we hypothesize by a reasonable restoration of a missing part of the text, at Knossos as in control of a quantity of grain for a single-month (designated by the lunate "month" ideogram) in the amount of 10.2 whole units (= ca. 980 liters). Two other entries for individuals follow with the same scale of grain, the last (to an otherwise unattested individual known as *da-na-mo*) for around 11 GRA units (= 1,056 liters).

We can get some comparative sense of the scale by noting that the *pantektōn* on Pylos Fn 7 received as his individual compensation for a month 1 HORD unit. This would seem to suggest that the monthly allocations or held amounts on KN E 847 are significant rewards granted to the collector *a-no-qo-ta* and to *da-na-mo,* or are amounts to be used for distribution later at much larger scales of operation. We should stress again that whether these amounts of grain were intended to be for the personal use of the parties listed on KN E 847 or for some use relating to projects in which the palatial center itself had an interest we do not know.

We get other hints of mobilization either for agricultural or building purposes in texts that simply list the number of persons involved in specific locations. For example, the palatial center at Knossos had need of a text that records the following:

Knossos Am 826

.1 men of *a-pa-ta-wa* , *telestai* MAN 45[

.2 *tektones* MAN 5 [

The association of this many individuals of the higher landholding class (45 *telestai* or "service men") who are involved in *dāmos* affairs with 5 building-project supervisors (*tektones*) resembles the association on Pylos tablet Fn 7 of 1 *pantektōn* with 20 wall-builders and 5 sawyers. The regular numbers on KN Am 826 suggest that there existed, at the time the tablet was written, at or from *a-pa-ta-wa,* five working groups or teams of ten consisting each of 1 *tektōn* and 9 *telestai.*

[53] Palaima 2012a: 349–350.
[54] Olivier 2001: 142.

Besides "collectors" in the economic sphere and the *korestēres* and *prokorestēres* appointed by the palatial authorities who see to the economic and political interests, broadly defined, of the palatial centers, the individuals known as *hek^{w}etai* (whom we have called "mobilizers") appear to play a clear role in "military" mobilization in the Pylos *o-ka* tablets. However, these records do not have an explicit bearing upon or furnish information about the economic aspects of such activities.[55]

Nonetheless, the actions of the *hek^{w}etai* are related in some ways to economic mobilization. Take, for example, the simple text from Pylos An 1. It records some basic information: 30 rowers total drawn from five different communities (and listed against them in numbers 8, 5, 4, 6 and 7) are "going to the site of *Pleurōn*" (in my opinion best located somewhere in Messenia). Why would such a text be written? Again in my opinion,[56] An 1 is best explained as written not only to verify that a full crew of rowers is on their way to *Pleurōn*, but also so that the five small communities providing these rowers may have the fact of their contributions explicitly known to the palatial center so that their reduced manpower resources and their fulfillment of this service of providing rowers may be taken into consideration when deciding how to mobilize manpower for other work projects.

Unfortunately Knossos text B 1055 is laconic in content and also incompletely preserved. It is structured as a typical "census" of men under the overall tablet heading on line 1:

ko-no-si-jo , e-qe-ta ,

This two-word heading phrase is interpretable as a rubric declaration meaning either

knōsioi hek^{w}etai = the men listed hereon are "Knossian *hek^{w}etai*"

or

knōsiōi hek^{w}etāi = the men listed hereon are "for the Knossian *hek^{w}etās*".[57]

[55] Shelmerdine 2008:146–147, makes clear that the data of personnel mobilization and placement in the *o-ka* tablets are "not tied to any records of rations or equipment." Killen 2008: 180, declares that these texts "are concerned with military (or para-military) disposition" and are thus only economic in secondary or tertiary ways.

[56] Palaima 2011b:66, n. 28.

[57] That is, the *hek^{w}etās* has some kind of interests in them.

The tablet itself is too fragmentary to offer us solid reasons to choose among various alternative interpretations of the heading. The standard interpretation posits that the approximately 13 men who seem to be listed on the tablet singly by personal name may be the "Knossian *hek^w^etai*" in the nominative of rubric on line .1. It is then further proposed, not unreasonably as the Linear B tablets go, that the entry on line .9:

"so many men all totaled MAN 213"

refers to the aggregate total number of *hek^w^etai* who would comprise the full dossier made up of a number of other tablets, no longer preserved, giving names of *hek^w^etai* at other sites.[58] All totaled there would be 213 *hek^w^etai* operating at whatever number of sites were taken up in this dossier, with 13 of these *hek^w^etai* identified as being at Knossos. This at least gives us some sense of the scale at which the *hek^w^etai* were present within the economic system at Knossos, and helps us to see that individuals with this designation, too, were out in the regional landscape, perhaps at sites like Tylissos, *u-ta-no*, *se-toi-ja*, Phaistos and *ku-do-ni-ja* (Khania).[59] We should caution, however, that other interpretations of the text of B 1055 are possible and that two entire lines (.4-.5) are missing from this nine-line text.

Besides the individuals acting in the interests of the palatial centers to mobilize and maintain economic resources, animate and inanimate, and to manage work projects, there are also three other prestige groups that, like the *dāmos* in the sphere of local land use, are also involved in labor mobilization. These three are:

(1) the *ra-wa-ke-si-ja* = *lāwagesiā* (as securely restored on Knossos tablet As 1516), an organization responding to the authority of the *lāwagetās*;

(2) the *qa-si-re-wi-ja* = *g^w^asilewiā* (KN As 1516.12, PY Fn 50.1–.3 and Fn 867.3), bodies either made up of *g^w^asilēwes* or led by one of them in local village areas;

[58] Deger-Jalkotzy 1978: 94–96, who points out that the scribe who wrote B 1055, also may have written tablet B 807 which lists men from Tylissos (unknown quantity) and men from the site of *u-ta-no* (237), *i.e.*, on a similar scale of massed personnel as B 1088.

[59] Deger-Jalkotzy 1978: 96–97, opines that Linear B tablets attest to 200 or so chariots (Driessen 1995: 491–493, estimates 250 chariots and 500 horses attested in the Linear B records as under maintenance at Knossos) and that the fact that we have a total number of *hek^w^etai* recorded of a similar number "ist vielleicht kein Zufall."

(3) and *ke-ro-si-ja* = *geronsia* = later *gerousia* (Pylos tablet An 261.2–.17 and v. .1–.2 and .4–.7), councils of elders operating at the village level and organizing and mobilizing labor and the exploitation of other resources.[60]

It is instructive to focus on a single individual here within the Pylos records and how his role in the texts illuminates the complexity of economic operations. The person known as *a-pi-qo-ta*[61] occurs on three tablets. On one (Jn 431.6) of the tablets of the allocation of raw bronze to smiths in various locales, *a-pi-qo-ta* appears as a *qa-si-re-u* = *g^w^asileus*, a power figure within local communities with large status on this small-scale. He also appears as the possessor of a *geronsia* that has recorded against it 17 men. Finally there are five individually named men listed and recorded against the *geronsia* of *a-pi-qo-ta* on tablet An 261.13–17. Moreover, on the verso of An 261, the four different *geronsiai* are listed with a group of land-holding men known as *ka-ma-e-we*, i.e., the men who have to do with the special kind of landholding known as a *ka-ma*, a higher status of landholding that is associated with a specific obligation to perform work. By association then the 20, 18, 17 and 14 men recorded on An 261 by tablet-writers at the palatial center would likewise be fulfilling some kind of work obligation. Deger-Jalkotzy clarifies for us as well as one can what seems to going on here:[62]

> Both *qa-si-re-wi-ja* and *ke-ro-si-ja* designated groups of men who originated from the local level of the province of a Mycenaean kingdom. But while the operations of the *qa-si-re-wi-ja* seem to have been related to the organisation of labour at the economy *within* the Mycenaean palace system, *ke-ro-si-ja* remained outside the sphere. May we then assume that *ke-ro-si-ja* was a term which refers to the socio-political conditions of the local districts which were normally not mentioned by the central bureaucrats at Pylos?

She further posits that the *ke-ro-si-ja* consists of "senior members of a kin group who may have been the heads of descent groups."[63]

60 For a complete list of Mycenaean social units that to some degree control human activity and resources, see Palaima 2012b: 701. For the most up-to-date, thorough, perceptive and sensible discussion of textual data for the operation of Mycenaean *g^w^asilewiā* and *geronsia* in the context of Mycenaean palatial society, see Deger-Jalkotzy 1998–99.

61 Nakassis 2013: 209.

62 Deger-Jalkotzy 1998–1999: 75.

63 Deger-Jalkotzy 1998–1999: 80.

The difficulty here is to figure out what is meant by activities being inside and outside the Mycenaean palatial system. What is clear is that *a-pi-qo-ta* is a *g^w^asileus* and appears in palatial texts when the palace needs to distribute bronze to individuals who have other economic concerns, *e.g.*, herding. So far as our documentation indicates, however, neither *a-pi-qo-ta* nor any of his three peers on An 261 as "possessors" of a *geronsia*, is a palatial "mobilizer" (*hek^w^etās*); nor are any of the four classed as "collectors."

To be cautious, we might wonder whether this is simply the result of the grounds by which we identify and classify "collectors". If we were to classify the mobilization that is clearly taking place on tablet An 261 and related tablets as an economic operation, a case could be made for the designation of "collectors" to be used here. After all the latest individuals to be identified as collectors (those with interests in bronze smith work, olive oil production and middleman economic transactions) were once not recognized as such.[64]

I think in the end, it is best to avoid trying to make distinctions as to whether classes of individuals or persons holding particular statuses are inside or outside the palatial system. The palatial centers did "rule" their territories and the other power centers, local communities and persons residing or brought within their territories. We should concentrate on the entities and institutions and officials with which they interacted.

What the foregoing discussion has demonstrated is how all-encompassing the *politeia* of the Mycenaean palatial system was. But the nature of economic activity within the system and the terms upon which labor projects were conceived, implemented, worked upon and completed involved a broad range of actors and agents and interests. The palatial centers, it would seem, were aware of boundaries of authority, interest, obligation and benefit. But they seem not to have done away with local big men (*g^w^asilēwes*) or sib groups, clans and elders (*gerontes* and *geronsiai*). Each palatial center would have had long experience of negotiating such relationships and interactions with regional elites known as *hek^w^etai* and "collectors" in its own immediate district, before it became the paramount site of a region. As we have mentioned, too, the delicacy with which palatial centers like Pylos (and Knossos where the same titles are attested) approached such matters is underscored by the ideological message of the titles they use when they want to effect matters directly through their own appointees (*korestēres, prokorestēres* and *dāmokoroi*).

[64] Olivier 2001: 140 n. 111, 149–151.

BIBLIOGRAPHY

Abbreviations

AJA *American Journal of Archaeology*
ÖAdW Österreichische Akademie der Wissenschaften
C.S.I.C. Consejo Superior de Investigaciones Científicas

References

Aura Jorro, Francisco (1985), *Diccionario micénico* 1 (Madrid: C.S.I.C.).

— (1993), *Diccionario micénico* 2 (Madrid: C.S.I.C.).

Beekes, Robert (2010), *Etymological Dictionary of Greek*. Volumes 1 and 2 (Leiden and Boston: Brill).

Bennet, John (1985), "The Structure of the Linear B Administration at Knossos," *AJA* 89: 231–249.

— (2011), "The Geography of Mycenaean Kingdoms," in Duhoux and Morpurgo Davies 2011: 137–168.

Chadwick, John (1988), "The Women of Pylos," in T. Palaima and J.-P. Olivier (eds.), *Texts, Tablets and Scribes*, Minos Supplement 10 (Salamanca: University of Salamanca Press): 43–95

Chadwick, John and John T. Killen, Jean-Pierre Olivier, Anna Sacconi, Iannis A. Sakellarakis (eds.) (1986), *Corpus of Mycenaean Inscriptions from Knossos, Volume 1*. Incunabula Graeca 88 (Cambridge *etc.*: Cambridge University Press; Rome: Edizioni dell'Ateneo).

Chantraine, Pierre (2009), *Dictionnaire étymologique de la langue grecque.* New edition by J. Taillardat, O. Masson, J.-L. Perpillou, with Supplement by A. Blanc, C. de Lamberterie and J.L. Perpillou (Paris: Klincksieck).

de Fidio, Pia (2008), "Mycenaean History," in Duhoux and Morpurgo Davies 2008: 81–114.

Deger-Jalkotzy, Sigrid (1978), E-QE-TA. *Zur Rolle des Gefolgschaftswesens in der Sozialstruktur mykenischer Reiche.* Mykenische Studien 6 (Vienna: ÖAdW).

— (1998–99), "Working for the Palace: Some Observations on PY An 261," in J. Bennet and J. Driessen (eds.), *A-NA-QO-TA. Studies Presented to J. T. Killen* (*Minos* 33–34, Salamanca): 65–81.

Del Freo, Maurizio (2001), "Mycénien *pu-te-ri-ja* et le couple *ki-ti-me-na* / *ke-ke-me-na*," *Revue de philologie, de littérature et d'histoire anciennes* 75: 27–44.

Driessen, Jan (1995), "The arsenal of Knossos (Crete) and Mycenaean chariot forces," in M. Lodewijckx (ed.), *Archaeological and Historical Aspects of West-European Societies.* Acta Archaeologica Lovaniensia Monographiae 8 (Leuven: Leuven University Press): 481–498.

— (2008), "Chronology of the Linear B Texts," in Duhoux and Morpurgo Davies 2008: 69–79.

Duhoux, Yves (2008), "Mycenaean Anthology," in Duhoux and Morpurgo Davies 2008: 243–397.

— (2011), "Interpreting the Linear B records: Some Guidelines," in Duhoux and Morpurgo Davies 2011: 1–32.

Duhoux, Yves and Anna Morpurgo Davies, eds. (2008), *A Companion to Linear B: Mycenaean Greek Texts and Their World. Volume 1.* Bibliothèque des cahiers de l'Institut de Linguistique de Louvain 120 (Louvain-la-Neuve/Dudley, Mass: Peeters).

— (2011), *A Companion to Linear B: Mycenaean Greek Texts and Their World. Volume 2.* Bibliothèque des cahiers de l'Institut de Linguistique de Louvain 127 (Louvain-la-Neuve/Dudley, Mass: Peeters).

— (2014), *A Companion to Linear B: Mycenaean Greek Texts and Their World. Volume 3.* Bibliothèque des cahiers de l'Institut de Linguistique de Louvain 133 (Louvain-la-Neuve/Dudley, Mass: Peeters).

Galaty, Michael L. and William A. Parkinson (eds.) (2007), *Rethinking Mycenaean Palaces II.* 2nd edition. Cotsen Institute of Archaeology Monographs 60 (Los Angeles: Cotsen Institute of Archaeology).

Hope Simpson, Richard (2014), *Mycenaean Messenia and the Kingdom of Pylos.* Prehistory Monographs 45 (Philadelphia: INSTAP Academic Press).

Killen, John T. (1999), "Mycenaean *o-pa*," in S. Deger-Jalkotzy, S. Hiller and O. Panagl (eds.), *Floreant studia mycenaea.* ÖAdW, phil.-hist. Klasse, Denkschriften 274, vol. 2 (Vienna: ÖAdW): 325–342.

— (2008), "Mycenaean Economy," in Duhoux and Morpurgo Davies 2008: 159–200.

Loader, N. Claire (1998), *Building in Cyclopean Masonry with Special Reference to the Mycenaean Fortifications on Mainland Greece.* Studies in Mediterranean Archaeology Paperback 148 (Jonsered: Paul Åströms Förlag).

Melena, José L. (2014), "Mycenaean Writing," in Duhoux and Morpurgo Davies 2014: 1–186.

Nakassis, Dimitri (2006), *The Individual and the Mycenaean State: Agency and Prosopography in the Linear B Texts from Pylos.* Ph.D. dissertation, University of Texas, Austin.

— (2012), "Named Individuals and the Mycenaean State at Pylos," in P. Carlier, C. De Lamberterie, M. Egetmeyer, N. Guilleux, F. Rougemont and J. Zurbach (eds.), *Études mycéniennes 2010.* Biblioteca di "Pasiphae" 10 (Pisa/Rome: Fabrizio Serra): 269–283.

— (2013), *Individuals and Society in Mycenaean Pylos*. Mnemosyne Supplements, History and Archaeology of Classical Antiquity 358 (Leiden/Boston: Brill).

Nelson, Michael C. (2007), "Pylos, Block Masonry and Monumental Architecture in the Late Bronze Age Peloponnese," in J. Driessen and K. van Lerberghe (eds.), *Power and Architecture: Monumental Public Architecture in the Bronze Age Near East and Aegean.* Orientalia Lovaniensia Analecta 156 (Leuven: Peeters): 143–159.

Olivier, Jean-Pierre (2001), "Les collecteurs*: Leur distribution spatiale et temporelle*," in S. Voutsaki and J. T. Killen (eds.), *Economy and Politics in the Mycenaean Palace States.* Cambridge Philological Society Supplementary Volume 27 (Cambridge: Cambridge Philological Society) 139–159.

Palaima, Thomas G. (1989), "Perspectives on the Pylos Oxen Tablets," in Th. G. Palaima, C.W. Shelmerdine and P. Hr. Ilievski (eds.), *Studia Mycenaea (1988)*. Živa Antika Monographies no. 7 (Skopje): 85–124.

— (2003), "'Archives' and 'Scribes' and Information Hierarchy in Mycenaean Greek Linear B Records," in M. Brosius (ed.), *Ancient Archives and Archival Traditions* (Oxford: Oxford University Press): 153-194.

— (2004a), "Sacrificial Feasting in the Linear B tablets," in J. C. Wright (ed.), *The Mycenaean Feast.* (*Hesperia. The Journal of the American School of Classical Studies at Athens* 73.2): 217–246.

— (2004b), "Mycenaean Accounting Methods and Systems and Their Place Within Mycenaean Palatial Civilization," in M. Hudson and C. Wunsch (eds.), *Creating Economic Order: Record-Keeping, Standardization and the Development of Accounting in the Ancient Near East*, International Scholars Conference on Ancient Near Eastern Economies 4 (Bethesda, Maryland: CDL Press): 269–301.

— (2004c), "Syntax and Context as Tools for Interpreting Mycenaean Texts and Scribal Processes: Un 718, Ta 709 and K(1) 740," in T. Krisch, T. Lindner and U. Müller (eds.), *Analecta Homini Universali Dicata = Festschrift Oswald Panagl.* Stuttgarter Arbeiten zur Germanistik 421 (Stuttgart: Hans-Dieter Heinz): 268–278.

— (2006a), "*wanaks* and Related Power Terms in Mycenaean and Later Greek," in S. Deger-Jalkotzy and I. Lemos (eds.), *Ancient* Greece: *From the Mycenaean Palaces to the Age of Homer*. Edinburgh Leventis Studies 3 (Edinburgh: Edinburgh University Press): 53–71.

— (2006b), "FAR? or ju? and other interpretative conundra in the new Thebes Tablets," in S. Deger-Jalkotzy and O. Panagl (eds.), *Die Neuen Linear B-Texte aus Theben.* ÖAdW, phil.-hist. Klasse, Denkschriften 338 (Vienna: ÖAdW): 139–148.

— (2007), "Mycenaean Society and Kingship: *Cui Bono*? A Counter-Speculative View," in S.P. Morris and R. Laffineur (eds.), *Epos. Reconsidering Greek Epic and Aegean Bronze Age Archaeology.* Aegaeum 28 (Leuven: Peeters): 129–140.

— (2008), "The Significance of Mycenaean Words Relating to Meals, Meal Rituals, and Food," in L.A. Hitchcock, R. Laffineur and J. Crowley (eds.), *DAIS. The Aegean Feast.* Aegaeum 29 (Leuven: Peeters): 383–389.

— (2011a), "Scribes, Scribal Hands and Palaeography," in Duhoux and Morpurgo Davies 2011: 33-136.

— (2011b), "Euboea, Athens and Thebes: The Implications of the Linear B References," in D. W. Rupp, J. E. Tomlinson *et al.* (eds.), *Euboea and Athens: Proceedings of a Colloquium in Memory of Malcolm B. Wallace. Athens, 26-27 June 2009.* Publications of the Canadian Institute in Greece 6 (Athens: The Canadian Institute in Greece): 53–76.

— (2012a), "Security and Insecurity as Tools of Power in Mycenaean Palatial Kingdoms," in P. Carlier, C. De Lamberterie, M. Egetmeyer, N. Guilleux, F. Rougemont and J. Zurbach (eds.), *Études mycéniennes 2010.* Biblioteca di »Pasiphae« 10 (Pisa/Rome: Fabrizio Serra): 345–356.

— (2012b), "*Kosmos* in the Mycenaean Texts: The Response of Mycenaean 'Scribes' to the Culture of *Kosmos*," in M.-L. Nosch and R. Laffineur (eds.), *Kosmos: Jewellery, Adornment and Textile in the Aegean Bronze Age.* Aegaeum 33 (Leuven: Peeters): 697–703.

— (2014), "Harnessing *phusis*: The Ideology of Control and Exploitation of the Natural World as Reflected in Terminology in the Linear B Texts Derived from Indo-European *$^*b^heh_2u$-* 'Grow, Arise, Be' and *$^*h_2eg$-ro-* 'the Uncultivated Wild Field' and Other Roots Related to the Natural Environs," in R. Laffineur (ed.) *PHYSIS*, Aegaeum (Leuven: Peeters): 93–99.

Palmer, Ruth (1989), "Subsistence Rations at Pylos and Knossos," *Minos* 24: 89–124.

— (1992), "Wheat and Barley in Mycenaean Society," in J.-P. Olivier (ed.), *Mykenaïka.* Bulletin de Correspondance Hellenique Supplement 25 (Paris: de Boccard): 475–497.

— (1999), "Perishable Goods in Mycenaean Texts," in S. Deger-Jalkotzy, S. Hiller and O. Panagl (eds.), *Floreant studia mycenaea.* ÖAdW, phil.-hist. Klasse, Denkschriften 274, vol. 2 (Vienna: ÖAdW): 463–485.

— (2008), "How to Begin? An Introduction to Linear B Conventions and Resources," in Duhoux and Morpurgo Davies 2008: 25-68.

Pluta, Kevin (2011), *Aegean Bronze Age Literacy and Its Consequences.* Ph.D. dissertation, University of Texas, Austin.

Privitera, Santo (2014), "Long-Term Grain Storage and Political Economy in Bronze Age Crete: Contextualizing Ayia Triada's Silo-Complexes," *AJA* 118: 429–449.

Ruijgh, Cornelis J. (2011), "Mycenaean and Homeric Language," Duhoux and Morpurgo Davies 2011: 253–298.

Santillo Frizell, Barbro (1998), "Giants or Geniuses? Monumental Building at Mycenae," *Current Swedish Archaeology* 6: 167–184.

Shaw, Joseph W. (2009), *Minoan Architecture: Materials and Techniques*. Studi di archeologia cretese 7 (Padua: Bottega d'Erasmo).

Shelmerdine, Cynthia W. (1998), "Review of Aegean Prehistory VI: The Palatial Bronze Age of the Southern and Central Greek Mainland," *AJA* 101: 537–585.

— (2008), "Mycenaean Society," in Duhoux and Morpurgo Davies 2008: 115–158.

Shemerdine, Cynthia W. and John Bennet (2008), "Mycenaean States. Economy and Administration," in C.W. Shelmerdine (ed.), *The Cambridge Companion to the Aegean Bronze Age* (New York: Cambridge University Press): 289–309.

Wells, H. Bartlett (1974), "The Position of the Large Bronze Saws of Minoan Crete in the History of Tool Making," *Expedition* (Summer): 2–8.

Zangger, Eberhard (1994), "Landscape Changes around Tiryns during the Bronze Age," *AJA* 98: 189–212.

— (2008), "The Port of Nestor," in J.L. Davis (ed.), *Sandy Pylos*. 2nd edition (Princeton: American School of Classical Studies at Athens): 69–74.

11.

How the Organization of Labor shaped Civilization's Takeoff

Michael Hudson

University of Missouri, Kansas City and ISLET

> In the primitive economic situation ... there is, of course, no "solitary hunter," living either in a cave or otherwise, and there is no man who "makes by his own labor all the goods that he uses," etc. ... There is no reasonable doubt but that, at least since mankind reached the human plane, the economic unit has been not a "solitary hunter," but a community of some kind.
>
> Thorstein Veblen (1908/1919:184–185)

It is now more than a century since Veblen poked fun at armchair philosophers postulating a primitive idyll of rugged individuals making products to trade. Such scenarios are based on a "simple scheme of economic life ... to throw into the foreground, in a highly unreal perspective, those features which lend themselves to interpretation in terms of the normalised competitive system."[1]

These heuristic examples do not acknowledge a productive role for communal or public institutions. Palaces appear in a Hollywood version of Egyptian overseers whipping slaves to build pyramids—a blind alley leading to Oriental Despotism. The only role for government that such economic individualism recognizes is that of a burdensome overhead, waging war and providing special privileges for insiders. There is no thought of a bureaucracy innovating the commercial practices that in time became privatized.

By the time written records appear in the third millennium BC, labor had long been mobilized for large building projects that must have involved entire communities. From the early Neolithic through the

1 Veblen 1908/1919:183–184.

Bronze Age, this mobilization was organized on different principles from those of the modern world. In view of the ever-present option of flight, it must have been on a voluntary basis. Members of the community were self-supporting on the land, not obliged to compete to find work.

Also, the most archaic employment of labor could not have been based on barter or market sales of crops or handicrafts, because (apart from working to produce its own subsistence) labor initially was organized to construct public ceremonial sites and buildings, irrigation works, and to serve in the military. No exchange value was initially involved. And when free labor did come to be organized for commercial purposes, the process was innovated mainly by chieftains, temple and palace officials, whose fortunes emerged in a symbiotic relationship with these large institutions.

From ceremonial community-based labor to the corvée

This volume starts with Lamberg-Karlovsky's discussion of Göbekli Tepe (c. 10,000–9000 BC) of in southeastern Turkey. Its monumental architecture was built by hunter-gatherers drawn from what must have been a broad territory to spend decade after decade working to build the ritual center. Such centers hosted the major occasions for gatherings for the rituals that integrated archaic communities for selection of mates and customary gift exchange that in time would evolve into markets.

Four or five thousand years after Göbekli, populations came together at Avebury, Stonehenge and other ceremonial sites of the late Neolithic.[2] This still was long before profit-seeking trade or state coercion developed. Just who brought the large excavated volume of gazelle, auroch cattle and other animal remains that fed Göbekli's builders is not recorded. But no doubt a kindred organizational practice guided the mobilization of labor evolved to build Sumerian, Babylonian and Egyptian monuments and infrastructure.

The labor requisitioned for such projects did not produce goods for sale. But someone had to organize it. One of the byproducts of Neolithic monument building was thus a managerial class. This role originally

[2] No doubt their gatherings and feasts were coordinated by calendrical turning points based on the lunar and solar cycles so that widely scattered groups would know when to converge. The cosmology extends back to the Ice Age caves described by Alexander Marshack in our group's urbanization volume, Hudson and Levine 1999: 53.

would have been played by chieftains as calendar keepers and organizers, dealing with outsiders, and centralizing some forms of specialized labor in their own households. Already by Pre-Pottery Neolithic-B these men "held religious authority that legitimized their right to rule," Lamberg-Karlovsky explains. "Supernatural sanction, confirmed and certified by specialist practitioners, offered not only the legitimacy of rule, but the structure of order within the earliest villages." Social status was sanctified by authority centered on the individuals responsible for allocating resources, organizing rituals and mobilizing labor for building monuments or temples and other public works. Authorities "presided over ritual centers, the nascent forms of the later temples that became the focus of centralized political and economic power."[3]

So what was "produced" already in preliterate times at Tal-i-Bakun (c. 6000 BC) and Tell Abyad (c. 5500 BC), Stonehenge and Central Asia were not only public works and ceremonial centers but also control mechanisms and administrative hierarchies. By the Bronze Age this managerial class would become the main beneficiaries, controlling wealth via the temples and palaces to produce textiles, metal and elite goods for long-distance trade.

The Neolithic thus bequeathed to the Bronze Age a complex of socio-economic relationships: (1) food provisioning and the hosting of feasts, requiring (2) empowerment of a managerial class, with (3) customary crop rights and land tenure, evolving in time into outright property ownership. Initially this land tenure was a byproduct of (4) fiscal policy to allocate responsibility to mobilize labor, food and other resources.

Corvée labor as the primordial proto-tax defining land rights

Goelet defines corvée labor as "unpaid, unskilled manual labor exacted in lieu of taxation in the form of money or goods. … it generally entailed involuntary service and normally involved a great mass of people from a given locality." In Egypt, "the impressment was temporary and may have been based on a quota that local officials had to meet."[4] A common theme of the papers in this volume is that supplying such labor was the prototypical "tax" obligation, leading land tenure to be defined in fiscal terms. "The man responsible for the tax was the 'owner' as far as the state was

3 Lamberg-Karlovsky (this volume): 59.

4 Goelet (this volume): 531.

concerned."[5] Property "belonged" to its holders in the sense of having the right to administer it in order to meet public obligations.

This is the reverse of Locke's justifying land ownership by the labor that landlords put into the land by clearing and improving it. Land in Mesopotamia was plentiful but required irrigation, which was provided by the local community (or by a larger territory in the case of major canals). Land rights were linked to the holder's obligation to supply corvée labor for such work, as well as for the military. An crop and manpower surplus was extracted from landholders—as it was from merchants and entrepreneurs for their leasing or control of property, trade and palace enterprises.

To be sure, property holders always have had a tendency to break free from their fiscal and social obligations. The history of civilization has seen a constant struggle to link property rights to reciprocal social obligations to serve society's survival, growth and equity in the face of owners seeking to use their privileges and control the state itself in predatory and extractive ways.

Corvée labor and feasts

Steinkeller emphasizes the major problem for organizing labor prior to classical antiquity: a chronic labor shortage.[6] The problem was how to get self-sufficient cultivators to work at manual labor consisting largely of carrying baskets of earth and transporting building materials during the non-planting season.

No doubt maintaining Neolithic practice, corvée activities had to attract and hold their participants. For Babylonia, Richardson cites rulers emphasizing their efforts to promote "public joy" in corvée projects by "invest[ing] such occasions with an atmosphere of feasting and plenty." This made the tasks "something closer to a prebend, an opportunity, a festival" with the benefit of group membership and identity. Indeed, he asks:

[5] Eyre 2005: 174. Lehner adds: "Historically, the delegation of fiscal responsibility to the richest local residents has been normal in Egypt. … as holders of liturgies in the Ptolemaic period, or as village headmen (*shaykh/umda*) in later periods. They were personally responsible for the flow of revenues to the 'lords of the land'" (this volume, p. 496, n. 533).

[6] Goelet cites the corollary observation from Eyre 1999: 46 about land-holding in Egypt: there always seems to have been enough land available for cultivation, but "[l]and was valueless without people" (this volume, p. 535, n. 40.)

> Would it even be possible to create a corps of 'forced,' 'unfree' or 'semi-free' laborers to toil under adverse conditions—for no more than one week a year? Would workers who had toiled for 150 days of the year in the dirt and mud to grow barley for state and bare survival choose to resent a few days of collective labor, in the company of neighbors and with the prospect of feasting and song? Should we really imagine teams of tens of thousands groaning under the weight of massive building blocks under the stern eyes of whip-wielding overseers, when the average work-account text deals with teams of workers numbering fewer than two hundred?[7]

Richardson estimates that institutional building work in Babylonia "only comes to something like 4% of the farming work" needed for families on the land to produce their own sustenance—"not more than a week of work compared to six months of farming."[8] And most corvée labor was seasonal so as not to interfere with the crop cycle. In Egypt, the workers' town housing the specialized labor force that "worked hard on the pyramids (such as moving megaliths)" was, in Lehner's description, "a rather elite place of high-status royal service and possibly higher-quality recompense than recruits might have known in their home districts."[9]

This solution was akin to Veblen's *Instinct of Workmanship*. In contrast to what Richardson characterizes as "our very modern assumption that labor is a social and economic disutility,"[10] what was being built was not just monuments and palaces, but communal identity—a ceremonial expression of creativity—and great feasts and drinking parties when projects were completed (and probably in between). Lehner describes an Egyptian causeway scene showing "the completion of the king's pyramid by the dragging and setting of the capstone (pyramidion) with a celebration of feasting, singing, and dancing" by the work crews, "perhaps a special feast out of the many regular feasts that we know so well from tomb and temple texts ... We see racks of hanging meat, to be shared and consumed for the occasion."[11] Such feasts must have been a major source of meat in the diets of many Bronze Age corvée attendees—not to mention the drinking parties where vast amounts of beer were consumed!

[7] Richardson, this volume, pp. 298–299.
[8] Richardson, this volume, p. 297.
[9] Lehner, this volume, p. 499.
[10] Richardson, this volume, p. 238.
[11] Lehner, this volume, p. 468.

Public feasts continued in classical antiquity. In Homer's Odyssey, "Alcinous has the Phaeacians build a ship for Odysseus and promises a public feast and rations for the sailors, offering to reimburse the other lords for gifts to him through a levy on the demos. ... the treasurers (*tamiai*) of the temple of Athena, who managed sacred revenue, and the so-called 'ham-collectors' (*kolakretai*), [refer] to their original function apportioning shares at public feasts, who perhaps by the time Solon also collected city revenue and paid out money, for example, to travelling envoys."[12]

Some coercion obviously was at work. Ambitious Sumerian empire builders retained the loyalty of leading towns by granting exemption from the bala contribution, and the well-to-do hired stand-ins to perform their corvée duties. But Steinkeller sees a political byproduct of bringing labor from distant provinces by the Ur III period: "National building projects were an extremely important tool of political and cultural integration," a "nation-building" effort instilling an idea of proto-national solidarity as workers came to think of themselves as "fellow members of a united Babylonia."[13]

Local abuses of labor

Throughout history local authorities have sought to divert labor for their own purposes. Sometimes the central authority deters this power grabbing, as in England's Star Chamber in the 16th and 17th centuries against aggressive local nobility. But the Bronze Age "Intermediate Periods" saw central power wane vis-à-vis that of local clan heads, chieftains and "bigmen." Writing of Egypt's First Intermediate Period, Goelet finds that "the power of the local elites apparently outweighed that of the monarch. The end result was that the status of *mrt*-laborers and other lower class individuals generally had declined from being serfs bound to the land to becoming purchasable chattel."[14] The Horemheb and Nauri decrees show that

> Those who were 'corvéable' ... might be subject to the arbitrary control of some powerful local official acting on his own interests without state sanction. This was by no means a minor problem since the

[12] Monson 2014.

[13] Steinkeller, this volume, p. 143.

[14] Goelet, this volume, p. 549.

unauthorized removal of personnel appears as a central concern for the institutions to which they were attached …"[15]

Palaces remained dependent on local officials or contractors to supply labor, resulting in a political tug of war. Assyriologists have found a similar reliance of Ur III and Babylonian rulers on local clan heads or lu-gal "big-men" acting as contractors to supply labor and military support, especially in Mesopotamian "intermediate periods."

To assert palace claims on labor over local creditors, Enmetena, Urukagina, Ur-Nammu, Shulgi, the rulers of Hammurabi's Babylonian dynasty, Hurrian and Amorite rulers proclaimed debt moratoriums. These Clean Slates prevented creditors from holding labor in bondage that would have prevented their serving in the army or being called up for corvée labor. Rulers annulled agrarian "barley" debts, liberated bond-servants to return to their families, and returned crop rights to debtors who had pledged them to foreclosing creditors. Such royal proclamations provided the model for the Biblical Jubilee Year of Leviticus 25, as our volume on *Debt and Renewal in the Ancient Near East*[16] has documented. The effect was to re-start a ruler's reign with the economy in financial balance (although commercial "silver" debts were not covered by such proclamations).

No interest-bearing debt is found in the Linear B records, but a similar tension existed between the palace and local authorities. Palaima distinguishes Mycenaean palace administrators from "collectors" or "mobilizers" acting as entrepreneurial contractors. He suggests that mobilizing labor in the outlying areas relied on pre-existing systems headed by "local big men (*g^{w}asilēwes*) or *sib* groups, clans and elders (*gerontes* and *geronsiai*)."[17]

[15] Goelet elaborates: "In the Horemheb Decree, those people most directly affected by the abuses appear to have been the independent individuals typical of rural life such as fishermen, herdsmen, or the agricultural workers called nḥmw, who might be comparable to our notion of freemen. … All such edicts aimed to shelter people who were deemed to be working on the king's behalf, especially if they were on institutional lands. … it seems that the peasantry was often vulnerable to compulsion or even long-term subjugation by powerful individuals. This is hardly surprising, yet these edicts show that occasionally this vulnerability extended even to the wealthier stratum, including the administrative class, in the countryside" (this volume, pp. 562, 565).

[16] Hudson and Van de Mieroop 2002.

[17] Palaima, this volume, p. 643.

After palace control ended c. 1200 BC, local Greek power reverted to local heads. As our privatization volume has described, *basilai* managers disappear from palace records with the ending of Linear B documentation in 1200, and reappear around the 8th century BC as "kings" independent of central authority.[18] In this sense one can view classical antiquity as a long "intermediate period" of lapsed central control until Roman times.

From the corvée to commodity-producing enterprise

Steinkeller points out that Ur III "building narratives emphasize the fact that among the workers employed on such projects "no one received a higher or a lower wage," an indication of the remarkable—and quite unusual—degree of equality that existed among the participants of these undertakings."[19] Wages for major building projects "were very generous, since, apart from a monthly salary of between 30 and 60 liters of barley, they included a daily food allowance, consisting of 2 liters of bread, 2 liters of beer, and 2 shekels of fat," and often dates, cheese and sesame bran. By the neo-Babylonian period, Jursa reports: "While there were difference in the size of rations owing to age, there were few and far less pronounced distinctions on the basis of profession and rank."[20] Young apprentices received 60 liters of barley a month, unskilled labor 90 liters, and trained workers 180 liters. Remuneration for skilled labor was negotiable.

Meanwhile, the aims of production had been widening since the fourth millennium to include large-scale commodity production employing manual labor that was more dependent, and also specialized skilled labor and a managerial class. Southern Mesopotamia needed to trade to obtain metals and stone not found in local soils. Meeting this challenge required workshops to produce exports, mainly by dependent and proto-wage labor overseen by a temple or palace hierarchy, from foremen and scribe accountants to chief administrators. A merchant class was required to organize and conduct this trade, and also credit formalities to reimburse the large institutions for their advance of goods.

[18] See the *Introduction* by Hudson in Hudson and Levine 1996: 19.

[19] Steinkeller, this volume, p. 145.

[20] Jursa, this volume, p. 356.

Skilled and specialized craft labor and technology were centered in temple and palace workshops but also worked "off the books,"[21] evidently on a piecework basis for whoever could pay for their services. It seems that wives and daughters from the free community also earned money working at weaving or other handicrafts in addition to their household work on the land. Jursa's paper shows that private for-hire contracts became widespread by the Neo-Babylonian period. [Englund chart?]

The standard adult male wage of 2 sila per day seems to have remained remarkably stable over the millennia.[22] This stability reflects the fact that there was no labor "market" fluctuating in response to shifts in supply and demand, and no natural tendency for wages to reflect rising productivity or profit rates.

Textiles were Mesopotamia's major export[23] and the employment of non-slave labor is best typified by the widows and war orphans assigned to weaving and other handicrafts in its temple and palace workshops. In

21 But not altogether out of the cuneiform record. In his paper to this colloquium (not included in this volume), Johannes Renger, points out that *nadītu* are documented as hiring workers to tend their fields, and cites Weitemeyer 1962 and other studies. Regarding such informal labor, Goelet observes: "Once a member of the crew, that state (or royal) affiliation does not seem to have prevented the village's craftsmen from occasional work on their own behalf, even leading to an "informal workshop" for which they could produce funerary goods for other private individuals, separately from their regular activities on behalf of the state" (this volume, p. 568).

22 This was the equivalent of 1.6 to 2 liters of barley rations. Summarizing the points he outlined in 1989: 234–252, Johannes Renger's paper at the colloquium (not included in this volume) notes: "Over centuries the amount of the barley rations did not change. According to the Persepolis documents (4th cent. B.C.) the daily ration was still ca. 2 sìla. Even in the Mediterranean in the 16. cent. A.D. the annual provision for an able bodied worker was the same as in Mesopotamia in the 3rd and 2nd millennium." See also Scheidel, 2010: 425–462. The exception to normalcy occurred in emergencies such as when Lagash was attacked by Umma.

23 These were woven mainly by poorly paid female labor –full-time dependents ("widows and orphans") and also part-time labor employed by the large institutions. No doubt these women normally were dependent on the husbands. One finds even today low-wage female labor producing exports in Korea, where their husbands earn enough working in the domestic economy to subsidize such export production. For a discussion of Ur III textile production see Waetzoldt 1986:117–142, and Wright1996. Women also were employed in corvée construction work.

contrast to the public infrastructure created by corvée labor, commodity production for trade aimed at gaining a monetary surplus by what today's economists call profit centers.

Managerial innovation was as important as material technology. Above all, writing was required for account keeping. Babylonian training exercises called for calculating the labor time and hence food needs (easily converted into silver-value) for corvée labor to make bricks and construct walls, move earth and dig canals. From prehistoric Uruk to Ur III Babylonia we find a labor-time/dietary basis for economic planning by accountants calculating monthly food needs per worker, categorized by male, female, older and younger children.

Egyptian sources suggest that scribes were not from elite families. Their profession was independent from property owning. But their planning and writing functions helped support authority and economic control. In fact, only large complex institutions could have created the measures needed for market exchange to develop. Weights and measures, money and salaries had to be standardized, along with prices and remuneration rates, to schedule the flow of food and raw materials.

All this required cost accounting to regularize the distribution of food and raw materials. An administrative managerial calendar with equal 30-day months enabled grain disbursements to be convertible into bread equivalents, and into silver at standard ratios for accounting purposes, valued in terms of a common monetary denominator. These calculations were a prototype of modern input-output tables. So in addition to (1) writing, the resulting account keeping system involved (2) standardization of measures and weights to supply labor with food and raw materials, (3) cylinder seals to establish administrative responsibility for receipt of goods and their storage, and (4) a schedule of administered prices to monetize payments in barley, silver, copper and other basic commodities to the palace, its collectors and the rest of the community. Silver acted as money, the measure against which other commodities were valued, with fixed price ratios for grain, copper and other commodities involving payments to and within the temples and palaces.

These flows of food and materials required (5) a standardized administrative calendar of equal 30-day months to replace the lunar months of variable length. The sexagesimal (60-based) system of fractions provided the basis for denominating (6) calendrical weights and measures, and an easily calculated rate of interest on advances to merchants and entrepreneurs.

Unfree labor that lost its liberty and self-support land

Goelet states a principle for Egypt that also applies from Mesopotamia to Rome: "[T]he entire working class of Egyptian society—effectively 95 per cent of the population—was effectively unfree and bound to the orders of some superior from childhood right through old age."[24] But some labor was less free than others.

Widows and orphans taken out of the family-based context on the land wove textiles in temple workshops, remunerated at a set rate, making products for sale to obtain silver, tin and gold. Half a century ago Maurice Lambert described the Sumerian bureaucracy as instituting austerity to squeeze out an economic surplus.[25] Rations were minimized by Lagash's ruler Lugalanda when his nubanda administrator Eniggal restructured the accounting system during the city-state's war with Umma.[26] The dependent work force (which included some enslaved mountain girls) had little alternative but to submit, being dependent on the administration to provide food and shelter.[27]

Unlike the takeoff of modern capitalism, labor was not forced off its self-support land to seek a livelihood as landless wage earners. An ever-present option was not to remain in the community. Flight occurred in times of economic hardship or oppression, natural disasters, crop failure, drought or flooding. Fugitives from the land after 1600 BC in Babylonia joined bands as migrant workers or outlaws.[28] The word hapiru has been used to refer to such outcasts.

Slavery was not an important source of public labor in Egypt in the New Kingdom, except for war prisoners consigned to near-death work in the mines. Male slavery was relatively secondary, and often took the form of debt bondage that likely was subject to pharaonic amnesties as in Mesopotamia. Most bondservants and slaves in both regions were female house servants—the slave women and daughters pledged to work as year-round household servants for creditors (earlier volumes have pointed to debt bondage as a path of least resistance to obtain labor services.) But at least bondservants were liberated by royal Clean Slates enabling Near Eastern debtors to return to their families of origin.

24 Goelet, this volume, p. 571.
25 Lambert 1960 1–26, and 1961a 21–46.
26 Lambert1961b. 427–38.
27 Lambert 1966 34ff.
28 Renger 1970 [1972]: 167–182.

These amnesties ended by classical antiquity. And the condition of slaves worsened as their role shifted from that of family members to being put to work in large-scale agricultural and handicraft production. In Athens slaves were foreign, and public labor was drudgery performed mainly by non-citizen metics. Dispossessed Roman citizens became mercenaries, fighting to extend the empire that had expropriated them for debt. Industry was associated with servile labor, mainly by dependents forced into clientage on the estates of large landowners. "The very wages the laborer receives are a badge of slavery," wrote Cicero.[29] By imperial Roman times a quarter of the population was reduced to debt bondage or slavery, ending up being housed in barracks on landed estates as economic life de-urbanized.

To trace how the conditions of labor shaped economies, their property rights and fiscal policy over time, this colloquium has focused on eight major themes:

Theme 1: Steinkeller emphasizes that the labor problem down through the Bronze Age was a shortage, not a modern "reserve army of the unemployed" driven off the land. The organization of work to build basic infrastructure could not have been too coercive, because its participants would have run away. The corvée had to be organized with widespread assent. Lehner's report of large volumes of remains of slaughtered animals indicating great feasts for Egypt's pyramid builders seems to reflect long-standing practice throughout the ancient Near East.

Theme 2: Being organized communally in the first instance, the "output" of labor was not marketable or had exchange value. The work produced social value, creating ceremonial buildings, city walls, irrigation systems and roads as "social capital." Hence, modern supply and demand curves for labor and its remuneration rates based on the market value of its output are not relevant.

Third millennium temple and palace records show manual labor being paid at standardized rates, ranked by sex and age (and in time by occupation). The basis for most salaries was what adult men, women and children needed for basic sustenance. Schoolbook exercises calculated the food needed per worker, denominated in grain or bread equivalents directly convertible into standard weight units of silver money. By Neo-Babylonian times such wages were paid directly in silver.

[29] Cicero, *De officiis* I, 150f. "To work for a private employer was regarded as 'slavery,'" writes Humphreys (1978:147).

Theme 3: Although they were only a small part of the labor force, skilled craftsmen required a broad range of collateral support activities to supply raw materials, schedule their delivery and provide tools. This large scale required management, oversight, account keeping and credit, and therefore was centered in the temples and palaces (and on large estates whose owners usually were associated with the temples or the royal family).

Theme 4: Mesopotamian institutions and households obtained wealth largely by foreign trade, producing handicrafts and consigning them to merchants. Most trade was conducted by merchants via their positions in the temple or royal bureaucracies, precisely because these large institutions were catalysts for entrepreneurial trade and the major employers of skilled craft labor. But as temple and palace activities were increasingly privatized in the hands of merchants and leasors of land or public enterprises, the resulting mixed economies had what today would be called a conflict between public and private interest.

Theme 5: Labor-for-hire started as a marginal phenomenon. Well-to-do citizens could hire surrogates to perform their corvée duty—typically younger brothers or other relatives. Unlike manual labor for construction, handicraft work typically was remunerated on a piecework basis. Weavers worked at home, much like those in England before power looms were introduced.[30] But by neo-Babylonian times, piecework labor by skilled craftsmen became more frequent, as did seasonal harvesting work.

Theme 6: Agrarian and personal usury became a major means to obtain labor services through debt bondage, and in time to pry away land rights. Local "big-men," *tamkārum* merchants and palace collectors sought control of labor at the expense of central palace fiscal authority that sought to maintain land tenure rights/obligations as a means of assigning responsibility for providing corvée labor and service in the army.

Theme 7: Mesopotamia's large institutions were creditors not debtors. Most personal and agrarian debts took the form of obligations to these institutions for advances of agricultural inputs or consumer goods. Collectors in the royal bureaucracy charged usury on arrears for these advances. Such debts increased sharply in times of drought, flood-

30 Renger 1989:234f. cites the Law-book of Daduša from Ešnunna §14 stipulating wages paid based on the weight of a garment to be finished by bleaching or washing.

ing and military hostilities. Falling into debt became the major dynamic leading to economic inequality as citizens lost their personal liberty and land tenure rights. Rulers restored fiscal stability, corvée labor and military service—as well as the personal liberty of debtors—by proclaiming royal Clean Slates that rescued debtors from bondage by clearing away the personal debts, bond servitude and land forfeitures that had occurred since the last such edict.

Theme 8: The way in which debt problems were resolved became the major factor determining the status of labor. Enforcing debt claims led to creditor foreclosure on the liberty of debtors, and ultimately their land rights.

By the 8th century BC, Near Eastern commercial practices were brought westward to Mediterranean lands that lacked the traditions of entrepreneurial temples or royal Clean Slate edicts. The replacement of kingship and Clean Slates by oligarchies distinguishes classical Greece and Rome from earlier Near Eastern experience. Although the 7th century BC saw populist "tyrants" overthrow landed oligarchies, followed by Solon's banning of debt bondage for Athenian citizens, free populations became more debt-ridden. Foreclosure became a major means of obtaining dependent labor and ultimately monopolizing the land, driving the citizenry into clientage and bondage by the time of the Roman Empire. Meanwhile, landholders and creditors at the top of the economic pyramid managed to avoid tax obligations, impoverishing the domestic market. Demographic and commercial shrinkage ensued, stabilized only by medieval serfdom.

Conclusion

"In the beginning," performing communal work under the corvée and conscription in the military must have been seen by its participants as part of society's survival. It must have seemed natural for members of the community, citizens or "sons of the city" to work for what was viewed as common needs, such as building public monuments and city walls or digging local irrigation ditches.

The Bronze Age added new layers to the Neolithic mode of organizing labor. From the corvée to temple and palace workshops and the levies found in Sumer, Babylonia, Egypt and Mycenaean Greece developed account keeping largely to organize and provision labor. In tracing this evolution the present volume extends what has been a central theme of the five colloquia we have held over the past twenty years: the role played by chieftains, temples, palaces and other civic institutions in creating the preconditions for markets and enterprise to develop, and their subsequent privatization.

Mobilization of corvée labor was linked to the fiscal systems based on land tenure. Property rights were part of society's system of providing itself with public labor, by requiring landholding citizens provide service. Greece imposed public leiturgoi expenses on large landholders, and the Roman concept of class was defined by the landed wealth needed to outfit and support oneself at a given military rank. As late as medieval feudalism, William the Conqueror ordered compilation of England's Domesday Book in 1086 to assess the land's ability to pay a crop tax.

The modern world has dissociated landholding rights and wealth from such reciprocal responsibilities. The fiscal burden is being shifted increasingly onto labor, obliging consumers to pay sales taxes and, as employees, income tax and other wage set-asides, while facing rising indebtedness to obtain their basic needs. As occurred in late antiquity, the result is to polarize society economically and financially by forcing labor into deepening dependency.

Bibliography

Eyre, Christopher (1999), "Village Economy in Pharaonic Egypt," in A.K. Bowman and E. Rogan, (eds.), *Agriculture in Egypt from Pharaonic to Modern Times* (Proceedings of the British Academy 96). Oxford: 33–60.

— (2005), "How Relevant was Personal Status to the Functioning of the Rural Economy in Pharaonic Egypt?" in Bernadette Menu, (ed.), *La dépendence rurale dans l'Antiquité égyptienne et proche-orientale* (BdÉ 140), Cairo: 157–186.

Hudson, Michael and Baruch A. Levine (1999), eds., *Urbanization and Land Ownership in the Ancient Near East.* (Peabody Museum Bulletin 7). Cambridge, MA.

Humphreys, Sarah C. (1978), *Anthropology and the Greeks.* London.

Lambert, Maurice (1960), "La naissance de la bureaucratie," *Revue Historique* 224: 1–26.

— (1961a), "Le premier triomphe de la bureaucratie," *Revue Historique* 225: 21–46.

— (1961b), "Recherches sur la vie ouvriers," *Archiv Orientalni* 29: 427–438.

— (1966), "La Guerre entre Urukagina et Lugalzagesi," *Rivista degli Studi Orientali* 41: 29–66.

Marshak, Alex (1999), "Space and Time in Pre-agricultural Europe and the Near East: The Evidence for Early Structural Complexity," in Hudson and Levine 1999: 19–63.

Monson, Andrew (2014), Review of Hans van Wees, *Ships and Silver, Taxes and Tribute: A Fiscal History of Archaic Athens* (London; New York: 2013) in *Bryn Mawr Classical Review* 2014.08.42.

Weitemeyer, Mogens (1962), *Some Aspects of the Hiring of Workers in the Sippar Region at the Time of Hammurabi.* London.

Renger, Johannes (1989), "Zur Rolle von Preisen und Löhnen im Wirtschaftssystem des alten Mesopotamien an der Wende vom 3. zum 2. Jahrtausend v. Chr. Grundsätzliche Fragen und Überlegungen," *AoF* 16: 234–252.

Renger, Johannes (1972), "Flucht als soziales Problem," in D.O. Edzard (ed.), *Gesellschaftsklassen im Alten Zweistromland und in den angrenzenden Gebieten. XVIII. Rencontre assyriologique internationale, München, 29. Juni bis 3. Juli 1970.* Munich:167–182.

Scheidel, Walther (2010), "Real Wages in Early Economies: Evidence for Living Standards from 1800 BCE to 1300 CE," *JESHO* 53: 425–462.

Veblen, Thorstein (1908/1919), "Professor Clark's Economics," *Quarterly Journal of Economics* 23 (February 1908), reprinted in *The Place of Science in Modern Civilisation, and Other Essays.* New York: 180–230.

Waetzoldt, Hartmut (1986), "Compensation of Craft Workers and Officials in the Ur III Period," in M. A. Powell, *Labor in the Ancient Near East.* (American Oriental Series 68). New Haven: 117–142.

Wright, Rita (1996), ed., *Gender and Archaeology.* Philadelphia.

www.ingramcontent.com/pod-product-compliance
Lightning Source LLC
Chambersburg PA
CBHW071405230926
51846CB00001B/14
* 9 7 8 3 9 8 1 4 8 4 2 3 6 *